Lecture Notes in Computer Science 5535

Commenced Publication in 1973
Founding and Former Series Editors:
Gerhard Goos, Juris Hartmanis, and Jan van Leeuwen

Geert-Jan Houben   Gord McCalla
Fabio Pianesi   Massimo Zancanaro (Eds.)

User Modeling, Adaptation, and Personalization

17th International Conference, UMAP 2009
formerly UM and AH
Trento, Italy, June 22-26, 2009
Proceedings

 Springer

Volume Editors

Geert-Jan Houben
Delft University of Technology
PO Box 5031, 2600 GA Delft, The Netherlands
E-mail: g.j.p.m.houben@tudelft.nl

Gord McCalla
University of Saskatchewan
Saskatoon, Saskatchewan S7N 5E2, Canada
E-mail: mccalla@cs.usask.ca

Fabio Pianesi
Massimo Zancanaro
FBK-irst
via Sommarive 18, 38050 Povo, Italy
E-mail: {pianesi,zancana}@fbk.eu

Library of Congress Control Number: 2009928433

CR Subject Classification (1998): H.5.2, I.2, H.4, I.6, J.4, K.4, K.6

LNCS Sublibrary: SL 3 – Information Systems and Application, incl. Internet/Web
and HCI

ISSN   0302-9743
ISBN-10   3-642-02246-4 Springer Berlin Heidelberg New York
ISBN-13   978-3-642-02246-3 Springer Berlin Heidelberg New York

springer.com

© Springer-Verlag Berlin Heidelberg 2009
Printed in Germany

Typesetting: Camera-ready by author, data conversion by Scientific Publishing Services, Chennai, India
Printed on acid-free paper   SPIN: 12693795   06/3180   5 4 3 2 1 0

Foreword

Research on user modeling (UM) and personalization can be traced back to the early 1970s, but it was not until the mid-1980s that the community of researchers working on user modeling and user-adaptive systems started its own series of international meetings on UM. After three international workshops in 1986, 1990, and 1992, User Modeling was transformed into an increasingly prominent biennial international conference. Its sustainability was ensured by User Modeling Inc. (http://www.um.org), a professional organization of researchers that has solicited and selected bids to run the conference, nominated program chairs, and provided financial backing to UM conferences. Between 1986 and 2007, 11 UM conferences were held (including the three workshops just mentioned), bringing together researchers from many areas and stimulating the development of the field.

Since the early 1990s, the rapid growth of the World Wide Web and other new platforms has populated the lives of an increasing number of people with a great variety of computing systems. This rampant growth has tended to increase the need for personalization, a topic that more and more researchers and practitioners are addressing and that has given rise to several new conferences. Among them, another biennial series on Adaptive Hypermedia and Adaptive Web-Based Systems (Adaptive Hypermedia or AH for short) quickly established itself as a major forum and sister event to UM, running on alternate years with it. Between 2000 and 2008, five AH conferences were held. During this period, the increasing complexity and prominence of Web systems prompted the enlargement of the list of topics covered by the AH series. Similarly, UM researchers had in the meantime quickly embraced the Web, developing many personalized Web systems. As a result, the original differences between the UM and the AH series faded away, and it became evident that their audiences, contributors, and topics largely overlapped. On the basis of many suggestions, the two conferences have now been merged into a new annual series. As a reflection of its continuity with the two parent series, the new conference series has been named User Modeling,

Adaptation, and Personalization (UMAP). By agreement of UM Inc. and the
Steering Committee of the Adaptive Hypermedia series (AHSC), four members
of AHSC have joined the board of UM Inc., which will therefore be in a position
to continue providing support to the new conference series.

The merger took almost 2 years to realize, and now the proud parents, UM
and AH, are happy to deliver their healthy baby: UMAP 2009. It seems fitting that the first UMAP conference was organized by FBK-irst, which hosted
the first AH conference in the year 2000. And the beautiful town of Trento,
surrounded by the Alps, provided an inspiring setting for the celebration.

With this merger, UMAP has become the largest and most prominent conference in the broad area of adaptation and personalization. Every year, it will
provide a forum in which to present the most innovative and important research
results, to meet with fellow researchers and practitioners from different fields,
and to educate the next generation.

June 2009

Peter Brusilovsky
Anthony Jameson

Preface

The First International Conference on User Modeling, Adaptation, and Personalization (UMAP 2009) was held June 22-26, 2009, in Trento, Italy.

UMAP 2009 was not, however, the first conference on user modeling or adaptation. In fact, UMAP 2009 merged two vigorous biennial conference traditions—the User Modeling (UM) conference series and the Adaptive Hypermedia (AH) conference series–into one annual conference that is now the premier venue for research into all aspects of user modeling, adaptation and personalization. Hence UMAP 2009 was the 17th international conference on this subject, not the first. A companion foreword provides more insight into the rationale for integrating these two conference series and discusses the goals of the new merged conference.

For our part, as Program and General Chairs for UMAP 2009, we chose a diverse Program Committee (PC) to adjudicate the submissions to the Research Track. The PC members were selected from established leaders in both the AH and UM communities, as well as highly up-and-coming newer researchers. Each paper was reviewed by at least three PC members, and typically a fourth PC member acted as both reviewer and meta-reviewer to ensure full discussion of the strengths and weaknesses of the paper and to make sure that consistent and constructive feedback was provided to the authors. Papers were submitted in two categories: full and short. Full papers describe mature work in detail (up to 12 pages were allowed) and short papers describe new and promising research of interest to the community (up to 6 pages were allowed).

For the Research Track there were 125 submissions: 88 full papers and 37 short papers. Twenty-three of the full papers were accepted for oral presentation, as were six of the short papers. In addition, 18 papers (full and short) were accepted for poster presentation at the conference. This meant that 26.1% of the 88 papers submitted as full papers were accepted for full presentation, and 37.6% of the 125 overall submissions were accepted in some form.

In addition to the Research Track, UMAP 2009 also established an Industry Track, chaired by Peter Brusilovsky and Alejandro Jaimes. The Industry Track had its own Program Committee of internationally renowned researchers and practitioners. The Industry Track is an important acknowledgement of the increasing impact of UMAP research on many areas of application, as personalization and adaptation become key elements of many deployed software systems. Papers submitted to the Industry Track were reviewed by at least three members of the Industry Track PC to ensure both that they met high standards for UMAP research and that they were relevant to application. Overall, there were 12 papers submitted to the Industry Track, with 3 accepted for oral presentation and 1 accepted for poster presentation.

UMAP 2009 also had a Doctoral Consortium, chaired by Sandra Carberry, Brent Martin and Riichiro Mizoguchi, to provide constructive feedback to young researchers. An exciting set of workshops and two informative tutorials were selected by a committee chaired by Milos Kravcik and Antonio Krüger.

The tutorials were:

- Constraint-Based Tutoring Systems, by Antonija Mitrovic and Stellan Ohlsson;
- New Paradigms for Adaptive Interaction, by Krzysztof Gajos and Anthony Jameson.

The workshops were:

- Adaptation and Personalization for Web 2.0, organized by Carlo Tasso, Antonina Dattolo, Rosta Farzan, Styliani Kleanthous, David Bueno Vallejo, and Julita Vassileva;
- Lifelong User Modelling, organized by Judy Kay and Bob Kummerfeld;
- Personalization in Mobile and Pervasive Computing, organized by Doreen Cheng, Kinshuk, Alfred Kobsa, Kurt Partridge, and Zhiwen Yu;
- Ubiquitous User Modeling, organized by Shlomo Berkovsky, Francesca Carmagnola, Dominikus Heckmann, and Tsvi Kuflik;
- User-Centered Design and Evaluation of Adaptive Systems, organized by Stephan Weibelzahl, Judith Masthoff, Alexandros Paramythis, and Lex van Velsen.

In addition to all of these events, UMAP 2009 had three keynote speakers:

- Susan Dumais, Microsoft Research: Thinking Outside the (Search) Box
- Alessandro Vinciarelli, Idiap Research Institute: Social Computers for the Social Animal. State-of-the-Art and Future Perspectives of Social Signal Processing
- Vincent Wade, Trinity College Dublin: Challenges for the Multi-Dimensional Personalized Web

We would like to thank the many people throughout the worldwide UMAP community who helped in putting on UMAP 2009. We deeply appreciate the hard work of the chairs responsible for the Industry Track, the Doctoral Consortium, the Workshops, Tutorials, and Demonstrations, and the conference publicity, as well as the conscientious work of the Program Committee members and the additional reviewers. We also gratefully acknowledge our sponsors who helped provide funding and organizational expertise: User Modeling Inc., Fondazione Bruno Kessler (FBK-irst), the U.S. National Science Foundation, Microsoft Research and the Japanese Society for Artificial Intelligence.

Finally, we want to acknowledge the use of EasyChair for management of the review process and the preparation of the proceedings.

June 2009

Geert-Jan Houben
Gord McCalla
Fabio Pianesi
Massimo Zancanaro

Organization

Chairs

Program Co-chairs	Geert-Jan Houben, Delft University of Technology (The Netherlands)
	Gord McCalla, University of Saskatchewan (Canada)
Conference Co-chairs	Fabio Pianesi, FBK-irst (Italy)
	Massimo Zancanaro, FBK-irst (Italy)
Industry Co-chairs	Peter Brusilovsky, University of Pittsburgh (USA)
	Alejandro Jaimes, Telefonica R&D Madrid (Spain)
Doctoral Consortium Co-chairs	Sandra Carberry, University of Delaware (USA)
	Brent Martin, University of Canterbury (New Zealand)
	Riichiro Mizoguchi, Osaka University (Japan)
Workshop, Tutorial, and Demonstration Co-chairs	Milos Kravcik, Open University of the Netherlands (The Netherlands)
	Antonio Krüger, University of Münster (Germany)
Publicity Co-chairs	Anthony Jameson, FBK-irst (Italy) and DFKI (Germany)
	Chiara Leonardi, FBK-irst (Italy)

Research Track Program Committee

Elisabeth Andrè	University of Augsburg, Germany
Liliana Ardissono	University of Turin, Italy
Lora Aroyo	Free University of Amsterdam, The Netherlands
Helen Ashman	University of South Australia, Australia
Ryan Baker	Carnegie Mellon University, USA
Joseph Beck	Worcester Polytechnic University, USA
Nicholas Belkin	Rutgers University, USA
David Benyon	Napier University, UK
Mária Bieliková	Slovak University of Technology, Slovakia
Susan Bull	University of Birmingham, UK
Noëlle Carbonnell	Université Henri Poincaré, France

Luca Chittaro	University of Udine, Italy
Robin Cohen	University of Waterloo, Canada
Cristina Conati	University of British Columbia, Canada
Ricardo Conejo	University of Malaga, Spain
Owen Conlan	Trinity College Dublin, Ireland
Evandro Costa	Federal University of Alagoas, Brazil
Paul De Bra	Technical University Eindhoven, The Netherlands
Jose Luis Perez de la Cruz	University of Malaga, Spain
Vania Dimitrova	University of Leeds, UK
Peter Dolog	Aalborg University, Denmark
Ben du Boulay	Sussex University, UK
Serge Garlatti	Telecom Bretagne, France
Susan Gauch	University of Arkansas, USA
Cristina Gena	University of Turin, Italy
Abigail Gertner	The MITRE Corporation, USA
Brad Goodman	The MITRE Corporation, USA
Jim Greer	University of Saskatchewan, Canada
Dominikus Heckmann	Saarland University, Germany
Eelco Herder	L3S Research Center, Germany
Anthony Jameson	FBK-irst, Italy
Judy Kay	University of Sydney, Australia
Alfred Kobsa	UC Irvine, USA
Joseph Konstan	University of Minnesota, USA
Tsvi Kuflik	University of Haifa, Israel
Henry Lieberman	MIT, USA
Frank Linton	The MITRE Corporation, USA
Chee-Kit Looi	Nanyang Technological University, Singapore
Judith Masthoff	University of Aberdeen, UK
Lorraine McGinty	UCD, Ireland
Bhaskar Mehta	Google, USA
Alessandro Micarelli	University of Rome III, Italy
David Millen	IBM, USA
Antonija Mitrovic	University of Canterbury, New Zealand
Bamshad Mobasher	DePaul University, USA
Rafael Morales	University of Guadalajara, Mexico
Wolfgang Nejdl	University of Hannover, Germany
Jon Oberlander	University of Edinburgh, UK
Georgios Paliouras	NCSR Demokritos, Greece
Cécile Paris	CSIRO, Australia
Michael Pazzani	Rutgers University, USA
Daniela Petrelli	University of Sheffield, UK
Francesco Ricci	Free University of Bozen-Bolzano, Italy
Gustavo Rossi	La Plata National University, Argentina

Vittorio Scarano	University of Salerno, Italy
Daniel Schwabe	University of Rio de Janeiro, Brazil
Marcus Specht	Open University of the Netherlands, The Netherlands
Oliviero Stock	FBK-irst, Italy
Carlo Strapparava	FBK-irst, Italy
Yasuyuki Sumi	Kyoto University, Japan
Carlo Tasso	Universit degli Studi di Udine, Italy
Julita Vassileva	University of Saskatchewan, Canada
Fabio Vitali	University of Bologna, Italy
Vincent Wade	Trinity College Dublin, Ireland
Gerhard Weber	PH Freiburg, Germany
Stephan Weibelzahl	National College of Ireland, Ireland
Ross Wilkinson	CSIRO, Australia
Diego Zapata-Rivera	Educational Testing Service, USA
Ingrid Zukerman	Monash University, Australia

Industry Track Program Committee

Mauro Barbieri	Philips Research, The Netherlands
Mathias Bauer	mineway, Germany
Ron Bekkerman	HP Labs, USA
Daniel Billsus	Shopping.com, USA
Elizabeth Churchill	Yahoo! Research, USA
William J. Clancey	NASA, USA
Enrique Frias-Martinez	Telefonica Research, Spain
Gustavo Gonzalez-Sanchez	Mediapro R&D, Spain
Ido Guy	IBM Research, Israel
Ashish Kapoor	Microsoft Research, USA
Ravi Kumar	Yahoo! Research, USA
Paul Lamere	Sun Microsystems, USA
Greg Linden	Microsoft, USA
Jiebo Luo	Kodak Research Lab, USA
Francisco Martin	MyStrands, USA
Andreas Nauerz	IBM, Germany
Nuria Oliver	Telefonica Research, Spain
Igor Perisic	LinkedIN, USA
Jeremy Pickens	FXPAL, USA
Prakash Reddy	HP Labs, USA
Christoph Rensing	HTTC, Germany
John Riedl	University of Minnesota, USA
Monica Rogati	LinkedIN, USA
Doree Duncan Seligmann	Avaya Labs, USA
Xuehua Shen	Google, USA

Malcolm Slaney   Yahoo! Research, USA
Barry Smyth   UCD and ChangingWorlds, Ireland
Neel Sundaresan   eBay Laboratories, USA
Ryen White   Microsoft Research, USA
Cong Yu   Yahoo! Research, USA
Michelle Zhou   IBM Research, China

External Reviewers

Abel, Fabian   Miao, Chunyan
Barla, Michal   Millan, Eva
Biancalana, Claudio   Möller, Sebastian
Bohnert, Fabian   Novielli, Nicole
Buttussi, Fabio   Pan, Shimei
Cena, Federica   Pazzani, Michael
Champaign, John   Perisic, Igor
Costello, Edwin   Peroni, Silvio
Coyle, Loran   Pierrakos, Dimitrios
Desmarais, Michel   Pinto, Monica
Di Iorio, Angelo   Ranon, Roberto
Doody, John   Rodriguez-Fornells, Antoni
Durao, Frederico   Sansonetti, Giuseppe
Federico, Marcello   Sciarrone, Filippo
Gasparetti, Fabio   Tintarev, Nava
Giannakopoulos, Georgios   Torre, Ilaria
Greer, Jim   Tvarozek, Michal
Guerini, Marco   Vogiatzis, Dimitrios
Guzmán, Eduardo   Wu, Longkai
Kabassi, Katerina
Lester, James

Table of Contents

Invited Talks (Abstracts)

Peer-reviewed Papers

Social Computers for the Social Animal: State-of-the-Art and Future Perspectives of Social Signal Processing

Alessandro Vinciarelli

IDIAP Research Institute
Switzerland

Abstract. Following Aristotle, "Man is by nature a social animal; an individual who is unsocial naturally and not accidentally is either beneath our notice or more than human." This is more than an abstract philosophical statement if, twenty five centuries after, we observe that people have exactly the same social behavior whether they interact with a computer or with another person. Furthermore, there is evidence that users tend to appreciate more computers displaying social behaviors similar to those they appreciate in people. This body of evidence suggests that there is a gap between current, unsocial, computers and user expectations for social behavior.

Social Signal Processing (SSP) is the new, emerging, domain that aims at making computers as social as their human users by modeling people and groups involved in social interactions. The SSP approach focuses on analysis, understanding and synthesis of social signals, the complex aggregates of non-verbal behavioral cues through which people convey their attitude towards others (including machines) and social environments. The development of SSP technologies will help computers to adapt to users like people adapt to others (i.e. depending on the kind of interaction and social context), and to personalize their interface in terms of characteristics socially desirable for the users.

G.-J. Houben et al. (Eds.): UMAP 2009, LNCS 5535, p. 1, 2009.

Thinking Outside the (Search) Box

Susan Dumais

Microsoft Research
USA

Abstract. Search is the main entry point for an ever-increasing range of information, services, communications and entertainment. During the last decade, there have been tremendous advances in the scale of search systems and the diversity of available resources. Yet the methods used to represent searchers' information needs have changed very little. Search interfaces today look much the same as they did a decade ago. Searchers type a few words into a search box, and the search engine returns a long list of results. When the results fail to satisfy the searcher's information needs, they try again and again with little support from the search engine. In this talk I describe several efforts to improve easy and effectiveness of search by: modeling searchers' interests and activities over time, representing non-content attributes of information such as time or genre, and developing interaction techniques that enable searchers to articulate their information needs more effectively.

G.-J. Houben et al. (Eds.): UMAP 2009, LNCS 5535, p. 2, 2009.
© Springer-Verlag Berlin Heidelberg 2009

Challenges for the Multi-dimensional Personalised Web

Vincent Wade

Trinity College Dublin
Ireland

Abstract. Adaptive hypermedia and adaptive web research have been reasonable successful in researching personalisation in closed corpus content and to a much lesser extent in open corpus content. From a commercial perspective, web adaptivity has been more focused on adaptive content retrieval rather than adaptive content composition. However, personal use of the web extends far beyond just content, and encompasses many dimensions which need to be addressed concurrently e.g. tasks & activities, cultural preferences, and social interaction etc. We need to consider new directions and dimensions in personalised, adaptive web and how they can be addressed within the same personal experience. In this talk I will investigate key challenges involving integrated open corpus & service personalisation, cultural adaptivity (including multilingual personalisation), dialogue and simulation personalisation and the power of the crowd, which could greatly empower web users of the future. I will also consider emerging approaches to tackle these problems and examine what this might mean to current web based personalisation engines and platforms.

G.-J. Houben et al. (Eds.): UMAP 2009, LNCS 5535, p. 3, 2009.

Modeling User Affect from Causes and Effects

Cristina Conati and Heather Maclaren

Computer Science Department, University of British Columbia
2366 Main Mall, Vancouver, BC, V6T 1Z4
conati@cs.ubc.ca

Abstract. We present a model of user affect to recognize multiple user emotions during interaction with an educational computer game. Our model deals with the high level of uncertainty involved in recognizing a variety of user emotions by probabilistically combining information on both the causes and effects of emotional reactions. In previous work, we presented the performance and limitations of the model when using only causal information. In this paper, we discuss the addition of diagnostic information on user affective valence detected via an EMG sensor, and present an evaluation of the resulting model.

1 Introduction

Several studies have reported correlations between student affect and learning (see [1] for an overview) suggesting that educational systems may be more effective if they can trigger appropriate student affective states. Taking student affect into account could be especially beneficial for systems that, like educational (edu-) games, rely heavily on student emotional engagement to be effective. The long-term goal of our research is to devise emotionally intelligent agents for edu-games that model both student affect and learning, and generate adaptive interventions aimed at balancing the two [2]. In this paper, we focus on the model of student affect that we built for one such agent included in an edu-game on number factorization.

The model is based on a framework that uses Dynamic Decision Networks (DDN) to leverage information on both the possible causes and the observable effects of the user's affective reaction [2]. In previous work, we built the model's part that reasons from causes to emotions (*predictive model*) and found that it can achieve reasonable accuracy [3,20]. As expected, however, we also found limitations hard to overcome by using causal information only. In this paper, we investigate the instantiation of the part of the model that reasons from effects to emotions (*diagnostic model*) by monitoring the valence of the user emotional state (i.e., positive or negative) via an Electromyography (EMG) sensor. We show that this addition significantly improves model accuracy in detecting strong user emotions during the interaction.

While other work has looked at combining causal and diagnostic information for affect detection (e.g., [4-6]) to our knowledge ours is the first attempt to provide an explicit comparison between a model that uses both sources vs. a model that uses causal information only. This comparison is important to assess whether it is worthwhile using the potentially more costly and intrusive technology necessary to obtain diagnostic information on user behaviors, as opposed to causal information that can

G.-J. Houben et al. (Eds.): UMAP 2009, LNCS 5535, pp. 4–15, 2009.

be usually gathered from naturally occurring interaction events. Our approach is also unique with respect to using information on student goals as a source of causal evidence. McGuiggan et al. [6] proposed an affective student model that also includes goal-related information in its assessment. However, in their application goals are explicitly given to students, whereas in ours they are not, requiring the model to do goal recognition.

Another distinguishing feature of our work is that we consider multiple, rapidly changing and possibly overlapping emotions, as often experienced by students playing educational games. In contrast, most work on affect recognition has focused on detecting one specific emotion (e.g., [4-6]), lower-level affective measures of valence and arousal (e.g., [7,9]) or overall emotional predisposition over a complete interaction (e.g., [10, 11]). One exception is the work by D'Mello et al. [12], which used dialogue features as predictors of student's boredom, confusion, flow and frustration during interaction with a dialogue-based tutoring system. There are three main differences between this work and ours. First, in [12] the target emotions are treated as mutually exclusive, which they mostly are, with the exception perhaps of confusion and frustration. We try to capture potentially overlapping emotions, adding an additional level of complexity to the modeling task. Second, [12] targets longer-term states that some researchers may classify as *moods*, i.e., states that are less specific than simple emotions, less likely to be triggered by a particular stimulus, and lasting [10]. We see these longer-term affective states as being complementary to the more instantaneous emotions we focus on, as we discuss in a later section. Finally, the approach in [12] does not include an explicit representation of causes of affect, thus providing less information than our approach for an agent to decide how to best deal with the student's emotions.

We begin by describing our general framework for affective user modeling. Next, we introduce the edu-game we use as a test–bed for model development. We then summarize the performance of the predictive part of the model, and compare it with an extended model that includes data from an EMG sensor as diagnostic evidence on student affective valence. We conclude by discussing future work.

2 The Affect-Modeling Framework

Fig. 1 shows a high-level representation of two time-slices in our DDN-based framework for modeling user affect [2]. Each time slice represents the system belief over relevant elements of the world after an interaction event of interest, such as a user's action (left slice) or an action from an interface agent (right slice). As the figure shows, the network can combine evidence on both the causes and effects of emotional reactions to assess the user's emotional state after each event.

The sub-network above the nodes *Emotional States* is the predictive component of the framework, representing the relations between emotional states and their possible causes as described in the OCC cognitive theory of emotions [15]. According to this theory, emotions derive from one's appraisal of the current situation (consisting of events, agents, and objects) with respect to one's goals and preferences. For instance, depending on whether an event (e.g., the outcome of an interface agent's action) fits or does not fit with one's goals, one will feel either joy or distress in relation to the

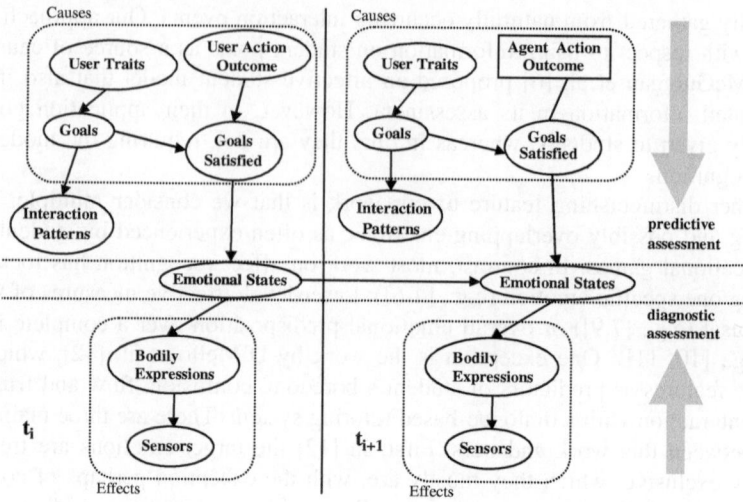

Fig. 1. High-level representation of the DDN for affective user modeling

event. If the current event is caused by a third-party agent, one will feel admiration or reproach toward the agent; if that agent is oneself, one will feel either pride or shame. Based on this structure, the OCC theory defines 22 different emotions.

We based our model on the OCC theory because its intuitive representation of the causal nature of emotions lends itself well to devising computational models that can assess not only which emotions a user feels but also why. Thus, an agent's ability to adequately respond to these emotions is enhanced. For instance, if the agent can recognize that the user feels a negative emotion because of something wrong the user has done (*shame* by OCC definition) it may provide hints aimed at making the user feel better toward herself. If the agent recognizes that the user is upset because of its own behavior (*reproach* by OCC definition), it may take actions to make amends. These specific interventions are not possible with approaches that cannot assess the reasons underlying user emotions (e.g., [12]). Another distinguishing feature of the OCC theory is that it mostly captures emotions that are instantaneous reactions to specific events, as opposed to the longer-term affective states such as *frustration, boredom, confusion* and *flow* targeted by other researchers. We see these states as complementary to those captured by the OCC model in that instantaneous emotions can contribute to creating longer-term affective states. Ideally, an affective user model should be able to capture all these different affective dimensions. However, we decided to focus initially on instantaneous emotions since by acting on them an agent can still impact longer terms affective states.

Our OCC-based DDN includes variables for goals that a user may have during the interaction with a system that includes an interface agent (nodes *Goals* in Fig. 1). The events subject to the user's appraisal are the outcomes of the user's or the agent's actions (nodes *User Action Outcome* and *Agent Action Outcome* in Fig. 1). Agent actions are represented as decision variables in the framework, indicating points where the agent decides how to intervene. The fit of events with user's goals is modeled by the node class *Goals Satisfied*, which in turn influences the user's *Emotional States* (we call this part of the model *appraisal-subnetwork*). Assessing user goals is not trivial, especially if asking the user about them during interaction is too intrusive, as is the case during game playing. Thus, our DDN also includes nodes (the *goal-assessment subnetwork*) to infer user goals from their interaction patterns and relevant traits (e.g., personality).

The sub-network below the nodes *Emotional States* is the model's diagnostic part, representing the interaction between emotional states and their observable effects. *Emotional States* directly influence user *Bodily Expressions*, which in turn affect the output of *Sensors* that can detect them. Our framework is designed to modularly combine data from any available sensor, and gracefully degrade in the presence of partial or noisy information. We used this framework to build an affective user model for an edu-game on number factorization, which we describe in the next section.

3 The Prime Climb Educational Game

Fig. 2. Prime Climb

Prime Climb is an educational game designed to help 6th and 7th grade students practice number factorization. Two players must cooperate to climb a series of mountains that are divided in numbered sectors (see Fig. 2). Each player should move to a number that does not share any common factors with her partner's number, otherwise she falls. Prime Climb includes a pedagogical agent that can both respond to explicit student help requests, and provide unsolicited hints when the student does not seem to be learning from the game

[13]. Currently the agent decides when and how to intervene based solely on a probabilistic model that assesses how the player's factorization knowledge evolves during game playing. We have evidence that this knowledge-aware agent can stimulate learning [13], but we believe that the agent could be more effective if it could respond to user emotions that we observed during game playing. These emotions include feelings generated by the player's performance in the game (i.e., *pride/shame* in the OCC theory) or by the agent's interventions (i.e., *admiration/reproach* in the OCC theory). Thus, the affective user model we are designing for Prime Climb assesses these emotions, as well as emotions towards game states (i.e., *joy/regret* in the OCC theory) to help the agent take both affect and learning into account when deciding how to act. While other emotions in the OCC model may be relevant, for instance emotions toward one's partner during game play, we decided to add more emotions only after verifying the viability of our approach with the six listed above.

We adopted an iterative design and evaluation approach in building the affective model, starting with the predictive part. In the next section, we briefly summarize the definition of this predictive part and results on its accuracy, to provide the basis for the extensions we describe later.

4   Definition and Evaluation of the Predictive Model

Many components of the predictive part of the Prime Climb's user model were derived from empirical evaluations [3, 20]. Based on student reports after game playing, we identified six high-level non-mutually exclusive goals (*Have Fun, Avoid Falling, Beat Partner, Learn Math, Succeed By Myself and Wanting Help*), represented by separate binary variables in the model. Note that while *Succeed By Myself* and *Wanting Help* intuitively seem mutually exclusive, we observed that they can in fact coexist for students who express a general preference to succeed by themselves but end up wanting help during especially challenging episodes. We then used interaction data to identify (i) the dependencies among student personality traits, goals and interaction patterns in order to define the goal assessment network; and (ii) the dependencies between the outcomes of student/agent actions and goal satisfaction in order to define the appraisal network. Each of the three emotion pairs in the appraisal network is represented by a binary node (*emotion-for-game, emotion-for-self and emotion-for-agent*, see figure 3 left). This structure was chosen because the two emotions in each pair are mutually exclusive and thus are best represented by a binary node; however, since students may simultaneously feel emotions in the different pairs, a separate node is required to represent each.

An evaluation of the predicted model [3, 20], showed that it performs reasonably well in capturing emotions towards the game (69.5% accuracy), but less so in capturing emotions towards the agent (56.6%), mainly because of problems in capturing regret. In-depth analysis showed that this inaccuracy is due to the model not being able to capture the shifts that some students experience between the goals *Succeed-by-myself* and *Wanting Help* at critical times of game playing. This confusion in turn causes the model to misinterpret how the user appraises the agent's interventions and the impact of user's appraisal on her affect toward the agent. The problem is a consequence of the fact that the model currently represents student goals as static. Modeling how goals evolve during interaction is a form of plan recognition, which is difficult to do without explicitly asking students about their goals. Thus, we decided to explore the alternative of improving the model by adding a diagnostic component that captures the player's affective valence via EMG sensors. We look at one sensor, as opposed to directly combining multiple sensors as others have done (see [14] for an overview), because we want to understand the potential of specific sensors as individual sources of affective information in this domain, with the long-term goal of modularly combining evidence in the diagnostic part of the model, depending upon which sensors are available/suitable to use.

5   Adding the EMG Signal to the Affective Model

EMG sensors measure muscle activity by detecting surface voltages that occur when a muscle is contracted. When placed on the corrugator muscle on the forehead, the signal gets excited by movements such as frowning and eyebrow raises. Previous studies (e.g., [16]) report that greater EMG activity in this area tends to be associated with expressions of negative affect. Thus, we decided to experiment with this source of diagnostic evidence, as a way to help the model capture instances of student's reproach. We incorporate this evidence into what we call from now on the *combined model*, as follows. We add two new nodes to each time slice: *Valence* and *Signal Prediction* (see Figure 3, left), both binary. The *Valence* node represents the combined model's overall prediction for the student's affective valence; the *Signal prediction* node encodes whether the EMG signal is positive/negative at a time of interest (as we describe in more detail in a later section). The conditional probability table (CPT) for *Valence* given *Emotional States* is defined so that the probability that valence is positive/negative is proportional to the number of positive/negative emotion nodes. The CPT for *Signal Prediction* given *Valence* represents the probability of observing an EMG prediction of positive or negative valence, given the student's actual affective valence. To instantiate this CPT, we ran a user study to collect both EMG evidence and accompanying affective labels, as described next.

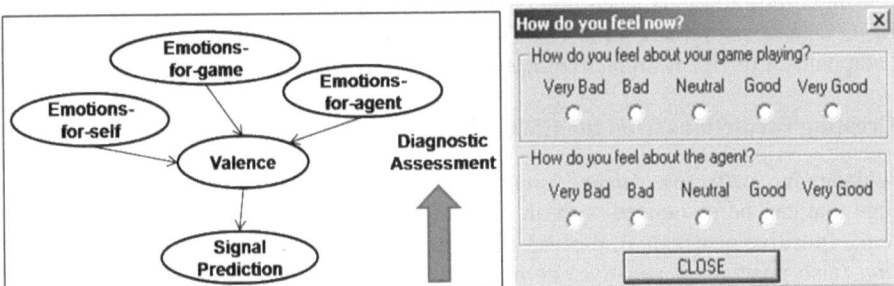

Fig. 3. Adding EMG data to the model (left); emotion self-report dialogue box (right)

Data Collection

Forty-one 6th and 7th grade students from two local schools participated in our study. The study took place in the schools, where for logistic reasons we were limited to a 30-minute session per student. An experimenter placed an EMG sensor on each participant's forehead, and showed a demo of Prime Climb with the emotion self-report mechanism described below. Participants were told that the game included an agent that would try to understand their needs and help them play the game better. The students were encouraged to provide their feelings whenever their emotions changed so that the agent could take them into account when providing help. Next, each participant played Prime Climb with an experimenter as a climbing companion. The experimenter was instructed to play as neutrally as possible, trying to avoid both making mistakes and leading the climb too much. This set up was adopted to avoid the strong emotions toward the partner that we often observed when students play together, given that our affective model currently does not model these emotions.

During game playing, the Prime Climb agent autonomously generated hints to help the student learn from the game, based on the existing model of student learning [13].

At any point during the interaction, students could volunteer information on their emotional states via the dialogue box shown in Figure 3 (right). If students tend not to volunteer self-reports, the dialog box pops up unsolicited, requiring students to input self-reports with a frequency adjusted to balance the amount of data collected and the level of interference generated. The emotion dialog box only elicits information on student emotions towards the game and the agent because dealing with three pairs of emotions turned out to be too confusing for our young subjects. The emotion-self-report approach (which we have used in several previous studies [3, 20]) was chosen because, during interaction with Prime Climb, user emotions are varied, ephemeral and rapidly changing, making it hard for our young users to describe their emotions after the interaction, as it has been done by other researchers. Another commonly used method to obtain affective labels is to have observers post-annotate videos of the interactions based on the users' visible reactions (e.g., [12]). However, when we tried to use this approach we found that observers often had a hard time discriminating among feelings with equal valence in our two different emotion pairs (e.g., reproach toward the agent vs. distress toward the game).

The log files from the study include all relevant game events (e.g., a student's successful climbs and falls, agent interventions), the student's reported emotions and the EMG signals sampled at 32 Hertz. These log files were analyzed to generate a set of datapoints of the form *<affective valence, signal prediction>*, as we describe next.

Creating Predictions from the EMG Signal

A datapoint *<affective valence, signal prediction>* is created for each event in the logs that can be associated with an emotion self-report, with value for *affective valence* (positive or negative) derived from that self-report and value for *signal prediction* (also positive or negative) computed by analyzing the EMG signal in the four seconds following the event. The period of four seconds was chosen based on [16], to allow for enough time to detect a response in the signal while avoiding recording the student's reaction to subsequent events. The analysis yielded 196 datapoints, which we used to instantiate the CPT for the *Signal Prediction* node in Figure 3 by calculating the frequencies of the various combinations of *signal prediction/affective valence* value pairs in the data set.

To obtain the values of *signal prediction* for our datapoints, we used the mean of the raw EMG signal as the base for signal analysis, because it is a measure that has consistently shown a reliable mapping with affective valence (e.g., [4,11]). The standard method for generating valence predictions from EMG is to compare the EMG signal over the interval of interest against a baseline recorded during a resting period before the experiment. Due to limitations on time with the students, in our study we could not set up an idle "resting time" that we could use as a baseline. Thus, we resorted to using as a baseline the mean of the EMG values recorded during the entire interaction. That is, given a datapoint associated with interface event e, the prediction produced by the EMG signal following e is computed as:

```
signal prediction(e) = positive
     if mean(EMG_e) < mean(EMG_all)   (1)
negative, otherwise.
```

where *EMG_e* is the set of EMG values recorded during the 4 seconds following *e* and *EMG_all* is the set of EMG values recorded during the entire interaction. Our choice of using the overall signal mean as a threshold for signal prediction is based on the experimenters' observations that many students experienced both positive and negative affect at some point during the interaction. Because negative affect is often associated with greater EMG activity in the forehead muscles [16, 17], the overall EMG mean of a student who experienced both positive and negative affect would be higher than the mean in those intervals where the student did not experience negative affect. This non-standard baseline is bound to misclassify students who experienced only positive affect during interaction. However, when we checked the performance of Equation 1 as a classifier for affective valence on our dataset, we found that this method could still allow us to add useful information to the model (see next section). Thus, we decided to continue with our investigation, by comparing the performance of the combined model with the predictive model described earlier.

6 Evaluating the Combined Model

Each model's performance is assessed via a simulator that replays event logs from Prime Climb interactions with that model. Model accuracy is computed via 100-fold random resampling, a cross-validation method commonly used with limited datasets [18]. We divided the evaluation into two steps. In the first step, we evaluate model performance on 83 datapoints obtained from self-reports that were either clearly positive or clearly negative. These are self-reports in which students indicated a positive (negative) emotion toward both game and agent, or in which one reported emotion was positive (negative) and the other was neutral; we will call these data points *clear-valence* from now on. In the second step, we analyze model performance on the less-investigated assessment of multiple emotions with unclear and possibly conflicting valence, represented in our dataset by 99 self-reports. We excluded from our analysis 14 reports that received neutral answers for both emotion questions. These points are certain to be misclassified by our models, which currently can't represent neutral affect.

The first step above, focusing on clear valence datapoints, is meant to verify whether we can replicate previous results from the literature on using the EMG on the corrugator muscle as valence predictor. These results were mainly obtained with clear valence affective states. As part of this step, we checked the performance of Equation 1 as a classifier for affective valence on the 83 clear-valence datapoints. The method achieved 89% accuracy in classifying datapoints with negative affective valence, indicating that, despite our less than ideal baseline, evidence from the EMG signal may still be a good detector of negative effect and help us improve the model's assessment of Reproach in the presence of clear valence emotions. As expected, Equation1 does not perform as well in classifying positive data points, reaching only 48% classification accuracy. Thus, any positive result obtained with this method should be considered as a lower bound on the potential of including EMG evidence in the Prime Climb model.

We tested model performance on clear-valence datapoints as follows. For each of the 100 folds in the cross-validation, we divided the set of students into a training and a test set of equal size using random selection. The clear-valence datapoints in the training set were used to define the CPT for the *Signal prediction* node in the combined model. The event logs in the test set were run through the simulator, first with the predictive and then with the combined model. For each data-point in the test-set, model prediction was compared with the corresponding self-reported emotion.We used an analogous procedure to test the models on datapoints with ambiguous valence (second evaluation step above).

Table 1. Accuracies on clear-valence data (†significantly different from predictive model)

	Accuracy %			N
	Predictive	Combined	Baseline	
Joy	74.80	79.10†	100	74
Distress	53.48	56.70	0.00	5
Macro Avg.	64.14	67.90†	50.00	
Micro Avg.	72.58	76.92†	91.03	
Admiration	83.49	83.18	100	67
Reproach	39.11	63.02†	0.00	9
Macro Avg.	61.30	73.10†	50.00	
Micro Avg.	76.86	79.2†	84.67	

For each emotion pair, we report model accuracy on both the positive and the negative emotion. Since there is a trade-off between these measures, we also need a measure of combined accuracy. Two common choices include micro-average (the percentage of cases correctly classified over all the test instances) and macro-average (the average of the accuracies for each class). Micro-averages are a commonly used measure of classification accuracy, but they produce a somewhat biased picture in the presence of classes with unbalanced size, because the accuracy over classes with few data-points is overshadowed by the accuracy over larger classes. Macro-averages are considered an adequate way to overcome this short-coming (e.g., [19]); they give fair weight to classes with few instances, when it is important that their instances are correctly detected. This is exactly the case in our work: we often see far fewer negative than positive data points (see Table 1), however, it is crucial for the model to detect these negative emotions since they may compromise the player's overall attitude towards the game. Given the nature of our dataset, macro-averages are a more appropriate measure of the model's overall accuracy, and so we will base our discussion on this measure. However, we report both micro- and macro- average for sake of completeness. We also report the performance of a standard baseline, i.e., a model that always predicts the most likely emotion. However, comparison with this baseline is not very meaningful, given the unbalance in our data. The baseline tends to have a high micro-average, because its perfect performance in capturing positive emotions off-balances its non-existent performance on the negative data points. Still, it would be hard to argue for a model that cannot capture negative affect, as reflected by its poor macro-average, consistently lower than those of both affective models.

Results

Clear-valence datapoints. We start by comparing the predictive and combined models on the clear-valence dataset. All measures of statistical significance are based on a two-tailed paired-samples t-test with $\alpha = 0.05$. As Table 1 shows, the combined model performs significantly better than the predictive model for Joy (t(99)=4.59, p<.001, d=.92) and Reproach (t(99)=8.84, p<.001, d=1.78). The increase in Reproach results in a significant increase of the model's macro average for emotions towards the agent (t(99)=8.62, p<.001, d=1.38), with a large effect size. The increase for Joy results in a significant increase of the model's macro average for emotions towards the game (t(99)=2.11, p=.038, d=.26), with small effect size.

Thus, we achieved our goal of improving the assessment of reproach by including diagnostic evidence in the model, at least for clear-valence datapoints. Essentially, when the student feels strong reproach and has no other conflicting emotion, the strong evidence of negative affect from the EMG sensor propagates to the *emotion-for-agent* node, overriding the more indirect (and incorrect) goal-based assessment from the causal part of the model. It is also encouraging to see that the poor performance of the EMG as a classifier for positive valence (see section 5) did not transfer to the combined model. In this case, the limitations of the EMG signal in detecting positive affect are compensated by the predictive model, with no negative, and actually some positive impact, on accuracy.

Ambiguous-valence datapoints. Accuracy results on the ambiguous-valence datapoints are not as encouraging. As Table 2 shows, there are significant decreases in both Joy (t(99)=-10.87, p<.001, d=-2.19) and Distress (t(99)=-2.55, p<.001, d=-.51). There is no relevant change for Reproach. The model's macro and micro-average for emotions towards the agent increase significantly (t(99)=8.03, p<.001, d=.84) because of an increase in admiration, but they are still below baseline accuracy. Although these results are disappointing, they are not surprising. Previous work showing the effectiveness of EMG in predicting valence usually investigated the mapping between EMG and clear valence emotions. Our ambiguous-valence data points, on the other hand, correspond to states were students reported mild or even conflicting emotions. Mild emotions are likely to generate more subtle facial expressions, difficult to capture by monitoring only the movements of the corrugator muscle. As for conflicting emotions, their overall valence may depend on which of the emotions involved is stronger. In our model, any evidence of overall valence coming from diagnostic data is propagated upwards to all the emotion pairs, biasing them in the same direction and causing a misclassification for any pair that had opposite valence, unless there is strong evidence coming from the causal model to correct the trend.

Table 2. Accuracies on ambiguous-valence data (†significantly different from predictive model)

	Accuracy %			N
	Predictive	Combined	Baseline	
Joy	83.66	75.15†	100	51
Distress	43.82	38.72	0.00	15
Macro Avg.	63.74	56.44†	50.00	
Micro Avg.	75.69	66.71†	79.35	
Admiration	58.58	71.70†	0.00	28
Reproach	25.36	25.11	100	33
Macro Avg.	42.11	48.41†	50.00	
Micro Avg.	42.67	49.10†	51.57	

The problem with capturing mild emotions is likely to be solved by increasing the model's ability to capture valence-related behaviors with the addition of other sensors linked with affective valence (e.g. an heart-rate monitor, EMG sensors on the frontalis muscle, or on the zygomatic major muscle). This solution, however, is unlikely to ease the problem with capturing conflicting emotions, because the problem is due to valence not carrying enough information to tease out the individual emotions. In this case, the only viable solution seems to be improving the accuracy of the diagnostic model, the only component that can provide direct information on the user's individual emotions.

7 Discussion and Conclusion

In this paper, we evaluated the addition of diagnostic information to an affective user model to detect players' emotions while interacting with Prime Climb, an edu-game for number factorization. The model combines information on causes and effects of users' affect to recognize multiple, possibly overlapping and rapidly changing emotions. While there are approaches to recognizing one specific user emotion or emotion valence/arousal, ours is one of the few models targeting the recognition of multiple emotions, and is unique in dealing with possibly overlapping emotions.

We have presented results of comparing a model that uses only causal information on game state, against a model that also includes information on user affective valence detected via an EMG sensor placed on the user's forehead. While approaches combining diagnostic and predictive inference have received substantial attention, our contribution is an ablation study that compares two versions of the model to understand the effects of each source of evidence. We showed that EMG information can significantly improve the model's accuracy in cases where the students' affective state has clear valence. Given that our method for signal processing relies on a less-than-ideal baseline, this result is a lower bound of what this approach can achieve. We also discussed the limitations of our approach in the presence of emotions with milder or conflicting valence, and presented two avenues of future work to overcome them. In particular, we are planning to (i) include other sources of valence information to detect emotional states expressed more subtly; and (ii) explore ways to capture the evolution of player goals during game playing, to refine the model assessment of conflicting emotions. We also plan to add sensors to capture arousal, so that the agent can gauge the actual impact of the user's emotions on game playing and learning. Other future work includes adding to the model the capability of assessing emotions toward a partner, and showing the effectiveness of an agent that has detailed information on user affect.

References

1. Craig, S.D., Graesser, A.C., Sullins, J., Gholson, B.: Affect and Learning: An Exploratory Look into the Role of Affect in Learning with AutoTutor. Journal of Educational Media 29 (2004)
2. Conati, C.: Probabilistic Assessment of User's Emotions in Educational Games. Journal of Applied Artificial Intelligence 16(7-8), 555–575 (2002)
3. Conati, C., Mclaren, H.: Data-driven Refinement of a Probabilistic Model of User Affect. In: Ardissono, L., Brna, P., Mitrović, A. (eds.) UM 2005. LNCS, vol. 3538, pp. 40–49. Springer, Heidelberg (2005)
4. Bosma, W., André, E.: Exploiting Emotions to Disambiguate Dialogue Acts. In: IUI 2004, Int. Conf. on Intelligent User Interfaces (2004)

5. Kapoor, A., Picard, R.W.: Multimodal Affect Recognition in Learning Environments. In: 13th Annual ACM Int. Conf. on Multimedia (2005)
6. McQuiggan, S., Lee, S., Lester, J.: Early Prediction of Student Frustration. In: 2nd Int. Conf. on Affective Computing and Intelligent Interactions (2007)
7. Zakharov, K., Mitrovic, A., Johnston, L.: Toward Emotionally Intelligent Pegadogical agents. In: Woolf, B.P., Aïmeur, E., Nkambou, R., Lajoie, S. (eds.) ITS 2008. LNCS, vol. 5091, pp. 19–28. Springer, Heidelberg (2008)
8. Thayer, R.E.: The biopsychology of mood and arousal. Oxford University Press, New Yok (1989)
9. Prendinger, H., Mori, J., Ishizuka, M.: Recognizing, Modeling, and Responding to Users' Affective States. In: Ardissono, L., Brna, P., Mitrović, A. (eds.) UM 2005. LNCS, vol. 3538, pp. 60–69. Springer, Heidelberg (2005)
10. Yannakakis, G.N., Hallam, J., Lund, H.H.: Entertainment Capture through Heart Rate Activity in Physical Interactive Playgrounds. User Modeling and User-Adapted Interaction 18(1-2) (2008)
11. Mandryk, R.L., Inkpen, K.M., Calvert, T.W.: Using Psychophysiological Techniques to Measure User Experience with Entertainment Technologes. Journal of Behavior and Information Technology 25 (2006)
12. D'Mello, S.K., Craig, S.D., Witherspoon, A.W., McDaniel, B.T., Graesser, A.C.: Automatic Detection of Learner's Affect from Conversational Cues. User Modeling and User-Adapted Interaction 18(1) (2008)
13. Conati, C., Zhao, X.: Building and Evaluating an Intelligent Pedagogical Agent to Improve the Effectiveness of an Educational Game. In: Proc. of IUI 2004, Int. Conf. on Intelligent User Interfaces, Island of Madeira, Portugal, pp. 6–13 (2004)
14. Kim, J., André, E.: Emotion Recognition Using Physiological and Speech Signal in Short-Term Observation. In: André, E., Dybkjær, L., Minker, W., Neumann, H., Weber, M. (eds.) PIT 2006. LNCS, vol. 4021, pp. 53–64. Springer, Heidelberg (2006)
15. Ortony, A., Clore, G.L., Collins, A.: The Cognitive Stucture of Emotions. Cambridge University Press, Cambridge (1988)
16. Lang, P., Greenwald, M., Bradley, M., Hamm, A.: Look at Pictures: Affective, Facial, Visceral, and Behavioral Reactions. Psychophysiology 30 (1993)
17. Scheirer, J., Fernandez, R., Picard, R.W.: Expression Glasses: A Wearable Device for Facial Expression Recognition. In: Proceedings of CHI 1999, Human Factors in Computer Systems, Pittsburgh, PA (1999)
18. Mitchell, T.: Machine Learning. McGraw-Hill, New York (1997)
19. Sebastiani, F.: Machine Learning in Automated Text Categorization. ACM Computing Surveys 34(1), 1–47 (2002)
20. Conati, C., Maclaren, H.: Empirically Building and Evaluating a Probabilistic Model of User Affect. User Modeling and User-Adapted Interaction (to appear)

Evaluating Web Based Instructional Models Using Association Rule Mining

Enrique García, Cristóbal Romero, Sebastián Ventura, and Carlos de Castro

Escuela Politécnica Superior. Universidad de Córdoba
14071 Córdoba, Spain
{egsalcines,cromero,sventura,cdecastro}@uco.es

Abstract. In this paper we describe an Integrated Development System for Instructional Model for E-learning (INDESIME) to create and to maintain instructional models using adaptive technologies and collaborative tools. An authoring tool has also been developed for helping to non-programming users to create Learning Management Systems (LMSs) courses that implement a specific instructional model. Data mining techniques are proposed to evaluate the e-learning courses generated from the model. We have tested the degree of effectiveness of our system using Moodle courses. The courses topics tested are based on the European Computer Driving Licence Foundation catalogue.

Keywords: instructional design, learning management systems, authoring tools and methods, data mining, association rules.

1 Introduction

The use of LMSs has grown considerably in the last years. These systems can offer a great variety of channels and workspaces to facilitate information sharing and communication between participants in a course. There are several types of LMSs: self-designed systems used by Universities, Colleges, Institutes; commercial products like WebCT [1], Blackboard [2], TopClass [3]; open source software (OSS) systems like Moodle [4], ILIAS [5], ATutor [6] among others.

Although LMSs provide useful tools for computer-supported collaborative learning (such as forums, chat rooms, discussion groups and e-mail), most of them show their contents and educational material to all students in the same way. At the same time, students are also completely free to choose their own learning pathway through the course, which is not necessarily the most effective one taking into account their previous knowledge or needs. One possible solution for this problem is the use of Adaptive and Intelligent Web-Based Educational Systems (AIWBES) [7]. These systems build a model for the objectives, preferences and knowledge of an individual user in order to adapt the system to his or her learning needs by means of Artificial Intelligence (AI) techniques from intelligent systems [8] such as machine learning and data mining. Examples of author tools are ELM-ART [9], InterBook [10], TANGOW [11], AHA [12] and ART-WEB [13] among others.

G.-J. Houben et al. (Eds.): UMAP 2009, LNCS 5535, pp. 16–29, 2009.

Another problem is that LMSs accumulate a vast amount of information which is very valuable for analyzing students' behavior and could create a gold mine. Educational Data Mining (EDM) [14] is an emerging discipline, concerned with developing methods for exploring the unique types of data that come from the educational context. In [14] the authors survey the application of data mining (clustering, classification and outlier detection; association rule mining and pattern mining; and text mining) to educational environments.

On the other hand, instructional design is a system or process of organizing learning resources to ensure that learners achieve established learning outcomes. From a designer's perspective, various models can be followed in the instructional design process [15]. Gros, B. [16] outlines the characteristics of more powerful instructional design models (IDM) that will facilitate multimedia authoring. Whereas much IDM focuses on cognitive skills and ignores the multi-perspective presentation of knowledge, the multimedia authoring tool tends to emphasize the presentation of knowledge without regarding developing cognitive skills. An effective IDM needs to combine the best of both worlds by using a more constructivist approach.

This paper presents the INDESIME (Integrated Development System for Instructional Model for E-learning). The novelty and originality of the INDESIME system is, on the one hand, the authoring tool component generates online courses, compatible with Moodle LMS, based on customizable instructional model that facilitates learner content parameterization and navigation design into a collaborative environment. And on the other hand, the data analysis component is designed to provide feed-back to the course author to how to improve the generated courses. An empirical evaluation of the approach is conducted by comparing it with a traditional one. We focused the evaluation on e-learning effectiveness from the students' point of view rather than the effectiveness of course modifications for the teacher. Finally, some examples of useful discovered association rules to improve the course are shown.

2 Problems When Implementing an Instructional Model for E-Learning

Theoretically, present-day technologies of information and communications are able to virtualize the entire process of education-learning. As with in-class education, e-learning also needs to use paradigms and didactic methods involving the identification of strategies, methods, tools, material, time and evaluation criteria, that together provide a unified process enabling one or more students to achieve the initially programmed educational objectives. However, in the case of e-learning there is no space-time element between the student and teacher, so these strategies and didactic methods must change, giving rise to what is known as the e-Didactics paradigm. According to [17], e-Didactics is the set of knowledge, processes and strategies intended to guarantee to one or more individuals the acquisition "at a distance" of competencies represented by specific didactic objectives, which are the didactics for e-learning.

A recent study carried out in the Universitat Oberta de Catalunya [18], which offers over 500 subjects in official university degrees, shows the tendencies in the instructional design of online learning programs. On analyzing these tendencies, the authors identify different types of activities used for the continuous evaluation of the learners. The results show the great efforts being made by teachers in terms of the conceptualization, design and elaboration of activities. Even so, these efforts were not rewarded since the activities were often not the most adequate ones for the students' needs. This was caused by a variety of factors; sometimes teachers did not have the tools for preparation or the necessary pedagogical assessment to allow them to carry out this task with the ease and adequacy desired, and other times there seems to have been a lack of criteria about how to plan the design of online evaluation as a system to evaluate the learning acquired with respect to the professional competencies desired.

On the other hand, the administration of learning objects (LO) is closely related to instructional design. In this sense a learning object is defined [19] as: a digital entity, self-contained and reusable, with a clear educational aim, made up of at least three internal and editable components: contents, learning activities and contextual elements. As a complement, the LO must have an (external) information structure to facilitate identification, storage and recuperation of metadata. However, in its recommendations about metadata, the IEEE [20] does not clarify how to classify them according to their use and relation to learning methods.

We have also considered it very advisable to analyse how concepts of LMS and AIWBES can be integrated, keeping in mind the main advantages of each one (Fig. 1) in order to obtain a more effective instructional design model for e-learning.

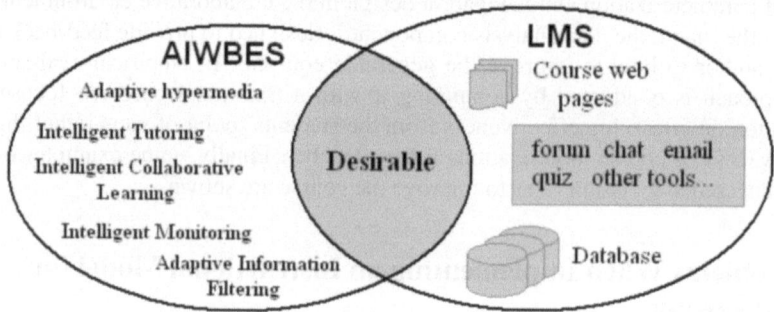

Fig. 1. Methodology for the continuous improvement of e-learning courses

Another aspect to be considered is the need to integrate continuous evaluation within the course design from the very beginning, thus covering the students' needs and building the knowledge process step by step. If this is difficult in normal class teaching, there are even more challenges when it is attempted in virtual courses or situations. It has been - and continues to be - difficult to get teachers to design online evaluation activities that are in conjunction with learning strategy criteria and whose validity can later be evaluated. In fact, we propose to use EDM for continuous empirical evaluation approach based on students' usage information.

In this sense, and given the necessary context of all the models available for instructional design that are characteristic of each institution, the idea is to systematize a flexible model that will grant enough freedom to professionals to design their own model based on the pedagogical articulation of multiple theories of learning. This articulation will allow the structure of contents to be selected according to the learning level to be developed, and will also allow the classification and selection of instructional design to comply with the objectives of a given company or organization. In short, whatever the need of the instruction designer, it can be resolved through a flexible model.

3 INDESIME: A System for Designing of Instructional Models

INDESIME is an integrated development system for the design of instructional models for e-learning, and the improvement of the e-learning courses generated with the model selected. The system is made up of two main components (Fig. 2): 1) the authoring tool, that implements the model and can generate the structure of an adaptive hypermedia course as the principle didactic resource of an online course along with other collaborating resources belonging to the LMS; and, 2) the data mining tool, that uses course information data provided by the students to detect any existing course problems, and show feed-back for improvement.

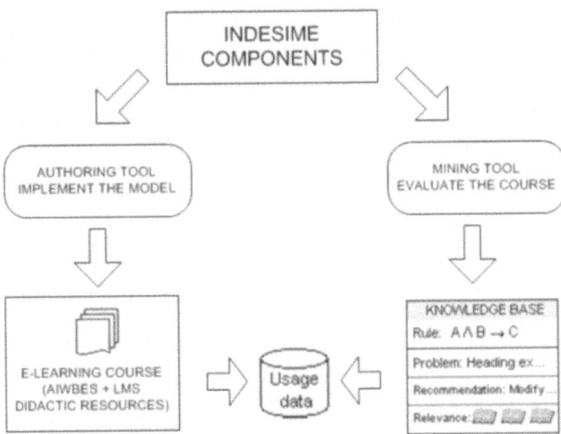

Fig. 2. INDESIME architecture

3.1 Authoring Tool Component

The authoring tool design is based on the reference model AHAM (Adaptive Hypermedia Application Model) [21]. The division into a Domain Model (DM), User Model (UM) and Adaptive Model (AM) allows a clear separation among the AHS components. In order to develop an adaptive model based on DM and UM, the course author needs to specify how the user's interaction with the system influences in the presentation of the information contained in the DM. This is done through the AM that allows manipulation of the links to adapt the contents to the user. In the specific design of INDESIME the functionality of the AHAM model has been widened to include information related to collaborative resources and communication tools in LMS like Forums, Chats, Quiz, among others. In order to do it, the authoring tool creates courses that are compatible with Moodle LMS. In fact, the generated course must executing inside the own Moodle environment.

3.1.1 The Domain Model

The domain model is divided into didactic units, which we have called Autostudy, and each one has the following modules:

Virtual classroom. It simulates student presence in the class. This module is divided into lessons and each one is divided into concepts with some type of scenarios or HTML pages. The students receive explanations about the current concepts, not only passive but also interactive explanations and afterwards, they carry out exercises helped by a virtual tutor.

Scenarios. By means of scenarios, the course designer can develop all the contents and apply what he considers to be the most adequate learning theory for the course. There are two types of scenarios: explanation and exercises. The scenarios can be created either using standard templates or by creating new ones. To design basic scenario templates, some of the main teaching models have been studied [16], so that, through basic scenarios, the author can implement an instructional model or combinations of various of them, depending on the profile of the course being created. Basic scenarios include such basic hypermedia elements as images, videos, text, and interactive animation in order to create scenarios such as tests, crosswords, gap-filling, problems, puzzle, crossword, drag-drop, among others.

Study. Students need to study and to practice when they finish the lesson. This is simulated by means of an exercise list at the end of each unit. In this module, the students will only be told if their answers are right or wrong, but they will not receive additional help unless they have a very high percentage of wrong answers.

Evaluation. This simulates an exam with an exercise list similar to that of the study section, but in this case students will not receive any help.

Glossary. The main definitions introduced in the concepts can be stored in an electronic dictionary that students can view whenever they want, except when they are doing the evaluation.

Finally, we have also included some didactic and collaborative resources in the domain model that we can find in LMSs in order to supplement the AutoStudy phase such as: document link, web link, task, forum, chat, quiz, among other tools.

3.1.2 The Adaptive Model

INDESIME implements an adaptive engine based on "link hiding" [12], so the user can only see content links that match her/his level of knowledge about the concept. This technique also avoids information overloads, limiting the size of the hyperspace. The user's level of prior knowledge is determined from initial questions at the beginning of each unit about the main topics studied in that unit. This level has been divided into three discreet values: low, medium and high. In this way, each student will see each units to his/her most appropriated level. However, it is need that the course designer has previously introduced/defined all the following data:

- The relationship between units, that is, which units are accessible from the current unit to create alternative navigation routes. When the course designer selects a unit, the program shows the others in order to establish relationships among them.
- The initial and final test of each unit.
- The difficulty level of each lesson and each exercise.

3.1.3 The User Model

The user model is formed by a set of general attributes, related to the user's identification, and a set of attributes associated to the user's progress in navigation through the course. Regarding the former, the attributes stored in an INDESIME course are one's address, age, sex and studies, as well as the user name and password to enter the course. The latter refers to how information about the student's navigation is recorded. Table 1 shows, on one hand, attributes related to adaptive hypermedia course which have been added to the Moodle database [4] as new tables. On the other hand, we can see attributes related to Moodle resources such as forum, chat, quiz, assignment, among others.

In order to simplify the development of new courses, we have developed an authoring tool, where the course's author can position each element of the domain model according to the instructional model that he/she wants to implement. Once the model is created, the author only must concentrate on preparing good contents.

Table 1. Different attributes related to user's navigation record

Level	Attribute	Description
Attributes related to adaptive hypermedia course		
Course	c_time	Time taken by the student to complete the course
	c_score	Average final score for the course
	c_attempts	Number of attempts before passing the course
Unit	u_lessons	Number of lessons in a unit
	u_time	Time taken by the student to complete a unit
	u_initial_score	Student's score in the unit pre-test
	u_final_score	Student's final score on completing the unit
	u_attempts	Number of attempts before passing the unit
Lesson	l_concepts	Number of concepts in the lesson
	l_time	Time taken by the student to complete the lesson
	l_diffic_level	Level of difficulty of the lesson
Exercise	e_time	Time taken by the student to complete the exercise
	e_score	Score obtained in the exercise
Attributes related to Moodle resources		
Forum	forum_read	Number of messages read in the forum
	forum_post	Number of messages posted in the forum
Chat	chat_messages	Number of messages sent in the chat room
Assignment	assign_score	Score in the assignment
Quiz	quiz_attempt	Total number of attempts in the quiz
	quiz_time	Total time taken in the quiz
	quiz_score	Score obtained in the quiz
Web link	link_visited	If the web link has been viewed
Doc link	doc_view	If the document has been viewed

The course structure definition in INDESIME is a compound of five steps: 1) Selection /creation of the instructional model template; 2) Definition of the course syllabus represented by units, lessons and concepts; 3) Configuration of learning objects where the user introduces scenario (web pages) parameters of each concept using graphics, text, audio or video templates; 4) Configuration of adaptive content to provide adaptation.

As we pointed out in section 3.1.2, our adaptive model implies that the course designer must specify some data. The final step is to append the learning management resources to the course syllabus according to the domain model proposed in section 3.1. The configuration parameters of each resource are the same ones that the professor would need to introduce if he/she were working directly with the LMS contained in the IMDESIME course. Therefore, what needs to be selected is a LMS that fulfils the requirements outlined in the model. We have choosen Moodle [4] due to is a well-known open-source LMS and it has been installed at universities and institutions all over the world. Introducing the parameters of Moodle LMS from the IMDESIME template has two main advantages: 1) the teacher can concentrate on preparing good content; 2) the teacher, from a sole interface, can create courses for Moodle that are adaptive, hypermedia, interactive and also take advantage of LMS.

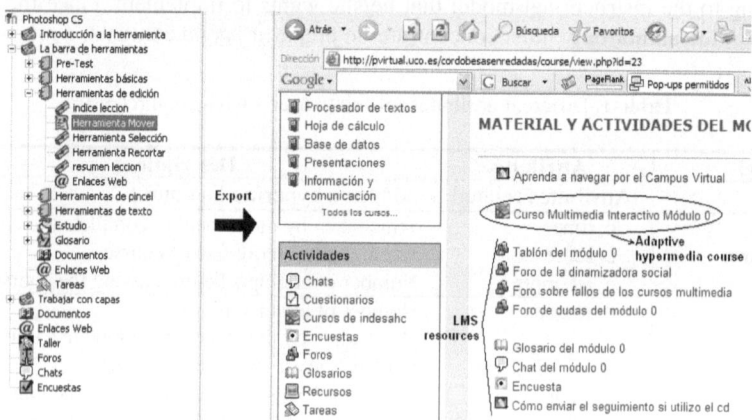

Fig. 3. A Moodle course example generated with IMDESIME

Once the concept edition is finished and all the Moodle resource parameters introduced, the course designer can publish the web-based course automatically (Figure 3). In the Moodle course generated, it is necessary to differentiate two main parts: on one hand, the adaptive hypermedia course compound for the units in the form of HTML pages, this being the main didactic resource the professor offers to the student, and on the other hand, the resources of Moodle itself, that were added automatically and supplement the IMDESIME course.

3.2 Mining Tool Component

In order to help teachers to evaluate and to improve the course generated by the authoring tool component of INDESIME, we propose to use a collaborative recommender system applied to education. We have used a hybrid recommender system based on collaborative filtering systems (CFS) and knowledge based systems (KBS) [25], in order to add a feedback stage in two ways. First of all, collaborative filtering will help to discover pertinent relationships among different teachers with similar profiles, each working with their own databases. The teacher profile is represented as a three-dimensional vector related with the following characteristic of his/her course: Topic (the area of knowledge, e.g. Computer Science or Biology); Level (level of the course, e.g. University, High School, Elementary or Special Education); and Difficulty (the difficulty of the course, e.g., Low or High). These similarities or useful relationships will be available to other teachers to assess in terms of applicability and relevance. Secondly, the knowledge database will be strengthened with experiences that, due to their significance, satisfy the needs of many teachers and therefore can give rise to increasingly effective recommendations.

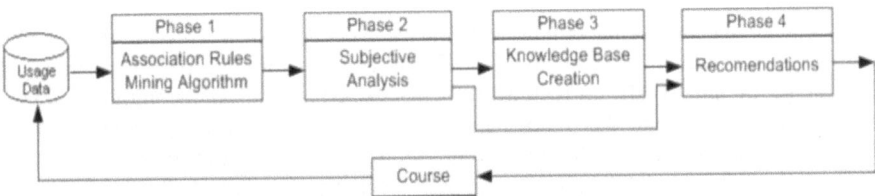

Fig. 4. Main phases of mining tool component

The main phases used in the mining tool architecture are (Figure 4):

- **Association rules mining:** This phase aims to find association rules on the data set generated as the students complete the course. Association rules are one of the most popular ways of representing discovered knowledge and describe a close correlation between frequent items in a database [22]. There are many association rule discovery algorithms but Apriori [23] is the first and foremost among them. However, in this phase we use an improved version of Apriori, called Predictive Apriori [24] because it does not require the user to specify such parameters as the minimum support threshold or confidence values; instead of this, the algorithm aims to find the N best association rules, which is a more intuitive parameter for a non-expert in data mining. Once the data has been pre-processed, it is used as input in the Predictive Apriori algorithm, the nucleus of this phase. Also, the teacher could select specific data and attributes in order to restrict the search domain. The output of this module (rules found) is then analyzed by the subjective analysis module.
- **Subjective analysis:** The association rules discovered by the mining algorithm must be evaluated to decide if they are relevant or not. This phase uses a subjective rule evaluation measure [25] to classify the rules as being expected or unexpected, comparing them with the rules stored in the knowledge base.
- **Knowledge base creation:** This phase combines collaborative filtering techniques with knowledge-based techniques to create and to manage the rules repository. The information in the knowledge base is stored in form of tuples (rule-problem-recommendation-relevance) which are classified according to a specific course profile. In order to avoid the cold-start issue of collaborative filtering systems, a group

of experts propose the first tuples of the repository and also vote on those tuples proposed by other experts. On the other hand, teachers could discover new tuples and these must be validated by the experts before being inserted in the repository.

- **Recommendations:** The expected rules found in phase 2 join the more intuitive tuples format mentioned in phase 3, and are then used in this last phase to show the teacher, more often than not a non-expert in data mining, some possible solutions to problems detected in the course. The teacher analyzes the recommendation and he determines if it is relevant or not. More information about recommendation can be consulted in [25].

4 Experimental Results

The effectiveness of INDESIME system can be measure from two points of view: 1) the perspective of the students with respect to how the instructional model implemented with the authoring component and delivery within a Moodle environment, influence the student's final results, and 2) the teacher's perspective, in terms of the percentage of apparently corrected problems, based on initial recommendations of mining tool component, that reappear in successive courses with different groups of students. We have focused the next experiments on the first point of view and showing how the information discovered can help teacher to improve the generated course. However, a more detailed experiment proposed by the authors about how to measure the effectiveness of recommendations can be consulted in [25].

In order to evaluate the instructional model and the authoring tool component, we have compared two courses which covered the same topic but, while one implemented using INDESIME with only online classes, the other one was delivered in face-to-face classes, called from here, TRADITIONAL learning style. During the 2004-2005 academic year, a pilot scheme was run in Spain called "*Cordobesas Enredadas*", aimed at increasing the technological literacy of women in rural areas. The experiment was based on 90 students from 3 towns in the Province of Cordoba. The following results include comparisons of the two course formats in the areas of course interaction and student satisfaction.

The course topics were based around the European Computer Driving Licence, which is based on the Linux operating system (Guadalinex distribution) and Open Office package (OpenOffice.org). These courses were officially approved by the University of Cordoba. The titles of the courses were as follows:

C1. Basic concepts of information technology
C2. Using the computer and managing files
C3. Word processing
C4. Spreadsheets
C5. DataBases / filing systems
C6. Presentation and drawing
C7. Information network services

The University of Cordoba and the Provincial Government signed a collaboration agreement for 2004-2005 in order to improve this pilot scheme. The project had the same title "*Cordobesas Enredadas*". The experiment included 47 towns in the

Province of Cordoba. Using the latest version of INDESIME, we have developed seven online courses corresponding to the ECDL. In Figure 5, we show the results comparing both approaches the TRADITIONAL or INDESIME. For this new experiment, we took into account the same towns that had participated in the previous experiment in order to compare the results.

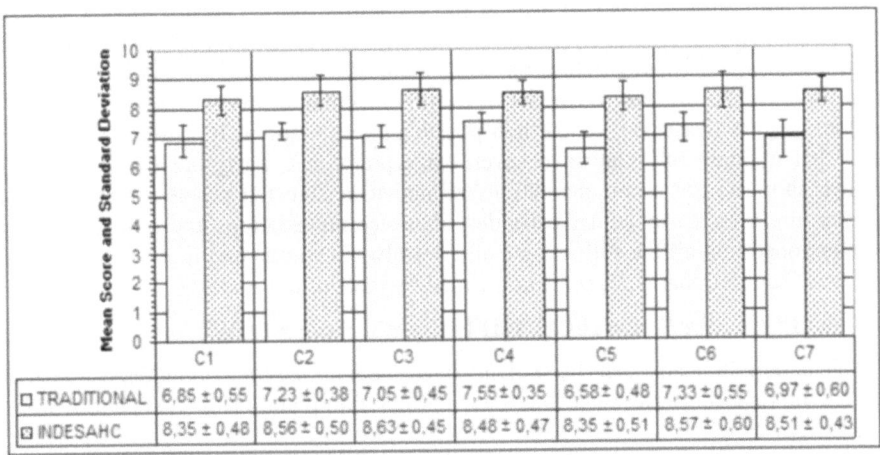

	C1	C2	C3	C4	C5	C6	C7
□ TRADITIONAL	6,85 ± 0,55	7,23 ± 0,38	7,05 ± 0,45	7,55±0,35	6,58± 0,48	7,33 ± 0,55	6,97 ± 0,60
□ INDESAHC	8,35 ± 0,48	8,56 ± 0,50	8,63±0,45	8,48 ± 0,47	8,35 ±0,51	8,57 ± 0,60	8,51 ± 0,43

Fig. 5. Experimental results for *"Cordobesas Enredadas"* project 2004-2005

By examining the mean values and standard deviation of the final score for the different courses, we observed that the new approach yielded higher mean scores than the traditional method. Furthermore, the p-values (< 0.05) calculated for each course show there was a significant difference between the means; hence we have concluded that the teaching-learning method used in the new courses is responsible for the difference.

4.1 Using Association Rule Mining to Improve the Generated Courses

The teacher or course author has a crucial role in our evaluation methodology because he/she can also guide the data mining search for association rules by imposing some restrictions or filters. The teacher can use his own knowledge and experience in education. For example, he/she can decide to use data about one specific unit, lesson or even a group of students, and whether or not to use information about times, score or participation in order to form rule antecedents and consequents.

As we have mentioned previously, our objective is to show a group of useful rules to the teacher, so that he/she can make decisions about which changes would improve the performance of the course. From a semantic point of view, our resulting rules match the following pattern:

IF *Time\Score\Participation* **AND ... THEN** *Time\Score\Participation*

Where *Time*, *Score* and *Participation* are thereby generic attributes referring to: the reading time for the course, units, lessons and exercises (HIGH, MEDIUM and LOW values); information on students' scores in the test and activities' questions

(HIGH, MEDIUM and LOW values); and lastly, participation refers to how the students have used the collaborative resources such as forum and chat (HIGH, MEDIUM and LOW values). Based on the rules discovered, the teacher can decide which of the relationships expressed are desirable or not, and whether or not to apply the recommendation in order to strengthen or weaken the relationship (namely changing or modifying the contents, structure and adaptation of the course, etc.).

The relationships that are shown in the rules discovered can refer to the course, units, lessons, or scenarios of concepts (namely instructional and activity pages related to concepts). Next, we describe some examples of the general patterns found in rules of interest, offering the teacher useful information about how to improve a course. We also describe some of their possible interpretations. It is important to highlight that a single rule can have several interpretations. Therefore the system will always show all the recommendations related to a detected problem, and it is the teacher him/herself who actually decides what recommendations to use. It should also be mentioned that all the following examples always correspond to rules with a high degree of support, that is, they are confirmed by most of the students.

IF *ExerciseTime* = HIGH **THEN** *ExerciseScore* = LOW

This pattern indicates that the students have spent a long time doing the exercise although the final score has been low. Two possible interpretations of this pattern are:

1) The wording of this exercise could be incorrect or ambiguous, giving place to several interpretations. In this case the teacher can correct the exercise's wording or eliminate it altogether if necessary.
2) The exercise is quite difficult and for this reason the students spend relatively more time than on other exercises, resulting in a lower score. In this case, the teacher will determine if the exercise is or is not in accord with the level of difficulty of the lesson.
3) The students were weak on prerequisite skills. In this case, the teacher should consult other higher level recommendations, such as the level obtained in the unit pre-test, in order to confirm that interpretation. From here on, we will present only those interpretations that could be difficult to detect and possibly to correct.

An example of this type of rule is:

IF (e_time [25] = HIGH) **THEN** (e_score[25] = LOW), supp. = 0.91, accur. = 0.82

This rule means that if students took a long time to complete exercise number 25, then they got a low score in this exercise. This rule can indicate that there is a problem with this specific exercise, which was part of the: "application use" subject; "first steps with the word processor" lesson; and "renaming and saving a document" concept. The exercise was an interactive video scenario in which the student had to simulate the necessary steps for completing an activity using the mouse. In this specific case, the question was confirmed to be ambiguous and interpretable in several ways, so the wording was changed. Other rules with a similar pattern were also found in multiple-choice or linking type questions.

IF *UnitForumParticipation* = LOW **THEN** *UniFinalScore* = HIGH

This pattern indicates that there was not much participation in the unit forum although the students obtained a high final score for the unit in question. Three possible interpretations of this pattern are:

1) The forum is not necessary for this unit, so the teacher can eliminate it.
2) There are problems concerning the tutors responsible for forum maintenance, so the teacher should analyze the causes of these problems in detail.
3) Strong students are more autonomous while weaker students are more inclined to use and consult the forum.

An example of this type of rule is:

IF (u_forum_read [2] = LOW) **AND** (u_forum_post [2] = LOW)
THEN (u_final_score [1] = HIGH), supp. = 0.85, accur. = 0.83

This rule shows that if students send or read few messages in forum 2 (unit 1), then they get a high score for this unit. This rule shows that the forum may not be necessary or that there were problems with it. This type of rule raises the issue about whether the forum is really necessary at certain levels of the domain hierarchy. In fact, the forum was removed in this case.

5 Conclusions and Future Work

In this paper, a system to develop instructional models for e-learning has been designed and implemented. This system integrates adaptive hypermedia techniques with the new communication and collaborative tools coming from learning management systems. Once implemented, and from there on, e-learning courses can be developed that, moreover, can be evaluated and improved using association rules mining. To make an efficient use of the model, the following didactic resources are included:

1) Didactic units, in order to create an adaptive hypermedia course based on the technique of hidden links, where the author can specify a set of prerequisites for access from one unit to another in order to organize the course in a tree, a net, a spiral, etc., according to what is considered most appropriate. Within each didactic unit there is a set of hypermedia scenarios that the author will use, depending on the type of course and the learning strategy preferred.
2) Collaborative Resources like Forums, Chats, Questionnaires, etc., that the author can include at course level or with each didactic unit.

Furthermore, an authoring tool has been developed for helping to non-programmer expert to create/maintain e-learning courses compatible with Moodle based on his/her instructional model. Association rule mining has been also proposed for providing feed-back to course author with useful information about how to improve the generated courses using the students' usage information. Experimental results, surveys and interviews have demonstrated the effectiveness of the system proposed, especially with technology-based courses using such equipment as computers.

Our future work will mainly focus on increasing the types of didactic resources available, to include a greater number of learning theories, as well as using standard metadata for e-learning like SCORM [26] that allows the creation and maintenance of a common knowledge base with a common vocabulary that can be shared by different communities of instructors or authors of e-learning courses.

Acknowledgments

The authors gratefully acknowledge the financial support provided by the Spanish department of Research under TIN2008-06681-C06-03 and P08-TIC-3720 Projects.

References

1. WebCT Inc. Learning management system WebCT (2005),
   http://www.webct.com/
2. BlackBoard Inc. Learning management system BlackBoard (2005),
   http://www.blackboard.com/
3. WBT Systems. Learning management system TopClass (2005),
   http://www.wbtsystems.com/
4. Dougiamas, M., et al.: Course management system MOODLE (2005),
   http://www.moodle.org/
5. Leidhold, W., et al.: Learning management system ILIAS (2005),
   http://www.ilias.de/ios/index-e.html
6. Gay, G., et al.: Learning management system ATutor (2005),
   http://www.atutor.ca/
7. Brusilovsky, P.: Adaptive and Intelligent Web-based Educational Systems. International Journal of Artificial Intelligence in Education 13, 159–169 (2003)
8. Brusilovsky, P., Schwarz, E., Weber, G.: ELM-ART: An intelligent tutoring system on World Wide Web. In: Lesgold, A.M., Frasson, C., Gauthier, G. (eds.) ITS 1996. LNCS, vol. 1086, pp. 261–269. Springer, Heidelberg (1996)
9. Brusilovsky, P., Schwarz, E., Weber, G.: ELM-ART: An intelligent tutoring system on World Wide Web. In: Third International Conference on Intelligent Tutoring Systems, pp. 261–269 (1995)
10. Brusilovsky, P., Eklund, J., Schwarz, E.: Web-based education for all: A tool for developing adaptive courseware. Computer Networks and ISDN Systems 30(1-7), 291–300 (1998)
11. Carro, R.M., Pulido, E., Rodrígues, P.: TANGOW. Computer Science Report, Eindhoven University of Technology. pp. 49–57 (1999)
12. De Bra, P., Calvi, L.: AHA! An Open Adaptive Hypermedia Architecture. The New Review of Hypermedia and Multimedia, vol. 4, pp. 115–139. Taylor Graham Publishers (1998)
13. Weber, G.: ART-WEB. University of Trier, Trier (1999)
14. Romero, C., Ventura, S.: Educational data mining: A survey from 1995 to 2005. International Journal Experts Systems with Applications 33(1), 135–146 (2007)
15. Reigeluth, C.: A new paradigm of instructional theory, vol. II. Lawrence Erlbaum Associates Inc., Mahwah (1999)
16. Gros, B., et al.: Instructional Design and the Authoring of Multimedia and Hypermedia Systems: Does a Marriage make Sense? Educational Technology 1(37), 48–56 (1997)
17. D'Angelo, G.: From didactics to e-didactics. E-learning paradigms, models and techniques. Liguori Editori (2007)

18. Guardià, L., Sangrà, A.: Instructional design and learning objects; towards a model for the design of online learning evaluation activities. In: Proceedings of the First Pluri-Disciplinary Symposium on Design, Evaluation and Description of Reusable Learning Contents, Guadalajara, Spain (2004)
19. Chiappe, A.: Modelo de diseño instruccional basado en objetos de aprendizaje. Universidad de la Sabana, Colombia (2006),
    http://oas.unisabana.edu.co/files/MDIBOA.pdf
20. Advanced Distributed Learning. Shareable content object reference model (SCORM): The SCORM overview (2005), http://www.adlnet.org
21. Wu, H., Houben, G.J., De Bra, P.: AHAM: A Dexter-based Reference Model for Adaptive Hypermedia. In: Proceedings of the ACM Conference on Hypertext and Hypermedia, Darmstadt, Germany, pp. 147–156 (1999)
22. Zheng, Z., et al.: Real world performance of association rules. In: Proceedings of the Sixth ACM-SIGKDD (2001)
23. Agrawal, R., Srikant, R.: Fast algorithms for mining association rules. Proceedings of 20th VLDB CVonf. Santiago de Chile (1996)
24. Scheffer, T.: Finding Association Rules That Trade Support Optimally against Confidence. Intelligent Data Analysis 9(4), 381–395 (2005)
25. García, E., Romero, C., Ventura, S., de Castro, C.: An architecture for making recommendations to courseware authors through association rule mining and collaborative filtering. UMUAI: User Modelling and User Adapted Interaction 19(1-2), 99–132 (2009)
26. Advanced Distributed Learning. Shareable content object reference model (SCORM): The SCORM overview (2009), http://www.adlnet.org

Sensors Model Student Self Concept in the Classroom

David G. Cooper[1], Ivon Arroyo[1], Beverly Park Woolf[1], Kasia Muldner[2], Winslow Burleson[2], and Robert Christopherson[2]

[1] University of Massachusetts, Department of Computer Science,
140 Governors Drive, Amherst MA 01003, USA
dcooper@cs.umass.edu
[2] Arizona State University, School of Computing and Informatics,
Tempe AZ 85287,USA

Abstract. In this paper we explore findings from three experiments that use minimally invasive sensors with a web based geometry tutor to create a user model. Minimally invasive sensor technology is mature enough to equip classrooms of up to 25 students with four sensors at the same time while using a computer based intelligent tutoring system. The sensors, which are on each student's chair, mouse, monitor, and wrist, provide data about posture, movement, grip tension, arousal, and facially expressed mental states. This data may provide adaptive feedback to an intelligent tutoring system based on an individual student's affective states. The experiments show that when sensor data supplements a user model based on tutor logs, the model reflects a larger percentage of the students' self-concept than a user model based on the tutor logs alone. The models are further expanded to classify four ranges of emotional self-concept including frustration, interest, confidence, and excitement with over 78% accuracy. The emotional predictions are a first step for intelligent tutor systems to create sensor based personalized feedback for each student in a classroom environment. Bringing sensors to our children's schools addresses real problems of students' relationship to mathematics as they are learning the subject.

1 Introduction

Traditionally, the User Model of an Intelligent Tutoring System (ITS) consists of registration information with or without statistics about interactions with the ITS [1,2]. Registration information often includes age, gender, class standing, teacher, and other static information about learners. A limitation of this approach is that the only dynamic information that the ITS uses is based on the performance of the students. With the use of non-invasive sensors, we have the opportunity to enhance user models with sensor data that is a natural byproduct of the student's interaction with the ITS. Though the cost of such sensors has previously made them less accessible for classroom deployment, recent strides have been made to address this limitation. Arizona State University (ASU), in

G.-J. Houben et al. (Eds.): UMAP 2009, LNCS 5535, pp. 30–41, 2009.

collaboration with the Affective Computing Group (ACG) at MIT, has developed 30 lower-cost versions of four sensors that have shown promise for their ability to detect elements of students' emotional expression. These sensors include a pressure sensitive mouse, a pressure sensitive chair, a skin conductance wristband, and a camera based facial expression recognition system that incorporates a computational framework that aims to infer a user's state of mind. At UMass Amherst, we have built on ASU's work by integrating the sensors and an Emotional Query intervention module with a traditional ITS user interaction based models to obtain the students' reported emotions as they interact with the tutor. This enables the User Model System (UMS) to compare sensor readings at the time of the emotional queries.

Ultimately we plan to have a UMS that models the student's interaction with an ITS in real-time and enables the ITS to intelligently tailor its behavior to a given student's needs. By personalizing the student's experience, the ITS can keep the student engaged and maintain or increase the student's interest and confidence in the subject. [3] is an example of having a character as part of the tutor giving non-verbal feedback, [4] is an example of a tutor that changes its feedback based on the tutor's emotional state in response to the student's emotion. For instance, a positive student emotional state elicits happiness in the tutor, which in turn rewards the student. In order to create the desired UMS, we have developed a platform comprised of three functional interacting components. These are (1) a sensor system for processing and integrating the sensor data described in Sec. 4, (2) a pedagogical engine for tutoring the student and collecting tutor data described in Sec. 2, and (3) a User Model system for integrating the sensor and tutor data to create a model of the student. We conducted three experiments using this framework in order to determine which sensor features have the best utility in terms of modeling students' perceived emotional state.

This paper describes our progress. Section 2 describes the Wayang Tutor and the student features that are used for the model. Section 3 describes related work. Section 4 describes the sensors that we use, their history, and the features for input to the User Model. Section 5 describes the integration of the sensor and tutor features. Section 6 describes the three studies performed to collect data for the user models. Finally, Section 7 discusses how the model can be used and ways to improve on the model we created.

2   The Tutor: Wayang Outpost

Our test-bed application for the experiments we describe in Sec. 6 was Wayang Outpost, a multimedia Intelligent Tutoring System (ITS) for geometry [5]. The tutoring software is adaptive in that it iterates through different topic sections (e.g. pythagorean theorem). Within each topic section, Wayang adjusts the difficulty of problems provided depending on past student performance. Students are presented with a problem and asked to choose the solution from a list of multiple choice options (typically four or five) as shown in Fig. 1.

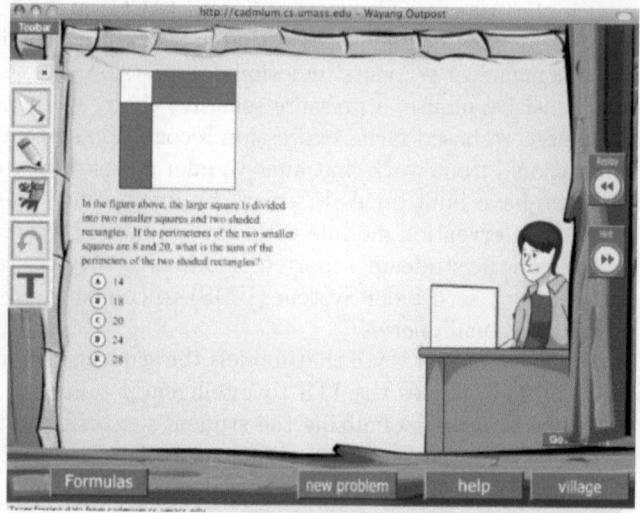

Fig. 1. An example problem presented by the Wayang system. Jake is on the lower right corner. The Hint Toolbar is on the right.

As students solve problems, they may ask the tutor for one or several multimedia hints, consisting of text messages, audio and animations. The software includes gendered learning companions that are actual "companions" only: they don't provide help; instead, they encourage students to use the help function; they have the capability of expressing emotions; and they emphasize the importance of effort and perseverance. Wayang has been used with thousands of students in the past and has demonstrated improved learning gains in state standard exams [5].

Wayang collects student interaction features in order to predict each student's level of effort on the problems presented. These features, described in Table 1, are derived from the tutor data that is sent to the UMS. The majority of the tutor features could be extracted from other tutor systems with similar structure including a clear delineation of when attempts are made to answer the problem. Some features of Wayang are more specific, such as the number of hints or whether a particular gendered learning companion was used.

3   Related Work

There are a number of systems that already exist that either use similar sensors, detect similar affective states, or incorporate both tutor data and sensor data in order to model the student's self reported emotion.

[6] uses a number of sensors to detect facial expressions, physiological features (heart rate, temperature, and skin conductance), and speech signals. The experiment uses 32 students simultaneously. Their application is to elicit emotional

Table 1. The nine tutor features below are selected along with the sensor features by using regression models to predict confidence, frustration, excitement, and interest. This table lists each tutor feature with an abbreviation and a definition.

Feature	Abbreviation	Definition
Solved On First	TsolF	Student's first attempt was correct.
Seconds to First Attempt	TsecF	Time in seconds to the first attempt.
Seconds to Solved	TsecS	Time in seconds to a correct attempt.
Number Incorrect	TNumInc	The number of incorrect responses.
Number of Hints	Thint	The number of hints the student selected.
Learning Companion (LC)	TLC	A value of 1 for LC and 0 for No LC
Group	TGroup	2 for Jake, 1 for Jane, 0 for Neither
Time In Session	TsesT	Time student has spent on interactive problems in the current session.
Time In Tutor	TtutT	Time student has spent on problems since the first use of the Tutor.

responses by the presentation of images rather than from using a tutor system. The emotions that they model are fear, anger, and frustration.

[7,8] use a 3-D learning environment as their tutoring system. The systems monitor heart-rate and skin conductance in addition to the student-tutor interactions. [7] creates a model of frustration, while, [8] creates a model of self-efficacy, i.e. the student's belief in producing a correct answer.

Other work such as [4] does not use sensors at all, but only uses self reports to determine emotional state. They use three emotional ranges to model the student: boredom vs. curiosity, distress vs. enthusiasm, and anxiety vs. confidence. With the model of the student, they then create a model of their tutor to have emotional states that guide the tutor's responses. The focus of this system is the repair rather than the detection of emotional states.

Much of the past research has focused on small populations of students or lab studies, while our research uses large groups of students in real school settings. This is relevant because much research has shown that students lose interest and self-confidence in math over the course of the K-12 school system [9,10,11]. Bringing sensors to our children's schools addresses real problems of students' relationship to mathematics as they are learning the subject. This brings new tools to address their frustration, anxiety and disinterest/boredom while learning.

4   The Sensors

4.1   Sensor History

The sensors used in this study are similar to sensors that have been used in previous studies done by the Affective Computing Group (ACG) at MIT, but we have invested considerable effort on decreasing the overall production cost and improving the non-invasive nature of the sensors. Below we describe how our sensors compare to earlier sensors as well as some of the past uses of such sensors.

Skin Conductance Bracelet. The current system used in our research employs the next generation of HandWave electronics [12], providing greater reliability, lower power requirements through wireless RFID transmission, and a smaller form. This smaller form was redesigned to minimize the visual impact and increase the wearable aspects of previous versions. ASU integrated and tested these electronic components into a wearable package suitable for students in classrooms. Our version reports at 1Hz.

Pressure Sensitive Mouse. ACG developed the pressure sensitive mouse. It uses six pressure sensors embedded in the surface of the mouse to detect the tension in a user's grip and has been used to infer elements of a user's frustration level [13]. Our endeavors replicated ACG's pressure sensitive mouse through a production of 30 units. The new design of the mouse minimized the changes made to the physical appearances of the original mouse in order to maintain a visually non-invasive sensor, while maintaining functionality.

Pressure Sensitive Chair. The chair sensor system was developed at ASU using a series of six force sensitive resistors as pressure sensors dispersed strategically in the seat and back of a readily available seat cover cushion. It is a greatly simplified version of the Tek-Scan Pressure system (costing around $10,000) used in [14,15]. This posture chair sensor was developed at ASU at an approximate cost of $500 per chair for a production volume of 30 chairs.

Mental State Camera. The studies in [14,15] utilized IBM Research's Blue-Eyes camera hardware. This is special purpose hardware for facial feature detection. In our current research we are using a standard web-camera to obtain 30fps at 320x240 pixels. The camera is placed on the monitor of each student's computer. This is coupled with the MindReader library from [16] using a Java Native Interface (JNI) wrapper developed at UMass. The interface starts a version of the MindReader software, and can be queried at any time to acquire the most recent mental state values that have been computed by the library. In the version used in the experiments, only the six mental state features were available, but in future versions we will have the Facial Action Units available as well. These six mental features have a 65% to 89% accuracy with 5 out of the six features reported at above 76% accuracy.

4.2   Sensor Features

In order to create effective user models, we want to select the best feature set for our classification of the user's emotional self concept. Given that we don't have a huge number of examples, it is important to use as few features as possible while still receiving the value from each sensor. Thus the data from each sensor has been aggregated in the case of the Mouse and the Chair, and processed into five mental states, in the case of the Camera. We are using the raw Skin Conductance values for the Bracelet. The sensor features that are used for the studies are summarized in Table 2. These are used in conjunction with tutor features described in Sec. 2.

Table 2. The ten sensor features below are summarized by their mean, standard deviation, min and max values and then these 40 summarized features are selected by using regression models to predict confidence, frustration, excitement, and interest. This table defines the abbreviations for each feature.

Source	Feature	Mean	Std. Dev.	Min	Max
Camera	Agreeing	CmeanA	CdevA	CminA	CmaxA
Camera	Concentrating	CmeanC	CdevC	CminC	CmaxC
Camera	Thinking	CmeanT	CdevT	CminT	CmaxT
Camera	Interested	CmeanI	CdevI	CminI	CmaxI
Camera	Unsure	CmeanU	CdevU	CminU	CmaxU
Mouse	Pressure	MmeanP	MdevP	MminP	MmaxP
Seat	Sit Forward	SmeanF	SdevF	SminF	SmaxF
Seat	Net Seat Change	SmeanS	SdevS	SminS	SmaxS
Seat	Net Back Change	SmeanB	SdevB	SminB	SmaxB
Bracelet	Skin Conductance	BmeanC	BdevC	BminC	BmaxA

The classifiers in [14] used a similar sensor set in order to predict whether a user would click a button indicating frustration. They used the mean values computed over the previous 150 second window from when clicking the frustrated button. Fourteen sensor features were used to make four classifier systems using data from 24 students. Each system performed better than a classifier always picking no frustration, but no classifier was more than 80% accurate.

In addition to predicting frustration, our model is meant to predict excitement, interest, and confidence. The sensor features considered in our analysis are described below.

Mouse Feature. From the six pressure values from the mouse, each having the range $[0, 1023]$, we compute the following feature:

$$mousePressure = \frac{\left(\begin{array}{l} leftMouseFront + leftMouseRear + \\ middleMouseFront + middleMouseRear + \\ rightMouseFront + rightMouseRear \end{array}\right)}{1023}, \quad (1)$$

which gives a potential range from $[0, 6]$, but empirically has the range of $[0, 2.5]$ in the High School (HS) study, and $[0, 1]$ in the two other studies.

Chair Features. We compute three features from the 6 chair sensors. The first two are based on the most useful features from [17]. These are the net change in pressure of the seat, and the net change in pressure of the back:

$$netSeatChange[t] = \left| \begin{array}{l} LeftSeat[t-1] - leftSeat[t] + \\ MiddleSeat[t-1] - middleSeat[t] + \\ RightSeat[t-1] - rightSeat[t] \end{array} \right|, \quad (2)$$

$$netBackChange = \begin{vmatrix} lastLeftBack & - & leftBack & + \\ lastMiddleBack & - & middleBack & + \\ lastRightBack & - & rightBack & \end{vmatrix}, \qquad (3)$$

The third chair feature is meant to determine if the student is sitting forward. From the three pressure values from the back of the chair, each having the range $[0, 1023]$, we compute the Sit Forward feature as follows:

$$sitForward = \begin{cases} 0 & \text{if } \begin{aligned} &leftBack & > & \quad 200 & \text{or} \\ &middleBack & > & \quad 200 & \text{or} \\ &rightBack & > & \quad 200 & \end{aligned} \\ 1 & \text{if } \begin{aligned} &200 & >= & leftBack & > -1 \text{ and} \\ &200 & >= & middleBack & > -1 \text{ and} \\ &200 & >= & rightBack & > -1 \end{aligned} \\ NA & \text{otherwise} \end{cases}, \qquad (4)$$

where NA is treated as no data.

Bracelet Feature. There are two values that we obtain from the wrist sensor, one is the battery voltage to inform us when the battery charge is low, and the other is the skin conductance in Microsiemens. Since there was no need to reduce the number of features, we processed basic statistics on the raw sensor values. In the future we plan to examine more sophisticated use of the skin conductance data such as the methods described in [8].

Mental State Camera Features. Of the six mental state features that the MindReader software identifies, we left out the disagree state, since agree and disagree are opposites. The five features we are left with are agreeing, concentrating, interested, thinking, and unsure. These mental states have a range from $[0, 1]$ as they are confidence values.

5   Feature Integration

In our framework, each feature source from each student is a separate stream of data. Hence we have five streams of data that each report asynchronously and at different rates. In order to merge all of the data sources, the wrist ID from each student, and a time of the report was needed from each source. An example of one client connected to our User Model Framework is shown in Fig. 2.

In our experiments, we used the logs rather than the sensor streams, since the streams are not yet informing a user model. In addition, the tutor does not yet create a stream of tutor data. Instead we used a database query to obtain the relevant tutor information, and fed it to the User Model System with the four sensor sources in order to time align the data and merge it with the correct student. The result is a database table with a row for every time stamp and wrist ID pair, and a column for each reported sensor value and tutor data value. Each cell in a row represents the latest report of the data source. If the data

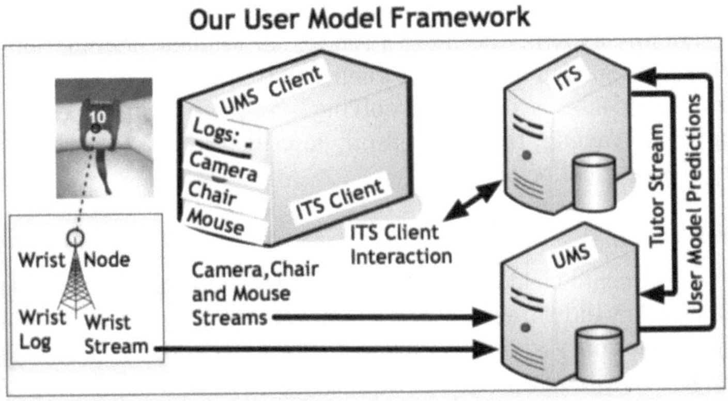

Our User Model Framework

Fig. 2. A student at the client computer puts on a bracelet and starts the two client programs indicating the wrist ID of the bracelet. The bracelet sends Skin Conductance data to the Wrist Node, then logs bracelet data from all of the students in the classroom. The User Model System (UMS) receives the bracelet data through the Wrist Stream. The UMS client performs the same task as the Wrist Node for each of the other three sensor sources. The ITS logs student interactions, and sends Tutor Data to the UMS. The data is time synced based on the client's system time. The UMS uses all available streams of data to make user predictions to improve the ITS Client interaction.

source has never reported or has not reported since the last tutor login or logout event with a corresponding wrist ID, then the value is -1 until the data source reports again. In this way the wrist IDs can be used by more than one student at separate time intervals, and the system will continue to work.

6 Experiments

We conducted three studies during Fall 2008 using our sensor system with Wayang Outpost. The HS study involved 35 students in a public high school in Massachusetts; the UMASS study involved 29 students in the University of Massachusetts; the AZ study involved 29 undergraduate students from Arizona State University. In the HS and UMASS studies, students used the software as part of their regular math class for 4-5 days, as it covered topics in the class. The AZ study was a lab study, where students would come to a lab in the university and use the software for one single session. Wayang worked the same way for all students, as introduced in Sec. 2, except for the fact that a student could be randomly assigned the female learning companion (Jane), the male learning companion (Jake) or no learning companion. In order to gather information on students' emotions, Wayang prompted students to report how they were feeling (e.g., *"how [interested/excited/confident/frustrated] do you feel right now?"*). Students answered this prompt by choosing one item from a five-point scale, where a three corresponded to a neutral value and the ends were labeled with extreme values (e.g., "*I feel anxious/ very confident*"). The queried emotion was randomly chosen, obtaining a report per student per emotion for most subjects. Wayang queried students on their emotions every five minutes, but did not interrupt students as they were solving a problem. During each student's interaction with Wayang, the four sensors described in Sec. 4 gathered data on his or her physiological responses.

6.1   Results

The three experiments yielded the results of 588 Emotional Queries from 80 students that include valid data from at least one sensor. The queries were separated into the four emotion variables as follows: 149 were about confidence/anxiety, 163 were about excitement/depression, 135 were about interest/boredom, and 141 were about frustration/no frustration. 16 of the student responses gave no answer to the Emotional Query. These results were used as examples for the Regression and the training and testing of the classification models.

In order to select a subset of the available features, a Stepwise Linear Regression was done with each of the emotions as the dependent variable, and tutor and sensor features as the independent variables. Since some students had missing sensor data, separate models were run pairing the Tutor Features with Sensor Features from one sensor at a time, and then finally with all of the Sensor Features. Results from the regression in Table 4 show that the best models for confidence, frustration, and excitement came from the subset of examples where all of the sensor data was available, and the best model for interest came from the subset of examples with mouse data available.

Table 3. Each cell corresponds to a linear model to predict emotion self-reports. Models were generated using Stepwise Regression, and variables entered into the model are shown in Table 4. The top row lists the feature sets that are available. The left column lists the emotional self-reports being predicted. R values correspond to the fit of the model (best fit models for each emotion are in bold). N values vary because some students are missing data for a sensor.

	Tutor only	Camera +Tutor	Seat + Tutor	Wrist + Tutor	Mouse + Tutor	All Sensors +Tutor	Best Sensor
Confident	$R = 0.44$ $N = 143$	$R = 0.61$ $N = 77$	$R = 0.48$ $N = 115$	$R = 0.40$ $N = 106$	$R = 0.48$ $N = 107$	**$R = 0.63$** **$N = 68$**	Camera
Frustrated	$R = 0.55$ $N = 138$	$R = 0.60$ $N = 78$	$R = 0.61$ $N = 105$	$R = 0.55$ $N = 109$	$R = 0.59$ $N = 102$	**$R = 0.62$** **$N = 67$**	Camera
Excited	$R = 0.39$ $N = 154$	$R = 0.40$ $N = 74$	$R = 0.45$ $N = 122$	$R = 0.39$ $N = 106$	$R = 0.45$ $N = 119$	**$R = 0.56$** **$N = 64$**	Seat+ Camera
Interested	$R = 0.42$ $N = 133$	$R = 0.56$ $N = 75$	$R = 0.53$ $N = 107$	$R = 0.36$ $N = 101$	**$R = 0.67$** **$N = 102$**	$R = 0.66$ $N = 62$	Mouse

Table 4 shows the features selected for each of the linear models. Looking at the best fitting models, highlighted in bold, it is interesting to see that at most two of the sensor sources and at most five of the available features are significant.

Table 4. This table lists the variables that the Stepwise Regression method selected as relevant, for each of the regression models in Table 3. Each of these features significantly contribute to the prediction of emotion self-reports ($p < 0.01$), and are listed in order of relevance (The feature at the top is the best predictor.) The abbreviations of these features are defined in Tables 1 and 2.

	Tutor context only	Camera + Tutor	Seat + Tutor	Wrist + Tutor	Mouse + Tutor	All Sensors + Tutor
Confident	TsolF Thint	TNumInc CminT CmaxC	TNumInc TsolF SdevF	TNumInc	TNumInc TsolF TsesT	**TNumInc** **CmaxC** **CmaxT**
Frustrated	TLC TNumInc Thint TsesT	TLC Thint TsesT CmaxI CminT	TLC TsesT TNumInc Thint	TLC Thint TsesT TNumInc	TLC TNumInc TsesT Thint TsecS	**CdevU** **TLC** **TsesT** **CminT** **Thint**
Excited	TGroup TNumInc	TNumInc CmeanI	TNumInc TGroup	TGroup TNumInc	TGroup TNumInc	**SmeanS** **CminI** **SmeanF**
Interested	TGroup	TGroup CminI Thint	TGroup	TGroup	**TGroup** **Thint** **MdevP** **MmaxP**	TGroup Thint CminI MmaxP

Table 5. This shows results of the best classifier of each emotional response. Accuracy of no classifier is a prediction that the emotional state is always not high. Values in parentheses include the middle values in the testing set as negative examples.

Classifier	True Pos.	False Pos.	True Neg.	False Neg.	Accuracy (%)	Accuracy (%) No Classifier
Confident All	28(28)	5(24)	10(16)	1(1)	86.36(63.77)	34.09(57.97)
Frustrated All	3(3)	0(0)	46(58)	7(7)	87.5(89.7)	82.14(85.29)
Excited Wrist	25(25)	9(37)	25(40)	5(5)	78.1(60.7)	53.12(71.96)
Interested Mouse	24(25)	4(19)	28(53)	7(7)	82.54(74.76)	50.79(69.90)

6.2   Cross Validation of the Linear Models

In order for the User Model system to give feedback to the ITS, the available sensor and tutor features can be put into a classifier and report when a user is likely to report a high value of a particular emotion. This likelihood could reduce and possibly eliminate the need for querying the user of their affective state. To test the efficacy of this idea, we made a classifier based on each linear model in the table. Rather than using the scale of one to five, the dependent variable of the classifier was 1 if the emotion level was high and -1 if the emotion level was not. Hence we used a classification threshold of 0 on the prediction.

For each model we performed leave-one-student-out cross validation. We recorded the number of True Positives, False Negatives, True Negatives, and False Positives at each test. Table 5 shows that the best classifier of each emotion in terms of Accuracy ranges from 78% to 87.5%. The best classification results are obtained by only training on examples that are not in the middle. This is likely the case because the middle values indicate indifference.

7   Discussion

We have presented a User Model framework to predict emotional self concept. The framework is the first of its kind – including models based on sensor data integrated with an ITS used in classrooms of up to 25 students. By using Stepwise Regression we have isolated key features for predicting user emotional responses to four categories of emotion. These results are supported by cross validation, and show improvement using a very basic classifier. The models from these classifiers can be used in future studies to predict a students' self-concept of emotional state on four ranges of emotion. These ranges are interest, frustration, confidence and excitement.

There are a number of places for improvement in our system. The first is that we used summary information of all of the sensor values. We may find better results by considering the time series of each of these sensors. In addition, the MindReader library can be trained for new mental states. This is one avenue of future work. Another place for improvement is to look at individual differences in the sensors. Creating a baseline for emotional detection before using the tutor system could help us to better interpret the sensor features.

Now that we have a basic User Model of students, the next step is to use this Model in the next experiments to send recommendations to the ITS. In order for this to be useful, the ITS needs to have some repair mechanisms based on the predictions from the User Model. Examples of this include encouragement, suggesting to the student to ask for a hint, and mirroring the emotion of the student.

Acknowledgments. We acknowledge contributions to the system development from Rana el Kaliouby, Ashish Kapoor, Selene Mota and Carson Reynolds. We also thank Joshua Richman, Roopesh Konda, and Assegid Kidane at ASU for their work on sensor manufacturing. This research was funded by awards from the National Science Foundation, 0705554, IIS/HCC *Affective Learning Companions: Modeling and Supporting Emotion During Teaching*, Woolf and Burleson (PIs) with Arroyo, Barto, and Fisher and the U.S. Department of Education to Woolf, B. P. (PI) with Arroyo, Maloy and the Center for Applied Special Technology (CAST), *Teaching Every Student: Using Intelligent Tutoring and Universal Design To Customize The Mathematics Curriculum*. Any opinions, findings, conclusions or recommendations expressed in this material are those of the authors and do not necessarily reflect the views of the funding agencies.

References

1. Koedinger, K.R., Anderson, J.R., Hadley, W.H., Mark, M.A.: Intelligent tutoring goes to school in the big city. International Journal of Artificial Intelligence in Education 8(1), 30–43 (1997)
2. Shute, V.J., Psotka, J.: Intelligent tutoring systems past, present and future. In: Jonassen, D. (ed.) Handbook of Research on Educational Communications and Technology. Scholastic Publications (1996)
3. Bailenson, J.N., Yee, N.: Digital chameleons. Psychological Science 16(10), 814–819 (2005)
4. Florea, A., Kalisz, E.: Embedding emotions in an artificial tutor. In: SYNASC 2005 (September 2005)
5. Arroyo, I., Beal, C., Murray, T., Walles, R., Woolf, B.P.: Web-based intelligent multimedia tutoring for high stakes achievement tests. In: Lester, J.C., Vicari, R.M., Paraguaçu, F. (eds.) ITS 2004. LNCS, vol. 3220, pp. 468–477. Springer, Heidelberg (2004)
6. Zhou, J., Wang, X.: Multimodal affective user interface using wireless devices for emotion identification, pp. 7155–7157 (2005)
7. McQuiggan, S., Lee, S., Lester, J.: Early prediction of student frustration. Affective Computing and Intelligent Interaction, pp. 698–709 (2007)
8. McQuiggan, S., Mott, B., Lester, J.: Modeling self-efficacy in intelligent tutoring systems: An inductive approach. User Modeling and User-Adapted Interaction 18(1), 81–123 (2008)
9. Royer, J.M., Walles, R.: Influences of gender, motivation and socioeconomic status on mathematics performance. In: Berch, D.B., Mazzocco, M.M.M. (eds.) Why is Math so Hard for Some Children, pp. 349–368. Paul H. Brookes Publishing Co., Baltimore (2007)
10. Catsambis, S.: The path to math: Gender and racial-ethnic differences in mathematics participation from middle school to high school. Sociology of Education 67(3), 199–215 (1994)
11. Tobias, S.: Overcoming Math Anxiety, Revised and Expanded. W.W. Norton & Company, New York (1995)
12. Strauss, M., Reynolds, C., Hughes, S., Park, K., McDarby, G., Picard, R.: The handwave bluetooth skin conductance sensor. In: Affective Computing and Intelligent Interaction, pp. 699–706 (2005)
13. Qi, Y., Picard, R.: Context-sensitive bayesian classifiers and application to mouse pressure pattern classification. In: Proceedings. 16th International Conference on Pattern Recognition, 2002, vol. 3, pp. 448–451 (2002)
14. Kapoor, A., Burleson, W., Picard, R.W.: Automatic prediction of frustration. International Journal of Human-Computer Studies 65(8), 724–736 (2007)
15. Burleson, W., Picard, R.W.: Gender-specific approaches to developing emotionally intelligent learning companions. IEEE Intelligent Systems 22(4), 62–69 (2007)
16. el Kaliouby, R.: Mind-reading Machines: the automated inference of complex mental states from video. PhD thesis, University of Cambridge (2005)
17. D'Mello, S., Picard, R.W., Graesser, A.: Toward an affect-sensitive autotutor. IEEE Intelligent Systems 22(4), 53–61 (2007)

Use and Trust of Simple Independent Open Learner Models to Support Learning within and across Courses

Susan Bull[1], Peter Gardner[1], Norasnita Ahmad[1], Jeffrey Ting[2], and Ben Clarke[1]

[1] Electronic, Electrical and Computer Engineering, University of Birmingham, UK
[2] Centre for Learning, Innovation and Collaboration, University of Birmingham, UK
{s.bull,p.gardner,nxa707,i.h.ting,b.j.clarke}@bham.ac.uk

Abstract. This paper introduces two independent open learner models (learner models that are accessible to user viewing), which are deployed alongside university courses to facilitate self-assessment skills, planning and independent learning. OLMlets is used in specific courses, while UK-SpecIAL, a modular extension to OLMlets, draws on the OLMlets learner models to display progress towards achieving learning outcomes applicable across courses. User logs demonstrate usage of each system, and questionnaire responses provide insight into the reasons for user trust in the environments.

Keywords: Open learner models, learner independence, user trust.

1 Introduction

Trust has been considered in a variety of fields. In psychology, for example, trust relates to personal qualities pertaining to the beliefs and expectations of the individual [1], whereas in sociology it tends to be regarded as a mutual relationship [2]. In human-computer interaction, an important question is whether a system inspires user confidence in its actions/decisions/recommendations, etc., to the extent that users will act on these [3]. In this paper our focus is on user trust in environments that open the learner model to the user, and use of such environments. A learner model that is open to learner inspection might help contribute to the development of student trust in a system, as users will be able to see (some of) the information on which it bases its inferences [4]. However, users will need to accept the information about their knowledge and understanding, if they are to act appropriately on the information that they find in their learner model. Accuracy of the model, utility of the model for promoting learning, and user trust in their learner model have all been identified as key features in open learner modelling in the SMILI Open Learner Modelling Framework [5]. We here aim to draw these components of the framework together. We define trust in this context as: "the individual user's belief in, and acceptance of the system's inferences; their feelings of attachment to their model; and their confidence to act appropriately according to the model inferences" [6]. Previous work suggests students view trust in this context in a similar way [7].

In student-centred learning, learners are encouraged to recognise their learning needs and manage their own learning, extending and deepening their knowledge using

G.-J. Houben et al. (Eds.): UMAP 2009, LNCS 5535, pp. 42–53, 2009.

a range of activities [8]. The U.K. Higher Education Academy encourages the development of metacognitive skills such as self-assessment and reflection in university education [9]. Externalising a system's model of the learner to the user, as well as helping to promote trust in a system's actions, can help prompt learner reflection and metacognitive skills [10]. Student self-knowledge is argued to be particularly important for self-directed learning or student-centred learning in the context of open learner models (OLM) [11]. This draws on key works on student reflection in the general education literature (e.g. [12],[13]).

Externalisation of user knowledge in an OLM can be simple or complex. Complex presentations can show hierarchical, prerequisite, conceptual and other relationships in or between knowledge (e.g. [11],[14],[15],[16],[17]), and can be a useful way to provide structured externalisations of learner knowledge in a domain-specific context. Simple model displays, whilst perhaps based on complex underlying learner models, use less complicated externalisations. The most common are 'skill meters' indicating the extent of current knowledge, mastery or understanding of a topic or concept, and have enjoyed widespread use in real settings (e.g. [18],[19],[20]), suggesting learners find them easy to interpret and useful as a learning support. Early investigations suggest simple learner model displays may be trusted by users, perhaps because it is clear to them, what the representations show [6]. User trust may be especially important when *independent* open learner models (IOLM) are used. IOLMs are OLMs that are the focus of an interaction, separate from the other, standard components of intelligent tutoring systems (domain and pedagogical model) [18]. Learner modelling occurs in the usual way (e.g. based on problem-solving attempts, responses to questions, help or hints requested, navigation, time on task). The user then accesses their learner model in order to determine how to proceed - i.e. the responsibility for the decisions in learning rests with the learner (see [11]). The IOLM approach aims specifically to promote metacognitive skills considered crucial to the development of successful and critical approaches to learning, as introduced above.

The OLMlets simple IOLM has been taken up by 2/3 of students across all courses in which it is available in the School of Electronic, Electrical and Computer Engineering, University of Birmingham. (Range: one 1/6 of students in an individual course, to all students taking a course, and this applies across all stages of the degrees [18].) In this paper we introduce a new component linked to OLMlets: UK-SpecIAL, which unites information about learning outcomes across courses in students' degrees. We investigate the utility of UK-SpecIAL in its situation of use with OLMlets.

In the following section we describe the requirements of U.K. engineering degrees, to present the pedagogical context within which our approach is deployed. In Section 3 we present OLMlets and UK-SpecIAL, and conclude with an evaluation of these systems in Section 4, considering levels of use and user trust. Whilst we describe a specific application, the approach may be relevant in a range of degree subjects.

2   Requirements of Engineering Degrees

In order to obtain accreditation for engineering degrees in the U.K., the UK SPEC Standard for Professional Engineering Competence [21] must be demonstrated. UK

SPEC covers five broad areas: (i) underpinning science and mathematics; (ii) engineering analysis; (iii) design; (iv) economic, social and environmental context; (v) engineering practice. Each of these areas is further broken down into specific learning outcomes for students, for example, "engineering analysis" includes: "ability to apply and integrate knowledge and understanding of other engineering disciplines to support study of their own engineering discipline"; "understanding of engineering principles and the ability to apply them to analyse key engineering processes". "Engineering practice" includes: "awareness of nature of intellectual property and contractual issues"; "ability to work with technical uncertainty". These learning outcomes differ from the format commonly used within courses to describe intended learning outcomes to students (e.g. "on successful completion of this module you will be able to: design.../select.../solve..." (see [22])). The UK SPEC learning outcomes have been interpreted specifically for electrical, electronic and computer engineering degrees by the U.K. Institution of Engineering and Technology (IET) [23].

Figure 1 illustrates how several courses contribute to a single UK SPEC learning outcome, showing first year courses that contribute to UK SPEC learning outcome: "Knowledge and understanding of scientific principles and methodology necessary to underpin their education in their engineering discipline, to enable appreciation of its scientific and engineering context, and to support their understanding of historical, current, and future developments and technologies". This learning outcome has been interpreted by the IET for degrees in its area of specialism as learning outcome B1. (The text associated with each course in Figure 1 is taken from that IET detail.)

Figure 2 shows as an example, the full set of UK SPEC learning outcomes to which a specific first year course, EE1A: Digital Logic and Microprocessor Systems, contributes. Again, words from the IET interpretation of UK SPEC are included to show which particular aspects of each learning outcome are addressed.

Figure 3 gives an example of the overall picture across all the years of the programme, by showing which courses contribute to the UK SPEC learning outcome "Understanding use of technical literature and other information sources". The IET interprets this as B22, requiring students to demonstrate "Familiarity in obtaining, searching and interpreting technical literature and other documentation from various sources". This is a clear example where it would be unrealistic to expect that the learning outcome to be addressed, would be met and demonstrated within a single course. Furthermore, there are differences in the ways in which these courses contribute to this learning outcome, as the courses are quite diverse. For example, in the first year course EE1A: Digital Logic and Microprocessor Systems, students need to make use of manufacturers' technical data sheets for microprocessors in order to complete laboratory assignments and exam questions. In the second year EE2H2: Personalisation and Adaptive Systems course, students engage with the literature on user modelling and adaptive hypermedia in order to inform (and provide justification for) their own questions and designs for adaptive systems with various functions (e.g. recommending products, supporting learning, tailoring information presentation [24]). Courses beginning with 'EE1' indicate first year courses; 'EE2', second year courses; and 'EE3', third year courses. For BEng undergraduate students, the third year is their final year of study. For MEng undergraduate students, the fourth year is their final year. In Figure 3 we have omitted the relevant fourth year courses (except for the individual project), for clarity.

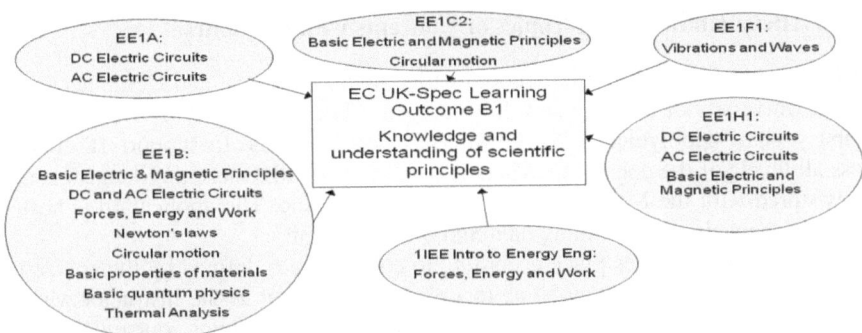

Fig. 1. Contribution of first year courses to UK SPEC learning outcome B1

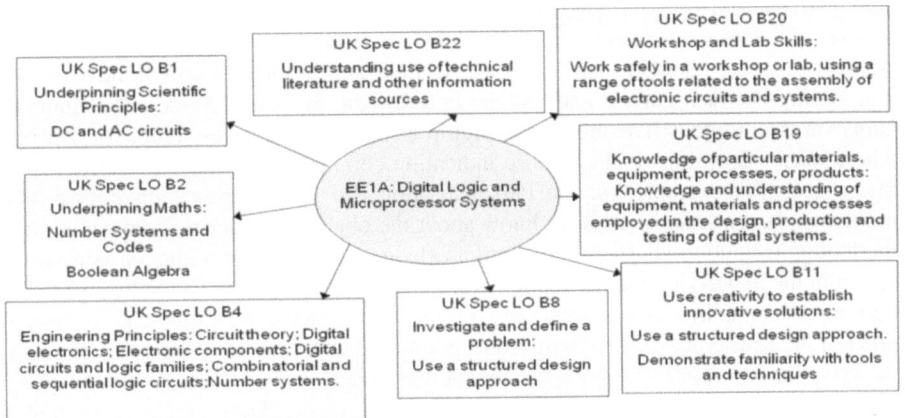

Fig. 2. UK SPEC learning outcome to which course EE1A contributes

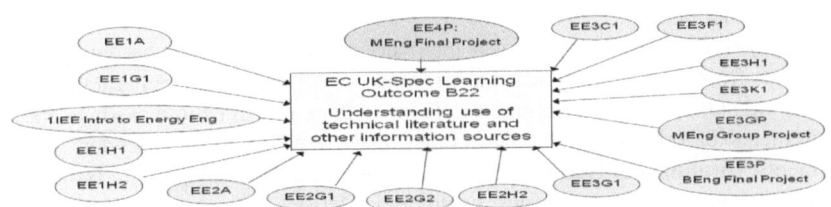

Fig. 3. Courses in all years that contribute to UK SPEC learning outcome B22

3 Simple Open Learner Models within and across Courses

This section presents (i) OLMlets, an IOLM used within courses; and (ii) UK-SpecIAL, an IOLM that shows progress towards learning outcomes across courses in a degree, based on UK SPEC.

3.1 OLMlets: Knowledge of Topics or Concepts within a Course

OLMlets has been in use in the School of Electronic, Electrical and Computer Engineering, University of Birmingham, for four years. Trialled initially in five courses in its first year of deployment [25], OLMlets is now available to support 18 courses across all levels of the degree. OLMlets is written in the PHP scripting language, and data is stored with the MySQL relational database engine. The application is hosted via an Apache web server running on a Sun Solaris system.

Learner modelling takes place according to course topics defined by the course instructor [25]. These topics may be as focussed or as general as the instructor wishes. For example, the second year Personalisation and Adaptive Systems course uses broad topics based on Jameson's user modelling classification: functions of user models; user properties modelled; obtaining user model information; user modelling techniques [24]; and other general user modelling issues including the differences between adaptable and adaptive systems. The first year Introduction to Circuits, Devices and Fields course defines more focussed areas, for example: electron and hole motion in a semiconductor; the relationship between electric field and voltage in simple devices; the relationship between current and voltage in a resistor. For each course, modelling occurs over the previous five attempts at multiple choice questions on a topic or concept, where response options include those indicating common errors or misconceptions in the subject. For example, for the Personalisation and Adaptive Systems course: that recommender systems necessarily know about the objects they are recommending (the modelling technique must be content/knowledge-based). Each topic or concept is stored in the underlying learner model with a figure in the range 0-1 to indicate level of current understanding of the topic; and a figure in the range 0-1 to indicate the likelihood of the learner holding each misconception defined by the instructor. Weighting of the contribution of each response in the learner model, across the last five attempts at questions on a topic or concept, increases by 0.3 each time. Thus, greater weighting is given to the most recent attempts. The modelling is necessarily simple, as OLMlets is used in a variety of courses having different structures and different conceptual relationships, and can be used in any subject for which appropriate multiple choice questions can be defined.

Figure 4 shows two ways to access the overview of their knowledge level available to students from within a course, in a first year course addressing general engineering and writing skills, which is designed to help students transfer these skills to meet the requirements of other courses. The course uses five topics (open-ended academic arguments; Birmingham Harvard referencing format; general plagiarism issues; ethics and professional engineering issues; health and safety).

Colour is used in the 'skill meters' view of the learner model to indicate strength of knowledge, gaps or problematic knowledge and misconceptions (brief descriptions of misconceptions can be obtained by clicking on the 'misconceptions' link - shown in Figure 4 for topic 2). The second set of skill meters indicates the learner's current knowledge, and the first set, the knowledge expected by the instructor for the present stage of the course. The 'boxes' view also uses colour: various shades of green to indicate strength of knowledge in the large boxes for each topic, and equivalent shading for the smaller boxes underneath each large box, to show the instructor's current expectations. (The 'Q' icons lead to further questions on a topic; the 'M' icons to course materials on the topic.) In total there are five views, also: graph, ranked list in table form, and text overview of knowledge level [25]. The purpose of the multiple views is to allow the learner to select the format that most suits them, based on previous findings suggesting that students may have differing preferences for the presentation format of their learner model contents [15].

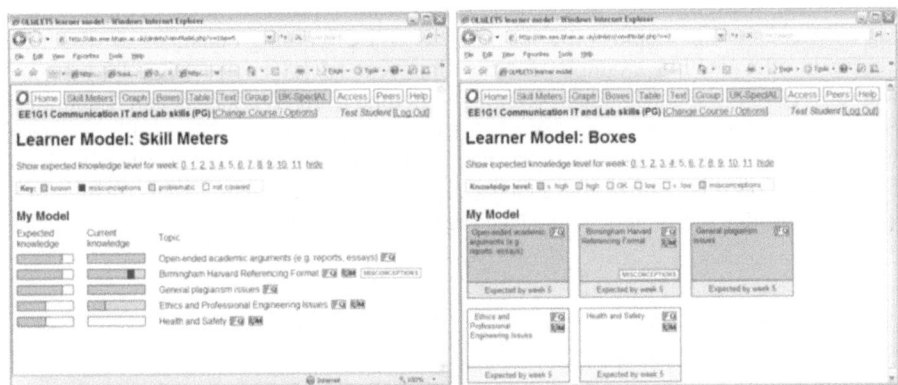

Fig. 4. The OLMlets open learner model (knowledge of topics or concepts within a course)

Students can choose to release their learner model to instructors and/or peers, in named or anonymous form. They may view the learner models of those people who have made their model available, alongside their own model.

3.2 UK-SpecIAL: UK SPEC Learning Outcomes across Courses

Forms of assessment using e-learning have been argued as useful additional support in today's outcomes-focused or objectives-focused educational systems [26]. For example, in engineering EASIMAP [27] maps UK SPEC learning outcomes to achievements, with reference to lecturers' assessment of a student's learning (learning outcomes are included on a grid, and student progress towards these is indicated after assessments have been completed). UK-SpecIAL (UK SPEC Independent Adaptive Learning) follows a complementary approach, focussed on formative assessment and helping students to identify their learning needs. The approach stresses the learner's current understanding as represented in their learner model, as a starting point for them to note any gaps in their knowledge and in their progress towards achieving the UK SPEC learning outcomes. This aims to help inform their decisions on how to focus their efforts across courses. In line with many other IOLMs, a primary purpose is to promote reflection, and encourage the development of independent learning skills and responsibility for one's own learning, but it also aims to address the problem of students sometimes not understanding how the various components of their degree fit together, at the time they are studying them [28].

UK-SpecIAL was developed as a modular extension to the OLMlets web application. It draws on the OLMlets learner models described above. The model data for each of the topics in an OLMlets course is averaged, resulting in a single figure (in the range 0-1) for each course. This figure is translated to the colour scheme in Figure 5 for presentation to the user: shading indicates the overall level of understanding of a course in a 'boxes' view; each course is then listed under the UK SPEC learning outcome to which it contributes. A course is listed as many times as the number of learning outcomes to which it applies (see Figure 6 for the relationship between OLMlets and UK-SpecIAL). Thus users can see immediately, which courses contribute to which learning outcomes, and their own relative progress in each course. Clicking on a course title displays the specific UK SPEC learning outcomes to which the course is relevant. For example, for the first year EE1A course Digital Logic and Microprocessor Systems, under learning outcome B20 Workshop and Laboratory Skills, the following is shown: "Work safely in a workshop or lab, using a range of tools related to the assembly of electronic circuits and systems" (illustrated in Figure 5). Clicking on this course title under a different learning outcome will display text applicable to that learning outcome (see Figure 2 for examples).

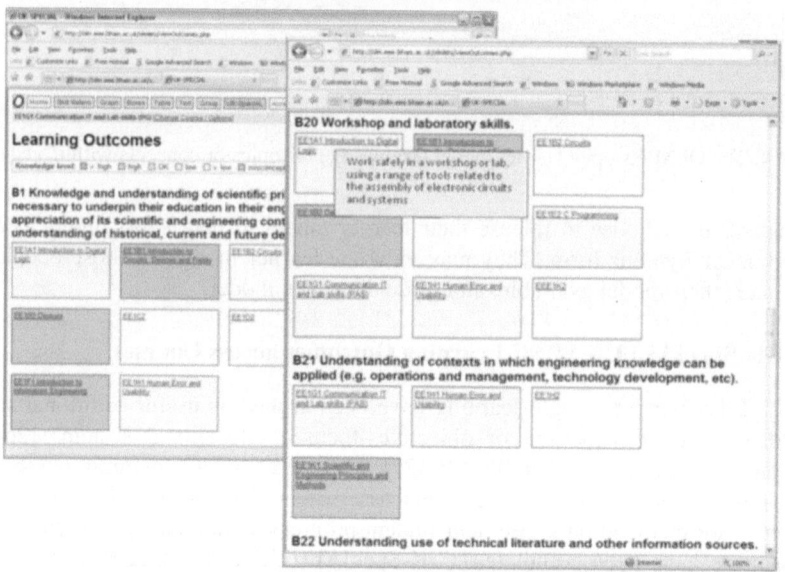

Fig. 5. The UK-SpecIAL open learner model (UK SPEC learning outcomes across courses)

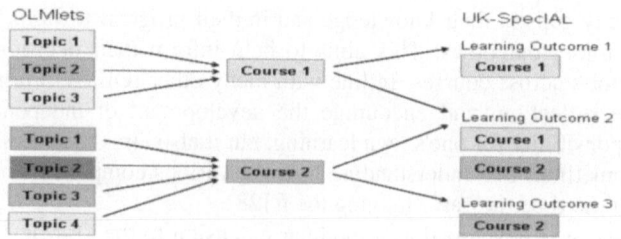

Fig. 6. OLMlets and UK-SpecIAL

4   Use and Trust of OLMlets and UK-SpecIAL

This section introduces the results of use of OLMlets and UK-SpecIAL across a term in first year courses, and student trust in the two systems.

4.1   Participants, Materials and Methods

Participants were 86[1] first years in Electronic, Electrical and Computer Engineering, University of Birmingham, U.K. Students were familiar with OLMlets from several courses. UK-SpecIAL was briefly introduced in a lab session in one of the courses (n=69). Students used the systems in their own time as they felt appropriate, during a term. The OLMlets learner models were assessed at the end of 2 courses (contributing 7% and 10% to the course mark), but use was optional in the other 6 courses. Interactions are automatically recorded, and provide an anonymous user log. Table 1 gives an example of an access to UK-SpecIAL by user 955, from OLMlets course 25. The unique user number is automatically assigned on creation of an account.

Questionnaires were completed in one of the courses. Responses were on a 5-point scale: 5 strongly agree, 4 agree, 3 neutral, 2 disagree, 1 strongly disagree, with space for additional comments. 23of the 66 students responded to an email sent a few weeks after the course, for consent to use their questionnaire data in this research.

Table 1. Example from user log

event_id	time	user_id	course_id	event_type	field_1
316463	2008-11-29 16:17:44	955	25	8	UK-SPECIAL

4.2   Results

Table 2 shows log data across all OLMlets courses in which students were registered (mean 4, median 4, range 1-6). 86 students attempted questions. The greatest use was in one of the courses that assessed the learner models, and the other course with assessed models had the third highest usage level, amonst the first year courses. Users attempted 577 questions on average (median over 400). The individual learner models were accessed on average 400 times (median over 300), by nearly all users (n=84). 54 also compared their knowledge to instructor expectations (mean 19.5, median 14.5 times), available in 5 courses; and 79 accessed UK-SpecIAL (mean 6.7, median 5). 66 accessed UK-SpecIAL multiple times. (Of these, mean access was 8, median 6.) 42 released their models to others; 44 viewed peer models that were accessible to them.

The mean and median figures in Table 3 show most students claimed to understand their OLMlets model, believed it an accurate representation of their understanding, and found it helpful in identifying their knowledge. Students claimed to trust the OLMlets information in general, and specifically because they could see its inferences about their knowledge, because they could make comparisons between their own

---

[1] This figure includes data from a *demo user* (that interacted minimally), that was not removed because of anonymous logs; and users who were not first years who may have registered by mistake, or may have been revising first year content. (There are 82 current first years.)

knowledge and that of other users and, in particular, because they could compare their current understanding against the expectations for the current stage of the course.

Table 4 shows that most students also understood the UK-SpecIAL information, considered it reasonably accurate and felt it helped them identify their knowledge, but to a lesser extent than OLMlets. They judged it useful to help identify relationships (of learning outcomes across courses, between their courses and UK SPEC, and between UK SPEC and the requirements for professional engineering). Overall levels of trust in UK-SpecIAL were very high. Students generally agreed that they trusted UK-SpecIAL because they could see the system's inferences, because of its clear relationship to UK SPEC, and because they could see relationships between courses.

Table 2. Use of OLMlets and UK-SpecIAL

Log Data: First Year Courses	Total	Mean	Median	Range
Questions attempted (n=86)	50745	577	428	4 - 2025
Viewing own model in OLMlets (n=84)	34793	400	316	1 - 1336
Viewing instructor expectations in OLMlets (n=54)	1053	19.5	14.5	1 - 120
Viewing UK-SpecIAL (n=79)	522	6.7	5	1 - 39

Table 3. Trust in OLMlets

Questionnaire Item: OLMlets	Mean	Median	Range
Understood learner model information	4.5	4	4-5
Learner model information was accurate	4.0	4	3-5
Helped identify knowledge (within first year courses)	4.5	5	3-5
Trust because can see system's inferences about oneself	3.8	4	1-5
Trust because can compare to instructor's expectations	4.2	5	1-5
Trust because can compare to other users	3.7	4	1-5
Overall trust in OLMlets learner model information	4.2	4	1-5

Table 4. Trust in UK-SpecIAL

Questionnaire Item: UK-SpecIAL	Mean	Median	Range
Understood learner model information	3.8	4	1-5
Learner model information was accurate	3.5	4	1-5
Helped identify knowledge (across courses)	3.9	4	1-5
Identify relationships: learning outcomes across courses	4.3	4	3-5
Identify relationships: courses/UK SPEC	4.3	4	2-5
Identify relationships: UK SPEC/professional engineering	4.2	4	2-5
Trust because can see system's inferences about oneself	3.9	4	2-5
Trust because relates to UK SPEC	4.0	4	1-5
Trust because demonstrates relationships between courses	3.9	4	1-5
Overall trust in UK-SpecIAL learner model information	4.4	5	3-5

The following are examples of typical open-ended comments about UK-SpecIAL:
o It is very important to know the uk-spec because it let me know many skills and required knowledge necessary to become a professional engineer. This allows

students to know and set their goals easily with this in place. Tendency of students not knowing why they are studying their modules will be greatly reduced.

o The point I find particularly important is how UK-SpecIAL relates to each module and then allows a student to see how the different modules fit together to provide a broad knowledge spectrum. This helps to prevent students seeing each module as a completely separate entity and allows them to gain a better overall view.

o It is exciting to find out how the learning outcomes from my course meet the requirements of employers which leads to a professional career in engineering.

4.3 Discussion

As an aim of our IOLMs is to encourage learner independence, we have not attempted to measure learning gains: we expect successful use of the systems to prompt study away from the environments, and students would not necessarily feel a need to verify their knowledge if they were confident in their independent study [18]. Nevertheless, students made extensive use of OLMlets in their first year courses, attempting well over 500 (mean), 400 (median) questions, and frequently accessed their individual learner models. Nearly two thirds also compared their knowledge to the instructor's expectations for the current stage of the course, in the courses in which this was available (mean 19.5, median 14.5 times). 92% of students accessed UK-SpecIAL during the term; 77% multiple times – even though only 80% of the users had been introduced to it. Students may also choose to release their learner model to others, which can be useful to those who like to work collaboratively or competitively. 49% released their models; 52% viewed peer models. Because the logs were anonymous, we do not know whether students used OLMlets in all courses in which it was available to them. However, there is sufficient use to suggest a simple IOLM can support learning over the duration of a set of courses, in students' own time: students would unlikely interact to this extent unless they perceive some benefit.

When a user can see the contents of their learner model, their beliefs about its accuracy and the extent to which they can interpret the representations, may affect their use of it. These issues relate to trust. Questionnaire responses suggest students did understand the representations in OLMlets in particular (also indicated by usage levels), considered them accurate, and useful in helping to identify their knowledge. The figures were a little lower for UK-SpecIAL. Students also claimed to trust both IOLMs. A key feature in engendering trust appears to be the ability to compare knowledge to instructor expectations. This allows users to not only determine their knowledge state, but also whether their current knowledge is 'acceptable'. Comparison of one's own model to peer models was also a feature contributing to trust. As only half the students used peer models, the existence of this information may be sufficient to contribute to user trust in this kind of system. That users can see relationships between courses, and to their future professions, also appears important. Students had a high level of trust in UK-SpecIAL despite needing to check progress with it only a few times in the term, and despite their lower confidence in its accuracy. Because of the infrequent need to refer to UK-SpecIAL, comments were also sought. The (typical) comments show users understood the purpose: e.g. they could explain its relationship to professional engineering, and relationships between their courses.

Based on the results, we suggest that simple IOLMs for use in and across courses can be found beneficial, and will be used in practice. As expected, use was high when models were assessed. However, in one course that did not assess the learner models, use was higher than in one of the courses that did assess them. Within a course an IOLM can help users pinpoint specific areas on which to focus their study; and an IOLM drawing together information from several courses can help users understand how components of their degree fit together. While UK-SpecIAL is specifically for engineering, the general approach could be applicable to a variety of disciplines.

Of course, the fact that questionnaire data came from a subset of users means that responses may not reflect the views of the whole group. However, we believe that there was sufficient use to warrant further study of use and trust of IOLMs in real settings. In particular, given the result for UK-SpecIAL, it seems important to investigate the relationship between perceived accuracy of the model and user trust.

5 Summary

This paper has presented OLMlets and UK-SpecIAL: independent open learner models to promote learner reflection and learner independence within courses, and a greater understanding of how courses fit together to build the 'bigger picture' of their degree and how this relates to their future professions. Usage logs showed that both systems were used by students, and questionnaire responses indicated that users trusted them. We therefore suggest that a similar approach may be useful in comparable university departments to promote metacognitive skills and independent learning by students outside lecture, lab and other scheduled sessions; and recommend investigation into whether the approach may generalise to other subjects.

Acknowledgments. UK-SpecIAL is funded by the UK Higher Education Academy Engineering Subject Centre (Ref: MPF 0806).

References

1. Robinson, S.L.: Trust and Breach of the Psychological Contract. Administrative Science Quarterly 41, 574–599 (1996)
2. Lewis, J.D., Weigert, A.: Trust as Social Reality. J. Social Forces 63, 967–985 (1985)
3. Madsen, M., Gregor, S.: Measuring Human-Computer Trust. In: Gable, G., Viatle, M. (eds.) 11th Australasian Conference on Information Systems, vol. 53 (2000)
4. Tanimoto, S.: Dimensions of Transparency in Open Learner Models. In: LeMoRe Workshop, Artificial Intelligence in Education 2005, pp. 100–106 (2005)
5. Bull, S., Kay, J.: Student Models that Invite the Learner In: The SMILI Open Learner Modelling Framework. Int. J. of Artificial Intelligence in Education. 17(2), 89–120 (2007)
6. Ahmad, N., Bull, S.: Do Students Trust their Open Learner Models? In: Nejdl, W., Kay, J., Pu, P., Herder, E. (eds.) AH 2008. LNCS, vol. 5149, pp. 255–258. Springer, Heidelberg (2008)
7. Ahmad, N., Bull, S.: Learner Trust in Learner Model Externalisations. In: Artificial Intelligence in Education 2009, IOS Press, Amsterdam (in press)
8. Land, S.M., Hanaffin, M.J.: Student-Centered Learning Environments: Foundations, Assumptions, and Implications. In: 18th Proceedings of Selected Research and Development Presentations at the 1996 National Convention of the Association for Educational Communications and Technology, Indianapolis, IN, pp. 394–400 (1996)

9. Higher Education Academy/Juwah et al. Enhancing Student Learning Through Effective Formative Feedback (2004), http://www.heacademy.ac.uk
10. Bull, S., Kay, J.: Metacognition and Open Learner Models. In: Workshop on Metacognition and Self-Regulated Learning in Educational Technologies. Int. Tutoring Systems (2008)
11. Kay, J.: Learner Know Thyself: Student Models to Give Learner Control and Responsibility. In: Halim, Z., Ottomann, T., Razak, Z. (eds.) Int. Conference on Computers in Education, AACE, pp. 17–24 (1997)
12. Boud, D.: Promoting Reflection in Learning: a Model. In: Boud, D., Keogh, R., Walker, D. (eds.) Reflection: Turning Experience into Learning, Kogan Page, London, pp. 18–40. Nichols Pub., New York (1985)
13. Schon, D.: The Reflective Practitioner. Basic Books, USA (1983)
14. Dimitrova, V.: StyLE-OLM: Interactive Open Learner Modelling. Int. J. of Artificial Intelligence in Education 13(1), 35–78 (2003)
15. Mabbott, A., Bull, S.: Alternative views on knowledge: Presentation of open learner models. In: Lester, J.C., Vicari, R.M., Paraguaçu, F. (eds.) ITS 2004. LNCS, vol. 3220, pp. 689–698. Springer, Heidelberg (2004)
16. Perez-Marin, D., Alfonseca, E., Rodriguez, P., Pascual-Neito, I.: A Study on the Possibility of Automatically Estimating the Confidence Value of Students' Knowledge in Generated Conceptual Models. J. of Computers 2(5), 17–26 (2007)
17. Zapata-Rivera, J.D., Greer, J.E.: Interacting with Inspectable Bayesian Models. Int. J. of Artificial Intelligence in Education 14, 127–163 (2004)
18. Bull, S., Mabbott, A., Gardner, P., Jackson, T., Lancaster, M., Quigley, S., Childs, P.A.: Supporting Interaction Preferences and Recognition of Misconceptions with Independent Open Learner Models. In: Nejdl, W., Kay, J., Pu, P., Herder, E. (eds.) AH 2008. LNCS, vol. 5149, pp. 62–72. Springer, Heidelberg (2008)
19. Mitrovic, A., Martin, B.: Evaluating the Effect of Open Student Models on Self-Assessment. Int. J. of Artificial Intelligence in Education 17(2), 121–144 (2007)
20. Weber, G., Brusilovsky, P.: ELM-ART: An Adaptive Versatile System for Web-Based Instruction. Int. J. of Artificial Intelligence in Education 12, 351–384 (2001)
21. Engineering Council. UK Standard for Professional Engineering Competence, The Accreditation of Higher Education Programmes (2004),
    http://www.engc.org.uk/documents/Accreditation_HE_Progs.pdf
22. Biggs, J., Tang, C.: Teaching for Quality Learning at University. McGraw Hill, OUP (2007)
23. Institution of Engineering and Technology (IET). Handbook of Learning Outcomes for BEng and MEng Degree Programmes (2006), http://www2.theiet.org
24. Jameson, A.: Adaptive Interfaces and Agents. In: Jacko, J.A., Sears, A. (eds.) Human-Computer Interaction Handbook, 2nd edn., Lawrence Erlbaum Publishers, Mahwah (2007)
25. Bull, S., Quigley, S., Mabbott, A.: Computer-Based Formative Assessment to Promote Reflection and Learner Autonomy. Engineering Education 1, 8–18 (2006)
26. Buzzetto-More, N.A., Alade, A.J., Panda, D.: Using e-Learning to Drive a Student Learning Outcomes Based Assessment Program. In: Buzzetto-More, N.A. (ed.) Advanced Principles of Effective e-Learning, pp. 213–244. Informing Science Press, CA (2007)
27. Maddocks, A.: EASIMAP: A Coherent Approach to the Assessment of Learning Outcomes on Engineering Degree Programmes. Engineering Education 2(2), 26–32 (2007)
28. Avitabile, P., McKelliget, J., Van Zandt, T.: Interweaving Numerical Processing Techniques in Multisemester Projects. In: American Society for Engineering Education Annual Conference & Exposition, American Society for Engineering (2005)

Narcissus: Group and Individual Models to Support Small Group Work

Kimberley Upton and Judy Kay

School of Information Technologies, University of Sydney, Sydney, NSW 2006,
Australia
{kupt2870,judy}@it.usyd.edu.au

Abstract. Long term group work by small teams is a central part of
many learning and workplace activities. Widespread group support tools
such as wikis, version control systems and issue tracking systems are an
invaluable aid for groups. They also have the potential to provide evidence for valuable models of the group activity. This paper describes
Narcissus, designed as a new way to improve group-work by exploiting
evidence from use of such group-work tools, to create a visual presentation of a *group model*. The *Narcissus* models and interfaces were designed
to help groups function more effectively. It helps individuals see how well
they are contributing to the group. It enables groups to assess contributions relative to plans. And it helps facilitators identify problems. The
Narcissus interface supports scrutability and control over its models. We
report a four part evaluation of *Narcissus*: *individual level* with 23 students; *group level* by 5 groups; *facilitator level* with 5 facilitators; and
fine grained study with 8 students. Results indicate that all these groups
were able to understand and use *Narcissus* and that they considered it
effective in modelling the group activity in useful ways. They particularly valued the support for scrutability. Key contributions of this work
are the creation of a *scrutable* and user controlled group model to support group work and to provide a new form of navigation interface for a
complex groupware site.

1   Introduction

Working effectively in groups is hard, particularly for projects that span months.
Yet long term group activity is central to many workplace projects [10]. It also
has an important role in education on two levels. One of these is the recognition
that development of students' skills in group work is important. Secondly, there
are learning benefits from working in groups [2,6,11]. It is natural then that we
have seen the emergence of many online tools designed to help groups collaborate
more effectively over long periods. For example, the growth in wikis has enabled
even large groups to work over long periods. Indeed, a range of online tools is
increasingly being used to support collaboration.

G.-J. Houben et al. (Eds.): UMAP 2009, LNCS 5535, pp. 54–65, 2009.

These tools present a promising potential for modelling individuals and groups and then exploiting these models to support group activity. Over long periods of use, groups typically generate large amounts of content and huge traces of electronic activity and interaction. However, this overwhelming amount of detail is of limited value because it is hard for group members to see the big picture. This means that individual team members cannot readily see how well they are contributing. At the group level, it is difficult to use these electronic traces to help the group determine if it is functioning effectively. In a setting where there are group facilitators, the situation is even more challenging: they need to get a big picture understanding and yet, unlike the individuals in the group, they do not have intimate knowledge of the actual details of any of the work done. This means that they cannot make use of the electronic traces to see the progress of the group.

Our approach has been to explore ways to analyse the electronic traces to create group models that can operate as *mirrors* which enable the individuals and teams to see their progress. Mirroring is the technique of presenting team members with a visual summary of their own activities in order to support reflective learning. We take inspiration from other visualisations that create social translucence for groups [1,4,13]. However, that work explored supporting large groups or those using chat for social reasons. This is very different from our prime concern, long term work by small groups, as is typical in workplaces.

The context of our research is a senior level capstone software development project which runs over a semester. Teams of around five students use *Trac* [3], an open-source web-based project management system. It has three key parts, each tightly integrated via hyperlinks. The *wiki* supports communication and documentation, *Subversion* is for source code management, and the *ticket system* supports task management and reporting software bugs. Assessment takes account of both the quality of the software produced and the group management. Students are also required to reflect on their group processes. Drury et al. [2] discuss the importance of reflection in overcoming lack of knowledge and experience in group work. This points to the value of mirroring tools to support reflection, both by individuals and as a group activity.

The next section reviews related work, explaining how it has informed this work and how *Narcissus* differs from it. We then present the user view of *Narcissus* followed by our evaluation experiments, their results and conclusions.

2   Related Work

In some of the key work on mirroring, there has been promising progress. Erickson's social translucence feedback tool [4] facilitated group interaction. For example, individuals who tended to dominate chat sessions became aware of this and modified their behaviour. This is precisely the goal of our mirroring approaches. In work somewhat closer to our own, the CodeSaw [5] temporal visualisation of collaborative software development was valuable for observing trends in source code contributions and a limited amount of communication. Also close to our work, with a focus on students in a software project course, Soller et al. [12] made use of online chat tools to support group work. The interface was specially modified, making it feasible to use Speech Act Theory to analyse the nature of group interaction. However, no work has involved the multiple media of our context, based on a state-of-the-art collaboration tool as we wanted to use. Nor did we wish to restrict students to artificial interfaces with special sentence starters or similar. So, we needed to take a different approach.

Some of our own foundation work resulted in a set of high level overview visualisations [7,8], one of which was called the *Wattle Tree*, a visualisation representing the activity of group members over time. Kay et al. [7] conducted a theoretical evaluation of this approach in terms of the *Big Five* theory of small group work [10]. We have built upon that work, taking a similar overall approach to building the group model, in making use of very simple measures as the evidence of activity: lines of text added to wiki pages, lines of committed code to *Subversion* and counts of ticket activities. While these measures are clearly very simple, by making them a very rough measure of the actual contributions made by each group member, we can readily explain the way that the model was built. It also facilitates the design of interfaces for users to control the way the group model is created.

Based on our previous experience, we formulated several new goals for supporting groups by building group models of activity on a state-of-the-art collaboration tool. One key new goal for *Narcissus* was to be readily extensible to additional media. Previous work cited above dealt with a single medium, with the exception of our Wattle tree which could handle the three basic media in Trac but would not readily extend to other new media. A second core goal was that the new visualisation of the group model should be scrutable, meaning that it enables group members to see the precise evidence that contributed to each part of the visualised group model. Beyond this, we wanted to provide user control, such that the presentation of the model in the visualisation can be controlled by the user. This is important to take account of the variability in levels of activity by different groups and individuals within them as well as the potentially diverse reasons that group members may have for studying the model. Another key new goal for *Narcissus* was to make it serve as a form of navigation of the vast collections of content within the group-work site. Essentially the visualised group model provides a new way for an individual to determine which parts of the group activity are important to them. Once they determine this, we wanted them to be able see the activity that contributed to any part of the visualised model. This goes beyond previous work described above but it is critical if the high level visualisation is to be easily used to scrutinise the Trac site to see why certain behaviours are observed. For example, if one person suddenly appears to be very active on the wiki, it is important to be able to easily see just what they did. Similarly, if an individual has very modest contributions, they may still be very valuable and may represent a large amount of work: hence it is important to have direct access to the actual contributions in order to see this.

3   Narcissus

Figure 1 illustrates the structure of the *Narcissus* group model displays and their associated support for scrutinising the model. It is for an actual group, but all names are anonymised. The very top shows the group name, in this case, it is Group Z. Next are hyperlinks to the three views: group, project, and ticket. In each of these, the left side of the page is the main visualisation of the group's model. All three views have a time-line down the left hand side, with the most recent date at the top. The *information panel* on the right provides a legend and additional details and navigation as discussed below.

3.1   Group View

The *Group View* is the main display of the group model and it is the default view. It has a vertical column for each member of the group. In this figure, the models for 5 team members are displayed. The user can customise the display to include just those team members they wish. This is useful for ensuring only interesting parts of the group model appear. For example, students would typically exclude models for tutors and clients.

The activities of each group member are mapped along the column. The media correspond to different colours and positions; leftmost, in purple is the wiki, next in blue is Subversion, and the third is tickets in green. The legend at the top of the information panel explains this.

The level of activity on a resource for a given day is given a discrete score from one to four, with four the highest. The score determines whether a square is pale or brightly coloured. Grey indicates there was no activity on that resource on that day, by that group member. For example, Figure 1 shows that member4 (second column from the right) on the most recent day (the top row) had moderate activity on the wiki and using tickets, and no activity committing data to Subversion. The middle column for this member is entirely grey, except on the bottom two rows, indicating that they have had no Subversion activity for 18 of the 20 days shown.

At the bottom of the columns is an *aggregate summary* of activity for each group member. The coloured bars indicate the total level of activity for each group member. The grey bars indicate the average level for the group. These bars are semi-transparent, so activity above average appears as a bright coloured tip, and below average has a grey tip. For example, Figure 1 shows that member2 was more active on the wiki and Subversion than the group average (indicated because their coloured bar is longer than the group one for the group), but less active on tickets than the group average. The aggregate summaries enable a user to compare the overall activity of each group member. Figure 1 shows that member1 was the most active on Subversion, and member4 the least active.

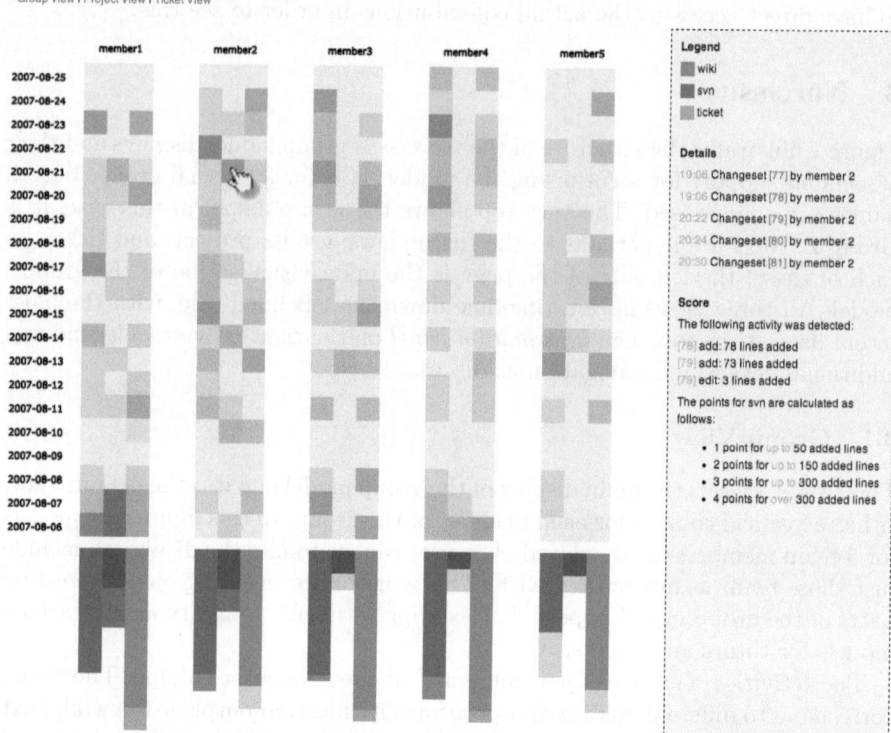

Fig. 1. The group view showing 20 days of activity of a group. *Narcissus* is structured with the visualisation on the left and an information panel on the right. Links for selecting one of three views are provided along the top.

3.2   Project View

The *project view* displays a single vertical column summarising the combined activity of all group members. As with the group view described above, each day is mapped vertically from bottom to top, each resource is indicated by a different colour (explained in the legend), and the level of activity is indicated by the brightness of the colour. Grey indicates that there was no activity on that resource on that day, by any member of the group.

Unlike the group view, the project view does not provide an aggregate summary on the bottom. Since the group as a whole is considered, a total does not provide any more information than an average. The average level of activity for each resource is depicted by the width of each resource column. The average is relative to the span of the project, not to the number of group members. This is important for two reasons. First, activity must be maintained throughout the project. Secondly, the average is less sensitive to extreme group members. If one group member is under-performing, or conversely, dominating the group, their activity will not skew the average as it can in the group view.

3.3 Ticket View

Tickets are key for managing the group, providing rich and important information associated with tasks. The *ticket view* displays a history of ticket activity for each group member. The lifespan of each ticket is plotted according to the group member who is responsible for the task associated with the ticket. The ticket view helps show the distribution of tasks amongst group members, which group members allocate tasks or maintain tickets, and point to other important behaviours, including evidence of collaboration.

3.4 Scrutability and User Control

The term scrutability refers to the design of a system so that a user can scrutinise it to determine why it behaves in the way it does. In the context of the *Narcissus* group model visualisation, users can see a model of each team member's activity. If the user is able to understand the underlying process that generated this model, then the model is scrutable. Such scrutability is important for ensuring that users can appreciate just what the model means. But it is also a foundation for user control. In the case of *Narcissus*, we consider that the user should be able to control the ways that activity data is interpreted to build the group model.

The activities are measured differently for each resource. Contributions to the wiki and Subversion repository are measured according to the number of added lines. Tickets are scored according to the type of activity, such as creating, accepting, and resolving tickets, as well as adding comments at different stages of the task. This establishes another motivation for making the model scrutable: the underlying measures of the visualisations are very simple and it is important that this is clear to the users.

As discussed earlier in this section, *Narcissus* models activity on a 4 level discrete scoring system. In the spirit of making *Narcissus* models scrutable, we provide explanations of the way activity evidence is interpreted, such as the metrics outlined above. In the case of Figure 1, the scoring is explained in the right-hand information panel. This shows that the model has 4 levels of activity, corresponding to up to 50, 150, 300 or above 300 lines added on this medium. The user can control this, altering these thresholds which serve to interpret the evidence available for the model. This means that the user can decide on the cut points in terms of levels that they wanted modelled. In different situations and at different times, a user may want to set quite different levels.

Narcissus provides another form of scrutability by linking each part of the displayed model directly to the actual evidence used to infer the activity shown in the model. All three views provide this form of scrutability. The user can click on any component of the visualised model to see the evidence associated with it. For example, the hand cursor in Figure 1 shows where the user has clicked on a Subversion square for member2. This causes the display of the particular details shown in the right hand information pane, showing details of the five change-sets committed by member2 on that day. The user can click on blue link with the number 77 to display the actual change-set, a display within the Trac system, showing the additions and deletions to the source code in that commit action.

There are corresponding links to the details for the other media. In all cases, the activities listed in the details sections provide a blue hyperlink to the actual activity on Trac. For the case of wiki activity, this is a hyperlink to the wiki page. Each ticket activity has a hyperlink to the ticket page, and Subversion activity has a hyperlink to the change-set, as just discussed. The links to Trac have three roles. One of these is scrutability. They also enable users to review the actual activities listed on the information panel, and make a qualitative judgement about the contributions that have been made. The third role is as a new means of navigation around the Trac site. Essentially, the *Narcissus* models show what the group has been doing on each of the media over the duration of the project and the user can explore interesting or potentially problematic aspects of the group's work by scrutinising the site, via the links from the *Narcissus* models.

3.5   Implementation

The implementation of *Narcissus* involves extracting the desired data from Trac then generating a group model which is presented in an active visualisation interface. The prototype was tested on Mozilla Firefox 2.0.0.9 on Mac OS X. *Narcissus* was written in Python to leverage the plugin support from Trac, and Quartz, a 2D and PDF drawing library for Mac OS X. It is available as a plugin for the Trac site, and accessible from the Trac menu bar once installed. This means that the visualisation is available to the user in real time.

4   Evaluation

The key evaluation goals were to assess *Narcissus*' effectiveness in assisting individual students and groups to reflect, to see how the group is performing and then to find relevant details via the interactive facilities. Another key goal was to assess how well *Narcissus* supported facilitators, especially in identifying indicators of likely problems in group and individual performance.

4.1   Experiments

Two groups of participants were recruited. Students came from the 2007 second semester capstone software project course and they participated near the end of the course. The facilitators were unfamiliar with the projects from that semester but had played that role at other times. This means they are familiar with the challenges of facilitating groups but they had to rely solely on the *Narcissus* model visualisations to gain insights into the performance of the students; they had no other knowledge of the groups. This is a challenging but useful test of *Narcissus* because it is important that facilitators be readily able to identify potential problems with minimal time investment.

The approach was to observe users as they learn and explore the interface, and allow the participants to provide a qualitative assessment. The experiments began with use of *Narcissus*, aided by an interactive tutorial. Then participants completed a questionnaire. The questionnaire included questions that required the participants to analyse the visualised group model.

The experiments used real student data from the current semester. Participants were provided with approximately three months of data, from the start of the project until the day of the experiment. The decision to use real data was to make the experiment as authentic as possible, and engage the participants. Students were provided with the data from their own project, which included changes to the wiki, changes to the ticketing system, and change-sets committed to the repository. Facilitators were provided with the data from all five project groups from this semester.

Essentially, there were four parts in the evaluation: *fine grained individual study* with 8 students; *group level* by 5 groups; *individual level* with 23 students; and *facilitator level* with 5 facilitators.

Fine grained individual study. In this experiment, participants used *Narcissus* to observe recent project activity and report on their own behaviour in relation to the group. From each of the five project groups 1-2 students participated in this experiment, 8 in all.

Group and individual level study. This experiment asked participants to work collectively, using *Narcissus* to reflect on aspects of their group processes. All five of the project groups, with 23 individuals, participated. Their questionnaire had three Likert items [9] about the suitability of *Narcissus* for real use. Participants also rated *ease of use* and *effectiveness* of the interface on a scale of 1 to 6, 6 being the highest rating.

Facilitator study. In this experiment, participants used *Narcissus* to identify and give examples of concerning groups or students. Five experienced facilitators participated.

4.2   Results

Of the three experiment categories, the group experiment most closely resembled real-world use. Students were able to work as a group to reflect on their group processes, and these reflections could then in turn be used in their final report. Although the experiment itself was not related to their assessment in the unit of study, their participation rewarded them with additional evidence for reflection which they could use for assessment.

We first report the results of the five groups. All worked through the tutorial effectively and then make use of the visualisations to answer the questionnaire. Figure 2 shows the ratings of ease of use and effectiveness (described to participants as 'the ability for groups to use the visualisations to identify their strengths; and areas of potential improvement as a group'). All five groups found *Narcissus* easy to use. All but one gave *Narcissus* an ease-of-use rating of 5, one giving a rating of 4, resulting in an average rating of 4.8. Furthermore, all groups gave *Narcissus* a rating of 4 or 5 for effectiveness.

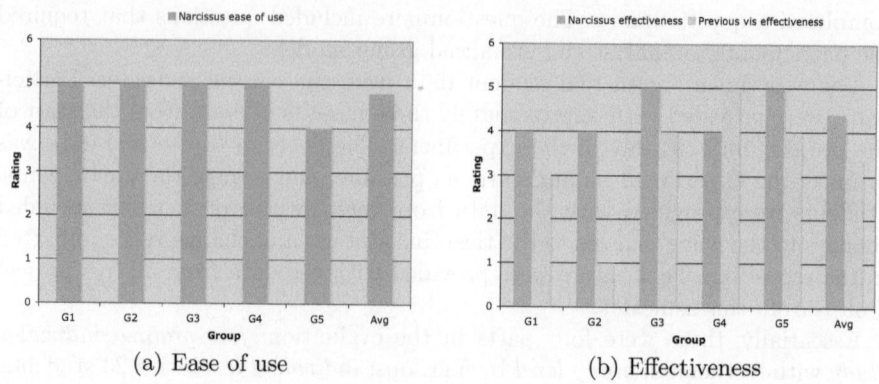

(a) Ease of use   (b) Effectiveness

Fig. 2. Group ratings of the ease of use and effectiveness of *Narcissus*

Table 1. Summary of task results from the student questionnaire, for students S1 .. S8

	S1	S2	S3	S4	S5	S6	S7	S8
Group view reflects activity	Y	Y	Y	Y	Y	N	Y	Y
Project view reflects activity	Y	N	Y	Y	Y	N	Y	Y
Project view useful for recent activity	Y	Y	Y	Y	Y	N	Y	Y
Overall preference	G	A	G	P	A	G	G	G

Key: G = group view; P = project view; A = all three views

In the other two experiment categories, all participants were able to successfully complete the tasks included in the questionnaire. Each student identified his/her personal level of activity using the group view, the overall level of group activity using the project view, and a range of behaviour regarding ticket use by examining the ticket view.

Table 1 details the results of the tasks in the student questionnaire, showing that students agreed that the group and project views accurately reflected activity, the project view was useful for viewing recent activity, and the preferred view overall was the group view.

The facilitators used *Narcissus* to successfully identify both groups and students of concern. They reported that the group view, like that in Figure 1, was the most useful for completing this task. Interestingly, all five facilitators were observed to scroll straight to the aggregate summary when comparing the group view across the different groups. Three participants reported that the project view was useful in addition to the group view. One participant said of the project view, "[the] relative performance of groups is clear."

Table 2 shows the comments made by the groups, and facilitators as they reviewed the visualisations for each group. The rightmost column shows the

Table 2. Comparison of observations made by groups and facilitators in the user study, as well as those my by the co-ordinators of the unit of study

	Group Reflections	Facilitators' Observations	Co-ordinator's Assessment
Group 1	Periods of inactivity, low overall activity.	Concerned about low overall activity.	Weaker group that improved, but made poor use of Trac.
Group 2	Well functioning group.	Concerned that one group member is dominating.	Very strong group, with an excessively active leader.
Group 3	Overall consistent activity, well distributed among group members.	No concerns.	Strong group, good split of work.
Group 4	Well functioning group.	Concerned about one or two of the group members.	Strong group with some under-performing group members.
Group 5	Well functioning group, no improvement needed.	Concerned about low overall activity.	Consistently weak group and modest individual work.

independent assessment of each group made by the course co-ordinator, after grading the full semester's material and devoting considerable time to reviewing the full work of each group, as part of the assessment process. It is striking that the facilitators were able to quickly draw conclusions about the groups and these correspond closely to the course co-ordinator's knowledge. For the student groups, the reflections seemed to be excessively positive which may well be due to their unwillingness to share admissions of problems.

Students and facilitators were both asked what they thought of the scrutability of *Narcissus*. There was an overwhelmingly positive response to this feature; all participants agreed that the active models and links down to the full details were useful. One of the students liked the links to Trac, remarking that it gave evidence for the *Narcissus* model's representation of activity. Three students and two facilitators noted that they valued the links to Trac. One facilitator found the link to Trac extremely useful for examining the quality of contributions, and another facilitator found it useful for identifying, then scrutinising abnormally large levels of activity, particularly source code committed to the repository.

Students and facilitators were also asked what they thought of the scrutable score section, and whether they found it useful. All but one student agreed that the detailing of the score calculation was useful, although there were caveats. One student felt it was only needed at the outset, to confirm fairness. Another student found it useful but only as a rough guide. Another student noted that counting added lines was a weak measure, but valued the explanation.

The facilitators responded very positively to the scrutable scoring model. One facilitator thought it was useful to know the nature of each activity, and why certain activities were scored highly. Another facilitator was interested in understanding busy periods, and mentioned that knowing how the system works offers a sense of security. One participant thought the scoring system, coupled with the drill down interactivity, was crucial:

> "Scrutability [is] very important for non-repudiability – while a [visualisation] may indicate something is wrong, if it is not scrutable, discovering how to amend the problem is difficult. Worse, students may blame the visualisation for misrepresenting their work."

The evaluation showed that while *Narcissus* is useful for students to identify their strengths and potential areas of improvement, facilitators identified many concerning behaviours that students did not. Furthermore, the inverse was true when facilitators identified concerning behaviour that could be explained by extenuating circumstances. In either case, this shows important promise as it means that *Narcissus* provides facilitators with indicators of concerning behaviour. They can then readily drill down to see the actual details. If it turns out that there is a problem, the facilitator is able to intervene early enough to remedy the situation.

5   Conclusion

Narcissus was designed to support long term group-work based on the Trac collaborative software platform. As Trac has the same collaborative elements that are widely used for long term collaboration, our approach has broad applicability. Essentially, *Narcissus* makes it possible for group members and facilitators to gain understanding of the way the group has been operating. It does this by presenting a group model of long term group-work activity.

Our evaluations demonstrate *Narcissus* was usable, supporting reflection on the way that each team member was contributing to the group. The students liked the interface, particularly for navigation. However, they understated group problems. By contrast, facilitators could quickly see how the groups were performing. This is a valuable foundation for identifying problems and helping groups address them early.

Narcissus uses simple measures of activity. Our evaluations indicate that, although participants recognised limitations of these, the active interface to the group model meant that they could scrutinise the evidence used to build the model. From this, they could apply much more informed and subtle reasoning to determine whether unusual patterns of activity indicated problems.

Project groups and other team-based work have a very large role in the workplace and in education. Our evaluations were in an educational context, but the groups were doing authentic large-scale team programming tasks. Our evaluations indicate that *Narcissus* offers a usable and useful tool for student reflection and for facilitators to identify problems. Importantly, it demonstrates that a scrutable group model visualisation can provides a new mechanism for navigating a large, sophisticated and complex groupware site.

Acknowledgments. We thank the Australasian Apple University Consortium for its support of this project with their generous Honours Scholarship.

References

1. Donath, J.: A semantic approach to visualizing online conversations. Communications of the ACM 45(4), 45–49 (2002)
2. Drury, H., Kay, J., Losberg, W.: Student satisfaction with groupwork in undergraduate computer science: Do things get better? In: ACE 2003: Proceedings of the fifth Australasian conference on Computing education, pp. 77–85. Australian Computer Society, Inc., Darlinghurst (2003)
3. Edgewall Software. The Trac Project (2008), http://trac.edgewall.org/ (verified, 2008-02-01)
4. Erickson, T., Kellogg, W.A.: Social translucence: an approach to designing systems that support social processes. ACM Transactions on Computer-Human Interaction 7(1), 59–83 (2000)
5. Gilbert, E., Karahalios, K.: CodeSaw: A social visualization of distributed software development. In: Baranauskas, C., Palanque, P., Abascal, J., Barbosa, S.D.J. (eds.) INTERACT 2007. LNCS, vol. 4663, pp. 303–316. Springer, Heidelberg (2007)
6. Johnson, D.W., Johnson, R.T.: Positive Interdependence: Key to Effective Cooperation. In: Interaction in cooperative groups: The theoretical anatomy of group learning, p. 174 (1992)
7. Kay, J., Maisonneuve, N., Yacef, K., Reimann, P.: The big five and visualisations of team work activity. In: Ikeda, M., Ashley, K.D., Chan, T.-W. (eds.) ITS 2006. LNCS, vol. 4053, pp. 197–206. Springer, Heidelberg (2006)
8. Kay, J., Maisonneuve, N., Yacef, K., Reimann, P.: Wattle tree: What'll it tell us? Technical Report 582, The University of Sydney (January 2006)
9. Likert, R.: A technique for the measurement of attitudes. Archives of Psychology 140, 55 (1932)
10. Salas, E., Sims, D.E., Burke, C.S.: Is there a "Big Five" in Teamwork? Small Group Research 36(5), 555–599 (2005)
11. Slavin, R.E.: Cooperative learning: theory, research and practice. Prentice-Hall, Englewood Cliffs (1990)
12. Soller, A.L.: Supporting social interaction in an intelligent collaborative learning system. International Journal of Artificial Intelligence in Education 12(1), 40–62 (2001)
13. Xiong, R., Donath, J.: Peoplegarden: Creating data portraits for users. In: UIST 1999: Proceedings of the 12th annual ACM symposium on User interface software and technology, pp. 37–44. ACM Press, New York (1999)

Social Navigation Support for Information Seeking: If You Build It, Will They Come?

Rosta Farzan and Peter Brusilovsky

Intelligent Systems Program
University of Pittsburgh
Pittsburgh, PA, 15260
rosta@cs.pitt.edu, peterb@mail.sis.pitt.edu

Abstract. Navigating through the ever-changing information space is becoming increasingly difficult. Social navigation support is a technique for guiding users to interesting and relevant information by leveraging the browsing behavior of past users. Effect of social navigation support on users' information seeking behavior has been studied mostly from conceptual basis or under natural experiments. In the current work, we have designed and conducted a controlled experiment to investigate the effect of social navigation support through a multifaceted method. This paper reports on the design of the study and the result of log data, subjective evaluation, and eye movement data analysis.

1   Introduction

Social Navigation emerged into a popular research area at the crossroads of two active research fields - personalized information access and social Web. Social navigation assists users browsing through Web resources by applying "community wisdom" distilled from the actions of earlier users. This navigation support most frequently comes in the form of visual cues indicating, for example, which of the available links were picked by the majority of similar users [22], or which pages were being explored by other users at the moment [14].

Despite the popularity of social navigation ideas [11], very few studies of social navigation systems can be found in the research literature. The majority of research done in the field falls into two categories of (1) Conceptual structure which focus on theoretical discussion of social navigation phenomena and design aspects with little or no focus on evaluation; and (2) Natural experiments that rely solely on observations of the effect of social navigation on the users' navigation behavior in the system under study rather than manipulating variables in controlled experiments. As a result, while there is a popular belief that social navigation support (SNS) is powerful and helpful, we know very little about the value of various social navigation approaches. Moreover, we are not sure whether the users of social navigation systems follow social navigation cues or these cues are simply ignored. In our past research [7], we attempted to present some evidence that social visual cues are noticed and used. Our results, however, were based on user log data collected during a long-term classroom study and can be

G.-J. Houben et al. (Eds.): UMAP 2009, LNCS 5535, pp. 66–77, 2009.

considered rather as the first step in exploring the impact of social navigation on user behavior. The click-stream collected in the user logs caused us to rely on secondary evidence about user attention to visual cues. A user click on an annotated link may be caused by the usefulness of the link, not the attached social cue. At the same time, the lack of a click does not really mean that the visual cue was not noticed - the link could be simply less relevant to the user in a specific context.

The work presented in this paper attempted to explore on a deeper level the impact of social navigation cues on users' information seeking behavior. We have designed a controlled experiment to assess the following questions: Do the users notice social navigation cues? Do the provided cues affect and change their link selection? Do the visual cues become more useful under time pressure when the user has little time to make a proper navigation decision? The experiment focused on a factual information seeking task designed for a lab study. We observed users' information seeking behavior with and without SNS and time constraint. We extended observational and log data by using eye-tracking. Eye tracking data provides information about users' areas of interest and attention and helps to closely examine the effect of social navigation cues on users' information seeking behavior.

The rest of the paper explains the design of the study and presents part of the results of the study. We conclude with a discussion of the results and their implications for the design of similar systems and plans for the future work.

2   Background

User navigation can be called social when it is driven by the actions from one or more advice providers [5]. In its classic form, social navigation attempts to visualize the aggregated or individual actions of a user community to help future users navigate through complex information spaces such as the Web. Social navigation in information spaces as well as the term social navigation were introduced by Dourish and Chalmers as "moving towards cluster of people" or "selecting objects because others have examined them" [5]. However, the idea of social navigation is frequently traced back to the pioneer Edit Wear and Read Wear systems [10]. Hill and Hollan introduced the idea of physical wear in the domain of document processing as "computational wear". Computational wear is the visualization of the history of authors' and readers' interactions with a document. The visualization of the history enables the new users to quickly locate the most viewed or edited parts of the document.

The systems Juggler [4] and Footprints [22] are classical examples which used social navigation to help users navigating in two kinds of information spaces - a Web site and a text-based virtual environment. Both systems attempted to visualize traces to guide future users. Wexelblat and Mayes [22] introduced the idea of interaction history for digital information which is taken from extensive use of history traces in the physical world. Footprints provides contextualized navigation through usage of several interface features such as maps, path views, annotations,and sign posts. Juggler is an educational tool which combines a text-based virtual environment (known as MOO) and a Web browser. Juggler highlights major navigation paths through different textual bulletin boards (rooms) and adds the computational wear to each bulletin boards by showing the number of times it was accessed. Juggler also supports a direct form of social navigation by encouraging users to directly recommend useful resources (such as URLs) to each other. Another example of a system with several forms of social navigation is KALAS [21], a food recipe system. It provides a history-enriched environment by visualizing the aggregated trail of users through the environment. The trail includes the comments left by the users as well as information about the number of users who have downloaded a recipe. KALAS supports direct social navigation by displaying currently logged on users in each section of the system and allowing real-time chat among the users. Implementation of social navigation goes beyond these classical examples. Growth of social information access applications on the Web over the last decade suggests social navigation as a response to problem of disorientation on the Web [20], [15], [6].

While the idea of social navigation has widely been implemented, evaluation of the effect of social navigation support is a less explored area. Evaluation methodologies used to evaluate information seeking tools can be employed to achieve deeper insight into the effectiveness and strength of social navigation support. Recently researchers in the field of information retrieval have been attracted to utilizing eye tracking for better understanding of users' search behavior and to model users and their interests beyond log analysis and queries they type in. Accurate viewing is only possible in 1-2 degrees of visual angle. As a result, gaze direction is a reliable indicator of the focus of attention.

Eye movement data are typically divided into fixations and saccades. Fixations are relative pauses of eye movements over an informative region of interest while saccades are the rapid eye movements between the fixations [19]. The main methodology employed in interface evaluation using eye-tracking is through dividing the interface into predefined areas of interest [8] and collecting users' eye movement on those areas. Number of fixations, location of fixations, fixation duration, and cumulative fixation time are some of the most commonly used measures in evaluation of computer interfaces using eye-tracking [18], [12]. Joachims et al [13] extended the work on assessing the reliability of implicit feedback by detailed analysis of users' decision making process through the use of eye tracking. They analyzed users' fixations on the search results page to understand how to associate users' decision process with their clickthrough actions and how to generate feedback from clicks. In a similar study, Cutrell and Guan [3] used eye tracking to investigate how users attend to different parts of web search results and whether users' search strategies are different for navigational versus informational tasks. Specifically, they were interested on assessing the effect of snippet length on how people use Web search. Chi et al [2] studied the eye-gaze behavior of subjects to understand how highlighting keywords and sentences containing highly relevant conceptual keywords (ScentHighlights) affected subjects' reading behavior. They were interested in assessing whether highlighting is successful in directing users' attention while skimming the text. They analyzed users' initial fixations and eye behavior, and percentage of fixations on highlighted areas.

3   Study of Social Navigation Support

In the current work, we explored the role of several factors on the added value of SNS. We designed an experiment to investigate the circumstances under which SNS can help users in an information exploration task. In the experiment, we controlled the presence of SNS and time to complete the task. We were specifically interested in investigating the effect of time pressure on the usage of SNS.

3.1   Task

The study investigated the effect of SNS on a factual information seeking task which is known as the most common type of information seeking task on the Web [17]. The participants were asked to respond to several questions by finding facts in a very large collection of relevant and irrelevant news articles from multiple sources. In our past work, we developed a set of search tasks (topics) for this collection and collected passage-level ground truth for each topic [9]. Each topic contains an overarching task theme and up to 10 different (but related) factual questions. Over the course of the study the participants worked with four topics of our collection solving four different search tasks. For each search task they were given a one-page task description providing a brief background to the task scenario and a list of questions to answer (a subset of 10 questions). To minimize the impact of topics, we tried to pick the topics with a similar difficulty level. We used data from a related prior study to judge the difficulty level of the topics [1]. We used criteria such as number of relevant documents in the corpus, average number of relevant documents returned by users, and number of questions to match the difficulty level of the topics.

3.2   Interface

For our study, we developed an information exploration system with social navigation. Figure 1 shows the main interface of the system. It is similar to other search engines in which the user enters a query and the results are returned sorted by the relevance to the query. In addition to this traditional interface, the experimental version of the system offers two kinds of social navigation support. First, the search results are annotated with social navigation cues. The cues are based on two types of user activities: reading and highlighting. The human icon represents the amount of reading activity for the associated document and the annotation icon represents the amount of highlighting done in the document. The level of the filling color represents the density of the activity with a higher level of filling representing the higher number of activities. Mousing over the icons shows the details about the number of visits or number of highlights.

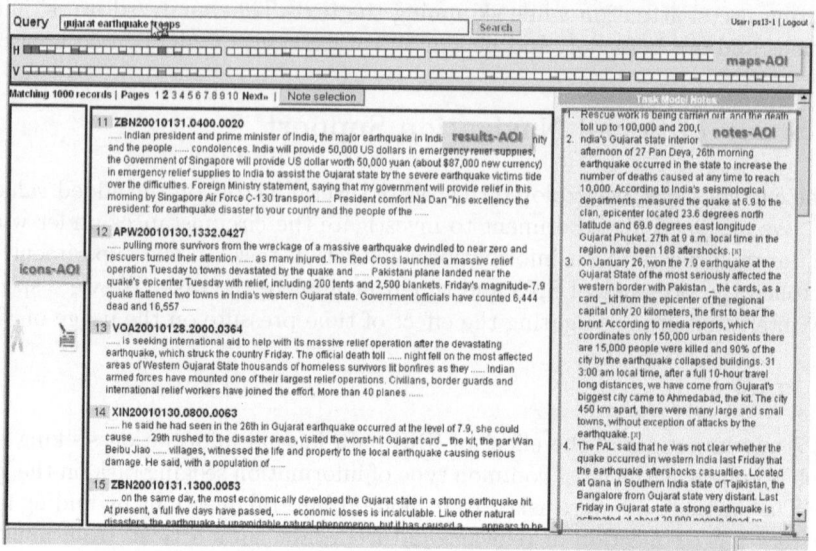

Fig. 1. Search Interface (with eye tracking areas of interest)

Second kind of social navigation support is offered by "social maps". Social maps are two tables at the top of the page, representing highlighting and visiting activities for the current 100 documents. Each cell in the table is associated with the document with the same rank as the cell number; i.e. first one is associated with the first document in the list. Users can directly access the document by clicking on the map cell. The filling level of the cell represents the magnitude of the activity. If the cell is empty, it means the associated document has not been visited or highlighted by anyone. The social maps provide information beyond 10 documents returned on each page of search results. They were designed to help users have broader picture of the results in an easy way.

A panel on the right side of the interface shows the list of notes (passages) collected by the current user. To collect notes, users can highlight and save a passage either directly from a snippet shown for each returned document in the list of search results or from the full text of the article, which the user can open by clicking on the document title. The passages saved from this document by past users will be highlighted providing another level of SNS. Figure 2 shows an example of the full text of the article. At this view, SNS is offered by showing the part of the text highlighted by past users. By default, other users' highlighted passages are shown (in pink). Users can choose to ignore that information and view their own highlighted passages (in yellow).

Social Navigation Support. The system provided SNS through augmenting search results with icons, social maps, and previously highlighted parts of the text. In real life, social navigation cues are generated from the activity of all past users. However, this is not good for a controlled study since every new

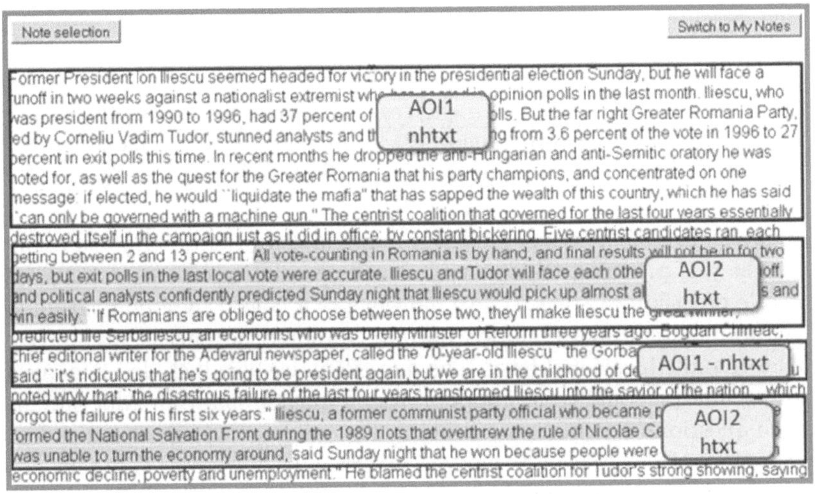

Fig. 2. Full text of the article (with eye tracking areas of interest)

user may see more cues than past users. To avoid this, in our study we used
"frozen" social cues generated from the activity of users from a prior study [1].
For each topic, the data includes the activities of three distinct users. To make
the task more realistic, we divided the questions for each topic into two sets
with the criteria of decreasing within-cluster similarity and increasing between-
cluster similarity. This simulated a collaborative task which is divided among
the members of a group. We calculated the similarity of two questions based
on the shared number of documents which included the response to each of the
questions. To cluster the questions, we calculated the similarity of questions for
every possible distinct combination of five questions in a set. We selected the sets
with the highest between-cluster similarity and lowest within-cluster similarity.
This means that SNS will guide the users to the right articles but the highlighted
parts of the articles are not necessarily responses to questions in their task. SNS
was not updated with the interaction history of the participants throughout the
study. This ensured that all users have the same opportunity of getting support
from social navigation cues.

3.3   Study Design

The study has a two-by-two design as shown in Table 1. It follows a complete
random design in which the order of conditions and topics are selected randomly. Under *no time constraint* condition the participants had 15 minutes and
under *time constraint* they had seven minutes. *NO-SNS* condition had no social
navigation cues. The interface looked the same as Figure 1 but with no social
navigation icons and no social maps. Also, when they looked at the full article,
there was no option to view passages highlighted by prior users.

Table 1. Study design - conditions

		SNS	
		Yes (SNS group)	No (no-SNS group)
Time Constraint	Yes (tc group)	Topic 1	Topic 2
	No (no-tc group)	Topic 3	Topic 4

The procedure of the study was at follows: first a brief description about the experiment was provided. Next an eye tracking calibration was done to ensure reasonable precision in tracking eye movements followed by a demographic and skill questionnaire which included questions about the participants' age, gender, major, and educational level. The questionnaire also included five questions measuring interpersonal trust adopted from a questionnaire by Mooradian et al [16]. The questions are shown in Table 2. The response to all questions had five choices ranging from "Strongly agree" to "Strongly disagree". Different parts of the interface were explained thoroughly to all subjects and they all went through a training session to become familiar with the interface before starting the main task. Each session included the main task and a subjective evaluation of the participants' satisfaction with the system.

Table 2. Interpersonal Trust Questionnaire

#	Question
1	I tend to be cynical and skeptical of others' intentions
2	I believe that most people will take advantage of you if you let them
3	If I got into difficulties at work I know my colleagues would try and help me out
4	I can trust the people I work with to lend me a hand if I needed it
5	Most of my peers can be relied upon to do as they say they will do

4   Evaluation

We recruited 15 participants from students at the University of Pittsburgh from several different disciplines including engineering, information science, life sciences, and humanities. Participants were paid for their participation in the study. To limit the variability of linguistic abilities, we recruited native English speakers. Nine out of 15 participants were female. Their age ranged from 20 to 35 with the average age equal to 24 ($\sigma=5$).

4.1   Eye Tracking Data Analysis

We defined two main stimuli, "search result" and "text" as shown in Figure 1 and Figure 2. *Search result* stimulus includes four areas of interest (AOIs) (1) Icons, (2) Maps, (3) Results, and (4) Notes. We were interested to measure the percentage of fixations and gaze time on AOI1 and AOI2 to assess the influence of SNS on users' search behavior. The *text* stimulus includes two AOIs: (1)

not highlighted text (AOI1-nhtxt) and (2)highlighted text (AOI2-htxt). Here, we were interested in measuring the percentage of fixations and gaze time on highlighted parts of the text to assess the influence of presenting prior users' highlights on current users' reading and highlighting behavior. Due to time constraints we analyzed eye movements data of five participants out of 15 who went through the experiment.

4.2 Statistical Analysis

Since the study deals with correlated data we performed hypothesis testing with models designed for correlated data. We fitted three types of models with respect to the distribution of the response variable and goodness of fit: (1) Linear, (2) Negative Binomial, and (3) Gamma.

4.3 Hypotheses and Results

The main goal of the evaluation was to assess the effect of SNS on participants' search behavior specifically with and without time constraint. The following are the main research questions we have tried to address in the analysis of the study:

- Q1 - Were participants more likely to click on documents augmented with social navigation cues? Were they more likely to follow SNS under time pressure?
- Q2 - Are eye movement data going to be different in terms of following social navigation cues under time constraint?
- Q3 - How much of the participants' highlighting and reading behavior was influenced by already highlighted text?

Question 1. To answer the first question, we calculated the average percentage of clicks on documents with and without SNS icons for each subject and we conducted repeated measure analysis to check whether there is a difference in terms of number of clicks. The result shows a significant effect of social navigation cues: documents augmented with cues were accessed significantly more (Wald χ^2=24.16, df=1, p-value<.001). Additionally, the result shows a significant effect of *SNS* condition and significant interaction of *SNS* and social navigation cues which means augmented documents were accessed more under *SNS* condition (SNS: Wald χ^2=4.70, df=1, p-value=.030, SNS×augmented: Wald $\chi^2$6.86, df=1, p-value=.009). We emphasize that under the *no-SNS* condition, the participants were not aware of which documents could have been augmented. This result is important to show that augmented documents are not just the important documents that would have been accessed even if not augmented. There is marginal significance of time pressure which suggests participants were slightly more likely to click on augmented documents under the *time constraint* condition (Wald χ^2=3.14, df=1, p-value=.076).

Question 2. We hypothesized that users under time pressure will be in more need of navigation support and will make more use of SNS. Number of fixations and total gaze time on the social navigation icons and social navigation maps can be an indication of how much they have utilized those navigation supports. We calculated the percentage of fixation count and gaze time on those AOIs while users were looking at search results. The average percentage is shown in Figure 3. The result shows a similar number of fixations and amount of gaze time over social navigation icons and a higher number of fixations and amount of gaze time on social navigation maps under the *no time constraint* condition.

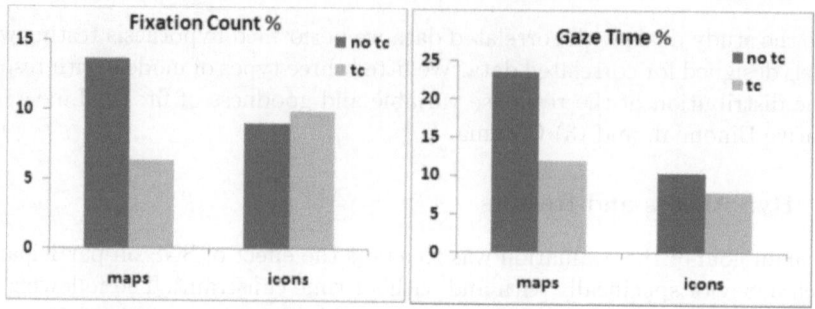

Fig. 3. Average percentage of fixations and gaze time on social navigation AOIs

This is an interesting result which does not match our expectation. This can be due to the fact that users under the *time constraint* condition had time to check very few articles and they might have mainly relied on the rank of search results. They still relied on social navigation cues integrated with the ranked list and checked the icons. However, they did not have enough time to explore anything (like social navigation maps) beyond highly-ranked results. In fact, our data shows that under the *time constraint* condition participants selected articles from significantly higher (numerically lower) ranking (Average rank: no-tc=4.2, tc=1.8).

Question 3. As we mentioned before, the highlighted text was not entirely related to questions the current participants were working on; instead there were responses to similar questions. We were interested in assessing how much the reading and highlighting behavior of participants were affected by those highlights and whether there is going to be a large overlap between their collected passages and highlighted passages. To answer this question, we calculated the percentage of overlapping notes for each participant as number of characters overlapping the highlighted area divided by total length of notes selected by that participant. On average, there was 9.3% overlap under *time constraint* condition (σ=.04) and 5.7% overlap under *no time constraint* condition (σ=.09). There is no significant effect of the condition on the average overlap. The result suggests that while the users were slightly influenced by highlights, they did not just select notes from highlighted areas. Our eye-tracking data supports the same result. The average percentage of fixation count is significantly higher on not highlighted text as compared to highlighted text(htxt-AOI:μ=18.92, nhtxt-AOI:μ=80.51,

Wald χ^2=37.014, df=1, p-value<.0001). The result shows that users did not only focus on highlighted text and spent considerable amount of time reading not highlighted text. It suggests that SNS helped the participants to get to the relevant documents, but within a document they relied on their own judgment.

4.4 Subjective Evaluation

We conducted a survey after each session to evaluate users' subjective opinions about the system. The first five questions were the same after all sessions: they asked about general usability of the system and whether the users had enough time to perform the task.

The result shows that, under all four conditions, it was quite easy to find relevant documents and passages. However, under the *NO-SNS* and *time constraint* condition, the participants were less happy with the output of the system for answering the questions (There is a marginal significance interaction of SNS and time constraint - wald χ^2 2=3.03, df=1, p-value=.08). While our eye movements and click-stream data shows that the participants did not necessarily utilize social navigation cues more under time pressure, this result suggests that presence of social navigation cues was somehow reassuring for them.

Additionally, the survey after the *SNS* conditions collected the users' opinion about SNS. The questions are shown in Table 3. The possible response to all questions ranged from 1 (not at all) to 5 (extremely).

Table 3. Subjective evaluation - SNS related questions

Question
1 Did you find it useful to know what documents were selected by other users?
2 Did you find it useful to know what documents were highlighted by other users?
3 Did you find it useful to view passages highlighted by other users?
4 Did you find it useful to know the number of times each document was visited?
5 Did you find it useful to know the number of times each document was highlighted?
6 The tables on top of the page were designed to facilitate navigating to documents highlighted or visited by other users. Did you find it useful?

As mentioned earlier, as part of our demographic questionnaire, we measured participants' interpersonal trust level. We divided the participants into high trust and low trust levels based on their responses to those questions. Eight participants were in the low trust level and seven in the high trust group. We were interested to determine any effect of interpersonal trust on their judgment of the usefulness of SNS. Figure 4 shows the average responses to the SNS-related questions of the questionnaire. The response is divided into four groups depending on the trust level and time constraint. The result suggests that participants with higher interpersonal trust levels are more satisfied with SNS, particularly under time constraint.

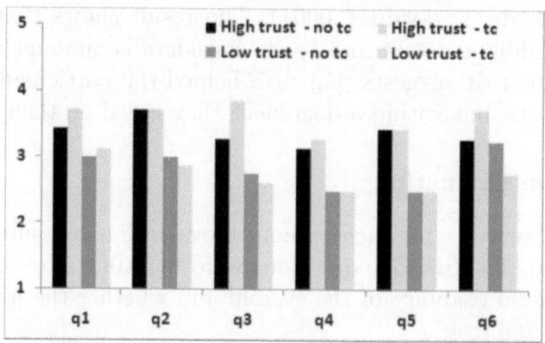

Fig. 4. Average responses to SNS related questions in the subjective evaluation

5 Discussion and Future Work

In the current work, we presented a multifaceted study of SNS in a controlled experiment designed for factual information seeking tasks. The result of the study confirms that social navigation cues affect users' search behavior and users pay attention to social navigation cues and follow those cues for finding information. However, contrary to our expectation, time constraint did not increase the applicability of SNS and traditional navigational support such as search rank proved to be more reliable for users. The result also shows that personal characteristics such as interpersonal trust affects the perception of usefulness of SNS. This should to be taken into account for user modeling applications. Moreover, our result suggests that the snowball effect often associated with social navigation can be avoided if the systems offer users sufficient information to make their own informed judgement. In our study, the participants did not select part of the text just because it was highlighted by prior users and even though the highlights were slightly relevant to their task.

An element missing in the current study is assessing the effect of SNS on the quality of the performed task. For our future work, we will look into evaluating the effect of SNS on the relevancy of collected information to the task. Moreover, we will extend our eye movement data analysis to a larger number of users to to assess our current observations with larger amount of data.

References

1. Ahn, J., Brusilovsky, P., He, D., Grady, J., Li, Q.: Personalized web exploration with task models. In: Proceedings of the 17th international conference on World Wide Web (2008)
2. Chi, E.H., Gumbrecht, M., Hong, L.: Visual foraging of highlighted text: An eye-tracking study. In: Jacko, J.A. (ed.) HCI 2007. LNCS, vol. 4552, pp. 589–598. Springer, Heidelberg (2007)
3. Cutrell, E., Guan, Z.: What are you looking for? an eye-tracking study of information usage in web search. In: Proceedings of the SIGCHI conference on Human factors in computing systems (2007)

4. Dieberger, A.: Supporting social navigation on the world wide web. International Journal of Human-Computer Interaction 46, 805–825 (1997)
5. Dourish, P., Chalmers, M.: Running out of space: Models of information navigation. In: Proceedings of HCI 1994 (1994)
6. Dron, J.: Termites in the schoolhouse: Stigmergy and transactional distance in an e-learning environment. In: Cantoni, L., McLoughlin, C. (eds.) Proceedings of World Conference on Educational Multimedia, Hypermedia and Telecommunications, Chesapeake, VA, pp. 263–269. AACE (2004)
7. Farzan, R., Brusilovsky, P.: Annotated: A social navigation and annotation service for web-based educational resources. New Review in Hypermedia and Multimedia 14(1), 3–32 (2008)
8. Goldberg, J.H., Kotval, X.P.: Computer interface evaluation using eye-movement: methods and constructs - its psychological foundation and relevance to display design. International Journal of Industrial Ergonomics (1999)
9. Brusilovsky, P., Ahn, J., Grady, J., Farzan, R., Peng, Y., Yang, Y., He, D., Rogati, M.: An evaluation of adaptive filtering in the context of realistic task-based information exploration. Information Processing and Management 44(2), 511–533 (2008)
10. Hill, W.C., Hollan, J.D., Wroblewski, D., Mccandless, T.: Edit wear and read wear. In: Bauersfeld, P., Bennett, J., Lynch, G. (eds.) Proceedings of the SIGCHI conference on Human factors in computing systems, pp. 3–9 (1992)
11. Höök, K., Benyon, D., Munro, A.J. (eds.): Designing Information Spaces: The Social Navigation Approach. Springer, Berlin (2003)
12. Jacob, R.J.K., Karn, K.S.: Eye tracking in human computer interaction and usability research: ready to deliver the promises (section commentary). The mind's eye: cognitive and applied aspects of eye movement research, 573–605 (2003)
13. Joachims, T., Granka, L., Pan, B.: Accurately interpreting clickthrough data as implicit feedback. In: SIGIR 2005 (2005)
14. Kurhila, J., Miettinen, M., Nokelainen, P., Tirri, H.: Educo - a collaborative learning environment based on social navigation. In: De Bra, P., Brusilovsky, P., Conejo, R. (eds.) AH 2002. LNCS, vol. 2347, pp. 242–252. Springer, Heidelberg (2002)
15. Millen, D.R., Feinberg, J., Kerr, B.: Dogear: Social bookmarkin in the enterprise. In: Proceedings of CHI (2006)
16. Mooradian, T., Renzl, B., Matzler, K.: Who trusts? personality, trust and knowledge sharing. Management Learning 37(4), 523–540 (2006)
17. Morrison, J., Pirolli, P., Card, S.K.: A taxonomic analysis of what world wide web activities significantly impact people's decisions and actions. In: Proceedings of CHI 2001 (2001)
18. Poole, A., Ball, L.J.: Eye Tracking in Human-Computer Interaction and Usability Research: Current Status and Future Prospects. In: Encyclopedia of Human Computer Interaction. Information Science Reference (2006)
19. Rayner, K.: Eye movements in reading and information processing: 20 years of research. Psychological Bulletin 124, 372–422 (1998)
20. Smyth, B., Balfe, E., Freyne, J., Briggs, P., Coyle, M., Boydell, O.: Exploiting query repetition and regularity in an adaptive community-based web search engine. User Modeling and User-Adapted Interaction 14(5), 383–423 (2004)
21. Svensson, M., Höök, K., Laaksolahti, J., Waern, A.: Social navigation of food recipes. In: Proceedings of CHI, Seattle, April 2001. ACM, New York (2001)
22. Wexelblat, A., Maes, P.: Footprints: History-rich tools for information foraging. In: Proceeding of ACM Conference on Human-Computer Interaction (CHI 1999), pp. 270–277. ACM Press, New York (1999)

Performance Evaluation of a Privacy-Enhancing Framework for Personalized Websites*

Yang Wang and Alfred Kobsa

Donald Bren School of Information and Computer Sciences
University of California, Irvine, U.S.A.
{yangwang,kobsa}@ics.uci.edu

Abstract. Reconciling personalization with privacy has been a continuing interest in the user modeling community. In prior work, we proposed a dynamic privacy-enhancing user modeling framework based on a software product line architecture (PLA). Our system dynamically selects personalization methods during runtime that respect users' current privacy preferences as well as the prevailing privacy laws and regulations. One major concern about our approach is its performance since dynamic architectural reconfiguration during runtime is usually resource-intensive. In this paper, we describe four implementations of our system that vary two factors, and an in-depth performance evaluation thereof under realistic workload conditions. Our study shows that a customized version performs better than the original PLA implementation, that a multi-level caching mechanism improves both versions, and that the customized version with caching performs best. The average handling time per user session is less than 0.2 seconds for all versions except the original PLA implementation. Overall, our results demonstrate that with a reasonable number of networked hosts in a cloud computing environment, an internationally operating website can use our dynamic PLA-based user modeling approach to personalize their user services, and at the same time respect the individual privacy desires of their users as well as the privacy norms that may apply.

1 Introduction

Since personalized websites collect personal data, they are subject to prevailing privacy laws and regulations if the respective individuals are in principle identifiable (see [1] for a comprehensive review of privacy issues in personalization). Internationally operating websites are particularly affected since a large number of countries extend the applicability of their privacy laws to operators and personal data flows beyond their national boundaries. Moreover, in order to encourage users to interact with personalized sites and thus benefit from the full potential of personalization, personalized systems should also cater to each user's current privacy preferences. That is to say, a user can have varying privacy preferences on different sites, and at different times on the same site, and thus each site should be able to treat the same user differently depending on

* This research has been supported through NSF grant IIS 0308277 and a Google Research Award. We would like to thank Scott Hendrickson, Eric Dashofy, André van der Hoek and the UMAP09 reviewers for their helpful comments.

G.-J. Houben et al. (Eds.): UMAP 2009, LNCS 5535, pp. 78–89, 2009.

her current privacy preferences. In [2] we illustrated that these privacy constraints may affect not only the data that may be collected by the personalized website, but also the admissibility of personalization methods for processing personal data.

The resulting combinatorial complexity of these privacy constraints make them hard to cope with. We therefore proposed a novel approach based on software product line architecture that models the variability in both the privacy and personalization domains, and allows the configuration of the employed personalization methods to be dynamically tailored to each user at runtime, considering both the prevailing privacy norms and the user's current privacy preferences. This flexible approach not only helps address the complexity of building personalized systems, but also strongly supports their evolution: as new privacy and personalization concerns arise, they can be added to the product line architecture in a modular manner [3,4].

One major concern about our approach is its performance since dynamic architectural reconfiguration during runtime is usually resource-intensive. Will it be practically possible to deploy such a dynamic system in a contemporary internationally operating website? In this paper, we describe four variant implementations of our system and an in-depth performance evaluation under realistic workload conditions. Our work stands in the tradition of similar attempts in the past to gauge the performance of user modeling tools through simulation experiments (e.g., [5,6,7]). It is however also substantially different from prior evaluations due to the fact that the workload is not induced by user requests (such as web page requests) or requests from software processes (such as user-adaptive applications or personalization methods), and that the aspired goal is not a user modeling tool that performs personalization tasks efficiently. Rather, the workload is induced by the initiation of new user sessions, and the goal is the efficient instantiation of user-modeling architectures that meet the privacy constraint of each individual user.

In the remainder of this paper, we will first briefly recap our privacy-enhancing user modeling framework in Section 2. We then describe the setup of our performance evaluation, such as the simulated parameters and workload, in Section 3. Thereafter, we present different implementations of our approach in Section 4, the performance evaluation of these implementations in Section 5, discussions of the results in Section 6, and conclusions in Section 7.

2   Our Privacy-Enhancing User Modeling Framework

In order to enable personalized web-based systems to respect users' individual privacy constraints, Kobsa [8] proposed a user modeling framework that encapsulates different personalization methods in individual components and, at any point during runtime, ensures that only those components that comply with current privacy constraints can be used. We adopted a Product Line Architecture (PLA) approach to implement this design. A PLA is an architectural representation for a set of related products. It includes core elements present in all product architectures, and variation points where variations exist among individual product architectures [9]. Each variation point is guarded by a Boolean expression that specifies the conditions under which an optional component should be included in a particular product architecture [10]. A particular product architecture can be selected out of a product line architecture by resolving the Boolean guards of each variation point at design-time, invocation-time or run-time [11].

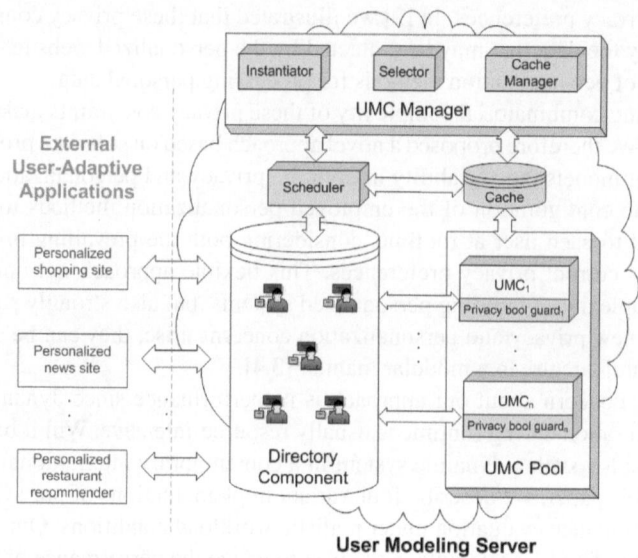

Fig. 1. Distributed dynamic privacy-enhancing user modeling framework

2.1 Framework Overview

Figure 1 shows an overview of our framework[1]. It consists of external user-adaptive
applications, an LDAP-based user modeling server (UMS) [12], a user modeling component (UMC) manager, a Scheduler and a cache database. External user-adaptive applications can retrieve user information from the UMS so as to personalize services to
their end users, and can submit additional user information to the UMS. The UMS includes a Directory Component and a pool of UMCs. The Directory Component hosts
a repository of user models, storing users' characteristics and their individual privacy
preferences. The UMC Pool contains a set of UMCs, each encapsulating one or more
personalization methods (e.g., collaborative filtering). UMCs make inferences about
users based on existing information in the user models and then add the derived user
information to the user models [2].

To enable PLA operations (e.g., product architecture selection), the UMC Manager
was added to the UMS. The enhanced UMS was then modeled as a PLA, in which the
Directory Component and the UMC Manger were core components, and UMCs were
optional components. Each UMC is guarded by a Boolean expression that represents
privacy conditions under which the respective UMC may operate. Each privacy condition is expressed by a Boolean variable (e.g., Combining_Profile == true). As such,
we use these Boolean variables bearing privacy semantics to represent users' privacy
preferences as well as applicable privacy regulations. In practice, the values of these
Boolean variables can come from the evaluation of privacy conditions expressed in a
privacy policy language (see [13] for a discussion of these languages).

---

[1] The shaded parts are our privacy-related additions to the user modeling server described in
   [12].

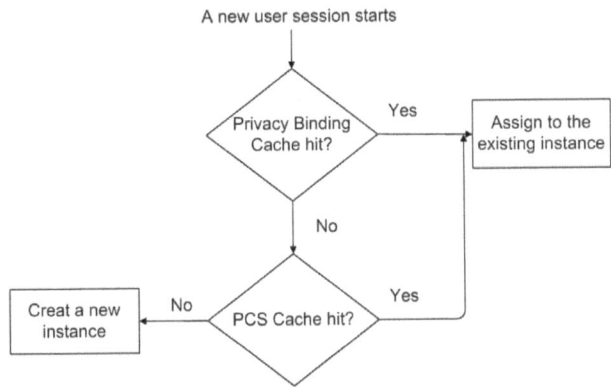

Fig. 2. Multi-level caching mechanism

In the following, we will describe the UMC Manager in more detail and then discuss distribution issues.

2.2   UMC Manager

The UMC Manager was implemented to support PLA selection and instantiation as well as our caching mechanism. It consists of the following components:

Selector. When a new user session begins, the Selector takes the PLA and the privacy bindings relating to the new session as inputs. Privacy bindings are name-value pairs for the Boolean guards in the PLA, e.g., Combining_Profile = false which would represent that the user or some privacy norm relating to the user session disallow the merging of profiles relating to the same user. The Selector selects a particular product architecture out of the PLA by resolving the Boolean guards associated with each optional component in the PLA using the current privacy bindings. It expresses the chosen architecture through a binary Privacy Constraint Satisfaction (PCS) vector [3] whose n^{th} element represents whether or not the nth UMC may be included in the selected product architecture.

Instantiator. The Instantiator takes a PCS as input and creates a runtime system instance for the product architecture. The total number of different PCS vectors ($2^{TotalUMCs}$) equals the theoretical maximum of instances that may be created.

Cache Manager. We designed a multi-level caching strategy that is shown in Fig. 2. The Cache Manager controls caches of both individual users' privacy bindings and their associate PCS vectors (i.e., the results of the PLA selection). More specifically, when a new user session starts, the Cache Manager checks the privacy binding cache whether the system has an existing user session with the same privacy bindings (i.e., a user with identical privacy norms and individual privacy preferences). If it finds one, the new session will be assigned to the same system instance as the existing session. If no such binding can be found, the Cache Manager will further check the PCS cache since a PCS may meet the constraints of more than one privacy binding. Only if no such PCS can be found either, the Instantiator will start a new instance for this user session. More details about our runtime dynamism mechanism can be found in [3].

2.3   Distributed Framework

In order to cope with potentially millions of concurrent users, the enhanced UMS needs to be distributed. In Fig. 1, the cloud denotes the distribution of processing over a network of machines. Distribution of the LDAP-based Directory Component and the UMC Pool have been addressed in [12]. We also distribute the UMC Manager over a network of hosts, each having a stand-alone copy of the UMC Manager. In addition, we add a Scheduler in the framework to assign incoming user sessions to various hosts, and a database to store the privacy binding cache and the PCS cache.

3   System Implementation

In this section, we describe the implementations of major components and operations in our framework (the first two were varied in the different conditions of our experiment).

3.1   PLA Representation, Selection and Instantiation

As explained above, our privacy-enhancing user modeling framework was designed as a PLA. Therefore, the core of the framework involves the following tasks: generation of a PLA for the system architecture, selection of UMCs based on the bindings of the privacy Boolean guards, and instantiation of the selected architecture for the user modeling system.

ArchStudio-based Implementation. In our preliminary implementation [3], we adapted functionalities from ArchStudio 3 [14] to perform the above tasks. ArchStudio 3 is an architecture-centric development environment, built on the C2 architectural style [15]. It provides excellent support for PLA modeling and development. This system has been meanwhile upgraded to ArchStudio 4 [16], built on the Myx architectural style [17]. The Myx style provides better system performance because it allows unmediated synchronous procedure calls between components in the architecture. In the C2 style, component interactions are always asynchronous and mediated by connectors. We therefore chose ArchStudio 4 for our final test system and implemented it in the Myx style (we call it the Myx version).

Our Customized Implementation. The standardization and extensibility of the XML-based PLA representation come at a price: XML processing can be expensive and thus affect the overall system performance. This is especially the case when the PLA has a large number of components. Therefore, we designed a light-weight alternative to the xADL 2.0 representation, called PLA Object Notation (PLAON). It contains an array of component objects. Each optional component object stores its privacy Boolean guard in an array, each element representing a privacy Boolean variable. Privacy bindings are in turn stored as a binary array, each element denoting the binding for a privacy Boolean variable. Our customized selector can then use the privacy binding array to resolve the

Boolean guard array. Again the results of the selection will be a PCS vector, implemented as a binary array. Our customized instantiator reads from the PCS array to start components whose values in the PCS array are 1. Since our customized implementation represents the PLA semantics in a succinct object notation and omits any XML processing, we expect it to perform better than the original Myx-based implementation.

3.2 Multi-level Caching

Caching is the other factor that we vary in our experiment. As described earlier, if two users have the same privacy bindings, or the same PCS vectors after selection, then they can share the same user modeling system instance. This reuse would save the system from performing unnecessary architectural selections and instantiations in such cases.

3.3 Resource-Aware Scheduling

Since hosts can have different hardware and networking characteristics in our distributed framework (e.g. different amounts of memory), the scheduler needs to take this heterogeneity into account, so as to optimize the overall system performance. When a host becomes available, it will connect and register itself with the Scheduler. The scheduler keeps track of all the registered hosts, their computing capabilities (right now we only consider the memory size), and the number of user sessions that each host is currently serving. When a new user session is initiated, the Scheduler first checks with the Cache Manager to see if any system instance can be reused for this session. If not, it would select the lightest-loaded host that can still handle this session with its resources. This resource-aware scheduling was used in all conditions of our experiment.

4 Experimental Design and Procedures

4.1 Controlled Variables

Since we suspected that the XML-based Myx implementation described in Sect. 3.1 would perform poorly, we aimed at contrasting it with the two optimization methods described in Sect. 3.1 and 3.2 through the following 2-factorial design: (Myx vs. Customized) × (Non-caching vs. Caching).

4.2 Simulation Parameters

Since we anticipated that a very large network of machines will be needed to handle real-world large-scale applications that was unavailable to us, we identified a reasonable number of 3000 maximum users per host in pre-trials and simulated such a single host on a PC. The other parameters of our experiment were chosen based on our analysis of international privacy laws and their impacts on personalized systems [18,19,2], as well as the user modeling literature:

- Total number of UMCs in the PLA: 10.
- Total number of different privacy constraints: 100.

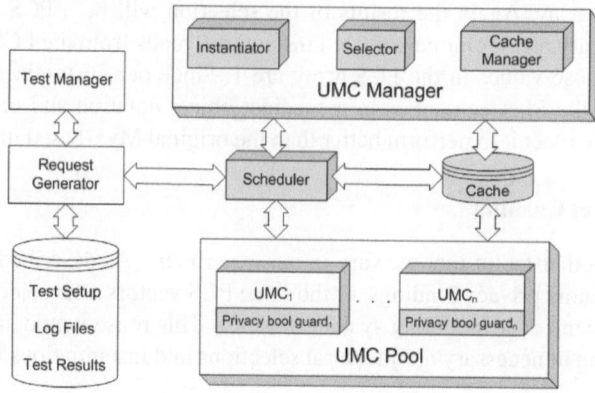

Fig. 3. Testbed architecture

- Simulated number of user sessions per host: 3000.
- Average arrival rate of unique visitors per host per second: 0.5.
- Number of variables in the privacy Boolean guards of each UMC: 5.

We randomly chose 5 out of the total 100 privacy constraints for each UMC and randomly generated the privacy bindings (true or false) for each user session.

Previous work such as [20,21] has empirically shown that the arrival of new user sessions at a website largely follows a Poisson process[2]. To compare the four conditions of our experiment on a common basis, we pre-generated Poisson-distributed session arrival times with a mean rate of 0.5 users per second, and used them in all experiments.

4.3 Testbed

Figure 3 depicts the overall testbed architecture. The performance evaluation of the LDAP-based Directory Component and the UMC Pool in [12] had already demonstrated that they scale well and can be deployed to high-workload commercial applications. To be able to measure the performance of the PLA selection and instantiation in isolation, we omitted the Directory Component and created functionless dummy implementations for all UMCs, thereby realistically assuming that those components would run on different hosts anyways when deployed in practice. We added a Test Manager to control experiments, a Request Generator to generate user sessions, and a MySQL database to store the test setup, logs and results. The whole testbed except for the database was implemented in Java, complied in Java 1.6, and run in the HotSpot Java Virtual Machine on a PC platform with two 3.2 GHz processors, 3 GB of RAM, and a 150 GB hard disk.

---

[2] Chlebus and Brazier [21] found two separate regions of time in a day, each lasting several hours and having a different average arrival rate. They therefore suggests that the arrival rate rather follows a non-stationary Poisson process, i.e. consists of more than one Poisson process, each with its own rate. Those results are not likely to apply to internationally operating sites though on which we largely focus.

4.4 Procedures

The Test Manager first reads the test setup from the database and informs the Request Generator to generate simulated user sessions and associated privacy bindings. The Request Generator reads the session arrival times from the database and starts sending user sessions to the Scheduler. The Scheduler chooses a host to handle the session. The host then performs the PLA selection and instantiation (in the Cache conditions, PLA selection and/or instantiation may be skipped, depending on the type of cache hit – see Sect. 2.2). Once the session has been assigned to a runtime system instance, the assignment is written into the cache if a cache is used. When all user sessions have been handled, log files and test results are written into the database.

For every user session, we measure three values:

Handling time, which is the period between the Request Generator sending the session to the Scheduler, and the session being assigned to a runtime instance.

Reuse rate of runtime instances, which considers the total number of user sessions and of instances currently in the system, has a range of $[0, 1)$ and is calculated as
$$\frac{Total\ Sessions - Total\ Instances}{Total\ Sessions}$$

Performance improvement (percentage), which compares the system performance of the original implementation (Myx implementation without caching) with that of an enhanced implementation. For a given number of users handled, this value has a range of $[0, 1)$ and is calculated as
$$\frac{\sum TotalHandlingTimeOriginalVersion - \sum TotalHandlingTimeEnhancedVersion}{\sum TotalHandlingTimeOriginalVersion}$$

5 Evaluation Results

5.1 Handling Time Per User Session

Figure 4 plots the handling times for each user session in the four implementations, and indicates the means and standard deviations. We can see that the customized versions perform better than the Myx versions, that our multi-level caching mechanism improves both versions, and that the customized version with caching performs best. The average handling time per user session is less than 0.2 seconds for all versions except the Myx implementation without caching.

We also analyzed the spikes of the handling time in Fig. 4 and disconfirmed that they were correlated with bursts in the arrival rate. Based on an analysis of the logs created by our experimental testbed we found that the main reason for the delay lies in Java's indeterministic thread scheduling. Requests to handle a new session, select an architecture, and instantiate an architecture each creates a new thread, and occasionally one of the threads gets switched out of processing and later switched back in. One can notice that in the Myx version without caching, high handling times increase towards the end of the experiment. This is because the machine almost ran out of heap space, and the Java Virtual Machine kept switching threads. A good remedy for these effects of indeterministic thread switching is to shorten the processing time, which is confirmed by the substantial decrease of such delays in the conditions in which the customized version and/or caching have been used.

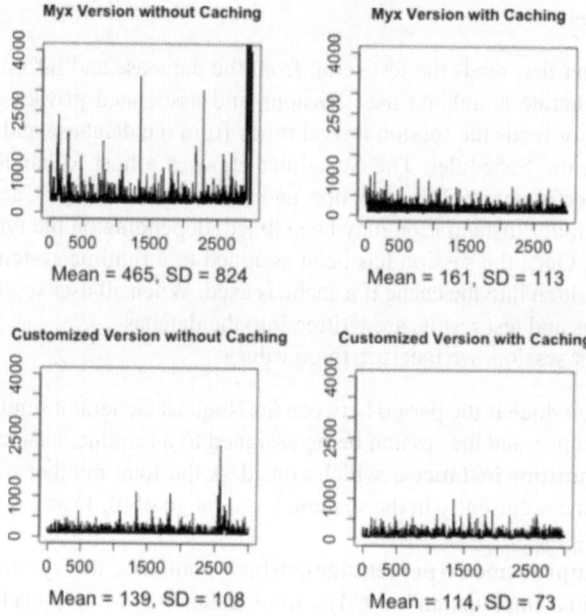

Fig. 4. Handling time for each user session (milliseconds)

5.2   Runtime Instance Reuse Rate

Figure 5(a) plots the runtime instance reuse rates for the two caching versions (in the non-caching versions, no instances are being reused). The reuse rates for the caching versions increase degressively as the cumulative number of user sessions increases. The two curves are very similar because both versions use the same caching scheme; the small variations are due to the true randomness of privacy Boolean guard and privacy binding generation.

5.3   Performance Improvement

Figure 5(b) plots the performance gain of our three improved versions in comparison to the baseline Myx version without caching. The curve at the bottom (gain from Myx version with caching) goes up as expected: the cache size increases with an increasing number of users, and hence the hit rate and thus the performance gain increase. The curve in the middle (gain from customized version without caching) is always above the first curve, meaning that the gains through customization are larger than through caching. As expected, this difference becomes smaller with increasing number of users and thus cache hits. The topmost curve shows the gains from both caching and customization. While the combined effect is always higher than each single effect, it is unfortunately not additive. While with increased number of users the gains through caching increase, each hit "cancels out" the gains through customization which will not be invoked in such a case. Larger cache sizes still cause performance gains as is demonstrated by the slightly increasing distance between the middle and upper curve.

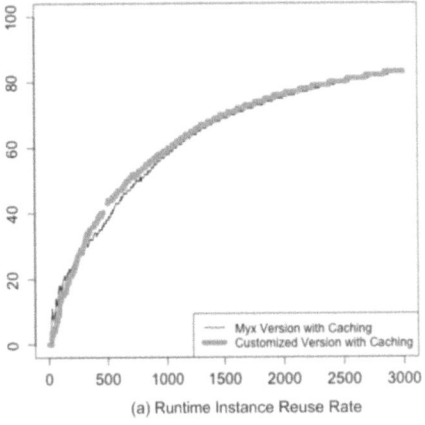
(a) Runtime Instance Reuse Rate

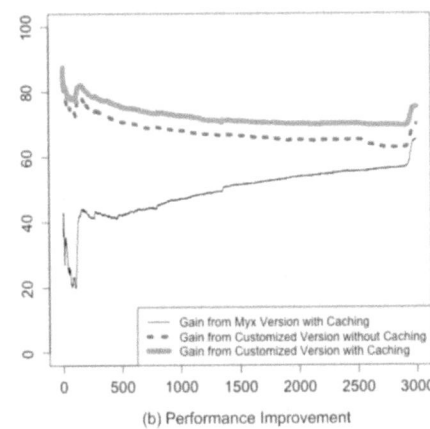
(b) Performance Improvement

Fig. 5. Instance reuse and performance improvement (both in %), by cumulative number of users

This differential however grows far less than the slope of the lowermost curve which represents the gains through caching for the non-customized Myx version.

6 Discussion

Performance Improvement. The evaluation results show that both our customization and caching improve the performance. The customized versions use a light-weight PLA representation, which consumes less memory and enables faster PLA selection and instantiation than the XML-based Myx versions. The multi-level caching mechanism saves time and resources that would otherwise be spent on creating new runtime instances. Under the current completely random assignment of privacy guards and bindings, the probability of a privacy binding cache hit is $1/2^{TotalConstraints}$ (about 7.9e-31), while the probability of a PCS cache hit is $1/2^{TotalUMCs}$ (about 9.8e-4). Therefore, the vast majority of instance reuses came from the PCS cache hits.

Practical Implications. The average arrival rate of new visitors in the current experiment setup is 0.5. In contrast, Yahoo.com which Alexa currently ranks No. 1 worldwide in terms of traffic seems to have a daily reach of close to 30 million unique visitors [22]. This roughly translates into an average arrival rate of 350 users per second. Because of its modular approach, our framework would be able to handle this workload in a cloud-computing paradigm [23]. If we continue using our average arrival rate of 0.5 visitors for each node, then we can handle Yahoo-sized traffic with a cloud that consists of 700 nodes on average. Therefore we believe that with sufficient support from a cloud computing environment, our approach can scale well to serve internationally operating websites, which would profit most from our privacy-enhancing framework. As a reminder though, this number does not include the nodes that would be required to run the Directory Component, the User Modeling Component, and the Web server.

Limitations of the Evaluation. Privacy bindings are randomly assigned to sessions in our simulation, and hence their variations are evenly distributed across users. In reality though, users' individual privacy preferences are likely to gravitate towards typical preferences, countries may have typical combinations of privacy bindings, and visitors from certain countries may be more frequent than from others. The hit rate in the privacy binding cache is likely to be higher in this more realistic scenario with uneven distribution, and the number of generated different instances lower than in our simulation, both of which reduces the memory load. Another limitation is that the experiments were conducted on a single PC platform. When the user modeling server is distributed in a cloud computing environment, the Scheduler and the cache database are likely to be overloaded, and therefore will need to be distributed as well.

7   Conclusions

Reconciling privacy and personalization in internationally operating websites is a challenging problem that no other existing work seems to address. Our PLA-based approach is aimed at filling this gap, but its resource-intensive PLA selection and instantiation process put the overall system performance into question. In this paper we discussed four implementations of our approach and evaluated their performance in a simulation experiment. Our study shows that our light-weight customized implementation performs better than the original PLA implementation (the Myx version), that our multilevel caching mechanism improves both versions, and that the customized version with caching performs best. The average handling time per user session is less than 0.2 seconds for all versions except the Myx version. Overall, our results demonstrate that with a reasonable number of networked hosts in a cloud computing environment, an internationally operating website can use our dynamic PLA-based user modeling approach to personalize their user services and at the same time respect the individual privacy desires of their users as well as the applicable privacy norms.

References

1. Kobsa, A.: Privacy-enhanced web personalization. In: Brusilovsky, P., Kobsa, A., Nejdl, W. (eds.) Adaptive Web 2007. LNCS, vol. 4321, pp. 628–670. Springer, Heidelberg (2007)
2. Wang, Y., Kobsa, A.: Respecting users' individual privacy constraints in web personalization. In: Conati, C., McCoy, K., Paliouras, G. (eds.) UM 2007. LNCS, vol. 4511, pp. 157–166. Springer, Heidelberg (2007)
3. Wang, Y., Kobsa, A., van der Hoek, A., White, J.: PLA-based runtime dynamism in support of privacy-enhanced web personalization. In: SPLC 2006, pp. 151–162. IEEE Press, Los Alamitos (2006)
4. Wang, Y., Hendrickson, S.A., van der Hoek, A., Taylor, R.N., Kobsa, A.: Modeling PLA variation of privacy-enhancing personalized systems (2009) (submitted for publication)
5. Kobsa, A., Fink, J.: Performance evaluation of user modeling servers under real-world workload conditions. In: Brusilovsky, P., Corbett, A.T., de Rosis, F. (eds.) UM 2003. LNCS, vol. 2702, pp. 143–153. Springer, Heidelberg (2003)
6. Carmichael, D.J., Kay, J., Kummerfeld, B.: Consistent modeling of users, devices and sensors in a ubiquitous computing environment. User Modeling and User-Adapted Interaction 15(3-4), 197–234 (2005)

7. Zadorozhny, V., Yudelson, M., Brusilovsky, P.: A framework for performance evaluation of user modeling servers for web applications. Web Intelli. and Agent Sys. 6(2), 175–191 (2008)

8. Kobsa, A.: A component architecture for dynamically managing privacy constraints in personalized web-based systems. In: Dingledine, R. (ed.) PET 2003. LNCS, vol. 2760, pp. 177–188. Springer, Heidelberg (2003)

9. Clements, P., Northrop, L.: Software Product Lines: Practices and Patterns. Addison-Wesley, New York (2002)

10. van der Hoek, A., Rakic, M., Roshandel, R., Medvidovic, N.: Taming architectural evolution. In: 9th ACM Symp. on the Foundations of Softw. Eng., pp. 1–10 (2001)

11. van der Hoek, A.: Design-time product line architectures for any-time variability. Sci. Comp. Prog., special issue on Softw. Variability Mgmt. 53(30), 285–304 (2004)

12. Kobsa, A., Fink, J.: An LDAP-based user modeling server and its evaluation. User Modeling and User-Adapted Interaction 16(2), 129–169 (2006)

13. Wang, Y., Kobsa, A.: Privacy-enhancing technologies. In: Gupta, M., Sharman, R. (eds.) Social and Organizational Liabilities in Information Security, pp. 203–227. IGI Global (2009)

14. ArchStudio: Archstudio 3 (2005),
http://www.isr.uci.edu/projects/archstudio/

15. Taylor, R.N., et al.: A component- and message-based architectural style for GUI software. IEEE Trans. Softw. Eng. 22(6), 390–406 (1996)

16. Dashofy, E., Asuncion, H., Hendrickson, S., Suryanarayana, G., Georgas, J., Taylor, R.: Archstudio 4: An architecture-based meta-modeling environment. In: ICSE 2007: Intl. Conf. on Softw. Eng., pp. 67–68. IEEE Computer Society, Los Alamitos (2007)

17. ArchStudio: Myx (2008),
http://www.isr.uci.edu/projects/archstudio/myx.html

18. Wang, Y., Chen, Z., Kobsa, A.: A collection and systematization of international privacy laws, with special consideration of internationally operating personalized websites (2006),
http://www.ics.uci.edu/~kobsa/privacy

19. Wang, Y., Kobsa, A.: Impacts of privacy laws and regulations on personalized systems. In: Kobsa, A., Chellappa, R., Spiekermann, S. (eds.) Proceedings of PEP 2006, CHI 2006 Workshop on Privacy-Enhanced Personalization, pp. 44–46. ACM, New York (2006)

20. Bhole, Y., Popescu, A.: Measurement and analysis of HTTP traffic. Journal of Network and Systems Management (2005)

21. Chlebus, E., Brazier, J.: Nonstationary poisson modeling of web browsing session arrivals. Information Processing Letters 102(5), 187–190 (2007)

22. Alexa: Yahoo traffic details (2009),
http://www.alexa.com/data/details/traffic_details/yahoo.com

23. Buyya, R., Yeo, C.S., Venugopal, S.: Market-oriented cloud computing: Vision, hype, and reality for delivering it services as computing utilities. In: 10th IEEE Intl. Conf. on High Perf. Comp. and Comms., pp. 5–13. IEEE Computer Society, Los Alamitos (2008)

Creating User Profiles from a Command-Line Interface: A Statistical Approach

José Antonio Iglesias, Agapito Ledezma, and Araceli Sanchis

Universidad Carlos III de Madrid,
Avda. de la Universidad, 30, 28911 Leganés (Madrid), Spain
{jiglesia,ledezma,masm}@inf.uc3m.es

Abstract. Knowledge about computer users is very beneficial for assisting them, predicting their future actions or detecting masqueraders. In this paper, an approach for creating and recognizing automatically the behavior profile of a user from the commands (s)he types in a command-line interface, is presented.

Specifically, in this research, a computer user behavior is represented as a sequence of UNIX commands. This sequence is transformed into a distribution of relevant subsequences in order to find out a profile that defines its behavior. Then, statistical methods are used for recognizing a user from the commands (s)he types. The experiment results, using 2 different sources of UNIX command data, show that a system based on our approach can efficiently recognize a UNIX user. In addition, a comparison with a HMM-base method is done.

Because a user profile usually changes constantly, we also propose a method to keep up to date the created profiles using an *age*-based mechanism.

1   Introduction

Would it not be interesting to recognize a computer user and to know how (s)he will behave after (s)he types a few commands?

Recognizing the behavior of others in real-time is significant in different tasks, such as to predict their future behavior, to coordinate with them or to assist them. In order to act efficiently, humans usually try to recognize the behavior of others. New theories claim that a high percentage of the human brain capacity is used for predicting the future, including the behavior of other humans [1].

Specifically, computer user modeling is the process of learning about ordinary computer users by observing the way they use the computer. This process needs the creation of a *user profile* that contains information that characterizes the usage behavior of a computer user. Experience has shown that users themselves do not know how to articulate what they do, especially if they are very familiar with the tasks they perform. Computer users, like all of us, leave out activities that they do not even notice they are doing. Thus, only by observing users we

G.-J. Houben et al. (Eds.): UMAP 2009, LNCS 5535, pp. 90–101, 2009.

can model his/her behavior correctly [2]. However, the construction of effective computer user profiles is a difficult problem because of the following aspects: human behavior is usually erratic, and sometimes humans behave differently because of a change in their goals.

In recent years, significant work has been carried out for profiling computer users. In this research, an approach for profiling and recognizing *general* user behavior profiles is proposed. This approach is called **ABCD** (*Agent Behavior Classification based on Distributions of relevant subsequences of commands*) and can be applied for creating and recognizing any behavior represented by a sequence of commands (or events). *ABCD* creates a user profile as a distribution of relevant subsequences and then statistical methods are applied for recognizing a given sequence of commands.

However, for evaluating *ABCD*, the UNIX operating system environment is used. The creation of the UNIX user profiles from a sequence of UNIX commands should consider the sequentiality of the commands typed by the user and the temporal dependencies. In a human-computer interaction by commands, the sequentiality of these commands is essential for the result of the interaction. This aspect motivates the idea of automated sequence learning for computer user behavior classification; if we do not know the features that influence the behavior of a user, we can consider a sequence of past actions to incorporate some of the historical context of the user. This aspect is taken into account in the HMM-based methods, so we will compare *ABCD* with a method which uses HMMs for modeling users. Finally, once the user has been classified, relevant actions can be done, however this task is not addressed in this paper.

This paper is organized as follows: Section 2 provides a brief overview of the background and related work relevant to this research. Our approach (*ABCD*) is explained in detail in section 3. Section 4 describes the experimental setting and the experimental results obtained. Section 5 compares the obtained results with a very well know technique (HMMs). The proposal for making *ABCD* adaptive is detailed in Section 6. Finally, Section 7 contains concluding remarks.

2   Background and Related Work

Different methods have been used to find out relevant information in the computer user behavior in different computer areas:

Discovery of navigation patterns: Spiliopoulou and Faulstich [3] present the *Web Utilization Miner WUM*, a mining system for discovering interesting navigation patterns in a web site. *WUM* prepares the web log data for mining and the language *MINT* mining the aggregated data according to the directives of the human expert. This work is complementary to "Footprints" tool, which focuses on the visualization of frequently accessed patterns and on the identification of pattern types that may be of importance [4].

Web recommender systems: Macedo et al. [5] propose a system (*WebMemex*) that provides recommended information based on the captured history of navigation from a list of known users. *WebMemex* captures information such as IP addresses, user Ids and URL accessed for future analysis.

Web page filtering: Gody and Amandi [6] present a technique to generate readable user profiles that accurately capture interests by observing their behavior on the Web. The proposed technique is built on the *Web Document Conceptual Clustering* algorithm, with which profiles without an a priori knowledge of user interest categories can be acquired.

Computer security: Pepyne et al. [7] describe a method using queuing theory and logistic regression modeling methods for profiling computer users based on simple temporal aspects of their behavior. In a similar area (intrusion detection problem), Coull et al. [8] propose an algorithm that uses pair-wise sequence alignment to characterize similarity between sequences of commands. The algorithm produces an effective metric for distinguishing a legitimate user from a masquerader. Schonlau et al. [9] investigate a number of statistical approaches for detecting masqueraders.

Although there is lot of work that focuses on user profiling in a specific environment, it is not clear that they can be transferred to other environments. However, the approach proposed in this research (*ABCD*) can be used in any domain in which a user behavior can be represented as a sequence of commands or events. Therefore, as sequences are very relevant in human skill learning and reasoning [10], the problem of user profile classification is examined as a problem of sequence classification. According to this aspect, Horman and Kaminka [11] present a learner with unlabeled sequential data that discover meaningful patterns of sequential behavior from example streams. Lane and Brodley [12] present an approach based on the basis of instance-based learning (IBL) techniques, and several techniques for reducing data storage requirements of the user profile.

3   ABCD: Agent Behavior Classifier Based on Distributions of Relevant Subsequences of Commands

Although *ABCD* can be applied for creating and recognizing any behavior profile represented by a sequence of commands, this research is focused on creating computer user profiles from a command-line interface. Specifically, *ABCD* is detailed using the UNIX commands environment.

ABCD, as other behavior modeling methods [13], uses a library in which all the different user profiles recognized are stored. Then, a matching of the sequence to classify with the *Profile-Library* is done. Thus, *ABCD* is divided into two phases:

1. **Construction of the User Behavior Profiles:** In this phase, the sequences of commands typed by different UNIX users are analyzed and the corresponding profiles are created and stored in the *Profile-Library*. This process is detailed in Section 3.1.

2. **User Classification:** The goal of this phase is to classify a *new* sequence
of commands typed by a user into one of the profiles created in the previous
phase. Section 3.2 explains the proposed statistical classification method.

3.1 Construction of the User Behavior Profiles

In this phase, the first step is to extract the significant pieces of the sequence
of commands that can represent a pattern of behavior. When a user types a
command, it usually depends on the previous typed commands and it is related
to the following commands. According to this aspect, and as it was used in [14],
in order to get the most representative set of subsequences from the acquired
sequence, the use of a ***trie* data structure** [15] is proposed. This structure is
also proposed in [16] to learn a team behavior and in [17] to classify the behavior
patterns of a *RoboCup* soccer simulation team.

The construction of a user profile from a single sequence of commands is
done by a three steps process: 1. Segmentation of the sequence of commands, 2.
Storage of the subsequences in a *trie*, and 3. Creation of the user profile. These
steps are detailed in the following 3 subsections.

In order to clarify the process for creating a UNIX user profile, let us consider
the following sequence as example: $\{ls \rightarrow date \rightarrow ls \rightarrow date \rightarrow cat\}$.

Segmentation of the sequence of commands: Firstly, the sequence is segmented in subsequence of equal length from the first to the last element. Thus,
the sequence $A = A_1 A_2 ... A_n$ (where n is the number of commands of the sequence) will be segmented in the subsequences described by $A_i ... A_{i+length}$ $\forall$
$i, i = [1, n\text{-}length + 1]$, where *length* is the size of the subsequences created and determines how many commands are considered as dependent. In the rest of the
paper, we will use the term *subsequence length* to denote the value of this length.

In the proposed sample sequence ($\{ ls \rightarrow date \rightarrow ls \rightarrow date \rightarrow cat\}$), let 3 be
the subsequence length, then it is obtained: $\{ls \rightarrow date \rightarrow ls\}$ and $\{date \rightarrow ls$
$\rightarrow date\}$ and $\{ls \rightarrow date \rightarrow cat\}$.

Storage of the subsequences in a *trie*: The subsequences of commands are
stored in a *trie* in a way that all possible subsequences are accessible and explicitly represented. In the proposed *trie*, a node represents a command, and its
children represent the commands that follow it. Also, each node keeps track
of the number of times a command has been inserted on to it. As the dependencies of the commands are relevant in the user profile, the subsequence
suffixes (subsequences that extend to the end of the given sequence) are also
inserted.

Considering the previous example, the first subsequence ($\{ls \rightarrow date \rightarrow ls\}$) is
added as the first branch of the empty *trie* (Figure 1a). Each node is labeled with
the number 1 (in square brackets) which indicates that the command has been
inserted in the node once. Then, the suffixes of the subsequence ($\{date \rightarrow ls\}$ and
$\{ls\}$) are also inserted (Figure 1b). Finally, after inserting the 3 subsequences
and its corresponding suffixes, the completed *trie* is obtained (Figure 1c).

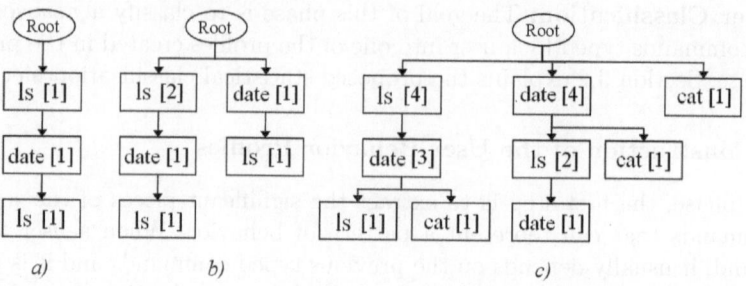

Fig. 1. Steps of creating an example trie

Creation of the user profile: For this purpose, **frequency-based methods** are used. Specifically, to evaluate the relevance of a subsequence using *ABCD*, its relative frequency or support [18] is calculated. In this case, the **support** of a subsequence is defined as the ratio of the number of times the subsequence has been inserted into the *trie* to the total number of subsequences of equal size inserted. Calculating this value, the *trie* is transformed into a set of subsequences labeled with its corresponding support value. This structure is represented as a distribution of relevant subsequences. Once a user behavior profile has been created, it is stored in the *Profile-Library* with an identification name.

In the previous example, the *trie* consists of 9 nodes; therefore, the profile consists of 9 different subsequences which are labeled with its support (Figure 2).

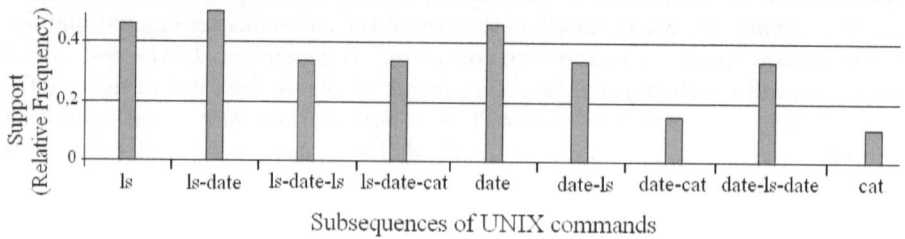

Fig. 2. Distribution of subsequences

3.2   User Recognition

In this second phase, a *new* sequence of commands typed by one of the users previously analyzed must be classified. It means that given an observed sequence E typed by a user and a set of user behavior profiles $P = \{up_1, up_2, ..., up_n\}$ stored in the *Profile-Library*, the goal of this phase is to determine into which profile $up_i \in P$ the sequence E belongs to.

Firstly, the distribution of relevant subsequences of the *new* sequence (input) is created by applying the process explained in the previous section. Then, it is matched with all the profiles stored in the *Profile-Library*. As both profiles are represented by a distribution of values, a statistical test is applied for matching these distributions. A non-parametric test (or distribution-free) is used because this kind of tests does not assume a particular population distribution. The proposed test applied for matching two behaviors is a **modification of the Chi-Square Test** for two samples.

To apply the proposed test, the sequence to classify (input) is considered as an observed sample and the profiles stored in *Profile-Library* are considered as the expected samples. Then, this test compares the observed distribution with all the expected distributions objectively and evaluates whether a deviation appears.

The *Chi-Square Test* compares the two sets of support values in which *Chi-Square* is the sum of the terms $\frac{(Obs-Exp)^2}{Exp}$ calculated from the observed (*Obs*) and expected (*Exp*) distributions. However, using this test, all the expected values are compared but if an observed value is not represented in the expected distribution, it is not considered. Also, the number of subsequences in an expected distribution is usually very large, so this kind of comparison can be very time-consumed. In order to solve these *problems*, the way to compare the two distributions is modified to the sum of the terms $\frac{(Exp-Obs)^2}{Obs}$.

An important advantage of the proposed test is its rapidity because only the observed subsequences are evaluated. However, there is no penalty for the expected relevant subsequences which do not appear in the observed distribution.

Using this test, a value that indicates the deviation between the observed and the stored profile is obtained. This deviation needs to be calculated with all the profiles stored in *Profile-Library* and the profile that obtains the lowest deviation value indicates the closer similarity. Also, the number of terms to sum in each comparison is always the same: number of subsequences of the observed profile. It means that the degrees of freedom (*dof*) are the same in all the comparisons with the expected behavior profiles. Otherwise, a normalization of the results according to the *dof* should be done.

As example, let us consider that the sequence that represents the observed behavior is: $\{ls \rightarrow date \rightarrow cpp\}$. Figure 3 shows the comparison between the previous expected distribution (*Expected Profile 1*) and the observed distribution (*Observed Profile*). Obtaining the support value of each subsequence in Figure 3, the deviation value in this example is: $\frac{(0,44-0,33)^2}{0,33} + \frac{(0,5-0,5)^2}{0,5} + \frac{(0,44-0,33)^2}{0,33} + \frac{(0-1)^2}{1} + \frac{(0-0,5)^2}{0,5} + \frac{(0-0,33)^2}{0,33}$.

4   Experimental Setup and Results

For evaluating *ABCD* in the UNIX environment, we have used 2 different sources of UNIX data with different number of users to classify:

- **Set of 9 UNIX Users:** Data[1] drawn from the command histories of 9 UNIX computer users at Purdue University over 2 years [19]. Each user file contains from about 10000 to 60000 commands.

---

[1] ML Repository: http://archive.ics.uci.edu/ml/datasets/UNIX+User+Data

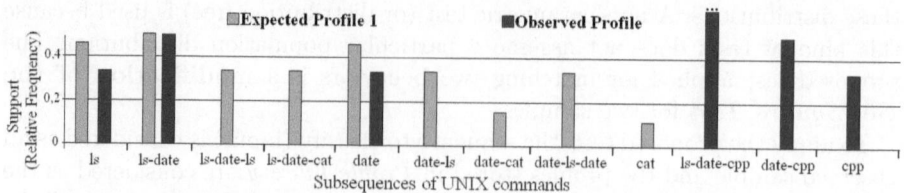

Fig. 3. Observed and Expected Comparison Example

- **Set of 50 UNIX Users:** Data[2] used in the masquerade-detection studies done by Schonlau et al. [9]. In Schonlau research, commands from other users are interspersed as masqueraders data. In our research, the 50 users data are used without these commands interspersed. Each user file contains 15000 commands.

In both cases, the data is drawn from *tcsh* history files and pre-processed to remove filenames, user name, directory structures, etc. Command names, flags, and shell meta characters have been preserved. However, this analysis is only based on two fields: *Command name* and *User Identification*. Thus, a user is identified by a set of commands concatenated by date order; for example the first 10 commands of the *User1* in the *50 Users set* are: *cpp, sh, xrdb, cpp, sh, xrdb, mkpts, env, csh, csh*.

4.1   Experimental Design

In order to measure the performance of the proposed classifier using the above data, the well-established technique cross-validation is used. For this research, **10-fold cross-validation** is used: We remove a 10% of the commands from the initial data of each user and the corresponding *distributions* are calculated (*Training Distributions*). Then, the portion of data originally taken out of each user data is analyzed and its corresponding distribution is created (*Test Distribution*). Using the proposed statistical method, these distributions are compared and the user is classified. As 10-fold cross validation is used, this process is repeated 10 times per user.

The number of UNIX commands analyzed per user is very relevant for the classification result. Therefore, we have performed several experiments with different number of UNIX commands (50, 100, 500, 1000 and 5000) per user. These commands are selected from the last commands typed by a user. Also, in the phase of behavior model creation, the length of the subsequences in which the original sequence is segmented (used for creating the *trie*) is a relevant parameter: Using a longer length, the time consumed for creating the *trie* and the number of relevant subsequences in the corresponding distribution increase drastically. In the experiments presented in this paper, 3 different segmentation values for the sequence (subsequence lengths) are evaluated: 3, 5 and 10.

---

[2] Schonlau web page: http://www.schonlau.net/intrusion.html

4.2   Results

In this research, a UNIX command sequence (*Test Distribution*) is classified into the user behavior (*Training Distribution*) with the smallest deviation. Also, the classification process generates a ranked list with the most likely users at the top. Although there are users whose behavior is quite similar, in the proposed experiments, the classification is correct only if the user who typed the sequence of commands to classify holds the first position of the ranking list.

The results are listed in Table 1. The classification rate is the ratio of the number of correct classifications made and the standard deviation measures the dispersion of the classification results according to the obtained ranking list.

Table 1. Classification Results using ABCD. 9 and 50 Users.

		ABCD Classifier Results			
		Set of 9 UNIX Users		Set of 50 UNIX Users	
Number of commands	Subseq Length	Classification rate %	Standard Deviation	Classification rate %	Standard Deviation
50	3	80,00	1,40	48,20	8,99
	5	78,89	1,34	48,80	7,73
100	3	80,00	0,96	53,40	8,42
	5	76,67	1,08	51,40	9,81
	10	78,89	0,83	54,80	6,99
500	3	90,00	1,08	64,00	9,16
	5	91,11	1,27	64,20	10,17
	10	86,67	1,49	63,80	12,48
1000	3	87,78	1,53	72,00	10,14
	5	87,78	1,30	71,20	10,49
	10	81,11	1,84	69,00	11,69
5000	3	85,56	1,23	75,80	12,05
	5	87,78	1,30	76,60	12,26
	10	84,40	1,54	75,00	12,64

We can see from the *Set of 9 Users* results (Table 1) that even with 50 commands (45 per training and 5 per testing), the classification rate is very high (around 80%). The results obtained with different subsequence lengths for creating the *trie* (3, 5 and 10) show that the higher classification rates are not obtained using a higher length. The higher classification rate is usually obtained using subsequences of length 5; this number determines the number of commands considered as dependent for a UNIX user.

According to the *Set of 50 Users* results (Table 1), the classification rate is smaller because of the high number of users to classify. In this case, this rate increases considerably with increasing the number of commands for training and testing. Using 5000 commands (4500 for training and 500 for testing), the classification rate is higher than 75% and if we can get more than 900 commands for training, the classification rate is higher than 70%.

5 *ABCD* vs. HMMs

Recent researches have demonstrated the effectiveness of *Hidden Markov Models* (HMMs) for information extraction and they are very used in speech recognition. However, HMMs can efficiently deal with time-sequential data and can provide time-scale invariability as well as learning capability for recognition. Therefore, HMMs are also used in the environment we propose in this research. HMMs have been used for recognizing automated robot behaviors [20] and recently, for behavior understanding from video streams [21]. In addition, Lane [22] demonstrates the use of HMMs for user profiling in the domain of anomaly detection using a data set very similar to the set used in our research. An improved HMM-based method for this purpose is proposed in [23].

For this reason, to evaluate the results shown in the previous section, we compare them with a **classifier based on HMMs**. A HMM is a finite set of states, each of which is associated with a probability distribution [24]. Transitions among the states are governed by a set of probabilities called transition probabilities. In a particular state an observation can be generated, according to the associated probability distribution (it is only the observation, not the state visible to an external observer).

To define a HMM completely, the following elements are needed: 1) Number of observation symbols in the alphabet, M. 2) Number of states of the model, K. 3) A state transition probabilities matrix, A. 4) A probability distribution in each of the states, B. 5) The initial state distribution, Π.

In order to classify the behavior of UNIX users using a HMM-based method, **a HMM is created for each user** as follows: The number of observation symbols (M) is the number of different commands typed by the user. The number of states of the model (K) is an open question in the use of HMMs for modeling but its choice is important because it affects the potential descriptiveness of the HMM. In our research, according to the study done in [22] and in order to compare the *ABCD* and HMM results; the number of states of a HMM corresponds with the *subsequence length* used in *ABCD* for creating the *trie*.

The toolkit Umdhmm [25] was used to create each HMM (UNIX user behavior model) from the corresponding training data files. After creating the HMMs, the *Forward Algorithm* is used to calculate the probability of an observed UNIX user sequence (*Test HMM*) given a user model (*Training HMM*). The sequence of commands is classified into the HMM with the highest likelihood.

Table 2 shows the results using a classifier based on HMMs and using the same data than in the previous experiments (Section 4). These results show that with a low number of commands for training, a classifier based on HMMs gets a low classification rate. Thus, using HMMs we need a high number of commands to get similar results to the obtained using *ABCD*. However, creating the user models with more than 5000 commands, the classification rate is usually *a bit* better using HMMs. Even so, the difference in the classification rate between *ABCD* and HMMs in the *Set of 50 users* is very significant. It is remarkable the high classification rate obtained by *ABCD* using a low number of commands (for training and classifying). For areas such as computer intrusion detection,

Table 2. Classification Results using HMMs. 9 and 50 Users.

| | | HMMs Classifier Results | | | |
| | | Set of 9 UNIX Users | | Set of 50 UNIX Users | |
Number of commands	Subseq Length	Classification rate %	Standard Deviation	Classification rate %	Standard Deviation
50	3	52,22	2,23	30,40	14,08
	5	54,44	2,06	32,40	14,72
	10	54,44	2,08	34,80	15,02
100	3	64,44	1,49	39,40	8,72
	5	61,11	1,53	40,00	8,58
	10	62,22	1,60	40,40	8,94
500	3	63,33	1,22	42,20	6,19
	5	68,89	1,30	48,20	6,03
	10	66,67	1,26	51,20	5,86
1000	3	63,33	1,20	46,20	4,69
	5	68,89	1,32	49,20	4,55
	10	66,67	1,09	53,20	4,47
5000	3	80,00	1,05	54,20	3,89
	5	82,22	0,90	58,20	3,53
	10	88,89	0,97	62,20	3,45

this aspect is really important because the detection can be done when the user only has typed a few commands and the set of users is small.

6   Future Work: ABCD Adaptative

A widely acknowledged challenge in the *ABCD* is how to accurately profile a user while his/her behavior changes constantly. Thus, a user profile should be frequently revised to keep it up to date. To solve this problem, we propose a technique used by Angelov and Zhou. [26] for analyzing the quality of the rule base in an on-line fuzzy system. This technique uses the **moment when the information is obtained**.

Applying this technique in *ABCD*, the subsequences typed by a user are indexed with a number that indicates the *moment* they were read. This value can be considered as an integer from 1 (the first subsequence read) to the number of subsequences read. Using this value, the *Age* of a subsequence can be calculated. This *Age* value indicates how old a subsequence stored in a user profile is. The formula for calculating this value is shown in Equation 1.a.

$$\textbf{a. } Age_s(t) = t - \frac{\sum_{i=1}^{N_s(t)} I_s(i)}{N_s(t)} \; ; \qquad \textbf{b. } \overline{Age(t)} = \frac{1}{R} \sum_{j=1}^{R} Age_i(t) \qquad (1)$$

where t is the current time instant; s represents a certain subsequence; $Age_s(t)$ denotes the *Age* of the subsequence s in the moment t; $N_s(t)$ is the number

of times the subsequence s was read until the moment t and $I_s(i)$ denotes the
moment of the subsequence s when it was read for i^{th} time.

Using this value, the distribution of subsequences that represents a user profile
can be **updated on-line**. Thus, the *Age* of each subsequence can be calculated
and compared with the *mean Age* that is determined in Equation 1.b.

These values can be used for removing older subsequences that were used by
a user but during a long period of time they have been omitted. Also, major
shifts in the user behavior can be detected using the *Age* value.

7   Conclusions

This paper presents an approach (*ABCD*) for profiling and classifying computer
users from a command-line interface. The sequence of commands typed by user is
segmented and stored in a *trie* data structure, and the relevant subsequences are
evaluated by using a frequency-based method. Then, a user profile is represented
by a distribution of relevant subsequences and a modification of the *Chi-square
Test* for two samples is proposed for recognition of users. In addition, as the
behavior of a user can change constantly, we also propose a technique to updated
these profiles by calculating the *Age* of each subsequence and removing the no
relevant ones.

ABCD has been evaluated with real-data analyzing two different data sources
which have different numbers of users: 9 and 50 UNIX users. A large set of experiments were conducted and the obtained results by using the *ABCD* are
very satisfactory. The comparison of *ABCD* with a classifier based on HMMs
shows that the proposed technique is more suitable in the environment evaluated, mainly when the training data is small. These results are very encouraging
because analyzing few commands, a user (and his/her behavior) can be recognized and then, different actions in the computer system, (such as to monitor,
analyze and detect abnormalities, assist the user, predict his/her future actions
or detect masqueraders) can be executed. However, *ABCD* is generalizable and
it could be evaluated in many other different domains (the only constraint is
that the behavior can be represented as a sequence of commands or events).

Finally, if we want to analyze hundreds (or thousands) of users, *ABCD* can
be easily modified for clustering users with similar profiles. This aspect could be
implemented using *Evolving Systems* [27] and it is proposed for future work.

References

1. Mulcahy, N.J., Call, J.: Apes save tools for future use. Science 312(5776), 1038–1040 (2006)
2. Hackos, J.T., Redish, J.C.: User and Task Analysis for Interface Design. Wiley, Chichester (1998)
3. Spiliopoulou, M., Faulstich, L.C.: Wum: A web utilization miner. In: Proceedings of EDBT Workshop WebDB 1998, pp. 109–115. Springer, Heidelberg (1998)
4. Wexelblat, A.: An environment for aiding information-browsing tasks. In: Proc. of AAAI Spring Symposium on Acquisition, Learning and Demonstration: Automat- ing Tasks for Users. AAAI Press, Menlo Park (1996)

5. Macedo, A.A., Truong, K.N., Camacho-Guerrero, J.A., da GraÇa Pimentel, M.: Automatically sharing web experiences through a hyperdocument recommender system. In: HYPERTEXT 2003, pp. 48–56. ACM, New York (2003)
6. Godoy, D., Amandi, A.: User profiling for web page filtering. IEEE Internet Computing 9(4), 56–64 (2005)
7. Pepyne, D.L., Hu, J., Gong, W.: User profiling for computer security. In: Proceedings of the American Control Conference, pp. 982–987 (2004)
8. Coull, S.E., Branch, J.W., Szymanski, B.K., Breimer, E.: Intrusion detection: A bioinformatics approach. In: Omondi, A.R., Sedukhin, S.G. (eds.) ACSAC 2003. LNCS, vol. 2823, pp. 24–33. Springer, Heidelberg (2003)
9. Schonlau, M., Dumouchel, W., Ju, W.H., Karr, A.F.: Theus, Computer Intrusion: Detecting Masquerades. Statistical Science 16, 58–74 (2001)
10. Anderson, J.: Learning and Memory: An Integrated Approach. John Wiley and Sons, New York (1995)
11. Horman, Y., Kaminka, G.A.: Removing biases in unsupervised learning of sequential patterns. Intelligent Data Analysis 11(5), 457–480 (2007)
12. Lane, T., Brodley, C.E.: Temporal sequence learning and data reduction for anomaly detection. In: CCS 1998, pp. 150–158. ACM, New York (1998)
13. Riley, P., Veloso, M.M.: On behavior classification in adversarial environments. In: DARS, pp. 371–380
14. Iglesias, J.A., Ledezma, A., Sanchis, A.: Sequence classification using statistical pattern recognition. In: Berthold, M.R., Shawe-Taylor, J., Lavrač, N. (eds.) IDA 2007. LNCS, vol. 4723, pp. 207–218. Springer, Heidelberg (2007)
15. Fredkin, E.: Trie memory. Comm. ACM 3(9), 490–499 (1960)
16. Kaminka, G.A., Fidanboylu, M., Chang, A., Veloso, M.M.: Learning the sequential coordinated behavior of teams from observations. In: Kaminka, G.A., Lima, P.U., Rojas, R. (eds.) RoboCup 2002. LNCS, vol. 2752, pp. 111–125. Springer, Heidelberg (2003)
17. Iglesias, J.A., Ledezma, A., Sanchis, A., Kaminka, G.A.: Classifying efficiently the behavior of a soccer team. In: Burgard, W., et al. (eds.) Intelligent Autonomous Systems 10. IAS-10, pp. 316–323 (2008)
18. Agrawal, R., Srikant, R.: Mining sequential patterns. In: Eleventh International Conference on Data Engineering, Taipei, Taiwan, pp. 3–14 (1995)
19. Blake, C., Newman, D.J., Hettich, S., Merz, C.: UCI repository of machine learning databases (1998)
20. Han, K., Veloso, M.: Automated robot behavior recognition applied to robotic soccer. In: IJCAI 1999 Workshop on Team Behaviors and Plan Recognition (1999)
21. Chung, P.-C., Liu, C.-D.: A daily behavior enabled hidden markov model for human behavior understanding. Pattern Recognition 41(5), 1572–1580 (2008)
22. Lane, T.: Hidden Markov Models for Human-computer interface modeling. In: Proceedings of IJCAI 1999 Workshop on Learning About Users, pp. 35–44 (1999)
23. Lane, T., Brodley, C.E.: An empirical study of two approaches to sequence learning for anomaly detection. Machine Learning 51(1), 73–107 (2003)
24. Bengio, Y.: Markovian models for sequential data. Neural Computing Surveys 2, 129–162 (1999)
25. Kanungo, T.: Umdhmm: A hidden markov model toolkit. In: Extended Finite State Models of Language. Cambridge Univ. Press, Cambridge (1999)
26. Angelov, P., Zhou, X.: Evolving fuzzy-rule-based classifiers from data streams. IEEE Transactions on Fuzzy Systems 16(6), 1462–1475 (2008)
27. Angelov, P.: Rule-based Models: A Tool for Design of Flexible Adaptive Systems. Springer, Heidelberg (2002)

Context-Aware Preference Model Based on a Study of Difference between Real and Supposed Situation Data

Chihiro Ono[1], Yasuhiro Takishima[1], Yoichi Motomura[2], and Hideki Asoh[3]

[1] KDDI R&D Laboratories, Inc. 2-1-15 Ohara Fujimino Saitama, 356-8502, Japan
{ono,takisima}@kddilabs.jp
[2] Digital Human RC, AIST, 2-41-6 Aomi, Koto-ku Tokyo 135-0064 Japan
[3] Intelligent Systems RI, AIST, 1-1-1, Umezono, Tsukuba, Ibaraki 305-8568 Japan
{y.motomura,h.asoh}@aist.go.jp

Abstract. We propose a novel approach for constructing statistical preference models for context-aware recommender systems. To do so, one of the most important but difficult problems is acquiring sufficient training data in various contexts/situations. Particularly, some situations require a heavy workload to set them up or to collect subjects under those situations. To avoid this, often a large amount of data in a supposed situation is collected, i.e., a situation where the subject pretends/imagines that he/she is in a specific situation. Although there may be difference between the preference in the real situation and the supposed situation, this has not been considered in existing researches. Here, to study the difference, we collected a certain amount of corresponding data. We asked subjects the same question about preference both in the real and the supposed situation. Then we proposed a new model construction method using a difference model constructed from the correspondence data and showed the effectiveness through the experiments.

Keywords: preference modeling, context-awareness, recommender systems, statistical modeling.

1 Introduction

Modeling users' preferences is a key technology for various personalized applications, such as recommender systems [1, 3, 14], intelligent user interface, and one-to-one marketing. Recently, "context-awareness" has become one of the most important research issues when constructing preference models. One reason for this is that the diversification of contexts/situations in which the user uses the service, e.g. in town or at home, as well as the diversification of the services and related items, has skyrocketed together with the surge in Internet access via PDAs and cellular phones. These trends revealed that users' preferences dramatically change based on the context/situation. For example, movie preferences may change depending on the mood or the persons accompanying the users.

We proposed a novel method for constructing context-aware preference models using Bayesian networks [9, 10] and implemented a movie recommender system on

G.-J. Houben et al. (Eds.): UMAP 2009, LNCS 5535, pp. 102–113, 2009.

cellular phones using the model [12]. There, complex relations among users' profiles, contents' attributes, and situation attributes are modeled with a Bayesian network.

In constructing such context-aware statistical preference models, one of the most important but difficult problems is acquiring considerable training data in various situations. In particular, some situations require a heavy workload to set them up or to collect subjects capable of answering the inquiries involved. As an example, let us consider a food recommender system that recommends food such as curry rice and beef bowl through cellular phone display by using users' information. The system should treat such conditions as "a user is choosing food in hot weather when feeling tired and hungry." To collect training data for such situation, the model constructor should make subjects tired and hungry, and gather them on a hot day.

As a way of reducing this difficulty, a small amount of data in a real situation is simply collected, or a large amount of data is collected in a supposed/imagined situation, i.e., a situation where the subject pretends/imagines being in the specific situation to answer inquiries, instead of setting up a real situation and putting them into it. Collecting answers in the supposed situations requires a much lighter workload than setting up a real situation. Although the data acquired in the supposed situation may differ from that acquired in a real situation, the difference is not taken seriously in existing researches and is usually neglected.

To solve the problem, we have been exploring a novel way of constructing preference model using both real situation data and supposed situation data. As the first step, we proposed simple methods to obtain a better preference model and confirmed the performance improvement against existing approaches through the experiments regarding food preference [11]. However, the difference between the preferences under the real and the supposed situation has not been investigated sufficiently.

In this research, to analyze the difference and propose better methods, we collected a certain amount of corresponding data. That is, we asked subjects the same question about preference both in the real and the supposed situation. Firstly, we designed a questionnaire to collect corresponding real/supposed situation data. Then we modeled the difference of rating between the real and supposed situation, and proposed a new method to precisely predict the rating under the real situation. We confirmed the effectiveness through the experiments.

The rest of this paper is organized as follows. Section 2 describes the problem and our solution and related works are described in Section 3. Section 4 and Section 5 describe data acquisition in the food preference domain. Section 6 describes the difference of preference between the real and the supposed situation and Section 7 provides model improvement methods. Section 8 presents model evaluation, while Section 9 presents discussion and a conclusion.

2 Issue and Solution

2.1 Statistical Preference Model

There has been an abundance of research on constructing statistical preference models. In most of it, the problem of constructing the statistical preference model is formalized as modeling the conditional probability distribution $P(V|U, C, S)$ to predict the value V from U, C, and S. Here, U represents a set of users' attribute variables, such as age, sex, etc. C represents a set of the target contents' attribute variables, for example, category, calorie, fat, salt, etc. for foods. S represents a set of user situation/context variables such as hungry, tired etc. for food recommendations, and V denotes the user's preference/rating of a given content within a given context.

2.2 Issue

To construct context-aware statistical preference models, we should acquire a considerable amount of training data in various situations. However, as described above, it is often difficult to collect data under real conditions, because we have to set up a real situation and collect subjects capable of answering the question in such situations.

To reduce the difficulty, we have been exploring a novel approach of combining supposed situation data and real situation data [11]. So far, we have proposed two model improving methods – the model modification method and inference result modification method – and confirmed performance improvement against models constructed with only supposed situation data or real situation data through the experiments regarding food recommendation. However, the difference between the data acquired in the real situation and that acquired in the supposed situation has not been analyzed in detail.

2.3 Solution

To clarify the difference, we designed an internet questionnaire survey and collected a certain amount of corresponding data in the real and supposed situation. That is, we asked subjects the same question about preference both in the real and the supposed situation. Consequently, we obtained pairs of real and supposed situation data that have exactly the same situational attributes, user attributes, and item attributes. Using the corresponding data, we can calculate the difference of preference between the supposed and real situation. We construct a statistical model for predicting the difference from user attributes, item attributes, and situational attributes. Then we propose a new method of modeling the preference under real situation by combining the difference model and the preference model constructed with only supposed situation data.

3   Related Works

In the context of preference modeling and recommender systems [1, 3, 14] our works are the first attempt to focus on, analyze, and utilize the difference between the preference under the supposed situation and that under the real situation.

In the broader context of statistical modeling/learning, the problem of constructing a better model by combining data from the target domain with a data from the related but not identical domain is investigated under several names such as "model adaptation," "domain adaptation," "learning to learn," "multi-task learning," and so forth [2, 4, 16].

As an example, in speech recognition systems, speaker adaptation of acoustic model is used to improve the performance of the system for a specific user by combining a large amount of speech data from unspecified users and a small amount of data from the specific target user [6]. Topic adaptation of language models in the area of speech recognition and text mining is another example [5, 15].

Recently, the research on such problems has become a hot topic in statistical learning and many interesting methods for improving the model performance have been proposed [17]. However, most of them start from some assumptions on the relation between the target and the related domain. Collecting a certain amount of corresponding data and analyzing/modeling the difference has not yet been conducted.

4 Food Recommendation

Our target domain is food recommendation. We are currently developing a food recommender system for cellular phone users. When someone is at a food court offering various food services, a system that recommends a dish regarding their preference and context is convenient. Fig.1 shows the flow of a recommendation process. Firstly, a user sends a request for recommendation based on the situation attributes (degree of hunger, degree of fatigue, and daily temperature) through his/her cellular phone. Subsequently, the recommender system merges the registered user attributes with the input user situational attributes, calculates the probability of the user rating for each candidate food and composes a recommendation list of foods according to the probability of positive ratings.

In the system, a Bayesian network is used to model the joint probability distribution $P(V, U, C, S)$ and calculate the probability of the user rating under a specific situation $P(V \mid U, C, S,)$. In a Bayesian network, each random variable is represented as a network node, and the network links represent dependencies between variables. Conditional independences between variables are represented by the entire network structure and used for a more efficient probabilistic inference [7, 8, 13].

The recommender system may receive user feedbacks, and periodically, the system re-learns the parameters of the Bayesian network model using feedback data to increase the precision of the recommendation.

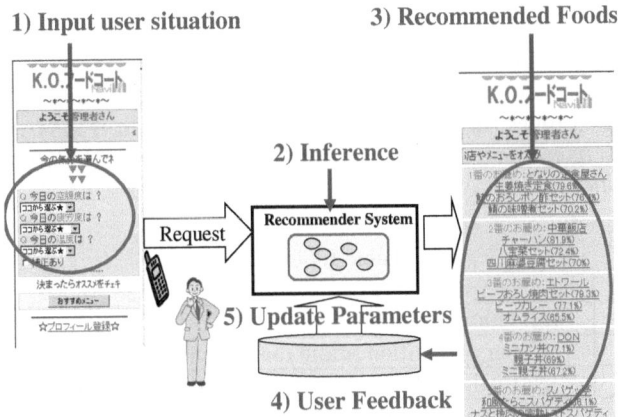

Fig. 1. Flow of recommender system

5 Data Acquisition Method

To acquire the corresponding data, we designed two stage Internet questionnaire surveys. In [11], we dealt with three attributes of user's situations (degree of hunger,
temperature, degree of fatigue). In this research, however, we concentrate on the degree of hunger as the target situation attribute because it is easy to get subjects with
various degrees of hunger even in an internet survey, and it is also easy to judge the
degree of hunger subjectively for the survey subjects.

The first questionnaire survey was conducted from 16th to 17th in December 2008.

- Number of subjects: 746
- Number of foods: 20
- Queries:
  - Query group 1: about user demographic and lifestyle attributes: 44 attributes
    such as age, gender, and occupation, brand loyalty, time and expenditure on lei-
    sure.
  - Query group 2: about user attributes regarding food appreciation: 19 attributes
    such as food category preference (3-grade scale for each attribute).
  - Query group 3: about rating of several foods and reasons of the rating for each
    food under the real and supposed situations depicted in Table 1: 1 total rating
    (3-grade scale from very satisfied to not satisfied at all) and 19 reasons (impres-
    sions of the food such as salty, easy to eat, etc.) (3-grade scale for each reason).
- Each subject rated foods and answered the queries concerning the reasons for the
  rating 15 times: in 3 situations (1 real situation and 2 supposed situations *that are
  different from the real situation*) and 5 foods for each situation.

The second questionnaire survey was conducted from 22nd to 24th in December
2008.

- Number of subjects: 268 (All subjects in the second questionnaire survey answered
  the first questionnaire survey).
- Number of foods: 20 (The same as the first survey).
- Queries:
  - Query group 3 in the first questionnaire.
  - Each subject rated foods and answered the queries concerning the reasons for
    the rating 15 times: In 3 situations (1 real situation *that is different from that
    in the first questionnaire*, and 2 supposed situations *that are different from the
    real situation*).

Table 1. Situations

ID	Situation
S1	Hungry condition: more than 6 hours since previous meal
S2	Normal condition: 3 to 5 hours since previous meal
S3	Full condition: 0 to 2 hours since previous meal.

From the result of both surveys, we chose 212 subjects by filtering out unreliable subjects. All of them answered both questionnaires. This means that each subject rated 5 foods in 6 situations; 2 different real situations and 4 supposed situations. Within the 4 supposed situations, 2 situations have the same corresponding one as the real situations. Combining the ratings, we obtained 2,120 corresponding data and 2,120 independent supposed situation data. The data is summarized in Fig.2.

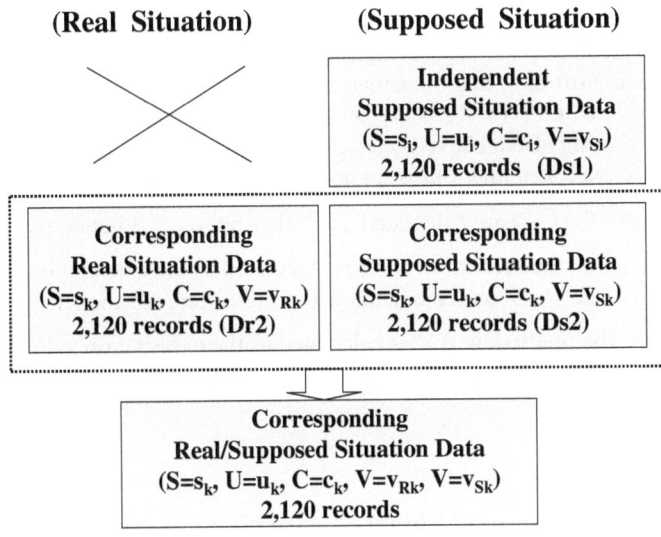

(Real Situation)   **(Supposed Situation)**

Independent
Supposed Situation Data
$(S=s_i, U=u_i, C=c_i, V=v_{Si})$
2,120 records (Ds1)

Corresponding
Real Situation Data
$(S=s_k, U=u_k, C=c_k, V=v_{Rk})$
2,120 records (Dr2)

Corresponding
Supposed Situation Data
$(S=s_k, U=u_k, C=c_k, V=v_{Sk})$
2,120 records (Ds2)

Corresponding
Real/Supposed Situation Data
$(S=s_k, U=u_k, C=c_k, V=v_{Rk}, V=v_{Sk})$
2,120 records

Fig. 2. Data set

6   Difference of Preference between Real and Supposed Situation

From the corresponding data Dr2 and Ds2 we calculate the difference of the rating $V'=V_R-V_S$. Table 2 shows the frequency of each value of the difference in 2,210 corresponding data. About 45% of the subjects rated menu differently under the real and under the supposed situations. 16% of the subjects rated menu higher under the real situation while 29% of the subjects rated menu higher under the supposed situation. We applied both paired t test and Wilcoxon signed rank test to the data, and confirmed that the difference of ratings is significant even at 1% confidence level. We conclude that the difference actually exists.

Table 2. Frequency of each value of the difference

-2 (Supposed situation data rated higher)	-1	0	1	2 (real situation data rated higher)
226(11%)	388(18%)	1,169(55%)	256(12%)	81(4%)

7 Model Construction Methods

7.1 Model Improvement Method Using the Difference Model

We propose a new method of constructing the preference model using a difference model.

[Proposed method: Difference modeling]. Firstly, the supposed situation model is constructed using all supposed data (Ds1 and Ds2). Here we exploit a Naive Bayes classifier for modeling the probability, which predicts the rating from the user attributes, the menu attributes, and the situational attribute. Then using the difference data consisting of S, U, C, V' ($= Vr - Vs$), the difference model that models $P(V', U, C, S)$ is constructed using also a Naive Bayes classifier (See Fig. 3).

In the inference step, the following procedure is executed:

Step1: $P(Vs \mid S, U, C)$ are calculated using the supposed situation model. Using this probability, $\hat{V}s$, the prediction of Vs is calculated as the expectation value.

Step2: $P(V' \mid S, U, C)$ are calculated using the difference model. Using this probability, $\hat{V}'$, the prediction of V' is calculated as the expectation value.

Step3: Prediction of rating under the real situation $\hat{V}_R$ is calculated as

$$\hat{V}_R = \hat{V}_S + \hat{V}'$$

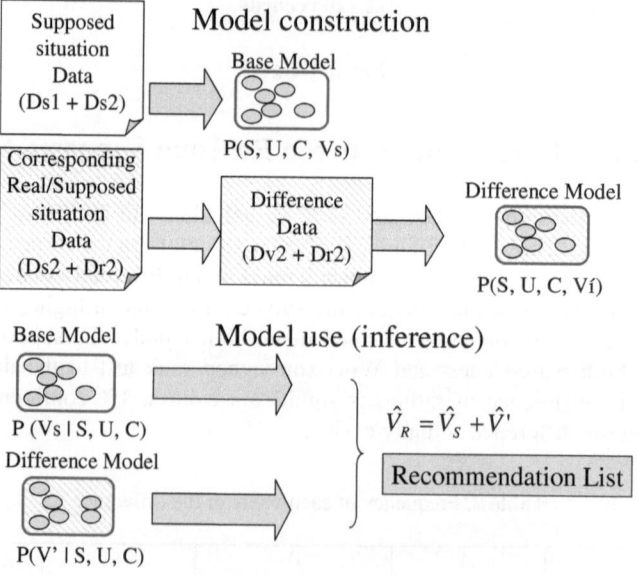

Fig. 3. Proposed Method

7.2 Model Improvement Methods in Previous Research

For comparison, we also applied the two model improvement methods proposed in our previous research [11].

[Method 1: Model modification] To modify and/or integrate a supposed situation's model parameters with a real situation's model parameters. Firstly, a supposed situation model is constructed using all the supposed situation data. Subsequently, using the same model structure as the supposed situation model, model parameters are re-estimated with the real situation data. Then by taking weighted sum of the re-estimated parameters and parameters in the supposed situation model, we get the adapted model (See Fig. 4 Method 1).

When the model is represented as a Bayesian network, each CPT (Conditional Probability Table) in the network is obtained by taking the weighted sum of the CPT in the real situation model and the CPT in the supposed situation model as:

$$P(x \mid pa(x)) = \alpha Pr(x \mid pa(x)) + (1 - \alpha) Ps(x \mid pa(x))$$

Here, $Pr(x|pa(x))$ denotes the CPT attached to variable x in the real situation model. $pa(x)$ is the set of parent nodes of x. $Ps(x|pa(x))$ denotes the corresponding CPT in the supposed model. α is the weight value and determined by try and error using training and test data.

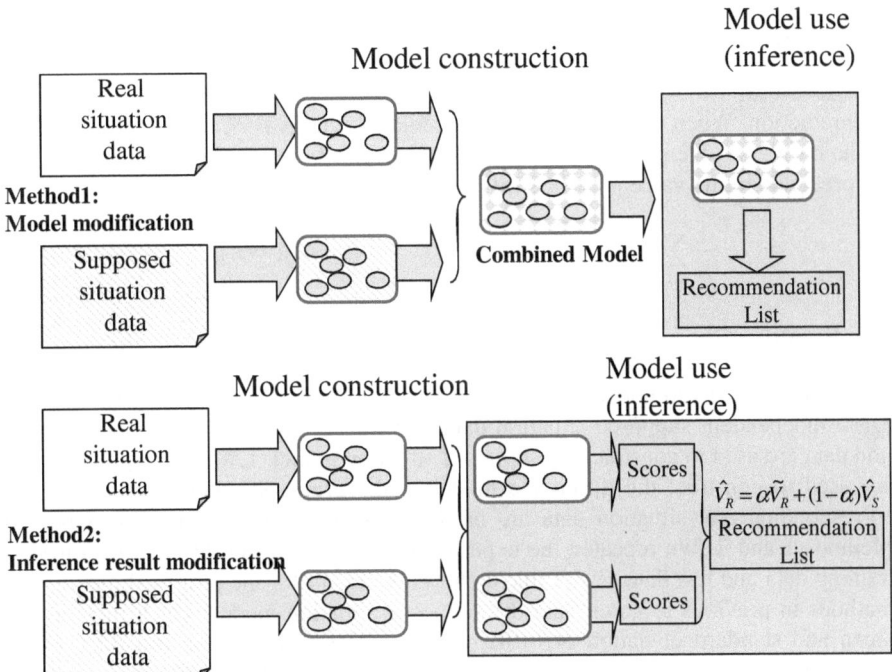

Fig. 4. Methods in Previous Research: Method 1 and Method 2

[Method 2: Inference Result Modification]. To modify and/or integrate an inference result of a supposed situation model with an inference result of a real situation model. Firstly, two models are constructed using all the supposed situation data, the real situation data, respectively. Subsequently, the predicted preference value from the supposed situation model is modified and/or integrated with the value from the real situation model. This procedure is similar to the previous one. Here, instead of smoothing parameters in the model, we propose simply taking the weighted sum of the output from two models (See Fig. 4 Method 2). We denote the output from the supposed situation model as $\hat{V}_S$ and the output from the real situation model as $\tilde{V}_R$. Then the combined output is:

$$\hat{V}_R = \alpha \tilde{V}_R + (1-\alpha)\hat{V}_S$$

When the model is linear relative to the parameters, it becomes equivalent to Method 1. However, if the model is non-linear, such as in a Bayesian network, then the result differs.

8 Evaluation

The constructed models are evaluated according to the accuracy of their preference predictions.

8.1 Evaluation Criteria

As a measure of the prediction accuracy, we used the mean squared error (MSE) of the prediction. When the total number of predicted ratings is N, the number of values of the rating is r, the correct rating value of User i to Food j in Situation k is p_{ijk}, and the predicted rating value is v, the MSE can be formulated as:

$$\frac{1}{N}\sum_{ijk}(p_{ijk} - \sum_{v=1}^{r}vP(V = v \mid U = i, C = j, S = k))^2.$$

8.2 Results

We divided the 2,120 corresponding data into 1,908 training data and 212 test data. 2,120 independent supposed situation data and 1,908 corresponding supposed situation data are used to construct the supposed situation model. 1,908 corresponding data are used to construct the difference model in the proposed method whereas 1,908 corresponding real situation data are used to construct the real situation model in Methods 1 and 2. We repeated the experiments 10 times using different divisions of training data and test data sets. Table 4 shows the result for the proposed method and methods in previous research, and the supposed situation model, which includes the mean and standard deviation of MSE scores against real-situation test data. Fig. 5 shows box-and-whisker plot of MSE score. A box shows the upper and lower quartiles and the median. A whisker shows the upper and lower extremes. We applied the paired t-test to compare the MSE values against the supposed situation model. Here, we confirmed that the improvements of the MSE scores against the supposed situation model are significant even at the 1% confidence level for all three methods. The differences between the three methods are not significant.

Although the MSE score of the proposed method is similar to the scores of Methods 1 and 2, for both methods, the optimal value of weighting parameter α should be selected for each dataset. Conversely, the proposed method does not need to tune the weighting parameter α. Thus, the proposed method is superior to the previous methods.

Table 4. Mean and Standard Deviation of MSE score

Model	Mean	Std Dev
Supposed situation model	0.787	0.0455
Method 1	0.740	0.0489
Method 2	0.740	0.0486
Proposed method	0.743	0.0552

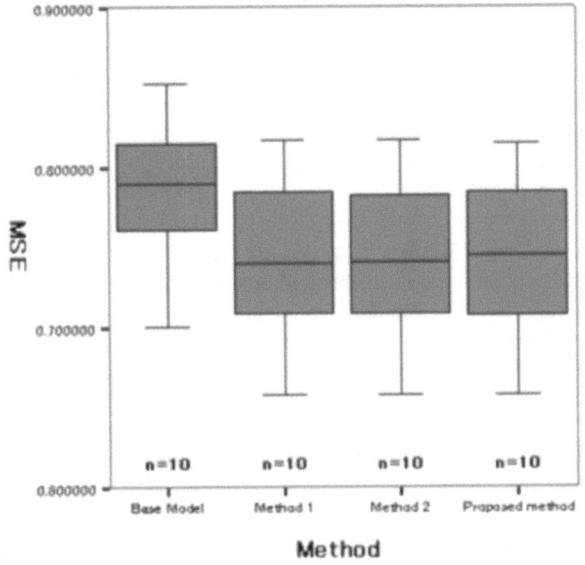

Fig. 5. Box-and-whisker plot of MSE score

9 Discussion and Conclusion

In this paper, we propose a novel way to construct statistical preference model based on the study of the difference between the real and the supposed situation data. To clarify the difference between the preference in a real situation and a supposed situation, we collected a certain amount of corresponding data. We confirmed the effectiveness of the proposed method through experiments. The proposed methods can be easily extended to other types of classifiers such as SVM, Neural Networks, etc. other than the Bayesian network.

In the previous research, we dealt with three situations (degree of hunger, temperature, degree of fatigue). In this research, we focused on the degree of hunger as a situational attribute because corresponding data could be collected easily through an internet survey. The proposed method is applicable to other situational attributes with similar characteristics.

It is interesting issue to frame this work in the context of Burke's classification of hybrid user modeling techniques [3]. The method 2 above, as an example, can be categorized as a kind of "Weighted" hybridization in the classification.

Although we focused on the food preference in this paper, the idea and the methods are applicable to other domains. We hope to conduct data acquisition and experiments in other domains in future.

Acknowledgments. We are grateful to Dr. Shigeyuki Akiba, President and CEO of KDDI R&D Laboratories, Inc. for his continuous support of this study. This work was supported in part by JSPS KAKENHI 20650030.

References

1. Adomavicius, G., Tuzhilin, A.: Toward the next generation of recommender systems: a survey of the state-of-the-art and possible extensions. IEEE Trans. on Knowledge and Data Engineering 17(6), 734–749 (2005)
2. Baxter, J.: A model of inductive bias learning. Journal of Artificial Intelligence Research 12, 149–198 (2000)
3. Burke, R.: Hybrid recommender systems: Survey and experiments. User Modeling and User-Adapted Interaction(UMUAI) 12(4), 331–370 (2002)
4. Daume III, H., Marcu, D.: Domain adaptation for statistical classifiers. Journal of Artificial Intelligence Research 26, 101–126 (2006)
5. Gildea, D., Hofmann, T.: Topic-based language models using EM. In: Proc. of the 6th European Conference on Speech Communication and Technology (EUROSPEECH 1999), vol. 5, pp. 2167–2170 (1999)
6. Huang, X., Acero, A., Hon, H.-W.: Language modeling. In: Spoken Language Processing: A Guide to Theory, Algorithm, and System Development, ch. 11, pp. 545–590. Prentice Hall, Englewood Cliffs (2001)
7. Jensen, F.V.: Bayesian Networks and Decision Graphs. Springer, Heidelberg (2001)
8. Motomura, Y.: Bayesian network construction system: BAYONET. In: Proc. Tutorial on Bayesian Networks, pp. 54–58 (2001) (in Japanese)
9. Ono, C., Kurokawa, M., Motomura, Y., Asoh, H.: A. Context-aware movie preference model using a Bayesian network for recommendation and promotion. In: Conati, C., McCoy, K., Paliouras, G. (eds.) UM 2007. LNCS, vol. 4511, pp. 247–257. Springer, Heidelberg (2007)
10. Ono, C., Motomura, Y., Asoh, H.: A study of probabilistic models for integrating collaborative and content-based recommendation. In: Working Notes of IJCAI 2005 Workshop on Advances in Preference Handling (2005)
11. Ono, C., Takishima, Y., Motomura, Y., Asoh, H., Shinagawa, Y., Imai, M., Anzai, Y.: Context-Aware Users' Preference Models by Integrating Real and Supposed Situation Data. IEICE Transactions on Information and Systems E91-D(11), 2552–2559 (2008)

12. Ono, C., Kurokawa, M., Motomura, Y., Asoh, H.: Implementation and Evaluation of a Movie Recommender System Considering both Users' Personality and Situation. IPSJ Journal 49(1), 130–140 (2008) (in Japanese)
13. Pearl, J.: Probabilistic Reasoning in Intelligent Systems: Networks of Plausible Inference. Morgan Kaufmann Publishers, San Francisco (1988)
14. Resnick, P., Varian, H.R.: Recommender systems. Communications of the ACM 40(3), 56–58 (1997)
15. Seymore, K., Rosenfeld, R.: Large-scale topic detection and language model adaptation. Technical Report CMU-CS-97-152, School of Computer Science, Carnegie Mellon University (1997)
16. Thrun, S., Pratt, L. (eds.): Learning to Learn. Kluwer Academic Publishers, Dordrecht (1998)
17. Video Lectures of the workshop at the NISP 2006 conference, Learning when test and training inputs have different distributions, DIFFERENT 2006 (2006),
    `http://videolectures.net/different06_whistler/`

Modeling the Personality of Participants During Group Interactions

Bruno Lepri, Nadia Mana, Alessandro Cappelletti, Fabio Pianesi,
and Massimo Zancanaro

FBK-irst
via Sommarive 18 Povo, Italy
Tel.: +39-0461-314570
{lepri,mana,cappelle,pianesi,zancana}@fbk.eu

Abstract. In this paper we target the automatic prediction of two personality traits, Extraversion and Locus of Control, in a meeting scenario using visual and acoustic features. We designed our task as a regression one where the goal is to predict the personality traits' scores obtained by the meeting participants. Support Vector Regression is applied to thin slices of behavior, in the form of 1-minute sequences.

Keywords: Personality Modeling, Support Vector Regression, Adaptivity, Group Interactions.

1 Introduction

Personality is the complex of all the attributes - behavioral, temperamental, emotional and mental - that characterize a unique individual. Humans have the tendency to understand and explain other humans' behavior in terms of stable properties that are variously assorted on the basis of the observation of everyday behavior. In this sense, the attribution of a personality and its usage to infer about the others is a fundamental property of our naïve psychology and therefore it is an important aspect in social interaction.

In everyday intuition, the personality of a person is assessed along several dimensions: we are used to talk about an individual as being (non-)open-minded, (dis-)organized, too much/little focused on herself, etc. Several existing theories have formalized this intuition in the form of multi-factorial models, whereby an individual's personality is described in terms of a number of more fundamental dimensions known as traits, derived through factorial studies. A well known example of a multi-factorial model is the Big Five [1] which owes its name to the five traits it takes as constitutive of people's personality:

1. Extraversion vs. Introversion (sociable, assertive, playful vs. aloof, reserved, shy);
2. Emotional stability vs. Neuroticism (calm, unemotional vs. insecure, anxious);
3. Agreeableness vs. Disagreeable (friendly, cooperative vs. antagonistic, faultfinding);

G.-J. Houben et al. (Eds.): UMAP 2009, LNCS 5535, pp. 114–125, 2009.

4. Conscientiousness vs. Un-conscientiousness (self-disciplined, organized vs. inefficient, careless);
5. Openness to experience (intellectual, insightful vs. shallow, unimaginative)

Despite some known limits ([2]; [3]), over the last 50 years the Big Five has become a standard in Psychology. Experiments show that personality traits influence many aspects of task-related individual behavior (e.g. leadership ability [4], attitude toward machines [5]) and also the attitude toward some basic dimensions of adaptivity [6].

Although in some applications it would be possible to acquire personality information by asking the users directly ([7];[8]), in other cases it would be very helpful to do it automatically. For instance, social network websites could analyze text messages to try to mach personalities and increase the chances of a successful relationship [9]. Tutoring systems could be more effective if they could adapt themselves to the learner's personality [10]. Some studies proved that users' evaluation of conversational agents depends on their own personality ([11];[12]). Consequently, a requirement for such systems to adapt to the users' personality, like humans do, is emerging ([13]; [14]). Because of its relevance in social settings, information on user' personality could be useful in personalized support to group dynamics [15].

The work presented in this paper intends to contribute to the specific task of the automatic analysis of people's personality during social interaction through the analysis of acoustic and visual features. We focus on two personality traits: Extraversion and Locus of Control.

Extraversion, one of the Big Five traits, is the quantity and intensity of a subject's interpersonal reactions, emotional expressiveness, and sociability. Correlation has been shown between extraversion and verbal behavior, in particular with prosodic features: higher pitch and higher variation of the fundamental frequency [16], fewer and shorter silent and filled pauses, and higher voice quality and intensity [17]. Moreover, studies on the differences between the communication styles of introverts and extroverts suggest that the latter speak more and more rapidly, with fewer pauses and hesitations [18].

Locus of Control (LoC) reflects a stable set of belief about whether the outcomes of one's actions are dependent upon what the subject does (internal orientation) or on events outside of her control (external orientation) [19]. That is, LoC measures whether causal attribution [20] for one's behavior or beliefs is made to oneself or to external events or circumstances. It has been used as an empirical tool in several domains; for instance, it was shown that people, who feel they are the source or cause of their own attitudes and behaviors (internal LoC), tend to see the computer as a tool that they can control and use to extend their capabilities [21]. On the other hand, those who attribute their own behavior or attitudes to external factors (external LoC) are much prone to regard computers as an autonomous, social entity with which they are need to interact.

In this work, we employ regression analysis on a set of acoustic and visual features extracted from a 1-minute slice of the interaction to predict the values of Extraversion and LoC that a given participant would score on a validated questionnaire.

In relevant respects, the task is similar to the one we, as humans, are routinely involved in when judging about strangers' personality from very short behavioral sequences. Those "intuitions", based on so-called thin slices of behavior, and the process they come by have been the subject of extensive investigation by social psychologists in the last years [23].

2 Previous and Related Works

In [24] the relative frequency of function words and of word categories based on Systemic Functional Grammar are used to train Support Vector Machines (SVMs) with linear kernel for the recognition of Extraversion and Emotional Stability. The data concerning the two personality traits were based on self-reports.

In [25] and [26] the recognition of personality in dialogue is examined. Later, classification, regression and ranking models were applied to the recognition of the Big Five personality traits and self-reports data were compared with observed one [27]. The usefulness of different sets of (acoustic and textual) features, suggested by the psycholinguistic and psychosocial literature, were systematically examined. Mairesse et al.'s work shows that Extraversion is the easiest personality trait to model from spoken language and that prosodic features play a major role. At the same time, their results turn out to be closer to those based on observed personality than on self-reports.

In [28] Naive Bayes and SVMs with linear kernel were trained on a corpus of personal weblogs, using n-gram features extracted from the dataset, for four of the Big Five traits. A major finding of Oberlander and Nowson's work is that the model for Agreeableness was the only one to outperform the baseline. Their personality data were obtained through self-reports.

We are not aware of any attempt to predict personality traits in a social setting besides our previous work [29] in which we used SVM to classify the level of Extraversion and LoC of the participants in 3 classes: low, medium and high.

3 The Mission Survival Corpus

For this study, we used a multimodal corpus of multi-party meetings in which groups of four people were involved in a social interaction (see [30] for a more comprehensive description), the so-called Mission Survival Task (MST), often used in experimental and social psychology to elicit decision making processes in small groups [31]. The MST task consists reaching a consensus on ranking a list of 12 specific items useful to allow survival after a plane crashing. First each participant expresses his/her own personal opinion and then the group discusses each individual proposal, weights the decision and finally ranks the 12 items according to their importance for survival.

Audio was recorded through close-talk microphones worn by each participant and through one omni-directional microphone placed in the middle of the table. Eight cameras recorded the visual context, four from the corners of the room and the other four from the closer walls surrounding the table.

The corpus consists of audio and video recordings of 12 meetings for a total of over 6 hours. Annotations of speech activities and 3D tracking of body activities were automatically extracted, as described below.

The personality traits of all participants were collected by means of standard questionnaires validated on the Italian language, namely the Italian version of Craig's Locus of Control of Behavior scale [32], and the part of Big Marker Five Scales related to the Extraversion dimension [33].

The former is composed by 17 items, with a rating scale from 0 to 5 points, while the Extraversion questionnaire is composed by 10 items, with a rating scale from 1 to 7. The individual LoC and Extraversion scores, characterizing personality traits of each participant, were obtained by summing the points of each item. The mean of the LoC scores for our sample is 27 (standard deviation 7.67; variance 58.86), while for the Extraversion the mean is 46 (standard deviation 8.02; 64.30). Both are consistent with Italian distribution reported by the validation studies above.

4 Feature Extraction

The goal of the learning task is to predict the scores on the two traits of each individual participants in the context of the social interaction. We therefore extracted a number of acoustic and visual features for all the participants and we modeled the learning task as a regression on the combinations of the vector representing the acoustic and visual features of the individual target, combined with the vectors representing the features of the other participants.

4.1 Acoustic Features

Using the speech feature extraction toolbox, developed by the Human Dynamics group at Media Lab[1], we extracted 22 acoustic features from the audio recordings.

The speech features were computed on a 1-minute audio windows. As suggested by previous works ([34], [35] and [36]), 1-minute size is large enough to compute the features in a reliable way, while being small enough to capture the transient nature of social behavior. Table 1 lists the set of acoustic features extracted from the audio corpus. Their relevance for the analysis of human behavior in social setting was discussed by [37]. They grouped them in four classes measuring vocal signals in social interactions: 'Activity', 'Emphasis', 'Influence', and 'Mimicry'. These four classes of features are honest signals, sufficiently expensive to fake that they can form the basis for a reliable channel of communication, and they can be used to predict and explain the human behavior in social interactions.

Emphasis is often considered a signal of how strong is the speaker's motivation. Moreover, the consistency of emphasis (the lower the variations, the higher the consistency) could be a signal of mental focus, while variability may signal an openness to influence from other people. Emphasis is measured by the variation in prosody, i.e. pitch and amplitude. For each voiced segment, the mean energy, frequency of the fundamental format and the spectral entropy are extracted (F1, F2, F3, F4, F5, F6 and F8). The mean-scaled standard deviation of these extracted values is then estimated by averaging over longer time periods (F9, F10, F11, F12, F13, F14 and F16).

---

[1] http://groupmedia.media.mit.edu/data.php

Table 1. Extracted acoustic features (Mean and Standard Deviation calculated on 1 minute)

LABELS	ACOUSTIC FEATURES	Sel_F		Sel_B	
		Extra	LOC	Extra	LOC
F1 - E	Mean Formant Frequency (Hz)	*		* ▲	* ▲
F2 - E	Mean Confidence in formant frequency	*		* ▲	* ▲
F3 - E	Mean Spectral Entropy			▲	* ▲
F4 - E	Mean of Largest Autocorrelation Peak	* ▲		* ▲	*
F5 - E	Mean of Location of Largest Autocorrelation Peak	*		* ▲	* ▲
F6 - E	Mean Number of Autocorrelation Peaks	▲		▲	▲
F7 -A	Mean Energy in Frame	*	* ▲	* ▲	* ▲
F8 - E	Mean of Time Derivative of Energy in Frame	*	*	* ▲	* ▲
F9 - E	SD of Formant Frequency (Hz)	* ▲		* ▲	
F10 - E	SD of Confidence in formant frequency			* ▲	
F11 - E	SD of Spectral Entropy	* ▲	▲	* ▲	* ▲
F12 - E	SD of Value of Largest Autocorrelation Peak	* ▲	▲	* ▲	▲
F13 - E	SD of Location of Largest Autocorrelation Peak	*		* ▲	* ▲
F14 - E	SD of Number of Autocorrelation Peaks		*	▲	* ▲
F15 - A	SD of Energy in Frame	* ▲		* ▲	* ▲
F16 - E	SD of Time Derivative of Energy in Frame	*		* ▲	▲
F17 - A	Average length of voiced segment (seconds)			▲	* ▲
F18 - A	Average length of speaking segment (seconds)	*		* ▲	▲
F19 - A	Fraction of time speaking	* ▲		* ▲	*
F20 - A	Voicing rate	*		* ▲	▲
F21 - I	Fraction speaking over	*		* ▲	*
F22 - M	Average number of short speaking segments	*		* ▲	* ▲

*= features for the target subject, and ▲ = features for the other subjects selected by the two correlation-based selection procedures.

Activity, meant as conversational activity level, usually indicates interest and excitement. Such level is measured by the z-scored percentage of speaking time (F7, F17, F18, F19 and F20). For this purpose, the speech stream of each participant is first segmented into voiced and non-voiced segments, and then the voiced ones are split into speaking and non-speaking.

Influence, the amount of influence each person has on another in a social interaction, was measured by calculating the overlapping speech segments (F21). Influence is a signal of dominance. Moreover, its strength in a conversation can serve as an indicator of attention. It is difficult, in fact, for a person maintain the rhythm of the conversational turn-taking without paying attention to it.

Mimicry, meant as the un-reflected copying of one person by another during a conversation (i.e. gestures and prosody of one are "mirrored" by the other), is expressed by short interjections (e.g. "yup", "uh-huh",) or back-and-forth exchanges consisting of short words (e.g. "OK?", "done!"). Usually, more empathetic people are more likely to mimic their conversational partners: for this reason, mimicry is often used as an unconscious signal of empathy. Mimicry is a complex behavior and therefore difficult to computationally measure. A proxy of its measure is given by the z-scored frequency of these short utterances (< 1 second) exchanges (features F22).

4.2 Visual Features

Regarding the visual context, we mainly focused on few features related to the energy (fidgeting) associated with head, hands and body (see Table 2).

Table 2. Extracted visual features, related to Head, Hands, and Body

LABELS	ACOUSTIC FEATURES	Sel_F		Sel_B	
		Extra	LOC	Extra	LOC
F23	Head fidgeting		*	▲	* ▲
F24	Hands fidgeting			▲	▲
F25	Body fidgeting	*		*	*

The fidgeting features have been automatically annotated by employing the MHI (Motion History Images) techniques [38], which use skin region features and temporal motions to detect repetitive motions in the images and associate such motions to an energy value in such a way that the higher the value, the more pronounced the motion.

5 Modelling Personality Traits Using Support Vector Regression

It is a tenet of this study that personality shows up in social behavior, and that our acoustic and visual features are appropriate to form the 'thin slices' an automatic system can exploit to predict personality traits. Our goal is therefore to model and predict personality traits by considering the behavior of a subject in a 1-minute temporal window; a task similar to that of a psychologist asked to assess personality traits based on thin slices of behavior.

A regression approach was exploited, based on Support Vector Regression (SVR) [39]. Similarly to Support Vector Classification, it produces models that only depend on a subset of the training data, thanks to the cost function that ignores any training data closer to the model prediction than a threshold ε. Moreover, SVR ensures the existence of a global minimum and the optimization of a reliable generalization bound. In ε-SVR the goal is to find a function $f(x)$ that has at most ε deviation from the target for all the training data and at the same time is as flat as possible [40].

We used an ε-SVR with a Radial Basis Function (RBF) kernel. The cost parameter C, the kernel parameter γ and the threshold ε were estimated through the grid technique by cross-fold validation using a factor of 10.[2]

5.1 Experimental Design

Personality can be assessed in two different manners, depending on the role social context is assigned. One might argue that the sole consideration of the target subject' behavior (her thin slices) is enough: the way she/he moves, the tone and energy of her/his voice, etc., are sufficiently informative to get at her personality. A different view maintains that personality manifestation/assessment is sensitive to the social context: the same behavior might have a different import if produced in a given social environment than in another. We formulate the following hypothesis:

Hypothesis 1. The consideration of the social context improves personality assessment.

For our purposes, the social context is encoded through thin slices of the other members of the group.

A second hypothesis we investigate is that personality assessment can be made more economical by limiting the analysis to subsets of the features discussed above. In this paper the following two feature selection procedures are investigated.

Correlation-based feature selection. The correlation-based feature selection technique [41] selects a subset of features that highly correlate with the target value and have low inter-correlation. This method is used in conjunction with a search strategy, typically Best First that searches the features subset space through a greedy hill-climbing strategy with backtracking. The search may start with an empty set of features and proceed forward (forward search) or with the full set of features and go backward (backward search), or proceed in both directions.

We used the backward and the forward search, applying them both to the features of the target subject and to those of the other members of the group. Table 3 and Table 4 report the results of the two selection procedures for the two personality traits. It can be noticed that the forward search (Sel_F) produces a much larger subset of features for Extraversion than for LoC. The backward search (Sel_B), in turn, yields more numerically balanced subsets/

ANOVA-based Feature Selection. ANOVA-based feature selection was performed only on the acoustic features of the target subject, by comparing their means through ANOVA: each feature was treated as a dependent variable in two between-subject analysis of variance, with factor Extraversion (3 levels: L, score<-1σ, M, -1σ≤score≤1σ; H, score>1σ) and LoC (3 levels: L, M, H); significance level was p<.05. No adjustment for multiple comparisons was performed, in order to have a more liberal test. Only the features for which the analysis of variance reported significant results were retained, for the each factor, namely: F1, F2, F6, F14, a subset of the

---

[2] We used the LibSVM tool, available at http://www.csie.ntu.edu.tw/~cjlin/libsvm/

Emphasis class, and F21, the Influence feature, for Extraversion, and F1, F6, F14, the same subset of the Emphasis class apart for the mean energy, and F22, the Mimicry feature, for LoC.

We formulate the following hypothesis.

Hypothesis 2. The selected subsets improve the performance

A within-subject design was exploited to address the two hypotheses, with factors 'Target' and 'Others', each relating to different arrangements of the target subject's (Target) and of the other participants' (Others) features.

- 'Target' has 3 levels: (i) All features (AllFeat); (ii) the features obtained by means of the correlation-based approach (either Sel_F or Sel_B, see below); (iii) the features provided by the Anova-based procedure (Sel_A).

- 'Others' has 4 levels: the same three as for Target, plus a level corresponding to the absence of any features for the other participant (No_Feat). The presence of this level allows to address the contextual hypothesis discussed above.

For each experimental condition, the training instances included the average values of the relevant acoustic and visual feature, computed over a 1-minute window. The analysis was conducted through a leave-one-out procedure. At each of the 48 folds, training was conducted on the data of all but one subject, who was used for testing.

6 Results

Our figure of merit is the squared regression error, $SSEER=(y_{obs}-y_{pred})^2$. Results are compared to those obtained by the base model that always returns the average (27 for LoC and 47 for Extraversion. Its mean SSERR are 59.70 (SD=60.14) for LoC and 63.63 (SD=93.35) for Extraversion.

T-tests (p<.05 with Bonferroni corrections) were first conducted comparing the performance of the features obtained by means of the forward (Sel_F) and backward (Sel_B) search for the correlation-based method in the following conditions: (SEL_F, No_Feat) vs. (Sel_B, No_Feat); (SEL_F, All_Feat) vs. (Sel_B, All_Feat); (Sel_F, Sel_F) vs. (Sel_B, Sel_B); (All_Feat, Sel_F) vs. (All_Feat, Sel_B). The two sets of features never produced significant differences for Extraversion, while Sel_B was consistently superior to Sel_F for LoC. Hence, in the following we will consider only Sel_F for Extraversion and Sel_B for LoC.

A repeated measure analysis of variance for Extraversion revealed only a Target main effect ($F_{1.435, 47}=6.802$, p=.004, with Greenhouse-Geisser correction). According to pairwise comparisons on Target's marginals, Target=All_Feat is significantly lower than the other two levels (p<.0001). Finally, all the conditions with Target=All_Feat have SSERR values that are not pairwise statistically different (t-tests, p<0.05, Bonferroni correction). Hence, no condition is better than (All_Feat, No_Feat) and there is no evidence that the exploitation of the context (as encoded by the Others' features) improves the results. In other words, both Hypothesis 1 and Hypothesis 2 cannot be maintained. Finally, (All_Feat, No_Feat) is better than the baseline.

Table 3. Average SSERR and standard deviations for Extraversion

		Others				
		No_Feat	All_Feat	Sel-B	Sel_A	
Target	All_Feat	19.45 (58.38) *	25.04 (69.98) *	24.13 (61.41) *	26.20 (72.45) *	23.78 (65.69)
	Sel-B	34.09 (68.65)	44.64 (80.93) *	26.63 (69.45) *	45.92 (80.23)	37.05 (75.21)
	Sel_A	35.02 (76.09) *	39.63 (115.06)	49.48 (84.57)	40.57 (102.43) *	41.27 (95.89)
		29.53 (67.99)	36.44 (90.46)	33.41 (72.84)	37.56 (85.79)	

* = conditions that are significantly better than the baseline.

Table 4. Average SSERR and standard deviations for LoC

		Others				
		No_Feat	All_Feat	Sel_F	Sel_A	
Target	All_Feat	17.78 (45.11) *	11.87 (30.23)	12.58 (32.17)	15.85 (30.03)	14.52 (36.38)
	Sel_F	33.82 (56.42)	27.35 (60.58) *	13.07 (34.91)	39.65 (54.27)	28.47 (53.00)
	Sel_A	33.23 (50.94)	29.73 (94.92)	53.32 (59.90)	26.39 (61.33)	35.69 (69.09)
		28.31 (51.22)	22.98 (67.31)	26.32 (47.82)	27.30 (52.44)	

* = conditions that are significantly better than the baseline.

Another repeated measure ANOVA for LoC produced both Target ($F_{1.546, 47}$=12.362, p<.0001) and Target*Others ($F_{1.815, 47}$=4.838, p<0.05) effects. Concerning marginals, Target=All_Feat is better than the others (pairwise t-tests, p<0.05, Bonferroni correction). The interaction is due to Others=Sel_B that produces very low SSERR values in two cases out of three (see Table 3). Conditions (All_Feat, All-Feat), (All_Feat, Sel_B) and (Sel_B, Sel_B) do not pairwise statistically differ, provide the best results and are all better than the baseline. Hence, for LoC both Hypothesis 1 and Hypothesis 2 are verified, the latter limited to a few cases.

7   Discussion and Conclusions

This paper aims to contribute to advance the state of the art in user modeling by demonstrating the feasibility of exploiting personality traits. We based our approach on the assumption that a) personality shows up in the course of social interaction and b) that thin slices of social behavior are enough to allow personality traits classification. The first assumption was realized by exploiting classes of acoustic features encoding specific aspects of social interaction (Activity, Emphasis, Mimicry, and Influence) and three visual features (head, body, and hands fidgeting). As to the second, we considered 1-minute long behavioral sequences. The resulting task for the regression model is similar to that of an expert (e.g., a psychologist) that must provide a personality assessment of strangers based only on short sequences of their behavior.

Based on those assumptions, we designed and executed a regression study addressing two hypotheses: a) that two simple feature selection procedures could provide a smaller, but still effective, subset of features, and b) that the encoding of the social contexts (in the form of the other group members' features) could contribute to regression performance. The data analysis shows that the two traits we have considered behave differently concerning those hypotheses. In the case of Extraversion, no feature selection procedure provided results that were no worse than those obtained by means of All_Feat for the target subject, and there was no evidence that the consideration of the interaction context improve performance. LoC, in turn, seems more capable of taking advantage of one of the feature selection procedure (Sel_B) and, what is more, there are clear signs that LOC's manifestation (and/or understanding by an external observer) improves if the social context is considered.

We believe that, if confirmed by further studies, these differences are of some theoretical and practical importance: theoretically, the different contextual sensitivity of Extraversion and LoC is probably a reflection of deep differences between these two traits: Extraversion is more directly linked to (certain) behavioral manifestations than LoC, for which the social context acts a moderating factor. Practically, our study not only shows the feasibility of automatically assessing personality traits based on thin slices of behavior; it also indicates which features (sub)sets are more appropriate: all our honest features (limited to the target subject) for Extraversion; the Sel_B subset for both the target and the context, in the case of LoC.

Given these initial encouraging results, several research directions disclose, in particular in the direction of providing more comprehensive personality assessments that can be actually used in realistic setting—e.g., by considering the full set of Big Five scales, or traits that, much as LoC, have been shown to affect the relationship between humans and machines (e.g., Computer Anxiety). Conceivably, this move might require considering other context types, beyond the social ones. Traits such as, e.g., Conscientiousness, might be better detectable during the execution of specific task types, while others, e.g., Computer Anxiety, might better show up when confronted with new tasks and/or pieces of technology. Last, but not least, there comes the important task to connect personality traits to behaviors, attitudes and beliefs of interest in a given scenario for the purposes of personalization and adaptation. One might, therefore, inquiry which interaction style and/or specific product choice are more appropriate to people exhibiting a given level personality profile, and then use this information to adapt the system behavior.

References

1. John, O.P., Srivastava, S.: The Big five trait taxonomy: History, measurement and theoretical perspectives. In: Pervian, L.A., John, O.P. (eds.) Handbook of personality theory and research. Guilford Press, New York (1999)

2. Eysenck, H.J.: Dimensions of personality: 16, 5 or 3? criteria for a taxonomic paradigm. Personality and Individual Differences 12(8), 773–790 (1991)
3. Paunonen, S.V., Jackson, D.N.: What is beyond the Big Five? plenty! Journal of Personality 68(5), 821–836 (2000)
4. Hogan, R., Curphy, G.J., Hogan, J.: What we know about leadership: Effectiveness and personality. American Psychologist 49(6), 493–504 (1994)
5. Sigurdsson, J.F.: Computer experience, attitudes toward computers and personality characteristics in psychology undergraduates. Personality and Individual Differences 12(6), 617–624 (1991)
6. Graziola, I., Pianesi, P., Zancanaro, M., Goren-Bar, D.: Dimensions of Adaptivity in Mobile Systems: Personality and People's Attitudes. In: Proceedings of Intelligent User Interfaces IUI 2005, San Diego, CA (2005)
7. John, O.P., Donahue, E.M., Kentle, R.L.: The "Big Five" Inventory: Versions 4a and 5b. Tech. rep., Berkeley: University of California, Institute of Personality and Social Research (1991)
8. Costa, P.T., McCrae, R.R.: NEO PI-R Professional Manual. Psychological Assessment Resources, Odessa, FL (1992)
9. Donnellan, M.B., Conger, R.D., Bryant, C.M.: The Big Five and enduring marriages. Journal of Research in Personality 38, 481–504 (2004)
10. Komarraju, M., Karau, S.J.: The relationship between the Big Five personality traits and academic motivation. Personality and Individual Differences 39, 557–567 (2005)
11. Reeves, B., Nass, C.: The Media Equation. University of Chicago Press, Chicago (1996)
12. Cassell, J., Bickmore, T.: Negotiated collusion: Modeling social language and its relationship effects in intelligent agents. User Modeling and User-Adapted Interaction 13, 89–132 (2003)
13. Funder, D.C., Sneed, C.D.: Behavioral manifestations of personality: An ecological approach to judgmental accuracy. Journal of Personality and Social Psychology 64(3), 479–490 (1993)
14. McLarney-Vesotski, A.R., Bernieri, F., Rempala, D.: Personality perception: A developmental study. Journal of Research in Personality 40(5), 652–674 (2006)
15. Pianesi, F., Zancanaro, M., Not, E., Leonardi, C., Falcon, V., Lepri, B.: Multimodal Support to Group Dynamics. Personal and Ubiquitous Computing 12(2) (2008)
16. Scherer, K.R.: Personality markers in speech. In: Scherer, K.R., Giles, H. (eds.) Social Markers in Speech, pp. 147–209. Cambridge University Press, Cambridge (1979)
17. Mallory, P., Miller, V.: A possible basis for the association of voice characteristics and personality traits. Speech Monograph 25, 255–260 (1958)
18. Furnham, D.: Language and Personality. In: Giles, H., Robinson, W. (eds.) Handbook of Language and Social Psychology. Winley (1990)
19. Rotter, J.B.: Generalized Expectancies for Internal versus External Control of Reinforcment. Psychological Monographs 80 (1, Whole N. 609) (1965)
20. Heider, F.: The psychology of interpersonal relations. Wiley, New York (1957)
21. Johnson, R.D., Marakas, G., Plamer, J.W.: Individual Perceptions Regarding the Capabilities and Roles of Computing Technology: Development of The Computing Technology Continuum of Perspective. Ms. (2002)
22. Ambady, N., Rosenthal, R.: Thin slices of expressive behaviors as predictors of interpersonal consequences: A meta-analysis. Psychological Bulletin 111, 256–274 (1992)
23. Kenny, D.A.: Interpersonal perception: A social relations analysis. Guilford Press, New York (1994)
24. Argamon, S., Dhawle, S., Koppel, M., Pennbaker, J.: Lexical predictors of personality type. In: Proceedings of Interface and the Classification Society of North America (2005)

25. Mairesse, F., Walker, M.: Automatic recognition of personality in conversation. In: Proceedings of HLT-NAACL (2006a)
26. Mairesse, F., Walker, M.: Words mark the nerds: Computational models of personality recognition through language. In: Proceedings of the 28th Annual Conference of the Cognitive Science Society, pp. 543–548 (2006b)
27. Mairesse, F., Walker, M.A., Mehl, M.R., Moore, R.K.: Using Linguistic Cues for the Automatic Recognition of Personality in Conversation and Text. Journal of Artificial Intelligence Research 30, 457–500 (2007)
28. Oberlander, J., Nowson, S.: Whose thumb is it anyway? Classifying author personality from weblog text. In: Proceedings of the Annual Meeting of the ACL, pp. 627–634. Association for Computational Linguistics, Morristown (2006)
29. Pianesi, F., Mana, N., Cappelletti, A., Lepri, B., Zancanaro, M.: Multimodal Recognition of Personality Traits in Social Interactions. In: Proceedings of ICMI 2008, Chania, Crete, Grecia (2008)
30. Mana, N., Lepri, B., Chippendale, P., Cappelletti, A., Pianesi, F., Svaizer, P., Zancanaro, M.: Multimodal Corpus of Multi-Party Meetings for Automatic Social Behavior Analysis and Personality Traits Detection. In: Proceedings of Workshop on Tagging, Mining and Retrieval of Human-Related Activity Information, at ICMI 2007, International Conference on Multimodal Interfaces, Nagoya, Japan (2007)
31. Hall, J.W., Watson, W.H.: The Effects of a normative intervention on group decision-making performance. Human Relations 23(4), 299–317 (1970)
32. Farma, T., Cortivonis, I.: Un Questionario sul "Locus of Control": Suo Utilizzo nel Contesto Italiano (A Questionnaire on the Locus of Control: Its Use in the Italian Context). Ricerca in Psicoterapia 2 (2000)
33. Perugini, M., Di Blas, L.: Analyzing Personality-Related Adjectives from an Eticemic Perspective: the Big Five Marker Scale (BFMS) and the Italian AB5C Taxonomy. In: De Raad, B., Perugini, M. (eds.) Big Five Assessment, pp. 281–304. Hogrefe und Huber Publishers, Göttingen (2002)
34. Lepri, B., Mani, A., Pentland, A., Pianesi, F.: Honest Signals in the Recognition of Functional Relational Roles in Meetings. In: Proceedings of AAAI Spring Symposium on Behavior Modelling, Stanford, CA (2009)
35. Pentland, A.: A Computational Model of Social Signaling. In: Proceedings of the 18th International Conference on Pattern Recognition (ICPR 2006), vol. 1, pp. 1080–1083 (2006)
36. Stoltzman, W.: Toward a Social Signaling Framework: Activity and Emphasis in Speech. MEng. Thesis, MIT (2006)
37. Pentland, A.: Honest Signals: how they shape our world. MIT Press, Cambridge (2008)
38. Chippendale, P.: Towards Automatic Body Language Annotation. In: Proceedings of the 7th International Conference on Automatic Face and Gesture Recognition - FG 2006, Southampton, UK, pp. 487–492. IEEE, Los Alamitos (2006)
39. Drucker, H., Burges, C.J.C., Kaufman, L., Smola, A.J., Vapnik, V.: Support Vector Regression Machines. In: Advances in Neural Information Processing Systems 9 NIPS, pp. 155–161. MIT Press, Cambridge (1997)
40. Smola, A.J., Schölkopf, B.: A Tutorial on Support Vector Regression. Statistics and Computing (2003)
41. Hall, M.A.: Correlation-based Feature Selection for Machine Learning. Ph.D dissertation, Department of Computer Science, University of Waikato (1999)

Predicting Customer Models Using Behavior-Based Features in Shops

Junichiro Mori[1], Yutaka Matsuo[1],
Hitoshi Koshiba[2], Kenro Aihara[2], and Hideaki Takeda[2]

[1] The University of Tokyo, Tokyo, Japan
jmori@ipr-ctr.t.u-tokyo.ac.jp,
matsuo@biz-model.t.u-tokyo.ac.jp
[2] National Institute of Informatics, Tokyo, Japan
{hkoshiba,aihara,takeda}@nii.ac.jp

Abstract. Recent sensor technologies have enabled the capture of users' behavior data. Given the large amount of data currently available from sensor-equipped environments, it is important to attempt characterization of the sensor data for automatically modeling users in a ubiquitous and mobile computing environment. As described herein, we propose a method that predicts a customer model using features based on customers' behavior in a shop. We capture the customers' behavior using various sensors in the form of the time duration and the sequence between blocks in the shop. Based on behavior data from the sensors, we design features that characterize the behavior pattern of a customer in the shop. We employ those features using a machine learning approach to predict customer attributes such as age, gender, occupation, and interest. Our results show that our designed behavior-based features perform with F-values of 70–90% for prediction. We also discuss the potential applications of our method in user modeling.

1 Introduction

Modeling the context for adapting to users is increasingly garnering interest in studies of user modeling and adaptive hypermedia. Numerous studies have addressed recognition and modeling of a user's external context, for example one's location, physical environment, and social environment, to provide context-aware information. Although "context" is a slippery notion [1], it is promising if we can recognize and adapt to aspects of users such as their activities, general interests, and current information needs [2]. Such user models are useful for adaptive context-aware information services in ubiquitous and mobile computing.

Recently, location information has become widely available in both commercial systems and research systems. The development of recent sensor devices such as Wi-Fi, Bluetooth, low-cost radio-frequency tags, and associated RFID enable us to obtain location-based information support in various situations and environments. One early and famous project was Active Badge [3]. Since that work, numerous studies of users' activity recognition and location-aware applications have been developed using location and other sensory information in the context of ubiquitous and mobile systems [4–8].

G.-J. Houben et al. (Eds.): UMAP 2009, LNCS 5535, pp. 126–137, 2009.

Although user models are sometimes assumed implicitly in these studies, several studies in recent years have proposed user models for ubiquitous computing. Heckmann proposes the concept of *ubiquitous user modeling* [9]. He proposes a general user model and context ontology GUMO and a user model and context markup language *UserML* that lay the foundation for inter-operability using Semantic Web technology. Carmichael et al. proposes a user-modeling representation to model people, places, and things for ubiquitous computing, which supports different spatial and temporal granularity [10]. Automatically obtaining such ubiquitous user models from currently available location and other sensory information will help realize adaptive context-aware information services in ubiquitous and mobile environments. As discussed in [11], user modeling and behavior recognition are mutually complementary: given a more precise user model, we can more precisely guess the user behavior, and vice versa.

As described in this paper, we propose a method to predict user attributes from location information. In particular, we specifically examine the location information of customers in a shop. We conducted an experiment to obtain empirical data from an actual shop with more than 100 users. We capture customers' behavior in the form of time duration in a block and the sequence between blocks in the shop using sensors of various types. Based on the behavior data, we design several features that characterize the behavior pattern of a customer in the shop. We employ those features with a machine learning approach to learn customer attributes such as age, gender, occupation, and interests. Consequently, our method can automatically predict a user model of a new user coming to the environment. We show that some attributes are likely to be predicted using behavior-based features with F-values of 70–90%. The method is useful in ubiquitous and mobile environments for adaptive context-aware information services because it obtains user models automatically from location information.

This paper is organized as follows. In the next section, we describe related work. We introduce our sensors and describe sensor data in Section 3. The proposed method to predict user attributes from location information is explained in Section 4. Analyses of the results are made in Section 5. Finally, we discuss potential applications of our method in user modeling and conclude the paper in Section 6.

2 Related Work

With recent advancements of sensor devices, numerous studies have addressed the use of location and other sensory information. Although most studies have specifically examined recognition of users' activity [3–5], some studies have recently addressed the issue of user modeling with location information [6–8]. Most of these studies have employed knowledge-related features for modeling a user, which require an explicit and a-priori built representation of the domain knowledge. In contrast, some studies have investigated modeling a user with features obtained non-intrusively such as observation of the behavior history and patterns [12, 13] using statistical user modeling techniques [14, 15]. Matsuo et al. proposed a similar method to predict user attributes using sensor information [11]. However, they employed only simple location history as the feature from sensors, whereas we design and combine several features to characterize behavior patterns, which in turn improves the performance for prediction.

Several studies in recent years have sought to model users for development of ubiquitous computing [9, 10, 16]. Heckmann proposes the concept of *ubiquitous user modeling* [9] including a general user model and context ontology GUMO and a user model, and a context markup language *UserML* that lay the foundation for interoperability using Semantic Web technology. Carmichael et al. proposes a user-modeling representation to model people, places, and things for ubiquitous computing. That mode of representation supports different spatial and temporal granularity [10]. Among various user-modeling dimensions, we mainly focus on long-term attributes such as age, gender, occupation, and interests. Kobsa lists frequently found services of user-modeling, some of which use users' long-term characteristics such as knowledge, preference, and abilities [17]. Jameson discusses how different types of information about a user, ranging from current context information to the user's long-term attributes, can contribute simultaneously to user adaptive mechanisms [18]. In the ontology GUMO, long-term user model dimensions are categorized as demographic information such as age group and gender, personality and characteristics, profession and proficiency, or interests such as music or sports. Some are basic and are therefore domain-independent, although others are domain-dependent. Our method contributes to the population of such existing user models by obtaining user attributes automatically.

3   Behavior Data from Sensors

This section presents a description of our sensors and experiments to collect sensor and user data for designing useful features to predict user models. In our experiment, we obtain the location information of customers in a shop using sensors of various types. The shop is virtually divided into multiple blocks. We represent the behavior data of a customer in the form of the time duration in each block and the sequence from one block to another.

3.1   Sensors

In our experiment, we use the following sensors of four types as shown in Fig. 1 to capture location information of customers in the shop:

- **IC card:** each participant in the experiment is delivered an Integrated Circuit card (IC card). The IC card readers are attached to the shelves in the shop. The participants can hold the IC card over the reader on the shelf if they would like to record their checking the goods on the shelf.
- **RFID and Wireless:** each participant also receives a mobile device that includes active Radio Frequency Identification (RFID) and wireless functions. The device is sufficiently compact that the participant can dangle it around the neck. Active RFID readers and wireless access points are installed in the shop to detect signals from the devices.
- **Video camera:** Video cameras are also installed in the shop to record participants' motions. The system identifies each participant by analyzing participants' facial images in the record video data.

Fig. 1. Sensors to capture location information of customers in the shop

Fig. 2. Outline view and virtual blocks in the shop where sensor data are collected

Data from these sensors are integrated to estimate the time duration in each block and the sequence from one block to another in the shop. Using the integrated sensor data, we can capture users' locations and transitions between blocks with accuracy of 90%. For our research, we assume that users' location information is estimated properly with our sensors.

3.2   Data Acquisition and Representation

To collect the sensor data, we conducted an experiment at a general shop in a city area that is visited by a wide range of people from youth to seniors. We installed five IC card readers, three active RFID readers, nine RFID reference tags, three wireless access points, and five video cameras in the shop. In all, 109 men and women participants

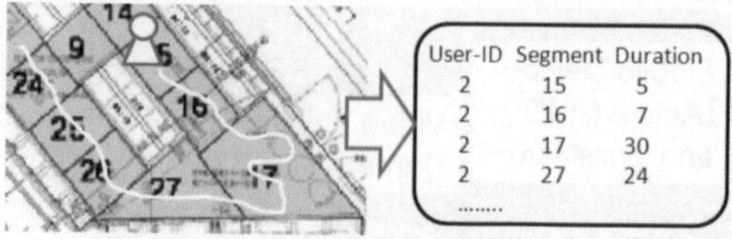

Fig. 3. Customers' behavior data based on their location information

Fig. 4. Interface of the system that enables users to create their Blog based on their location history in the shop

from their late teens to their forties were enrolled in the experiment. Each participant was provided an IC card and a mobile device. The participants were instructed to walk around the shop freely according to their personal interests towards the goods.

The shop is divided into several virtual blocks of about a meter square, as shown in Fig. 2. In our experiment, the granularity of the blocks are decided so that each block represents a certain kind of goods in the shop. We had seventeen blocks in total. Based on customers' location information from the sensors, we represent their behavior data as the time duration in each block and the sequence from one block to another. To estimate the time duration and the sequence, we integrate the location information captured from individual sensors. Then, we obtain behavior data of each participant as shown in Fig. 3. The time duration is counted by seconds.

3.3 Online System

We provided the participants with an online system during the experiment. The online system automatically generates a personalized Blog template that includes points of

interest from one's record of a IC card and one's location history from the sensor data
(Fig. 4). The participant can freely edit the Blog template and create a Blog during the
experiment. We obtained participants' subjective sentiment related to the shop or its
goods on this Blog system.

4   Predicting a Customer Model

In this section, we propose our method to predict a customer model consisting of several user attributes. The customer model is predicted using a machine learning approach
with features based on customers' behavior in the shop. We first describe our customer
model to be predicted. Then, we explain the design of customers' behavior-based features to be used for our machine learning method.

4.1   Customer Model

Table 1 shows that we define our customer model using four attributes (*age*, *gender*,
occupation, and *interest*). The attributes of *age*, *gender*, and *occupation* were obtained
from the questionnaire that each participant filled out before the experiment.

Table 1. List of user attributes and their values in a customer model

attribute	value (ratio)
age	10s (1.8%), 20s (43.1%), 30s (37.6%), 40s (17.4%)
gender	men (54.1%), women (45.9%)
occupation	office worker (58.7%), student (24.8%),
	housekeeper (10.1%), other (6.4%)
interest	interested (45.8%), disinterested (54.2%))

The final attribute *interest* was obtained from the Blog system that we provided for
participants during the experiment. The Blog contains each participant's subjective sentiment related to the shop or its goods. We manually checked the Blog contents and
counted both positive comments and negative comments for each participant. According to the sums of respective positive comments and negative comments, we classified
each participant according to whether he or she was interested in the shop and its goods,
which then defined that participant's *interest*.

4.2   Behavior-Based Features

We now describe our feature design for predicting our customer model. In the shop, a
customer was able to take behavior patterns of several types. Although some customers
might remain in places which interest them, others might stroll around the shop seeking
something interesting for them. Our sensor data capture such different behavior patterns
of individual customers in the form of the time duration in each block in the shop and the
sequence between blocks. We can design several features that characterize customers'
behaviors in the shop given the sensor data. In our research, we specifically examine
the following intuitive features based on customers' behaviors.

- **binary**: whether a customer visits a block or not.
- **frequency**: how many times a customer visits a block.
- **duration**: how long a customer is in a block[1].
- **sequence**: how often a customer moves from one block to another.

Matsuo proposed a method to infer user properties from sensor data as a text categorization problem by converting the sensor data into a sensor-user matrix, which resembles a document-by-word matrix. In line with this approach, we build the following matrices of two types: a user-block matrix (left) and a user-block transition matrix (right).

	b_1	...	b_j	...	b_m
u_1	v_{11}	...	v_{1j}	...	v_{1m}
...	...	...	...	...	...
u_i	v_{i1}	...	v_{ij}	...	v_{im}
...	...	...	...	...	...
u_n	v_{n1}	...	v_{nj}	...	v_{nm}

	$t_1 : b_1 \rightarrow b_2$	...	$t_j : b_o \rightarrow b_p$	...	$t_l : b_s \rightarrow b_m$
u_1	w_{11}	...	w_{1j}	...	w_{1l}
...	...	...	...	...	...
u_i	w_{i1}	...	w_{ij}	...	w_{il}
...	...	...	...	...	...
u_n	w_{n1}	...	w_{nj}	...	w_{nl}

Denoting the number of users as n and the number of blocks as m, the user-block matrix is an $n \times m$ matrix $U \times B$ and the user-block transition matrix is an $n \times l$ matrix $U \times T$ where l is the number of combination of bordering blocks. We denote v_{ij} as the element of $U \times B$ and w_{ij} as the element of $U \times T$. Furthermore, **binary, frequency,** and **duration** are derived from $U \times B$ and **sequence** derived from $U \times T$ by defining v_{ij} and w_{ij} as follows:

- **frequency**: $v_{ij} = freq(u_i, b_j)$ where $freq(u_i, b_j)$ is the number of visits of a user u_i at a block b_j.
- **binary**: $v_{ij} = \begin{cases} 1 \text{ if } freq(u_i, b_j) > 0 \\ 0 \text{ otherwise} \end{cases}$
- **duration**: $v_{ij} = dur(u_i, b_j)$ where $dur(u_i, b_j)$ is the time of stays of users u_i at blocks b_j.
- **sequence**: $w_{ij} = seq(u_i, t_j : b_o \rightarrow b_p)$ where $seq(u_i, t_j : b_o \rightarrow b_p)$ is the number of transitions of a user u_i from a block b_o to a block b_p.

For **frequency, duration**, and **sequence**, we normalized the weight for each feature by cosine normalization so that the feature weights fall in the [0,1] interval and the feature vectors become equal in length. The normalization is defined as $weight_{ij}^{normalized} = weight_{ij}/\sqrt{\sum_{i=1}^{m}(weight_{ij})^2}$. Thereby, we generated three other features that we call **n-frequency, n-duration**, and **n-sequence**.

4.3 Prediction

Given the customer model and the feature set, our task is now to predict each attribute in the customer model using the feature set. For each attribute in the customer model, we trained a learner that predicts the attribute given a set of training examples that includes a set of feature values corresponding to the certain value of the attribute. Although

---

[1] If a customer comes back to a block, we count this stay as another time of duration.

some attributes take multiple values, we solve the two-class problem for every attribute because the distribution of each value of some attribute is biased. For example, for *occupation*, 58.7% of subjects are classiable as "office workers". Thereby, we train the learner for *occupation* using the training examples of positive and negative classes and solve the two-class problem of classifying people into those who are office workers and those who are not. Similarly, we train the learner for *age* to classify people into those who are in their teens and 20s or 30s and 40s. Regarding *gender* and *interest*, they are also solved as two-class problems because they originally have two classes.

We employ a support vector machine (SVM) as a learner, which creates a hyperplane that separates the data into two classes with the maximum-margin [19]. The SVMs tend to be fairly robust to overfitting. In addition, there is a theoretically motivated "default" choice of parameter setting [20]. The SVM is often used to learn the categorization problem that is our case reduced from our user modeling problem. We employ a radius basis function (RBF) kernel, which performs well in our preliminary experiments. The SVM performance is evaluated using five-fold cross validation.

5   Evaluation and Results

5.1   Attribute Prediction

Performance of the learner for each attribute are shown with Recall, Precision, and *F*-value in Table 2. The *F*-value is a geometric average of recall and precision, defined as *F*-value $= (2 \times \text{Recall} \times \text{Precision})/(\text{Recall} + \text{Precision})$. For example, if we use **frequency** as a feature to predict the *age* of a customer, the recall is 0.74, meaning that we can classify 74% of people with the *age* having a certain value.

On average, the *F*-value is about 62%, precision is about 60%, and recall is about 70%. However, the performance of the learner varies depending on the attribute to be predicted. For *age*, *gender*, *occupation*, and *interest*, the *F*-values are as high as 0.67, 0.71, 0.79, and 0.62, respectively, with about 0.44–0.98 recall and 0.51–0.74 precision. Depending on the attribute, the performance varies as much as 0.2 points, which indicates that some attributes are predicted and others are difficult to predict. We claim that we must carefully select the attribute to be applied for personalized information services if we use the automatically obtained user model from location information in ubiquitous and mobile environments.

The learner performance also varies depending on the feature. For *age*, **n-duration** has the highest *F*-value and **frequency** is the second best. Regarding *gender*, **n-sequence** is the best and **frequency** is the second. For *occupation*, **frequency** is the best and **n-duration** is the second. Finally, teh **n-sequence** is the best and **frequency** is the second for *interest*. Overall, normalization seems to function effectively for **duration** and **sequence**. The learner based on **frequency** performs well for every attribute. However, some features are useful for predicting particular attributes. Our results show that attributes such as *age* and *occupation* can be predicted effectively using features such as **frequency** and **n-duration** whereas *gender* can be predicted effectively with **n-sequence**. Selecting appropriate behavior features depending on the attribute to be predicted is important to obtain a user model from location information. Although

Table 2. Performances of prediction for respective attributes depending on the feature

age					gender			
Feature	F-value	Precision	Recall		Feature	F-value	Precision	Recall
frequency	0.62	0.55	0.74		frequency	0.68	0.69	0.70
n-freq	0.46	0.50	0.50		n-frequency	0.66	0.56	0.84
bin	0.56	0.61	0.54		binary	0.50	0.52	0.54
duration	0.60	0.61	0.60		duration	0.44	0.51	0.44
n-duration	0.67	0.61	0.78		n-duration	0.52	0.58	0.54
sequence	0.59	0.55	0.68		sequence	0.67	0.66	0.76
n-sequence	0.60	0.54	0.72		n-sequence	0.71	0.71	0.78
average	0.58	0.55	0.65		average	0.59	0.60	0.65
frequency & duration & sequence	0.58	0.60	0.58		frequency & duration & sequence	0.69	0.64	0.8

occupation					interest			
Feature	F-value	Precision	Recall		Feature	F-value	Precision	Recall
frequency	0.79	0.69	0.98		frequency	0.59	0.58	0.62
n-frequency	0.69	0.66	0.80		n-frequency	0.58	0.58	0.62
binary	0.68	0.57	0.86		binary	0.55	0.55	0.60
duration	0.78	0.74	0.83		duration	0.48	0.51	0.50
n-duration	0.78	0.72	0.89		n-duration	0.57	0.54	0.64
sequence	0.76	0.70	0.91		sequence	0.55	0.56	0.60
n-sequence	0.73	0.67	0.87		n-sequence	0.62	0.59	0.74
average	0.74	0.67	0.87		average	0.56	0.55	0.61
frequency & duration & sequence	0.75	0.69	0.94		frequency & duration & sequence	0.70	0.67	0.78

interest seems difficult to predict compared with other attributes, the combination and selection of features improve the performance, as described in the following section.

5.2   Feature Selection

The results show that behavior-based features are effective to predict some attributes. We were able to further assume that combining features such that they represent behavior patterns in a more detailed way would improve the performance. Although it is difficult to represent overall behavior patterns using only our simple features, combining those features represents customers' behavior more precisely than any single feature. For example, combination of the duration and the sequence can represent a user moving and stopping. The **frequency & duration & sequence** in Table 2 shows the performance of a learner with combined features. For *age*, *gender*, and *occupation*, a learner with the combined features does not perform better than using the best performance feature. On the other hand, the combined features improve the performance of a learner for *interest* as much as 0.08 points from the best performance feature and 0.14 points from average performance. Moreover, *interest*, which shows a customer's positive or negative attitude towards the shop or its goods seems affected by overall

Table 3. Performance of prediction for *interest* depending on feature selection

interest

Feature	F-value	Precision	Recall
frequency & duration & sequence	0.70	0.67	0.78
profile (age, gender, occupation, marriage, etc.)	0.74	0.74	0.73
frequency & duration & sequence + profile	0.70	0.72	0.74
selected features	0.72	0.72	0.74

behavior patterns rather than partial behavior patterns. Some attributes are clearly better predicted by the combined behavior-based features.

In addition to our behavior-based features, we were able to design various features using other information sources. For example, if we were able to know user demographic data such as *age*, *gender*, and *occupation* beforehand, we could use those attributes as features to predict *interest*. In our experiment, each participant filled out a questionnaire that enabled us to derive user profile data such as age, gender, marriage, occupation, and PC proficiency. Based on the profile data, we design the profile-based features for predicting *interest*. As presented in Table 3, a learner with profile-based features performs better than the combined features. The combination of profile-based features and behavior-based features does not perform better than the profile-based features. The features from the user profile are clearly effective to predict *interest*. However, behavior-based features can predict *interest* with comparable performance of the user-model based features. This is important for modeling a user in a ubiquitous and mobile environment, where it is often difficult to obtain user information beforehand. Our behavior-based features, which are obtainable from the sensors in the environment, are useful to predict some user attributes like *interest* without knowing the user information.

For this purpose, several feature selection strategies to determine a proper set of features among many features have been proposed [21]. As portrayed in Table 3, the performance of a learner with selected features is better than the combination of all possible features. It is also comparable with the performance of profile-based features. Feature selection provides a set of weighted behavior-based features; consequently the weighted features give information about which behavior on a certain location is for the prediction. This information can be used for installing sensors so that the important location, the particular block in our case, is properly detected. From a practical perspective, such information is useful for arranging displays in a shop or for controlling customers' flow in the shop.

6   Discussion and Conclusion

Although we focused on predicting a customer model using features based on customers' behavior in a shop, our method is not limited in such environment. Our method is applicable to a sensor-equipped environment which could provide a user's simple behavior history as described in this paper. By predicting a user model of a new visitor to the environment such as a shop and museum, we can offer personalized information services to the visitor. In particular, many researchers have examined systems using the user model from location information to improve a museum visitor's experience by recommending points of interest and personalizing the delivered content [7, 8]. Our method can be adopted easily to such existing systems by providing the user model from location information. Some studies use the user model ontology to provide such context-aware services [6]. Importantly, our method contributes to the population of existing user modeling ontologies for ubiquitous computing such as those of GUMO [9].

Because we provide an online system that helps a user create a Blog based on his or her behavior data during our experiment, our method can facilitate creation of a user-adaptive "Lifelog" by predicting whether the user liked a certain point in one's behavior history or not. Lifelog is fundamentally a dataset composed of one or more media forms that record the same individual's daily activities [22]. A main challenging issue is how to extract meaningful information from the huge and complex data which are captured continuously and accumulated from multiple sensors. Our method can tackle the issue by predicting what events, states, or places are interesting or important for a user and summarizing the useful records.

This paper has presented a proposal of a method to predict user attributes from location information. In particular, we described our specific examination of the location information of customers in a shop. We designed several features that characterize the behavior pattern of a customer in the shop. Machine learning techniques were applied to learn the pattern between the features and customer's attributes such as age, gender, occupation, and interests. Our results show that some user attributes are well predictable with behavior-based features. The results also show that the selection and the combination of features are important to predict some attributes. In future work, we will employ more complicated features that characterize various types of behavior patterns for predicting user models.

Acknowledgements

This research was supported by the Information Grand Voyage Project from the Japanese Ministry of Economy, Trade and Industry. The authors thank our cooperated partners on the project, NEC Corporation and Tokyu Corporation, for providing the opportunity and the infrastructure to conduct the experiment. The authors also appreciate the cooperation of all experiment participants.

References

1. Dourish, P.: What we talk about when we talk about context. Personal and Ubiquitous Computing 8(1) (2004)
2. Jameson, A., Kruger, A.: Preface to the special issue on user modeling in ubiquitous computing. User Modeling and User-Adapted Interaction (3–4) (2005)
3. Want, R., Hopper, A., Falcao, V., Gibbons, J.: The active badge location system. ACM Transactions on Information Systems 10(1), 91–102 (1992)
4. Wilson, D.H.: The narrator: A daily activity summarizer using simple sensors in an instrumented environment. In: Proc. UbiComp 2003 (2003)

5. Liao, L., Fox, D., Kautz, H.: Location-based activity recognition using relational markov networks. In: Proc. IJCAI 2005 (2005)
6. Hatala, M., Wakkary, R.: Ontology-based user modeling in an augmented audio reality system for museums. User Model. User-Adapt. Interact. 15(3-4), 339–380 (2005)
7. Petrelli, D., Not, E.: User-centred design of flexible hypermedia for a mobile guide: Reflections on the hyperaudio experience. User Model. User-Adapt. Interact. 16(1), 85–86 (2006)
8. Stock, O., Zancanaro, M., Busetta, P., Callaway, C.B., Krüger, A., Kruppa, M., Kuflik, T., Not, E., Rocchi, C.: Adaptive, intelligent presentation of information for the museum visitor in peach. User Model. User-Adapt. Interact. 17(3), 257–304 (2007)
9. Heckmann, D.: Ubiquitous Use Modeling. Ph.d thesis, University of Saarland (2005)
10. Camichael, D.J., Kay, J., Kummerfeld, B.: Consistent modelling of users, devices and sensors in a ubiquitous computing environment. User Modeling and User-Adapted Interaction 15(3-4), 197–234 (2005)
11. Matsuo, Y., Okazaki, N., Izumi, K., Nakamura, Y., Nishimura, T., Hasida, K., Nakashima, H.: Inferring long-term user properties based on users' location history. In: IJCAI, pp. 2159–2165 (2007)
12. Zancanaro, M., Kuflik, T., Boger, Z., Goren-Bar, D., Goldwasser, D.: Analyzing museum visitors' behavior patterns. In: Conati, C., McCoy, K., Paliouras, G. (eds.) UM 2007. LNCS, vol. 4511, pp. 238–246. Springer, Heidelberg (2007)
13. Bohnert, F., Zukerman, I., Berkovsky, S., Baldwin, T., Sonenberg, L.: Using collaborative models to adaptively predict visitor locations in museums. In: Nejdl, W., Kay, J., Pu, P., Herder, E. (eds.) AH 2008. LNCS, vol. 5149, pp. 42–51. Springer, Heidelberg (2008)
14. Webb, G.I., Pazzani, M.J., Billsus, D.: Machine learning for user modeling. User Model. User-Adapt. Interact. 11(1-2), 19–29 (2001)
15. Zukerman, I., Albrecht, D.: Predictive statistical models for user modeling. User Modeling and User-Adapted Interaction 11, 5–18 (2001)
16. Niu, W.T., Kay, J.: Pervasive personalisation of location information: Personalised context ontology. In: Nejdl, W., Kay, J., Pu, P., Herder, E. (eds.) AH 2008. LNCS, vol. 5149, pp. 143–152. Springer, Heidelberg (2008)
17. Kobsa, A.: Generic user modeling systems. User Modeling and User-Adaptied Interaction 11, 49–63 (2001)
18. Jameson, A.: Modeling both the context and the user. Personal Technologies 5 (2001)
19. Vapnik, V.: The Nature of Statistical Learning Theory. Springer, Heidelberg (1995)
20. Joachims, T.: Text categorization with support vector machines: learning with many relevant features. In: Nédellec, C., Rouveirol, C. (eds.) ECML 1998. LNCS, vol. 1398, pp. 137–142. Springer, Heidelberg (1998)
21. Chen, Y.W., Lin, C.J.: Combining SVMs with various feature selection strategies. Springer, Heidelberg (2006)
22. Kleek, M.V., Shrobe, H.E.: A practical activity capture framework for personal, lifetime user modeling. In: Conati, C., McCoy, K., Paliouras, G. (eds.) UM 2007. LNCS, vol. 4511, pp. 298–302. Springer, Heidelberg (2007)

Investigating the Utility of Eye-Tracking Information on Affect and Reasoning for User Modeling

K. Muldner[1], R. Christopherson[2], R. Atkinson[2], and W. Burleson[1]

Arizona State University, School of Computing and Informatics/Arts, Media and Engineering[1], Psychology of Education[2], Tempe, Arizona
{Katarzyna.Muldner,rmchris3,Robert.Atkinson,Winslow.Burleson}@asu.edu

Abstract. We investigate the utility of an eye tracker for providing information on users' affect and reasoning. To do so, we conducted a user study, results from which show that users' pupillary responses differ significantly between positive and negative affective states. As far as reasoning is concerned, while our analysis shows that larger pupil size is associated with more constructive reasoning events, it also suggests that to disambiguate between different kinds of reasoning, additional information may be needed. Our results show that pupillary response is a promising non-invasive avenue for increasing user model bandwidth.

1 Introduction

Increasing model *bandwidth*, i.e., the amount and quality of information available to a user model, without disrupting a user's interaction with an adaptive system is a key user modeling challenge [1]. Arguably, the higher the level of the information to be captured, the more complex a user model's construction becomes, because it may require sophisticated Artificial Intelligence (AI) techniques and innovative sensing devices. Thus, it is increasingly critical to show that (1) it is feasible to capture the necessary user states (*feasibility* requirement) and (2) the the increased model complexity improves system usability (*usability* requirement).

Here, we focus on the feasibility requirement, by investigating the utility of pupillary data provided by an eye tracker for informing a user model on high-level user states related to affect and reasoning style. Information on how a user is feeling and/or reasoning can be highly valuable, as it enables an adaptive system to respond appropriately to the user's needs and preferences. For instance, users engage in frustrating tasks on a computer significantly longer after an empathetic computational response (e.g., [2]); learning outcomes are improved when computational tutors provide tailored prompts to foster *meta-cognitive* skills, i.e., domain-independent reasoning abilities (e.g., [3]). However, information on high-level states is rarely observable and so challenging to obtain unobtrusively. A promising avenue corresponds to innovative sensing devices, which capture users' physiological responses that are a natural by-product of their interaction

G.-J. Houben et al. (Eds.): UMAP 2009, LNCS 5535, pp. 138–149, 2009.

with an adaptive system. For instance, D'Mello and Graessor [4] rely on machine learning to show that dialog and posture features can discriminate between affective states of boredom, confusion, flow and frustration. Burleson et al. [5] show that a learning companion, based on a model incorporating information from a pressure mouse, posture chair, video camera, and skin conductance bracelet, impacts students' motivation and attitudes towards the companion.

There is also work exploring how information on gaze patterns from an eye tracker can inform a user model, for instance to determine (1) attention shifts and/or focus [6,7]; (2) high-level reasoning via *self-explanation* [8], the process of explaining and clarifying instructional material to oneself [9]. Another branch of eye-tracking research focuses on pupil dilation. In tightly-controlled experimental settings, there is a clear link between mental effort and pupil dilation [10,11] and affect and pupil dilation [10,12], where affective responses and mental effort increase pupil size. However, these evaluations rely on an experimental protocol where the context is far removed from what a natural interaction with an adaptive system might entail. For instance, subjects categorize emotionally charged words [12], or listen to affect-induced audio at controlled time intervals [13]. When transferred to more realistic applications, there have been mixed results with respect to reliability of pupil information. Several attempts to find a link between reading difficulty and mental effort have failed (e.g., [14,15]), although Igbal et al. [14] did find that pupil size increased with more difficult file manipulation tasks. Conati et al. [8] failed to find a link between pupillary response and self-explanation, which is presumably associated with mental effort, and so pupil size. Clearly, more work is needed assessing the link between mental effort, affect and pupil response, and its utility for user modeling. Our research is a step in this direction.

As our test-bed application, we rely on the Example Analogy (EA)-Coach [16,17], an adaptive learning environment we developed that supports meta-cognition during example-based learning. Although a formal evaluation of the EA-Coach showed that in general, it effectively fosters meta-cognition [17], it also suggested that some students require more support than is currently provided by the system. Thus, we would like to extend the tutor with affective and meta-cognitive scaffolding, to help all students learn effectively from APS. Given that this scaffolding will be based on the EA-Coach user model, as the first step, we have been investigating ways to increase the model's bandwidth to provide adequate information on the relevant student states.

We begin with an introduction to the EA-Coach and its user model. We then describe the user study we conducted to evaluate whether affect and reasoning style impacts pupillary response. After we present our results, we conclude and provide suggestions for some future work.

2   The EA-Coach

The Example-Analogy (EA) Coach [16,17] is an adaptive learning environment that fosters meta-cognitive skills during *analogical problem solving* (APS),

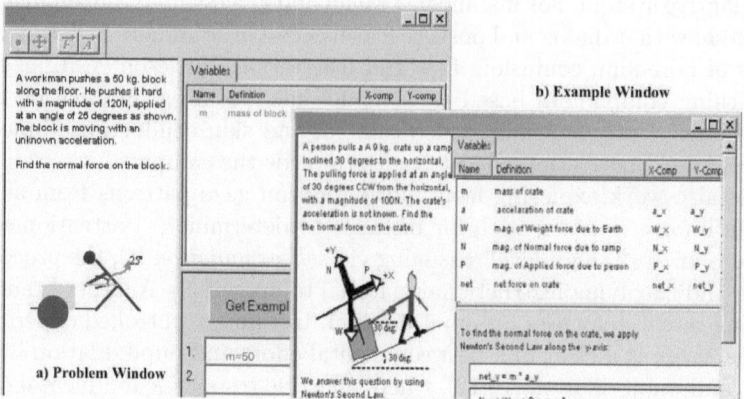

Fig. 1. The EA-Coach Interface: (a) problem window and (b) example window

i.e., using examples to aid problem solving, in the target domain of introductory Newtonian physics. Two meta-cognitive skills that are relevant to APS and therefore targeted by the EA-Coach include:

- *min-analogy*: solving the problem on ones own as much as possible instead of by copying from examples [18]
- *explanation-based learning of correctness (EBLC)*: a form of self-explanation that involves using ones existing common sense, overly general and/or domain knowledge to infer new rules that explain how a given example solution step is derived [19].

The EA-Coach includes an interface that students use to solve problems and refer to examples (see Fig. 1(a) and (b), respectively). To solve problems, students draw free-body diagrams and type equations in the problem window (see Fig. 1a). The EA-Coach does not constrain input of the problem solution, and students may enter the solution steps in any order and/or skip steps. The tutor provides immediate feedback for correctness on students' problem-solving entries, by coloring correct vs. incorrect entries red or green, respectively. It also informs students when it can not interpret their problem entries, but does not provide any other feedback or hints (e.g., related to physics).

While working on a problem, a student can ask for an example (via the 'Get Example' button, see Fig. 1a). In response, the EA-Coach adaptively selects the one from its example pool that has the best potential to help the student solve the problem and learn from doing so, and presents it in the example window (see Fig. 1b). Example selection is accomplished by a decision-theoretic process that we described in [17]; a key aspect of this process is EA-Coach user model. During selection, the model generates a *prediction* of how (1) student characteristics and (2) similarity between the problem and a candidate example will impact min-analogy and EBLC, and subsequent learning and problem solving outcomes. Once an example is presented to a student, the model relies

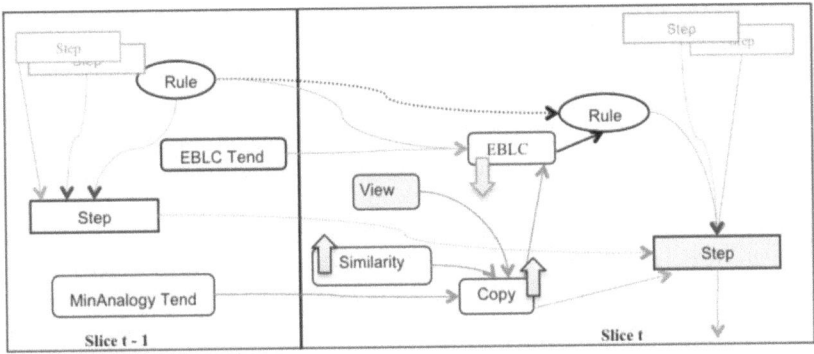

Fig. 2. Fragment of the EA-Coach User Model

on the same sources of information (problem/example similarity, student characteristics), as well as a student's interface actions, to update its *assessment* of the student. This assessment enables the EA-Coach to track how the student's knowledge and meta-cognition evolve as a result of interacting with the tutor. The same model structure is used during both modes (prediction, assessment).

2.1 The EA-Coach User Model

The EA-Coach user model [17,20] corresponds to a dynamic Bayesian network, a fragment of which is shown in Fig. 2. The network's backbone consists of nodes representing the solution steps for the problem the student is currently solving, and the domain rules deriving those steps (see *Step* and *Rule* nodes in Fig. 2), as well as two nodes to model meta-cognitive tendencies (see *EBLCTend* and *MinAnalogyTend* nodes in Fig. 2). For each problem-solving action being modeled, the network also includes nodes accounting for the impact of the example on the APS process (see Fig. 2, slice t), as follows: (1) *similarity* nodes, to capture the similarity between the target problem and example; (2) *copy* nodes, to capture the probability that a student generated the corresponding solution step by copying from the example; (3) *EBLC* nodes, to capture the probability that a student self-explained the corresponding rule from the example with EBLC; (4) *view* nodes representing whether a student viewed the corresponding example step[1]. When a student generates a solution step in the EA-Coach interface, the model enters this and example-viewing information as evidence (see shaded *Step* and *View* nodes in slice t in Fig. 2), and subsequently updates its belief in how the student reasoned (copied vs. self-explained through EBLC). For instance, in Fig. 2, slice t, a high problem/example step similarity increases the probability of copying, which decreases the probability of EBLC and so learning of

---

[1] View nodes are only included during assessment mode; the viewing information is provided by a *masking* interface that covers the example solution and is uncovered by moving the mouse over a region; this interface is not shown in Fig. 1 and was not used in the evaluation described in Section 3.

the corresponding rule. Note that the EA-Coach model has low bandwidth - for instance, the only explicit information on if and how a student self-explained with EBLC corresponds to whether the student viewed the related step in the example window and/or her subsequent problem-solving entry.

When we evaluated the EA-Coach, we found that in general, the tutor encouraged students to engage in the target meta-cognitive behaviors of min-analogy and EBLC [17]. However, the evaluation also showed that some students need more explicit scaffolding than what is currently provided by the system. Therefore, we have been working on designing this support. Since both affect and meta-cognition play a key role in the learning process, we are exploring incorporating affective support into the EA-Coach, as well as enriching its current level of meta-cognitive support. In order for this new scaffolding to be tailored to a student's needs, a challenge relates to how the model can obtain the necessary information, while at the same time preserving the free nature of the interaction with the EA-Coach.

3   Experiment: User Study

The aim of our study was to explore the utility of information derived from sensing devices for modeling high-level user states related to affect and reasoning style. Here, we focus our analysis on data coming from one sensor: an eye tracker. The study participants were 15 university students, who were either in the process of taking a first year university physics course, or had taken a physics course in high school, but had not taken any higher-level physics courses. This was the strategy used in the study methodology in [17], on which this study is directly based. The rationale behind this requirement was to include subjects who have had some exposure to physics, but who were not so expert as to find the physics problems trivial to solve, as we felt that this would provide less varied data. Subjects were either (1) payed for their participation (five subjects) or (2) given extra credit for a course they were enrolled in (ten subjects).

Each study session was conducted separately. During a session, a participant was introduced to the EA-Coach interface, calibrated an eye tracker, and used the EA-Coach to work on two Newton's Second Law problems of the type shown in Fig. 1[2]. For each problem that subjects solved with the EA-Coach, they were given the choice of accessing an example, which was provided by the EA-Coach. The similarity between the problem/example pairs was manipulated, so that for one of the problems, subjects received a more similar example with respect to the target problem than for the other problem (following the method described in [17]). By providing two different scenarios (high + low similarity), we hoped to maximize opportunities for subjects to express a wide range of affective and reasoning behaviors. The order of both the problems and the similarity type (low, high) was fully counterbalanced. Subjects were told that they had 60 minutes per problem, but that could stop before that if they wished.

[2] Prior to and following a session, participants were also asked to fill in questionnaires to assess their physics and self-regulation knowledge.

As subjects worked with the EA-Coach, a Tobii T60 eye tracker captured their gaze information. This eyetracker is a non-intrusive model that is fully integrated into a 17" monitor and so from a participant's perspective, it appears as a regular computer screen. To calibrate the eye tracker, participants were asked to focus on a series of 16 dots on the computer screen; this phase took approximately one minute. We also captured other physiological data using a set of non-invasive sensors, but this data analysis is in progress and is not reported here (the sensors included a bracelet to measure skin conductance, a pressure mouse and a pressure pad placed on subjects' chair, see [21]).

To obtain information on how subjects were reasoning and feeling during the study, we asked subjects to verbalize their thoughts and feelings via talk-aloud protocol [22], extended to include affect, as in [23]. The verbal data, along with subjects' eye gaze patterns and interface actions, was recorded via the Tobii system as video files; the EA-Coach logged all interface actions as text files.

3.1   Data Preparation: Coding the Transcripts

To investigate how users' affect and reasoning related to physiological responses, we needed data from our study on both kinds of events. To obtain this data, we first transcribed the video files, including subjects' actions, utterances and time stamps when they occurred. We then devised a coding scheme for identifying in the protocols instances of reasoning (e.g., self-explanation) and affect (e.g., happy).

The *reasoning* portion of the coding scheme (see Table 1, bottom) is based on one from a previous study we ran [17]. We coded utterances as *self-explanation* if subjects expressed a conclusion about a domain-specific principle related to physics [3]. We coded utterances as *analogy* if subjects expressed something about the relation between the problem and example and/or copied from an example (see Table 1 for examples), but did not provide indications of any other kind of reasoning beyond the analogy[4]. Finally, we included an *'other reasoning'* code because we wanted to capture instances when subjects expressed some reasoning, albeit too shallow to be classified as self-explanation, but that did involve more than just a straight comparison of problem/example constants via analogy (see Table 1 for examples). Note that while self-explanation is a highly constructive reasoning activity that correlates with positive learning outcomes (e.g., [9]), reasoning via analogy is associated with a lack of learning [18]; likewise, in our classification, *'other reasoning'* is a less constructive form of reasoning, as compared to *self-explanation*.

The *affect* portion of the coding scheme (see Table 1, top portion) is new and is based on several iterations through the data to solidify the codes. We originally planned on developing fine-grained categories of affect (e.g., 'happy', 'excited',

---

[3] We did not distinguish between different types of self-explanation (e.g., EBLC-based vs. other) because as a first step, we wanted to analyze in general if and how pupillary response relates to self-explanation.

[4] A simple comparison of problem/example constants is not a self-explanation, as it does not involve a conclusion about a domain-specific principle.

Table 1. Protocol Codes

Affective Codes:

Code	#	Description	Sample Verbalizations
Positive	68	subject expresses positive affect related to happy or excited state	" and i got it right and that makes me really happy", "oh that's exciting", "HOORAY", "now I feel good"
Negative	69	subject expresses feeling negative affect related to frustration	"now I'm mad", "oh my god this is irritating", "NO!!! not correct ", "Darn it!! "
Shame	20	subject expresses feeling shame or remorse	"I really do feel like such an idiot", "I fail ... sorry I took so long"
Confusion	29	subject expresses confusion	"I'm feeling confused", " maybe it wants me to draw the horizontal ... I can' understand"

Reasoning Codes:

Code	#	Description	Sample Verbalizations
Self-explanation	39	subject explains or clarifies a physics-related concept	'since it is accelerating I know all the forces added together don't equal zero", "it would be zero because it is ... there is no x component"
Analogy/Copy	180	subject draws a comparison between problem and example and/or copies but provides no additional inference/reasoning	"and their a is acceleration of block which is my mouse", "mag of the normal force... so this is e_y on mine"
Other Reasoning	106	subject expresses some shallow reasoning that is not a self-explanation or pure analogy	" well in this picture it is pulling it horizontally and then... 90 plus 40 ... 130?"

'angry'). However, while subjects would sometimes clearly express a particular type of affect (e.g., "I feel happy" or "I'm irritated"), they would also at times express affect through a single phrase like "NO!!" or "HOORAY!". While in the latter case, the general direction of the affect, i.e,. positive or negative, was clear from the tone and the term used (e.g., "NO!" used to express negative affect), it was more difficult to unambiguously identify the precise emotion expressed. Therefore we broadened the affective categories so that *positive* codes included instances when subjects indicated feeling excited, happy, or generally good (see Table 1 for examples). The *negative* codes included instances when subjects explicitly expressed irritation or frustration, and/or expressed a negative utterance like "darn it!" that related to frustration (see Table 1 for examples).

The coding scheme described above was applied by the first author to classify the data in the verbal protocols, returning to the video files as needed. Overall, 186 instances of *affect* codes and 325 instances of *reasoning* codes were identified (see Table 1).

3.2   Results

As mentioned above, here we focus on data coming from the eye tracker, and in particular, on pupillary response. Given that there tends to be variability among subjects in terms of baseline pupil size, we used Z-scores to normalize pupil sizes among participants (i.e., *normalized pupil value = (original pupil value - mean pupil size) / standard deviation*, as in [8]). We then associated each coded utterance in the transcripts with the normalized eye tracker data and the EA-Coach logs by standardizing the time stamps in the three sources of data (transcript files, EA-Coach logs, eye tracker logs).

To analyze the data, we originally intended to rely on repeated-measures analysis of variance and/or paired t-tests as appropriate, i.e., depending on the number of levels of the independent variable in question (method A, *within-subjects* analysis). An alternative technique involves using one-way ANOVA (method B, *between-subjects* analysis). Each approach suffers from a limitation. Method A can suffer from data sparseness, since not all subjects necessarily express all types of affect and/or reasoning. This reduces the sample size thereby decreasing power and increasing the chance of a type 2 error (i.e., failing to find an effect when one does in fact exist). The alternative is to use method B, as in for instance [8]. However, the set of data points associated with a given code are not independent, which increases the chance of a type 1 error (i.e., finding an effect when there in fact is none) if method B is used. Given these considerations, we decided to conduct both types of analyses, to triangulate across findings. We will now present the results, starting with findings pertaining to affect.

Results on Affect. To investigate the relationship between pupillary response and affect, we calculated the mean pupil size during the time period a subject expressed an affective response of the type we identified (see Table 1, top). We considered a five second time span, starting at the point when the utterance began (this threshold is similar to that used in related work, e.g., [24]).

We begin with the results from the within-subjects analysis. As anticipated, we found that each subject did not express every type of affective response, leaving missing data entries. When we included the *confusion* or *shame* affective codes in the analysis, we were left with only six subjects that expressed all four types of affect we identified in our analysis. Therefore, we decided to conduct the analysis on the *positive* and *negative* instances of affect only, since this was the only combination that left us with more than six data points. This analysis involved ten students; for each student, we calculated the mean pupil size associated with *positive* and *negative* events, respectively. A paired-samples t-test showed that *affect* had a significant effect on pupillary response($t(9)$=2.294, p = 0.047): on average, pupil size was smaller when subjects expressed negative affect, as compared to positive affect (0.0208 vs. 0.3876, respectively).

Recall that the EA-Coach provides immediate feedback for correctness by coloring subjects' entries red or green in the interface. Many of our subjects' affective responses related to entries they generated in the EA-Coach interface, and in particular were responses to an entry being correct or incorrect. Consequently, we wanted to investigate whether entry correctness (or lack of) was driving the affective results. To do so, we compared the mean pupil size five seconds after correct and incorrect entries. We did not find a significant impact of correctness (i.e., correct vs. incorrect entries) on pupillary response ($t(14)$=0.508, p=0.620).

As far as the between-subjects analysis is concerned, the ANOVA revealed a significant main effect of *affect* on pupillary response (F(3,182) = 4.057, p = 0.008). We then conducted Bonferroni post hoc pairwise comparisons to identify which affective responses differed significantly from one another. The only comparison that revealed a significant difference corresponded to the pair *positive-negative* affect (p=0.006), where mean pupil size was smaller for *negative* than *positive* (-0.0913 vs. 0.3214), thereby confirming the within-subjects analysis.

Results on Reasoning. To investigate the relationship between pupillary response and how subjects reasoned during the study, we calculated the mean pupil size during the time period a subject engaged in one of the three types of reasoning we identified in the transcripts (*self-explanation, analogy, 'other reasoning'*, see Table 1, bottom). For this analysis, we considered a 15 second time span, starting at the point when the utterance began (this threshold was found to disambiguate self-explanation and lack of in [8]).

We begin with the within-subjects results. As was the case with the affective data, each subject did not express each type of reasoning. Nine subjects did express all three types; for each student, we calculated the mean pupil size for each type of reasoning (*self-explanation, analogy* and *'other reasoning'* events). Since the *reasoning* variable has three levels, we conducted a repeated measures analysis of variance. The results revealed a significant main effect of *reasoning* on pupillary response (F(2,8)=3.63, p=0.047). Given that post-hoc tests are not recommended for within subjects analysis, we followed the method proposed in [25] and conducted pairwise comparisons to identify how the three types of *reasoning* varied from one another. We found that pupil size was significantly bigger for *self-explanation* than *'other reasoning'* (0.4074 vs. -0.0661, respectively; t(9)= -2.382, p=0.04). We also found that pupil size was bigger for *self-explanation* than *analogy*, but this did not reach significance (0.4074 vs. -.0210, respectively; t(9)=1.744, p=0.115). The difference between *'other reasoning'* than *analogy* was not significant (-0.0661 vs -0.0210, respectively, t(9)=0.395, p=0.702).

As was the case with the affect-related analysis, we wanted to investigate if our results were driven by subjects' problem-solving entries, and in particular the correctness (or lack thereof) of these entries. For this analysis, we also considered a 15 second window both prior to and following correct entries, and used paired samples t-tests to investigate differences in response between these two variables. We did not find a significant impact of correctness (or lack of) on pupillary response for either window (before, after).

As far as the between-subjects analysis is concerned, the ANOVA revealed a significant main effect of *reasoning* on pupillary response (F(2, 322) = 6.454, p = 0.002). We then conducted Bonferroni post hoc pairwise comparisons to identify which types of reasoning responses differed significantly from one another. These results showed that on average, (1) pupil size was significantly bigger for *self-explanation* than *'other reasoning'* (0.2311 vs. -0.0876, respectively; p=0.008) and (2) pupil size was significantly bigger for *analogy* than *'other reasoning'* (0.1195 vs. -0.0876, respectively; p=0.006). There was no significant difference in pupil size between *self-explanation* and *analogy*.

4 Discussion and Future Work

Our results show that pupillary response is a promising non-invasive avenue for increasing user model bandwidth. As far as affect is concerned, both the within and between subject analysis confirmed that subjects had significantly larger pupil size when they expressed positive affect, as compared to when they expressed negative affect. In contrast to tightly controlled experiments, our subjects were not induced to express affect, but rather expressed it as a natural by-product of the interaction with the EA-Coach. Their affective responses influenced pupil size, information that a user model could take into account when assessing affect, thereby allowing an adaptive application to tailor the interaction to a user's needs. Given that work in psychology shows pupil size increases for affective responses (e.g., [13]), our results indicate that subjects in our experiment experienced positive affect such as excitement more strongly than negative affect related to frustration. The context of our experiment, i.e., a pedagogical one, however, may have influenced particular affective responses, and so more investigation is needed to see how other, non-educational contexts impact pupillary responses. Another area in need of further research pertains to measuring affect. We found that talk-aloud protocol was not suited for performing fine-grained distinctions between affective states. In general, how to measure affect is a key challenge that is the subject of much research (e.g., see [26] for a review), but to date there is a lack of complete understanding related to this issue.

Our study also found support for the fact that how subjects reason impacts pupillary response. As we pointed out earlier, larger pupillary response has been associated with mental effort in tightly controlled experiments. We compared three types of reasoning: (1) *self-explanation*, a highly constructive reasoning activity, against (2) *analogy*, which included comparison of problem/example constants and/or copying from examples and which are not constructive activities, against (3) *other reasoning*. Since self-explanation is a more constructive type of reasoning than the other two, it should result in larger pupil size (as was for instance suggested in [8]). Both kinds of analyses we conducted did indeed confirm that self-explanation resulted in significantly larger pupil size than 'other reasoning'. However, we did not find a significant difference in pupil size between self-explanation and analogy episodes. In fact, our between-subjects analysis showed that analogy resulted in larger pupil size than 'other reasoning', something we did not expect, although this result was not confirmed by the within-subjects analysis. One reason why neither analysis found a difference between analogy and self-explanation is that analogy may actually require mental effort, *despite* the fact that it is a shallow reasoning style. We saw instances in the verbal protocols where subjects struggled aligning the problem/example constants (e.g., *"p underscore y... plus ... plus p [long pause] p is what p [another pause] applied by child applied force"* - a subject trying to substitute example-constant 'p' with one appropriate to her problem). These difficulties may have increased mental effort and thus pupil size. Our results suggest that the model may need additional information to disambiguate self-explanation and analogical reasoning. One way to do so could involve having the model analyze attention patterns in the interface: since analogy requires the comparison of problem/example constants, but self-explanation does not, including gaze pattern information could disambiguate self-explanation from analogy.

As our next steps, we plan to conduct additional analysis related to investigating further the difference between positive and negative affect, and identifying the mitigating factors driving this difference. Another relevant avenue of investigation relates to exploring the interaction between affect and cognition. There is evidence that subjects process information better when they in a positive affective state [27], and so it would be interesting to analyze if and how this occurred in our study. We also plan to analyze other aspects of data provided by the eye tracker (fixations and saccadic eye movements) to explore how they may inform a user model. We plan to rely on our findings both from this experiment and subsequent analysis to extend the EA-Coach user model to take into account eye-tracker information, and design affect and additional meta-cognitive support based on the revised model. We will subsequently evaluate how this support impacts the tutor's pedagogical effectiveness and usability.

References

1. VanLehn, K.: Student modeling. Foundations of Intelligent Tutoring Systems, 55–78 (1988)
2. Klein, J., Moon, Y.: This computer responds to user frustration: Theory, design, results, and implications. Interacting with Computers 14, 119–140 (2000)
3. Aleven, V., Koedinger, R.: An effective metacognitive strategy: learning by doing and explaining with a computer-based cognitive tutor. Cognitive Science 26(2), 147–179 (2002)
4. D'Mello, S.K., Picard, R.W., Graesser, A.C.: Towards an affect-sensitive autotutor. IEEE Intelligent Systems 22(4), 53–61 (2007)
5. Burleson, W.: Affective Learning Companions: Strategies for Empathetic Agents with Real-Time Multimodal Affective Sensing to Foster Meta-Cognitive Approaches to Learning, Motivation, and Perseverance. Ph.D thesis, MIT (2006)
6. Gluck, K., Anderson, J.: Cognitive architectures play in intelligent tutoring systems? In: Cognition and Instruction: Twenty-Five Years of Progress, pp. 227–262 (2001)
7. Qu, L., Johnson, L.: Detecting the learner's motivational states in an interactive learning environment. In: 12th International Conference on Artificial Intelligence in Education, pp. 547–554 (2005)
8. Conati, C., Merten, C.: Eye-tracking for user modeling in exploratory learning environments: an empirical evaluation. Knowledge Based Systems 20(6), 557–574 (2007)
9. Chi, M., Basssok, M., Lewis, M., Reimann, P., Glaser, R.: Self-explanations: How students study and use examples in learning to solve problems. Cognitive Science 13, 145–182 (1989)
10. Marshall, S.P.: Identifying cognitive state from eye metrics. Aviation, Space, and Environmental Medicine 78, 165–175 (2007)
11. Van Gerven, P.W.M., Paas, F., Van Merrinboer, J.J.G., Schmidt, H.G.: Memory load and the cognitive pupillary response in aging. Psychophysiology 41(2), 167–174 (2004)

12. Vo, M.L.H., Jacobs, A.M., Kuchinke, L., Hofmann, M., Conrad, M., Schacht, A., Hutzler, F.: The coupling of emotion and cognition in the eye: Introducing the pupil old/new effect. Psychophysiology 45(1), 130–140 (2008)

13. Partala, T., Surakka, V.: Pupil size variation as an indication of affective processing. Int. Journal of Human-Computer Studies 59(1-2), 185–198 (2003)

14. Iqbal, S., Zheng, X., Bailey, B.P.: Task-evoked pupillary response to mental workload in human-computer interaction. In: CHI 2004 extended abstracts on Human factors in computing systems, pp. 1477–1480 (2004)

15. Schultheis, H., Jameson, A.: Load in adaptive hypermedia systems: Physiological and behavioral methods. In: Adaptive hypermedia. Interacting with Computers, pp. 225–234 (2004)

16. Conati, C., Muldner, K., Carenini, G.: From example studying to problem solving via tailored computer-based meta-cognitive scaffolding: Hypotheses and design. Technology, Instruction, Cognition and Learning (TICL) 4(2), 139–190 (2006)

17. Muldner, K., Conati, C.: Evaluating a decision-theoretic approach to tailored example selection. In: IJCAI 2007, 20th International Joint Conference in Artificial Intelligence, pp. 483–488 (2007)

18. VanLehn, K.: Analogy events: How examples are used during problem solving. Cognitive Science 22(3), 347–388 (1998)

19. VanLehn, K.: Rule-learning events in the acquisition of a complex skill: An evaluation of cascade. The Journal of the Learning Sciences 1(8), 71–125 (1999)

20. Muldner, K.: Tailored Support for Analogical Problem Solving. Ph.D thesis, University of British Columbia (2007)

21. Dragon, T., Arroyo, I., Woolf, B.P., Burleson, W., el Kaliouby, R., Eydgahi, H.: Viewing Student Affect and Learning through Classroom Observation and Physical Sensors. In: Woolf, B.P., Aïmeur, E., Nkambou, R., Lajoie, S. (eds.) ITS 2008. LNCS, vol. 5091, pp. 29–39. Springer, Heidelberg (2008)

22. Ercisson, K., Simmon, H.: Verbal reports as data. Psychological Review 87(3), 215–250 (1980)

23. Craig, S., D'Mello, S., Witherspoon, A., Graesser, A.: Emote aloud during learning with autotutor: Applying the facial action coding system to cognitive-affective states during learning. Cognition and Emotion 22(5), 777–788 (2008)

24. Van Gerven, P., Paas, F., Van Merrienboer, J., Schmidt, H.: Memory load and the cognitive pupillary response in aging. Psychophysiology 41(2), 167–174 (2001)

25. Cardinal, R., Aitken, M.: ANOVA for the Behavioural Sciences Researcher. Routledge, London (2006)

26. Mauss, I., Robinson, M.: Measures of emotion: A review. Cognition & Emotion 23(2), 209–237 (in press)

27. Levens, S., Phelps, E.: Emotion processing effects on interference resolution in working memory. Emotion 8(2), 267–280 (2008)

Describing User Interactions in Adaptive Interactive Systems

Matthias Bezold

[1] University of Ulm, Institute for Information Technology, Ulm, Germany
[2] Elektrobit Automotive Software, Erlangen, Germany
matthias.bezold@uni-ulm.de

Abstract. The description of the user-system interaction plays a crucial role in adaptive interactive systems, since the adaptations depend on this description. User actions in interactive systems can be described as a sequence of events, which are created by input through input devices as well as by the system as reactions to these inputs. An interactive system can observe these events and thus extract information about the user's behavior. This paper presents a two-step approach for describing user behavior from sequences of basic events. First, user actions are recognized in the sequence of interaction events by means of previously trained probabilistic automata. Second, a task model describes the higher-level user activity as a hierarchical composition of these actions. Different kinds of adaptive support can be derived from this description of user behavior, such as recommending next interaction steps to the user.

1 Introduction

The number of features of interactive systems, such as digital TV systems or automotive dashboard systems, often increases when new versions are introduced [15]. At the same time, the users and thus the requirements become more diverse, e.g. when older people start using these systems. Adaptation [5] is an approach to cope with this increasing complexity and diversity by adapting the system to an individual user to better reflect the respective requirements. Adaptive interfaces can infer improvements of the system by observing user behavior, for instance recommending the most probable next action or highlighting the user's favorite item to help unexperienced users. In doing so, adaptations can increase the usability of interactive systems.

Describing user behavior plays a crucial role in adaptive interfaces. User behavior is – from a system's point of view – limited to what the system can observe: interactions between the user and the system. Perceptual sensors, such as cameras, microphones, or other physical sensors, are not available in most interactive systems. Further information, such as what the user is doing or thinking besides this interaction, can therefore not be observed, but only inferred with

G.-J. Houben et al. (Eds.): UMAP 2009, LNCS 5535, pp. 150–161, 2009.

```
1 [1180520776220] hw name={COMM_0x6e}
2 [1180520776220] event name={Start}
3 [1180520776220] state name={Session_Main}
4 [1180520776376] view name={WelcomeView}
```

Fig. 1. Exemplary log lines, showing a button press (line 1) and the reactions of the system to this input (lines 2–4)

a limited certainty. An accurate and comprehensive means for describing user actions based on the observations of the system is crucial for adaptive interfaces.

This paper presents an approach for describing user-system interactions from a sequence of basic events, defining higher-level user activity, and triggering adaptations derived from this information. The paper is organized as follows. First, Sect. 2 presents a method for extracting user actions from an event sequence by means of probabilistic automata, which are trained from annotated log data. Sect. 3 introduces task models as an approach for describing user activity as a hierarchy of user actions. Thereafter, Sect. 4 delineates how both techniques in combination provide a comprehensive description of the user-system interaction as a basis for executing adaptations. Sect. 5 reviews related work and an outlook to future work in Sect. 6 concludes this paper.

1.1 User Interactions as a Sequence of Events

User interactions in interactive systems are represented by a series of low-level events [2], such as key presses, speech utterances by the user, or system reactions, e.g. internal state changes. For example, if the user presses a red button on a remote control, a certain action is triggered, e.g. opening a result screen in a digital TV system. The low-level log data does not directly reveal which action was performed, i.e., a red button press can be observed, but not that it opens the result screen. Moreover, a speech utterance can open the same menu, creating a completely different log sequence for essentially the same action.

All events relevant for describing user-system interactions are represented in a common format: events have a time stamp, a type, and a set of parameters that depend on the event type, e.g. the name of the button that was pressed. These events originate either from a live interaction or from recorded log files. A short sequence of example events is shown in Fig. 1. User actions consist of subsequences of events, with an action being represented by different sequences, as was shown before. Therefore, user actions can be described by collecting these sub-sequences for every action.

Tasks describe the user's activity by combining user actions hierarchically. Task models [13] consist of a set of tasks and provide a comprehensive description of the user-system interaction at a more abstract level than basic interactions. A more detailed introduction to task modeling is given in Sect. 3. By extracting user actions from the interaction events and applying the actions to a task model, the system is enabled to follow the user's activity.

152   M. Bezold

1.2   The DICIT Project

The assessment of this approach was conducted with log data obtained during the evaluation of a prototype of the DICIT project. The DICIT project is an European FP6 project that develops a speech-enabled digital TV system [9]. The DICIT system supports distant-talking and natural language interaction.

The prototype provides the standard functionality of digital TV: A TV screen lets the user watch TV, change the channel and the volume. An electronic program guide (EPG) lets the user browse the TV program and select shows by changing a set of filters, such as time or channel. Moreover, programs can be put on a recording list. In addition, the user can change settings in a settings menu, such as switching on or off the speech output. All functions can be controlled either by remote control or speech. The system is based on a graphical interface; feedback to commands and help are given by speech output as well.

An evaluation was performed with 20 test subjects, where the users had to fulfill a number of tasks with remote control and speech interaction, covering all parts of the system. During the evaluation, extensive log data was collected, with the average length of these sessions being 24 minutes. The log files are sequences of user events; a short excerpt of a log file is given in Fig. 1, where a user presses a button (line 1) that causes different reactions of the system (lines 2-4). The log format reflects the structure of the events introduced in the previous section.

While the assessment was performed within the digital TV domain, this approach is general and therefore applicable to other interactive systems. However, an actual application to other domains is planned as future work.

2   Detecting User Actions in Event Sequences

In order to facilitate a comprehensive description of the user's actions, meaningful actions first have to be extracted from a sequence of meaningless basic events, hereby adding semantic information. A certain user action, such as selecting a channel in a digital TV system, can be represented by different sequences of events. This section describes how these subsequences can be extracted from longer sequences of events that represent a user-system interaction.

Our approach deals with systems that do not explicitly provide information about user actions, but only emit a sequence of basic events from the user-system interaction. Moreover, if a modification of the system is not feasible, a keyhole observation must be applied instead. Describing the sequences manually is tedious and error-prone and therefore not viable. Since the sequences that

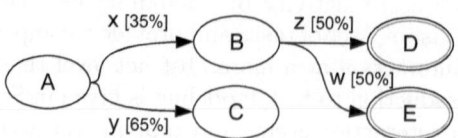

Fig. 2. An example of a probabilistic deterministic finite-state automaton

describe user actions can be quite different in length, hidden Markov models and artificial neural networks are not well-suited for this problem. Instead, we present an approach to describe user actions by means of probabilistic automata trained from annotated data. The model containing the automaton definitions is called interaction model.

2.1 Probabilistic Deterministic Finite-State Automata

Probabilistic deterministic finite-state automata (PDFA), described in detail by Vidal et al. [16,17], consist of states and transitions between these states. A state change is triggered by a certain event with a certain probability. An example is given in Fig. 2: In state "A", the event "x" triggering a transition to state "B" occurs with a probability of 35 %, whereas the event "y" going to state "C" occurs with a probability of 65 %. Every state has a probability of being a final state.

A state acceptor is one application of the state automaton that is used to determine if and with which probability an automaton matches a given sequence. Starting at the initial state, the respective transition for every element of the sequence is taken. If none is found, the automaton does not accept the sequence. Otherwise, this step is repeated until a final state is found. The probability of the accepted sequence for this automaton can be computed by multiplying the transition probabilities of all used transitions. Therefore, the acceptance probability of the automaton in Fig. 2 for the sequence (x, w) is 17.5 %.

A PDFA is generated from a set of sequences as follows (cf. [17]). Starting at an initial state, a transition and a new state are added to the automaton for each element of the sequence. If the transition already exists, its weight is increased instead. After the automaton is constructed, the probabilities of every transition can be computed from the transition weights.

2.2 Describing User Behavior Using PDFAs

In the following, the application of probabilistic automata to the problem of recognizing user actions represented by a set of event subsequences from a larger sequence of events is described. An overview of the workflow is given in Fig. 3. First, log data, e.g. collected during user tests, is annotated by assigning action classes that represent an action name to certain sections of the recording. A PDFA is created from the sequences associated with the respective annotations for every action class. Finally, an interactive system employs these PDFAs to

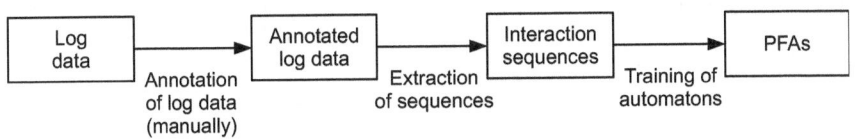

Fig. 3. The workflow of the probabilistic automaton approach for recognizing user actions

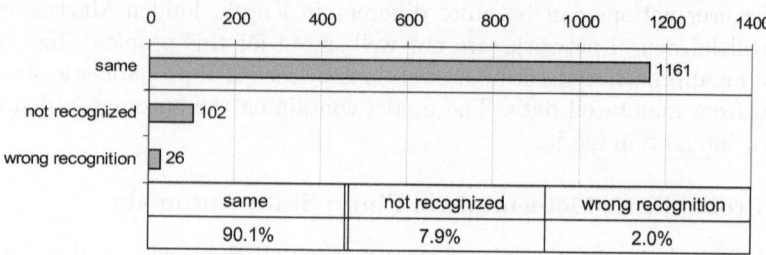

Fig. 4. Evaluation results of the PDFA matching with a test set of 10 log files and a total number of 1289 user actions

determine the user's current activity by applying the automata to live log data. In addition to identifying user actions, parameters of these actions are extracted, such as the name of the channel for a "channel change" action, thus allowing to model these values as well.

Annotating the log data and creating the PDFAs. In order to create the PDFAs for different action classes, annotations are created first using a custom graphical evaluation and annotation tool [18], which displays log events from a recorded session in timeline views. Sequences of events are marked in the timeline views and associated with an action class. Different representations are extracted for each class by assigning the same action class to different sequences.

Next, the annotated sequences are extracted from the log data and PDFAs created as described in Sect. 2.1, with every event corresponding to a transition. However, the context, i.e., the graphical screen or dialog state in which an action was performed, is relevant for some action classes. For instance, the red button has different meanings in different screens, e.g. opening the result list or recording an entry. On the other hand, the context should not be included for patterns that are the same in different areas of the system, such as scrolling. These events are differentiated by adding the context to the set of parameters for classes that require this information and the action class definition stores whether the context is needed.

Matching. The purpose of matching is to extract user actions from a log sequence. Successively, events are submitted to the PDFAs of the individual action classes. If an automaton accepts a sequence, an interaction of the respective type was detected. A match factor is computed for all PDFAs that matched a certain sequence and the pattern is accepted if the factor is above a certain threshold. Since the probabilities of the branches of long and complex patterns can be low and since longer patterns should be recognized preferably, the match probability is multiplied with a length factor to obtain the match factor. The element with the highest match factor is selected in case more than one match was found.

Evaluation. We performed an evaluation of this approach using log data from a prototype of the DICIT system, introduced in Sect. 1.2. 20 log files were annotated with information about user actions using a custom annotation tool

[18]. 10 sessions were used to train PDFA models and 10 used for the evaluation by submitting them to the matchers. In these recordings, 32 different action classes were identified, such as "show results" or "change channel". The sequence length of these action classes is between 1 and 64 events, with the average length being 3.1. On average, the sessions consist of 141 interactions.

The results of the comparison of the automatic and the manual annotations are shown in Fig. 4. A match rate of 90 % could be achieved. Differences can occur for several reasons. First, an action can be present in the manual annotation, but not in the automatic one (*not recognized*), i.e., an action did not occur in the training data. Using more training data can therefore reduce these kinds of errors. Second, a wrong class can be selected (*wrong recognition*), which occurs 26 times in the recordings. These errors can for instance occur if there are ambiguities in the annotations.

Therefore, PDFAs present a viable means for describing user actions from basic events. However, this approach has limitations. First, as all statistical approaches, it highly depends on the annotations, i.e., only patterns occurring in the annotated sessions can be recognized. In addition, the consistency of the annotations has an impact on the recognition accuracy: The more errors are in the annotations used for training the PDFAs, the lower the recognition rate will be. Moreover, actions that depend on the number and order of events are not reflected well by the statistical nature of this approach. For instance, the number of up and down key presses decides which element in a list is selected, but the probabilistic nature of the automata does not consider this well. As a solution for this problem, the selection of every list item would need to create a separate "list selection" event to make it applicable for this approach.

3 Describing User Tasks

Once the single user actions were extracted from the sequence of events, a task model provides a description of the user's activity at a higher level. Task modeling is an approach used in the development of interactive systems that describes the user-system interaction by means of a task model. The original use of task models is in the development, e.g. for an automatic creation of interfaces, or the evaluation of interactive systems [12]. Our work uses the task model in a different way: At runtime, the interactive system observes the user-system interaction and derives adaptation information accordingly by means of a task model.

3.1 Task Models

Task models are higher-order descriptions of user activity and consist of a set of tasks, with each task being hierarchically composed of user actions. One of the most well-known task modeling notations is ConcurTaskTrees (CTT) [13]. A CTT task model consists of a hierarchy of basic tasks, which can be user tasks, application tasks, interaction tasks, or abstract tasks. Different temporal

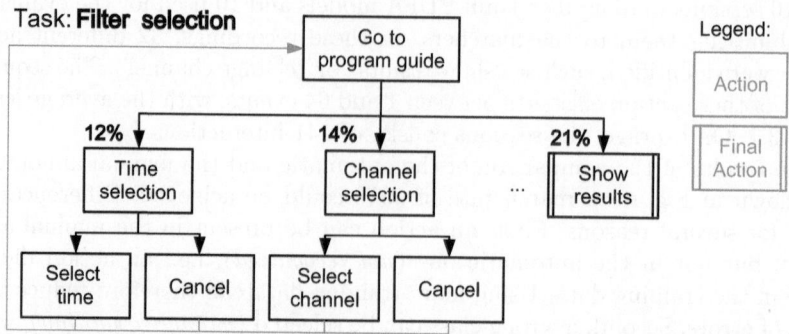

Fig. 5. An example task model that describe the user's activity when selecting a set of filter criteria in the DICIT system

operators define in which order these actions can be executed: in an arbitrary order (*interleaving*), one action enables another (*enabling*), iterative (*iteration*), optional (*optional task*), and others.

The task model used in this work is conceptually similar to CTT. However, it is limited to system and interaction tasks, because actions that do not involve an interaction with the system cannot be observed. User actions are grouped using sequences, with each action occurring in the given order, or alternatives, where only one of the actions occurs. These groups can be optional or iterative, i.e., can occur more than once. Actions can be marked as final, i.e., they terminate the current task. However, such final interactions can reference other tasks.

An example of a task is given in Fig. 5. In this notation, horizontal elements represent alternatives, whereas vertical ones represent sequences. This example task model is taken from the DICIT system and describes the selection of filter criteria in the electronic program guide. After selecting a set of criteria, such as time or a channel, the user can open the result screen, thus finishing the task.

The ConcurTaskTree Environment (CTTE) [11] is a graphical editing tool for the CTT notation. A converter allows using a subset of the CTT constructs for our system and supports the interleaving (mapped to "alternative"), enabling (mapped to "sequential"), iteration, and optional temporal relationships.

3.2 Using Task Models in Adaptive Systems

Despite being used for the development and evaluation of interactive systems, a task model can also provide valuable information about the current user-system interaction by instantiating it at runtime: Adaptations can be initiated based on information from the task model. Whenever an interaction step was detected (e.g. by means of the PDFAs discussed in Sect. 2), the task model information is updated accordingly, either advancing the activation information of a task, finishing a task, or starting a new one. For instance, if the user enters the electronic program guide, the task model activates the task "Filter selection" shown in Fig. 5. The task is completed when the user performs the "Show results" action. To ensure the validity of the task model at runtime, the context information, which is attached to the actions, is monitored. If it becomes invalid for some reason, the task is cancelled.

There are a number of applications of task models in adaptive interactive systems, which will be discussed in the remainder of this section. First, the most likely next step or sequence of steps can be predicted and adaptive assistance provided, for instance by help messages or by emphasizing parts of the interface. For example, if the user has already specified a value for time and channel in the model in Fig. 5, the system recommends the "Show results" command. The next section discusses how predictions for the next step can be made by means of a task model.

The task model also provides information about problems the user has when working with the system. If tasks switch frequently, e.g. between the "filter selection" and the "record" task (not shown), the system can infer that the user requires help and provide support accordingly.

Another information that can be derived form the task model is which features of the system have not been used by the current user. By marking used parts of the task model, this information is available directly. If information from other users is available, the task model can recommend features that were used by other users, but not by the current one.

Therefore, a task model provides a solid description of higher-level user behavior, from which different kinds of information can be derived to trigger adaptations.

3.3   Predicting the Next Action

This section presents two approaches for predicting the next action and compares them in an evaluation.

Enriching the task model with statistical information. Adding statistical information from user sessions to the task model facilitates predictions about the most probable next step. Past user interactions, either from the current user or others, are entered into the task model to gain information about which steps were taken most frequently. In Fig. 5, the probability of selecting a time value in the main menu is 12 %, 14 % for selecting a channel, and 21 % for opening the result screen.

This approach always predicts the same action for one location in the task model, although the action a user is going to perform depends on past interactions. Therefore, a second approach employs Markov chains to produce predictions that consider the interaction history.

Markov chains. Markov chains are a tool for modeling sequential processes and are based on the Markovian assumption, which states that the next step only depends on the previous one. In [14], first-order Markov chains are used for modeling link predictions in web sites. We apply this approach to user interactions.

First, an index is assigned to each action to be able to store actions in vectors and matrices. The interaction history H stores the last N=5 actions as a set of vectors h, in which only that index is set to 1 which represents the respective action. A matrix A stores the probabilities a_{ij} that action j follows action i. A prediction for the next interaction can be computed using formula (1).

$$s(t) = \sum_{j=1}^{N} d(j)h(t-j)A^j \tag{1}$$

$s(t)$ represents the next step and d is a dampening factor that decreases the weight of older elements.

The transition matrix T is trained as follows. If the last action was i and an action j occurs, the value t_{ij} of T is incremented by 1. The probability transition matrix A is computed directly from T by dividing each value by the sum of the respective row. The matrix can be initialized from recorded training data and updated with the interactions of the current session to better reflect the behavior of the current user. However, the prediction can return actions that are currently not valid according to the task model due to the statistical nature of the prediction. A combination of the initial prediction with the task model information ensures the validity of the prediction.

Evaluation. This section compares the prediction accuracy of the two approaches. Since behavior of real users is erratic, the prediction accuracy can never be 100 %. The same recordings as for the evaluation of the PDFAs were employed and again 10 sessions were used for training and 10 for testing. A prediction is made before every interaction and compared to the actual value.

Since predictions can only be made if a task is active in the task model, we investigated for what number of actions in a session this was the case, called "task model coverage". The coverage for the recordings was 99.3 %, i.e., the task model covers almost all of the interactions.

As can be seen in Fig. 6, the combined prediction is more accurate than the approach using only the statistical task model information. The error rate of Markov predictions that were invalid but corrected is 1.3 %. The computation time for the Markov prediction amounts to 8.3 ms and 0.2 ms for the task model prediction. Therefore, including the interaction history in the prediction improves the accuracy considerably.

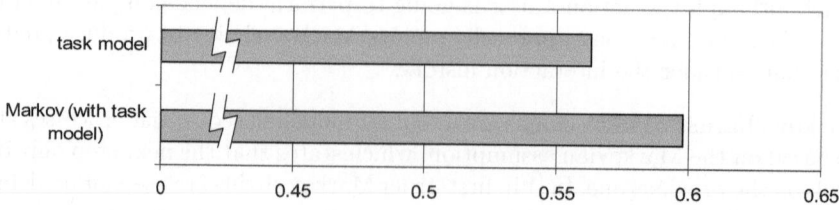

Fig. 6. Prediction probabilities for the next user action

4   Carrying Out Adaptations

In this section, we briefly summarize how the action model and task model are integrated into an interactive system and how the adaptation component carries out adaptations using these models. An interactive system sends live log data to a facility that records all relevant events and forwards them to the action model, which employs automata to recognize actions. These actions are in turn forwarded to the task model that tracks the active task. Predictions are made by combining the information from the task model with a Markov prediction (cf. Sect. 3.3).

Once a recommendation was computed, the adaptation component adapts the interactive system to convey this information to the user. Two sample adaptations were implemented in an adaptive prototype of the DICIT system. First, an adaptive help feature recommends an action to the user. For this purpose, a help icon is brightened when a prediction was made and the user can open a help screen. Second, a graphical button that triggers the predicted action is highlighted. For instance the "Show results" button in the main menu of the DICIT system is highlighted after the user has selected different filter criteria. The mapping information between actions and graphical elements was annotated to the button. Therefore, the presented user modeling approach provides a feasible basis for describing user behavior for this exemplary interactive system.

5   Related Work

This section reviews related work and compares it to the approach presented in this paper.

Different approaches for recognizing elements from sequences are available. Sequence mining [8] searches for frequent episodes in a sequence of events. However, a statement about the meaning of the discovered episodes is not made, but a comprehensive description of user behavior requires this information. Other techniques can be employed as well. For instance, user profiles are trained from user traces in Galassi et al. [4] by means of hidden Markov models for identifying users. Techniques exist for supervised classification, where models – such as Markov models or neural networks [10] – are trained from labeled data, but these are not well-suited for sequences of variable lengths, which the automata user in our approach reflect well.

Task knowledge for supporting a user is employed by Klug and Kangasharju [6]: The system observes the user's activity by instantiating a task model at runtime and generates an improved interface. Another system, an intelligent classroom [3], recognizes what the users are doing by means of a plan-based action description and supports users in performing these actions, e.g. by advancing slides during presentations. However, both systems do not derive explicit adaptations from the task model.

An overview of predictive statistical models, such as Markov models and Bayesian networks, is given in Zukerman and Albrecht [19]. A different approach is sequence prediction based on sequence mining, thus offering shortcuts for frequently executed action sequences (e.g. [7]), but this technique does not provide domain knowledge that can be employed for the adaptation presentation. Davison and Hirsh [1] present an example interface using action prediction: Based on a dataset of UNIX commands, a prediction of the user's next action is computed. However, a command line interface does not have separate screens and can therefore perform more global support.

6   Conclusions and Future Work

This paper presented an approach for modeling user behavior from basic events. First, user actions are extracted from a sequence of meaningless events by means of probabilistic automata, which are trained with labeled sessions. A task model tracks the user's activity, using user actions as building blocks, and triggers adaptations, such as recommending a next step to the user. An evaluation with a digital TV prototype showed the viability of this approach.

As future work, we plan to show the applicability of our approach to other domains than the digital TV example. Moreover, speech-based and multimodal interaction will be investigated more specifically. A user evaluation with adaptive systems based on the approach presented in this paper will be conducted to show not only the feasibility of this approach, but also the benefits for users. For this purpose, we will employ an adaptation framework that also comprises an implementation of the presented approach. The focus of this framework is on the connection between user behavior and adaptations.

References

1. Davison, B.D., Hirsh, H.: Probabilistic Online Action Prediction. In: AAAI Spring Symposium on Intelligent Environments 1998, pp. 148–154 (1998)
2. Dix, A., Finlay, J., Beale, R.: Analysis of User Behaviour as Time Series. In: Conference on People and Computers (HCI) 1992, pp. 429–444. Cambridge University Press, Cambridge (1993)
3. Franklin, D., Budzik, J., Hammond, K.: Plan-based Interfaces: Keeping Track of User Tasks and Acting to Cooperate. In: Intelligent User Interfaces (IUI) 2002, pp. 79–86. ACM, New York (2002)
4. Galassi, U., Giordana, A., Mendola, D.: Learning User Profile from Traces. In: SAINT Workshops 2005, pp. 166–169. IEEE Computer Society, Washington (2005)
5. Jameson, A.: Adaptive Interfaces and Agents. In: Human-computer Interaction Handbook, 1st edn., pp. 305–330. Erlbaum, Mahwah (2003)
6. Klug, T., Kangasharju, J.: Executable Task Models. In: Task Models and Diagrams (TAMODIA) 2005, pp. 119–122. ACM, New York (2005)
7. Liu, J., Wong, C.K., Hui, K.K.: An Adaptive User Interface Based On Personalized Learning. IEEE Intelligent Systems 18(2), 52–57 (2003)
8. Mannila, H., Toivonen, H., Verkamo, A.I.: Discovery of Frequent Episodes in Event Sequences. Data Mining and Knowledge Discovery 1, 259–289 (1997)

 9. Matassoni, M., Omologo, M., Manione, R., Sowa, T., Balchandran, R., Epstein, M.E., Seredi, L.: The DICIT Project: An Example of Distant-talking Based Spoken Dialogue Interactive System. In: Intelligent Information Systems (IIS) 2008, pp. 527–533. Academic Publishing House EXIT, Warsaw (2008)
10. Mitchell, T.: Machine Learning. McGraw Hill, New York (1997)
11. Mori, G., Paternò, F., Santoro, C.: CTTE: Support for Developing and Analyzing Task Models for Interactive System Design. IEEE Transactions on Software Engineering 28(8), 797–813 (2002)
12. Paternò, F.: Task Models in Interactive Software Systems. In: Chang, S.K. (ed.) Handbook of Software Engineering and Knowledge Engineering, vol. I. World Scientific Publishing Company, Singapore (2001)
13. Paternò, F., Mancini, C., Meniconi, S.: ConcurTaskTrees: A Diagrammatic Notation for Specifying Task Models. In: INTERACT 1997, pp. 362–369. Chapman & Hall, Boca Raton (1997)
14. Sarukkai, R.: Link Prediction and Path Analysis Using Markov Chains. Computer Networks 33(1-6), 377–386 (2000)
15. Thompson, D.V., Hamilton, R.W., Rust, R.: Feature Fatigue: When Product Capabilities Become Too Much of a Good Thing. Journal of Marketing Research 42, 431–442 (2005)
16. Vidal, E., Thollard, F., de la Higuera, C., Casacuberta, F., Carrasco, R.C.: Probabilistic Finite-State Machines-Part I. In: Pattern Analysis and Machine Intelligence, vol. 27, pp. 1013–1025. IEEE Computer Society, Washington (2005)
17. Vidal, E., Thollard, F., de la Higuera, C., Casacuberta, F., Carrasco, R.C.: Probabilistic Finite-State Machines-Part II. In: Pattern Analysis and Machine Intelligence, vol. 27, pp. 1013–1025. IEEE Computer Society, Washington (2005)
18. Wesseling, H., Bezold, M., Beringer, N.: Automatic Evaluation Tool for Multimodal Dialogue Systems. In: André, E., Dybkjær, L., Minker, W., Neumann, H., Pieraccini, R., Weber, M. (eds.) PIT 2008. LNCS, vol. 5078, pp. 297–305. Springer, Heidelberg (2008)
19. Zukerman, I., Albrecht, D.W.: Predictive Statistical Models for User Modeling. User Modeling and User-Adapted Interaction 11(1-2), 5–18 (2001)

PerspectiveSpace: Opinion Modeling with Dimensionality Reduction

Jason B. Alonso[1], Catherine Havasi[2], and Henry Lieberman[3]

[1] MIT Media Laboratory, Personal Robots
20 Ames St E15-468a, Cambridge MA 02139, USA
jalonso@media.mit.edu
[2] Brandeis University, Lab for Linguistics and Computation,
415 South Street, Waltham, MA 02454
havasi@cs.brandeis.edu
[3] MIT Media Laboratory, Software Agents
20 Ames St E15-384a, Cambridge MA 02139, USA
lieber@media.mit.edu

Abstract. Words mean different things to different people, and capturing these differences is often a subtle art. These differences are often "a matter of perspective". Perspective can be taken to be the set of beliefs held by a person as a result of their background, culture, tastes, and experience. But how can we represent perspective computationally?

In this paper, we present PerspectiveSpace, a new technique for modeling spaces of users and their beliefs. PerspectiveSpace represents these spaces as a matrix of users, and data on how people agree or disagree on assertions that they themselves have expressed. It uses Principal Component Analysis (PCA) to reduce the dimensionality of that matrix, discovering the most important axes that best characterize the space. It can then express user perspectives and opinions in terms of these axes. For recommender systems, because it discovers patterns in the beliefs about items, rather than similarity of the items or users themselves, it can perform more nuanced categorization and recommendation. It integrates with our more general common sense reasoning technique, AnalogySpace, which can reason over the content of expressed opinions.

An application of PerspectiveSpace to movie recommendation, 2-wit, is presented. A leave-one-out test shows that PerspectiveSpace captures the consistency of users' opinions very well. The technique also has applications ranging from discovering subcultures in a larger society, to building community-driven web sites.

1 Finding Perspective

The variations in people's beliefs and personalities lie at the heart of many common problems where people are trying to make use of information subject to opinion. People look at reviews of movies and products, but people don't always think the same way about them. An online forum of many users is often strewn with many disagreements, and users have difficulty navigating them to find the

G.-J. Houben et al. (Eds.): UMAP 2009, LNCS 5535, pp. 162–172, 2009.

useful commentary amongst the noise. This is especially true for newcomers to a forum, where the reputations of the regular contributors are unknown to entrants. What is needed here is a tool that lets people express themselves honestly and then captures even the subtle differences between people and the opinions in a conversation in a meaningful way.

PerspectiveSpace is an analysis of person-to-person interactions that explores the similarities and differences in what people believe by discovering descriptive axes on which people can be arranged. These belief patterns underlie the different "perspectives" that people may have, which can be taken to be the set of beliefs held by a person as a result of his or her background, culture, tastes, and experience. In addition to studying the varying beliefs of different social or cultural groups, PerspectiveSpace has applications in recommender systems in that it utilizes knowledge about how people think about the items being recommended.

2   Related Work

2.1   Common Sense

The roots of the PerspectiveSpace project lie in research into collecting and applying common sense knowledge. Open Mind Common Sense (OMCS)[1] is a project that seeks to collect a large body of common sense knowledge in natural language from volunteer contributors over the Internet. ConceptNet[2] is a semantic network designed to be a machine-usable representation of the corpus of knowledge captured by the OMCS project. The nodes of the semantic network are normalized strings of natural language, called "concepts," and these concepts are interconnected with labeled directed links.

AnalogySpace [3] is a new reasoning technique designed to work well on common sense knowledge, which is often vague, redundant, or inconsistent. Rather then compute logical truth, it is oriented towards computing less stringent notions such as similarity, plausibility, analogy, or position along a descriptive spectrum. AnalogySpace represents a space of knowledge as a matrix of concepts vs. features of these concepts. It uses the technique of Singular Value Decomposition (SVD) to reduce the dimension of this matrix, and find the most important descriptive axes that best account for variation in the data. AnalogySpace is computationally very efficient, since the SVD can be computed in advance, and semantic notions such as similarity can be easily computed at run time with basic vector mathematics.

The key insight that led us from AnalogySpace to PerspectiveSpace is that users of a system can be represented as an extra dimension in this matrix. Different users may or may not agree with any given assertion, which allows patterns in sets of beliefs or sets of users to emerge from the mathematical analysis. We observed that these patterns could be used to capture some notion of perspective, as it is generally understood in user modeling. Details of the mathematics, and the relationship between AnalogySpace and PerspectiveSpace, are further explained below.

2.2   Recommender Systems

Recommender systems are tools that look at the behavior (like purchasing activity) or direct input (like movie ratings) of a user to make an informed recommendation of content, products, or other entities in which the user would likely take an interest.

Recommender systems generally come in two types. First, those that are based on the direct characteristics of the product or item to be recommended. These represent each item as a feature vector, with features categorized in advance, and look for similarity between the user's vector of preferences, and individual items.

A second category of recommender systems is collaborative filtering, which is based on similarity between people, according to their history of selected items, and recommend other items selected by similar users. A notable example of collaborative filtering is the Tapestry project from Xerox PARC [4]. A more recent example that uses SVD is given in [5]. A variant, feature-guided collaborative filtering, represents the users and items using predefined feature vectors, as for the case of recommenders based on item characteristics.

PerspectiveSpace also can group users according to their similarity, but with greater sensitivity to subtle differences in beliefs. Rather than being based on their direct selection of items, it uses their beliefs about these items, and can discover emergent patterns of these beliefs. Different users may select the same item for different reasons, or users who have similar beliefs may nonetheless select different items. Thus PerspectiveSpace operates at a finer grain than traditional collaborative filtering. It holds the potential for more nuanced recommendation, and can deliver better insight into why these recommendations were chosen.

2.3   Sentiment Analysis

Opinion mining and sentiment analysis are disciplines very closely related to PerspectiveSpace. Morinaga et al. even used PCA to find associations between products and natural-language opinion terms that describe them [6]. A recent survey of these fields [7], however, makes it very clear that the field focuses on finding a general affinity score for a given product using information extracted (mined) from free text. In particular, emphasis is given to reducing the semantics of free text to either a "positive" or "negative" opinion. The survey discusses treatment of reviewer reliability, but that treatment appears perfunctory and is secondary to establishing the affinity score. Furthermore, there does not appear to be much treatment of characterizing and differentiating reviewers as is typically done with recommender systems.

3   Methodology

3.1   From AnalogySpace to PerspectiveSpace

AnalogySpace, mentioned above, is a transformation of the scored assertions (concepts crossed with features, giving scores) in ConceptNet that yields a compressed vector for each concept or feature, permitting elementary linear operations to be used to perform calculations on semantic similarity [3]. PerspectiveSpace, which is separate from but related to AnalogySpace, is a transformation of the ratings people assign to statements that gives a compressed vector for each statement and person. The axes of these vectors represent significant variations which can be used to characterize different subcultures.

There are a couple notable properties of the SVD that are important to PerspectiveSpace. One is that the principle components found (termed "axes" in the lingo of AnalogySpace and PerspectiveSpace) are ordered in decreasing significance, and that degree of significance is measured by its singular value. The most significant axis divides the data into the two most divisive sets of items and their properties, summarizing groups of properties with a single varying parameter. In the case of PerspectiveSpace, this varying parameter tends to be either a divisive issue or a set of beliefs neither held nor contradicted by groups of people not falling on the axis. Subsequent axes divide and describe the data along successively less significant but empirically independent parameters. Each of these varying parameters can be take to describe a group of properties holistically. Another important property is that the discovered axes are orthogonal, which means that each successively less significant axis describes successively more subtle variations in the data. In appropriate circumstances, the most subtle variations can be taken to be noise, which can then be removed to make sensible interpolations of missing data.

3.2   Creating a PerspectiveSpace

As an example for motivating many of the computation steps in calculating PerspectiveSpace, we introduce 2-wit, a recommender system that recommends reviews of products in the consumer market (in this example, movies), which is distinctly different from the traditional approach of recommending products themselves. First, we will discuss the initial data set and matrix for a PerspectiveSpace analysis, then the normalization and decomposition.

Collecting the Data. The collection of data for PerspectiveSpace must have four features:

1. contributors must be able to express their beliefs in succinct, natural language assertions;
2. agreement and disagreement between contributors on their assertions must be readily and frequently ascertained;
3. each contribution must be linked to the identity of the contributor; and
4. each contributor may only issue one rating per assertion, though that rating may be altered over time.

It should be noted that assertions are, in general, structured with "tags" and "statements." A tag is a simple indication of what the contributor thinks about the statement. In the simplest of implementations, the only tag available is "agree," which indicates whether or not the contributor believes the statement is

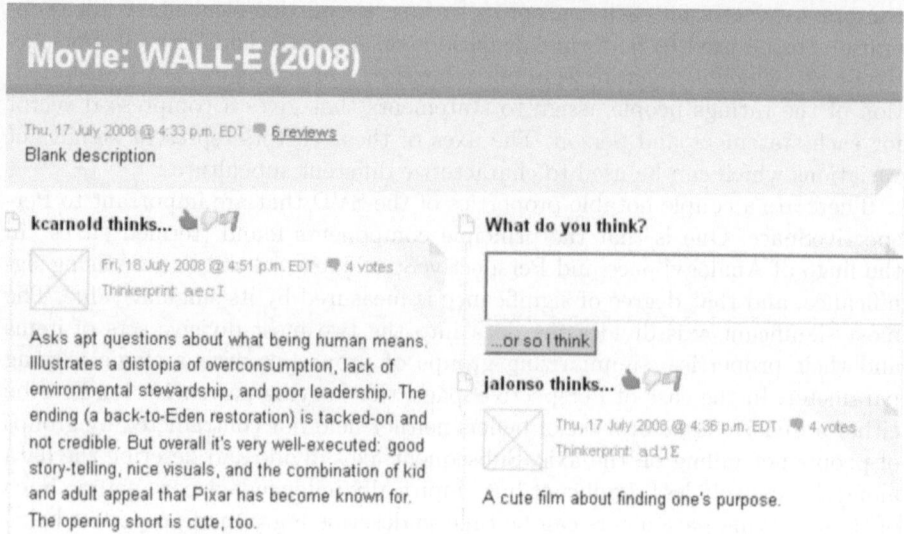

Fig. 1. A screenshot of the 2-wit collection interface

true. In the case of 2-wit, each statement is a review made of a particular movie. The tags in 2-wit are "agree," for indicating that the contributor either agrees (positive rating) or disagrees (negative rating) with a statement, and "junk" for indicating that the contributor believes the statement is obscene, spam, or otherwise generally useless in the opinion of the contributor.

In the case of 2-wit, the interface (see figure 1) presents logged-in users with a simple box for entering one or more reviews or otherwise short commentaries on a movie. All of the reviews entered by other users are visible for consideration, and there are three icons at the top of each review for users to click to express their opinion of each review: a green thumbs-up (agree), a red thumbs-down (disagree), and a yellow flag (junk).

Constructing the matrix. The construction of PerspectiveSpace begins with the preparation of a ratings matrix, which is denoted as M_R in this paper.

The rows of M_R are person-tag pairs, its columns are assertions or statements, and its values are ratings. M_R is also sparse, which is an important consideration for the normalization methods discussed in section 3.2, and it influences the choice of SVD implementation. The sparse matrix is populated such that $M_R[(i, k), j]$ is positive if and only if person i gave statement j with tag k a rating of agreement, negative with a rating of disagreement, and zero with no rating or a neutral rating.

By coupling tags with people in this manner, an SVD can detect patterns where one group of people tend to make or believe statements that another group tends to believe are junk (or otherwise assign a different tag). As such, the matrix describes the statements (columns) in terms of what people think of them with rows like "Alice agrees" and "Bob thinks is junk".

Normalization. The matrix M_R is normalized to obtain $\hat{M}_R$. In the context of PerspectiveSpace, this process reshapes the data set going into the SVD, while altering its semantics as little as possible, so as to maximize the effectiveness of the algorithm.

Sparse mean-shifting. PCA methods generally require that zero-mean vectors be prepared before performing an SVD[8]. Given that PerspectiveSpace data sets are usually sparse, some attention must be paid to the shifting of the terms, as the sparse SVD methods used do not permit the use of nonzero unpopulated entries. The result is that the shifts take only non-zero columns into account.

This approach, unfortunately, places undue emphasis on negative ratings. In the OMCS corpus, for example, 75% to 80% of the assertions are considered true when reviewed by human judges, and so most of the ratings made by contributors are ratings of agreement. This means that very few ratings by a person, if any, are negative. Mean shifting thus increases the magnitude of the negative ratings significantly, while diminishing the magnitude of the many positive ratings. Possibly even more damaging is that people who have only rated things positively will have no non-zero values in their rows of $\hat{M}_R$.

What is needed is another way to bring the mean rating per person to zero without introducing an imbalance.

Unity magnitude. Magnitude normalization methods in PerspectiveSpace were inherited from the methods used in constructing AnalogySpace. Though they do not accomplish the zero-mean property typically used with PCA, they improve the quality of the discovered axes by preventing the most significant axes from being dominated by the most populated rows and columns of the input matrix. When AnalogySpace is prepared without magnitude normalization, the most significant axes simply described the concepts for which OMCS had the most data[3]. In terms of 2-wit, a user who rates 100 reviews would overpower the user who rates 10 reviews in the data set, such that the user who rated 100 reviews would likely establish an axis unto himself/herself. Unity magnitude normalization rescales the input values, so users can readily establish their positions in PerspectiveSpace without simply granting the most prolific users their own axes. This is important, as the data collection process places no constraints on the relative number of ratings obtained from each person.

An immediately apparent limitation of unity magnitude normalization is that rows of the input matrix with very little content, which would describe a person (in PerspectiveSpace) who contributed a single rating, would have just as much influence in the formation of axes as rows with a lot of content. The solution adopted in AnalogySpace, and subsequently adopted in PerspectiveSpace, was to add a constant term in each row to make the magnitude of the normalized row vary with the magnitude of the initial row.

This normalization model works as follows, with b as the "base parameter" to be added to each row to diminish insignificant rows and $\mathbb{P}_A$ as the set of assertions (that is, all of the columns of M_R):

$$\hat{M}_R[i,j] = \frac{M_R[i,j]}{\sqrt{b + \sum_{j'' \in \mathbb{P}_A} M_R[i,j'']^2}} \tag{1}$$

Complementary ratings. Under the complementary (or "mirrored") ratings model, every assertion was matched with a complementary, opposite assertion. That is, for every rating a person gives a normal assertion, the person is modeled to give the opposite rating to the complementary assertion. This ensures that the average rating given by a user is always zero without placing undue bias on any particular assertion. As such, the artifacts that appear as a result of using unity magnitude normalization methods disappears.

This approach can be taken to the logical extreme by having complementary users in addition to complementary assertions.

Combined magnitude normalization with mirrored ratings. The final normalization method chosen for 2-wit, and recommended for any PerspectiveSpace preparation, was a combination of mirroring and unity magnitude normalization. Mirroring is applied first to ensure that the average value in each row of the resultant matrix is zero. Applying unity magnitude normalization (with $b = 2.0$) does not alter the zero-mean property of the matrix.

Performing the decomposition. Once a normalized matrix is obtained, a singular value decomposition (SVD) is taken using the Lanczos algorithm, yielding U, Σ, and V^T

$$\hat{M}_R \approx U \Sigma V^T \tag{2}$$

U gives the coordinates of each user in PerspectiveSpace, while V gives the coordinates of each assertion in the same space.

4   2-Wit

2-wit, whose name is a contraction of "What Will I Think," is a web-based system that collects opinions people have about movies and suggests, to each user, opinions from other users that he or she might agree with.

The 2-wit implementation, used as an example above, was designed to give people a social space where they could share their opinions on the movies they've seen, with the general expectation that they could also rely on each other to help make decisions on movies to see in the future. Though the interface was designed to emphasize the social nature of the system, it is not a social networking system that allows people to declare "friends" or "groups" as contemporary social networking sites like Facebook permit.

The movie review domain was chosen as for any two people in the same society, there are likely to be at least a few movies that they have both seen. At the same time, people's tastes and opinions of movies are sufficiently varied to make a range of trends readily detectable. As such, even a small number of contributors was expected to produce usable results.

4.1   Using 2-Wit to Evaluate PerspectiveSpace

A variation of the leave-one-out test was performed to test the interpolative abilities of PerspectiveSpace in the 2-wit implementation. The presumed usage scenario for the 2-wit movie system is that a user considering movies that he or she has not seen would search for reviews that he or she would agree with. With this in mind, the traditional leave-one-out test was extended to leave out one user-movie pair per trial. As such, all ratings a particular user gave for reviews of a particular movie were removed for the duration of the trial, and recall was defined in terms of the number of reviews for which the user's rating could be properly estimated. The test, accordingly, is dubbed "leave-some-out."

In determining viable user-movie pairs for the leave-some-out test, the test skipped the degenerate case of reviews where only one user provided a rating in trials testing the applicable user and the relevant movie. Finally, the case of users who commented on only one movie was also avoided, as there were no grounds for an SVD to interpolate ratings for such users.

Given these restrictions, it was determined that exactly 61 user-movie pairs were viable as trials for the evaluation, and so the evaluation covers all possible user-movie pairs rather than a random subset. This test was also repeated with varying values of k, which determines the number of axes that should be computed and used for the analysis.

4.2   Results

The results are shown in table 1. For the purposes of this evaluation, "hits" are defined as the number of trials in which the user's rating of a movie review was successfully interpolated by taking the dot product of the PerspectiveSpace vectors for the person and the review (a process called perspective projection) with a threshold $\tau = 0.01$. "Misses" are defined similarly where the rating was predicted opposite to the the correct value. "Undecided" is defined as the number of reviews for which the magnitude of the predictive rating was smaller than τ, where there is insufficient confidence to make a reasonable estimate of a user's acceptance or rejection of the movie review. The "% decided" represents the fraction of reviews for which a confident estimation was made, while "% correct" represents the portion of *the decided reviews* for which the correct estimation was made.

The results are positive in that 2-wit performed substantially better than chance in estimating the opinions that users would have about movies. Given any user-movie pair for testing, the leave-some-out test appropriately excluded all reviews the user made of any assertion about the movie. It is further interesting to note that the best performance was obtained with $k = 4$—a reasonable interpretation of this phenomenon is that the omission of lower-ranking axes removed noise from the data set, particularly excluding "information" that specifically worked to diminish properly-interpolated ratings for which there was no direct measurement.

Table 1. Results of the 2-wit evaluation with $\tau = 0.01$

Tags	k	Hits	Misses	Undecided	Cumulative % decided	% correct	Average % decided	% correct
all	4	215	74	88	77	74	76	78
	8	215	74	88	77	74	78	74
	16	150	81	146	61	65	63	66
agree	4	93	46	43	76	67	76	71
	8	92	42	48	74	69	75	69
	16	58	45	79	57	56	60	59
junk	4	122	28	44	77	81	76	84
	8	123	32	39	80	79	81	79
	16	92	36	66	66	72	65	71

5   Other Applications Using PerspectiveSpace

PerspectiveSpace has also been used in other applications. It was used by the Common Sense Computing Initiative to identify and combat malicious or disruptive users. When contributors rate statements for truth, such as in OMCS, one can find the class or classes of users which tend to be at odds with more trusted users. This is also useful for discovering when a user has created multiple accounts which he uses only to agree with his primary account or bolster his ratings[9].

SlantExplorer, an application prototype, is a web-based interface for navigating the conflicting opinions that underlie or are otherwise applicable to a document. SlantExplorer is designed as a tool for composing expository documents or for assisting users trying to draft document summaries. By considering the perspectives that people can take on a document, SlantExplorer can help identify portions of a document of interest to people belonging to particular groups or backgrounds [9].

6   Perspectives for Understanding an Increasingly Connected Society

In addition to recommender systems, the potential application domains for PerspectiveSpace fall into four major categories: characterizing societies, detecting microtheories, and community-driven content.

6.1   Characterizing Societies

PerspectiveSpace offers many opportunities for the identification and study of behavior pattern within a larger community. PerspectiveSpace can tie into the AnalogySpace family of language analysis tools and together they offers a means for the systematic study of jargon usage, dialects, and belief patterns related to culture or subculture. In more general terms, PerspectiveSpace is a tool for opinion analysis, which has direct applications in marketing and political settings.

With care, these "opinions" can be applied toward understanding the language of particular groups of people (or characterizing people by the language they use) in natural language processing applications. A simple example of this application would be useful in common sense reasoning. Since people of different countries and cultures speak the same language, it would be useful to isolate which users were representative of which cultures.

Natural language processing applications can use PerspectiveSpace to help model the language patterns of people dynamically by generating perspectives representative of a speaker from the language he or she uses, including jargon and idioms. If the PerspectiveSpace were constructed from a semantic resource, these perspectives could be used in later processing steps to aid with understanding the semantics underlying a statement. Given, for example sentences like "Soda is a carbonated beverage" and "Pop is a carbonated beverage," a system can learn that a particular group of people using the word "pop" might be significantly more likely than other groups to mean a carbonated beverage rather than a small explosive sound.

6.2   Pseudo-microtheories

Microtheories are consistent subsets of larger bodies of assertions, usually descriptive of a specific domain of knowledge. They are usually understood and discussed in the context of formal reasoning systems: the Cyc project, for example, is a body of common sense knowledge professionally-crafted into the form of formal, logical assertions[10].

Principle perspectives, by virtue of their discovery process, tend to identify assertions that are believed or disbelieved in tandem by people. This correlation between assertions appears to imply that the assertions are consistent and related to each other, which make these assertions like microtheories. We hesitate to call these assertions "microtheories" as this discovery process does not represent assertions in predicate logic or show how one assertion can be derived from others, and these are expected in contemporary notions of "microtheories."

6.3   Community-Driven Content

PerspectiveSpace offers a variety of interesting possibilities for applications that use community-driven content, which share the feature that people can contribute to and navigate a body of knowledge on which not every user would agree. PerspectiveSpace has been tested using the Open Mind Common Sense project[9] and could be utilized in other websites such as Slashdot[11] and Wikipedia[12].

The use of perspective projection can allow contributors and browsers of a community-driven content project to work in a space of assertions that are compatible with their particular belief patterns. For a contributor, this would allow him or her to build upon existing statements in greater detail and comfort. For a browser, this would allow him or her to explore content in a self-consistent form.

Subculture detection, on the other hand, can help a contributor or browser identify and understand the major sides of an argument as well as the prevailing agreements underlying a discussion.

Using perspective projection and subculture detection, both contributors and browsers can easily explore different perspectives. PerspectiveSpace gives them the tools they need to consider counter-arguments and differing opinions.

References

1. Singh, P.: The public acquisition of commonsense knowledge. In: Proceedings of AAAI Spring Symposium: Acquiring (and Using) Linguistic (and World) Knowledge for Information Access. AAAI, Menlo Park (2002)
2. Havasi, C., Speer, R., Alonso, J.: Conceptnet 3: a flexible, multilingual semantic network for common sense knowledge. In: Recent Advances in Natural Language Processing (2007)
3. Speer, R., Havasi, C., Lieberman, H.: AnalogySpace: Reducing the dimensionality of common sense knowledge. In: Proceedings of AAAI 2008 (July 2008)
4. Goldberg, D., Nichols, D., Oki, B.M., Terry, D.: Using collaborative filtering to weave an information tapestry. Commun. ACM 35(12), 61–70 (1992)
5. Sarwar, B.M., Karypis, G., Konstan, J.A., Reidl, J.T.: Application of dimensionality reduction in recommender system–a case study. In: WebKDD 2000 Workshop (2000)
6. Morinaga, S., Yamanishi, K., Tateishi, K., Fukushima, T.: Mining product reputations on the web. In: KDD 2002: Proceedings of the eighth ACM SIGKDD international conference on Knowledge discovery and data mining, pp. 341–349. ACM, New York (2002)
7. Pang, B., Lee, L.: Opinion mining and sentiment analysis. Foundations and Trends in Information Retrieval 2(1-2), 1–135 (2008)
8. Smith, L.: A tutorial on Principal Components Analysis, vol. 51, p. 52. Cornell University, USA (2002)
9. Alonso, J.B.: PerspectiveSpace. S.M. thesis, Massachusetts Institute of Technology. Program in Media Arts and Sciences (2008)
10. Lenat, D.: Cyc: A large-scale investment in knowledge infrastructure. Communications of the ACM 11, 33–38 (1995)
11. SourceForge, Inc.: Slashdot: News for nerds, stuff that matters. Slashdot web site (2008), http://slashdot.org/
12. Wikimedia Foundation, Inc.: Wikipedia, the free encyclopedia. English language Wikipedia web site (2008), http://en.wikipedia.org/

Recognition of User Intentions for Interface Agents with Variable Order Markov Models

Marcelo G. Armentano[1] and Analía A. Amandi[2]

[1] ISISTAN Research Institute, Fac. Cs. Exactas, UNCPBA
Campus Universitario, Paraje Arroyo Seco, Tandil, 7000, Argentina
[2] CONICET, Consejo Nacional de Investigaciones Científicas y Técnicas, Argentina

Abstract. A key aspect to study in the field of interface agents is the need to detect as soon as possible the user intentions. User intentions have an important role for an interface agent because they serve as a context to define the way in which the agents can collaborate with users. Intention recognition can be used to infer the user's intentions based on the observation of the tasks the user performs in a software application. In this work, we propose an approach to model the intentions the user can pursue in an application in a semi-automatic way, based on Variable-Order Markov models. We claim that with appropriate training from the user, an interface agent following our approach will be able both to detect the user intention and the most probable sequence of following tasks the user will perform to achieve his/her intention.

1 Introduction

Interface Agents [Maes, 1994] are computer programs designed to assist human users in their computer-based tasks in a personalized manner. This kind of agent is able to learn interests, preferences, priorities, goals and needs of a user aiming at providing him/her proactive and reactive assistance in order to increase the user's productivity regarding to the application at issue.

With the aim of assisting a user of a software application, interface agents not only have to learn the user's preferences and habits regarding the use of the application itself, but should also consider what his/her intention is before initiating an interaction with the user. Considering the status of a user's attention (i.e. his/her intention or the goal he/she is pursuing) and the uncertainty about the user's intentions are critical factors for the effective integration of automated services with direct manipulation interfaces [Horvitz et al., 1998]. A correct detection of the user's intention will avoid the agent interrupting the user in an improper moment. Users generally don't want to be interrupted while working on a specific task, unless this interruption is strongly related to the task they are performing [Whitworth, 2005]. By considering the user's intention the agent will be able to answer to his/her requirements always in the realm of his/her current intention. As a result, we must build agents capable of detecting the

G.-J. Houben et al. (Eds.): UMAP 2009, LNCS 5535, pp. 173–184, 2009.

user's intention so that it can predict opportune moments for gaining the user's attention.

In this work we propose an approach to automatically obtain a model of the user intentions in a software application to allow a posterior detection of those intentions. This model aims at being considered by an interface agent as a context that represents the user's focus of attention in a particular moment in the use of the application. The interface agent can use this knowledge to assist the user in the context of his/her intentions and, moreover, to find a suitable moment to initiate an interaction with him/her (that is, when the agent is quite sure of his/her intention). However, how the agent uses the detected intention to assist the user is out of the scope of our work.

The rest of this work is organized as follows. Section 2 describes some related work in the area and the problems detected in existent approaches. Next, in Section 3 we describe our approach to the problem of modeling and detecting a user's intention. In Section 4 we present the experiments we performed to validate our proposal. Finally, in Section 5, we present our conclusions.

2   Problem Overview

Intention recognition in this context can be defined as the process of inferring a *user* intentions based on the observation of the actions he/she performs in a *software application*. Intention recognition is a special case of plan recognition in which only the intention of the user, but not the associated plan is predicted. A complete plan recognition process is a more complex and time requiring task. In the domain of an interface agent, such as in many other domains, it is preferable a fast detection of just the user's intention than a slower detection of the complete plan needed to fulfill his/her intention.

The basic idea beyond the intention recognition process is to narrow the number of possible goals the agent believes the user is pursuing. This task is accomplished by observing the actions the user performs. For example, when starting a scheduling application, the user can have any goal $G_1, G_2, \cdots, G_n$. Now, if the agent observes that the user performs certain task, like selecting "Add new contact" in the application menu, the set of goals is reduced to those in which the task performed is included as a particular step (for example, organizing an event with the new contact as a participant, or sending a email to him/her). If the next task observed is "Compose new email", the set of candidate intentions can be further narrowed. Note that even if there is only one candidate intention, the agent will not always be absolutely sure that the user really has that intention. This way, each time the user performs an action in the application, the set of candidate intentions might be reduced and/or some intention will be more probable than others.

The basic algorithm to accomplish plan or intention recognition seems to be straightforward; however, most of previous approaches to the problem fail in three main aspects. The first problem that makes many previous approaches to the problem of plan recognition unsuitable for interface agents is that plan libraries are usually hand-coded by a domain expert [Kautz, 1991] [Charniak and Goldman, 1993] [Horvitz et al., 1998] [Lesh et al., 1999]. Building a plan library is a tedious and error prone task and the success of a plan recognizer firstly relies on the correctness and completeness of the plan library itself. For this reason, in the recent years researchers have put special attention in the acquisition of plan libraries by constructing models that capture regularities in the user behavior. Nevertheless, most of this research was conducted to learn the parameters of the model, such as probabilities, while the structure of the model itself remained fixed [Nguyen et al., 2005] [Duong et al., 2006] [Liao et al., 2007]. On the other hand, few efforts were put on the task of learning plan libraries from the interaction history of a user with a software application and the proposed approaches are limited in the kind of plan structures that they are able to model [Bauer, 1999] [Gorniak and Poole, 2000] [Garland; and Lesh, 2002]. Behavior usually differs from one user to another and a predefined structure of plans may not fit a specific user behavior. For these reasons, the automatic acquisition of plan libraries is desirable.

Second, one of the most important problems that an interface agent faces when inferring the user's intention is the uncertainty related to the moment in which the user starts a new plan to achieve a new goal, that is how does the agent become aware that the user has already achieved one goal and started pursuing a new one? This issue is not usually addressed by many approaches to the problem of plan recognition, and they consider only one "session", which starts with the first observed action and ends when the algorithm recognizes the user's intention. In an interface agent environment, the user will repeatedly start pursuing new goals in the application, with no preplanned behavior. Moreover, the user can even change his/her intention without completing his/her previous goal. This problem is usually tackled by restricting the memory of the plan recognizer so that it only considers the most recent tasks performed by the user, or it considers each task for only a fixed interval of time and then they are completely disregarded [Brown, 1998] [Waern, 1996].

Another issue to take into account is that users usually follow several intentions at a time. Consequently, a plan recognizer used by an interface agent should be able to manage the realization of multiple user intentions simultaneously. Plan recognizers that limit themselves to one-at-a-time intentions are not suitable in the interface agents domain. Related to this issue is the execution of noisy tasks. Noisy tasks are tasks that the user performs but that do not belong to his/her main goal, such as checking the current time while answering an email. Predictions of a plan recognizer should not be highly affected by the presence of such kind of tasks.

Although there are many approaches to the problem of plan recognition, no previous approach is able to manage all the issues stated in this section. In the next section we present our approach to deal with all these aspects of an intention recognition system for interface agents.

3   Proposed Approach

3.1   Learning an Intention Model from Examples

Markov models are a natural way of modeling sequences of actions observed along time. In its simplest form, a Markov chain is a stochastic process with the Markov property. Having the Markov property means that, given the present state, future states are independent of the past states. In other words, the description of the present state fully captures all the information that could influence the future evolution of the process. Future states will be reached through a probabilistic process instead of a deterministic one. At each step the system may change its state from the current state to another state, or remain in the same state, according to a certain probability distribution. The changes of state are called transitions, and the probabilities associated with various state-changes are called transition probabilities.

Markov chains of fixed order are a natural extension in which the future state is dependent on the previous m states. Although this extension is beneficial for many domains, there are some main drawbacks in the use of these models. First, only models with very small order are of practical value since there is an exponential grow in the number of states of Markov chains as their order is increased. Second, for sequences of tasks performed by a user to achieve an intention, the probability of the next performed task is not always determined by the same fixed number of previous tasks. There is usually a variable length previous "context" that determines the probability distribution of what the user may perform next.

Hidden Markov Models are an alternative way of modeling natural sequences. Although these models are a powerful and popular representation, there are theoretical results concerning the difficulty of their learning [Ron et al., 1996].

Variable Order Markov (VOM) models arose as a solution to capture longer regularities while avoiding the size explosion caused by increasing the order of the model. In contrast to the Markov chain models, where each random variable in a sequence with a Markov property depends on a fixed number of random variables, in VOM models this number of conditioning random variables may vary based on the specific observed realization, known as *context*. These models consider that in realistic settings, there are certain realizations of states (represented by contexts) in which some past states are independent from the future states conducting to a great reduction in the number of model parameters.

Algorithms for learning VOM models over a finite alphabet Σ attempt to learn a subclass of Probabilistic Finite-state Automata (PFA) called Probabilistic Suffix Automata (PSA) which can model sequential data of considerable complexity. Formally, a PSA can be described as a 5-tuple $(Q, \Sigma, \tau, \gamma, \pi)$, where Q is a finite set of states, Σ is the task universe, $\tau : Q \times \Sigma \to Q$ is the transition function, $\gamma : Q \times \Sigma \to [0, 1]$ is the next task probability function, where for each $q \in Q$, $\sum_{\sigma \in \Sigma} \gamma(q, \sigma) = 1$, $\pi : Q \to [0, 1]$ is the initial probability distribution over the starting states, with $\sum_{\sigma \in \Sigma} \pi(q) = 1$.

A PFA is a PSA if the following property holds. Each state in a PSA M is labeled by a sequence of tasks with finite length in Σ^* and the set of sequences S labeling the states is suffix free. Σ is the domain task universe, that is the finite set of tasks that the user can perform in the domain. A set of sequences S is said to be suffix free if $\forall s \in S$, $Suffix^*(s) \cap S = \{s\}$, where $Suffix^*(s) = \{s_i, \cdots, s_l | 1 \leq i \leq l\}$ is the set of all possible suffixes of s, including the empty sequence e. For every two states q_1 and $q_2 \in Q$ and for every task $\sigma \in \Sigma$, if $\tau(q_1, \sigma) = q_2$ and q_1 is labeled by a sequence s_1, then q_2 is labeled by a sequence s_2 that is a suffix of $s_1 \cdot \sigma$.

In contrast to N-order Markov models, which attempt to estimate conditional distributions of the form $Pr(\sigma|s)$, with $s \in \Sigma^N$ and $\sigma \in \Sigma$, VOM algorithms learn such conditional distributions where context lengths $|s|$ vary in response to the available statistics in the training data. Thus, PSA models provide the means for capturing both large and small order Markov dependencies based on the observed data. In [Armentano, 2008] we proposed an algorithm for learning such models in an incremental way.

For learning a user's intention model we follow a Programming By Example (PBE) [Lieberman, 2001] approach in the sense that the user will teach the agent what sequence or sequences of tasks he/she usually performs when he/she has a given intention. However, unlike the classic programming by demonstration approach, our aim is not to create a program that allows the agent to perform repetitive tasks on behalf of the user, but to detect the user's intention that lead him/her to perform a set of tasks.

Learning the user's intention model by example has the main advantage that we do not need any additional information of the domain being modeled more than the tasks that can be performed in the domain. The agent will be able to learn regularities in the user's behavior just by analyzing the examples given by the user. This way the agent will be able to learn any intention the user may have in the domain, just by giving an example of how to fulfill this intention.

By using the examples provided by the user, the agent will build a PSA model for each goal the user can pursue in the domain. When a new example for an existent model is provided, it may correspond to an alternative way of reaching the same goal, so the corresponding model is updated to reflect this fact.

3.2   Recognizing a User's Intentions

To perform plan recognition, the agent will have a PSA model for each goal for which it was trained by means of examples provided by the user. By having a separate model for each goal, the agent will be able to track several goals that are being pursued simultaneously by the user.

Conventionally, to compute the probability assigned by a PSA k to a given sequence of observations, we should compute $P_{\text{PSA}_k}(r) = \prod_{i=1}^{N} \gamma(s_{i-1}, r_i)$, where $\gamma(s_{i-1}, r_i)$ is the probability value assigned in state s_{i-1} to the observed task r_i, and will select the PSA that assigns the maximum probability as the PSA corresponding to the user's intention. However, as the user continues performing tasks, the total cumulative probability value assigned by each PSA will become smaller and smaller as we are multiplying values in the range $(0, 1]$. Furthermore, we must consider the uncertainty related to the moment in which the user starts a new plan to achieve a new goal. The agent will be faced with a continuous stream of tasks and should be able to recognize changes in the user's current intention. Moreover, the plan recognition process should not be affected by the execution of noisy tasks. The problem we are facing is not a classical problem of classification as we do not predict a "class" (intention) after observing a complete sequence of performed tasks. In our domain, the interface agent should be able to predict the most probable intention after each performed task, and the limit between sequences of tasks corresponding to different intentions is often fuzzy.

To tackle this problem we use an *exponential moving average* on the prediction probability $\gamma(s, \sigma)$ at each step in each PSA as the predicted value for each corresponding user intention. Moving averages are one of the most popular and easy to use tools to smooth a data series and make it easier to spot trends. An exponential moving average (EMA) [Hunter, 1986] is a statistic for monitoring a process that averages the data in a way that gives less and less weight to data as time passes. The weighting for each step decreases exponentially, giving much more importance to recent observations while still not discarding older observations entirely. By the choice of a weighting factor $0 \leq \lambda \leq 1$, the EMA control procedure can be made sensitive to a small or gradual drift in the process. Alternatively, λ may be expressed in terms of N time periods, where $\lambda = \frac{2}{N+1}$.

EMA_t expresses the value of the EMA at any time period t. EMA_1 is set to the a priori probability of the first observed task σ. Then, the computation of the EMA at time periods $t \geq 2$ is done according to equation 1

$$EMA_t = \lambda \gamma_{PSA_i}(s, \sigma) + (1 - \lambda)EMA_{t-1} \tag{1}$$

The parameter λ determines the rate at which *older* probabilities enter into the calculation of the EMA statistic. A value of $\lambda = 1$ implies that only the most recent measurement influences the EMA. Thus, a large value of λ gives more weight to recent probabilities and less weight to older probabilities; a small value of λ gives more weight to older probabilities. The value of λ is usually set between 0.2 and 0.3 [Hunter, 1986] although this choice is somewhat arbitrary and should be determined experimentally.

To sum up, the plan recognition process works as follows: as the user performs tasks in the application at issue the agent will keep making the corresponding state transitions in each PSA and computing the exponential moving average of the transition probability of the performed tasks given each PSA. At each step, the agent will own a probabilistically ranked set of PSAs which correspond to the most probable intentions the user may have at each moment.

The problems we pointed out in Section 2 are then solved with our approach. The uncertainty related to the moment in which the user starts a new plan to achieve a new goal is managed by the exponential moving average by giving more importance to recent observations than to older ones. The rate at which previous intentions are forgotten is controlled by parameter λ of the EMA calculation.

The fact that users usually pursue several goals at a time is managed by keeping a set of PSA models, one for each goal the user can try to accomplish. With each task performed by the user, a transition is made in every model. Noisy tasks are also considered as the prediction of each PSA is computed as an EMA. Again, how much this task influences the prediction is controlled by parameter λ of the EMA calculation. Finally, personalization of the plan library is implicit in our approach, as it is the user who gives examples on which his/her intentions are and how to achieve each of them.

4   Experimental Evaluation

In the experiments shown in this section we evaluate two different metrics. The *Error* for a model q given an observed task sequence $Seq = \sigma_1, \cdots, \sigma_N$ is computed as the sum of the absolute differences between the value assigned for each model with respect to the higher value assigned by all the PSAs, as shown in Equation 2

$$error_q(Seq) = \frac{\sum_{i=1}^{N} |q(\sigma_i) - q_{best}(\sigma_i)|}{\sum_{i=1}^{N} q_{best}(\sigma_i)} \quad (2)$$

On the other hand, the *Convergence* is a metric that indicates how much time took the recognizer to converge in what the current user goal was. If from the time step t to the time step corresponding to the last performed task the algorithm predicted correctly the actual user goal, the convergence is computed as shown in Equation 3. The time step t is called *convergence point*.

$$convergence_q(Seq) = \frac{N - t + 1}{N}, \quad (3)$$
$$not\ best_q(\sigma_{t-1}),$$
$$best_q(\sigma_j), \forall j\ t \leq j \leq N$$
$$where \quad best_q(\sigma_i) = \begin{cases} 1\ if\ q(\sigma_i) = q_{best}(\sigma_i) \\ 0\ otherwise \end{cases} \quad (4)$$

4.1   Recognition in the Presence of Noisy Tasks

The purpose of the experiments described in this section is to test the ability of the proposed model to perform well in the presence of noisy tasks. We considered three kinds of "noise" that can be observed while performing plan recognition: *Omitted tasks* (tasks that were observed in a training sequence and that are not executed in the recognition process), *Inserted tasks* (tasks that were not observed in a training sequence and are observed during the execution of a sequence corresponding to a given intention) and *Replaced tasks* (tasks that were performed in the place of another task that was expected for a given intention).

To test the influence of the length of the task sequences corresponding to the intentions being modeled in the accuracy of the predictions, we run different experiments for different sequences length. For each experiment we used sequences of a fixed length for training 20 PSA models. Each sequence was generated randomly from a set of 26 abstract tasks. Then we altered each training sequence by introducing different combinations of noise, both in amount and kind to build 25 testing sequences for each model and each combination of noises. The noise was introduced in amounts varying from 0 to 90 percent of the length of the sequence and in the three different kinds detailed above.

Figure 1 shows a comparison between the mean error for different values of λ for sequences of length 5, 15, 25 and 50. We did not compute convergence in this case because our goal is to evaluate individual sequences so that we can have a better perception of the influence of noise. We can observe that with few amount of noise present in the testing sequences, longer sequences lead to lower error in the prediction for any value of λ. However, as we increase the noise we introduce in the testing sequences there is a strong dependence on the value selected for λ and the length of sequences for the error of the predictions. As a general observation, we can state that higher values of λ make the system predict shorter sequences better than longer sequences, while lower values of λ make the system predict better longer sequences of tasks. For long sequences, it is suggested that the value of λ has to be reduced to 0.1 to obtain better results. However, for sequences of length 5, the value of λ that leads to lower error in the predictions is 0.3. This result is due to the fact that a lower value for the smoothing constant will take into consideration a history longer than 5 tasks, and this will include tasks not belonging to the current user intention.

4.2   Prediction of Consecutive Intentions

In this section we will analyze the amount of tasks the plan recognizer needs to observe to detect a change in the user intention (convergence) and how the execution of consecutive plans affects the error of the plan recognizer. We used the same set of 20 PSA models as in the previous experiments. For testing, we generated 50 sequences by concatenating sequences belonging to a set of η models selected randomly for each case. We experimentally set $\lambda = 0.9$, since we obtained better results with this value of the smoothing constant.

Figure 2 shows a comparative plot of the values obtained for convergence and error metrics for different sequence lengths when 3, 10 and 20 successive intentions were simulated.

We can observe that there is a fall in convergence, that is more notorious for shorter sequences, when we increase the number of successive intentions simulated. For longer sequences, however, there is almost no change in the value for this metric for 10 and 20 successive intentions. The convergence point is risen to 1.60, 2.02, 2.06 3.45 for sequences of length 5, 10, 15 and 25 respectively and for both cases of 10 and 20 successive intentions; for 10 successive intentions using sequences of length 50 the convergence point obtained is 7.55 tasks and for 20 successive intentions 7.9. For the error metric, on the other hand, the value obtained is higher as we simulate more successive intentions, but the difference tends to be smaller for longer sequences of tasks.

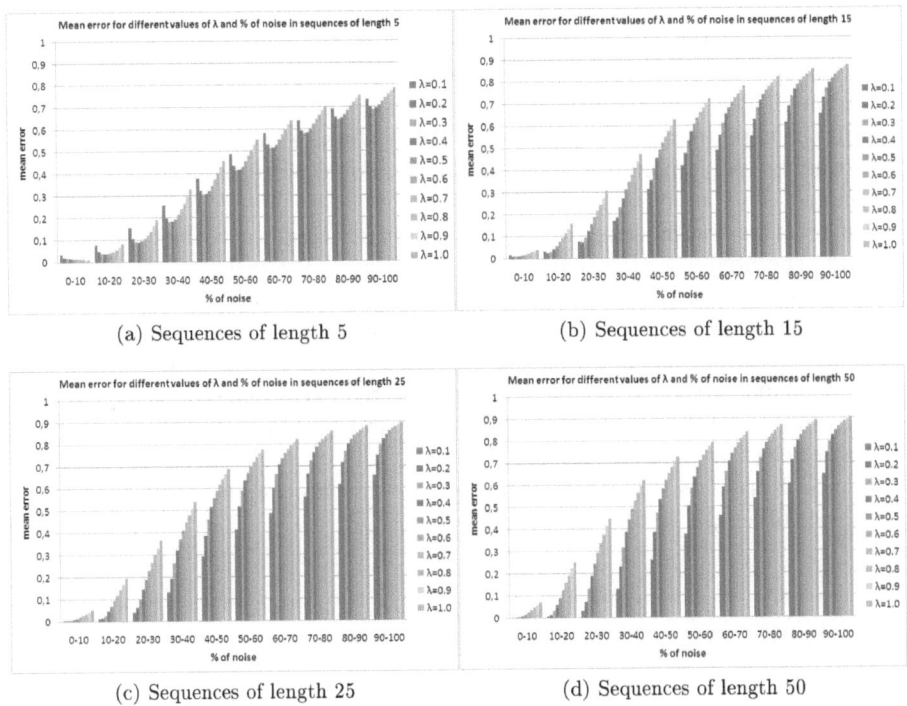

(a) Sequences of length 5

(b) Sequences of length 15

(c) Sequences of length 25

(d) Sequences of length 50

Fig. 1. Average error for different sequences length and different values of the smoothing constant

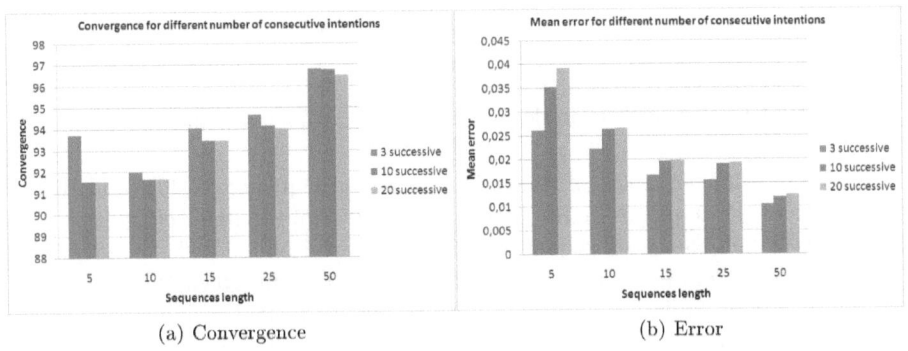

(a) Convergence

(b) Error

Fig. 2. Metrics values for different number of consecutive simulated intentions

4.3   Prediction of Interleaved Intentions

In this section we will describe another series of experiments performed to analyze the behavior of the plan recognizer when the user performs tasks belonging to different intentions.

The set of models used are the same we used the previous section. We varied two variables in these experiments: the number of simultaneous models being tested η and the percentage of tasks performed before changing the current intention ζ. The smoothing constant λ was set experimentally to a value 0.9. For all the experiments η was varied to take values in the set $\{2, 3, 5\}$ and ζ to take "chunks" corresponding to the 20, 40, 60 and 80 percent of the length of the sequences.

For creating testing sequences we randomly selected a subset of the 20 models and generated a testing sequence by interleaving the tasks belonging to each model in this subset, taking chunks of a specified size each time. We also randomly selected the next model from which to take tasks, not considering the same model used immediately before. The last chunk remained usually shorter than the chunk size ζ. When this was the case, the performance of the recognizer usually decreased. For each combination of η and ζ we repeated the experiment 50 times selecting different models.

Figure 3 presents the values obtained for convergence and error metrics for sequences of length 5, 10, 15, 25 and 50.

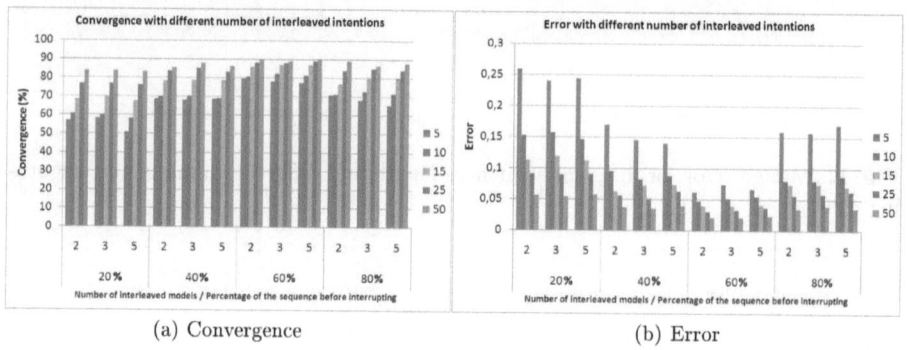

(a) Convergence   (b) Error

Fig. 3. Metrics values for interleaved intentions for different sequences length

Notice that for sequences of length 5 by using subsequences of 20% and 80% of the length of the sequence highly increases the error of the plan recognizer. This is due to the fact that a subsequence of 20% leads to isolated tasks (sequences of length 1). This represents a very uncommon situation in which the user would alternate between different intentions performing one task of each one. Sequences of length 1 are not sufficient to activate the memory of the model. Something similar happens with 80% of the sequence length; we will have a subsequence of length 4 and a sequence of length 1 would be left (the last task in the sequence). In general, we can observe that the number of simultaneous models considered in the experiments does not have a major influence in the resultant values for the error and convergence metrics. We can observe that there is a general better behavior of the recognition algorithm for both metrics for the case of chunks with size $\zeta = 60\%$. The reason for this is that this is the test case with a better equilibrium in the sizes of the chunks that lead to a better performance.

A final observation from the graphics presented in Figure 3 is that our plan recognizer predict longer sequences better. We obtained an error lower than 5% and a convergence of more than 80% for the best case of sequences of length 50 for all tested cases of interleaved intentions, and an error lower than 25%, with a convergence of more than 50% for the worst case of sort sequences of length 5.

One advantage we found for our plan recognizer is that there is no need to "remember" which was the last task performed before interrupting the current intention and start pursuing a different goal. Subsequences of the sequences used to train a model lead to correct predictions, although we do not start executing the sequence from its beginning.

5   Conclusions and Discussion

In this article, we presented an approach to model and recognize a user's intentions from the unobtrusive observation of his interaction with a software application. We propose the use of Variable Order Markov models to model each user intention and the use of an exponential moving average to tackle the evolution of the process through long user sessions. We evaluated our proposal with promising results. However, there is still a challenge that need further study that is the way the user will provide the system with training examples for building the intention models needed by the agent. Currently, we are evaluating our approach in a concrete application domain, using data collected from the observation of real users.

References

[Armentano, 2008]Armentano, M.G.: Recognition of User Intentions with Variable-Order Markov Models. Ph.D thesis, Universidad Nacional del Centro de la Provincia de Buenos Aires. Argentina (2008)

[Bauer, 1999]Bauer, M.: From interaction data to plan libraries: A clustering approach. In: IJCAI 1999: Proceedings of the Sixteenth International Joint Conference on Artificial Intelligence, pp. 962–967. Morgan Kaufmann Publishers Inc., San Francisco (1999)

[Brown, 1998]Brown, S.: A Decision Theoretic Approach for Interface Agent Development. Ph.D thesis, Faculty of the Graduate School of Engineering of the Air Force Institute of Technology Air University (1998)

[Charniak and Goldman, 1993]Charniak, E., Goldman, R.P.: A bayesian model of plan recognition. Artificial Intelligence 64(1), 53–79 (1993)

[Duong et al., 2006]Duong, T.V., Phung, D.Q., Bui, H.H., Venkatesh, S.: Human behavior recognition with generic exponential family duration modeling in the hidden semi-markov model. In: International Conference on Pattern Recognition, vol. 3, pp. 202–207 (2006)

[Garland; and Lesh, 2002]Garland, A., Lesh, N.: Learning hierarchical task models by demonstration. Technical report, Mitsubishi Electric Research Laboratories (2002)

[Gorniak and Poole, 2000]Gorniak, P., Poole, D.: Building a stochastic dynamic model of application. In: Boutilier, C., Goldszmidt, M. (eds.) Sixteenth Conference on Uncertainty in Artificial Intelligence (UAI 2000), Stanford University, Stanford, California, USA, pp. 230–237. Morgan Kaufmann, San Francisco (2000)

[Horvitz et al., 1998]Horvitz, E., Breese, J., Heckerman, D., Hovel, D., Rommelse, K.: The Lumière project: Bayesian user modeling for inferring the goals and needs of software users. In: Cooper, G.F., Moral, S. (eds.) Proceedings of the Fourteenth Conference on Uncertainty in Artificial Intelligence, pp. 256–265. Morgan Kaufmann, San Mateo (1998)

[Hunter, 1986]Hunter, J.S.: The exponentially weighted moving average. Journal of Quality Technology 18(4), 203–209 (1986)

[Kautz, 1991]Kautz, H.: A formal theory of plan recognition and its implementation. In: Allen, J.F., Kautz, H.A., Pelavin, R., Tenenberg, J. (eds.) Reasoning About Plans, pp. 69–125. Morgan Kaufmann Publishers, San Mateo (1991)

[Lesh et al., 1999]Lesh, N., Rich, C., Sidner, A.L.: Using plan recognition in human-computer collaboration. In: International Conference on User Modeling (UM 1999), pp. 23–32. Mitsubishi Electric Research Laboratories (1999)

[Liao et al., 2007]Liao, L., Patterson, D.J., Fox, D., Kautz, H.A.: Learning and inferring transportation routines. Artificial Intelligence 171(5-6), 311–331 (2007)

[Lieberman, 2001]Lieberman, H.: Your Wish Is My Command: Programming by Example. Morgan Kaufmann, San Francisco (2001)

[Maes, 1994]Maes, P.: Agents that reduce work and information overload. Communications of the ACM (1994)

[Nguyen et al., 2005]Nguyen, N.T., Phung, D.Q., Venkatesh, S., Bui, H.H.: Learning and detecting activities from movement trajectories using the hierarchical hidden markov model. In: IEEE Computer Vision and Pattern Recognition or CVPR, pp. 955–960. IEEE Computer Society, Los Alamitos (2005)

[Ron et al., 1996]Ron, D., Singer, Y., Tishby, N.: The power of amnesia: Learning probabilistic automata with variable memory length. Machine Learning 25(2-3), 117–149 (1996)

[Whitworth, 2005]Whitworth, B.: Polite computing. Behaviour and Information Technology 24(5), 353–363 (2005)

[Waern, 1996]Wærn, A.: Recognizing Human Plans: Issues for Plan Recognition in Human-Computer Interaction. Ph.D thesis, Royal Institute of Technology (1996)

Tell Me Where You've Lived, and I'll Tell You What You Like: Adapting Interfaces to Cultural Preferences*

Katharina Reinecke and Abraham Bernstein

Department of Informatics, University of Zurich
Binzmhlestr. 14, 8050 Zurich, Switzerland
{reinecke,bernstein}@ifi.uzh.ch

Abstract. Adapting user interfaces to cultural preferences has been shown to improve a user's performance, but is oftentimes foregone because of its time-consuming and costly procedure. Moreover, it is usually limited to producing one uniform user interface (UI) for each nation disregarding the intangible nature of cultural backgrounds. To overcome these problems, we exemplify a new approach with our culturally adaptive web application MOCCA, which is able to map information in a cultural user model onto adaptation rules in order to create personalized UIs. Apart from introducing the adaptation flexibility of MOCCA, the paper describes a study with 30 participants in which we compared UI preferences to MOCCA's automatically generated UIs. Results confirm that automatically predicting cultural UI preferences is possible, paving the way for low-cost cultural UI adaptations.

Keywords: Cultural User Modeling, Personalization, Localization.

1 Introduction

Today, the number of localized software and web applications underline the growing awareness that considering culture in user interface (UI) design is the key to improvements in work efficiency and user satisfaction – and thus, to customer loyalty in global marketplaces [1,2]. The design process is typically done in all conscience of the target nation(s) by conducting ethnographical analyses. However, due to this time-intensive endeavor, the manual localization of UIs has proven to be prohibitively expensive. If software manufacturers are willing to invest this money, another problem remains: the problem of assigning one interface to a whole nation. In today's globalized world, it is highly contradictory to restrict culture to country borders. In fact, although a person's culture is certainly influenced by his or her country of residence, other aspects such as former stays in other countries, the parents' nationality, or religion also strongly impact the dynamic nature of cultural background [3].

In this paper we propose to address this problem by an automated customization of the UI, using a rule base to transform a user's cultural model into a personalized UI. In order to reduce the time needed for the initial information acquisition, we show how a small number of initial questions are already enough to predict user preferences and provide a suitable first adaptation of the UI. To illustrate this approach, we have developed

* This work was partly supported by research fellowship no. 53511101 of the University of Zurich, and research grant no. 2322 of Hasler Foundation.

G.-J. Houben et al. (Eds.): UMAP 2009, LNCS 5535, pp. 185–196, 2009.

MOCCA, an application that can adapt ten different aspects of its UI (not counting language) with 39'366 combination possibilities altogether. In addition to presenting the technical implementation of the flexible interface generation, this paper also evaluates MOCCA's core functionality: the adaptation rules that are responsible for the resulting UIs.

In the following, we shortly present related work and its limitations before explaining the basics of our approach. Next, we introduce our test application MOCCA, detailing on its adaptation possibilities with visible effects for the user, and the technical processes in the back-end. We then discuss our experiment, following with a discussion of the results and their general implications for other culturally adaptive systems.

2 Related Work

Many studies have shown that localization increases user satisfaction and work efficiency; however, many researchers have acknowledged that it is not sufficient for culturally ambiguous users in our globalizing world [4]. While there have been attempts on cultural user modeling - mostly confined to the area of international e-learning applications [5] - the major problem of groundbreaking research in this area seems to be the classification of culture: How can we define culture in order to derive culturally-based preferences for UIs? Hofstede was one of the first researchers to develop a cultural classification with the five dimensions Masculinity (MAS), Uncertainty Avoidance (UAI), Power Distance (PDI), Individualism (IDV), and Long Term Orientation (LTO) [6]. Although often criticized for theorizing culture as a national concept [7], his classification has been successfully applied to the field of Human-Computer Interaction (HCI) [8]. According to Hofstede, who originally developed the dimensions for international business communication, the dimension *Uncertainty Avoidance*, for example, reveals the extent of which people are willing to deal with uncertain and unstructured situations. In the field of HCI, different studies have demonstrated that it also relates to whether users like a non-linear navigation, or prefer consistent applications [2,4,8]. Likewise, all of Hofstede's dimensions have been mapped to certain aspects of UIs [9,10,11], and his dimensions have been proven useful for predictive purposes [12]. Apart from the need for an applicable classification of culture, an approach to cultural adaptivity also requires extremely flexible UIs. So far, adaptive systems have been mostly developed for different types of learners [13], disabilities [14,15], or know-how [16,17,18]; however, none of these approaches cater for all the needs of users with different cultural backgrounds, such as a versatile positioning of UI elements, varying degrees of colorfulness, or different levels of guidance.

3 Procedure for Cultural Adaptivity

We propose to overcome the problems of manually localized UIs by automatically adapting them to a user's cultural background. For first-time users, an application inquires about the user's current and former residences, as well as about the respective durations. For each of these countries, the application retrieves the dimensions from a cultural user model ontology. Since previous user model ontologies were mostly domain-specific and did not include cultural information, we developed the Cultural User Model Ontology *CUMO* [19], which contains information such as different places of residence, the parents' nationality, languages spoken, or religion. Furthermore, CUMO contains information about Hofstede's five dimensions and their values [6]. However, the scores assigned to a user and his cultural dimensions are not static to everybody residing in the same country, and thus, do not resemble a "national culture", as suggested by Hofstede [6]. Instead, we take into account all places of residence and calculate their influence on the user's dimensions according to the duration of the user's stay at those places [12]:

$$influenceOfCountry_N = \frac{monthlyDurationOfStayInCountryN}{ageInMonths} \qquad (1)$$

Retrieving Hofstede's values ($countryScore_H$) for the relevant countries from CUMO, we are able to calculate the user's new dimensions with a weighted average:

$$userDimScore_H = \sum_{i=1}^{N} countryScore_H * influenceOfCountry_i \qquad (2)$$

(where H is Hofstede's dimension 1 to 5; N the number of countries the user has lived in, and $countryScore_i$ is the Hofstede score for the respective country.)

The $userDimScore_H$s are further discretized into low, medium, and high according to their distance to the world average scores stored in CUMO. Each adaptable aspect of the application now has a set of rules that associate the user's classification with a UI directive influencing the application's interface. Thus, after obtaining the user's cultural classification from CUMO, the application can look up the corresponding adaptation rules and apply them.

After these first predictions on the user's preferences, we offer two refinement possibilities: (1) The user can manually provide more information about his cultural background, and (2) the application tracks the user interaction, such as mouse movements and clicks. From both, we are able to derive refining adaptations. For example, if the user hovers the mouse pointer over a certain area without clicking for a certain time, we infer that she needs support on which actions to perform next.

4   MOCCA: A Culturally Adaptive To-Do Tool

We have developed a culturally adaptive web application called MOCCA, which is a web-based to-do list tool that allows users to manage their tasks online. Its goal is to automatically adapt to the cultural preferences of its users. This *user-specific adaptation* is in contrast to the country-specific adaptation of usual localized applications. But how flexible does MOCCA really need to be? What interaction elements need to be adaptable? To answer these question, we looked at the influence of culture on UI perception, compiled a list of general *adaptation guidelines*, and evaluated them in a survey [12]. According to these adaptation guidelines, various UI aspects need to be adaptable to users' cultural backgrounds, the most obvious being date and time formats, language, and the reading direction. These evident aspects are easily changed: the reading direction, for example, 'only' requires to re-align text and elements (such as the navigation) to the left or to the right. However, it is also said to impact the visual attention on the UI [20]. Thus, elements that cannot be arranged centrally but still need the user's attention should be placed in the lower left corner (for right-to-left readers), or in the lower right corner (for left-to-right readers). Consequently, MOCCA offers full alignment of all interface elements to the left or to the right (as shown in Figures 1(a) and 1(b)).

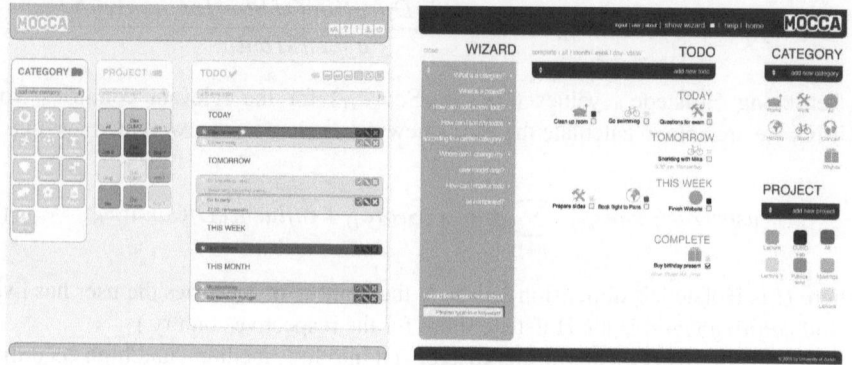

(a) MOCCA with left-alignment, flat navigation, and color-coded to-dos with high structuring

(b) MOCCA with right-alignment, high information density, flat navigation, and an adaptive wizard

Fig. 1. Example interfaces for MOCCA

Cultural differences in perception also necessitate other adaptations that are oftentimes too subtle to be included in conventional localization. For example, in a neural fMRI study Gutchess et al. found that Western cultures attend to individual objects more than people from Asia who usually concentrate on object correlations [21]. Their findings coincide with our adaptation guidelines, which suggest to highly structure objects for users with a high score for the dimension Long Term Orientation. Hence, MOCCA offers different levels of content structuring by spatializing objects and color-coding elements that belong together (see Figure 1).

Even more subtle differences in perception are concealed in Hofstede's interpretation of culture. Many researchers have concentrated on the influence of his cultural dimensions on HCI and found that a low score in the dimension Uncertainty Avoidance, for example, suggests a strong preference for a high information density. High Individualism, in contrast, indicates that the user favors color-coordinated interfaces with fewer gadgets, such as blinking animations, whereas a high Power Distance Index relates to the requirement for a higher level of support [12]. Accordingly, MOCCA has to be able to include an easier navigation with more buttons (Figure 1(a)), or intensify user support with a wizard (1(b)), to name a few.

Summarizing, MOCCA has to be extremely flexible in the composition of different UI elements - more flexible, than required for previous adaptive systems (cf. Related Work). In the following, we therefore discuss how we implemented this flexibility in MOCCA and introduce the most important adaptation rules.

4.1   Technical Details and Adaptation Rules

In order to fulfill the requirements, MOCCA has to be sufficiently flexible to allow the exchange of each UI element with alternative placements. To model the 'space' of possible solutions, the different compositions of UI elements, their dependencies among each other, their types (e.g. navigation or header), and their representations (for different scores in a certain dimension) were modeled in an application-specific *adaptation ontology*, which defines the adaptable parts of the UI.

MOCCA considers nine aspects of the interface, each of which can be adapted to either a low, medium, or high score of the dimension they are associated with (see Table 1). In addition, it can adapt itself to the users reading direction (i.e., left-to-right or right-to-left) resulting in a total of $3^9 * 2 = 39'366$ possible combinations of UI elements. As an example, consider a user with a cultural background of high Uncertainty Avoidance and a right-to-left writing direction (e.g., as applicable to some people in Japan). For such a user MOCCA would trigger the rule if (UAI = high) then show wizard associated with the interface aspect 'Support' (number 8 in Table 1), resulting in a UI

Table 1. Adaptable Interface Aspects

No.	Interface aspect:	Effects:	Linked with dimension
1	Information Density	Amount of information visible at first sight, level of hierarchy in the information representation.	Long Term Orientation (LTO)
2	Navigation	Structures the navigation in a range from nested menu items such as in a tree, to a flat navigation.	Power Distance (PDI)
3	Workflow I	Presence and accessibility of functions, e.g. whether buttons are always visible or can be activated on mouse-over.	Power Distance (PDI)
4	Workflow II	Integration of functions with the interface, e.g. whether other items are still accessible or the user is forced to concentrate on the current operation.	Uncertainty Avoidance (UAI)
5	Structure	Different levels of structure for the interface, e.g. grouped information, accentuated affiliations.	Individualism (IDV)
6	Colorfulness	Influences whether the user interface presentation uses many different colors or is rather homogeneously colored.	Individualism (IDV)
7	Brightness & Contrast	Saturation and contrast of colors, e.g. complementary colors.	Masculinity (MAS)
8	Support	Amount of on-site support the user receives, e.g., wizards versus tool tips.	Uncertainty Avoidance (UAI)
9	Help text	Error messages and general help, e.g. strict or friendly instructions.	Power Distance (PDI)
10	Alignment	Alignment of all interface elements to the user's reading direction.	Reading Direction

akin to the one shown in Figure 1(b). In the case of a low Uncertainty Avoidance and low Individualism the wizard would not be shown and the rule `if (IDV = low) then color-code to-dos` would result in an interface comparable to Figure 2(d).

In order to place the elements, MOCCA relies on placement information in the adaptation ontology, which includes the preferred precise location, preferred general area (in case of conflict), extent of the element, priority, and association with the cultural dimension for each UI element. All elements have to be dynamically composed into a grid layout. MOCCA first retrieves all possible interface elements from the adaptation ontology. For each UI aspect it then chooses the most appropriate element comparing the user's cultural preference stored in CUMO with the ones of the elements stored in the adaptation ontology. Next, all elements are tentatively placed in their preferred location on a temporary UI grid. In case two elements are associated with the same or overlapping locations, the priority tag in the adaptation ontology decides which element takes precedence and which one needs to be moved. The elements are then placed according to the free locations within their preferred general area. The result of this operation is a non-overlapping two dimensional layout of the culturally appropriate UI elements, which MOCCA then generates as an AJAX UI.

Apart from the dynamic placement of suitable UI elements, MOCCA has further adaptation possibilities with an overall effect on all elements, such as color schemes, languages, or left/right alignment. The choice of these *meta elements* is made on the basis of their categorized instances in the adaptation ontology with the same procedure that has been described for the UI elements.

5   Experiment

We have conducted an experiment on the adaptations in MOCCA comparing a user's interface choices to MOCCA's automatically generated UI. Thus, the experiment evaluated the adaptation rules (our *predictions*).

5.1   Method

Participants. 30 participants (mean = 28.7 y, sd = 3.9 y, 7 female) from the local university campus took part, all had high computer literacy, and university education. The majority had lived in > 2 countries (mean # = 2.5), 22 were non-Swiss nationals, but had lived in Switzerland for at least 9 months (avg. 3.4 y, sd = 4.3 y). Only 3 of 8 Swiss participants had always lived in Switzerland and/or did not have foreign parents.

Apparatus. The experiment was carried out using paper-based UI mock-ups in shades of gray, so that participants were able to choose their preferred layout without the complexity and limitations of a UI design tool. The gray-scale UI elements prevented influencing the participants' preferences by the chosen colors – which is often a decisive aspect of UI acceptance and preference. Each participant was presented with a paper computer screen and the different UI elements. Participants were able to see all three UI representations for each task at once and arrange them freely.

Procedure. Participants were asked to put themselves into the position of a UI designer, and reflect on their own experiences with UIs. They were encouraged to think aloud throughout the test, take their time to choose between the elements, as well as further ask questions for clarification. Throughout the test, we recorded what participants were saying to be able to retrace the train of thought for their choices. The experimenter then explained the application purpose, and its main aspects. The experiment consisted of eight tasks (one for each interface aspect), the participant chose between three interface elements each. Prior to each task, we briefly explained the differences of the three choices, complying to a precise description to keep the explanation consistent and neutral. Participants then had to place the chosen element within an outline of the MOCCA interface. The tasks were presented in the same order, however, we counterbalanced the presentation of the different choices of UI elements between participants. All arrangements of the UI were photographed. Participants also filled out a short questionnaire about age and gender, current and former residences, durations in years and months, and nationality of parents. A small incentive was given for time.

Hypotheses. (1) Hofstede's dimensions can be used as a basis for predicting UI preferences of culturally ambiguous users; (2) certain dimensions (see Table 1) yield a better prediction rate for particular interface aspects than others; (3) the majority of incorrect predictions deviate by only 1 (instead of 2).

Test Design and Analysis. We used a within-subjects design with the following factors and levels: (1) *Cultural Background:* 5 dimensions x 3 subdivisions each (low, medium, high). (2) *General User Details:* age, gender, computer literacy, (3) *Interface elements:* eight elements with three options each, (4) *Participants:* 30.

For comparing the choice (= our dependent measures) of a UI element for each task by the user and the system, we first entered the information from the questionnaire into MOCCA and its user modeling component, receiving a classification of his cultural background into low, medium, or high for each of the five dimensions. We subsequently simulated MOCCA's adaptations by looking up the corresponding adaptation rule and the resulting UI. The participants' choices (with a range of three *low, medium, high* according to the allocation of the interface element representation in the adaptation ontology) were then compared to the adaptation rules. The probability of guessing the participant's choice was $p = 1/3$. An example: if MOCCA calculated the participant's Uncertainty Avoidance Index to be high, but this participant chose the UI element assigned to the category low, we noted a deviation of 2 (=the maximum deviation). Experimentally, we tested three of our eight interface aspects on two dimensions in order to find out whether other cultural dimensions might be more suitable to predict preferences for certain interface aspects: Task 1 (Information Density) and task 3 (Workflow I) were additionally assigned to the dimension Uncertainty Avoidance, and task 8 (Support) to the dimension Power Distance.

Adjustment of Data. We excluded task no. 5 from analysis after the majority of participants made a choice contradictory to their oral statements. After inquiring about the reason for their choice afterwards, most participants stated that the design of the version assigned to a low PDI was slightly confusing. In fact, most people who had a low PDI actually chose the opposite version. Overall, the version for high PDIs was preferred by 14 participants, which was different to the fairly even distribution of choices we achieved testing other interface aspects. After this adjustment, the following section reports on data of 7 tasks performed by 30 participants, adding up to 210 choices altogether.

5.2 Results and Discussion

MOCCA's adaptation rules accurately predicted the users' preferences for all seven tasks at the significance level of at least 5% ($\chi^2 = 44.08, 7.6, 9.89, 15.38, 3.92, 5.61, 3.92$; $p = 3.14e^{-11}, .006, .002, 8.80e^{-5}, .048, .018, .048$; $d.f = 1$). We achieved an average deviation of .46 over all dimensions and tasks. The number of correct predictions lay between 15 and 27 (mean = 18, sd = 4.23) with a correct prediction rate of 60.95 %. The number of false predictions with a deviation of 1 lay between 2 and 15 (mean = 9.1, sd = 4.07), and the false predictions with a deviation of 2 ranged from 0 to 6 (mean = 2, sd = 2.23). Table 2 shows a summary of the prediction results relating to the percentages of correct predictions, and ones with a deviation of 1 or 2. While we are not so much concerned about the prediction errors with a deviation of 1, the 6.67 % cases with a deviation of 2 are indeed critical. In practice, offering such an interface to users with opposing preferences without any alternatives could mean that these users refrain from using the application. It confirms the need for intervention possibilities that allow the user to choose alternatives in case of a not suitable initial adaptation.

Distribution of Choices. Participants' choices were almost evenly distributed over the three interface options: elements assigned to a low score were chosen 72 times, the ones for a normal score 76 times, and the elements for a high score 62 times. Thus, participants went for the "extremes" in 134 cases out of the 210 choices ($\approx 64\%$). The distribution of the users' scores for each cultural dimension related to this phenomenon.

Prediction of User Interface Aspects. In the following, we describe the most remarkable results for each UI aspect separately (cf. Table 2):

The *information density* proved to be very well-predictable with the dimension Long Term Orientation. For 90 % of all participants we were able to anticipate the correct choice. As shown in Figure 2(c), for example, participant 27 chose a UI with a high information density (color-coded to-dos with symbols) and a low level of hierarchy in

Table 2. Summary of the results (in %)

Interface aspect	Tested with dimension:	Correct Predictions	Deviation of 1	Deviation of 2
Information Hierarchy	LTO	90	6.67	3.33
Navigation	PDI	56.67	36.67	6.67
Workflow I	PDI	60	40	0
Workflow II	UAI	66.67	30	3.33
Colorfulness	IDV	50	36.67	13.33
Brightness & Contrast	MAS	53.33	26.67	20
Support	UAI	50	50	0
Average		60.95	32.38	6.67

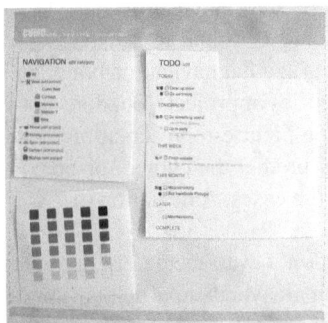

(a) The UI as chosen by Participant 3 (PDI = low, IDV = high, MAS = high, UAI = normal, LTO = low).

(b) MOCCA's UI for Participant 3.

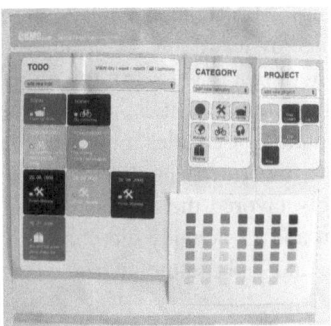

(c) The UI as chosen by Participant 27 (PDI = high, IDV = low, MAS = high, UAI = low, LTO = high).

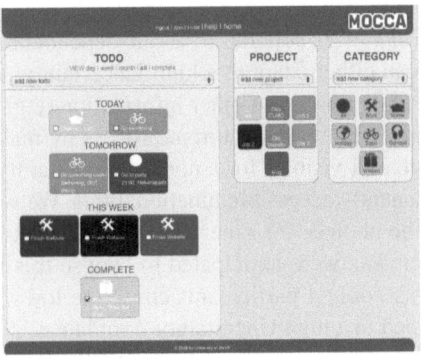

(d) MOCCA's UI for Participant 27.

Fig. 2. The self-built interface and the interface generated by MOCCA for two different participants

information presentation (permanently visible notes). MOCCA was able to correctly predict this choice (Figure 2(d)). In contrast, participant 3 chose the UI designed for normal Long Term Orientation (Figure 2(a)), which shows less information at first sight by being less encoded with colors and symbols (Figure 2(b)). MOCCA, however, was not able to correctly predict her choice basing its prediction on a low Long Term Orientation with scarce to-dos and unfolding notes (Figure 2(b)). Nonetheless, a comparison of the two pictures shows that the deviation of 1 in the cultural dimension had only a small effect on the overall UI design. Altogether, a deviation of 1 occurred in 6.67 % of the cases. For 3.33 % of all participants, MOCCA provided for a low information density (as shown in Figure 2(b)), whereas the participant showed a preference for the opposite, a high information density as in Figure 2(d). We did not find any cases where participants preferred a low information density although predicted to favor the opposite.

We provided three *navigation choices*: (1) A tree navigation as shown in Figure 2(b) allows to nest categories and projects and is bound to a list view of the to-dos in order to be able to sort this list accordingly; (2) a flat navigation bound to a list view of the to-dos restricts users to clicking on categories or projects, but does not allow nested sorting; and (3) a flat navigation bound to the picture-representation of to-dos, as shown in Figure 2(d). We were able to correctly predict the choice for 56.67 % of participants, and had a deviation of 1 in 36.67 % of the cases. A deviation of 2 was rare with 6.67 %.

The accessibility of functions for the task *Workflow I* was accurately predicted for 60 % of the participants. Thus, we were able to anticipate whether participants preferred a "hidden" accessibility of functionalities, reaching them only on mouse-over (for a low PDI), or a constant accessibility, with two differing degrees of information density (for a normal and a high PDI). For 40 % of the participants we failed the correct prediction with a deviation of 1; however, none of the participants chose the interface variant deviating from our prediction completely (0 % with a deviation of 2).

Workflow II adhered to a self-dependent handling of procedures: MOCCA's interface can either adapt to a high Uncertainty Avoidance by leading users through a process while obscuring other information (e.g. when adding a new to-do), force the user to concentrate on the current process by making other functionalities inaccessible (although still visible) for a normal Uncertainty Avoidance, or enables more freedom by permanently accessible functionalities. We were able to correctly predict 66.67 %. Unlike the choices for other tasks, participants strongly favored the normal version (20 participants were anticipated to choose this version and 17 actually did choose it). In contrast, only 4 participants chose the low version, and 7 chose the interface element assigned to a high Uncertainty Avoidance.

Tasks 5 and 6 (*Colorfulness* and *Brightness & Contrast*) were expected to strongly related to each other: Participants who chose a colorful interface (low Individualism) were thought to prefer bright colors (high Masculinity). Likewise, the choice of an interface with matching colors (high Individualism) was expected to implicate the choice of a pastel-colored interface with less contrast (low Masculinity). However, 14 participants chose either low/low, or high/high; hence the poor result for these two aspects.

MOCCA provides *support* from short tool-tips (low Uncertainty Avoidance), a more comprehensive help-on-demand after hovering the mouse over different question marks on the UI, to an extensive wizard. To our surprise, all five users who we had expected to choose the wizard because of their high Uncertainty Avoidance Score, instead chose the normal version and rejected the wizard. At this point, it might be important to consider the level of computer literacy, as well as the level of difficulty of the application into the design of the adaptation rules. However, although all users had a high computer literacy and had used to-do applications previously, only five participants chose the tool-tip designed for users with a low Uncertainty Avoidance Score. Instead, the majority (20 participants) preferred the more comprehensive help-on-demand. The high number tending to the middle variant of support explains why we had 0 % with a deviation of 2, but 50 % with a deviation of 1.

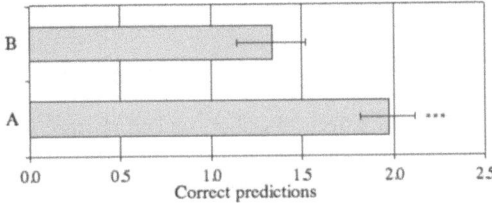

Fig. 3. Predictions based on the initial dimensions (A) result in significantly (***, $p < 1e - 7$) more correct predictions than using alternative dimensions (B) for three interface aspects

Suitability of Alternative Dimensions for Prediction. Certain aspects of the UI could not be clearly linked to one dimension only, as their effect on UI performance is partly ambiguous. We therefore replaced the dimensions responsible for triggering the UI elements for three different tasks. Task 3 and 5 (Workflow I and Support) were newly predicted with the dimension Uncertainty Avoidance (instead of LTO and PDI), and task 8 was newly predicted with the Power Distance Index (instead of UAI). The dimensions that were initially linked to certain interface aspects in the adaptation rules were demonstrated to be more suitable for prediction (t-test, $p < 1e - 7$) than the same test with alternative dimensions (see Figure 3 where column A refers to the initial dimensions as listed in table 1 and column B is the result for the alternative dimensions). This further reinforces hypothesis 2 in that the dimensions incorporated in our adaptation rules effect the assigned aspects of the UI, and that the result of our prediction cannot be reproduced by randomly choosing alternative dimensions.

6   Conclusion and Future Work

In the age of a global software industry the cultural differences in UI preferences become increasingly important. We have introduced a new approach to convert knowledge about a user's cultural background into predictions of UI preferences. We exemplified our approach in the test application MOCCA, which is able to adapt the user interaction to the user's cultural background. In addition, this paper succinctly discussed the interaction between the application-independent cultural user model ontology, the adaptation rules, and the application-specific adaptation ontology.

In order to substantiate the approach, we conducted an evaluation with 30 participants of different cultural backgrounds, demonstrating a high significance in accurately predicting UI preferences ($\chi^2_{(1,N=30)}$, $0.05 < p > 3.14e^{-11}$ across all 7 task). With that, we showed that an automated generation of suitable UIs for different cultural preferences is feasible, providing a basis for future approaches to cultural adaptivity. Our future work includes usability evaluations of MOCCA in different countries in order to assess whether its adaptations actually result in an increased work efficiency. We plan to evaluate both the initial UI, as well as the ongoing adaptations that result from the continuous prediction, detection, and correction of mistakes of the initial adaptation with the help of the user interaction tracking.

References

1. Sheppard, C., Scholtz, J.: The Effects of Cultural Markers on Web Site Use. In: CHI 1999. ACM Press, New York (1999)
2. Ford, G., Gelderblom, H.: The Effects of Culture on Performance Achieved through the use of Human Computer Interaction. In: SAICSIT 2003, pp. 218–230 (2003)
3. Rhoads, K.: The Culture Variable in the Influence Equation. In: The Public Diplomacy Handbook (2008)
4. Kamentz, E., Womser-Hacker, C.: Defining Culture-Bound User Characteristics as a Starting-Point for the Design of Adaptive Learning Systems. Journal of Universal Computer Science 7(9) (2003)
5. Kamentz, E., Mandl, T.: Culture and E-Learning: Automatic Detection of a Users' Culture from Survey Data. In: IWIPS 2003, pp. 227–240 (2003)
6. Hofstede, G.: Culture's Consequences: Comparing Values, Behaviours and Organisations Across Nations. Sage Publications Inc., Thousand Oaks (2003)
7. McSweeney, B.: Hofstede's Model of National Cultural Differences and Their Consequences. Human Relations 55(1), 89–118 (2002)
8. Baumgartner, V.: A Practical Set of Cultural Dimensions for Global User-Interface Analysis and Design. Diploma Thesis, Fachhochschule Joanneum (2003)
9. Marcus, A., Gould, E.: Cultural Dimensions and Global Web Design: What? So What? Now What? In: CHI 2000. ACM Press, New York (2000)
10. Dormann, C., Chisalita, C.: Cultural Values in Web Site Design (2002), http://www.cs.vu.nl/~martijn/gta/docs/Hofstede-dormann.pdf
11. Hodemacher, D., et al.: Kultur und Web-Design: Ein empirischer Vergleich zwischen Grossbritannien und Deutschland. In: Mensch & Computer 2005 (2005)
12. Reinecke, K., Bernstein, A.: Predicting User Interface Preferences of Culturally Ambiguous Users. In: CHI 2008. ACM Digital Library, New York (2008)
13. Henze, N.: Personalization Services for e-Learning in the Semantic Web. In: Workshop on Adaptive Systems for Web-Based Education (2005)
14. Stephanidis, C., et al.: Adaptable and Adaptive User Interfaces for Disabled Users in the AVANTI project. In: 5th Int. Conf. on IS&N. Springer, Heidelberg (1998)
15. Gajos, K., Wobbrock, J., Weld, D.: Improving the Performance of Motor-Impaired Users with Automatically-Generated, Ability-Based Interfaces. In: CHI 2008. ACM Press, New York (2008)
16. Shneiderman, B.: Promoting Universal Usability with Multi-Layer Interface Design. In: CUU 2003, pp. 1–8. ACM Press, New York (2003)
17. Schmidt, K., et al.: On Enriching Ajax with Semantics: The Web Personalization Use Case. In: Franconi, E., Kifer, M., May, W. (eds.) ESWC 2007. LNCS, vol. 4519, pp. 686–700. Springer, Heidelberg (2007)
18. Hurst, A., Hudson, S., Mankoff, J.: Dynamic Detection of Novice vs. Skilled Use Without a Task Model. In: CHI 2007. ACM Press, New York (2007)
19. Reinecke, K., Reif, G., Bernstein, A.: Cultural User Modeling With CUMO: An Approach to Overcome the Personalization Bootstrapping Problem. In: Workshop on Cultural Heritage on the Semantic Web, ISWC (2007)
20. Bergen, B., Chan, T.: Writing Direction Influences Spatial Cognition. In: 27th Annual Conference of the Cognitive Science Society (2005)
21. Gutchess, A., Welsh, R., Boduroglu, A., Park, D.: Cultural Differences in Neural Function Associated with Object Processing. Cognitive, Affective, and Behavioral Neuroscience 6(2), 102–109 (2006)

Non-intrusive Personalisation
of the Museum Experience

Fabian Bohnert and Ingrid Zukerman

Faculty of Information Technology, Monash University
Clayton, VIC 3800, Australia
{fabian.bohnert,ingrid.zukerman}@infotech.monash.edu.au

Abstract. The vast amount of information presented in museums is often over-whelming to a visitor, making it difficult to select personally interesting exhibits. Advances in mobile computing and user modelling have made possible technology that can assist a visitor in this selection process. Such a technology can (1) utilise non-intrusive observations of a visitor's behaviour in the physical space to learn a model of his/her interests, and (2) generate personalised exhibit recommendations based on interest predictions. Due to the physicality of the domain, datasets of visitors' behaviour (i. e., visitor pathways) are difficult to obtain prior to deploying mobile technology in a museum. However, they are necessary to assess different modelling techniques. This paper reports on a methodology that we used to conduct a manual data collection, and describes the dataset we obtained. We also present two collaborative models for predicting a visitor's viewing times of unseen exhibits from his/her viewing times at visited exhibits (viewing time is indicative of interest), and evaluate our models with the dataset we collected. Both models achieve a higher predictive accuracy than a non-personalised baseline.

1 Introduction

Cultural heritage spaces such as museums offer a vast amount of information. However, a visitor's receptivity and time are typically limited, posing the challenge of selecting personally interesting exhibits to view within the available time. Advances in mobile computing and user modelling provide the opportunity to assist a visitor in this selection process — by means of personalised mobile technology. Such a technology can (1) utilise non-intrusive observations of a visitor's behaviour in the physical space to learn a model of his/her interests, and (2) generate personalised exhibit recommendations based on interest predictions. The physicality of the domain poses practical challenges for developing predictive user models. For example, datasets of visitors' behaviour in the museum (i. e., visitor pathways) are difficult to obtain prior to deploying mobile technology (e. g., positioning technology).

In this paper, we describe a computer-supported methodology that we used to manually collect a dataset of visitor pathways in Melbourne Museum (Melbourne, Australia), and the dataset we obtained. We then present two collaborative models for predicting a visitor's viewing times of unseen exhibits from his/her viewing times at visited exhibits:

G.-J. Houben et al. (Eds.): UMAP 2009, LNCS 5535, pp. 197–209, 2009.

(1) a memory-based nearest-neighbour collaborative filter, and (2) a model-based approach utilising the theory of Gaussian spatial processes. Our models were evaluated with the dataset we collected, by comparing their predictive accuracy with that of a non-personalised baseline. Both models attain a higher predictive accuracy than the baseline, with our spatial process model outperforming the nearest-neighbour collaborative filter.

The paper is organised as follows. In Section 2, we outline related research. Section 3 describes our methodology for collecting visitor pathways in a physical museum and the dataset we obtained, followed by Section 4 where we discuss our models for predicting a visitor's viewing times. Section 5 summarises the results of our evaluation, and in Section 6, we discuss ways to utilise our predictive models in a personalised museum handheld guide. We conclude in Section 7.

2   Related Research

Personalised guide systems in physical domains have often employed adaptable user models, which require visitors to explicitly state their interests in some form. For example, the *GUIDE* project [1] developed a handheld tourist guide for visitors to the city of Lancaster, UK. It employed a user model obtained from explicit user input to generate a dynamic and user-adapted city tour, where the order of the visited items could be varied. In the museum domain, the *CHIP* project [2] investigates how Semantic Web techniques can be used to provide personalised access to digital museum collections both online and in the physical museum, based on explicitly initialised user models.

Less attention has been paid to predicting preferences from non-intrusive observations, and to utilising adaptive user models that do not require explicit user input. In the museum domain, adaptive user models have usually been updated from a user's interactions with the system, with a focus on adapting content presentation, rather than predicting and recommending exhibits to be viewed. For example, *HyperAudio* [3] dynamically adapted the presented content and hyperlinks to stereotypical assumptions about a user, and to what a user has already accessed and seems interested in. The augmented audio reality system for museums *ec(h)o* [4] treated user interests in a dynamic manner, and adapted its user model on the basis of a user's interactions with the system. The collected user modelling data were used to deliver personalised information associated with exhibits via audio display. The *PEACH* project [5] developed a multimedia handheld guide which adapts its user model on the basis of both explicit visitor feedback and implicit observations of a visitor's interactions with the device. This user model was then used to generate personalised multimedia presentations.

These systems, like most systems in the museum domain, rely on knowledge-based user models in some way, and hence, require an explicit, a-priori engineered representation of the domain knowledge. In contrast, our research investigates non-intrusive statistical user modelling and recommendation techniques that do not require such an explicit domain knowledge representation [6].

3   Data Collection and Dataset

This section describes our methodology for collecting a dataset of visitor pathways (Section 3.1), and the dataset we obtained (Section 3.2).

(a) Melbourne Museum – Ground level   (b) Melbourne Museum – Upper level

Fig. 1. Visitor pathway visualised on a site map of Melbourne Museum

3.1 Data Collection Methodology

The GECKO project endeavours to develop user modelling techniques which rely on non-intrusive observations of users' behaviour in physical spaces [7]. Developing such non-intrusive user modelling and personalisation techniques for museums requires datasets about visitor behaviour in the physical museum space (i. e., visitor pathways). Datasets that are suitable for the development phase can be obtained by manually tracking museum visitors. Such a data collection methodology is clearly inappropriate for model deployment, but it facilitates model development by eschewing issues related to technology selection and instrumentation accuracy.

In the museum domain, traditional manual tracking methodologies include using printed site maps and a stopwatch to record visitors' pathways and the time spent at various exhibits [8]. However, depending on the required level of detail and frequency of events, such logging techniques can overwhelm a tracker, potentially yielding tracking errors. Additionally, they require a substantial transcription effort to digitise the data. This motivated us to develop a computer-supported methodology for recording museum visitors' time-annotated pathways. Hence, in the framework of the GECKO project, we developed two Java-based tools for manual tracking and visualisation of datasets, GECKO*tracker* and GECKO*visualiser* respectively.

– GECKO*tracker* is a clickable interface showing a digitised site map of the physical space encoded in the *Scalable Vector Graphics (SVG)* file format. GECKO*tracker* resides on portable computers carried by (human) trackers — one tracker follows one museum visitor at a time. When following a visitor, a tracker logs the visitor's position by clicking on the map, while the computer clock delivers the time. A 'viewing event' is registered when the tracker clicks on an exhibit. Figure 1 depicts the site map for Melbourne Museum, together with one of the visitor pathways we collected.

– GECKO*visualiser* is used for post-collection visualisation and analysis of the gathered data. It supports different views of the data (e. g., showing a pathway or the distribution of viewing times) in two linked formats: visualisation on the site map (Figure 1) and textual log. GECKO*visualiser* was used to gain a better understanding of our dataset, and to correct obvious mistakes made by our trackers.

Museums such as Melbourne Museum display thousands of exhibits distributed over many separate galleries and exhibitions. However, normally visitors do not require recommendations to travel between individual, logically related exhibits in close physical proximity. Rather, they may prefer recommendations regarding physically separate areas. In order to gather data for assessing predictive models that support appropriate recommendations, we grouped Melbourne Museum's individual exhibits into semantically coherent and spatially confined *exhibit areas*. This task, which was performed with the assistance of museum staff, yielded 126 exhibit areas.

GECKO*tracker* was used by 16 trackers in total, comprising university students and museum staff. Feedback from trackers and other museum staff indicates that they value our software. The trackers particularly liked the software's ease of operation. Feedback regarding the digital maps of the museum indicates that our maps encode sufficient information for the trackers to correctly identify exhibit areas — a key requirement for accurate tracking. Feedback from participants shows that most visitors did not feel disturbed by a tracker following them through the museum. In fact, some participants stated that quite early into their visit, they forgot that they were being tracked (despite being approached at the start of the visit to obtain their approval).

3.2   Dataset

Using GECKO*tracker*, we recorded the pathways of over 170 visitors to Melbourne Museum from April to June 2008. We restricted ourselves to tracking first-time adult visitors travelling on their own, to ensure that neither prior knowledge about the museum nor other visitors' interests influenced a visitor's decisions about which exhibits to view. Prior to the data collection, we briefed our trackers on the usage of the tracking tool, the layout of the museum, and its digital representation on the site map. Additionally, we clarified what should be considered a viewing event. After the data collection, the visitor pathways were post-processed using GECKO*visualiser*. For instance, we removed mis-clicks reflecting viewing events that could not have possibly occurred, e. g., visitor transitions from one end of the museum to the other and back within a few seconds, or transitions outside the museum walls and back. We also removed incomplete visitor pathways, e. g., due to a laptop running out of battery, or a visitor leaving unexpectedly. The resulting dataset comprises 158 complete visitor pathways in the form of time-annotated sequences of visited exhibit areas, with a total visit length of 291:22:37 hours, and a total viewing time of 240:00:28 hours. The dataset also contains demographic information about the visitors, which was obtained by means of post-visit interviews conducted by our trackers. In total, we obtained 8327 viewing durations at

Table 1. Dataset statistics

	Mean	Stddev	Min	Max
Visit length (hrs)	1:50:39	0:47:54	0:28:23	4:42:12
Viewing time (hrs)	1:31:09	0:42:05	0:14:09	4:08:27
Exhibit areas / visitor	52.70	20.69	16	103
Visitors / exhibit area	66.09	25.36	6	117

the 126 exhibit areas, yielding an average of 52.7 exhibit areas per visitor (41.8% of the exhibit areas). Hence, on average 58.2% of the exhibit areas were not viewed by a visitor. This indicates that there is potential for pointing a visitor to relevant but unvisited exhibit areas. Table 1 summarises further statistics of the dataset.

Clearly, the deployment of non-intrusive personalised visitor support in a museum requires suitable positioning technology to track visitors, and models to infer visitors' interests. Although our dataset was obtained manually, it provides information that is of the same type as information inferable from sensing data. Additionally, the results obtained from experiments with this dataset are essential for model development, as they provide an upper bound for the predictive performance of our models.

4   Viewing Time Prediction from Non-intrusive Observations

In an information-seeking context, people usually spend more time on relevant information than on irrelevant information, as viewing time correlates positively with preference and interest [9]. Hence, viewing time can be used as an indirect measure of interest. We propose to use log viewing time (instead of raw viewing time), due to the following reasons. When examining our dataset (Section 3.2), we found the distributions of viewing times at exhibits to be positively skewed (we use the terms 'exhibit' and 'exhibit area' synonymously in the remainder of this paper). Thus, the usual assumption of a Gaussian model did not seem appropriate. To select a more appropriate family of probability distributions, we used the *Bayesian Information Criterion (BIC)*. We tested exponential, gamma, normal, log-normal and Weibull distributions. The log-normal family fitted best, with respect to both number of best fits and average BIC score (averaged over all exhibits). By transforming all viewing times to their log-equivalent, we obtained normally distributed data. This transformation fits well with the idea that for high viewing times, an increase in viewing time indicates a smaller increase in the modelled interest than a similar increase in the context of low viewing times.

In this section, we propose two models for predicting a visitor's (log) viewing times from non-intrusive observations of his/her (log) viewing times at visited exhibits: a memory-based nearest-neighbour collaborative filter [10] (Section 4.1), and a model-based approach based on the theory of Gaussian spatial processes [11] (Section 4.2).

4.1   Nearest-Neighbour Collaborative Filter

Our *Collaborative Filter Model (CFM)* for predicting a visitor's viewing times of unseen exhibits is a nearest-neighbour collaborative filter [10]. The predictive model is built by first collecting all observed log viewing times into a matrix of size $m \times n$, where m is the cardinality of the set V of all visitors, and n is the cardinality of the set I of all exhibits (we use $v \in V$ to denote a visitor, and $i \in I$ to denote an exhibit). To ensure that varying exhibit complexity does not affect the similarity computation for selecting the nearest neighbours (viewing time increases with exhibit complexity), we then normalise all these values by calculating exhibit-wise z-scores. That is, we normalise the log viewing time of a visitor for an exhibit by subtracting its log viewing time mean $\bar{r}_{\cdot i}$ and dividing by its standard deviation σ_i. The resultant normalised log viewing times r_{vi}, which are stored in a matrix R of size $m \times n$, may be regarded as implicit ratings given by visitors to exhibits.

We calculate $\tilde{r}_{ai}$, a personalised prediction of a current visitor a's unobserved (normalised log) viewing time r_{ai}, from the values in R as follows (we unnormalise afterwards to obtain a log viewing time):

$$\tilde{r}_{ai} = \bar{r}_{a\cdot} + \frac{\sum_{v \in N(a,i)} s_{av}\left(r_{vi} - \bar{r}_{v\cdot}\right)}{\sum_{v \in N(a,i)} |s_{av}|}, \tag{1}$$

where $\bar{r}_{a\cdot}$ denotes the current visitor a's average normalised log viewing time, $N(a,i)$ is the set of nearest neighbours, and s_{av} is the similarity between visitors a and v (calculated using Pearson's correlation coefficient on the normalised log viewing times of visitors a and v). The set of nearest neighbours $N(a,i)$ for the current visitor a and exhibit i is constructed by (1) calculating s_{av} for all visitors v who viewed exhibit i, and (2) selecting the visitors most similar to current visitor a — those for whom $|s_{av}|$, the absolute similarity to visitor a, is above a certain threshold. When calculating $\tilde{r}_{ai}$, we use a weighted mean of deviations from each neighbour's average normalised log viewing duration $\bar{r}_{v\cdot}$ in order to neutralise viewing behaviour differences between visitors. This weighted mean is then added to the current visitor's average normalised log viewing time $\bar{r}_{a\cdot}$. Our experiments suggest that these calculations should be performed only after enough evidence has been gathered for obtaining a good estimate of $\bar{r}_{a\cdot}$. In our case, this happens after 20 observations. Prior to that, we estimate r_{ai} using only a (personalised) similarity-weighted mean of the r_{vi}s.

Whenever a similarity-weighted personalised prediction is not possible (e. g., when the set of nearest neighbours is empty), we estimate r_{ai} using an unweighted average of the deviations from the neighbours' (normalised log viewing time) means [10]:

$$\tilde{r}_{\cdot i}^a = \bar{r}_{a\cdot} + \frac{\sum_{v \in N(\cdot,i)} \left(r_{vi} - \bar{r}_{v\cdot}\right)}{|N(\cdot,i)|},$$

where $N(\cdot,i)$ denotes the set of visitors who viewed exhibit i. As above, we use a simple (non-personalised) mean of the r_{vi}s for less than 20 observations in visitor a's profile.

We added further modifications from the literature to improve *CFM*'s performance. For instance, we use *significance weighting* [10] to decrease the influence of nearest neighbours whose similarity value is computed from a small number of co-viewed exhibits. We also employ *shrinkage to the mean* [12], which has been shown to often improve statistical estimation, whenever we compute a personalised prediction of r_{ai} (replacing Equation 1):

$$\hat{r}_{ai} = \tilde{r}_{\cdot i}^a + \omega \left(\tilde{r}_{ai} - \tilde{r}_{\cdot i}^a\right), \tag{2}$$

where $\omega \in [0,1]$ is chosen such that an error measure of choice is minimised. We use the *mean absolute error (MAE)* (Section 5.1).

4.2 Gaussian Spatial Process Model

Spatial statistics is concerned with the analysis and prediction of geographic data [11]. Utilising spatial processes, the field deals with tasks such as modelling the associations between observations made at certain locations, and predicting values at locations where no observations have been made. The assumption made for spatial processes, that correlation between observations increases with decreasing site distance, fits well with our scenario, where viewing times are usually more correlated the more related exhibits are. Hence, by introducing a notion of spatial distance between exhibits to functionally specify this correlation structure, we can use spatial process models for predicting viewing times. We use $s_1, \ldots, s_n$ to denote the locations of exhibits $i, j \in I = \{1, \ldots, n\}$ in a space providing such a distance measure, i.e., $\|s_i - s_j\|$. This distance measure can be easily obtained for the museum domain. That is, museums are carefully themed by curatorial staff, such that closely-related exhibits are in physical proximity. Based on this observation, we hypothesise that physical walking distance between exhibits is inversely proportional to their (content) similarity. Thus, we use physical walking distance as our distance measure between exhibits. Specifically, our SVG file-based representation of the museum (Section 3.1) was used to calculate the walking distances by mapping the site map onto a graph structure which preserves the physical layout of the museum (i.e., preventing paths from passing through walls or ceilings). We normalised the resulting distances to the interval $[0, 1]$.

Typically, for a visitor $v \in V$, we have viewing times for only a subset of I, say for n_v exhibits. Denoting a visitor's log viewing time vector with r_v, we collect all observed log viewing times into a vector $r = (r_1, \ldots, r_m)$ of dimension $\sum_{v=1}^{m} n_v$.[1] Associated with each exhibit i is a log viewing time mean $\bar{r}_{\cdot i}$ and a standard deviation σ_i. Let $\mu = (\bar{r}_{\cdot 1}, \ldots, \bar{r}_{\cdot n})$ be the vector of mean log viewing times, and $\sigma = (\sigma_1, \ldots, \sigma_n)$ the vector of standard deviations. Furthermore, μ_v and σ_v are the vectors of means and standard deviations respectively for only those exhibits viewed by a visitor v. For example, if visitor 1 viewed exhibits 2, 3, 7 and 9, then $\mu_1 = (\bar{r}_{\cdot 2}, \bar{r}_{\cdot 3}, \bar{r}_{\cdot 7}, \bar{r}_{\cdot 9})$ and $\sigma_1 = (\sigma_2, \sigma_3, \sigma_7, \sigma_9)$.

Similarly to spatial processes, our *Spatial Process Model (SPM)* assumes a special correlation structure between the viewing times of different exhibits. In our experiments, we use a powered exponential [11]:

$$\rho(\|s_i - s_j\|; \phi, \nu) = \exp\left(-(\phi\|s_i - s_j\|)^\nu\right),$$

where $\phi > 0$ and $0 < \nu < 2$. That is, $\rho(\|s_i - s_j\|; \phi, \nu)$ models the correlation between the log viewing times of exhibits i and j. Let $H(\phi, \nu)$ be a correlation matrix with components $(H(\phi, \nu))_{ij} = \rho(\|s_i - s_j\|; \phi, \nu)$ collecting all these correlations, and let $H_v(\phi, \nu)$ denote a visitor v's correlation matrix (dimension $n_v \times n_v$). That is, $H_v(\phi, \nu)$ corresponds to $H(\phi, \nu)$ having removed those rows and columns that correspond to unvisited exhibits. Also, let $\theta = (\mu, \sigma, \tau^2, \phi, \nu)$ be a vector collecting the $2n + 3$ model parameters, where τ^2 denotes the variance of non-spatial error terms necessary to fully specify the model (they model non-spatial variation in the data).

---

[1] The information in r is the unnormalised equivalent of the information in R (Section 4.1).

Then, modelling the data using Gaussian spatial processes (a detailed derivation appears in [13]), r given θ is multivariate normal of dimension $\sum_{v=1}^{m} n_v$. As the viewing times of different visitors $v = 1, \ldots, m$ are independent, the model simplifies to

$$r_v \mid \theta \sim \mathcal{N}(\mu_v, \Sigma_v) \text{ for all } v = 1, \ldots, m, \tag{3}$$

where $\Sigma_v = \sigma_v 1_{n_v} H_v(\phi, \nu) \sigma_v 1_{n_v} + \tau^2 1_{n_v}$ is a visitor v's covariance matrix, and 1_{n_v} is the identity matrix of dimension $n_v \times n_v$.

Given the model parameters $\theta = (\mu, \sigma, \tau^2, \phi, \nu)$, our model is fully specified. We employ Bayesian inference using SPM's likelihood function derived from Equation 3 to estimate θ from r (in particular, we use *slice Gibbs sampling* [14]). This solution offers attractive advantages over the classic frequentist approach, such as the opportunity of incorporating prior knowledge into parameter estimation via the prior distribution, and capturing the uncertainty about the parameters via the posterior distribution.

We can now use multivariate normal theory to predict a current visitor a's log viewing times of unseen exhibits, say $r_{a,1}$, from a vector of observed viewing times $r_{a,2}$. This is because $(r_{a,1}, r_{a,2}) \mid \theta$ is normally distributed (similarly to Equation 3). If we use the following notation

$$\begin{bmatrix} r_{a,1} \\ r_{a,2} \end{bmatrix} \mid \theta \sim \mathcal{N} \left(\begin{bmatrix} \mu_{a,1} \\ \mu_{a,2} \end{bmatrix}, \begin{bmatrix} \Sigma_{a,11} & \Sigma_{a,12} \\ \Sigma_{a,12}^T & \Sigma_{a,22} \end{bmatrix} \right),$$

then the conditional distribution $p(r_{a,1} \mid r_{a,2}, \theta)$ is normal with mean vector and covariance matrix

$$\begin{aligned} \hat{r}_{a,1} &= \mathbb{E}(r_{a,1} \mid r_{a,2}, \theta) = \mu_{a,1} + \Sigma_{a,12} \Sigma_{a,22}^{-1} (r_{a,2} - \mu_{a,2}), \\ \text{Cov}(r_{a,1} \mid r_{a,2}, \theta) &= \Sigma_{a,11} - \Sigma_{a,12} \Sigma_{a,22}^{-1} \Sigma_{a,12}^T, \end{aligned} \tag{4}$$

where $\hat{r}_{a,1} = \mathbb{E}(r_{a,1} \mid r_{a,2}, \theta)$ represents a personalised prediction of the log viewing times $r_{a,1}$. Additionally, a measure of confidence in this prediction can be derived from $\text{Cov}(r_{a,1} \mid r_{a,2}, \theta)$, e. g., by using the variances on the diagonal of this matrix.

Being a model-based approach, SPM offers advantages over memory-based techniques such as CFM. For instance, the model parameters $\theta = (\mu, \sigma, \tau^2, \phi, \nu)$ have a clear interpretation, and the confidence measure provided by the model supports an informed interpretation of the model's predictions. Additionally, recommendation generation is sped up by uncoupling the model-fitting phase from the prediction phase.

5 Evaluation

We describe the experimental setup in Section 5.1, and discuss our results in Section 5.2.

5.1 Experimental Setup

We used the dataset discussed in Section 3.2 to evaluate the predictive performance of our models CFM and SPM (Section 4). For our experiments, we ignored travel time between exhibits, and collapsed multiple viewing events of one exhibit into one event.

Due to the relatively small size of our dataset, we used leave-one-out cross validation. That is, for each visitor, we trained the models with the data from 157 of the 158 visit trajectories, and used the withheld visit pathway for testing. For *CFM*, we evaluated several thousand parameterisations (e. g., varying the maximum number of nearest neighbours and the shrinkage weight ω), and used the best-performing one for our final experiments. As mentioned above, *SPM*'s model parameters θ were estimated from the training data using slice Gibbs sampling [14]. For *CFM*, we computed predictions of a visitor's log viewing times of unseen exhibits from the (normalised) log viewing times of the nearest neighbours (Equation 2). For *SPM*, log viewing times were predicted by conditioning a multivariate normal distribution (Equation 4), using the parameter estimates for θ to instantiate the model. In addition to *CFM* and *SPM*, we implemented a baseline *Mean Model (MM)* which predicts the log viewing time of an exhibit i to be its (non-personalised) mean log viewing time $\bar{r}_{.i}$.

We performed three types of experiments: *Individual Exhibit*, *Progressive Visit* and *Recommendation Potential*.

- **Individual Exhibit (IE).** *IE* evaluates predictive performance for a single exhibit. For each observed visitor-exhibit pair (v, i), we removed the log viewing time r_{vi} from the vector of the visitor's log viewing durations, and computed a prediction $\hat{r}_{vi}$ from the other observations. This experiment is lenient in the sense that all available observations except the observation for exhibit i are kept in a visitor's viewing duration vector.
- **Progressive Visit (PV).** *PV* evaluates performance as a museum visit progresses, i. e., as the number of viewed exhibits increases. For each visitor, we started with an empty visit, and iteratively added each viewed exhibit to the visit history, together with its log viewing time. We then predicted the log viewing times of all yet unvisited exhibits.
- **Recommendation Potential (RP).** *RP* assesses the recommendation potential of our models, i. e., it gives an indication as to whether our models can discover unvisited but personally interesting exhibits. We predicted the log viewing times of all unvisited exhibits for each visitor, given his/her complete visit history. We then counted the predicted log viewing durations that were significantly above the corresponding exhibit's average log viewing time $\bar{r}_{.i}$. For this purpose, we used the 95% credible interval around $\bar{r}_{.i}$.

For the first two experiments, we used the *mean absolute error (MAE)* to measure predictive accuracy as follows:

$$\text{MAE} = \frac{1}{\sum_{v \in V} |I_v|} \sum_{v \in V} \sum_{i \in I_v} |r_{vi} - \hat{r}_{vi}|,$$

where I_v denotes a visitor v's set of exhibits for which predictions were computed. For *IE*, we calculated the total MAE for all visitors and all exhibits; and for *PV*, we computed the MAE across the yet unvisited exhibits for all visitors for each time fraction of a visit (to account for different visit lengths, we normalised all visits to a length of 1).

Figure 2 shows a plot of the relationship between the shrinkage weight ω and the MAE for *CFM*. To obtain the plot, we used the best-performing *CFM* parameterisation

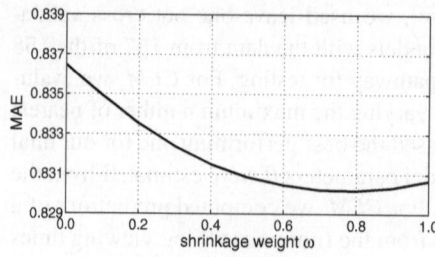
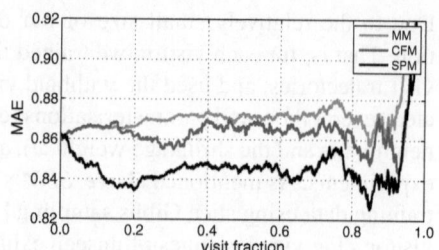

Fig. 2. *CFM* performance
(shrinkage weight vs. MAE)

Fig. 3. Model performance
for the *PV* experiment (MAE)

and varied ω over $[0, 1]$. For each ω, we averaged the MAEs obtained for the *IE* and *PV* experiments. The mimimum MAE is achieved for $\omega \approx 0.75$. This value of ω was used in our comparative evaluations.

5.2   Results

For the *IE* experiment, *CFM* outperforms *MM*, achieving an MAE of 0.7868 (stderr 0.0068). *SPM* outperforms both *MM* and *CFM*, achieving an MAE of 0.7548 (stderr 0.0066). The performance differences are statistically significant with $p \ll 0.01$ (upper portion of Table 2, column 'log t MAE').

Computing MAEs with respect to log viewing times penalises errors for higher viewing times less than errors for lower viewing times, which is reasonable in our context. To illustrate the meaning of our results in terms of raw viewing times, we give a few exhibit-specific MAEs (calculated as for the *IE* experiment, but on raw viewing times). The lower portion of Table 2 shows these values for five exhibit areas A to E, which were selected on the basis of the variability of their viewing times and locations in Melbourne Museum (marked in Figure 1). The first column in Table 2 designates the exhibit area, the second and third column the mean and standard deviation of the distribution of viewing times for this area (in seconds) respectively (we used the parameters of the fitted log-normal models to compute estimates of the means and standard deviations), and the last column shows the MAE with respect to log viewing times. In addition, for each exhibit area, we split the data at the median of the fitted log-normal model, separating low and high viewing times. We then computed the MAEs for each half separately (fourth and fifth columns). As expected, the MAEs for the lower half are smaller than the MAEs for the upper half. For instance, *CFM* achieves an MAE of 52.6 seconds for the low viewing times at area C (29.7% of the mean), and 118.7 seconds for the high viewing times (67.1% of the mean). For *CFM*, the average MAE (when averaged over the five exhibits) as a percentage of mean exhibit viewing time is 26.2% for the lower half, and 66.4% for the upper half. In contrast, *SPM* achieves 23.9% and 63.0% respectively.

The performance of *SPM*, *CFM* and the baseline *MM* for the *PV* experiment is depicted in Figure 3. *CFM* outperforms *MM* slightly (statistically significantly for visit fractions 0.191 to 0.374 and for several shorter intervals later on, $p < 0.05$). There is a significant improvement in performance for *SPM*, compared to both *MM* and *CFM*

Table 2. Model performance for the *IE* experiment (MAE)

Exhibit area	Viewing time Mean Stddev			lowerMAE Mean (Stderr)	upperMAE Mean (Stderr)	log *t* MAE Mean (Stderr)
Total *MM*						0.8618 (0.0071)
Total *CFM*						0.7868 (0.0068)
Total *SPM*						0.7548 (0.0066)
Area A	220	246	*CFM*	60.8 (6.3)	119.1 (12.4)	0.6024 (0.0492)
			SPM	53.2 (5.8)	111.4 (11.5)	0.5513 (0.0463)
Area B	115	156	*CFM*	29.8 (4.0)	84.4 (11.1)	0.6844 (0.0590)
			SPM	26.9 (3.7)	76.4 (10.7)	0.6245 (0.0588)
Area C	177	240	*CFM*	52.6 (6.5)	118.7 (19.2)	0.7038 (0.0587)
			SPM	42.8 (5.4)	110.7 (18.0)	0.6308 (0.0531)
Area D	87	149	*CFM*	20.7 (2.7)	64.9 (11.3)	0.8066 (0.0733)
			SPM	20.6 (3.3)	60.6 (10.7)	0.7588 (0.0719)
Area E	75	125	*CFM*	18.1 (3.5)	47.0 (10.8)	0.7896 (0.1118)
			SPM	18.1 (3.5)	49.3 (10.1)	0.7921 (0.1047)

(statistically significant for visit fractions 0.019 to 0.922, $p < 0.05$). Drawing attention to the initial portion of the visits, *SPM*'s MAE decreases rapidly, whereas the MAE for *MM* and *CFM* remains at a higher level. Generally, the faster a model adapts to a visitor's interests, the more likely it is to quickly deliver personally useful recommendations. Such behaviour in the early stages of a museum visit is essential in order to build trust in the system's recommendations, and to guide a visitor in a phase of his/her visit where such guidance is most likely needed. As expected, *MM* performs at a relatively constant MAE level. For *CFM* and *SPM*, we expected to see a relative improvement in performance as the number of visited exhibits increases. However, this trend is rather subtle. Additionally, for all three models, there is a performance drop towards the end of a visit. We postulate that these phenomena may be explained, at least partially, by the increased influence of outliers on the MAE as the number of exhibits remaining to be viewed is reduced with the progression of a visit. This influence in turn offsets potential gains in performance obtained from additional observations. Our hypothesis is supported by a widening in the standard error bands for all models as a visit progresses, in particular towards the end (not shown in Figure 3 for clarity of presentation).

For the *RP* experiment, we obtained the following results. Per visitor (on average), *CFM* discovers 29.3 exhibits with predicted viewing times that are significantly higher than the average. This corresponds to 37.0% of the predictions per visitor (on average). In comparison, *SPM* predicts 23.6 such exhibits (30.1% of the predictions). These numbers indicate that our models discover exhibits which visitors appear to be interested in but did not view. As *SPM* significantly outperforms *CFM* with respect to predictive accuracy, *SPM*'s percentage is most likely a more realistic estimate of the true potential of our models with respect to visitor support. A more conclusive interpretation requires a further, more rigorous investigation.

6   Discussion

Recommender systems have often been employed in virtual (i. e., non-physical) domains, where personalised recommendations are directly derived from predicted ratings, e. g., by recommending the items with the highest ratings. In contrast, in a physical domain, the transition from predicting a visitor's interests to recommendation generation is not trivial, as we do not want to recommend exhibits that visitors are going to see anyway. We suggest the following approach to address this problem. Firstly, use the predictions generated by interest-based predictive models (Section 4) to build a list of areas in the museum that a visitor is likely to be interested in, e. g., by determining whether a predicted interest is significantly higher than the (non-personalised) average interest. Secondly, form a list of exhibits from a location-based prediction of a visitor's pathway through the physical museum [7]. Then, after merging the lists appropriately, one can recommend exhibits that a visitor may be interested in but is likely to overlook. This approach requires a strategy for merging the lists, e. g., whether locations that a visitor is likely to visit anyway should be included (to help build trust in the system) or excluded (to avoid over-communication). The modality of the presentation, e. g., visualised on a site map or provided in textual or audio form, should be taken into account when selecting the exhibits to be recommended.

7   Conclusions and Future Work

In this paper, we proposed a computer-supported methodology that we used to collect pathways of visitors to Melbourne Museum. We presented two collaborative models for predicting a visitor's viewing times of unseen exhibits from his/her viewing times at visited exhibits — a memory-based nearest-neighbour collaborative filter (called *CFM*), and a model-based approach utilising the theory of Gaussian spatial processes (called *SPM*). Our models were evaluated with the dataset we collected. Our results show that both models attain a higher predictive accuracy than a non-personalised baseline, with *SPM* outperforming the other models. Additionally, in the realistic *Progressive Visit* setting, *SPM* rapidly adapts to observed visitor behaviour, addressing the *new-user problem* of collaborative approaches.

In the future, we intend to investigate ways of hybridising *SPM* by incorporating content-based exhibit features into our distance measure. We also plan to combine our models with a model that predicts a visitor's pathway (i. e., a sequence of exhibits), and develop strategies for delivering useful personalised recommendations about exhibits.

Acknowledgements. This research was supported in part by grant DP0770931 from the Australian Research Council. The authors thank Carolyn Meehan and her team from Museum Victoria for fruitful discussions and their support; and David Abramson, Jeff Tan and Blair Bethwaite for their assistance with using their computer cluster.

References

1. Cheverst, K., Mitchell, K., Davies, N.: The role of adaptive hypermedia in a context-aware tourist guide. Communications of the ACM 45(5), 47–51 (2002)
2. Aroyo, L., Stash, N., Wang, Y., Gorgels, P., Rutledge, L.: CHIP demonstrator: Semantics-driven recommendations and museum tour generation. In: Aberer, K., Choi, K.-S., Noy, N., Allemang, D., Lee, K.-I., Nixon, L., Golbeck, J., Mika, P., Maynard, D., Mizoguchi, R., Schreiber, G., Cudré-Mauroux, P. (eds.) ASWC 2007 and ISWC 2007. LNCS, vol. 4825, pp. 879–886. Springer, Heidelberg (2007)
3. Petrelli, D., Not, E.: User-centred design of flexible hypermedia for a mobile guide: Reflections on the HyperAudio experience. User Modeling and User-Adapted Interaction 15(3-4), 303–338 (2005)
4. Hatala, M., Wakkary, R.: Ontology-based user modeling in an augmented audio reality system for museums. User Modeling and User-Adapted Interaction 15(3-4), 339–380 (2005)
5. Stock, O., Zancanaro, M., Busetta, P., Callaway, C., Krüger, A., Kruppa, M., Kuflik, T., Not, E., Rocchi, C.: Adaptive, intelligent presentation of information for the museum visitor in PEACH. User Modeling and User-Adapted Interaction 18(3), 257–304 (2007)
6. Albrecht, D.W., Zukerman, I.: Special issue on statistical and probabilistic methods for user modeling. User Modeling and User-Adapted Interaction 17(1-2) (2007)
7. Bohnert, F., Zukerman, I., Berkovsky, S., Baldwin, T., Sonenberg, L.: Using interest and transition models to predict visitor locations in museums. AI Communications 21(2-3), 195–202 (2008)
8. Diamond, J.: Practical Evaluation Guide – Tools for Museums and Other Informal Educational Settings. AltaMira Press (1999)
9. Parsons, J., Ralph, P., Gallager, K.: Using viewing time to infer user preference in recommender systems. In: Proc. of the AAAI Workshop on Semantic Web Personalization (SWP 2004), pp. 52–64 (2004)
10. Herlocker, J.L., Konstan, J.A., Borchers, A., Riedl, J.T.: An algorithmic framework for performing collaborative filtering. In: Proc. of the 22th Annual Intl. ACM SIGIR Conf. on Research and Development in Information Retrieval (SIGIR 1999), pp. 230–237 (1999)
11. Banerjee, S., Carlin, B.P., Gelfand, A.E.: Hierarchical Modeling and Analysis for Spatial Data. Chapman & Hall/CRC, Boca Raton (2004)
12. James, W., Stein, C.M.: Estimation with quadratic loss. In: Proc. of the Fourth Berkeley Symp. on Mathematical Statistics and Probability, vol. 1, pp. 361–379 (1961)
13. Bohnert, F., Schmidt, D.F., Zukerman, I.: Spatial processes for recommender systems. In: Proc. of the 21st Intl. Joint Conf. on Artifical Intelligence (IJCAI 2009) (2009)
14. Neal, R.M.: Slice sampling. The Annals of Statistics 31(3), 705–767 (2003)

Assessing the Impact of Measurement Uncertainty on User Models in Spatial Domains

Daniel F. Schmidt, Ingrid Zukerman, and David W. Albrecht

Faculty of Information Technology
Monash University, Clayton 3800, Australia
{daniel.schmidt,ingrid.zukerman,david.albrecht}@infotech.monash.edu.au

Abstract. This paper examines the problem of uncertainty due to instrumentation in user modeling systems within spatial domains. We consider the uncertainty of inferring a user's trajectory within a physical space combined with the uncertainty due to inaccuracies in measuring a user's position. A framework for modeling both types of uncertainties is presented, and applied to a real-world case study from the museum domain. Our results show that this framework may be used to investigate the effects of layout in a gallery, and to explore the degradation in the predictive performance of user models due to measurement error. This information in turn may be used to guide the curation of the space, and the selection of sensing technologies prior to instrumenting the space.

1 Introduction

Advances in mobile computing and sensing technology have enabled the instrumentation of physical spaces in order to track the movements of people and model their behaviour [1,2]. Typically, these systems are implemented by equipping the space or the users with sensing technology, and applying machine learning or probabilistic techniques to build user models from logged sensor input [3,4]. In principle, this approach appears to be sound. However, in practice it may be error prone, and hence expensive, as the selected sensor technology or configuration may turn out to be inadequate for the task. Further, compared to virtual spaces, physical spaces pose additional challenges to user modeling, owing to the inaccuracies inherent in sensory observations.

In this paper, we propose a framework for investigating the impact of different sensing technologies on the predictive performance of user models *prior* to deploying a particular technology. To this effect, we simulate sensor logs of users, and compare the predictive performance of a user model derived from these logs with that of a user model derived from perfect observations. Our framework was implemented in the context of the Marine Life Exhibition at Melbourne Museum (Figure 1(a)), where the derived models were used to predict exhibits viewed by museum visitors (the perfect observations were obtained by manually recording the exhibits actually viewed by visitors [5]). These predictions will eventually be used by a recommendation system that suggests exhibits of interest.

G.-J. Houben et al. (Eds.): UMAP 2009, LNCS 5535, pp. 210–222, 2009.

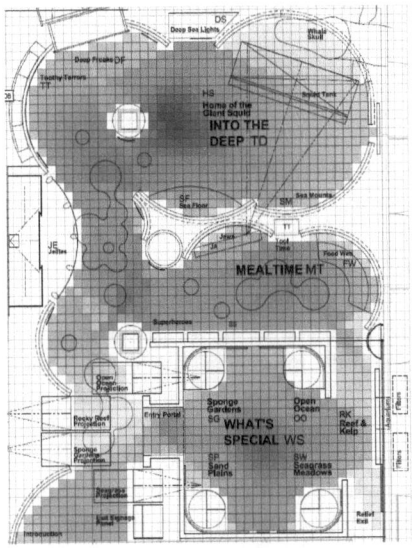

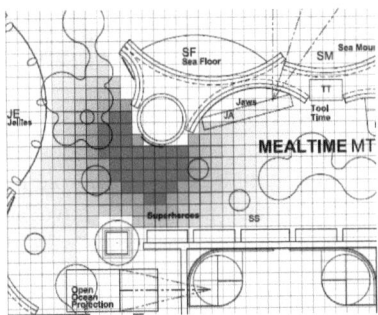

(a) Entropy mapping of the exhibition: darker colour indicates higher entropy.

(b) Probability of viewing exhibit 'Eat or be Eaten' from a square: darker colour indicates higher probability.

Fig. 1. The Marine Life Exhibit at Melbourne Museum

Our approach requires the following models: (1) a predictive user model of exhibits to be viewed, which also provides an upper bound of performance; (2) a spatial viewing model representing positions from which each exhibit can be seen; and (3) models of sensor characteristics for different types of sensors. Our predictive model is built from logs obtained by manually tracking the exhibits viewed by visitors [5]. To link this information to logs that can be obtained from sensors, we first need to infer a plausible viewing position for each exhibit; we employ the spatial viewing model to make this inference. Owing to sensor inaccuracies, a visitor's position recorded by a sensor may differ from his/her actual position. The nature and magnitude of this difference depends on the type of sensor (and even on the specific sensor). Models of sensor behaviour are needed to incorporate such distortions into the inferred position of a visitor.[1]

This paper is organized as follows. Sections 2-4 describe our three models. Section 5 describes the integration of the predictive user model and the spatial viewing model to generate synthetic pathways through the exhibition and predict viewed exhibits from positional information. The results of our evaluation are presented in Section 6, followed by concluding remarks.

---

[1] In principle, we could manually record a person's position and viewed exhibit directly. However, our experience shows that recording two separate information items at the same time places an excessive burden on human trackers, making their logs more error prone. More importantly, one of our objectives is to produce useful insights from a relatively small amount of easily recorded information.

2   Predictive User Model

There is a range of statistical models used in collaborative systems for predicting users' interests from observed behaviour, e.g., [6,7,8]. These systems have focused on making predictions in the virtual rather than the physical space. The body of work pertaining to building predictive models from sensory observations in physical spaces is more reduced, e.g., [3,4,5], with [5] being the main proponent of such models for the museum domain.

Our approach requires a user model that exhibits good predictive performance, and can be easily sampled from to generate synthetic visitors (Section 5.1). In this paper, we have adopted Bohnert *et al.*'s *Transition Model* to represent visitors' movements between exhibits in a museum [5]. This model is a stationary 1-stage Markov model, where $P_{i,j}$ approximates the probability of moving from exhibit i to exhibit j ($i, j = 1, \ldots, M$ and M is the number of exhibits). The Transition Model has a reasonable predictive performance on a homogeneous exhibition, such as Marine Life, where visitors' behaviour is mainly determined by the layout of the exhibition [5] (a hybrid model combining interest with transitions outperforms a pure Transition Model, but it includes a non-parametric component, which makes sampling more difficult).

The main issue in fitting the Transition Model is estimating the transition probabilities from the available traces. The *sparse data problem* (also known as the 'small n, large p' problem) occurs when there is a small number of data points n compared to the number of parameters p to be estimated (in our case $p = M^2$, $M = 22$ exhibits, and $n = 317$ total exhibits viewed by 44 visitors). As a result of this problem, many transitions between exhibits have zero observed counts. Hence, estimating transition probabilities using a method such as Maximum Likelihood will lead to zero transition probabilities for these transitions (even when there is no physical reason for this to happen).

To overcome the sparse data problem, we employ a Bayesian approach, where our prior distribution over the possible transition probabilities $(P_{i,1}, \ldots, P_{i,M})$ from a particular exhibit i is given by a Dirichlet distribution, $\mathrm{Dir}(\alpha_i, \ldots, \alpha_i)$ (i.e., all the parameters have been set to α_i). The posterior distribution of these transition probabilities is given by another Dirichlet distribution, $\mathrm{Dir}(n_{i,1} + \alpha_i, \ldots, n_{i,M} + \alpha_i)$, where $n_{i,j}$ is the number of times a user was observed to have moved from exhibit i to j. To estimate the probabilities $P_{i,j}$ it is common to employ the mean *a posteriori* estimates

$$\hat{P}_{i,j} = \frac{n_{i,j} + \alpha_i}{N_i + M\alpha_i} \tag{1}$$

where $N_i = \sum_{k=1}^{M} n_{i,k}$ is the total number of times visitors viewed exhibit i, and α_i can be interpreted as the number of *a priori* observed counts per exhibit.[2]

However, as Hausser and Strimmer [9] point out, there is no general agreement regarding the value of α_i. Moreover, they demonstrate that for a small n and

---

[2] α_i is often assigned a single value, in which case it is called a 'flattening constant'.

large p, in terms of Mean Square Error, a better estimate of $P_{i,j}$ is obtained by choosing the α_i for an exhibit i to be

$$\alpha_i = \frac{N_i \left(1 - \sum_{k=1}^{M} \hat{\theta}_{i,k}^2\right)}{M \left(\sum_{k=1}^{M} \hat{\theta}_{i,k}^2 + (N_i - 1) \sum_{k=1}^{M} \left(1/M - \hat{\theta}_{i,k}\right)^2 - 1\right)} \tag{2}$$

where $\hat{\theta}_{i,j} = n_{i,j}/N_i$ denotes the Maximum Likelihood estimate of the transition probability from exhibit i to exhibit j.

3   Spatial Exhibit Viewing Model

One of the most interesting and difficult aspects of instrumenting a space such as a museum is inferring abstract concepts, such as interest or intention, from measured coordinates. In the museum domain, the time a visitor spent viewing an exhibit is treated as proportional to his/her interest, and thus provides a form of implicit rating, which can then be used by a recommender system. Therefore, in order to infer interest from measurements, one must be able to infer which exhibit is being viewed by a visitor when standing in a particular place.

Our approach consists of building a probabilistic model of the viewing areas for each exhibit in the physical space. To facilitate this, we divided the physical space into a grid. The dimensions of the grid were chosen to balance level of detail with computational expense (a fine-grained grid provides a lot of detail, but its integration into a viewing model is computationally expensive). The actual grid size we chose is $61 \times 47 = 2,867$ squares, where a square is about 30cm $\times$ 30cm.

At each square we placed a multinomial distribution which represents the probability that a visitor standing at that square is observing each exhibit. Figure 1(b) illustrates this distribution for the 'Eat or be Eaten' exhibit in the Marine Life Exhibition — the darker squares indicate a higher probability of viewing the exhibit from there. We now need to specify the probability of viewing each exhibit from each square. This was done as follows. We observed visitors' behaviour in the Marine Life exhibition, and for each exhibit, marked out areas on the grid where people stood most often to view the exhibit. These high probability areas (the darkest in Figure 1(b)) were assigned an unnormalized probability of 1. The probability of the remaining areas was determined by making $G(i; x, y)$ – the unnormalized probability of viewing exhibit i from square (x, y) – proportional to the distance between square (x, y) and the closest high-probability square (x_h, y_h) as follows

$$G(i; x, y) \propto \exp\left(-\frac{(x - x_h)^2 + (y - y_h)^2}{\lambda_i}\right)$$

where λ_i is chosen to control the rate of decay. This parameter, which may differ for each exhibit, reflects how large the viewing areas are in the physical space, and must be chosen by the space modeler. Based on our observations, we chose the same λ_i (= 3) for all the exhibits $(i = 1, \ldots, M)$, as the gallery space was quite homogeneous.

Clearly, squares from which it is not physically possible to view an exhibit should have a zero probability associated with them. This is handled by simply marking the squares that correspond to walls, and setting $G(i; x, y)$ to zero if a straight line cannot be drawn from square (x, y) to any of the exhibit squares.

The final probability of viewing exhibit i from square (x, y) is estimated by normalizing over all the exhibits

$$P(i|x, y) = \frac{G(i; x, y)}{\sum_{j=1}^{M} G(j; x, y)} \tag{3}$$

An interesting use of our viewing model is for assessing the clutter in a gallery. For each square in the gallery, we have an M-state multinomial distribution over the M exhibits (i.e., a list of probabilities that a visitor standing at that square is observing each exhibit). We represent the clutter at each square by the entropy of this multinomial. Specifically, the entropy $H(\mathbf{P})$ of an M-nomial with probabilities $\mathbf{P} = (P_1, \ldots, P_M)$ is given by $H(\mathbf{P}) = -\sum_{j=1}^{M} P_j \log P_j$. $H(\mathbf{P})$ is maximized when all exhibits are equally likely to be viewed, and is minimized when one $P_j = 1$ and the rest are zero (i.e., there is no uncertainty). Figure 1(a) illustrates the entropy of each viewing square in the Marine Life Exhibition; dark shading indicates high entropy, and light shading indicates low entropy.

4   Sensor Models

The final component of the user modeling system is the sensor model. This component allows us to simulate real-life sensing technologies that are required to deploy a predictive model in a physical space. Ideally, a sensor model should be simple enough to easily integrate into a user modeling system, and also abstract enough to be able to represent a wide range of real-life sensing possibilities. A suitably abstract sensor model would allow different types of sensing technologies to be simulated by changing several parameters. Our basic model is that the measured coordinates (x', y') are a realization of a random variable whose probability distribution depends on the true location (x, y) and the type of sensor technology deployed. This distribution should be chosen to represent the behaviour of some real-life sensor technology. Below we propose models for indoor GPS, RFID tags and accelerometers. Our evaluation is based on our indoor GPS model (Section 6).

Indoor GPS or localization technologies. We adopt a simple model whereby the (x, y) coordinates are distorted by additive Gaussian noise. Under this regime, the *measured* coordinates are found by sampling from a bivariate normal distribution $N((x, y), \mathbf{C})$ with mean (x, y) and covariance $\mathbf{C}$. Usually one can assume that the accuracy is the same in all directions, and so we can make the simpler model choice $\mathbf{C} = \sigma^2 \mathbf{I}$, where $\mathbf{I}$ is the identity matrix, and σ is a constant that is chosen to reflect the expected accuracy of the device. For example, if the GPS is nominally accurate to within ν meters, and the (x, y) coordinates are measured in meters, then $\sigma = \nu/2$ would be a suitable value, as such a choice places the bulk of the probability mass within the circle defined by $x^2 + y^2 = \nu^2$.

RFID-tag arrays. An array of RFID tags positioned through the physical space can be modeled in a similar fashion to an indoor GPS. Given an array of active RFID tags, the physical space is divided into a set of (possibly overlapping) cells that are covered by the RFID tags — each cell potentially spanning several squares. When a user (wearing a passive RFID tag) moves into a cell, and the active RFID is activated, the system is aware of the user's approximate position. The uncertainty of the user's exact (x, y) position within a cell may be modeled by treating the measured (x', y') as a Gaussian distribution $N((a_k, b_k), \mathbf{C}_k)$, where (a_k, b_k) are the coordinates of the center of the cell covered by active RFID tag k, and the covariance matrix $\mathbf{C}_k$ is chosen to approximate the area of the cell. A more refined model of a user's position may be devised by treating the different cells as discrete states in a Markov model, and noting that a user's likely (x, y) position on entering a cell depends on the previous cell s/he was in (and thus, the direction from which s/he moved into the new cell). However, the Gaussian model will be insufficient to represent this extra information.

Accelerometer based sensing. The behaviour of accelerometer-based technology may be modeled as a state-space evolution of (x, y) coordinates with suitable Gaussian process noise over acceleration (rather than position, as for the previous devices). In order to model the behaviour of accelerometer-based technology, we need to simulate trajectories of users' (x, y) coordinates through the physical space. Such trajectories should include a sequence of points in the path between two consecutively visited exhibits, and the time required to traverse this path. The path may be approximated using a shortest path algorithm, and the traversal time may be approximated using average speeds of visitors and the length of the path. This information enables the calculation of acceleration vectors $(\ddot{x}, \ddot{y})_t$ at each time t along the trajectory. Thus, given a starting position $(x, y)_0$, the *measured* positions of the user (x', y') evolve over time according to the state-space equations

$$(x', y')_{t+\delta} = (x', y')_t + (\dot{x}', \dot{y}')_t \delta \tag{4}$$

$$(\dot{x}', \dot{y}')_{t+\delta} = (\dot{x}', \dot{y}')_t + (\ddot{x}', \ddot{y}')_t \delta + \varepsilon_t \tag{5}$$

where ε_t is distributed as $N((0, 0), \mathbf{C})$, and $\mathbf{C}$ is a suitable covariance matrix representing the noise due to imperfect measurement of acceleration.

A major problem with acceleration-based tracking is *measurement drift*. That is, this technology produces relative positions (in contrast with absolute positions generated by GPS and RFID tags). Hence, the noise distorting the acceleration measurements will cause the estimated positions to increasingly drift away from the truth; the longer the sequence of acceleration measurements, the bigger the expected drift. This problem may be alleviated by deploying several absolute positioning devices (e.g., RFID tags) around the space, and using them to reset a user's position when s/he moves past them.[3]

5   Integrating the User Model with the Viewing Model

The Transition Model presented in Section 2 is based on precise knowledge of the last exhibit viewed by a visitor. However, if information on the visitor's behaviour is being automatically gathered by instruments, then all that is available is a sequence of (possibly distorted) (x, y) coordinates. Assuming that there exists some criterion for detecting that a visitor is stationary (and hence viewing an exhibit), we can decompose the complete (x, y) sequence into a sub-sequence of *stationary* (x, y) coordinates (at present, we do not model 'hovering' around an exhibit). From these, we must attempt to infer which exhibit the visitor is viewing, and then employ our user model to predict which exhibit the visitor will view next on the basis of this information.

Recall that our manually gathered data consists of a sequence of viewed exhibits (rather than (x, y) coordinates). Hence, in order to make predictions from (x, y) coordinates, we must first generate positional pathways from information regarding viewed exhibits. We generate synthetic pathways, driven by the predictive user model, rather than pathways tailored to the 44 observed users. This is done to ensure that any deterioration in predictive performance can be attributed to the use of positional coordinates (instead of precise exhibits) and to sensing distortion due to instrumentation error. Synthetic users were also generated by [11] for plan-based activities in the virtual space. However, their objective was to generate new, plausible users, while ours is to filter out prediction errors made by the user model.

5.1   Generating User Pathways

We generate realistic synthetic trajectories for the Marine Life Exhibition as follows. We first use the Transition Model (Section 2) to generate a tour (ordered list) of viewed exhibits, and then apply our spatial viewing model (Section 3) to transform this list of exhibits to a sequence of plausible spatial coordinates within the physical space (these coordinates are subsequently distorted by measurement error).

Generating a tour. The Transition Model proposed in Section 2 assumes that the primary driving force behind a tour is the layout of the gallery, and that the probability that a visitor moves to an exhibit depends entirely on the last exhibit viewed. As mentioned above, this model yields reasonable predictions for

---

[3] If a Kalman filter [10] is used to estimate a user's current position from the state-space model (Equations 4 and 5), the effect of resetting a user's position to within the accuracy provided by an RFID tag may be naturally incorporated into the Kalman filtering process by setting the covariance matrix of the Kalman-filter state estimate to the covariance matrix of the RFID-tag noise model.

our dataset. Also, Markov models are easy to sample from, thus facilitating the generation of synthetic tours. Our tours begin at a (fictitious) 'start' position, with the first viewed exhibit being drawn from the possible transitions from this position; the next exhibit is drawn from the transition probabilities of the first exhibit, and so on, until a (fictitious) 'end' exhibit is drawn.

The generated tours depend on the estimates of the transition probabilities obtained in Section 2. Due to the small amount of data used to estimate the multinomial distributions that comprise the Transition Model, these estimates have a large variance. This variance is not taken into account when point estimates, such as those in Equation 1, are employed to define the multinomial distributions from which samples are drawn. To overcome this problem, we use the complete Bayesian predictive distribution to generate tours, as follows. For each exhibit i in a tour, we first sample $\phi_1, \ldots, \phi_M$ from the Dirichlet distribution $\mathrm{Dir}\,(n_{i,1} + \alpha_i, \ldots, n_{i,M} + \alpha_i)$ for the exhibit ($n_{i,j}$ and α_i are given in Section 2), and then sample the next exhibit from the multinomial distribution $\mathrm{Multi}(\phi_1, \ldots, \phi_M)$. For small samples sizes, if one was to use a point estimate to generate tours, the resulting tours would contain less variability than warranted by the data. The full predictive distribution takes this overdispersion into account, yielding tours with higher variability.

Generating User Coordinates. Once a tour of exhibits has been generated, we need to place the visitors in physical (x, y) coordinates within the gallery in a plausible fashion. We employ Bayes' theorem to produce the probability of a visitor being at square (x, y) conditioned on the fact that s/he has been viewing exhibit i, where $x = 1, \ldots, 61$ and $y = 1, \ldots, 47$ (Section 3). This yields

$$P(x, y|i) = \frac{P(i|x, y)\pi(x, y)}{\sum_x \sum_y P(i|x, y)\pi(x, y)}$$

where $P(i|(x, y)$ is obtained from Equation 3.

It remains to specify a prior distribution $\pi(\cdot)$ over the possible (x, y) positions where a visitor may be standing. Assuming a simple prior of ignorance, whereby every square is equally likely to be occupied by a visitor, we obtain

$$P(x, y|i) = \frac{P(i|x, y)}{\sum_x \sum_y P(i|x, y)} \qquad (6)$$

Now, given that a synthetic visitor is viewing exhibit i, we just need to sample from a multinomial distribution representing all the squares in the space to determine a square occupied by the visitor.

5.2   Predicting Exhibits from Positional Information

When a visitor stands in a particular location, there is some uncertainty regarding which exhibit s/he is viewing. The more exhibits are in close proximity (i.e., the more cluttered is an exhibit area), the higher the uncertainty. We consider two approaches for inferring viewed exhibits from positional information in light of this uncertainty: *Argmax* and *Weighted*.

- **Argmax** selects the most probable exhibit given the coordinates (x, y) of the user, i.e.,

$$j\text{max} = \underset{j \in \{1,...,M\}}{\arg \max} \{P(j|x,y)\} \tag{7}$$

  The Transition Model is then used to estimate the probability of the next exhibit i assuming that the current exhibit being viewed is $j\text{max}$

$$\hat{P}(i|x,y) = P_{j\text{max},i} \tag{8}$$

- **Weighted** employs the Transition Model to estimate the probability of going to the next exhibit i from each other exhibit in the gallery, and calculates a weighted average of these probabilities on the basis of the probability of viewing each exhibit from coordinates (x, y).

$$\hat{P}(i|x,y) = \sum_{j=1}^{M} \{ P(j|x,y) \times P_{j,i} \} \tag{9}$$

We expect the differences in the performance of Argmax and Weighted to be greatest when the (x, y) coordinates are in areas of high uncertainty, i.e., areas with many exhibits. When only one exhibit is feasibly viewable from a particular (x, y) coordinate, the two predictors are expected to coincide (Section 6).

6   Evaluation

We first review the data collection process, followed by a description of our experiments and the results we obtained.

6.1   Data Collection

As mentioned above, our framework was evaluated on data obtained from the Marine Life Exhibition at Melbourne Museum (Figure 1). The dataset, which was gathered manually, consists of tour traces from 44 visitors (Section 2). These traces contain an ordered list of the exhibits viewed by each visitor, and the time spent at each exhibit (which is not used in our models, but is necessary for assessing interest [5]). There are $M = 22$ exhibits in the Marine Life Exhibition, and on average, a visitor viewed 7.2 exhibits. We augmented the exhibit list with fictitious 'start' and 'end' exhibits in order to naturally incorporate an initial and final event into our predictive model.

The data for the viewing model were obtained separately from the user modeling data. This was done by observing the movements of visitors to the Marine Life Exhibition as they viewed the exhibits, and manually annotating a grid-divided map of the gallery to record their positions (Section 3).

6.2   Experimental Setup

We conducted two experiments as follows. First we evaluated the performance of our two position-based prediction models, Argmax and Weighted (Section 5.2), compared with the performance obtained by the Transition Model alone, i.e., from direct observations of the exhibits viewed. We then introduced distortions modeled by our indoor GPS sensor model (Section 4) into the position-based predictive models in order to examine the effect of sensor inaccuracy on predictive performance. For both experiments we generated 1000 synthetic tours as described in Section 5.1.

6.3   Results

Figure 2(a) shows the results obtained by the three predictive models, Argmax, Weighted and Transition Model, in terms of the average log-loss of the predictions made at each of the 22 exhibits (i.e., the negative-log of the probability with which the exhibit actually viewed next was predicted). This average, which is calculated over all the synthetic visitors, summarizes how well the predictive models perform at each exhibit. The curve is plotted in order of decreasing predictive performance of the Transition Model, and the crosses mark exhibits for which the difference between the Argmax and Weighted models is statistically significant at the 0.05 level. For the position-based models, this plot was produced on the basis of the (x, y) coordinates where each synthetic visitor 'stood' to view each exhibit in his/her tour. The predictions made by the Transition Model were obtained directly from viewed exhibits. These predictions represent an upper bound on predictive performance (lower bound on log-loss).

In general, the Weighted method outperforms the Argmax method. When Weighted does better than Argmax, as for Exhibit 19 ('Tool Time') and 21 ('Deep Freaks'), the difference is quite substantial. In contrast, when Argmax outperforms Weighted, as for exhibit 18 ('Sea Floor'), the difference is rather marginal. It is worth noting that the viewing areas for both 'Tool Time' and 'Deep Freaks' have a significant amount of overlap with the viewing areas of other exhibits, while 'Sea Floor' is quite separate from its neighbour 'Sea Mounts'. Thus, these models behave according to the expectations set out in Section 5.2.

The effect of instrumentation accuracy on predictive performance was tested with respect to indoor GPS — the instrumentation option being considered at present by Melbourne Museum. We calculated the average predictive accuracy of our models under various levels of sensor noise (the average was computed over all the exhibits in all the tours). The predictive accuracy of a model was calculated by scoring 1 if one of the top-3 most probable exhibits was viewed next, and 0 otherwise. We chose top-3 (rather than top-1) because top-1 ignores the fact that top probabilities are often quite similar in our scenario. Figure 2(b) shows the degradation in the predictive performance of the Weighted and Argmax models as a function of increasing sensor error ν (Section 4). The true prediction error baseline, which is obtained when the viewed exhibit is known, is 0.54

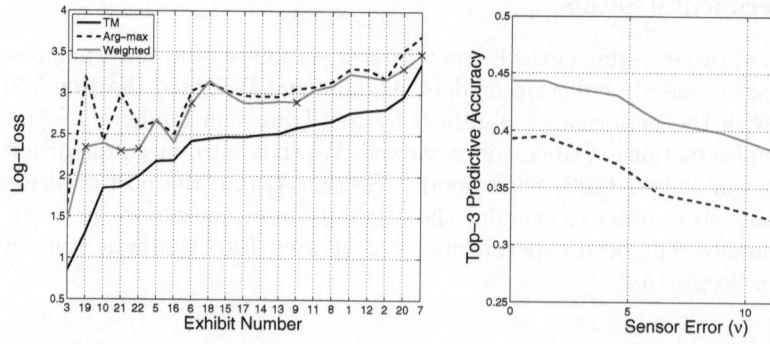

(a) Log-loss at each exhibit, plotted in decreasing order of predictive performance of the Transition Model.

(b) Degradation in predictive performance for indoor GPS for the Weighted and Argmax models.

Fig. 2. Results for the Marine Life Exhibition at Melbourne Museum

on average (0.32 for top-1 accuracy),[4] compared with 0.44 for Weighted and 0.39 for Argmax when $\nu = 0$. This drop in performance as one changes from precise observations to positional observations may be largely attributed to the clutter in the gallery (recall that error due to the predictive model has been filtered out, since this model is also used to generate the synthetic pathways). Our results show that performance degrades slowly as sensor error increases. For instance, an error of $\nu = 5$ squares (1.5 meters) results in only approximately 10% drop in performance. This indicates that a fairly inaccurate sensor technology or a fairly coarse instrumentation of the museum space may be suitable, which can significantly lower instrumentation costs. At the same time, more accurate predictive user models may be necessary to improve the baseline predictive performance, possibly in combination with a reduction in the clutter of certain exhibit areas.

7   Conclusion and Future Work

We have offered a framework for investigating the impact of sensing technologies on the predictive performance of user models in physical spaces. Our framework combines a predictive user model with a spatial viewing model to produce pathways of synthetic users from a relatively small dataset. It then incorporates simulated sensing distortions from different types of instruments. This framework was applied to a small, real-life dataset obtained from Melbourne Museum. Our results show that the Weighted position-based predictive model outperforms the Argmax model, and that the Weighted model can attain tolerable predictive performance, even in the presence of a substantial sensory distortion.

---

[4] The predictive performance of the baseline model is lower than that in [5] due to our sampling approach, which generates tours with higher variability.

There are several interesting avenues for further investigation. Firstly, we propose to implement models of the other positioning devices mentioned in Section 4, viz RFID tags and accelerometers. In addition, in order to improve the realism of our models we intend to do the following.

- Devise a more accurate spatial viewing model by considering particular restrictions of museums. For example, our model could reduce the probabilities of squares that are too close to walls or exhibits, and take into account size of exhibits (bigger exhibits are more likely to be viewed from farther away than smaller exhibits). The association of suitable attributes with exhibits will in turn enable the application of machine learning techniques to learn models of viewing areas for new exhibits.
- Combine a tour generated from a predictive user model and the (x, y) coordinates generated from the spatial model into a dynamic trajectory through the physical space (rather than just stops at particular exhibits). This requires the derivation of a path between exhibits (e.g., by using a shortest-path algorithm), and a suitable stopping criterion to determine when a visitor has paused to interact with an exhibit or is 'hovering' around the exhibit. This criterion could be based on factors such as the direction and velocity of a visitor's approach to a particular square.

Acknowledgements. This research was supported in part by a grant from the Monash Research Fund and grant DP0770931 from the Australian Research Council. The authors thank Carolyn Meehan and the staff of Melbourne Museum for their assistance in data collection and museum mapping, and Fabian Bohnert for his help with the modeling task.

References

1. Hightower, J., Borriello, G.: Location systems for ubiquitous computing. IEEE Computer 34(8), 57–66 (2001)
2. Carmichael, D.J., Kay, J., Kummerfeld, B.: Consistent modelling of users, devices and sensors in a ubiquitous computing environment. User Modeling and User-Adapted Interaction 15(3-4), 197–234 (2005)
3. Horvitz, E., Apacible, J., Sarin, R., Liao, L.: Prediction, expectation, and surprise: Methods, designs, and study of a deployed traffic forecasting service. In: UAI 2005 – Proceedings of the 21st Conference on Uncertainty in Artificial Intelligence, Edinburgh, Scotland, pp. 275–280 (2005)
4. Philipose, M., Fishkin, K.P., Perkowitz, M., Patterson, D.J., Fox, D., Kautz, H., Hahnel, D.: Inferring activities from interactions with objects. IEEE Pervasive Computing 3(4), 50–57 (2004)
5. Bohnert, F., Zukerman, I., Berkovsky, S., Baldwin, T., Sonenberg, L.: Using interest and transition models to predict visitor locations in museums. AI Communications – Special Issue on Recommender Systems 21(2-3), 195–202 (2008)
6. Resnick, P., Iacovou, N., Suchak, M., Bergstrom, P., Riedl, J.: GroupLens: An open architecture for collaborative filtering of Netnews. In: CSCW 1994 – Proc. of the 1994 ACM Conf. on Computer Supported Cooperative Work, pp. 175–186 (1994)

7. Herlocker, J.L., Konstan, J.A., Borchers, A., Riedl, J.: An algorithmic framework for performing collaborative filtering. In: SIGIR 1999 – Proceedings of the 22nd Annual International ACM SIGIR Conference on Research and Development in Information Retrieval, pp. 230–237 (1999)
8. Bell, R., Koren, Y., Volinsky, C.: Chasing $1,000,000: How we won the Netflix progress prize. ASA Statistical and Computing Graphics Newsletter 18(2), 4–12 (2007)
9. Hausser, J., Strimmer, K.: Entropy inference and the James-Stein estimator (November 2008), http://arxiv.org/abs/0811.3579
10. Gelb, A.: Applied Optimal Estimation. MIT Press, Cambridge (1974)
11. Blaylock, N., Allen, J.: Generating artificial corpora for plan recognition. In: Ardissono, L., Brna, P., Mitrović, A. (eds.) UM 2005. LNCS, vol. 3538, pp. 179–188. Springer, Heidelberg (2005)

SoNARS: A Social Networks-Based Algorithm for Social Recommender Systems

Francesca Carmagnola, Fabiana Vernero, and Pierluigi Grillo

Dipartimento di Informatica, Università di Torino
Corso Svizzera 185; 10149 Torino, Italy
{carmagnola,vernerof,grillo}@di.unito.it

Abstract. User modeling systems have been influenced by the overspread of Web 2.0 and social networks. New systems aimed at helping people finding information of interest and including "social functions" like social networks, tagging, commenting, inserting content, arose. Such systems are the so-called "social recommender systems". The idea at the base of social recommender systems is that the recommendation of content should follow user's preferences while social network just represents a group of users joined by some kind of voluntary relation and does not reflect any preference. We claim that social network is a very important source of information to profile users. Moving from theories in social psychology which describe influence dynamics among individuals, we state that joining in a network with other people exposes individuals to social dynamics which can influence their attitudes, behaviours and preferences.

We present in this paper *SoNARS*, a new algorithm for recommending content in social recommender systems. SoNARS targets users as members of social networks, suggesting items that reflect the trend of the network itself, based on its structure and on the influence relationships among users.

1   Introduction

Users are finding it increasingly difficult to locate the right information at the right time. This is known as information overload problem. Recommender systems have emerged as an important response to this problem [13,1,14]. Recommender systems form a specific type of information filtering technique that attempts to predict and present items (movies, music, books, news, images, web pages) a user may be interested in.

Typically, a recommender system compares the user's profile to some reference characteristics which may be from the information item (content-based approach) or from the user's social environment (collaborative filtering approach). Collaborative filtering is the most widely used technique for recommender systems. In such systems the generation of high-quality recommendations for a target user is facilitated by leveraging the preferences of communities of similar users. Indeed, the collaborative filtering method takes advantage of the collaborative world moving from the idea that every user contributes with her ratings to the overall performance of the system. In such systems the only relation among users which is taken into account to produce recommendations is user similarity while no attention is given to the social relations among users [15].

G.-J. Houben et al. (Eds.): UMAP 2009, LNCS 5535, pp. 223–234, 2009.
© Springer-Verlag Berlin Heidelberg 2009

From about 2001 onwards, social relations have been included in many web sites. We have assisted at a wide revolution in recommender systems user experience. Recommender systems are no longer centered only on completing a finding task or making sales. With the deployment of social networking systems and the overspread of Web 2.0 the user is no more isolated but part of a *social context* meant as a *network of users*. Besides those systems that already considered the social relations of a user through group modeling, new systems arose. These can be defined as "social recommender systems", i.e. systems aimed at helping people finding information of interest (like recommenders do) and including "social functions" like social networks, tagging, commenting, inserting content. Some social recommender systems like LastFm, Findory, Memigo, del.icio.us, Tailrank, are even more "social" since the concept of social network as a network of users is crucial and most of their functions are related with it. Hence, in social recommender systems users are proposed, on the one hand, recommended content and, on the other hand, they can browse the content of the social network, e.g. in LastFm, users can access the playlist music of the users belonging to their social network.

However, in all such systems the starting idea is that the recommendation of content is performed simply on the basis of user's preferences/interests and the social network just represents a group of users joined by some kind of voluntary relation and does not reflect any preference. In terms of recommendations, in social recommender system (see Section 2) social networks are used, at most, to suggest content on the basis of the similarity among the users partaking the social network.

On the contrary, we claim that social networks are a very important source of information to profile users. Moving from theories in social psychology which describe influence dynamics among individuals, we state that joining in a network with other people exposes individuals to social dynamics which can influence their attitudes and behaviours. Therefore we assume that individuals become interested in topics or subjects that do not necessarily match their personal preferences and tastes, but that reflect those of their social network.

We propose a Social Networks-based Algorithm, which we called SoNARS, for recommending content in social recommender systems, both content-based and collaborative filtering. SoNARS targets users as members of social networks, suggesting items that reflect not only preference/interest, like in traditional recommender systems, but also the trend of the network itself, based on its structure and on the influence relationships among users.

The paper will first position our work in the relevant literature (Section 2), and will then give an overview of the social psychology theories we have referred to define our research (Section 3). Section 4 will present the Sonars algorithm in detail. In Section 5 we describe the evaluation of the algorithm, using Facebook as test bed social system. Finally Section 6 concludes the paper and points at future research directions.

2   Related Work

Since 2006 onwards, the rise of Web 2.0 and Social Web has brought people to interact with other users, their content and tags to find information and to connect with other people. In recommender systems some works have started to merge adaptation and Web 2.0. Dourish and Chalmers [4] and Farzan and Brusilovsky [5] use social annotation to provide social navigation support; Van Setten et al. [18] suggest that tags can become part of the user profile and Carmagnola et al. [3] exploit tagging in order to infer knowledge about the user.

Besides these works, systems that accompany the recommendation of content to social networks, namely *social recommender systems*, have become very popular (e.g. Pandora[1] LastFm[2], Findory[3], Memigo[4], and Tailrank[5]). Moreover, the KeepUp recommender system [19] applies an algorithm which exploits the *implicit social networks* based on shared interests which are created as a side-effect of recommendation processes; in this approach, users can "converse" with their peers and manually adjust their neighbors' influence in determining recommendations.

However, to the authors knowledge, none of the existing social recommender systems deeply investigate the behaviour of users in social networks for recommendations. All these systems use a collaborative filtering approach, more specifically a person-to-person approach, to create for each user a social network of unknown others who nevertheless have shared tastes, and through whose preferences information can be filtered on user's behalf. Like in conventional collaborative filtering approaches, that whilst they may list "people like you", they are generally aimed towards informing the user that "people like you also liked X". Indeed, recommendations are based on user's preferences and social networks are used just to assess user's preferences based on the similarity among the user and the other members of her social network.

In other words, social networks allow users to access new interesting information but they are not considered for their influence on user interests, which appear to be "given".

The work of Granovetter [7] highlighted how social networks can serve as a source of new information to which an individual may not otherwise have access.

Based on that, Health and Motta [8], following the principle that knowing who in the social network knows what, and who is the most trustworthy source of information on that topic is often the greatest challenge in seeking information or recommendations, propose an approach for generating trust profiles for members of a user's social network, in the context of word of mouth recommendation seeking.

Differently from our approach, they focus on investigating how to exploit social networks to judge the competence and trustworthiness of people the user knows, as she has greater background knowledge of their relevant traits in a particular domain.

On the contrary, we move from social network analysis [16] and social psychology theories [17] which describe influence dynamics among individuals (Section 3) to support the idea that the mere fact of taking part into social relationships may cause individuals to modify their attitudes and behaviours. Following the the principle of *homophily* [12] we state that we are likely to have more in common with members of our social networks than with other members of the population, and more likely to like what

---

[1] www.pandora.com

[2] www.last.fm

[3] http://findory.com

[4] http://memigo.org

[5] http://tailrank.com

they like, independently by our preferences, and by the competence and trustworthiness in a particular domain of the network members.

Therefore, the algorithm we propose can be used by social recommender systems to suggest items not only on the basis of user's preference/interest, like in traditional social recommender systems, but also considering the trend of the user's social network, its structure and the influence relationships among users.

3   Social Background

Several theories in social psychology describe influence dynamics among individuals. Since we defined social networks based on social relationships, stating that such a relationship exists between individuals A and B if A performs an action which refers to or has an effect on user B [16] (e.g., A peruses B's user profile, as far as the domain of social websites is concerned), we can claim that joining in a network with other people exposes individuals to social dynamics which can influence their attitudes and behaviours. More specifically, we can therefore hypothesize that individuals become interested in topics or subjects that do not necessarily match their personal pre-existing preferences and tastes, but that reflect those of the network.

In the following, we briefly sketch three complementary theories of social influence [17] (*Social conformity* (3.1), *Social comparison* (3.2), and *Social facilitation*, (3.3)) which have been considered for the definition of our algorithm.

3.1   Social Conformity

The classical theory of social influence states that people belonging to a group usually experience a "pressure to conform", namely, they tend to change their attitudes and behaviours to match the expectations of the other members (*normative influence*). Conformity can be often limited to exterior, observable features and fail to alter the underlying principles. According to psychology literature, conformity, far from being an irrational process based on "suggestion", is a conscious and rational social dynamic aimed at allowing people to build an objective and shared vision of the world. Indeed, when they are required to make a decision or judgment, or to build a theory about some phenomenon, people take into consideration all the available information, regarding, on the one hand, their own perceptions and opinions and, on the other hand, social information coming from relevant others -that is, other members of the group.

In such a scenario, individuals who deviate from the vision advocated by the majority represent a sort of obstacle for the group to jointly achieve its goals and are therefore exposed to explicit or implicit pressure to conform; in case such pressure is not effective, they are usually excluded from the group itself.

As a consequence, people should be interested in topics which reflect the "shared vision of the world" of the groups they belong to, so that they can conform to it, at least superficially, and act as fully-integrated group members.

3.2   Social Comparison

People actively seek information about the opinions of others in order to evaluate how they compare and to correctly form their own attitudes and behaviours. In fact, after that social comparison has occurred, people usually act so that they minimize any differences they may have found. Social comparison most often occurs when people lack objective means for evaluation, being in a state of uncertainty about what they should be thinking or doing; in addition, the effects of social comparison are especially evident if people compare themselves to individuals who can be considered somehow similar to them (e.g., for their age or abilities), since these represent good comparison points.

In contrast with conformity, in social comparison processes the influenced individual plays an active role; moreover, in this case influence is not normative, but informative (*social proof*). As a consequence, people who are new to a certain context or are not expert of certain domain should be interested in topics which reflect the opinions of other individuals in their network, since these represent useful information for them to form their own attitudes.

3.3 Social Facilitation

Social facilitation occurs when people are encouraged in performing a certain target behaviour as a consequence of the physical or virtual company of other people; in other words, if they can observe others performing the same behaviour and are conscious that these people are also observing them.

In contrast with the previously exposed theories, social facilitation dynamics can influence the level of motivation, involvement, frequency and effectiveness, but do not refer to behaviours for which a certain individual had no pre-existing interest.

As a consequence, people who are interested in a certain topic, but lack strong motivation, should appreciate information showing that other people in their network share their interest, since this encourages and motivates them.

4 SoNARS: The Social Networks-Based Algorithm for Social Recommender Systems

Typically, the recommender module produces a ranked list of domain items tailored to the user preferences and interests, where such parameters can be estimated considering different approaches. More specifically, in collaborative recommenders interests and preferences are inferred on the basis of "person to person" similarity, while in content-based recommenders they are inferred on the basis of the match between the attributes of the item and the attributes of the user profile. Finally, hybrid recommenders use both user similarity and usage data [2,9].

On the contrary, the algorithm we propose exploits foremost social psychology theories (Section 3) to assess the interest of a target user x for an item to be recommended as a function i) of how much every user y in the target user's social network likes that item, *independently* of the similarity between the target user x and user y, and ii) of the strength of the relation among the target user x and user y. The idea at the basis of the algorithm is that the mere fact of taking part into social relationships may cause individuals to modify their attitudes and behaviours and they are more likely to be interested in what people belonging the their social network like, independently of their real preferences. Therefore, we consider that an item is likely to be recommended to a target user all the more another user in a deep relation with the target one in her social network likes the item.

The SoNARS algorithm takes into consideration the level of interest a certain item i has for each person y in the network of the target user x, balancing this value based on the strength of the relationship between x and y.

In particular, the total score $(Score_i)$ is computed for item i and with respect to the target user x based on the following formula:

$$Score_i = \frac{\sum_{y=1}^{|users|} (Score_{iy} * R_{xy})}{\sum_{y=1}^{|users|} R_{xy}} \quad (1)$$

The formula sums up the results of the product of $Score_{iy}$ and R_{xy}, calculated for each user y. $Score_{iy}$ is the partial score indicating the level of interest item i has for user y and is determined considering the actions user y performed with respect to item i, such as clicking, posting, tagging, bookmarking and tagging. R_{xy} is the value indicating the strength of the relationship between the target user x and user y. The total sum is then divided by the term $\sum_{y=1}^{|users|} R_{xy}$, that is the total weight of all the relationships between the target user x and each user y in her network. $\sum_{y=1}^{|users|} R_{xy}$ represents therefore the *activism level* of user x in her social network.

It is clear from the formula that such a score need not be calculated for each item, since items for which no partial score $Score_{iy}$ exists relative to some user y for whom the value R_{xy} is positive can be automatically excluded. In other words, only the items on which at least one user y actually performed some actions (e.g., clicking, posting or tagging) can be taken into consideration by the SoNARS algorithm.

Notice that the measure of $Score_i$ as above defined, can be used by social recommender systems purely or such a value can be merged with the score of the actual interest of user x on item i, based on users' similarity or by monitoring user and usage data, as discussed in Section 6.

The following sections present how we estimate i) the strength of the relationship between x and y (Section 4.1) and ii) the level of interest a certain item i has for each person y in the network of the target user x (Section 4.2).

4.1 R_{xy}

R_{xy} represents the strength of the relation among the target user x and every user y of the target user's social network.

Before describing how we assess R_{xy}, let us explain how we conceive the network of the target user. According to network analysis, networks allow to represent relationships among people, which are usually heterogeneous and may vary according to several parameters such as their content, duration and frequency [16]. Moreover, they may or may not be mutual and they may be direct as well as indirect (e.g., actors A and B are directly connected if a tie exists between them; they are indirectly connected if A has some relationship with a third actor C and C is tied to B).

A social network can be effectively represented by means of a graph G = (V, E), where V is a set of nodes, corresponding to the actors, and E is a set of arcs, corresponding to the relationships which tie a couple of actors [16].

In our analysis, networks are defined as ego-centric networks where the target user x plays the role of focal node and the other nodes represent the users in relation with x[6]. In such a network, R_{xy} is the measure of the strength of the relation among the target user x and an actor y in her network. In the graph G representing the social network, R_{xy} is the length of every arc E joining x to other nodes. The higher is R_{xy}, the shortest is the path connecting x and y. But how can we measure the strength of the relation among a couple of users in a social recommender system? Since we define social networks based on social relationships, we claim that a relation between individuals x and y exists if x performs an action which refers to or has an effect on user y. Therefore, the more actions x performs on y, the higher R_{xy} will be. Thus, R_{xy} can be calculated by counting all the actions performed by x over y. In our case-study application (Section 5), as well as in many other social websites, a user is allowed to provide users of her social network with comments, messages, tags, invitations to take part to a virtual group, and so on.

Moreover, we considered that different actions may provide different pieces of evidence about the actual strength of the relation among x and y. The weights have been assigned based on the ideas expressed by Kobsa et al. [10] and our experience with iCITY [3].

R_{xy} is measured applying the following formula:

$$R_{xy} = \frac{\sum_{i=1}^{|actions|} (count_{xy}(i) * actionWeight(i))}{\sum_{i=1}^{|actions|} actionWeight(i)} \qquad (2)$$

For each action type i, $(count_{xy}(i)$ is the total number of actions of type i performed by user x over user y and $actionWeight(i)$ is the weight of the action type i. The formula sums up the results of the product of $count_{xy}(i)$ and $actionWeight(i)$, calculated for each action type i; i ranges from 1 to $actions$ that is total number of action types we consider. Normalization is given dividing by $actionWeight(i)$ which represents the sum of the weights of all action types.

4.2 $Score_{iy}$

$Score_{iy}$ represents the level of interest a certain item i has for user y. This score is function of the actions user y performed on item i. Actions are considered in number and type, moving from the idea that actions reveal interest.

$Score_{iy}$ is derived by applying the following formula:

$$Score_{iy} = \frac{\sum_{a=1}^{actions} \frac{count(a_i)*AW(a)}{\sum_{j=1}^{items} count(a_j)}}{actions} \qquad (3)$$

---

[6] For simplicity, we consider only direct relationships between the target user and the tied actors.

where, given the item i and the user y, (a_i) is action of type h that user y can perform over item i, while $AW(ah)$ is the weight associated to an action (a) accordingly to [3]. Finally, (a_j) is the action of type h related to item j. The obtained value is then divided by $actions$, that is the total number of action types.

A distinct value $Score_{iy}$ must be calculated for each item i on which a given user y has performed at least one action. In addition, such calculations must be repeated for all users y belonging to the network of the target user x.

5   Experimental Evaluation

Starting from our assumption that users are likely to be influenced by the network they belong to, the experimental evaluation we conducted aimed at assessing SoNARS algorithm with respect to its capacity to provide users with interesting contents. To this respect, we needed to understand if the recommended contents actually reflect the structure and influence dynamics in the social network of the target user or if we missed to consider some important parameters. Moreover, we were interested in understanding how relevant network recommendations actually are for users: this would be fundamental to assign a correct weight to this kind of recommendations if the network-based part of SoNARS algorithm were to be coupled with a traditional one, in order to provide users with contents which depend both on their own interests and on network dynamics.

Subjects. We selected a group of 45 subjects (20-50 years old, 21 females and 24 males) among the users of Facebook[7], according to an availability sampling strategy. Facebook was chosen as a test-bed since it is a very popular website where we could observe real social networks. All the selected subjects were considered target users.

Procedure. The experimental procedure consisted of two main steps: first, we identified the social networks of the target users and, after that, we generated recommendations for them with SoNARS algorithm. We opted for Facebook groups as items to recommend, for two reasons. First, Facebook groups can be compared to contents to be recommended in recommender systems; second, the huge number of groups per target user (approximately 210) suggests that users are probably pursued in subscribing to a group for other reasons besides their personal interests. Groups exist for very different subjects (from politics, to sport, to fun), organizations and geographical areas and consist in pages where users can post their contributions (e.g., comments and photos). Users can subscribe to groups in order to receive updates about their activities in their Facebook home page. We thought that groups are relevant contents with respect to social network dynamics since they actually aggregate people.

Social networks were constructed by parsing the target users' personal pages in order to identify i) all the persons with whom they interacted and ii) all the actions they performed which refer to or have an effect on another user. Each action was assigned a different weight based on the ideas expressed by Kobsa [10] and our past experience with iCITY DSA [3]. In particular, we considered the actions and the weights reported in the following in order to compute the value of R_{xy} for each person belonging to the network of the target users.

---

[7] http://www.facebook.com/

Comment: Weight = 0.6
Send Message: Weight = 0.9
Tag photo: Weight = 0.5
Group invitation: Weight = 0.6
Event invitation: Weight = 0.6

The complete list of the groups a certain user subscribed to was retrieved from the home page of all the people in the network of the target users and the corresponding partial score $Score_{iy}$ was computed for each group. For simplicity, as a special case of the formula we proposed, we only considered the action of subscribing, which was assigned a weight equal to 1. The total score $Score_i$ was then calculated for each group, considering each target user and her network separately from the others. Notice thet we kept trace of the users who had subscribed to the various groups. Recommendations for each taget user were generated by sorting the corresponding groups in descending order, according to their score.

Experimental task. Recommended groups were presented to the target users by means of a web interface in the style of Facebook pages, displaying the first thirty elements in the recommendation list (see Figure 1) and clearly indicating the names of the users who had already joined the various groups. Notice that the complete list of recommended groups could be retrieved by selecting the "Show all" link, as it normally happens in Facebook when long lists of groups have to be displayed. Target users were asked to indicate the groups they would like to subscribe to.

Performance measurement. We used *precision* and *recall*, which are popular performance measures in the domain of recommender systems [9], as well as *accuracy*, commonly used in machine learning. To evaluation purposes, we considered to be actually "recommended" only the first thirty groups in the recommendation list, since these are the items with the highest values for $Score_i$, that is, those which best reflect network dynamics. "Correctly recommended" groups are the recommended groups the target user would like to subscribe to. Groups "chosen by the user" (used in computing recall) are the groups the user would like to subscribe to, independently of the fact that they were actually recommended or not. As far as accuracy is concerned, true positives are represented by the correctly recommended groups, while true negatives are represented by the groups which were neither recommended (that is, the groups which were not displayed in the first page), nor chosen by users.

Performance results. The values we obtained were 0.67 for precision, 0.5 for recall and 0.8 for accuracy. In interpreting these results, notice that all the groups we propose are recommended, since they were all selected through SoNARS algorithm, according to the actions that users belonging to the social network of the target user performed on them; however, each group is assigned a specific score which reflects its esteemed relevance. When visualizing recommendations, we sort them in descending order according to their score and display 30 groups per page, so that the first 30 groups should be the most relevant to the target user. As explained in "Performance measurement", in computing precision, recall and accuracy we only considered the groups displayed in the first page as recommended.

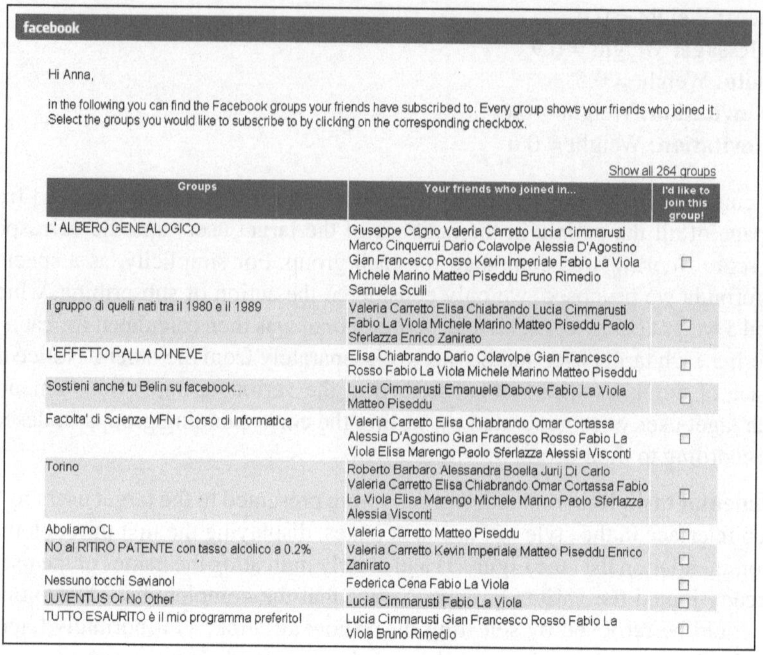

Fig. 1. The web interface used for the evaluation of SoNARS

Precision (0.67), which is probably the most interesting measure when evaluating recommending tasks, is quite satisfactory. This value suggests that network recommendations are actually interesting for users, so that they choose various groups among those displayed in the first page. Notice that the precision value could have been partially biased by the experimental task itself: as a matter of fact, users have been required to choose the Facebook groups they would like to subscribe to. This could have led users to provide *socially desiderable answers* [11], that is to choose those groups about significant and appreciable topics (like for the group "Say no to violence on children"), regardless of their social networks members subscriptions.

Accuracy (0.8) is definitely good, indicating that the algorithm tends to recommend groups that users actually choose and not to recommend groups that they do not choose. However, notice that target users selected on average 15 groups, consequently, the high value for accuracy is largely determined by the contribution of true negatives.

Notice that precision and accuracy are interdependent measures, since the number of correctly recommended groups is used to compute both. In examining the results for these measures, we must take into consideration the hypothesis that the relatively high number of correctly recommended groups is partially due to our visualization strategy, which presents the recommended groups in a prominent position. Users may have selected interesting groups in the first pages and then got tired and failed to carefully examine the whole list, therefore missing potentially interesting groups at the end.

The relatively low value for recall (0.5), which evaluates the capacity of providing a large number of correct recommendations, can be explained by the fact that the 30 recommended groups represented on average only one seventh of the complete list, which potentially contained many other relevant items (e.g., groups displayed in the second page probably had high values of $Score_i$ for most target users).

As a final remark, consider that our evaluation only considered network-based recommendations, while users' personal interests were not taken into account.

6   Conclusion and Future Work

The paper has proposed a new Social Networks-based Algorithm, called SoNARS, for recommending content in social recommender systems, both content-based and collaborative filtering. With respect to the related work, our algorithm estimates user's preferences and interests not only considering the actual user's preference/interest, like in traditional social recommender systems, but also considering the trend of the user's social network, its structure and the influence relationships among users.

The approach at the basis of SoNARS moves from social psychology theories which support the idea that the mere fact of taking part into social relationships may cause individuals to modify their attitudes and behaviours. In other words, we state that users are likely to have more in common with members of their social networks than with other individualsn, and more likely to like what they also like, independently of their real preferences and of the competences and trustworthiness of the network members.

In the immediate future work we plan to exploit SoNARS into iCITY [3], a social content-based recommender system we developed recently. Such an integration is aimed at investigating how network- and interest-based recommendations could be properly coupled in order to improve recommendations of relevant contents to users. Moreover, we will lead a further evaluation which integrates also a qualitative approach to collect explicit feedback from participants.

Regarding the algorithm, at the current stage it does not consider that a person's social network consists of acquaintances from different contexts. To improve SoNARS, we are working on modeling the relationship between two people by taking into account their shared context through FOAF [8].

As a final point, let us consider that in social recommender systems, and in social networks in general, calculating values of users trustworthiness and reputation is a very popular issue. In the social networks community several trust propagation mechanisms have been proposed. They are used to provide a trust value to a directly known user (e.g. [6]), as well as to all the users of the network. From this perspective, Heath and Motta [8] define a trust model by eliciting a set of dimensions typically used by people to determine the trustworthiness of recommendation sources, such as the user experience, expertise and affinity to her. At the current stage, SoNARS does not take into account trust. In the long run, we aim at investigating how trust and reputation can affect the strength of the relationships among users in her social network, how they both influence users preferences and interests, and how this can be estimated in SoNARS.

---

[8] http://www.foaf-project.org/

References

1. Breese, J., Heckerman, D., Kadie, C.: Empirical analysis of predictive algorithms for collaborative filtering. In: Conference on Uncertainty in Artificial Intelligence (1998)
2. Burke, B.: Hybrid recommender systems: Survey and experiments. User Modeling and User-Adapted Interaction 12(4), 331–370 (2002)
3. Carmagnola, F., Cena, F., Console, L., Cortassa, O., Gena, C., Goy, A., Torre, I., Toso, A., Vernero, F.: Tag-based user models for social multi-device adaptive guides. In: User Modeling and User-Adapted Interaction (2008)
4. Dourish, P., Chalmers, M.: Running out of Space: Models of Information Navigation. In: Cockton, G., Draper, S.W., Weir, G.R.S. (eds.) People and Computers IX, Proceedings of HCI 1994, Glasgow, Scotland. Cambridge University Press, Cambridge (1994)
5. Farzan, R., Brusilovsky, P.: Annotated: A social navigation and annotation service for web-based educational resources. In: Proceedings of the World Conference on E-Learning in Corporate, Government, Healthcare, and Higher Education, E-Learn 2006, Honolulu, Hawaii, pp. 2794–2802 (2006)
6. Golbeck, J., Mannes, A.: Using trust and provenance for content filtering on the semantic web. In: Proc. of Workshop on Models of Trust for the Web, at 15th International World Wide Web Conference WWW 2006, Edinburgh, UK, May 22-26 (2006)
7. Granovetter, M.S.: The strength of weak ties. The American Journal of Sociology 78, 1360–1380 (1973)
8. Heath, T., Motta, E.: Ease of interaction plus ease of integration: Combining web2.0 and the semantic web in a reviewing site. Web Semantics 6(1), 76–83 (2008)
9. Herlocker, J., Konstan, J., Terveen, L.G., Riedl, J.T.: Evaluating collaborative filtering recommender systems. ACM Transactions on Information Systems 22(1), 5–53 (2004)
10. Kobsa, A., Koenemann, J., Pohl, W.: Personalized hypermedia presentation techniques for improving online customer relationships. The Knowledge Engineering Review 16(2), 111–155 (2001)
11. Livolsi, M.: L' Italia che cambia. La Nuova Italia (1993)
12. Mcpherson, M., Lovin, L.S., Cook, J.M.: Birds of a feather: Homophily in social networks. Annual Review of Sociology 27(1), 415–444 (2001)
13. O'Sullivan, D., Wilson, D., Smyth, B.: Improving case-based recommendation: A collaborative filtering approach. In: Craw, S., Preece, A.D. (eds.) ECCBR 2002. LNCS, vol. 2416, p. 278. Springer, Heidelberg (2002)
14. Resnick, P., Iacovou, N., Suchak, M., Bergstrom, P., Riedl, J.: Grouplens: An open architecture for collaborative filtering of netnews. In: Proceedings of the ACM Conference on Computer Supported Cooperative Work, CSCW 1994, pp. 175–186. Chapel Hill, NC (1994)
15. Resnick, P., Varian, H.: Recommender systems. Introduction to special section of Communications of the ACM 40(3) (March 1997)
16. Scott, J.P.: Social Network Analysis: A Handbook. SAGE Publications, Thousand Oaks (2000)
17. Turner, J.C.: Social Influence. Brooks/Cole, Pacific Grove (1991)
18. Van Mark, S., Brussee, R., van Vliet, H., Gazendam, L., van Houten, Y., Veenstra, M.: On the importance of "who tagged what". In: Wade, V.P., Ashman, H., Smyth, B. (eds.) AH 2006. LNCS, vol. 4018, pp. 552–561. Springer, Heidelberg (2006)
19. Webster, A., Vassileva, J.: The keepup recommender system. In: Konstan, J.A., Riedl, J., Smyth, B. (eds.) RecSys, pp. 173–176. ACM, New York (2007)

Grocery Product Recommendations from Natural Language Inputs

Petteri Nurmi, Andreas Forsblom, and Patrik Floréen

Helsinki Institute for Information Technology HIIT
P.O. Box 68, FI-00014 University of Helsinki, Finland
firstname.lastname@cs.helsinki.fi

Abstract. Shopping lists play a central role in grocery shopping. Among other things, shopping lists serve as memory aids and as a tool for budgeting. More interestingly, shopping lists serve as an expression and indication of customer needs and interests. Accordingly, shopping lists can be used as an input for recommendation techniques. In this paper we describe a methodology for making recommendations about additional products to purchase using items on the user's shopping list. As shopping list entries seldom correspond to products, we first use information retrieval techniques to map the shopping list entries into candidate products. Association rules are used to generate recommendations based on the candidate products. We evaluate the usefulness and interestingness of the recommendations in a user study.

1 Introduction

According to user studies, between 50% and 75% of customers use shopping lists for major shopping visits [1,2]. The shopping list serves various functions; among other things, it can be used to aid budgeting, or to plan the shopping event [3]. More interestingly, the shopping list also serves as an expression and indication of customer needs and interests. Accordingly, shopping lists can be used as input for recommendation techniques. For example, we could suggest additional grocery products, use the recommendations to rank special offers or to remind the user about products that might have been forgotten. This paper focuses on the first of these tasks, recommending additional products to purchase.

The way people normally write shopping lists contrasts with the way stores maintain information. Most people use generic expressions (e.g., "milk", "carrots") whereas stores tend to use structured formats that refer to product level information. Before additional products can be recommended, we must map the items on the user's shopping list into products within the store. This paper describes a methodology that combines information retrieval techniques with collaborative filtering. We first use a grocery retrieval engine, described in our previous work [4,5], to map the shopping list items to potential products. Collaborative filtering techniques are then used to recommend additional products based on the retrieved products. We evaluate our techniques in a user study.

G.-J. Houben et al. (Eds.): UMAP 2009, LNCS 5535, pp. 235–246, 2009.

The rest of the paper is organized as follows: Sec. 2 describes our grocery retrieval engine. Sec. 3 describes the methods we use to recommend products, as well as how we integrate grocery retrieval with recommendations. Evaluation of our techniques is discussed in Sec. 4. Related work is discussed in Sec. 5. Finally, Sec. 6 concludes the paper.

2   Background

2.1   Dataset

Our system has been built using shopping basket data from a major store in Helsinki, Finland. The data includes all grocery purchases made by customers using loyalty cards during the calendar year 2007. The data includes 12.6 million products bought in 1.2 million shopping baskets by 140,000 different customers.

The store chain uses a hierarchical taxonomy of the about 20,000 different grocery products. The taxonomy contains four levels, but the topmost two category levels were overly generic and we only consider the two lowest levels in the rest of the paper. The hierarchy has about 1000 elements on the lowest level and more than 200 on the second lowest level.

2.2   Grocery Retrieval Engine

In order to map shopping list entries into candidate products, we utilize a grocery retrieval system that we have built as part of our earlier work [4,5]. The system takes as an input a natural language query (e.g, milk) and returns a ranked list of candidate products that match the query. We use a ranking formula that combines textual features, i.e., product name and category name, with product popularity information, i.e., how often the product has been purchased. More specifically, we use the following formula:

$$
\begin{aligned}
relevance(product|item) &= p(product|item) \\
&\propto \log p(product) + \log p(item|product) \\
&\approx \log p(product) + \lambda BM25(product|item), \quad (1)
\end{aligned}
$$

where λ is a weight term and BM25 is the BM25 Okapi function for a query term. We use a multinomial distribution with a Dirichlet prior to model $p(product)$. The BM25 Okapi function is given by [6]:

$$
BM25(product|item) = \sum_{j \in item} \log \frac{N - n_j + 0.5}{n_j + 0.5} \frac{(\alpha + 1)f_j}{f_j + \alpha\left((1 - b) + bL\right)}. \quad (2)
$$

Here n_j is the number of product names where word j appears, f_j is the term frequency of word j and N is the total number of products. The variable L is the normalized document length, i.e., the length of the current item divided by the average item length (in words). Finally, the parameters α and b are predefined constants; see [6] for details.

The grocery retrieval system was constructed using the data described in Sec. 2.1. The category information is utilized in the ranking so that products matching both in product name and category name receive higher ranks than other products. In order to achieve this behavior, we use a weighted extension to BM25 that replaces the term and document frequencies in Eq. 2 with weighted linear sums [7]:

$$n'_j = dm_j + n_j$$
$$f'_j = dc_j + f_j \qquad\qquad (3)$$

Here d is a weight term, m_j is the number of category names where word j appears and c_j is the term frequency of word j. See [4,5] for more details about the system and the techniques we use.

3   Recommending Grocery Products

3.1   Recommending Techniques

Similarly to most of existing work (see Sec. 5), our recommendations are based on association rules. We consider two types of rules. First, we consider rules that capture associations between products. Secondly, we consider so-called generalized association rules, which utilize the product taxonomy (see Sec. 2.1) in the mining process and capture associations where the items can be on any level of the taxonomy [8]. Generalized association rules also use the taxonomy to prune redundant rules. In the rest of this paper we use the term non-generalized association rules to refer to the former class of rules.

In order to mine generalized association rules, we first expand the transaction data by including category information for the products that are part of a transaction. As described in Sec. 2.1, we consider two category levels per product. After expanding the transactions, we use a standard association rule mining algorithm on the data. In our case we use the freely available Apriori implementation by Borgelt [9]. We experimented with various support and confidence thresholds. The quality of the rules seemed to be a smaller problem than the amount of rules. If the support and confidence values are not small enough, the association rule mining will not discover any rules for most products. Because of this, we use relatively low support and confidence thresholds. In the experiments we use 0.01% ($\approx$ 120 transactions) as the support threshold and 5% as the confidence threshold. As we calculate recommendations for an individual product, we consider only rules that contain a single item both in the body (antecedent) and the head (consequent) of the rule (e.g., $A \Rightarrow B$).

The resulting rules contain many redundant ones that need to be pruned. We consider two pruning criteria. First, we remove all trivial rules, i.e., rules that correspond to relations in the original taxonomy (e.g., milk $\Rightarrow$ skimmed milk). Secondly, we prune rules that are not interesting with respect to the taxonomy structure; see Appendix A for a definition of interestingness and how to compute it. The pruning step significantly reduces the number of rules. For example, mining association rules from the expanded transaction data using the above mentioned support and confidence thresholds resulted in 565, 302 rules. The pruning step reduced this to 65, 930 rules. After pruning the rules, we calculate the lift[1] of each rule and store the rules in a database. A similar process is used for the non-generalized association rules.

The actual recommendations are calculated using individual items on the user's shopping list. The first step is to map the item to a product or a list of products using the grocery retrieval engine described in Sec. 2.2. Assume, for now, that only the topmost retrieval result is considered. The use of multiple retrieval results is discussed in the next section. Let j denote the topmost product. With the non-generalized association rules we retrieve from the database rules that contain product j in the body of the rule. With the generalized association rules we consider rules whose body matches either product j or one of the categories to which it belongs. We go through the top k rules in descending lift order and use the rule head to make recommendations. If the rule head is a product, we recommend that product. When the rule head is a category, we recommend the most popular product from that category. In the experiments we recommend five products per item, i.e., we set $k = 5$. This choice is motivated by our target application and device. The recommendations have been integrated into Ma$$iv€, an intelligent mobile shopping assistant that we are currently constructing [10]. Ma$$iv€ has been designed for Nokia E61i devices and visualizing more than five recommendations would force the user to scroll the screen in order to see all recommendations.

3.2   Using Multiple Retrieval Results for Recommendations

Using only a single retrieval result can make the recommendations sensitive to the performance of the grocery retrieval engine and to limit the set of products that can be recommended. In this section we discuss how to overcome this issue by considering multiple retrieval results in the recommendation process.

A naïve approach is to consider the top k retrieval results as a candidate set and use rules whose body matches any of the products in the candidate set to recommend products. This approach naturally works only if the top k retrieval results are approximately equally relevant. User evaluations that we have conducted using our grocery retrieval system and Lemur[2] suggest that this is not the case [4,5]. According to the user evaluations, around 80% of products are relevant at the topmost ranks whereas only around 70% of products at rank five are relevant. Hence, we should take the relevance scores of the retrieval results into account.

A popular approach for integrating scores from multiple systems is to use a (weighted) linear combination. As discussed by Burke [11], a weighted linear combination is meaningful only when the relative values of the different systems can be meaningfully compared. In our case, both the lift and the retrieval results

---

[1] The lift of rule $A \Rightarrow B$ is defined as $\frac{P(A,B)}{P(A)P(B)}$.

[2] http://www.lemurproject.org/ [Retrieved: 2008-06-03].

are ratios and hence they can be meaningfully compared. The lift is, by definition, an odds ratio whereas the ranking formula in Eq. 1 corresponds to a scaled and translated log-odds ratio[3]. We use the following formula to integrate multiple retrieval results into the recommendation process:

$$\text{score}(\text{product}|\text{item}) =$$
$$\text{relevance}(\text{product}|\text{item}) + \log\left(\text{lift}(\text{product})\right). \quad (4)$$

The user evaluations also indicated that there are seldom more than five relevant products for a query. For this reason, we do not consider more than five retrieval results in the experiments.

4 Evaluation

4.1 Experiment Setup

We have evaluated our techniques in a user study. The study was conducted using an online interface that showed users a list with eleven shopping list items. For each product we showed five recommendations and asked the users to rate the suitability and interestingness of the recommendations on a five-point Likert scale (1 = not suitable at all, 5 = very suitable). We define a suitable recommendation to be a product that the users would consider purchasing together with the corresponding shopping list item. An interesting recommendation is defined as a product that the user finds suitable, but that (s)he does not immediately think of buying together with the corresponding item. These definitions were visible to the users during the study.

The shopping list items that were shown to the users were randomly selected from a manually constructed list of seed items. In order to construct the seed list, we first sampled 800 products from the database according to the products' purchase frequencies. Next we manually examined each product in the sample and mapped it into a form that could potentially appear in a shopping list. For example, the product `cucumber domestic 1kg` was mapped to `cucumber`. Some of the products could not be meaningfully mapped and we dropped them. The final list contained 762 items, of which 495 were unique.

We consider four methods in the evaluation. As a simple baseline we include recommendations that are based on the most popular products. We also consider two techniques that utilize non-generalized association rules. The first of these uses a single information retrieval result together with rules that are sorted by lift. The second method is otherwise the same, but it uses five retrieval results. The retrieval results are combined with the lift values using Eq. 4 in Sec. 3.2. The final method is based on generalized association rules with a single retrieval result. All methods were used with the same support (0.01%) and confidence thresholds (5%).

---

[3] The BM25 Okapi is known to correspond to the log-odds ratio of relevant documents and non-relevant documents [12].

We used the different methods to generate recommendations as follows: generalized association rules (Generalized) were used for four items, non-generalized rules with one retrieval result (Assoc-1) were used for three items, the non-generalized rules with five retrieval results (Assoc-5) were user for three items and the most popular products (Frequent) were used for one item. The item allocation and the order of items were randomized. Users were not told which method was used to generate recommendations or even that different recommendation techniques were used. The study was conducted using an intercept method at the public premises of a university building. Each participant evaluated a single shopping list, i.e., 11 products, and was given candy for participation. In total, we collected 28 participants and 1470 subjective evaluations[4].

4.2   Metrics

We selected the normalized discounted cumulative gain (NDCG) as the evaluation measure. While the NDCG is not commonly used to evaluate recommendation techniques, it is widely used for evaluating information retrieval results and it has several properties that make it well suited for our setting [13]. The most important properties are that (i) NDCG is able to handle non-binary relevance assessments, (ii) it discounts results at lower ranks and (iii) it allows penalizing cases where a method fails to recommend any products.

Let $r_{i,j}$ denote the rating that the user assigns to the rank j recommendation for item i. The *discounted cumulative gain* (DCG) at rank j equals:

$$DCG[j] = \begin{cases} r_{i,j} & j = 1 \\ DCG[j-1] + r_{i,j} & 1 < j < b \\ DCG[j-1] + r_{i,j}/\log_b(j) & j \geq b \end{cases} \qquad (5)$$

where b defines the base of the logarithm that is used to discount results. Smaller logarithm bases cause a sharper discounting. We used the natural logarithm, which means our results are discounted from rank three onwards. The results of the different items are summed to form a total score.

Let $\widehat{r}_{i,j}$ denote the maximum possible value of $r_{i,j}$. In our case $\widehat{r}_{i,j} = 5$. By replacing $r_{i,j}$ in Eq. 5 with $\widehat{r}_{i,j}$ for all i and j, we obtain a so-called *ideal DCG* value. As the name suggests, the ideal DCG measures how well the system could perform in the ideal case. The normalized discounted cumulative gain (NDCG) is defined as the DCG divided by the ideal DCG vector. In our case the ideal DCG corresponds to the vector $(5, 10, 14.55, 18.16, 21.26)$ times the number of products for which recommendations have been evaluated.

4.3   Results and Discussion

Users consistently assigned higher ratings for usefulness than for interestingness. The different association rule methods were approximately equal in terms

---

[4] Sometimes the methods fail to generate enough recommendations and hence we do not obtain user evaluations for all possible items or ranks.

Table 1. Mean scores for the different methods

Method	Usefulness	Interestingness
Baseline	2.06	2.06
Assoc-1	2.97	2.76
Assoc-5	2.98	2.50
Generalized	3.13	2.77

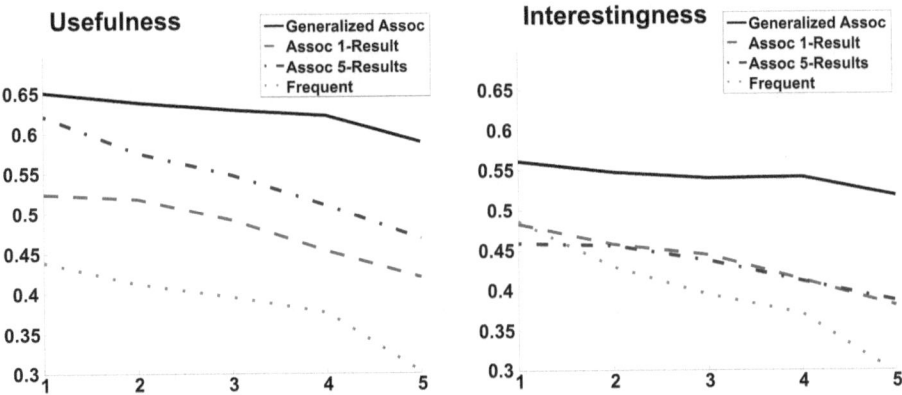

Fig. 1. Results of the user evaluation. The value on the y-axis indicates the normalized discounted cumulative gain and the value on the x-axis corresponds to the rank of the recommendation. The discounting has been performed using the natural logarithm. Higher values are better, the range of values is [0, 1]. A difference of 0.1 in NDCG value corresponds to a difference of 0.5 in ratings.

of average ratings; see Table 1. However, the mean scores are somewhat misleading because they do not consider the distribution of ratings or missing recommendations.

Figure 1 shows a plot of the NDCG values at different ranks. The non-generalized association rules with a single retrieval result (Assoc-1) often fail to recommend any products (18.6% of recommendations missing), which explains the lower NDCG values despite the approximately equal average ratings. The non-generalized association rules with five retrieval results (Assoc-5) are able to recommend products at all ranks (8.9% of recommendations missing), but the quality of the recommendations rapidly decreases at lower ranks. In terms of interestingness, the non-generalized association rules are not able to improve on the baseline. The generalized association rules are clearly the best method. The quality of the recommendations is consistent across different ranks and the method is able to recommend products in 92% of cases.

We also separately analyzed the distribution of the users' ratings; see Fig. 2. For the non-generalized association rules, the distributions followed a decreasing exponential curve, whereas for the generalized association rules the distributions

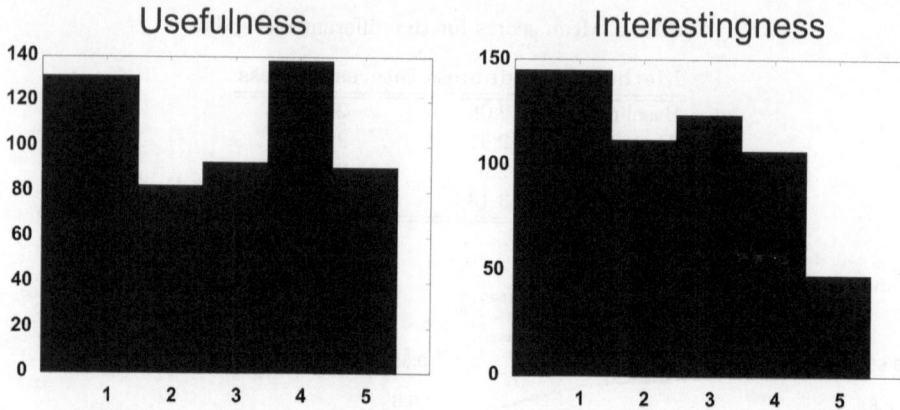

Fig. 2. Distribution of users' ratings for the generalized association rules. The x-axis indicates the rating and the y-axis indicates the number of times the rating was given.

were bimodal. One of the modes was positive or neutral (value 4 for usefulness and value 3 for interestingness) and the other one was negative (value 1 for both usefulness and interestingness). Accordingly, our results suggest that (i) users feel strongly about the recommendations and that (ii) our methods also often provide recommendations that users find useful.

4.4   Influence of Multiple Retrieval Results

In order to obtain a better understanding of how the number of retrieval results influences the recommendations, we conducted an offline analysis using the 495 unique seed list items (see Sec. 4.1). In the analysis we varied the number of retrieval results and calculated the average lift of the recommendations. We considered both generalized and non-generalized association rules and the retrieval results were combined using Eq. 4 in Sec. 3.2.

The results of the analysis are shown in Table 2. As expected, the average lift values increase as the number of retrieval results increases. This result has two important implications for us. First, since the average lift of the recommendations increases, we can expect that the quality of the recommendations increases, or at least that it does not decrease. This implication is also supported by the user study: the usefulness of the non-generalized association rules increased as

Table 2. The average lift of the recommendations when the number of retrieval results is varied between one and five

# Results	Non-Generalized	Generalized
1	5.8	6.9
2	7.1	7.5
3	8.5	8.2
4	9.0	8.4
5	9.7	8.6

we increased the number of retrieval results while the interestingness remained the same. Accordingly, generalized association rules with multiple retrieval results should perform at least equally good as the generalized rules with a single retrieval result. The second implication relates to the use of Eq. 4 for combining retrieval scores with lift values. As the lift of the rules increases despite decreasing relevance scores, the comparison of the scores is meaningful and the use of Eq. 4 is justified.

5   Related Work

Most of the existing work on recommendations in the retail domain builds on association rule mining. For example, Brijs et al. [14] use association rule mining to discover frequent itemsets. The frequent itemsets are used together with an economic model to optimize product assortment decisions, i.e., which items to have on sale. Anand et al. [15] use association rule mining for designing cross-sales strategies. While association rules are the most popular technique, also other recommendation techniques have been suggested. For example, Vindevogel et al. [16] suggest using cross-price elasticities that can be modeled using multivariate time series techniques.

Many authors have considered the task of making personalized recommendations in the retailing domain. For example, Cumby et al. [17] predict shopping lists from the customer's recent transaction history. The predictions are used to remind about forgotten products and to target promotions. A combination of a top-N predictor and a simple discriminative classifier (Winnow, Perceptron or C4.5) is shown to achieve F-scores slightly over 0.40. Demiriz [18] uses a two-phased process to recommend products. The first phase consists of association rule mining, after which the recommendations are re-ranked taking into consideration the similarity of products and the confidence of the discovered rules. Adomavicius and Tuzhilin [19] discover association rules for individual customers and propose a validation layer that allows experts to easily investigate and validate the discovered rules.

Also some prototypes of intelligent mobile assistants integrate recommendation techniques. For example, the SMMART system uses content-based filtering for location-based marketing [20]. Another example is the SmartPad system which allows customers to prepare grocery orders remotely [21,22]. In SmartPad, a combination of association rule mining and cluster analysis is used to make recommendations. Association rules are used to determine relationships between product categories in the product domain. Cluster analysis is simultaneously applied on the customer domain to identify customers with similar spending histories. Users are then matched with a cluster and cluster-specific lists of popular products are used to recommend products from categories that are presumed relevant according to the association rules.

Our work differs from earlier work in three main aspects. First, instead of using customer transaction history, we make recommendations based on the customer's shopping list. While transaction history indicates the user's general interests, the shopping list items indicate his/her current needs. Secondly, while most of existing work has focused on accurate recommendations, we focused on recommendations that users find useful and interesting. Finally, another novel aspect of our work is that we make recommendations from natural language inputs.

6   Summary and Discussion

We described methods for making grocery product recommendations from shopping list inputs expressed in natural language. Our techniques combine information retrieval techniques with association rule recommendations. We evaluated our techniques in a user study. The results indicate that generalized association rules provide more useful recommendations than non-generalized rules, and that they are more robust with respect to information retrieval results. In terms of future work, our goal is to investigate the usefulness of the recommendations in a field setting.

Acknowledgments

The authors are grateful to Joonas Kukkonen for helping with the user study. The authors are thankful to their present and past colleagues in the project. This work was supported by the Finnish Funding Agency for Technology and Innovation TEKES, under the project Personalised Ubiservices in Public Spaces. The work was also supported in part by the ICT program of the European Community, under the PASCAL2 network of excellence, ICT-216886-PASCAL2. The publication only reflects the authors' views.

References

1. Bassett, R., Beagan, B., Chapman, G.E.: Grocery lists: connecting family, household and grocery store. British Food Journal 110(2), 206–217 (2008)
2. Thomas, A., Garland, R.: Grocery shopping: list and non-list usage. Marketing Intelligence & Planning 22, 623–635 (2004)
3. Block, L.G., Morwitz, V.G.: Shopping lists as an external memory aid for grocery shopping: Influences on list writing and list fulfillment. Journal of Consumer Psychology 8(4), 343–375 (1999)
4. Nurmi, P., Lagerspetz, E., Buntine, W., Floréen, P., Kukkonen, J.: Product retrieval for grocery stores. In: Proceedings of the 31st Annual International ACM SIGIR Conference on Research and Development in Information Retrieval, pp. 781–782. ACM, New York (2008)
5. Nurmi, P., Lagerspetz, E., Buntine, W., Floréen, P., Kukkonen, J., Peltonen, P.: Natural language retrieval of grocery products. In: Proceedings of the 17th ACM Conference on Information and Knowledge Management (CIKM 2008). ACM, New York (2008)

6. Robertson, S., Walker, S., Beaulieu, M.M., Gatford, M., Payne, A.: Okapi at TREC-4. In: NIST Special Publication 500-236: The Fourth Text REtrieval Conference (TREC-4), pp. 73–96 (1995)
7. Robertson, S., Zaragoza, H., Taylor, M.: Simple BM25 extension to multiple weighted fields. In: Proceedings of the 13th ACM International Conference on Information and Knowledge Management (CIKM), pp. 42–49. ACM, New York (2004)
8. Srikant, R., Agrawal, R.: Mining generalized association rules. In: Proceedings of the 21st International Conference on Very Large Data Bases (VLDB), pp. 407–419 (1995)
9. Borgelt, C.: Efficient implementations of apriori and eclat. In: Proceedings of the 1st Workshop of Frequent Item Set Mining Implementations, FIMI (2003)
10. Nurmi, P., Boström, F., Floréen, P., Kukkonen, J., Lagerspetz, E., Peltonen, P., Saarikko, P.: Massive - an adaptive shopping assistant. In: Adjunct Proceedings of the 10th International Conference on Ubiquitous Computing (2008)
11. Burke, R.: Hybrid recommender systems: Survey and experiments. User Modeling and User Adapted Interaction 12(4), 331–370 (2002)
12. Sparck Jones, K., Walker, S., Robertson, S.E.: A probabilistic model of information retrieval: development and comparative experiments Part 1. Information Processing and Management 36, 779–808 (2000)
13. Järvelin, K., Kekäläinen, J.: Cumulated gain-based evaluation of ir techniques. ACM Transactions on Information Systems 20(4), 422–446 (2002)
14. Brijs, T., Swinnen, G., Vanhoof, K., Wets, G.: Using association rules for product assortment decisions: a case study. In: Proceedings of the fifth ACM SIGKDD international conference on Knowledge discovery and data mining (KDD), pp. 254–260. ACM, New York (1999)
15. Anand, S.S., Patrick, A.R., Hughes, J.G., Bell, D.A.: A data mining methodology for cross-sales. Knowledge-Based Systems 10(7), 449–461 (1998)
16. Vindevogel, B., der Poel, D.V., Wets, G.: Why promotion strategies based on market basket analysis do not work. Expert Systems with Applications 28, 583–590 (2005)
17. Cumby, C., Fano, A., Ghani, R., Krema, M.: Predicting customer shopping lists from point-of-sale purchase data. In: Proceedings of the tenth ACM SIGKDD international conference on Knowledge discovery and data mining (KDD 2004), pp. 402–409. ACM, New York (2004)
18. Demiriz, A.: Enhancing product recommender systems on sparse binary data. Data Mining and Knowledge Discovery 9(2), 147–170 (2004)
19. Adomavicius, G., Tuzhilin, A.: Using data mining methods to build customer profiles. IEEE Computer 34(2), 74–82 (2001)
20. Kurkovsky, S., Harihar, K.: Using ubiquitous computing in interactive mobile marketing. Personal and Ubiquitous Computing 10(4), 227–240 (2006)
21. Lawrence, R.D., Almasi, G.S., Kotlyar, V., Viveros, M.S., Duri, S.S.: Personalization of supermarket product recommendations. Data Mining and Knowledge Discovery 5, 11–32 (2001)
22. Kotlyar, V., Viveros, M.S., Duri, S., Lawrence, R.D., Almasi, G.S.: A case study in information delivery to mass retail markets. In: Bench-Capon, T.J.M., Soda, G., Tjoa, A.M. (eds.) DEXA 1999. LNCS, vol. 1677, pp. 842–851. Springer, Heidelberg (1999)

A   Interestingness of Generalized Association Rules

The definitions below follow [8]. Let $I = \{I_1, \ldots, I_n\}$ denote a set of items and let $\mathcal{T}$ denote a taxonomy on the items. We require that the taxonomy can be represented as a directed and acyclic graph. In our case the set of items corresponds to the union of all products and categories. We use lowercase letters to denote items, and uppercase letters to denote sets of items. The item $\widehat{x} \in I$ is an ancestor of item $x \in I$ if there is an edge from x to $\widehat{x}$ in the transitive closure of $\mathcal{T}$. In other words, when x is a product, $\widehat{x}$ is an ancestor of x when x belongs to category $\widehat{x}$. When x is a category, $\widehat{x}$ is an ancestor of x when x is a subcategory of $\widehat{x}$. A generalized association rule is an implication of the form $X \Rightarrow Y$, where $X \subset I, Y \subset I, X \cap Y = \emptyset$ and no item in Y is an ancestor of any item in X.

Let $X \Rightarrow Y$ be an arbitrary generalized association rule. The rules $X \Rightarrow \widehat{Y}, \widehat{X} \Rightarrow Y$ and $\widehat{X} \Rightarrow \widehat{Y}$, where we have replaced one or more items from X and Y with their ancestors, are called ancestors of rule $X \Rightarrow Y$. The rule $\widehat{X} \Rightarrow \widehat{Y}$ is a *close ancestor* of $X \Rightarrow Y$ if there is no rule $X' \Rightarrow Y'$ such that $X' \Rightarrow Y'$ is an ancestor of $X \Rightarrow Y$ and $\widehat{X} \Rightarrow \widehat{Y}$ is an ancestor of $X' \Rightarrow Y'$.

The expected support of $X \Rightarrow Y$ w.r.t. the rule $\widehat{X} \Rightarrow \widehat{Y}$ is defined as follows:

$$E_{\widehat{X} \Rightarrow \widehat{Y}}\left[Pr(X,Y)\right] = \frac{Pr(X)}{Pr(\widehat{X})} \times \frac{Pr(Y)}{Pr(\widehat{Y})} \times Pr(\widehat{X}, \widehat{Y}) \qquad (6)$$

The expected confidence of rule $X \Rightarrow Y$ w.r.t. the rule $\widehat{X} \Rightarrow \widehat{Y}$ is defined as:

$$E_{\widehat{X} \Rightarrow \widehat{Y}}\left[Pr(Y|X)\right] = \frac{Pr(Y)}{Pr(\widehat{Y})} \times Pr(\widehat{Y}|\widehat{X}). \qquad (7)$$

The expected support and confidence of X w.r.t. the rules $\widehat{X} \Rightarrow Y$ and $X \Rightarrow \widehat{Y}$ are defined analogously. A rule is called *R-interesting* with respect to an ancestor $\widehat{X} \Rightarrow \widehat{Y}$ if the support of the rule $X \Rightarrow Y$ is at least R times the expected support based on $\widehat{X} \Rightarrow \widehat{Y}$ or the confidence of the rule $X \Rightarrow Y$ is at least R times the expected confidence based on $\widehat{X} \Rightarrow \widehat{Y}$. Given a set of rules S, the rule $X \Rightarrow Y$ is *interesting* (in S) if it has no ancestors or it is R-interesting with respect to all of its close ancestors among its interesting ancestors. In the experiments we use $R = 1.1$ to detect interesting rules.

I Like It... I Like It Not: Evaluating User Ratings Noise in Recommender Systems

Xavier Amatriain, Josep M. Pujol, and Nuria Oliver

Telefonica Research

Abstract. Recent growing interest in predicting and influencing consumer behavior has generated a parallel increase in research efforts on Recommender Systems. Many of the state-of-the-art Recommender Systems algorithms rely on obtaining user ratings in order to later predict unknown ratings. An underlying assumption in this approach is that the user ratings can be treated as ground truth of the user's taste. However, users are inconsistent in giving their feedback, thus introducing an unknown amount of noise that challenges the validity of this assumption.

In this paper, we tackle the problem of analyzing and characterizing the noise in user feedback through ratings of movies. We present a user study aimed at quantifying the noise in user ratings that is due to inconsistencies. We measure RMSE values that range from 0.557 to 0.8156. We also analyze how factors such as item sorting and time of rating affect this noise.

1 Introduction and Motivation

A common approach to handle digital information overload is to offer users a personalized access to information. Recommender Systems (RS), for instance, automatically suggest new content that should comply with the user's taste. In the RS literature, these predictions of user preferences are typically obtained by means of approaches such as collaborative filtering – *i.e.* taking into account other users rating history in order to model the taste of peers – or content-based – *i.e.* using existing content descriptions to uncover relations between items. Regardless of the approach, these personalized services share a common concern: modeling the user's taste. Therefore, such systems need to somehow capture likes and dislikes in order to model or infer the user's preferences.

User preferences can be captured via either *implicit* or *explicit* user feedback. In the implicit approach [12], user preferences are inferred by observing consumption patterns. However, modeling user preferences on the basis of implicit feedback has a major limitation: the underlying assumption is that the amount of time that users spend accessing a given content is directly proportional to how much they like it. Consequently, explicit feedback is the favored approach for gathering information on user preferences. Although this approach adds a burden on the users and different users might respond differently to incentives [6], it is generally accepted that explicit data is more reliable in most situations.

The preferred method for capturing explicit preference information from users consists of rating questionnaires [1], where users are asked to provide feedback – via a

G.-J. Houben et al. (Eds.): UMAP 2009, LNCS 5535, pp. 247–258, 2009.

value point on a fixed scale – on how much they like some content. Typically, scales range from 0 or 1 to 5 or 10 and are quantized to integer values.

Approaches to inferring user preferences are evaluated on the basis of how well they can match a previously existing rating or anticipate future ones. However, little attention has been paid to how consistent users are in giving these ratings, how much input noise can be expected and how this noise can be characterized (see Section 2). The main contribution of this paper is a user study aimed at characterizing and quantifying the noise caused by user inconsistencies when providing ratings (see Section 4 for an overview of the experimental procedure and Section 5 for the results). This estimation is important because it represents a lower bound on the error of explicit feedback-based RS.

2   Related Work

The bias introduced in RS by noise in user ratings has been known for some time. Hill et al. [9] were aware of this issue and designed a small scale experiment to measure reliability in user ratings. They carried out a two trial user study with 22 participants and a time difference of 6 weeks between trials. Unfortunately, the noise in user ratings was a side issue in their overall study and they only reported pairwise correlations. Cosley et al. [4] carried out a similar experiment using a rate-rerate procedure with two trials on 212 participants. They selected 40 random movies in the center of the rating scale (*i.e.* 2,3 or 4 rating) that participants had already rated in the past – months or even years earlier, according to the authors. They reported participants being consistent only 60% of the time. In this study, the measured correlation between trials was 0.70. Herlocker et al. [8] discuss the noise in user ratings in their review of evaluating methods for RS. In particular, they introduce the concept of the "magic barrier" that is created by natural variability in ratings. The authors also highlight the importance of analyzing and discovering this inherent variability in recommender data sets and include it as a future line of work.

Mahony et al. [13] classify noise in RS into *natural* and *malicious*. The former refers to the definition of user generated noise provided in this paper, while the latter refers to noise that is deliberately introduced in a system in order to bias the results. Even though the focus of their work is on *malicious* noise, they do propose a de-noising algorithm that can be used to detect *natural* noise. Their baseline recommender algorithm reported a marginal improvement on a reduced data set once the ratings labeled as noise by the de-noising method are discarded.

To the best of our knowledge, the former are the only pieces of work in the literature on RS that explicitly address the problem of inconsistencies in user ratings. The work presented in this paper provides a more detailed study and in-depth analysis with the aim of characterizing the noise due to inconsistencies in user ratings.

3   Measures of Reliability in User Tests

Our effort to analyze and characterize noise and inconsistencies in user ratings is related to the concept of *reliability* of user tests from classical test theory. Reliability in this context is defined as the ratio of true score variance over the observed score variance. This ratio is used as a signal-to-noise measure of a given user test. Since true scores are unknown, it is not possible to compute reliability directly. However, there are methods to estimate it [10].

Of particular interest to us is the so-called *test-retest reliability*. This measure is often used in psychometry to quantify how reliable a particular "instrument" (*e.g.* survey or test) is [15]. The test-retest reliability is a function of the Pearson correlations between the different trials of the same test. However, it is not sufficient to compute the correlation between two different trials of the same test. As Heise explains [7], the correlation is aggregating two effects: the instrument's reliability and the stability of the user's judgements. That is, if we measure how much a user likes an item at two different times (separated by a month, for instance) and find a different rating, this could be due to either the reliability of the measure and the user's response or to the fact that the user's opinion has changed during that period. Therefore, three points in time are needed in order to distinguish between both effects. Once these are available, pairwise correlations r_{12}, r_{23}, and r_{13} can be computed to obtain (a) the overall reliability (Eq. 1), and (b) the stability in users' opinions from time x to time y, (s_{xy}) (Eq. 2).

$$r_{xx} = r_{12}r_{23}/r_{13} \qquad (1)$$

$$s_{12} = r_{13}/r_{23}; \quad s_{23} = r_{13}/r_{12}; \quad s_{13} = r_{13}{}^2/r_{12}r_{23} \qquad (2)$$

Note that neither of the related surveys reviewed in the previous section [9] [4] take into account the reliability and stability of their studies. This is especially problematic in the case of Cosle's *et al.* experiment where ratings might be separated by months.

4   Experimental Setup

The research questions that we wanted to address with our experiment are: *Q1:* Are users inconsistent when providing ratings? *Q2:* If so, how large is the error due to such inconsistencies? *Q3:* What are the factors that have an impact on user inconsistencies?

Apparatus and Procedure. We selected 100 movie titles from the Netflix Prize database [2]. The selection was done by using a stratified random sample on the movie popularity curve. We divided the 500000 movies in the database into 10 equal-density bins and random sampled 10 movies out of each bin – only 100 movies were selected in order to avoid user churn. By using this procedure, we obtained a sample that included a significant portion of unpopular movies that ensured an appropriate spread of the results.

Our experiment consisted of 3 trials (R_1, R_2, and R_3) of the same task: rating 100 movies via a Web interface. The three trials took place at different points in time, in order to assess the reliability of the user rating paradigm and to measure the variability of users. The minimum time difference between trials was set to 24 hours for the first and second and 15 days for the second and third. Users could stop and resume the trial at the same spot at any time.

User ratings were provided on a 1 to 5 star scale with a special crossed-out eye icon located on the left to indicate unseen movies. Information about the movie included title, year, director, cast and DVD cover. Users could follow a link to *IMDB*[1] if they needed further information.

We designed a two part test-retest experiment in order to discern the test reliability from the user's stability. In addition, we wanted to analyze whether the elapsed time between ratings and the order in which items were presented had any influence in the consistency of the participants' answers.

Participants were presented with movie titles in a predetermined sequential order so that the effect of the order of the responses could also be analyzed. Previous research has shown that sequential user tests generate what is known as the *assimilation/contrast effect* [14, 5]: a user is likely to give a lower rating to an item if the preceding one deserved a very high evaluation. However, if successive items are comparable in their ratings, the user is likely to assimilate the second item to the preceding one and give the same rating to both. In addition, and especially in the case of the first and second trials, we wanted to rule out the effect of any possible sequential memory effect (*i.e.* remembering the ratings from the previous trial and therefore not paying enough attention the next time). For these reasons, two different permutations of the movies were created: permutation 1 (used in trials 1 and 3) was a random order; and permutation 2 (used trial 2) ordered movies according to their popularity in Netflix.

One possible concern in our experiment design was the short elapsed time between our trials. Another concern was that the different order introduced in trial 2 could be introducing a hard-to-isolate confound. To address these issues, we ran a fourth trial, R_4, with a subset of our population (36 users) seven months after our original survey. The results are reported separately in section 5.4 as a final support to our hypothesis.

Participants. Participants were recruited via email advertisement in a large telecommunications company. A total of 118 distinct users completed the three trials in the study. The participants' age ranged from 22 to 47 years, with an average age of 31.2 years. Almost 90% of our participants were in the 22 to 37 age group and most of them were male (79.12%). This demographic group corresponds to the most active group in online applications such as RS [3].

Additionally, we collected data about their familiarity with the movie domain. Participants reported watching an average of 1.55 movies in the cinema, 3.8 TV movies, and 5.13 DVD movies per month. When asked about their familiarity with online rating systems, participants were somewhat unfamiliar with them (mean: 2.60 on a 5 point Likert scale). Finally, when asked about Web usage familiarity, our participants considered themselves to be proficient users, with an average of 4.74 on a 5 point Likert scale.

5   Results

In this section, we first compare the ratings obtained in our survey with the Netflix ratings for the same movies. We then present our results by evaluating the test-retest re-

---

[1] http://www.imdb.com

liability of the experiment as well as user stabilities. Finally, we analyze three variables that might play a role in determining user inconsistencies: (a) the rating scale, (b) the order in which the movies were presented; and (c) the moment of time when movies were rated[2].

Comparison to Netflix. The Netflix dataset is one of the most popular benchmarks in the RS community. Therefore and before further analysis, we compare the behavior of the participants in our experiment to that of Netflix' users. First, we compare the ratings obtained in our survey with those in Neflix. Figure 1 depicts the rating distribution of the three trials of the experiment, when compared to the Netflix ratings on the *same* 100 movies. Note how similar both rating distributions are. The main difference is that the Netflix data set distribution has a *higher* mean (*i.e.* Netflix users tend to rate the 100 movies with higher scores than the participants in our study). This observation might be due to several factors: Our experiment, as opposed to Netflix, asked users to rate movies that they did not explicitly choose to rate. In addition, our movie sample is biased towards non-popular movies, which in a different setting most users would have not rated. Finally, there might also be an effect of our biased demographics.

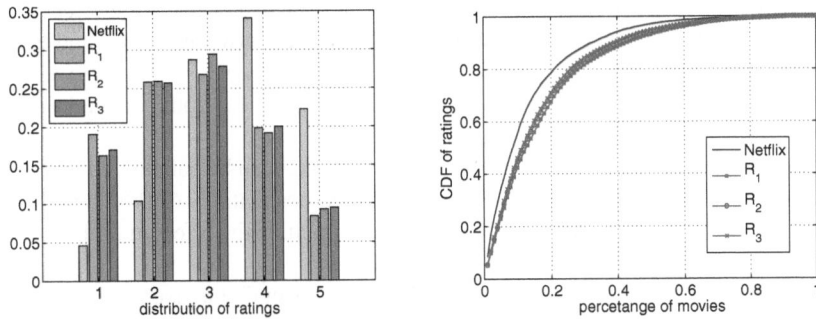

Fig. 1. User study data compared to Netflix. (a) Rating distribution in the 3 trials of our survey as compared to the Netflix data set. And, (b) Cumulative distribution of number of ratings by movie.

Next, we are interested in assessing whether our experiment design – *i.e.* having users rate movies in a batch – might be different enough from a real setting that would bias the results. In our experiment, we measure an average of 18.5 ratings per user in the worst case (first trial). If we analyze the Netflix dataset, we measure an average of 5.8 ratings per day (session). However, when we remove sessions with less than 4 ratings from the Netflix dataset, we measure an average of 20 movies per session, larger than in our study. Note that sessions not removed in this case (*i.e.* those with 4 or more consecutive ratings) account for 79.67% of the ratings in the Netflix dataset. Therefore, our experimental setting seems to be representative of high proportions of the Netflix dataset (and hence of similar real-life settings).

---

[2] In addition, and in order to rule-out a possible effect of our movie selection procedure, we computed all values for the 20% most popular movies, observing no significant difference.

5.1   Test-Retest Reliability and Stability

In order to compute the reliability of our test, we first compute the correlation coefficients between different trials, which result in $r_{12} = 0.8986$, $r_{23} = 0.9028$, and $r_{13} = 0.8783$. From these values and using Eq. 1, the overall reliability of our experiment is $r_{overall} = 0.924$. As a first conclusion, we observe that our test has high overall reliability – any value over 0.9 is usually considered "good" in classical test theory [11]. This result validates the procedure of asking users for their ratings – in the context of Web-based movie rating – as a good measure of whether they like/dislike **these** particular movies. A different question, that we will address later in our analysis, is whether this procedure is a good way to quantify user preferences. The overall reliability also sets an upper bound for a predictive algorithm based on this explicit user feedback.

Using Eq. 2, we compute the temporal pairwise stabilities to be: $s_{12} = 0.973$, $s_{23} = 0.977$, and $s_{13} = 0.951$. These stability factors are all high as well. This should be expected given the short times elapsed between trials: user preferences are not likely to change in two weeks. Also as expected, the lowest stability coefficient (s_{13}) corresponds to the longest time interval between trials (at least 15 days between trials 1 and 3). However, it comes as a surprise that the stability between trials 1 and 2 (at least 1 day apart) is slightly lower than the that between trials 2 and 3 (at least 15 days). Note that the stability coefficient might also be accounting for the user's "learning effect". Such intuition is supported by the fact that the stability effect between trials 1 and 2 is not closer to 1.0 – it is hard to imagine that the users opinions have changed in about 24 hours. The lower values in s_{13} could in fact be accounting for both change in opinion and a learning effect. We leave this issue to future work.

These inter-test correlations are the only measures that can be compared to the works of Hill et al. [9] and Cosley et al. [4], with reported correlations of 0.83 and 0.70 respectively (see Section 2). However, their measures include the effect of both reliability and stability.

Additionally, we are interested in measuring the impact that a given rating value has on the overall reliability. Therefore, we compute new reliability values by ignoring all triplets of ratings where at least one rating equals the value to remove. Removing ratings 2, 4, and especially 3, improves the reliability, yielding new values of 0.93, 0.925 and 0.95, respectively – as compared to the overall reliability of 0.924. On the other hand, removing extreme ratings (1 and 5) yields lower reliability – 0.88 and 0.89, respectively. This finding seems to indicate that recommender algorithms could benefit from giving lower weight or importance to ratings in the middle of the rating scale.

5.2   Analysis of Users Inconsistencies

Next, we shall study the inconsistencies of user ratings across different trials. Table 1 summarizes the results of the experiment when grouping the trials by pairs, where R_k corresponds to trial $k = 1, ..., 3$.

Let us define the aggregated rating of user u's ratings of movie m as a tuple $\langle r_k \rangle_{um}$, where r_k corresponds to the rating at trial R_k. Therefore, for a given user u and movie m we have vector of three ratings $\langle r_{um1} r_{um2} r_{um3} \rangle$, Note that there are user $\times$ movies tuples (*i.e.* $118 \times 100 = 11800$ in our case). A rating is considered to be *consistent* across trials, when all values of r_k are the same. Note that we are not interested in those tuples where all r_k are zeros, which is the value used to represent a *not-seen*.

Effect of "not seen" values. In order to analyze the effect that the "not seen" value has in our study, we consider two different subsets: a) the *intersection* or only tuples where all ratings are *seen* (> 0) and b) the *union*, where not seen values are included. For instance, ratings $\langle 4, 4, 5 \rangle_{um}$ would be inconsistent, because user u changed her evaluation of movie m from 4 to 5 in the last trial. This tuple, however, would be included both in the intersection and the union set. However, the tuple $\langle 4, 4, 0 \rangle_{um}$ would not be included in the intersection set, because one of the ratings is a *not-seen*.

Table 1. Summary of results on the pairwise comparison between trials. The first and second column contain the number of ratings in trials R_i and R_j. The third and forth column depict the number of elements in the intersection and the union for R_i and R_j. The intersection set contains ratings in which no element is *not-seen*, whereas the union set allows for *not-seen* elements. The last two columns report the root square mean error of the intersection and the union sets.

	$\#R_i$	$\#R_j$	#		$RMSE$	
			$\cap$	$\cup$	$\cap$	$\cup$
R_1, R_2	2185	1961	1838	2308	0.573	0.707
R_1, R_3	2185	1909	1774	2320	0.637	0.765
R_2, R_3	1969	1909	1730	2140	0.557	0.694

Table 1 summarizes the users' inconsistency results. For example, in R_1, users provide 2185 out of the potential 11800 ratings. Thus, 9615 positions in the rating matrix of R_1 are *not-seen* values. Without taking the actual value of the rating into consideration, the divergence in the number of ratings illustrates how users are not even able to consistently determine whether they have seen a movie or not. Only 1838 ratings in R_1 also appear in R_2 – the intersection. If we take the union, we obtain 2308 ratings. The results are similar on all pairs of trials. With these results, we are able to answer our first research question *Q1*.

RMSE due to inconsistencies. We shall now look at the inconsistencies due to a *different rating value* in different trials. We use the *root mean squared error* (RMSE) for easy comparison with previous and related work in the RS literature and in particular with the Netflix Prize threshold (*i.e.* desired RMSE of 0.8563) [2]. The right side of Table 1 contains the RMSE for the intersection and union sets across all trials.

The RMSE for the intersection sets ranges between 0.55 and 0.63, depending on the trials. Note that the previously computed stability is inversely correlated with the RMSE. The most stable comparison is between R_2 and R_3, 0.977, which gives the smallest RMSE (0.5571).

In the case of the union sets, we replace the *not-seen* value with the average rating for that movie. The RMSE is now higher as it is accounting for two types of user inconsistencies: inconsistencies in labeling as *seen or not-seen* and inconsistencies in the actual values. The RMSE ranges from 0.694 to 0.765 in this case.

Note that these values of RMSE represent a lower bound of the RMSE that could be achieved by a RS built from the data in our study. Therefore, and in the context of our study, current RS algorithms would not be able to predict the movie ratings with lower RMSE that the ones described in Table 1 (unless they are overfitting the training data). Of course, the particular RMSE values are dataset dependent. With this analysis, we address our second research question Q2.

5.3   Variables That Have an Impact on User Inconsistencies

In order to answer our third research question (Q3), we analyze the variables that might play a role in increasing the likelihood of user inconsistencies. In particular, we explore the impact that the rating scale, item order and user input speed might have on inconsistencies.

Rating Scale Effect.   In the initial reliability analysis presented in Section 5.1, we showed that removing 2 and 3 star ratings yields higher reliability. We shall now investigate this further by analyzing which are the most common inconsistencies. Figure 2a shows the probability of inconsistency by the value of the rating between pairwise trials (R_1,R_2), (R_2,R_3) and (R_1,R_3). In other words, the probability that if users gave a rating of X in trial R_i, they will give a different rating in trial R_j.

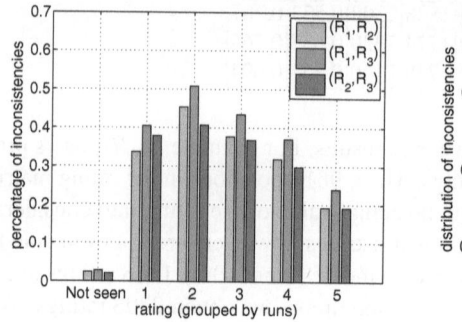 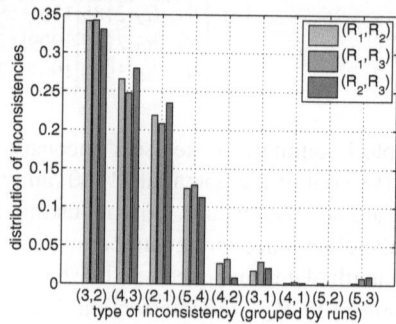

Fig. 2. Users Inconsistencies. (a) Percentage of inconsistencies by rating value and (b) Distribution of types of inconsistencies.

Note how ratings with extreme opinions (*i.e.* the lowest and highest ratings in the scale) are more consistent across different trials: the probability of inconsistencies is highest for 2 and 3 stars ratings. The average ratings in our study are 2.73, 2.79 and 2.79 for R_1, R_2 and R_3 respectively. Also note that the probability of inconsistency with *not-seen* is lower.

We shall investigate next what are the most common inconsistencies. Figure 2b depicts the distribution of inconsistencies by switching the score – note that the Figure does not include inconsistencies due to *not-seen* items. The two most common inconsistencies are due to a rating drifting between 2 and 3 (about 34%) and between 3 and 4 (25%). Ratings with a ±1 drift account for more than 90% of the inconsistencies.

Thus, ratings in the middle of the rating scale seem to be more prone to inconsistencies than extreme ratings. This observation makes intuitive sense for several reasons: First, extreme ratings have a lower or higher bound (*e.g.* you cannot get higher than 5). Also, users are probably more consistent about remembering very good and very bad movies, which somehow impacted them. Finally, extreme ratings seem to be less prone to assimilation and contrast effects. These intuitions, however should be further investigated in future work.

Item Order Effect. Next, we shall analyze the effect of time on user inconsistencies. Figure 3 depicts the inconsistencies as they appeared over time while participants filled out each of the surveys. Note that now inconsistencies are not computed by pairwise comparisons across trials, but reckoned across the three trials. In our analysis, we compute the *ground truth or valid* rating for each movie and participant as the rating that appears *at least twice* across the three trials. Thus, we assume that the trial with the different value is the one causing the inconsistency. Note that movies where the three ratings for the three trials are different from each other are discarded (they represent a 10.69% of the total).

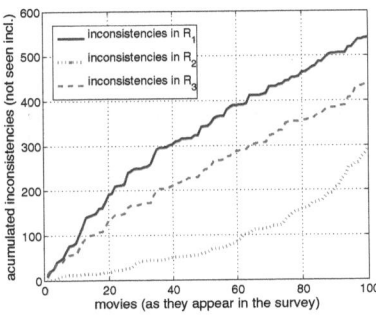 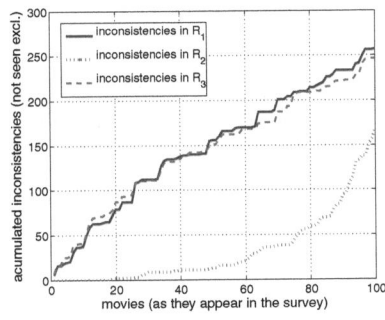

(a) Taking into account "not seen" values.   (b) "Not seen" values not taken into account.

Fig. 3. Accumulated error across movies. An error is assigned to R_i if its rating is different than the other R. The movies are set as they appear in R_0 and R_3.

Figure 3a shows the accumulated inconsistencies over time as movies were presented to the user, including inconsistencies due to *not-seen*. Figure 3b excludes the *not-seen* inconsistencies.

As Figure 3a illustrates, the first trial R_1 is responsible for most of the inconsistencies, followed by the third trial R_3. The decrease of inconsistencies in the last trial R_3 might be caused by the learning effect, as users would have undergone the survey twice before. However, when discarding the effect of the *not-seen* value (Fig. 3b), R_1 and R_3 exhibit a very similar behavior. This result suggests that a learning effect might only affect the consistency on discriminating between *seen* and *not-seen* movies.

Interestingly, the second trial R_2, which took place at least one day after R_1 and where the movies were sorted by increasing popularity, displays the lowest level of inconsistencies. The improvement in consistency in R_2 might be explained by several factors: First, the short time between trials – only 24 hours. However, neither the pairwise stability nor the RSME support this hypothesis. Therefore, it seems that the *order* in which the movies are presented (*i.e.* showing popular movies first) could be the factor for the consistency gain. Additionally, this result might be related to the minimization of the *contrast effect*, as similar movies are shown together.

To sum up and according to our experiment, a rating interface that groups movies that are likely to receive similar ratings should help minimize user inconsistencies.

User Rating Speed Effect. The data logs collected in the user study include the exact time at which each user rating was generated. This allows us to analyze how the speed with which users rate movies might affect their consistency.

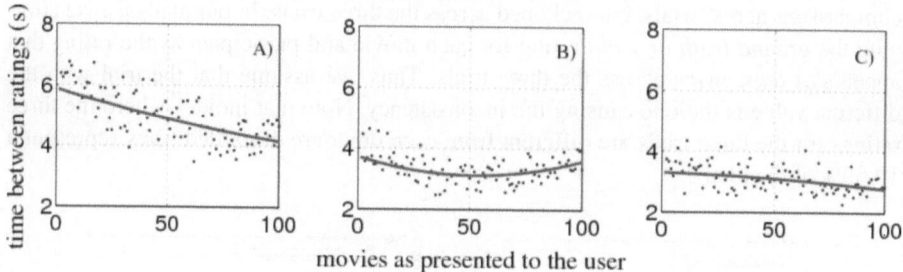

Fig. 4. Graphs depicting time between ratings for (a) R_1, (b) R_2, and (c) R_3. Note that all plots have the same temporal scale. The clicking time is always between 2 and 8 seconds. The average clicking time is 4.93, 3.30, 3.08 seconds for R_1, R_2 and R_3 respectively. For reference, a quadratic fit is also plotted as a line.

Figure 4 depicts the average evaluation time by movies where movies are sorted as they were presented to the user. Note how in the case of R_1 and R_3 (sorted at random), the evaluation time decreases as the survey progresses. This result makes intuitive sense, as users were probably getting tired or used to the setting. However, in the case of R_2 (Fig. 4.b), the evaluation time decreases at first, but then increases again during the last half of the survey. This behavior might be caused by the way the movies in R_2 were presented: users were fast in assessing unpopular movies, many of which they might not have seen, at the beginning of the survey. Then, when popular movies appear (and therefore probably seen by participants), users seem to spend more time thinking about the rating.

We measure an average rating time of 4.93, 3.30, and 3.08 seconds respectively for each of our trials. One might expect that faster clicking could introduce more inconsistencies due to input error. However, the percentage of inconsistencies per trial are 42.5%, 23.2%, and 32.3%. So, a shorter time between ratings does not imply more inconsistencies on the ratings.

5.4   Long-Term Errors and Reliability

In this section, we measure the reliability and RMSE of our experiment when removing the original R_2 trial and adding a new one (R_4). This new trial was conducted 7 months after $R3$, and using the same random movie permutation as R_1 and R_3. Therefore, we now have three trials with the same movie order, separated 15 days and 7 months respectively. Our goal is to evaluate if there are significant differences in the values because of the longer elapsed time and the removal of the different sorting in the intermediate trial.

First, and in order to rule out the effects of this smaller – and maybe biased – population, we recomputed the correlations, stability factors, reliability, and RMSE in the three original trials for this subset of 36 users, observing no significant differences with the original values reported for the entire population.

Using this new setting, we obtain an overall reliability of 0.8763 – compared to the original 0.924. Although this is only a 5% difference, we are now below the 0.9 threshold. This is an indication that this kind of rating surveys might not be an appropriate way to measure user preferences over a long period of time. Our new stability factors are measured as $s_{13} = 1.0025$, $s_{34} = 0.9706$, and $s_{14} = 0.9730$. Now, and as it would be expected, we see a much clearer trend: very high stability between the trials separated 15 days and significantly lower for any two trials separated by 7 months.

Finally, we measure our new RMSE values as $R_{13} = 0.6143$, $R_{14} = 0.6822$, and $R_{34} = 0.6835$ for the intersection, and $R_{13} = 0.7445$, $R_{14} = 0.8156$, $R_{34} = 0.8014$ for the union. First, we observe that the RMSE for trials separated by 7 months, is significantly larger than in the original setting (see Table 1, columns 6 and 7). In the original setting, we also measured lower values between consecutive trials, arguably due to the memory effect. However, when the elapsed time between consecutive trials is long enough (*e.g.* 7 months), this effect is no longer noticeable and the RMSE is larger for sessions separated a long time, regardless of whether they are consecutive or not. Note that if we want to measure the effect of both the long time interval plus a change in movie ordering, we can compute R_{24} – error between trial 2, sorted by popularity, and trial 4 with random order and conducted 7 monhts after. The measured RMSE is now 0.832.

6 Conclusions

In this paper, we have presented a user study aimed at quantitatively analyzing user inconsistencies in a movie rating domain. Since recommender systems commonly rely on user ratings to compute their predictions, inconsistencies in these ratings will have an impact on the quality of the recommendations. We believe that the characterization of these inconsistencies is of key importance in the RS field.

Our study shows that, although the reliability of the survey as an instrument and the stability of user opinions are high, inconsistencies negatively impact the quality of the predictions that would be given by a RS. The calculated RMSE between different trials ranged between 0.557 and 0.8156, depending on the elapsed time and whether the "not seen" ratings effect is ruled out. These RMSE values represent a lower bound (*magic barrier*) for any explicit feedback-based RS built from the data of our study unless overfitting to this data. We plan on carrying out additional studies in order to understand how well our results generalize to other domains and settings. It is interesting to note how close these values are to current state-of-the-art recommendation algorithms.

We have also presented a detailed analysis on the nature of user inconsistencies. Our main findings can be summarized as follows: (1) Extreme ratings are more consistent than mild opinions; (2) users are more consistent when movies with similar ratings are grouped together; (3) the learning effect on the setting improves the user's assessment on whether she has seen the movie, but not the stability of the rating itself; and (4) faster user clicking does not yield more inconsistencies.

We believe that these insights will benefit the design of RS, which could take this characteristic distribution of inconsistencies into consideration. Future work should validate how much our findings can be generalized across settings, datasets and domains. In addition, we plan on using the information gathered in this study to analyze how different recommendation algorithms behave to this type of noise and design strategies to overcome it.

Acknowledgments

This work has been partially funded by an ICREA grant from the Generalitat de Catalunya.

References

1. Adomavicius, G., Tuzhilin, A.: Toward the next generation of recommender systems: A survey of the state-of-the-art and possible extensions. IEEE Trans. on Knowl. and Data Eng. 17(6), 734–749 (2005)
2. Bennet, J., Lanning, S.: The netflix prize. In: Proc. of KDD Work. on Large-scale Rec. Sys. (2007)
3. Choicestream. Personalization Survey. Technical report, Choicestream Inc. (2007)
4. Cosley, D., Lam, S.K., Albert, I., Konstan, J.A., Riedl, J.: Is seeing believing?: how recommender system interfaces affect users' opinions. In: Proc. of CHI 2003 (2003)
5. Dijksterhuis, A., Spears, R., Lepinasse, V.: Reflecting and deflecting stereotypes: Assimilation and contrast in impression formation and automatic behavior. J. of Exp. Social Psych. 37, 286–299 (2001)
6. Harper, M., Li, X., Chen, Y., Konstan, J.: An economic model of user rating in an online recommender system. In: Ardissono, L., Brna, P., Mitrović, A. (eds.) UM 2005. LNCS, vol. 3538, pp. 307–316. Springer, Heidelberg (2005)
7. Heise, D.: Separating reliability and stability in test-retest correlation. Amer. Sociol. Rev. 34(1), 93–101 (1969)
8. Herlocker, J.L., Konstan, J.A., Terveen, L.G., Riedl, J.T.: Evaluating collaborative filtering recommender systems. ACM Trans. on Inf. Syst. 22(1), 5–53 (2004)
9. Hill, W., Stead, L., Rosenstein, M., Furnas, G.: Recommending and evaluating choices in a virtual community of use. In: Proc. of CHI 1995 (1995)
10. Lord, F.M., Novick, M.R.: Statistical theories of mental test scores. Addison Wesley, Reading (1968)
11. Murphy, K., Davidshofer, C.: Psychological testing: Principles and applications, 4th edn. Addison-Wesley, Reading (1996)
12. Oard, D.W., Kim, J.: Implicit feedback for recommender systems. In: AAAI Works. on Rec. Sys. (1998)
13. O'Mahony, M.P.: Detecting noise in recommender system databases. In: Proc. of IUI 2006 (2006)
14. Sherif, M., Hovland, C.I.: Social judgment: Assimilation and contrast effects in communication and attitude change. Yale University Press, New Haven (1961)
15. Torkzadeh, G., Doll, W.J.: The test-retest reliability of user involvement instruments. Inf. Manag. 26(1), 21–31 (1994)

Evaluating Interface Variants on Personality Acquisition for Recommender Systems

Greg Dunn[1], Jurgen Wiersema[2], Jaap Ham[3], and Lora Aroyo[4]

[1] Philips Research Europe, HTC 34, 5.006,5656 AE, Eindhoven, Netherlands
greg.dunn@philips.com
[2] Capgemini Nederland B.V., Papendorpseweg 100, 3528 BJ, Utrecht, Netherlands
jurgen.wiersema@capgemini.com
[3] Eindhoven University of Technology, P.O. Box 513, 5600 MB, Eindhoven, Netherlands
j.r.c.ham@tue.nl
[4] VU University Amsterdam, 1081 HV, Amsterdam, Netherlands
l.m.aroyo@cs.vu.nl

Abstract. Recommender systems help users find personally relevant media content in response to an overwhelming amount of this content available digitally. A prominent issue with recommender systems is recommending new content to new users; commonly referred to as the cold start problem. It has been argued that detailed user characteristics, like personality, could be used to mitigate cold start. To explore this solution, three alternative methods measuring users' personality were compared to investigate which would be most suitable for user information acquisition. Participants ($N = 60$) provided user ease of use and satisfaction ratings to evaluate three different interface variants believed to measure participants' personality characteristics. Results indicated that the *NEO interface* and the *CFG interface* were promising methods for measuring personality. Results are discussed in terms of potential benefits and broader implications for recommender systems.

Keywords: Recommender systems, adaptive systems, cold start, information acquisition, personality.

1 Introduction

This paper presents an evaluation of three innovative interface variants that obtain users' personality characteristics, such as those characteristics described by [1]. In doing so, this evaluation has explored how information acquisition of users' personality could be used in recommender systems. Recommender systems help users find personally relevant content in response to an overwhelming amount of content available through digital means [18, 19]. Despite evidence that user characteristics (e.g., age, gender, occupation) could help lessen the familiar cold start problem affiliated with recommender systems, few researchers have ventured into this area [11]. This apprehension might be due to perceived difficulty in obtaining these characteristics. This paper has incorporated research paradigms from psychology to suggest alternative

G.-J. Houben et al. (Eds.): UMAP 2009, LNCS 5535, pp. 259–270, 2009.
© Springer-Verlag Berlin Heidelberg 2009

techniques for measuring users' personality, which could be incorporated into various recommender systems to mitigate cold start.

The research background provided in this paper comes from the fields of recommender systems and personality. This is followed by a design rationale and process for three interface variants designed to measure personality, and by hypotheses for the experiment presented in this paper. The Method section describes how these interface variants were evaluated. Results of the experiment are then provided, followed by discussion and conclusions.

1.1 Background

It has been suggested that recommender systems imitate social techniques individuals use to get informed about novel experiences, commonly known as word-of-mouth [18]. For instance, individuals ask friends for suggestions regarding a good movie, music, restaurant, etc. While there are different types of recommender systems, the most successfully utilized are collaborative filtering (CF) systems [2, 6], which mimic word-of-mouth. Despite their success, one recognized issue with CF systems is cold start [11, 16, 20]. Cold start refers to difficulties encountered by recommender algorithms when a new item or user is added to a CF system. Research has often tried to address cold start by including content meta-data [e.g., 14, 16, 19, 20].

Alternatively, other researchers [e.g., 11] have suggested further improvements addressing cold start in CF systems can be gained via user characteristics (i.e., characteristics that are inherently part of the user). Though few researchers have tackled the cold start problem by leveraging users' characteristics, this research has shown promise [e.g., 11, 12, 15]. So far, this research has only looked at surface-level characteristics. Nonetheless, [11] argues that improvements to this research can be gained by measuring more detailed user characteristics. Personality is known to be a stable user characteristic [1, 9], which has been shown to reliably describe various personal habits and behaviors [3, 17]. This suggests that by incorporating detailed user characteristics, such as personality, it is possible to address the cold start problem and possibly improve prediction in current CF systems.

One identified and well-established model of personality within psychology is known Big Five model [9], which outlines five personality characteristics known as:

1. *Neuroticism* (N) – individual's propensity to feel fear, sadness, embarrassment, anger, guilt, and other emotions of negative affect.
2. *Extraversion* (E) – individual's propensity to be sociable, talkative, assertive, active, and prefer environments providing stimulation and excitement.
3. *Openness to Experience* (O) – individual's propensity toward intellectual curiosity, imagination, aesthetic and emotional sensitivity, and originality.
4. *Agreeableness* (A) – individual's propensity toward being altruistic, helpful, sympathetic, and empathetic toward others.
5. *Conscientiousness* (C) – individual's propensity toward cleanliness, orderliness, determination, and self-control.

The challenge when measuring personality for a CF system, however, is that users will likely give up if too much information is required from them when first starting to use such a system [16, 24]. According to [21], however, it is also important that why this user information and how it will be used is transparent to the user. So, these methods must try to solve cold start while requiring minimal effort from users, or in such a way that it is satisfying to users, and while making it clear to the user why this information is necessary.

There are two distinct ways to acquire information from the user: explicit and implicit [24]. Interfaces employing explicit user information acquisition ask questions that the user is required to answer. Interfaces employing implicit information acquisition simply acquire user information by observing users' behavioral patterns. Based on previous research [16, 24], it seems likely that implicit acquisition would be preferred by users because it requires less effort on their behalf. By developing and testing several methods that acquire user information, it provides the opportunity to investigate what is the best method for a CF system to measure more detailed user characteristics, such as personality. The following section describes the design rationale and process for each of the three interface variants that were tested to investigate this issue.

2 Design Rationale and Process

Three interface variants have been proposed: 1) the *NEO interface*, 2) the *Commons Fishing Game (CFG) interface*, and 3) the *Implicit Association Test (IAT) interface*.

2.1 The NEO Interface

The *NEO interface* was based on the Dutch NEO PI-R [7], acquired personality explicitly via 24 screens, each with ten statements numbered sequentially. The NEO PI-R is a well-established and reliable method to measure the Big Five [1]. Five radio buttons were placed beside each of the 240 statements. Using these buttons, participants rated their level of agreement on a scale from 1 (Strongly Disagree) to 5 (Strongly Agree). Responses were summed for each of the Big Five characteristics mentioned above. A minimum of 264 mouse-clicks was required to rate all items. Figure 1 gives a screenshot of the NEO interface.

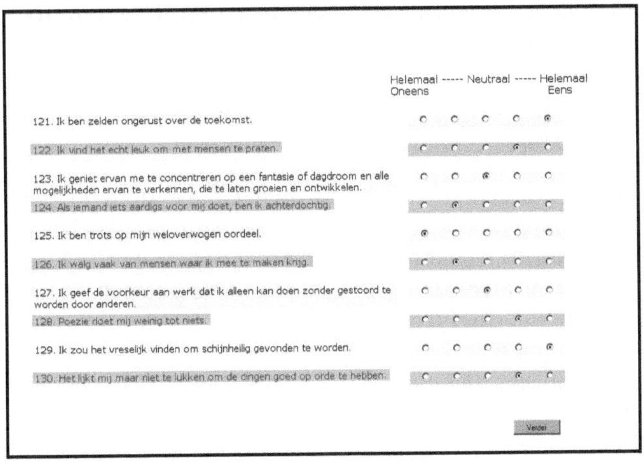

Fig. 1. Screenshot of the *NEO interface*

2.2 The CFG Interface

The second proposed interface variant was based on a common resources dilemma gaming paradigm employed by [10]. In this game, users are instructed to maximize the amount gathered from a common resource, which is shared amongst a group of players; collectively trying not to deplete this resource. Using 72 University students playing with a computerized resource dilemma interface, [10] showed that participants scoring high on *Extraversion* gathered more from the common resource in the first few rounds, than participants who scored low. Furthermore, participants scoring high on *Agreeableness* tended to gather less as the game went on compared to participants who score low. To closely follow the resource dilemma interface implemented by [10], the *CFG interface* adhered to the following procedure:

- Participants were told they were playing against 7 other participants and players for an unspecified number of rounds for an additional reward in the experiment; a €5.00 bonus to the winner.
- The interface was pre-programmed to last 16 rounds or once the common resource was depleted.
- Participants played against computer opponents.
- Each round, participants bid on how much of the common resource they would gather.

Fishing was arbitrarily used as the *CFG interface* theme. There were two scenarios provided in [10]'s experiment, one in which resource depletion was slow and one in which depletion was rapid. The *CFG interface* provided only one scenario (slow to rapid resource depletion), which was the only substantial change from [10]. This interface was first prototyped and pre-tested to ensure that participants understood the game play. Figure 2 provides a screenshot of the final *CFG interface* after usability issues found in pre-testing were corrected. The *CFG interface* used fish bids as its DV, which ranged from 0 to 10 units per round. Computer opponents bidding behavior was pre-programmed to withdraw random amounts from the resource with a pre-specified mean [10]. After bidding, the common fish resource diminished by the total number of fish bids gathered by all players, then replenished by 10%. Controls used in the *CFG interface* were a drop-down menu (fish bid amount) and a standard button. A minimum of 48 mouse-clicks was necessary to complete the game.

2.3 The IAT Interface

The third interface variant was based on implicit measures of personality [5, 22]. These measures compared reaction time to visual stimuli associated with contrasting personality descriptors. Compared to the *CFG interface*, the *IAT interface* is able to measure all of the Big Five personality characteristics. Results relating the IAT with explicit measures of the Big Five have been inconsistent [e.g., 5, 22]. There are, however, relatively few implicit tests that have been previously associated with personality measurement. So, the *IAT interface* was developed based on the work by [5] to explore the efficacy of this implementation in a recommender system.

The *IAT interface* was a Dutch adaption from [5]. Participants sorted descriptors related to a Big Five personality characteristic or its opposite. They went through five

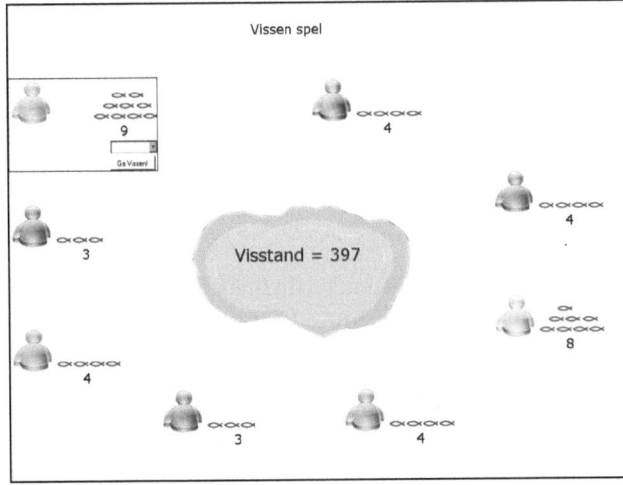

Fig. 2. Screenshot of the *CFG interface*

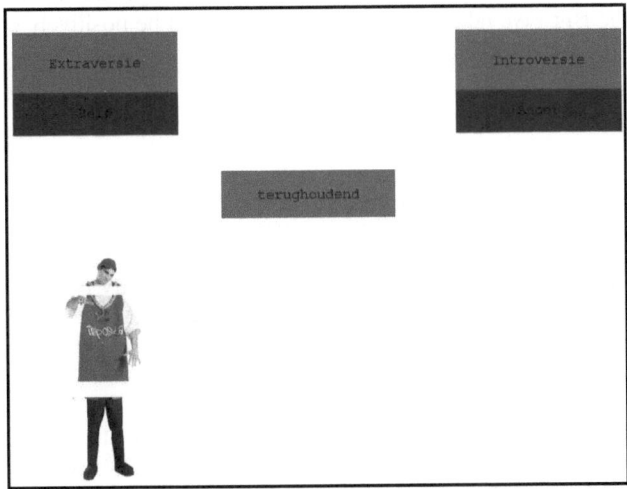

Fig. 3. Screenshot of the *IAT Interface*

conditions divided into six blocks, one condition for each characteristic. Four blocks were practice blocks, which allowed participants to familiarize themselves with correct and incorrect associations. Pictures were included in these blocks to make the interface more engaging. Participants' reaction times were not taken during this time. In the two remaining test blocks, participants were given personality trait descriptors (e.g., Outgoing) to associate with a given personality characteristic (e.g., Extraversion). Furthermore, in one test block the given personality characteristic was associated with self, while in the other test block, this characteristic was attributed to others (i.e., not self). The DV for the *IAT interface* was the difference in time (D_{time}) between categorization reaction times in one test block versus the other test block. Keyboard inputs collected reaction times (keys 'a' and 'k'). The interface was first prototyped and pre-tested to ensure that participants understood the task. Figure 3 provides a screenshot of the *IAT interface* after correcting usability issues found in pre-testing. A minimum of 840 key presses was necessary to complete this task.

3   Hypotheses

The first hypothesis (H1) reflects literature findings that suggest users will give up if too much effort is required when starting to use a recommender system [16, 24]. Given these findings, H1 states that both the *CFG interface* and the *IAT interface* will receive higher user acceptance ratings compared to the *NEO interface*.

The second hypothesis (H2) pertains to psychology literature that has related implicit measures of personality to the Big Five. The hypothesis for the *CFG interface* is based on [10]'s results. So, H2a states that participants' average bids in the *CFG interface* for the first three rounds will be positively correlated to *Extraversion*, while their average bids over all rounds will be negatively correlated with *Agreeableness*. Regarding the *IAT interface*, H2b is based on [5]'s findings and so, states that measurements of the Big Five taken by the *IAT interface* will be positively correlated with the same measurements taken by the *NEO interface*.

4   Method

4.1   Participants

Participants ($N = 60$; 40 male, 20 female) were recruited via a university participant database and advertisements distributed across the University campus. Participants' ages ranged from 16 to 62 with a mean age of 30 ($SD = 12.6$).

4.2   Materials

Participants completed the experiment using Pentium 4 computers with Windows XP. Monitors had a 1024x768 pixels screen resolution at 85 Hz. The *IAT interface* was created using E-Prime 2.0, while the remaining interfaces were created in C#. Beside the measures used to obtain personality via the three interface variants, participants also completed a measure of users' acceptance toward each of these interfaces:

- *Ease of Use and Satisfaction Questionnaire (USE)* consisted of 8 questions; 4 questions measuring participants' perceived ease of use (alpha = .89), and 4 questions measuring their satisfaction (alpha = .90) with the interface previously used. The questions were first developed by [23]. Each question was answered on a 7-point Likert scale ranging from 0 (Completely Disagree) to 6 (Completely Agree). For the current study, these questions were translated in Dutch with some changes in wording (i.e., "the system" in the English form specified the interface variant that participants just used, when translated into Dutch).

4.3 Procedure

The experiment was a counterbalanced within-groups design where participants were tested in groups ranging between 1 and 7 individuals ($M = 3.2$). After giving consent, participants were seated in separate testing rooms with a computer. Participants were informed that they would be provided with a series of interfaces, each with its own separate instructions. Participants were also told that these interfaces were constructed to gather their personality information for use by a recommender system. They were further informed that for one of the interfaces, they would be competing against other players for a €5.00 bonus, where the highest scorer would receive this bonus. Participants began the experiment by proceeding through interfaces inquiring about their age, gender, and education. Following this, participants then interacted with each of the three interface variants (*NEO, CFG, IAT*), presented in counterbalanced order. After each variant, they were given a screen with the USE questions measuring their perceived ease of use and satisfaction toward the preceding interface variant. Once the experiment was finished, participants were debriefed and received a €15.00 gift certificate, as well as the €5.00 bonus, regardless of their performance in the *CFG interface*.

5 Results

We compared interface variants in two ways: participants' preference toward each of these interface variants (H1), and personality measurement accuracy (H2).

The first comparison analyzed participants' user acceptance with each of the three interface variants. Acceptance scores were obtained via the USE questionnaire described in the Method section, which separated acceptance into participants' perceived ease of use and their satisfaction toward each interface variant. A MANOVA was done using this data, with interface variant as the repeated measures IV and the aggregated scores for perceived ease of use and satisfaction as our DVs. Figure 4 indicates mean scores for participants' perceived ease of use and satisfaction given interface variant. The MANOVA showed overall effects of interface variant ($F(4, 56) = 14.99, p < .001$, $\eta^2 = .52$), and subsequent univariate tests indicated differences in participants' perceived ease of use scores ($F(2, 118) = 17.71, p < .001, \eta^2 = .23$), and their satisfaction scores ($F(2, 118) = 14.62, p < .001, \eta^2 = .20$). Regarding ease of use, pairwise comparisons (Bonferroni) indicated that participants scored the *NEO interface* ($M = 20.62$, $SE = .412$) higher than both the *CFG interface* ($M = 17.43, SE = .668; p < .001$) and *IAT interface* ($M = 16.17, SE = .724; p < .001$). For satisfaction, pairwise comparisons (Bonferroni) indicated that participants scored the *NEO interface* ($M = 16.62, SE = .646$) and *CFG interface* ($M = 14.68, SE = .739$) higher than the *IAT interface* ($M = 12$, $SE = .760; p < .001$ and $p < .01$, respectively).

To better understand these findings, participants' mean times with each of the interface variants were compared. These means were compared in a 3-way ANOVA, with interface variant as the IV, and mean time as the DV. This ANOVA indicated a significant difference in participants' mean time depending on the interface variant, $F(2, 118) = 307.32, p < .001$. Pairwise comparisons (Bonferroni) indicated that participants' mean time with the *NEO interface* ($M = 21:54$ min, $SD = 6:39$ min.) was

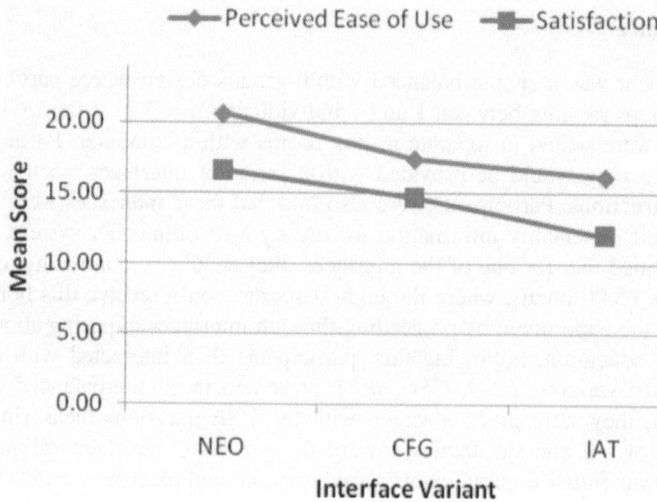

Fig. 4. Mean scores for participants' perceived ease of use and satisfaction given interface variant

Table 1. Personality correlations for the *NEO interface* compared to *CFG* and *IAT interfaces*

| | | NEO | | | | |
		N	E	O	A	C
C	1st 3 rounds	-	.29*	-	-.21	-
F						
G	All rounds	-	.38**	-	-.32*	-
	Neuroticism (N)	-.19	-	-	-	-
I	Extraversion (E)	-	-.24	-	-	-
A	Openness (O)	-	-	.09	-	-
T	Agreeableness (A)	-	-	-	-.23	-
	Conscientious-ness (C)	-	-	-	-	.11

* indicates $p < .05$, ** indicates $p < .01$.

greater than their mean time with the *IAT interface* ($M = 9:49$ min, $SD = 1:55$ min., $p < .001$), which in turn, was greater than their mean time with the *CFG interface* ($M = 5:51$ min, $SD = 1:28$ min, $p < .001$).

For the second comparison, Big Five measurements taken by the *NEO interface* were correlated to the measurements hypothesized to be similarly taken by the *CFG* and *IAT interfaces*. Table 1 shows the personality measurements correlations for the *NEO interface* compared to the *CFG* and *IAT interfaces*. Columns in this table provide each of the Big Five factors, as measured by the *NEO interface*. The first two rows provide the personality measurement correlations between the *NEO interface* and *CFG interface* (H2a). As mentioned in the Design Rationale and Process section, the *CFG interface* measured personality by using fish bid scores. Based on [10], these scores were separated by average fish bid score for the first three rounds and average fish bid score over all rounds. The last five rows provide the correlations between the

NEO interface and *IAT interface* (H2b). Only the correlations related to hypotheses are shown. As indicated in this table, the *NEO interface* measurement for *Extraversion* was positively correlated to both *CFG interface* measurements: average fish bids in the first three trials ($r = .29$, $p < .05$), and average fish bids across all trials ($r = .38$, $p < .01$). Furthermore, the *NEO interface* measurement for *Agreeableness* was negatively correlated to averaged fish bids across all trials ($r = -.32$, $p < .05$). There were no significant correlations between the *NEO interface* and *IAT interface* measurements for their matched Big Five factors.

6 Discussion

The goal of this study was to compare and gauge the value of the three interface variants believed to effectively obtain users' personality. Results suggest that the (explicit) *NEO interface* and the (implicit) *CFG interface* both show promise as a method to obtain users' personality, both in terms of personality measurement accuracy and participants' reported ease of use and satisfaction data. The remainder of this discussion expands on the interpretation of these results.

As previously stated, the (explicit) *NEO interface* and the (implicit) *CFG interface* both showed promise as an effective and preferred method to obtain users' personality. Based on the literature review, however, it was expected that implicit measures would be preferred by users because it required less effort on their behalf [16, 24]. So, it was somewhat surprising to see that the *NEO interface* received significantly higher perceived ease of use scores compared to the other two interface variants. The *NEO interface* required a minimum of 264 key presses compared to 840 for the *IAT interface*. Also, the *NEO interface* only used two types of buttons (radio and standard), while the *CFG interface* used more complex controls (e.g., a drop down menu) that increased the chance of errors made by participants. Thus, perhaps one reason the *NEO interface* received these higher scores from participants was because the interface complexity was simpler. More importantly, however, the *NEO interface* also received the highest scores from participants' satisfaction; though these scores were not significantly greater than the *CFG interface*. Some participants freely expressed after the experiment that the *NEO interface* seemed to have a clear purpose, while the purpose of *CFG* and *IAT interfaces* remained unclear. Given this, these findings might be explained by [21], who argue that recommender systems must be more transparent to users with respect to how they work. Thus, these results suggest that the *NEO interface*, an explicit measure of personality, was the most promising interface variant in terms of both users' perceived ease of use and satisfaction.

Even with participants' clear preference toward the *NEO interface*, the *CFG interface* has also shown promise. Specifically, participants' satisfaction scores toward the *CFG interface* were similar to the *NEO interface*, indicating that participants' seemed to be reasonably satisfied when interacting with this interface. In addition, significant correlations between personality measures taken by the *NEO interface* and *CFG interface* for participants' *Extraversion* and *Agreeableness*, suggest that it is possible to use this method to estimate personality. It would be necessary to somehow leverage the ability of the *CFG interface* to estimate these personality characteristics more accurately, however, before it would be sufficiently effective for practical applications, like a recommender system. Furthermore, ideas would have to be generated to create a game interface, like the *CFG interface*, which would be able to estimate more of the personality characteristics that could potentially be implemented in a recommendation system. Thus, it would seem promising to explore other game (theory) possibilities that could have practical applications to recommender systems.

When compared to the *NEO* and *CFG interfaces*, the *IAT interface* showed little promise in its current state as personality assessment tool. This interface received the lowest scores for both participants' perceived ease of use and their satisfaction scores. Again, post-experiment comments from participants suggested that they were sometimes frustrated by the implementation of the pictures in the *IAT interface*, which likely impacted their low satisfaction scores toward this interface. Worse still were the correlation results obtained between personality measurements taken by the *NEO interface* and *IAT interface*, which indicated that the *IAT interface* did not measure personality, or at least not the same characteristics as the *NEO interface*. While [5] found that the IAT measure sufficiently assessed the Big Five, our findings seem to agree with [22], who found inconsistent correlations between the IAT measures and their respective Big Five counterparts. Therefore, it is argued that the IAT measure is not robust enough to be adapted and used in a different context than that used in [5]. If this is the case, then it would mean that the IAT would be hard to simplify in order to reduce effort. This would further suggest that the *IAT interface* is an inefficient personality measurement tool, considering only about 10% of all trials in this interface are used for determining presence of personality traits.

In closing, should future technologies attempt to improve recommender or other adaptive systems by using detailed user characteristics, like personality, these findings suggest that such an interface should acquire this data in an explicit manner. At the very least, reasons and how such information would be used should be made explicit. Additionally, however, there do appear to be opportunities for satisfying and engaging interfaces emerging from game theory, which are able to estimate personality.

6.1 Limitations and Future Work

An obvious limitation of this work was that it did not formally test recommender performance against existing standards, such as current CF recommender systems [e.g., 14, 16, 19]. Future research could focus on evaluating the performance of personality-enhanced CF systems compared to similar recommender functions.

7 Conclusion

Three interface variants, which were believed to measure users' personality, were compared. Results suggested that the *NEO interface* and the *CFG interface* appear to be promising methods for such personality acquisition. While it was particularly surprising that the explicit measure (the *NEO interface*) seemed most preferred by users, this was likely due to the clear and transparent nature of the interface.

In closing, the results of this study suggest opportunities to create an interface that explicitly acquires personality characteristics in an interactive and engaging way, which can provide personality-based recommendations related to content.

Acknowledgments. We thank Marie Curie Actions for funding this research as part of the CONTACT project (FP6-008201). We would also like to thank Boris de Ruyter, William Green, and Marco Tiemann among others for their ideas and support.

References

1. Costa, P.T., McCrae, R.R.: NEO PI-R Professional Manual. In: Psychological Assessment Resources, Odessa, FL (1992)
2. Deshpande, M., Karypis, G.: Item-Based Top-N Recommendation Algorithms. ACM Transactions on Information Systems 22, 143–177 (2004)
3. Gosling, S.: Snoop: What Your Stuff Says About You. Profile Books, London (2008)
4. Greenwald, A.G., Nosek, B.A., Banaji, M.R.: Understanding and Using the Implicit Association Test: I. An Improved Scoring Algorithm. J. of Pers. and Soc. Psych. 85, 197–216 (2003)
5. Grumm, M., von Collani, G.: Measuring Big-Five Personality Dimensions with the Implicit Association Test – Implicit Personality Traits or Self-Esteem? Pers. and Ind. Diff. 43, 2205–2217 (2007)
6. Herlocker, J.L., Konstan, J.A., Terveen, L.G., Riedl, J.T.: Evaluating Collaborative Filtering Recommender Systems. ACM Transactions on Information Systems 22, 5–53 (2004)
7. Hoekstra, H.A., Ormel, J., de Fruyt, F.: NEO-PI-R/NEO-FFI Big Five Persoonlijkheids-vragenlijst: Handleiding. Harcourt Assessment, Lisse (2003)
8. Hofmann, T.: Latent Semantic Models for Collaborative Filtering. ACM Transactions on Information Systems 22, 89–115 (2004)
9. John, O.P., Srivastava, S.: The Big-Five Trait Taxonomy: History, Measurement, and Theoretical Perspectives. In: Pervin, L., John, O.P. (eds.) Handbook of Personality: Theory and Research, 2nd edn., pp. 102–138. Guilford, New York (1999)
10. Koole, S.L., Jager, W., van den Berg, A.E., Vlek, C.A.J., Hofstee, W.K.B.: On the Social Nature of Personality: Effects of Extraversion, Agreeableness, and Feedback about Collective Resource use on Cooperation in a Resource Dilemma. Pers. and Soc. Psych. Bulletin 27, 289–301 (2001)
11. Lam, X.N., Vu, T., Le, T.D., Duong, A.D.: Addressing Cold-Start Problem in Recommendation Systems. In: ICUIMC 2008, pp. 208–211. ACM Press, New York (2008)
12. Lekakos, G., Giaglis, G.M.: Improving the Prediction Accuracy of Recommendation Algorithms: Approaches Anchored on Human Factors. Int. with Comp. 18, 410–431 (2006)
13. McNee, S.M., Riedl, J., Konstan, J.A.: Making Recommendations Better: An Analytic Model for Human-Recommender Interaction. In: CHI 2006, pp. 1103–1108. ACM Press, New York (2006)
14. Nathanson, T., Bitton, E., Goldberg, K.: Eigentaste 5.0: Constant-Time Adaptability in a Recommender System Using Item Clustering. In: RecSys 2007, pp. 149–152. ACM Press, New York (2007)
15. Nguyen, A., Denos, N., Berrut, C.: Improving New User Recommendations with Rule-Based Induction on Cold User Data. In: RecSys 2007, pp. 121–128. ACM Press, New York (2007)
16. Rashid, A.M., Albert, I., Cosley, D., Lam, S.K., McNee, S.M., Konstan, J.A., Riedl, J.: Getting to Know You: Learning New User Preferences in Recommender Systems. In: IUI 2002, pp. 127–134. ACM Press, New York (2002)
17. Rentfrow, P.J., Gosling, S.D.: The Do Re Mi's of Everyday Life: The Structure and Personality Correlates of Music Preferences. J. of Pers. and Soc. Psych. 84, 1236–1256 (2003)

18. Resnick, P., Varian, H.R.: Recommender Systems. Comm. of the ACM 40, 56–58 (1997)
19. Sarwar, B., Karypis, G., Konstan, J., Riedl, J.: Item-Based Collaborative Filtering Recommendation Algorithms. In: WWW10, pp. 285–295. ACM Press, New York (2001)
20. Schein, A.I., Popescul, A., Ungar, L.H., Pennock, D.M.: Methods and Metrics for Cold-Start Recommendations. In: SIGIR 2002, pp. 253–260. ACM Press, New York (2002)
21. Sinha, R., Swearingen, K.: The Role of Transparency in Recommender Systems. In: CHI 2002, pp. 830–831. ACM Press, New York (2002)
22. Steffens, M.C., Schulze König, S.: Predicting Spontaneous Big Five Behavior with Implicit Association Tests. European J. of Psychological Assessment 22, 13–20 (2006)
23. Venkatesh, V., Morris, M.G., Davis, G.B., Davis, F.D.: User Acceptance of Information Technology: Toward a Unified View. MIS Quarterly 27, 425–478 (2003)
24. Zigoris, P., Zhang, Y.: Bayesian Adaptive User Profiling with Explicit and Implicit Feedback. In: CIKM 2006, pp. 397–404. ACM Press, New York (2006)

Context-Dependent Personalised Feedback Prioritisation in Exploratory Learning for Mathematical Generalisation

Mihaela Cocea and George Magoulas

London Knowledge Lab, Birkbeck College,
23-29 Emerald Street, WC1N 3QS, London, UK
{mihaela,gmagoulas}@dcs.bbk.ac.uk

Abstract. In this paper we address the problem of prioritising feedback on the basis of multiple heterogeneous pieces of information in exploratory learning. The problem arises when multiple types of feedback are required in order to address different types of conceptual difficulties, accommodate particular learning behaviours identified during exploration, and provide appropriate support depending on the learning mode (e.g. individual or collaborative learning) and/or the stage of the exploratory learning process. We propose an approach that integrates learners' characteristics and context-related information through a Multicriteria Decision-Making formalism. The outcome is a context-aware mechanism for prioritising personalised feedback that is tested in an exploratory learning environment for mathematical generalisation.

Keywords: context-dependent personalised feedback, feedback prioritisation, Analytic Hierarchy Process, Multicriteria Decision Making.

1 Introduction

In exploratory learning, tasks can be approached in many different ways and are often characterized by some key points the learner needs to address or be aware of. The actions of learners can indicate what they need help with, but their personal characteristics may not guarantee the effectiveness of help. Context could bring valuable information that would make help more appropriate and, thus, more effective. Context-awareness has been studied in a diversity of domains like artificial intelligence [1], ubiquitous computing [2], educational psychology [3] and recommender systems [4]. The definition of context is also diverse, varying from the wide social context to the specificity of network characteristics.

In this paper we present a context-dependent personalised feedback prioritisation mechanism using the Analytic Hierarchy Process [5], a popular method in Multicriteria Decision-Making [6]. In our approach context refers to the learning mode (i.e. individual or collaborative) and to the stages within a task. The approach is illustrated using an Exploratory Learning Environment (ELE) for mathematical generalisation and the prioritisations delivered by the proposed method are validated by experts in the field of mathematical education.

G.-J. Houben et al. (Eds.): UMAP 2009, LNCS 5535, pp. 271–282, 2009.

The paper is organised as follows. Section 2 briefly introduces adaptive feedback, mathematical generalisation and the system employed; Section 3 presents the multicriteria decision problem and the Analytic Hierarchy Process method. Section 4 includes examples of how this approach operates under different contextual requirements and discusses the results, and Section 5 concludes the paper.

2   Adaptive Feedback in Exploratory Learning for Mathematical Generalisation

Feedback is usually a response to the actions of a learner aiming to correct future iterations of the actions [7]. It includes information about what happened or did not happen as a consequence of the user's actions in relations to the goal [8]; this information is given to the users to compare their performance with the expected one [9] and to make use of it in the following attempt [8].

In exploratory learning, the freedom given to learners leads to situations when feedback is required on several aspects. This is also the case of *eXpresser*[1] [10] [11], which is an ELE for mathematical generalisation that aims to link the visual with the algebraic-like representation of rules. It enables constructions of patterns, creating dependences between them, naming properties of patterns and creating algebraic-like rules with either names or numbers. Some screenshots are displayed in Figure 1, illustrating the system, two constructions, the *properties list* of a pattern that is dependent on another one, the *properties list* of an independent pattern and two examples of *rules*.

The main area of the screen in Figure 1 displays two constructions. These are solutions of two learners working independently on a task called "footpath", which is typical in the UK curriculum. The task requires to find out the number of green tiles needed to surround *any* pattern of red tiles (representing the footpath). The components of *Construction 1* are displayed separately for ease of understanding; this construction has four patterns: (a) two compact rows of green (lighter colour) tiles and (b) two rows with gaps in between tiles: one green and one red (darker colour). The first two mentioned are the same, and consequently, have the same properties displayed in the *property list* of the highlighted row in *Construction 1*. The first property, i.e. number of iterations, shows that the pattern depends on the red one because the number of iterations of the green tiles is set to 'the number of red tiles multiplied by 2 plus 1'; the *T box* with the name *red* and the corresponding value of 3 is called an *icon variable* and is used to make a pattern dependent on another; the use of *icon variables* leads to general constructions, i.e. they work for any number of red tiles. The second property, *moving left*, is set to 1 and the third property, *moving down*, is set to 0, which makes the pattern a row; for the red pattern *moving left* is set to 2 and *moving down* is set to 0, which makes a row with gaps between the tiles. The last property establishes the number needed to colour all the tiles in the

---

[1] Developed in the context of MiGen Project, funded by the ESRC/EPSRC Teaching and Learning Research Programme (RES-139-25-0381); http://www.migen.org

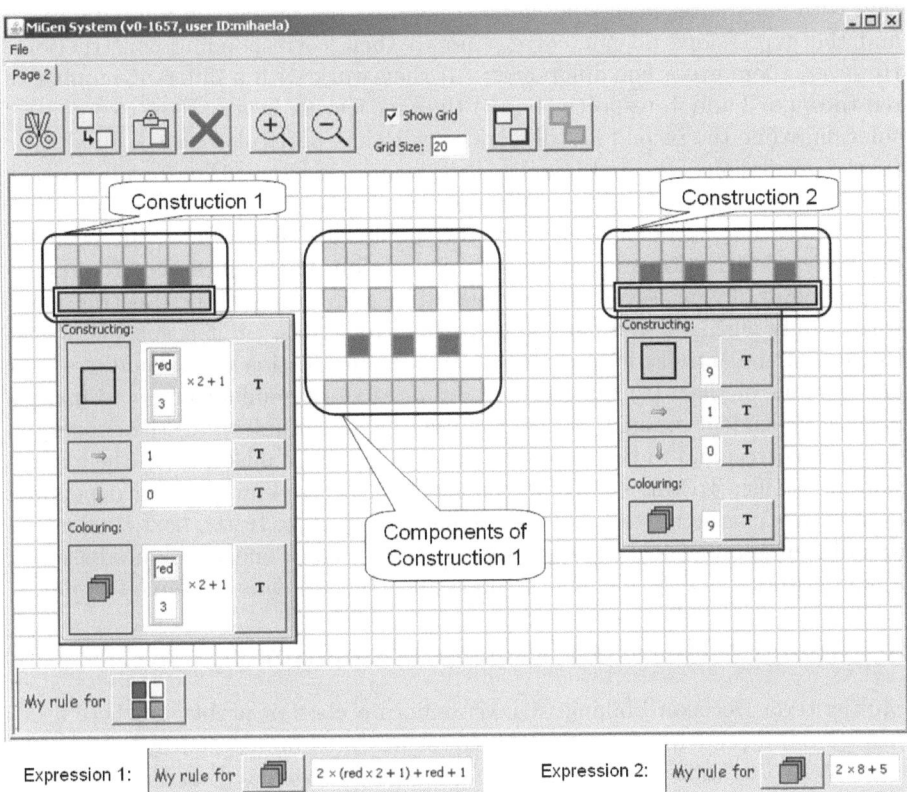

Fig. 1. eXpresser screenshots. The screenshot of the system includes a toolbar, an area for pattern construction and an area for defining rules; the toolbar (at the top) allows the following actions: cut, copy, paste, delete, zoom in, zoom out, show grid, grid size (changeable from here or using the zoom tools), group and ungroup; the main area has two constructions for the "footpath" task and two *property lists*; the components of *Construction 1* are also presented separately. The two screenshots at the bottom illustrate the rules defined by the learners who built the two constructions.

pattern; in the current case it is the same as the number of iterations in the pattern. However, if a pattern is a group of several tiles, this would not be the case anymore; for example, if a pattern is a group of three tiles and is iterated five times, the number required to colour it would be three times five.

Construction 2 is build in a similar fashion, but the compact rows of green tiles do not depend on the red pattern: the first property (number of iterations) from the *property list* is set to 9. At the bottom of Figure 1, two expressions corresponding to the two constructions are displayed. *Expression 1* uses the name *red* for the number of red tiles, while *Expression 2* is numeric.

In the constructions of Figure 1, both learners follow the same strategy in surrounding the footpath: two rows of tiles at top and bottom, and one row of tiles in the gaps of the red pattern; also, for both constructions, the row of green tiles with gaps in between (the middle one) does not depend on the red pattern and the expressions do not correspond to their corresponding constructions. However, there are a few differences: (a) they work with a different number of red tiles, i.e. 3 and 4, respectively; (b) the first learner is very close to a general solution, while the second is still working with the particular case of 4 red tiles; (c) the expression of the first learner (*Expression 1* in Figure 1) is already general, while the expression of the second learner (*Expression 2* in Figure 1) is numeric.

Construction 2 could be used at this point to illustrate how the need for feedback prioritisation emerges during exploration. In this instance, from pedagogical point of view, several issues need to be addressed: (a) the construction is correct only when the red pattern consists of four tiles, i.e. it is specific, whilst the aim of the activity is to create a general construction that would work for any number of tiles; (b) the learner may need to be reminded how to make a pattern dependent on another (i.e. the use of icon variables); (c) the expression does not correspond to the construction and contains a mistake; (d) the expression is specific. To this end, different types of feedback are needed depending on learner's characteristics and contextual information. In the next section, we describe an approach that leads to prioritising feedback on these issues based on a multicriteria decision making method called the *Analytic Hierarchy Process*.

3   Analytic Hierarchy Process Formalism

Multicriteria Decision Making (MDM) defines a class of problems where a decision from a predefined set of alternatives needs to be reached by taking into account two or more criteria. Each alternative is evaluated on the set of criteria; the outcomes provide a means of comparison between the alternatives that will facilitate a selection of one or more alternatives, or a ranking between them. Other purposes are classification of alternatives into groups (clustering) and group ranking [6]. Among the possible approaches of decision problems that correspond to this description are: statistical techniques, multi-attribute utility analysis, analytic hierarchy process, knowledge bases, mathematical models, etc.

MDM has many applications in fields where decisions need to be taken. The Analytic Hierarchy Process (AHP) is one of the most popular methods in MDM and is widely applied in a diversity of areas like logistics, military, manufacturing and health-care [12]. Frequently AHP is used in combination with other methods - a recent literature review [12] reports five main categories of tools integrated with AHP: (a) mathematical programming, (b) quality function development, (c) meta-heuristics, (d) SWOT analysis, and (e) data envelopment analysis. Four works related to higher education are reported in areas of IT-based project selection [13], teaching method selection [14], education requirement selection [15] and faculty course assignment [16].

In the area of learner/user modelling, AHP has been used in combination with fuzzy logic [17] for student diagnosis in an adaptive hypermedia educational system and in combination with Multi-Attribute Utility Theory (MAUT), another method from MDM, in recommender systems [18], where the evaluation function from MAUT is used to rate how well each alternative fulfills the decision criteria.

The AHP uses a hierarchy to represent a decision problem and to establish priorities between alternatives depending on a set of criteria involved in the decision process. It includes three main steps: (a) construction of the hierarchy; (b) analysis of priorities and (c) verification of consistency.

The *hierarchy* has the general structure presented in Figure 2. The highest level represents the *goal*, which, in our context, is personalised feedback. The second level includes the *criteria* based on which the decision should be taken; in our case, the criteria refer to the learning mode and the stage in the exploratory task. The third level includes the *alternatives* to be prioritised with respect to the criteria; the alternatives correspond to pedagogical aspects of mathematical generalisation. The first step includes a decomposition of the decision problem into parts defined by all relevant attributes; these attributes are arranged into hierarchical levels so as to reach the hierarchical structure presented in Figure 2.

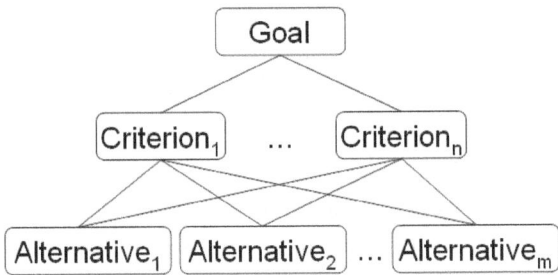

Fig. 2. Hierarchy in the Analytic Hierarchy Process

The analysis of *priorities* includes pairwise comparisons used to compute weights for the alternatives, which establish an order between them. This involves two steps: (a) decide priorities between criteria; (b) decide priorities between alternatives with respect to each criterion. The priorities take the form of matrices as in (1): one for the first step (priorities amongst criteria) and n for the second (priorities amongst alternatives) (a matrix for each criterion). For both types of matrices the values below the main diagonal are the reversed values from above the main diagonal, i.e. $c_{ji} = 1/c_{ij}, a_{ji} = 1/a_{ij}$, as the comparison result between objects A and B is reversed when the order changes (B and A).

$$C = \begin{bmatrix} 1 & c_{12} & \dots & c_{1n} \\ 1/c_{12} & 1 & \dots & c_{2n} \\ \dots & \dots & \dots & \dots \\ 1/c_{1n} & 1/c_{2n} & \dots & 1 \end{bmatrix}, \quad A^L = \begin{bmatrix} 1 & a_{12} & \dots & a_{1m} \\ 1/a_{12} & 1 & \dots & a_{2m} \\ \dots & \dots & \dots & \dots \\ 1/a_{1m} & 1/a_{2m} & \dots & 1 \end{bmatrix} \quad (1)$$

Each pair of criteria c_i and c_j has an associated value that specifies their relative importance. The values of $c_{ij}(1 \le i, j \le n)$ and $a_{ij}(1 \le i, j \le m)$ are determined using a scale from 1 to 9, where 1 means 'equally important' and 9 means 'extremely more important'. For example, $c_{ij} = 1$ means that the criteria c_i and c_j are equally important, $c_{ij} = 3$ means that c_i is more important than c_j

and $c_{ij} = 9$ means that c_i is extremely more important than c_j. The vales and meaning for the inverse pairs are: (a) $c_{ji} = 1$: c_j and c_i are equally important, (b) $c_{ji} = 1/3$: c_j is less important than c_i and (c) $c_{ji} = 1/9$: c_j is extremely less important than c_i.

The weight of each criterion is calculated using (2) and the criteria weight vector is obtained: $W = (w_1, w_2, \ldots, w_n)$.

$$w_i = \frac{\left(\prod_{j=1}^{n} c_{ij}\right)^{1/n}}{\sum_{i=1}^{n} \left(\prod_{j=1}^{n} c_{ij}\right)^{1/n}} \tag{2}$$

For the alternatives, a priority vector is calculated for each matrix (corresponding to a criterion) using the same equation (2). Thus priority vectors: $A(Cr_j) = (A_1(Cr_j), A_2(Cr_j), \ldots, A_m(Cr_j))$, $j = \overline{1,n}$ are obtained. Matrix A (3) results from combining the n priority vectors.

$$A = \begin{bmatrix} A_1(Cr_1) & A_1(Cr_2) & \cdots & A_1(Cr_n) \\ A_2(Cr_1) & A_2(Cr_2) & \cdots & A_2(Cr_n) \\ \vdots & \vdots & \ddots & \vdots \\ A_m(Cr_1) & A_m(Cr_2) & \cdots & A_m(Cr_n) \end{bmatrix} \tag{3}$$

By combining the criteria weights and the priority vectors the final alternatives priorities vector P with respect to all criteria is obtained using: $P = A * W$. More specifically, the priority for each alternative is calculated as: $p_i = A_i(Cr_1) * w_1 + A_i(Cr_2) * w_2 + \ldots + A_i(Cr_n) * w_n, i = \overline{1,m}$.

Consistency refers to the lack of logical contradictions in the pairwise comparisons; for example, if in a matrix the alternative x is more important than alternative y and less important than alternative z, and, at the same time, y is more important than z, there is an inconsistency (x is more important than z (by transitivity through y) and x is less important that z by direct comparison). To verify the *consistency* of the $n + 1$ pairwise comparisons matrices (n alternatives matrices and 1 criteria matrix), an approximation of the maximum eigenvalue for each matrix, denoted as λ_{max} (see Equation 4) is used to calculate the consistency index (CI). Equation (5) shows how to calculate CI for the criteria matrix and the n alternatives matrices.

$$\lambda_{max_j} = (\sum_{i=1}^{m} a_{i1}, \sum_{i=1}^{m} a_{i2}, \ldots, \sum_{i=1}^{m} a_{im}) *$$
$$(A_1(Cr_j), A_2(Cr_j), \ldots, A_m(Cr_j))^T, j = \overline{1,n} \tag{4}$$

$$\text{For criteria: } CI = \frac{\lambda_{max} - n}{n - 1}$$
$$\text{For alternatives: } CI_j = \frac{\lambda_{max_j} - m}{m - 1}, \quad j = \overline{1,m} \tag{5}$$

CI and the Random Consistency Index (RCI) are used to calculate the consistency ratio (CR) as: $CR = \frac{CI}{RCI}$. The values of the RCI [5] for 1 to 10 criteria are displayed in Table 1. Values of the consistency ratio below 0.10 indicate consistency, while greater values indicate the opposite. In the later case, revision of the pairwise comparisons is necessary.

Table 1. Values of RCI for $n = \overline{1, 10}$

n	1	2	3	4	5	6	7	8	9	10
RCI	0	0	0.58	0.90	1.12	1.24	1.32	1.41	1.45	1.49

The overall consistency of the hierarchy is a function of the consistency indexes of all pairwise matrices, the RCI for the number of criteria and number of alternatives and the weights of the criteria, as in (6).

$$CR = \frac{CI_{criteria} + w_1 * CI_{alt_{Cr_1}} + w_2 * CI_{alt_{Cr_2}} + \ldots + w_n * CI_{alt_{Cr_n}}}{RCI_n + w_1 * RCI_m + w_2 * RCI_m + \ldots + w_n * RCI_m} \quad (6)$$

Summarising, the AHP process involves three main steps: definition of the hierarchy, analysis of pairwise comparisons and verification of consistency. These are illustrated through scenarios in the following section.

4   AHP for Context-Dependent Personalised Feedback Prioritisation

Three scenarios are presented to illustrate the AHP process in the context of eXpresser and similar tasks to "footpath". The hierarchy of the AHP formalism is illustrated in Figure 3: the goal is to obtain feedback priorities; the criteria is the learning mode, i.e. individual or collaborative, and the stage in a task, i.e. specific and general. The alternatives are feedback on the following aspects: (a) correctness of construction (CC); (b) correctness of expression (CE); (c) construction-expression correspondence (C-E); (d) symmetry of construction (Sym); (e) generality of construction (CGen); (f) generality of expression (EGen); (g) use of icon variables (IV).

The pairwise comparisons between criteria and between alternatives vary depending on learner's (dynamic) characteristics: (a) level of experience (stored for

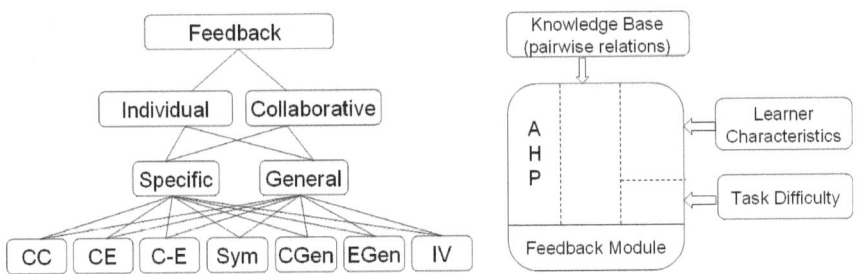

Fig. 3. AHP hierarchy   Fig. 4. Feedback module

each level of task difficulty), (b) arithmetics knowledge level and (c) preferred approach: from specific to general (S-to-G) or from general to specific (G-to-S). The feedback module (Figure 4) integrates this information together with information about task difficulty to retrieve sets of pairwise relations from the Knowledge Base. This generates different instantiations of the AHP process. To illustrate how AHP is going to operate in different situations, three scenarios are considered below (summarised in Table 2).

Table 2. Scenarios characteristics

Characteristics	Scenario 1	Scenario 2	Scenario 3
Mode	individual	individual	collaborative
Task difficulty	medium	medium	medium
Experience	low	medium	low&medium
Arithmetics	high	low	high&low
Approach	G-to-S	S-to-G	G-to-S&S-to-G

The constructions for the scenarios are displayed in Figure 1: *Constructions 1* and *2* are used in Scenario 1 and 2, respectively. In the collaborative scenario, i.e. Scenario 3, the learners who produced these constructions and their corresponding expressions are working together. The pairing for collaboration is made based on the similarity of the strategy [19] and the complementarity of approach and/or arithmetic level. A diagnosis of the learners' constructions [19] is carried out at the same time with the computation of feedback priorities. Combining these two sources, a decision is taken with regard to necessary and/or relevant.

Scenario 1. Feedback prioritisation is established by taking into consideration: (a) the individual learning mode, (b) the learner's characteristics mentioned in Table 2 and (c) *Construction 1* and *Expression 1* from Figure 1. The criteria pairwise comparison, the corresponding weights and consistency information are displayed in Table 3; the alternatives pairwise comparison with respect to the criteria (specific and general context), the priority vectors and the consistency measures are displayed in Table 4 and Table 5. The final priorities and the overall consistency are displayed in Table 6. From these tables, the numbers assigned by the designer of the AHP component are the criteria and the alternatives pairwise comparisons; the rest are computed using the formulas presented in Section 2.

As the learner prefers the general-to-specific approach, the top item for feedback is *icon variables* as they allow general constructions. The next two items to give feedback on are correctness of construction and its generality. *Construction 1* has two general components and a specific one, which indicates that the

Table 3. Criteria pairwise comparison, weights, and consistency

Criteria	Specific	General	Weights
Specific	1	1/2	0.33
General	2	1	0.67

$\lambda_{max} = 2.00$, $CI = 0$, $CR = 0$

Table 4. Alternatives pairwise comparison, priority vector with respect to the specific context, and consistency

Alternatives	CC	CE	C-E	Sym	CGen	EGen	IV	Priority vector
CC	1	2	2	5	2	3	1/2	0.22
CE	1/2	1	1/2	3	1/5	1/2	1/2	0.08
C-E	1/2	2	1	3	1/5	2	1/2	0.11
Sym	1/5	1/3	1/3	1	1/3	1/3	1/3	0.04
CGen	1/2	5	5	3	1	3	1/2	0.22
EGen	1/3	2	1/2	3	1/3	1	1/2	0.09
IV	2	2	2	3	2	2	1	0.23

$\lambda_{max} = 7.75$, $CI = 0.13$, $CR = 0.10$

Table 5. Alternatives pairwise comparison, priority vector with respect to the general context, and consistency

Alternatives	CC	CE	C-E	Sym	CGen	EGen	IV	Priority vector
CC	1	5	5	7	1	5	1/2	0.27
CE	1/5	1	1/2	7	1/5	2	1/3	0.08
C-E	1/5	2	1	3	1/3	3	1/3	0.10
Sym	1/7	1/7	1/3	1	1/3	3	1/3	0.05
CGen	1	5	3	3	1	2	1/2	0.19
EGen	1/5	1/2	1/3	1/3	1/2	1	1/5	0.04
IV	2	3	3	3	2	5	1	0.27

$\lambda_{max} = 7.82$, $CI = 0.14$, $CR = 0.10$

Table 6. Scenario 1: Feedback priorities and overall consistency

Alternatives	CC	CE	C-E	Sym	CGen	EGen	IV
Priorities	0.25	0.08	0.10	0.05	0.20	0.06	0.26

Overall $CR = 0.04$

learner has used icon variables, so no feedback on that is necessary; as the construction is correct, the first feedback to be provided will be on the generality of the construction, and more specifically, on the generality of the only specific component of the construction. From the AHP process, the next priorities are related to the expression: correspondence between construction and expression, correctness of expression and expression generality. The last two items are already in place, so no feedback on them is given. If in the previous step the learner has made the specific component general, the construction would correspond to the expression; if not, feedback would be provided to the learner to make sure the construction (partially general) corresponds to the expression (general).

Scenario 2. In this scenario, the prioritisation is computed for the individual learning mode, taking in consideration the learner's characteristics displayed in Table 2, *Construction 2* and its corresponding expression from Figure 1. The

Table 7. Scenario 2: Feedback priorities and overall consistency

Alternatives	CC	CE	C-E	Sym	CGen	EGen	IV
Priorities	0.310	0.108	0.130	0.194	0.092	0.060	0.106
Overall $CR = 0.03$							

procedure is applied as in Scenario 1; only the final feedback priorities and the overall consistency are reported in Table 7.

As the learner prefers a specific-to-general approach, the feedback addresses generality at the end. The first aspects to give feedback on are: the correctness of construction, its symmetry and the correspondence between construction and expression. The first two aspects are in place, so the feedback would be given on the correspondence between expression and construction. If the learner addresses this aspect and the new expression is $2 * 9 + 5$, the feedback on the following item, i.e. correctness of construction, becomes unnecessary. If the learner does not correct the expression accordingly, the feedback would address the correctness of expression, pointing out that the construction is correct and that the expression should correspond to the construction. So, feedback at this point includes the two interrelated aspects: the correctness of expression and the correspondence between construction and expression. Only after establishing the correctness of construction and expression for the specific case of 4 red tiles, the feedback will address the generality of the construction: the use of icon variables, the generality of construction, and, finally, the generality of expression.

Scenario 3. In the collaborative mode, the two learners are working together towards finding a general solution. The first leaner has a construction with 3 red tiles, while the second has a construction with 4 red tiles. Consequently, a specific approach on one side will lead to an inadequate construction on the other, which enforces the learners to work with the general. The feedback priorities for this particular collaborative situation are displayed in Table 8.

Table 8. Scenario 3: Feedback priorities and overall consistency

Alternatives	CC	CE	C-E	Sym	CGen	EGen	IV
Priorities	0.15	0.08	0.11	0.24	0.17	0.05	0.19
Overall $CR = 0.03$							

As the learners are 'forced' to work with the general, the first aspect to give feedback on is the symmetry of construction as, otherwise, it would be difficult to make it general – as both learners have symmetric constructions, this is not necessary. The next aspect to give feedback on is the use of icon variables; ideally, this feedback from the system would be replaced by the feedback of learner one to learner two, who has a specific construction. The next two aspects to be addressed are the generality and the correctness of the construction. For the same reason mentioned previously, the construction will be correct only when it is general, so generality is addressed first and correctness afterwards. The expression is dealt with at the end, starting from the correspondence with the construction, addressing its correctness and finally, its generality.

The priorities delivered by the AHP process were validated by two experts in the field of mathematical education who were aware of the way learners interacted with *eXpresser*. Both of them agreed on the prioritisation for the two individual situations, but there was one disagreement on the collaborative scenario. One expert agreed with the prioritisation delivered by the AHP process, while the other argued for the following order: IV, CGen, CC, Sym, C-E, CE and EGen. This order differs from the output of the AHP process by the fact that symmetry is moved from the first place to the fourth. The expert's argument for this was that they could build a construction that is correct and not symmetrical, but symmetry becomes important at this point because it would facilitate finding a general expression. On the other hand, the other expert argued that symmetry is important from the very beginning to facilitate the generality of construction (and then, the expression) because one of the learners prefers the specific-to-general approach and also has a low arithmetics ability; therefore, even if the other learner would be able to reach a general construction, though non-symmetrical, and to find a corresponding expression, for the other learner this would be difficult and hardly beneficial.

5   Concluding Remarks

In this paper we have presented a mechanism for personalised feedback prioritisation depending on the learning mode, i.e. individual or collaborative, the context within a task, i.e. specific or general, and the learner's characteristics. The way the mechanism operates was illustrated in two individual and one collaborative scenario. The feedback priorities for the individual mode were confirmed by two experts, whilst the priority given to *symmetry* in collaborative mode was considered by one of the experts as too high. One possible explanation for the diversity of the experts' opinion could be the added complexity of the collaborative mode, which is an issue that requires further investigation.

Acknowledgements

This work is partially funded by the ESRC/EPSRC Teaching and Learning Research Programme (Technology Enhanced Learning); Award no: RES-139-25-0381).

References

1. Akman, V., Bouquet, P., Thomason, R., Young, R.A. (eds.): CONTEXT 2001. LNCS (LNAI), vol. 2116. Springer, Heidelberg (2001)
2. Kwon, O.: The potential roles of context-aware computing technology in optimization-based intelligent decision-making. Expert Systems with Applications 31(3), 629–642 (2006)

3. Wang, S.S., Treat, T.A., Brownell, K.D.: Cognitive Processing About Classroom-Relevant Contexts: Teachers' Attention to and Utilization of Girls' Body Size, Ethnicity, Attractiveness, and Facial Affect. Journal of Educational Psychology 100(2), 473–489 (2008)

4. Anand, S.S., Mobasher, B.: Contextual Recommendation. In: Berendt, B., Hotho, A., Mladenic, D., Semeraro, G. (eds.) WebMine 2007. LNCS, vol. 4737, pp. 142–160. Springer, Heidelberg (2007)

5. Saaty, T.L.: The Analytic Hierarchy Process. McGraw-Hill, New York (1980)

6. Zopounidis, C., Doumpos, M.: Multicriteria classification and sorting methods: A literature review. European Journal of Operational Research 138(2), 229–246 (2002)

7. Mason, B.J., Bruning, R.: Providing feedback in computer-based instruction: What the research tells us (2001), http://dwb.unl.edu/Edit/MB/MasonBruning.html

8. Wiggins, G.: Feedback: how learning occurs (2008), http://www.authenticeducation.org/bigideas/article.lasso?artId=61

9. Johnson, D.W., Johnson, R.T.: Cooperative learning and feedback in technology-based instruction. In: Dempsey, J.V., Sales, G.C. (eds.) Interactive Instruction and Feedback, Educational Technology, Englewood Cliffs, NJ (1993)

10. Pearce, D., Geraniou, E., Mavrikis, M., Gutierrez-Santos, S., Kahn, K.: Using Pattern Construction and Analysis in an Exploratory Learning Environment for Understanding Mathematical Generalisation: The Potential for Intelligent Support. In: Gutierrez-Santos, S., Mavrikis, M. (eds.) Proceedings of the 1st International Workshop on Intelligent Support for Exploratory Environments, EC-TEL 2008 (2008)

11. Noss, R., Hoyles, C., Geraniou, E., Gutierrez-Santos, S., Mavrikis, M., Pearce, D.: Broadening the sense of 'dynamic': an intelligent system to support students' mathematical generalisation. The International Journal on Mathematics Education (2008) (submitted)

12. Ho, W.: Integrated analytic hierarchy process and its applications – A literature review. European Journal of Operational Research 186, 211–228 (2008)

13. Kwak, N.K., Lee, C.W.: A multicriteria decision-making approach to university resource allocation and information infrastructure planning. European Journal of Operational Research 110(2), 234–242 (1998)

14. Lam, K., Zhao, X.: An application of quality function deployment to improve the quality of teaching. International Journal of Quality and Reliability Management 15(4), 389–413 (1998)

15. Koksal, G., Egitman, A.: Planning and design on industrial engineering education quality. Computers and Industrial Engineering 35(3-4), 639–642 (1998)

16. Ozdemir, M.S., Gasimov, R.N.: The analytic hierarchy process and multiobjective 01 faculty course assignment. European Journal of Operational Research 157(2), 398–408 (2004)

17. Grigoriadou, M., Kornilakis, H., Papanikolaou, K.A., Magoulas, G.D.: Fuzzy Inference for Student Diagnosis in Adaptive Educational Systems. In: Vlahavas, I.P., Spyropoulos, C.D. (eds.) SETN 2002. LNCS (LNAI), vol. 2308, pp. 191–202. Springer, Heidelberg (2002)

18. Schmitt, C., Dengler, D., Bauer, M.: Multivariate Preference Models and Decision Making with the MAUT Machine. In: Brusilovsky, P., Corbett, A.T., de Rosis, F. (eds.) UM 2003. LNCS (LNAI), vol. 2702, pp. 297–302. Springer, Heidelberg (2003)

19. Cocea, M., Magoulas, G.: Combining Intelligent Methods for Learner Modelling in Exploratory Learning Environments. In: Proceedings of the 1st International Workshop on Combinations of Intelligent Methods and Applications, in conjunction with ECAI 2008, pp. 13–18 (2008)

Google Shared.
A Case-Study in Social Search*

Barry Smyth, Peter Briggs, Maurice Coyle, and Michael O'Mahony

CLARITY: Centre for Sensor Web Technologies
School of Computer Science and Informatics
University College Dublin, Ireland
{firstname.lastname}@ucd.ie

Abstract. Web search is the dominant form of information access and everyday millions of searches are handled by mainstream search engines, but users still struggle to find what they are looking for, and there is much room for improvement. In this paper we describe a novel and practical approach to Web search that combines ideas from personalization and social networking to provide a more collaborative search experience. We described how this has been delivered by complementing, rather than competing with, mainstream search engines, which offers considerable business potential in a Google-dominated search marketplace.

1 Introduction

For all the success of mainstream Web search engines, users still struggle to find the right information quickly. Poor search productivity is largely a result of vague or ambiguous queries [6, 8, 20], and there is considerable research on different ways to improve result selection and ranking. For example, researchers have looked at ways to bias search towards special types of information (e.g., people, research papers, etc.); see for e.g. [9]. Others have attempted to profile the preferences of searchers in order to deliver more personalized result-rankings [10, 11, 21]. Recently, other researchers have explored how to take advantage of the collaborative nature of search [1, 12, 14, 13, 17]. In our own research we have explored a collaborative approach to personalized Web search [4, 18, 19], profiling the preferences of communities of users, rather than individuals, and generating recommendations inline with community preferences; see also [7].

While results have been promising, little attention has been paid to the issue of deployment and it is difficult to see how these technologies can be successfully brought to mainstream search. We have previously explored different deployment options [2, 5] as a way to loosely integrate community-based search with mainstream search engines. However it has been clear for some time that neither approach is likely to work for consumer Web search: users want to search as normal using their favourite search engine. However, the recent arrival of

---

* This work is supported by Science Foundation Ireland under grant 07/CE/I1147.

G.-J. Houben et al. (Eds.): UMAP 2009, LNCS 5535, pp. 283–294, 2009.

browser plugins has presented a new opportunity to deliver third-party search technology, via the browser, on top of some underlying service like Google.

This paper describes how this has been achieved through a new commercial venture called HeyStaks (*www.heystaks.com*). HeyStaks places an emphasis on the potential for collaboration within Web search as a route to a better search experience; see also [1, 12, 14, 13, 17]. The key motivating insight is that there are important features missing from mainstream search engines. For example, recent studies highlight that for 30% of searches the searcher is looking for something that they have previously found, yet search engines like Google offer no practical support to help users re-find information. Similarly, for up to 70% of searches the searcher is looking for something that has recently been found by a friend or colleague [19]. And, once again, search engines like Google offer no support for the sharing of search results. Helping searchers to organise and share their search experiences could deliver significant improvements in overall search productivity. We describe how HeyStaks adds these missing collaboration features to mainstream search engines and present results from a recent usage analysis based on the initial beta deployment of the system.

2   HeyStaks

HeyStaks adds two basic features to any mainstream search engine. First, it allows users to create *search staks*, as a type of folder for their search experiences at search time. Staks can be shared with others so that their searches will also be added to the stak. Second, HeyStaks uses staks to generate recommendations that are added to the underlying search results that come from the mainstream search engine. These recommendations are results that stak members have previously found to be relevant for similar queries and help the searcher to discover results that friends or colleagues have found interesting, results that may otherwise be buried deep within Google's default result-list.

As per Fig. 1, HeyStaks takes the form of two basic components: a client-side *browser toolbar* and a back-end *server*. The toolbar allows users to create and share staks and provides a range of ancillary services, such as the ability to tag or vote for pages. The toolbar also captures search result click-thrus and manages the integration of HeyStaks recommendations with the default result-list. The back-end server manages the individual stak indexes (indexing individual pages against query/tag terms and positive/negative votes), the stak database (stak titles, members, descriptions, status, etc.), the HeyStaks social networking service and, of course, the recommendation engine. In the following sections we will briefly outline the basic operation of HeyStaks and then focus on some of the detail behind the recommendation engine.

2.1   System Overview

Consider the following example. Steve, Bill and some friends were planning a European vacation and they knew that during the course of their research they would use Web search as their primary source of information about what to

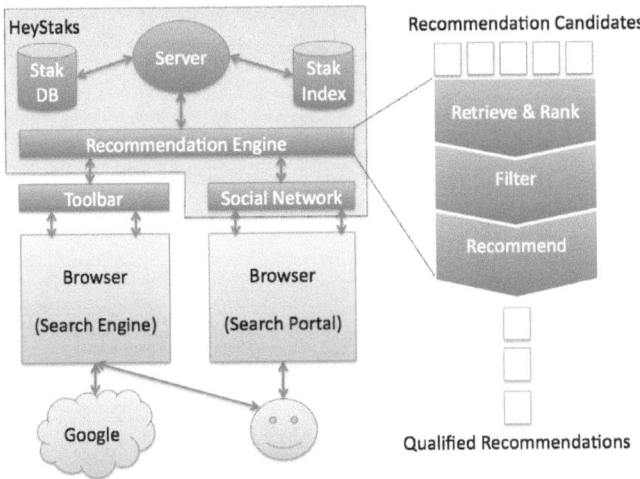

Fig. 1. The HeyStaks system architecture and outline recommendation model

do and where to visit. Steve created a (private) search stak called "European Vacation 2008" and shared this with Bill and friends, encouraging them to use this stak for their vacation-related searches.

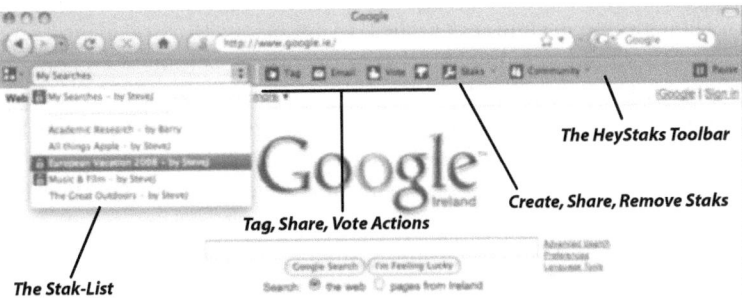

Fig. 2. Selecting a new active stak

Fig. 2 shows Steve selecting this stak as he embarks on a new search for "Dublin hotels", and Fig. 3 shows the results of this search. The usual Google results are shown, but in addition HeyStaks has made two promotions. These were promoted because other members of the "European Vacation 2008" stak had recently found these results to be relevant; perhaps they selected them for *similar* queries, or voted for them, or tagged them with related terms. These recommendations may have been promoted from much deeper within the Google result-list, or they may not even be present in Google's default results. Other relevant results may also be highlighted by HeyStaks, but left in their default Google position. In this way Steve and Bill benefit from promotions that are

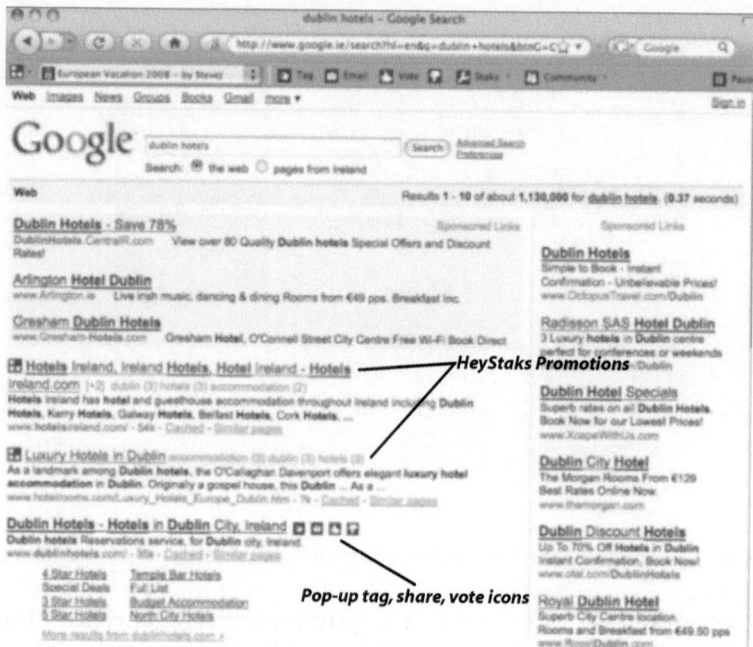

Fig. 3. Google search results with HeyStaks promotions

based on their previous similar searches. In addition, HeyStaks can recommend results from other related public staks as appropriate, helping searchers to benefit from the search knowledge that other groups and communities have created.

Separately from the toolbar, HeyStaks users also benefit from the HeyStaks *search portal*, which provides a social networking service built around people's search histories. For example, Fig. 4 shows the portal page for the "European Vacation 2008" stak, which is available to all stak members. It presents an activity feed of recent search history and a query cloud that makes it easy for the user to find out about what others have been searching for. The search portal also provides users with a wide range of features such as stak maintenance (e.g., editing, moving, copying results in staks and between staks), various search and filtering tools, and a variety of features to manage their own search profiles and find new search partners.

2.2   The HeyStaks Recomendation Engine

In HeyStaks each search stak (S) serves as a profile of the search activities of the stak members and HeyStaks combines a number of implicit and explicit profiling techniques to capture a rich history of search experiences. Each stak is made up of a set of result pages $(S = \{p_1, ..., p_k\})$ and each page is anonymously associated with a number of implicit and explicit interest indicators, including the total number of times a result has been selected (sel), the query terms $(q_1, ..., q_n)$ that led to its selection, the number of times a result has been tagged

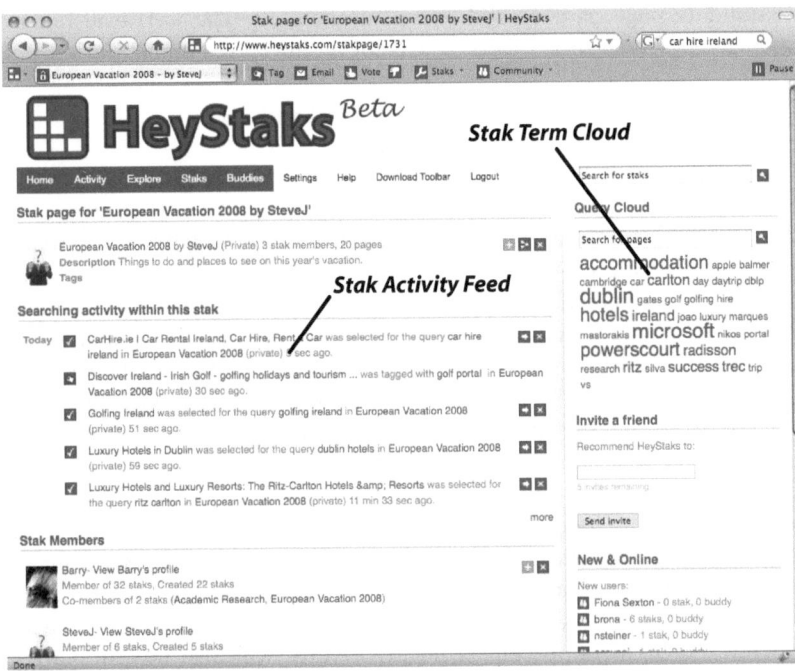

Fig. 4. The HeyStaks search portal provide direct access to staks and past searches

(tag), the terms used to tag it ($t_1, ..., t_m$), the votes it has received (v^+, v^-), and the number of people it has been shared with ($share$) (all explicit indicators of interest) as indicated by Eq. 1.

$$p_i^S = \{q_1, ..., q_n, t_1, ..., t_m, v^+, v^-, sel, tag, share\} \tag{1}$$

In this way, each page is associated with a set of *term data* (query terms and/or tag terms) and a set of *usage data* (the selection, tag, share, and voting count). The term data is represented as a Lucene (*lucene.apache.org*) index table, with each page indexed under its associated query and tag terms, and provides the basis for retrieving and ranking *promotion candidates*. The usage data provides an additional source of evidence that can be used to filter results and to generate a final set of recommendations. At search time, a set of recommendations is produced in a number of stages: relevant results are retrieved and ranked from the Lucene stak index table; these promotion candidates are filtered based on an *evidence model* to eliminate noisy recommendations; and the remaining results are added to the Google result-list according to a set of *recommendation rules*.

Retrieval & Ranking. Briefly, there are two types of promotion candidates: *primary promotions* are results that come from the active stak S_t; whereas *secondary promotions* come from other staks in the searcher's stak-list. To generate these promotion candidates, the HeyStaks server uses the current query q_t as a probe into each stak index, S_i, to identify a set of relevant stak pages $P(S_i, q_t)$.

Each candidate page, p, is scored using Lucene's *TF*IDF* retrieval function as per Equation 2, which serves as the basis for an initial recommendation ranking.

$$score(q_t, p) = \sum_{t \epsilon q_t} tf(t \epsilon p) \bullet idf(t)^2 \tag{2}$$

Evidence-Based Filtering. Staks are inevitably noisy, in the sense that they will frequently contain pages that are not on topic. For example, searchers will often forget to set an appropriate stak at the start of a new search session, and although HeyStaks includes a number of automatic stak-selection techniques to ensure that the right stak is active for a given search, these techniques are not perfect, and misclassifications do inevitably occur. As a result, the retrieval and ranking stage may select pages that are not strictly relevant to the current query context. To avoid making spurious recommendations HeyStaks employs an *evidence filter*, which uses a variety of threshold models to evaluate the relevance of a particular result, in terms of its usage evidence; tagging evidence is considered more important than voting, which in turn is more important than implicit selection evidence. For example, pages that have only been selected once, by a single stak member, are not automatically considered for recommendation and, all other things being equal, will be filtered out at this stage. In turn, pages that have received a high proportion of negative votes will also be eliminated. The precise details of this model are beyond the scope of this paper but suffice it to say that any results which do not meet the necessary evidence thresholds are eliminated from further consideration.

Recommendation Rules. After evidence pruning we are left with revised primary and secondary promotions and the final task is to add these *qualified recommendations* to the Google result-list. HeyStaks uses a number of different recommendation rules to determine how and where a promotion should be added. Once again, space restrictions prevent a detailed account of this component but, for example, the top 3 primary promotions are always added to the top of the Google result-list and labelled using the HeyStaks promotion icons. If a remaining primary promotion is also in the default Google result-list then this is labeled in place. If there are still remaining primary promotions then these are added to the secondary promotion list, which is sorted according to TF*IDF scores. These recommendations are then added to the Google result-list as an optional, expandable list of recommendations.

3   Empirical User Studies

In this section we examine a subset of 95 HeyStaks users who have remained active during the course of the early beta release of the toolbar and service. These users registered with HeyStaks during the period October-December 2008 and the results below represent a summary of their usage during the period October 2008 - January 2009. Our aim is to gain an understanding of both how users are using HeyStaks, and whether they seem to be benefiting from its search promotions. Because this is a study of live-users *in the wild* there are certain limitations about what we have been able to measure. There is no control group, for example, and it was not feasible, mainly for data privacy reasons, to analyse the relative click-through behaviour of users, by comparing their selections of default Google results to their selections of HeyStaks promotions. However, for the interested reader, our earlier work does report on this type of analysis in more conventional control-group laboratory studies [3, 4, 19].

3.1   On the Creation and Sharing of Search Staks

Key to the HeyStaks proposition is that searchers need a better way to organise and share their search experiences. HeyStaks provides these features but do users actually take the time to create staks? Do they share them with others or join those created by others?

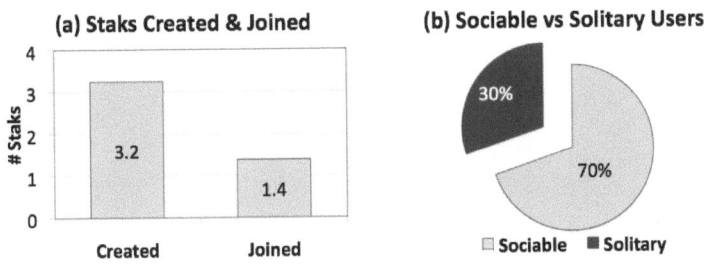

Fig. 5. (a) Average staks created and joined per user. (b) The percentage of *sociable* and *solitary* users.

During the course of the initial deployment of HeyStaks users did engage in a reasonable degree of stak creation and sharing activity. For example, as per Fig. 5, on average, beta users created just over 3.2 new staks and joined a further 1.4. Perhaps this is not surprising: most users create a few staks and share them with a small network of colleagues or friends, at least initially.

In total there were over 300 staks created on a wide range of topics, from broad topics such as travel, research, music and movies, to more niche interests including archaeology, black and white photography, and mountain biking. A few users were prolific stak creators and joiners: one user created 13 staks and joined another 11, to create a search network of 47 other searchers (users who co-shared the same staks). In fact on average, each user was connected to a search network of just over 5 other searchers by the staks that they shared.

The vast majority of staks were created as public staks, although most (52%) remained the domain of a single member, the stak creator. Thus 48% of staks were shared with at least one other user and, on average, these staks attracted 3.6 members. One way to look at this is as depicted in Fig. 5(b): 70% of users make the effort to share or join staks (*sociable* users); and only 30% of users created staks just for their own personal use and declined to join staks created by others (*solitary* users).

3.2   On the Social Life of Search

At its core HeyStaks is motivated by the idea that Web search is an inherently social or collaborative activity. And even though mainstream search engines do not support this, searchers do find alternative collaboration channels (e.g., email, IM, etc.) with which to partially, albeit inefficiently, share their search experiences. One of the most important early questions to ask about HeyStaks users concerns the extent to which their natural search activity serves to create a community of collaborating searchers. As users search, tag, and vote they are effectively producing and consuming community search knowledge. A user might be the first to select or tag a given result for a stak and, in this context, they have *produced* new search knowledge. Later, if this result is promoted to another user and then re-selected (or tagged or voted on), then this other user is said to have *consumed* that search knowledge; of course they have also produced search knowledge as their selection, tag, or vote is added to the stak.

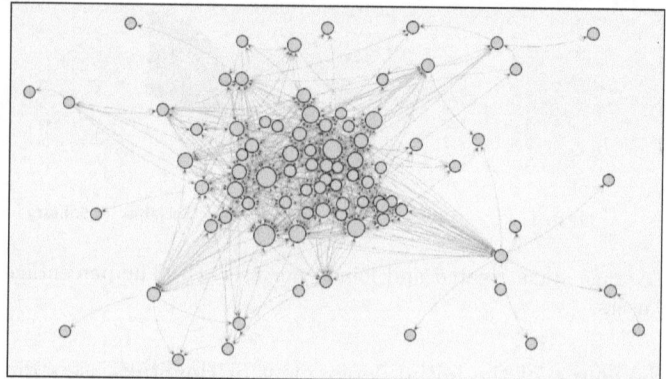

Fig. 6. A representation of the collaboration network among HeyStaks searchers

These relationships between the producers and consumers of search knowledge within staks effectively creates an implicit social network of search collaboration. Fig. 6 presents a visualization of this network of the beta users. Each node is a unique user and edges between nodes correspond to evidence for search collaboration. These edges are directed: an edge from *user A* (the producer) to *user B* (the consumer) signifies that *user B* has selected at least one of the search results that *user A* has been responsible for adding (through his/her own selections, tagging or voting activity) to a search stak that is shared between both users. Of course a single edge can (and typically does) reflect many collaboration instances between two users. In this example the diameter of the nodes reflects the *reputation* of the user in terms of their relative ability to help other users to search; however a detailed discussion of this reputation mechanism is beyond the scope of this paper.

Perhaps the first thing to notice is the extent of the collaboration that is evident among these users. From Fig. 6 we can see that the sharing of search knowledge is not limited to to a small clique of especially social searchers. In fact, far from it, the graph includes 85% of beta users meaning that 85% of users have engaged in search collaborations. The majority have consumed results that were produced by at least one other user, and on average these users have consumed results from 7.45 other users. In contrast 50% of users have produced knowledge that has been consumed by at least one other user, and in this case each of these producers has created search knowledge that is consumed by more than 12 other users on average.

These production/consumption statistics can be contrasted with more conventional social media participation levels, where less than 10% of users actively engage in the production of information [15]. In HeyStaks, the implicit nature of search knowledge production means that 50% of users are effectively contributing to the search knowledge as a side effect of their normal search habits.

Moreover, these collaboration instances are far from being one-offs. As mentioned above each edge typically relates to multiple instances of collaboration. One particular user has been helped by 18 other users during 286 searches. Another user has produced search knowledge that 27 users have found to be useful during 499 different searches.

3.3 Producers and Consumers

These data speak to the potential for HeyStaks as a collaboration platform for Web search. Clearly HeyStaks is capturing and harnessing a significant amount of natural search collaboration. In this section we dig a little deeper in to the nature of this collaboration from the perspective of an individual searcher.

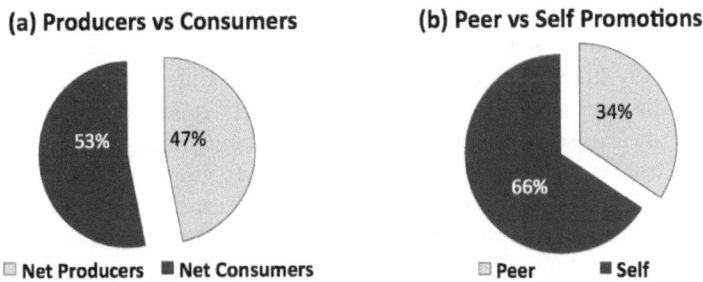

Fig. 7. (a) Average staks created and joined per user. (b) The percentage of *sociable* and *solitary* users.

One question we might ask is to what extent individual users tend to be producers or consumers of search knowledge. Are some searchers *net producers* of search knowledge, in the sense that they are more inclined to create search knowledge that is useful to others? Are other users *net consumers*, in the sense that they are more inclined to consume search knowledge that others have created? This data is presented in Fig. 7(a). To be clear a net producer is defined as a user who has helped more other users than they themselves have been helped by, where as a net consumer is defined as a user who has been helped by more users than they themselves have helped. The chart shows that 47% of users are net producers. Remember that, above, we noted how 50% of users have produced at least *some* search knowledge that has been consumed by some other user. It seems that the vast majority of *these* users, 94% of them in fact, are actually helping more people than they are helped by in return.

3.4 Peer vs. Self Promotions

So, we have found that lots of users are helping other users, and lots of users are helped by other users. Perhaps this altruism is limited to a small number of searches? Perhaps, most of the time, at the level of individual searches, users are helping themselves? A variation on the above analysis can help shed light on this question by looking at the source of promotions that users judge to be relevant enough to select during their searches.

Overall, the beta users selected more than 11,000 promotions during their searches. Some of these promotions will have been derived from the searcher's own past history; we call these *self* promotions. Others will have been derived from the search activities of other users who co-share staks with the searcher; we call these *peer* promotions. The intuition here is that the selection of self promotions corresponds to examples of HeyStaks helping users to *recover* results they have previously found, whereas the selection of promotions from peers corresponds to *discovery* tasks, where the user is benefiting from focused new content that might otherwise have been missed, or have been difficult to find; see [16].

Fig. 7(b) compares the percentage of peer and self promotions and shows that two-thirds of selected promotions are generated from the searcher's own past search activities; most of the time HeyStaks is helping searchers to recover previously found results. However, 33% of the time peer promotions are selected (and we already know that these come from many different users), helping the searcher to discover new information that others have found.

The bias towards self promotions is perhaps not surprising, especially given the habits of searchers, and especially during the early stages of stak development. The growth of most staks is initially led by a single user, usually the creator, and so inevitably most of the promotions are generated in response to the creator's own search queries. And most of these promotions will be self promotions, derived from the leader's own search activities. Many staks are not shared and so are only capable of making self promotions. As staks are shared, however, and more users join, the pool of searchers becomes more diverse. More results are added by the actions of peers and more peer promotions are generated and selected. It is an interesting task for future work to explore the evolution of a search stak and to investigate how stak content and promotions are affected as more and more users participate. Are there well-defined stages in stak evolution, for example, as self promotions give way to peer promotions? For now it is satisfying to see that even in the early stages of stak evolution, where the average stak as between 3 and 4 members, that 34% of the time members are benefiting from promotions that are derived from the activities of their peers.

4   Conclusions

In the late 1990's the world of Web search was transformed by the idea of using connectivity information to rank search results, and within a few short years Google's PageRank had rendered purely term-based approaches obsolete. Today, Web search is the primary mode of information access but there is still considerable room for improvement. We believe that social (or collaborative) search techniques have the potential to have a similarly transformative impact on current Web search, and in this paper we have described the result of one research project in this area which has now matured in to a commercial venture.

HeyStaks is designed to work with mainstream search engines. Users search as normal but benefit from new collaboration features, allowing searchers to better organise and share their search experiences. Moreover, HeyStaks harnesses the product of search collaboration to generate result recommendations that offer more focused results than the underlying search engine. We have presented the results of a recent deployment that highlight how many early users have adapted well to the collaboration features offered by HeyStaks: most users create multiple search staks to store their search experiences and 70% of users share staks with others. In turn, collaboration has begun to pay dividends for early HeyStaks users: 85% of users have benefitted from the search experiences of others and, on average, 34% of the time users are seen to select promotions that have originated from their peers. Perhaps most surprising is the degree to which users are actively engaged in the production of useful search knowledge, which forms the basis of collaboration. Unlike other forms of social media, where a minority of users ($< 10\%$) participate in production, we have found that more than half of HeyStaks users are involved in the creation of useful search knowledge.

References

1. Amershi, S., Morris, M.R.: Cosearch: a system for co-located collaborative web search. In: CHI, pp. 1647–1656 (2008)
2. Balfe, E., Smyth, B.: Case-based collaborative web search. In: Funk, P., González Calero, P.A. (eds.) ECCBR 2004. LNCS, vol. 3155, pp. 489–503. Springer, Heidelberg (2004)
3. Boydell, O., Smyth, B.: Enhancing case-based, collaborative web search. In: Weber, R.O., Richter, M.M. (eds.) ICCBR 2007. LNCS, vol. 4626, pp. 329–343. Springer, Heidelberg (2007)
4. Coyle, M., Smyth, B.: Supporting intelligent web search. ACM Trans. Internet Techn. 7(4) (2007)
5. Coyle, M., Smyth, B.: (web search) shared: Social aspects of a collaborative, community-based search network. In: Nejdl, W., Kay, J., Pu, P., Herder, E. (eds.) AH 2008. LNCS, vol. 5149, pp. 103–112. Springer, Heidelberg (2008)
6. Furnas, G.W., Landauer, T.K., Gomez, L.M., Dumais, S.T.: The vocabulary problem in human-system communication. Communications of the ACM 30(11), 964–971 (1987)
7. Glance, N.S.: Community Search Assistant. In: Proceedings of the International Conference on Intelligent User Interfaces, pp. 91–96. ACM Press, New York (2001)

8. Lawrence, S., Lee Giles, C.: Accessibility of Information on the Web. Nature 400(6740), 107–109 (1999)
9. Lawrence, S.: Context in Web Search. IEEE Data Engineering Bulletin 23(3), 25–32 (2000)
10. Liu, F., Yu, C., Meng, W.: Personalized Web Search for Improving Retrieval Effectiveness. IEEE Transactions on Knowledge and Data Engineering 16(1), 28–40 (2004)
11. Micarelli, A., Gasparetti, F., Sciarrone, F., Gauch, S.: Personalized search on the world wide web. In: Brusilovsky, P., Kobsa, A., Nejdl, W. (eds.) Adaptive Web 2007. LNCS, vol. 4321, pp. 195–230. Springer, Heidelberg (2007)
12. Morris, M.R.: A survey of collaborative web search practices. In: CHI, pp. 1657–1660 (2008)
13. Morris, M.R., Horvitz, E.: S^3: Storable, shareable search. INTERACT (1), 120–123 (2007)
14. Morris, M.R., Horvitz, E.: Searchtogether: an interface for collaborative web search. In: UIST, pp. 3–12 (2007)
15. Nielsen, J.: Participation inequality: Lurkers vs. contributors in internet communities (2006), http://www.useit.com/alertbox/participation_inequality.html
16. O'Day, V.L., Jeffries, R.: Orienteering in an information landscape: how information seekers get from here to there. In: Proceedings of the SIGCHI conference on Human factors in computing systems (CHI 1993), pp. 438–445. ACM Press, New York (1993)
17. Pickens, J., Golovchinsky, G., Shah, C., Qvarfordt, P., Back, M.: Algorithmic mediation for collaborative exploratory search. In: SIGIR, pp. 315–322 (2008)
18. Smyth, B.: A community-based approach to personalizing web search. IEEE Computer 40(8), 42–50 (2007)
19. Smyth, B., Balfe, E., Freyne, J., Briggs, P., Coyle, M., Boydell, O.: Exploiting query repetition and regularity in an adaptive community-based web search engine. User Model. User-Adapt. Interact. 14(5), 383–423 (2004)
20. Spink, A., Wolfram, D., Jansen, M.B.J., Saracevic, T.: Searching the web: the public and their queries. Journal of the American Society for Information Science and Technology 52(3), 226–234 (2001)
21. Teevan, J., Dumais, S.T., Horvitz, E.: Personalizing search via automated analysis of interests and activities. In: SIGIR 2005: Proceedings of the 28th annual international ACM SIGIR conference on Research and development in information retrieval, pp. 449–456. ACM Press, New York (2005)

Collaborative Filtering Is Not Enough? Experiments with a Mixed-Model Recommender for Leisure Activities

Nicolas Ducheneaut, Kurt Partridge, Qingfeng Huang, Bob Price,
Mike Roberts, Ed H. Chi, Victoria Bellotti, and Bo Begole

Palo Alto Research Center, 3333 Coyote Hill Road,
Palo Alto, CA 94304, USA
{nicolas,kurt.partridge,qingfeng.huang,bob.price,
michael.roberts,echi,victoria.bellotti,bo.begole}@parc.com

Abstract. Collaborative filtering (CF) is at the heart of most successful recommender systems nowadays. While this technique often provides useful recommendations, conventional systems also ignore data that could potentially be used to refine and adjust recommendations based on a user's context and preferences. The problem is particularly acute with mobile systems where information delivery often needs to be contextualized. Past research has also shown that combining CF with other techniques often improves the quality of recommendations. In this paper, we present results from an experiment assessing user satisfaction with recommendations for leisure activities that are obtained from different combinations of these techniques. We show that the most effective mix is highly dependent on a user's familiarity with a geographical area and discuss the implications of our findings for future research.

Keywords: Recommender systems, hybrid models, evaluation.

1 Introduction

The variety of opportunities available today makes it difficult to find items that suit an individual's tastes. On the Internet, people can enter search terms to seek items but this only works for items that a person knows how to describe in some form (usually simple keyword lists) and potentially misses a variety of items that the person might like if only she knew of them. To address this issue, recommendation systems use a model of a person's interests to suggest items that are likely to be close to an individual's tastes. They have proven effective at recommending content such as movies, books, music, and other kinds of products [18].

Early recommender systems were mostly designed for access from a personal computer [8, 10]. But more recently the explosion in the number of mobile devices has led researchers to examine how recommender systems should be designed for use on-the-go [15]. With mobility, recommender systems are used in contexts that change frequently, as the user moves about and engages in a variety of activities. The incorporation of this contextual information into the recommendation process has been identified as a central challenge for the recommender systems community [2]. As

G.-J. Houben et al. (Eds.): UMAP 2009, LNCS 5535, pp. 295–306, 2009.

such there has been some recent work to extend the power of recommender systems to leverage context [1] in the physical world primarily for providing tourist information (e.g., [6, 16]), as well as some early efforts at providing mobile restaurant recommendations (e.g., [17, 21]).

Another common thread in recommender systems research is the need to combine recommendations techniques to achieve peak performance [5]. Collaborative filtering is currently the most familiar and most widely implemented technique [13]. It aggregates ratings assigned to items by its users, recognizes commonalities between them on the basis of these ratings, and generates new recommendations based on inter-user comparisons. But a variety of other approaches are available: content-based, demographic, utility-based, and knowledge-based techniques have all been actively researched and combined [2, 5], with varying degrees of success. The challenge here is to find a combination of algorithms that would best satisfy a user, given her needs and circumstances.

We recently designed and implemented a mobile, leisure-time recommender system (codenamed Magitti) to address these two challenges. Magitti delivers recommendations that consider both the user's contextual data (location, weather, current reading patterns, etc.) and their tastes (see [3] for more detail on the system's implementation). To determine how to best combine all these information sources, we conducted experiments to find out how to make the most effective recommendations. In this paper, we present results from these experiments indicating which combination of recommender techniques might lead to the highest user satisfaction when using such mobile, context-aware recommender systems.

2 Magitti: Recommending Leisure

The prototype for Magitti serves needs broadly similar to those addressed by other mobile recommendation systems such as CitySearch, Yelp, and Zagat. In addition, Magitti performs sophisticated user modeling that combines various kinds of user preference data, contextual data, and activity inference. The activity inference mechanism, which is described elsewhere [3], infers which general category of information the user is most likely to be interested in. The categories are "EAT" (restaurants and cafes), "SHOP" (retail stores), "SEE" (theaters and museums), "DO" (parks and sporting events), and "READ" (news and lifestyle articles). The inference is not perfect, but the user can explicitly correct wrong inferences.

Once the activity category is determined, the recommender engine ranks the items in the chosen category by combining results from a variety of models to compute each item's *utility*. We adopt a hybrid approach [5] for the recommender in order to address the issues introduced by mobility and the leisure domain. Indeed, it has been proposed that different recommender algorithms are better suited to certain information seeking tasks. For instance, CF may generate more serendipitous recommendations, while a content-based recommender might produce more homogeneous results with high similarity [13]. Since Magitti needs to support both serendipitous discovery and directed search and planning, it makes sense to combine different recommendation techniques. A hybrid approach also allows us not only to integrate contextual models when such information is available, but also to return useful results when it is not.

Table 1. Models used to calculate the ranking of recommended items

Model Name	Details
Collaborative Filtering Model	Unknown ratings are estimated from user similarity on known ratings using the Pearson correlation coefficient.
Stated Preferences Model	Explicit preferences for attributes (e.g., "Japanese cuisine") are multiplied by a particular item's attributes, summed, and normalized.
Learned Preferences Model	Time-dependent attributes are learned from proximity to other items in historical traces for each user. E.g., frequent visits to Mexican restaurants would automatically infer a preference for them [3].
Distance Model	Utilities are scored according a thresholded exponential decay function of the distance from the user.
Content Preference Model	Keywords from viewed web-page content are extracted using TF/IDF [2], and item scores are determined using cosine similarity to the keywords in the item's text description.
Future Plans Model	Calendar entries and planning-related natural language expressions in messages influence particular attributes (e.g., the message "How about pizza tonight?")

Currently, Magitti combines the six models in Table 1. These models can be combined in a variety of ways. In the current implementation we use a simple weighted linear combination for its flexibility. With this approach, it is easy to perform post-hoc credit assignment and adjust the contribution of each model to the total utility accordingly [5]. This lets the recommender not only adapt to the results of the evaluation, but also, given enough time and data, learn a weight for each model that is independent of each model's time-varying parameters.

3   Evaluation

To better understand how to combine recommendation techniques to be most satisfying to users, we conducted a qualitative evaluation in which users assessed the usefulness and serendipity of recommendations obtained from these models, both individually and in various combinations.

3.1   Method

We recruited 16 participants through a mailing list internal to our organization (confidentiality agreements prevented us from recruiting external users). The participants were offered a $20 gift certificate for completing the evaluation. The participants ranged in age from 20 to 60 years old; 11 were male, 5 were female.

To facilitate participation and data collection we created a web-based system that reproduced the main features of Magitti's recommendation list. This way, participants were free to complete the evaluation tasks at work or from their home, at their own pace. We were also able to collect much more data than would have been possible in an *in situ* study. Since our focus was on the quality of recommendations and not on activity detection, we limited our content to information about one activity, eating, in order to allow comparison between lists of recommendations for the users.

The participants started by rating a list of local restaurants that they had already visited on a scale from 1 to 5. These ratings were necessary to bootstrap the CF model. Prior to the experiment, we had 20 members of our team and other employees rate the same set of restaurants, which produced enough comparison data to generate collaboratively filtered recommendations for each participant.

The participants then entered explicit preferences to be used by the Stated Preferences model. They were presented with a list of all possible attribute/value pairs available in our restaurant database and asked to assign a value to as many as they wished. The participants were told that scores should lie between 0 and 1.

After the initial setup phase we asked the participants to select one of five street locations and assume they were being teleported to it on the next coming Friday at 6pm to have dinner there. The locations were all well-known neighborhood dining "hotspots." The system then sequentially presented them with five different lists of ten restaurants, each generated by one or several of our algorithms. The restaurants were sorted in decreasing order of utility, and the algorithm used to generate the list and each restaurant's utility score was not shown to the participants. For each list, the participants answered "Would you be interested in dining at this restaurant?" using one of three choices: "(1) Definitely," "(2) Maybe," or "(3) Probably not." The participant could also decline to answer. We also asked them to say whether they had already been to each restaurant they chose to evaluate.

Beyond its name and address, our Web interface also displayed the following information about each entry, just like Magitti would: (1) its relative distance to the participant's chosen location, (2) the average past user ratings, (3) pricing information, and (4) (if available) three user comments. To help investigate various biases we also asked participants two questions about each list:

(1) "To what degree did the user comments affect your decision (from 1 [not at all] to 10 [very much])?"

(2) "To what degree did the existing ratings influence your decision (from 1 [not at all] to 10 [very much])?"

We also asked the participants to complete the same tasks for other locations among the five, if time permitted.

3.2 Algorithms Tested

The nature of our experiment prevented us from testing all the recommendation models available in Magitti. Models relying on historical information would have required extensive use of the mobile device to generate useful recommendations for the participants, which we could not achieve during the timeframe of this study. As such, we did not evaluate Learned Preferences and Future Plans. Moreover, privacy concerns about collecting participants' Web usage data prior to the experiment prevented us from bootstrapping the Content Preference Model. Without such data, the model is effectively deactivated. Consequently, the five algorithms studied were: 1) Collaborative filtering; 2) the Stated Preferences model; 3) the Distance model; 4) a mixed algorithm using (1-3) with even weights; 5) a mixed algorithm using (1-3) with respective weights of (0.2, 0.75, 0.25).

This set of algorithms is diverse and interesting for comparison purposes. CF is a good representative of a high-serendipity model with high dependence on user input. The Stated Preferences model is a good example of a static utility-based approach that produces results consistent with a user's explicit tastes, but without much variability. And finally the Distance model illustrates how contextual data (in this case, location) can be integrated with other recommendation techniques. The weights for Algorithm 5 were determined empirically by the experimenters after using the system over several months—they are closest to what we felt was the "ideal" combination, based on our usage patterns.

Magitti has a facility for automatically learning weights over time that maximizes the models that best predict the items that the user will select. However, it requires more usage data than we could conveniently collect for this study, and therefore the weights of each model were kept constant for the duration of each experimental session.

3.3 Results

Our 16 participants evaluated a total of 99 recommendation lists. Most completed the tasks for one location only, a few did two. Twelve (out of the 16) participants rated results generated by all five algorithms. This resulted in a total of 940 restaurant recommendation assessments. Some did not assess all items in a list, which was allowed by the protocol.

Usefulness of Recommendations. In order to evaluate the usefulness [13] of each algorithm we first computed its average "score" by assigning a value of 1 to "definitely", 0.5 to "maybe" and 0 to "probably not" for each user assessment of an algorithm's recommended items. Table 2 summarizes the results. The results indicate that CF seems to dominate, offering on average recommendations that are more likely to be followed than other algorithms. The difference is statistically significant, $F_{(2.3816)} = 13.0211$, $p < 0.01$.

Table 2. Average usefulness score for each algorithm

Algorithms	N ratings	Average	Variance
CF	110	0.75	0.13
PREFS	220	0.54	0.15
DISTANCE	200	0.43	0.15
ALL EQUAL	180	0.56	0.14
CUSTOM WEIGHTS	210	0.56	0.14

It is possible, however, that users might favor familiar places. To explore this possible confound we repeated the above analysis, this time excluding places that had already been visited (see Table 3). The results are again statistically significant, $F_{(2,3872)} = 3.4395$, $p < 0.01$. CF retains its edge but the effect is less dramatic than before.

Table 3. Average usefulness scores, excluding already visited locations

Algorithms	N ratings	Average	Variance
CF	46	0.57	0.14
PREFS	154	0.46	0.12
DISTANCE	139	0.37	0.13
ALL EQUAL	112	0.48	0.12
CUSTOM WEIGHTS	135	0.45	0.13

Table 4. Average number of items classified as "novel" by the participants

Algorithms	N users	Average	Variance
CF	8	4.25	5.36
PREFS	12	7.92	7.72
DISTANCE	11	6.55	3.47
ALL EQUAL	12	5.83	7.06
CUSTOM WEIGHTS	12	7.00	7.64

The Novelty Factor. While CF appears to stand out in terms of the usefulness of its recommendations, it did not generate as many novel recommendations as we had expected. The differences between Table 2 and Table 3 already pointed in this direction and we therefore decided to investigate the issue in more depth by computing the average number of novel items returned by each algorithm.

Table 4 clearly shows that CF yields the smallest number of novel items, despite its reputation as the most serendipitous algorithm [13]. The results are statistically significant, albeit a bit weaker than before: $F_{(2,5571)} = 2.8553$, $p < 0.05$. It is interesting to note that models based on distance or stated preferences greatly outperform CF. As a consequence the two mixed models also score higher on novelty since they mix the three other algorithms (CF, Preferences, and Distance) in various proportions. The custom weights model (0.2, 0.75, 0.25) scores much better than an even mix and it is even fairly close to the highest score (7.00 vs. 7.92). This confirms our intuition, based on system usage, about the overall balance that needs to be achieved between models to generate the most serendipitous recommendations, which was the main goal of our design. In particular, it looks like while CF is clearly useful (especially for people unfamiliar with an area) and needs to be taken into account, its overall contribution needs to be downplayed against more "static" models like stated preferences and distance to optimize novelty. But these results also show that this mix is still not ideal and could be further improved upon.

Another interesting discovery is that the number of items rated "definitely worth visiting" is inversely correlated with the number of novel items generated by an algorithm (r=0.79). This might be a reflection of some risk aversion from our participants when choosing restaurants: while exotic places are attractive, they might also disappoint. This is an interesting illustration of the tension created by mixing the results from heterogeneous models in the same list and potentially argues for more user control over which model should be on or off, as suggested by Schaefer et al [19].

Predictive Accuracy. We initially designed our system with a Model Weights Learner that automatically adjusts the contribution of each individual model based on a user's implicit feedback. However, this only works if at least some of the models predict a utility for an item that is close to the user's true rating of this item. We therefore looked into the predictive accuracy of each algorithm.

Table 5. Average error (deviation from user rating) for each algorithm and each participant. Cells are blank if too little data was available to compute the error.

	CF	PREFS	DISTANCE	ALL EQUAL	CUSTOM WEIGHTS
P1		0.21		0.05	0.01
P2	0.02	0.08	0.32		0.04
P3			0.34		-0.40
P4		-0.42	0.47	0.03	-0.17
P5		-0.35	0.23	-0.11	-0.63
P6	0.13				
P7		-0.22	0.29	0.00	-0.45
P8	0.25	0.02	0.21	-0.22	-0.12
P9	0.09	-0.10	0.16	-0.08	-0.15
P10	0.50	-0.06	0.48	0.24	-0.09
P11	-0.07	-0.08	0.24	-0.09	-0.38
P12	0.30	-0.71	0.38	-0.23	-0.50
P13		-0.42	0.48	-0.02	-0.39
P14	0.30	0.07	0.19	0.12	-0.08
P15				-0.06	-0.36
P16	-0.02	0.05	0.37	0.08	0.02
MEAN	0.17	-0.15	0.32	-0.02	-0.24
SD	0.19	0.26	0.11	0.13	0.21

Table 5 lists the average error for each algorithm and each participant. For each recommended item, we subtracted the user's assessment (by again mapping "definitely" to 1, "maybe" to 0.5, and "probably not" to 0) from the item's predicted utility. We then averaged these values over all items recommended by a given algorithm. This gives us a sense of how much an algorithm over- or underestimates item values.

Several interesting trends can be seen. First, it is clear that the accuracy of any algorithm varies greatly across users. For instance, the Stated Preferences model overestimates the value of items for P1 (0.21), but also underestimates the same value for P12 (-0.71). This is a clear argument in favor of a dynamic model weights learner that would adjust each model's contribution over time on a per-user basis (using the same examples, the learner should downplay Stated Preferences for P1, but increase its contribution for P12). Second, the average error across all participants indicates that some models tend to over- or underestimate a user's value of an item. For some algorithms this is not surprising: for example, the Distance model returns maximum utility (that is, 1 or close to it) for all items that are within range, but the probability that all of them will be useful to the user is low—consequently, the model often over-estimates the value of an item (mean error: 0.32). More surprisingly, it looks as if CF overestimates value overall (mean error: 0.17) while Stated Preferences underesti-mates (mean error: -0.15). The differences are statistically significant, $F(2.5306) = 19.1794$, $p<0.01$. Since the three models appear to "pull" in opposite directions, the algorithm mixing them all with equal weights is overall fairly accurate, deviating from a user's assessment by only -0.02 on average.

Influence of Comments and Ratings. Magitti does not limit itself to displaying a ranked list of recommended items based on information internal to each algorithm. As we mentioned earlier, the device's interface also displays the average user rating for each item, as well as detailed comments from other users. We wanted to assess the influence of this additional information on a user's final decision since earlier research shows it can have a significant impact [7].

Table 6. Average influence of comments and ratings for each user

| Participant | Influence of... | |
	COMMENTS	RATINGS
P1	2.5	1.7
P2	5.0	3.6
P3	6.0	1.0
P4	6.4	6.6
P5	6.5	2.5
P6	7.0	7.2
P7	7.7	3.8
P8	3.3	5.0
P9	2.9	1.1
P10	6.0	4.0
P11	7.0	1.0
P12	8.0	5.8
P13	6.0	4.8
P14	10.0	1.6
P15	6.0	1.7
P16	9.5	4.0
MEAN	5.7	3.2
SD	2.8	2.4

Table 6 summarizes our participants' answers to the two questions they received after assessing each recommendation list. Several interesting trends can be seen.

First, it looks as if comments have more influence than ratings (the difference is significant, $F(3.8893) = 46.4293$, $p<0.01$). It is clear that users pay attention to reviews written by other users and that these reviews affect their decision, probably not to the point of totally overriding an algorithm's ranking but still with some significance (the average reported influence is close to 6/10). The detailed nature of these reviews (many are several paragraphs long) and the fact that they come from human beings and not from the system probably both play a role in their impact. Conversely, a simple average rating is probably too limited to have a great influence.

Second, it is clear that the impact of this additional information varies greatly across users. For instance, while P1 claimed being almost "immune" to the effect of comments (2.5/10), P10 was greatly swayed by them (10/10). The differences between users are significant both for comments ($F(1.7885) = 8.1037$, $p<0.01$) and ratings ($F(1.7907 = 17.1247$, $p<0.01$). Again, this great variability illustrates how difficult it can be to satisfy all users with a "one size fits all recommender," which argues in favor of rich interfaces and dynamic, adjustable recommender systems.

Another way to look at the same data is to average the influence of comments and ratings by algorithm type rather than participants. This is shown in Table 7. There does not appear to be much variability across algorithms. The differences are not significant either for comments ($F(2.4685) = 0.6253$) or ratings ($F(2.4685) = 0.6373$). User-generated data like comments appear therefore to have a purely subjective influence that does not affect one type of recommender algorithm more than another.

Table 7. Average influence of comments and ratings for each recommender algorithm

Algorithms	COMMENTS	RATINGS
CF	5.2	2.5
PREFS	6.3	3.7
DISTANCE	5.1	3.2
ALL EQUAL	5.8	2.9
CUSTOM WEIGHTS	5.8	3.3

4 Discussion

Collaborative filtering algorithms have been at the core of most recommender systems for more than a decade. As we argued in our introduction, however, the move towards mobile and context-sensitive systems seems to require more complex, hybrid approaches. Our experiments provide evidence as to how much improvement these approaches provide, and what combination of models is most promising.

It is important to mention at first that CF, by itself, still generates recommendations rated as the most useful by our participants – a testament to the value of this algorithm and proof that simplicity is often a virtue. However, our data allowed us to refine this picture and shed light on CF's limitations for mobile and context-aware systems. In particular, it appears that CF is most useful for people unfamiliar with an area. This would make it particularly well suited to applications like a tourist guide.

The problem, however, is that overall, each individual algorithm has a tendency to under- or overestimate utility. Our data shows that, since they each pull in opposite directions, a mix of models with even weights tends to be fairly accurate and assigns a utility to each item that is close to a user's eventual rating. For users highly familiar with an area, such a mix of models generates recommendations that are as useful as CF alone, but more diverse. However, the most diverse and novel recommendations are obtained by combining the models using the custom weights we had chosen based on our own usage. While users would be less likely to follow-up on all of the recommendations from the latter algorithm (it is more error-prone), it is clearly the most serendipitous and probably closest to our design intentions.

Our analyses also clearly show that, to perform well, a hybrid recommender should be customized for each user. There is simply too much variability in the accuracy of each algorithm across users for a "one size fits all" approach to be satisfying. Moreover, our data also indicates that the eventual mix of models and their weights could benefit from a user's input in order to reduce the tension between getting items that are either too exotic or too familiar. This argues in favor of an automated approach to weights learning, but with the addition of transparency and control [9] so that the user can override some of the estimated parameters if desired.

Finally, it is worth noting the considerable influence that user-generated content, like comments about restaurants, can have on some users. For this subpopulation, it is almost as if the system could dispense with complex recommendation techniques in favor of user reviews, since the latter become the ultimate decision factor.

5 Conclusion

Mobile location-based systems are increasingly becoming a practical means for providing context-specific information. Recommending information takes the effort out of location-based information retrieval so that users need no longer shoulder the entire burden of searching for information relevant to them. The most effective solutions will likely combine explicit user input with implicit and/or contextual data.

To understand which combination might be the most useful, this paper has presented results from an evaluation of a context-aware recommendation system that uses a mixture of models to make recommendations. Our data indicates that, for systems targeted at users highly familiar with the intended geographical area of use, collaborative filtering alone is not enough. Indeed, our data shows that a hybrid approach combining collaborative elements with more static preferences and contextual data like a user's location has the potential to generate recommendations that are more novel and useful. However the contribution of each model to such a combination appears to be highly dependent on the user of the system, which argues in favor of an individual, automated model weights learner – provided the weights and types of models are made transparent to the user, in order to allow them to alter the mix of models if they feel the need. Indeed, the hybrid approach has the potential to generate results that are either too exotic (and therefore not acted upon) or too familiar (and therefore ignored). Putting the user in the loop would help ensure the right balance is achieved. The addition of user-generated content like restaurant reviews also helps put the recommendations into context, which some users find very influential.

We believe that these results are broadly applicable to the design of future mobile, activity-based recommendation systems. More research is needed to refine our understanding of the design of such systems—in particular, it would be interesting to conduct an experiment like ours on a larger scale, with the addition of other models, and over a longer usage period. While we plan to investigate these issues in future work, we also hope this paper inspires others researchers interested in the intersection between recommender systems, mobility, and context-awareness.

Acknowledgements. Dai Nippon Printing Co., Ltd. 'Media Technology Research Center' and 'Corporate R&D Division' sponsored this research. Diane Schiano conducted extensive analysis to provide the prior probabilities needed for bootstrapping our activity detection module.

References

[1] Adomavicius, G., Sankaranarayanan, S.S., Tuzhilin, A.: Incorporating contextual information in recommender systems using a multidimensional approach. ACM Transactions on Information Systems 23(1) (2005)

[2] Adomavicius, G., Tuzhilin, A.: Toward the next generation of recommender systems: a survey of the state-of-the-art and possible extensions. IEEE Transactions on Knowledge and Data Engineering 17(6), 734–749 (2005)

[3] Bellotti, V., Begole, J., Chi, E.H., Ducheneaut, N., Fang, J., Isaacs, E., King, T., Newman, M., Partridge, K., Price, B., Rasmussen, P., Roberts, M., Schiano, D., Walendowski, A.: Activity-based serendipitous recommendations with the Magitti mobile leisure guide. In: Proceedings of CHI 2008 (2008)

[4] Breese, J.S., Heckerman, D., Kadie, C.: Empirical analysis of predictive algorithms for collaborative filtering. In: Proceedings of UAI 1998, pp. 43–52. Morgan Kaufmann, San Francisco (1998)

[5] Burke, R.: Hybrid recommender systems: survey and experiments. User Modeling and User-Adapted Interaction 12(4), 331–370 (2002)

[6] Cheverst, K., Davies, N., Mitchell, K., Friday, A., Efstratiou, C.: Developing a context-aware electronic tourist guide: some issues and experiences. In: Proceedings of CHI 2000, pp. 17–24. ACM, New York (2000)

[7] Cosley, D., Lam, S.K., Albert, I., Konstan, J., Riedl, J.: Is Seeing Believing? How Recommender Systems Influence Users' Opinions. In: Proceedings of CHI 2003, pp. 575–592. ACM, New York (2003)

[8] Goldberg, D., Nichols, D., Oki, B.M., Terry, D.: Using collaborative filtering to weave an Information Tapestry. Communications of the ACM 35(12), 61–70 (1992)

[9] Herlocker, J., Konstan, J., Riedl, J.: Explaining collaborative filtering recommendations. In: Proceedings of CSCW 2000, pp. 241–250. ACM, New York (2000)

[10] Konstan, J., Miller, B., Maltz, D., Herlocker, J., Gordon, L., Riedl, J.: GroupLens: Applying Collaborative Filtering to Usenet News. Communications of the ACM 40(3), 77–87 (1997)

[11] Kurtenbach, G., Sellen, A., Buxton, W.: An empirical evaluation of some articulatory and cognitive aspects of "marking menus". Human Computer Interaction 8(1), 1–23 (1993)

[12] le Cessie, S., van Houwelingen, J.C.: Ridge estimators in logistic regression. Applied statistics 41(1), 191–201 (1992)

[13] McNee, S., Kapoor, N., Konstan, J.: Dont look stupid: avoiding pitfalls when recommending research papers. In: Proceedings of CSCW 2006, pp. 171–180. ACM, New York (2006)

[14] McNee, S., Riedl, J., Konstan, J.: Being accurate is not enough: how accuracy metrics have hurt recommender systems. In: CHI 2006 Extended Abstracts, pp. 1097–1101. ACM, New York (2006)

[15] Miller, B., Albert, I., Lam, S.K., Konstan, J., Riedl, J.: MovieLens Unplugged: Experiences with a Recommender System on Four Mobile Devices. In: Proceedings of HCI 2003. British HCI Group (2003)

[16] Poslad, S., Laamanen, H., Malaka, R., Nick, A., Buckle, P., Zipf, A.: CRUMPET: Creation of user-friendly mobile services personalised for tourism. In: Proceedings of 3G, pp. 26–28 (2001)

[17] Ricci, F., Nguyen, Q.N.: Acquiring and revising preferences in a critique-based mobile recommender system. IEEE Intelligent Systems 22(3), 22–29 (2007)

[18] Schafer, J.B., Konstan, J., Riedl, J.: Recommender systems in e-commerce. In: Proceedings of EC 1999, pp. 158–166. ACM, New York (1999)

[19] Schafer, J.B., Konstan, J., Riedl, J.: Meta-recommendation systems: user-controlled integration of diverse recommendations. In: Proceedings of CIKM 2002, pp. 43–51. ACM, New York (2002)

[20] Schiano, D., Elliott, A., Bellotti, V.: Tokyo youth at leisure: towards the design of new media to support leisure planning and practice. In: CHI 2006 Extended Abstracts, pp. 309–314. ACM, New York (2006)

[21] Tung, H.-W., Soo, V.-W.: A Personalized Restaurant Recommender Agent for Mobile E-Service. In: Proceedings of EEE 2004, pp. 259–262 (2004)

[22] Witten, I.H., Frank, E.: Data Mining: Practical machine learning tools and techniques. Morgan Kaufmann, San Francisco (2005)

Enhancing Mobile Recommender Systems
with Activity Inference

Kurt Partridge and Bob Price

Palo Alto Research Center, 3333 Coyote Hill Road,
Palo Alto, CA 94304, USA
{kurt.partridge,bob.price}@parc.com

Abstract. Today's mobile leisure guide systems give their users unprecedented help in finding places of interest. However, the process still requires significant user interaction, for example to specify preferences and navigate lists. While interaction is effective for obtaining desired results, learning the interaction pattern can be an obstacle for new users, and performing it can slow down experienced users. This paper describes how to infer a user's high-level activity automatically to improve recommendations. Activity is determined by interpreting a combination of current sensor data, models generated from historical sensor data, and priors from a large time-use study. We present an initial user study that shows an increase in prediction accuracy from 62% to over 77%, and discuss the challenges of integrating activity representations into a user model.

Keywords: Bayesian Inference, recommender systems, activity inference.

1 Introduction

In the past few years, people have increasingly relied upon electronic city-guides (such as Yelp, CitySearch, Zagat, Google and Yahoo! local search, and navigation systems such as Garmin and TomTom) to decide how to spend their leisure time. These guides typically give information such as venue name, category, location, description, and user reviews and rankings. People value these services. A recent study found that one quarter of mobile information needs were related to either discovering a point of interest, or getting directions to one [1]. However, the same study found that many of these users often found the interaction experience to be cumbersome and frustrating.

Recommender systems such as Netflix's for movies or Amazon's for online goods simplify the search process in other domains by building user models. However, these systems typically only model persistent user preferences. They do not capture the situational user preferences that might depend on location, time of day, weather, and other variables, which are critical for a mobile city leisure-time guide.

Contextual data, however, is not so easy for a recommender system to use. Models constructed directly from one context may not easily generalize to another. For example, visits to several different geographical regions are informative for new visits only if all these visits are recognized as belonging to a common pattern, such as going out for lunch. The multidimensional streams of contextual data are therefore more easily

G.-J. Houben et al. (Eds.): UMAP 2009, LNCS 5535, pp. 307–318, 2009.
© Springer-Verlag Berlin Heidelberg 2009

utilized if they are abstracted into a categorical variable that represents the user's activity, such as eating, shopping, etc. This approach allows a context-aware recommendation system to be factored into two parts, the first that recognizes the activity, and the second that uses the stream of the user's activities.

Of course, it is also possible for a user to explicitly specify their activity. However, this adds complexity to the system, which, as explained above, is a serious barrier for the average user. Furthermore, advertising systems, which must also select the best information for a particular situation, do not always have direct information about the user's activity of interest or the user's future activities of interest. Being able to automatically infer a user's current or future activity, however imperfectly, is valuable for such advertising systems.

In this paper, we show how to use activity inference to improve the recommendations of a mobile leisure guide. We describe a system, codenamed Magitti, that provides mobile recommendations through a thin mobile client supported by a backend server. The server predicts activity (such as eating or shopping) and preferences (such as fast food versus elegant dining) from the contextual data obtained from the client's low-level sensors. A user study demonstrates how the various activity-inference components work together and provides an initial indication of the accuracy of activity inference. We conclude with a number of lessons that we learned during the development and evaluation of the prototype.

2   Related Work

An early activity-based information retrieval system was Pepys [2]. It proposed using activity but did not explore how to detect it or built models from it. More recent applications specific to tourist guides take the user's location into account [3] but do not build rich models of user preferences. Modeling user preferences has been at the heart of recommender system research for over a decade [4]. Recently there has been considerable interest in recommenders that take the user's current context into account [5], however practical systems (such as CRUMPET [6] and COMPASS [7]) primarily use location, and do not infer and predict activity from a wider variety of contextual data sources.

A growing number of papers have investigated ways to answer the question "What are you doing now?" Some prominent work includes models for activity recognition [8], wearable systems [9], Conditional Random Fields using GPS data [10], and predictive systems using temporal patterns [11] and spatial patterns [12]. Activity based systems have been proposed for several purposes, including monitoring of the young or elderly, providing cognitive assistance, managing time, assessing interruptibility, conducting market research, improving advertisement targeting, and assisting transportation decisions. To our knowledge, our work is the first that aggregates many different kinds of information sources to determine activity for the purposes of leisure-guide recommendations.

3   System Overview

Magitti differs from existing leisure guides like Yelp and CitySearch by providing a highly customized experience that unobtrusively adapts both to the user's individual preferences and to the user's current contextual situation. Although the eventual target market is residents of large Japanese cities, the prototype was constructed and tested using content for Palo Alto, California.

The prototype comprises two parts. A mobile client runs on a mobile smartphone (WindowsMobile). The client gathers data about the user's physical context (GPS, time of day, user inputs, and weather) and her data context (content of emails sent/received, calendar, web pages and documents viewed, and applications used). This information is sent over a mobile data connection to a server. The server preprocesses the textual data, and then passes all data to two modules, the Activity Prediction Module and the Recommendation Module. The Recommendation Module is ultimately responsible for generating the recommendation using the activity generated by the Activity Prediction Module and using minimal additional information from the contextual data (such as distance to venues).

The general system architecture and recommendation module are discussed in other publications [13, 14]; this paper describes and evaluates the activity prediction module.

3.1 Activity Prediction

Magitti represents activity by a categorical variable that takes one of five values: "EAT" (eating at a restaurant), "SHOP" (shopping inside a store), "SEE" (passively enjoying entertainment such as a movie or sports event), "DO" (working out, attending special events), and "READ" (reading articles on the device). Although this representation covers only some leisure-time activities, it does correspond to classes of information that are typically sought from a leisure guide. We found them to be easily understood by first-time users [13]. An activity prediction is represented by a probability distribution over the possible activity types. The prediction thus provides an indication of the certainty the system has about its predictions, which helps the recommender module rank its item list.

A common approach to predicting activity is to collect labeled contextual data and apply machine learning techniques. However, the complexity of the input data, individual user variation, and need to produce accurate results "out-of-the-box" suggests instead that a structured model could leverage existing datasets such as national activity studies, land-use surveys, and local business directories. This strategy has been used by others (e.g., Krumm *et al.* [12]) in other domains.

Our structured model combines activity predictions from five separate primitive activity models, which are listed later in this section. The compartmentalization of models reflects the sources of data we were able to obtain, and allows each model to be independently constructed, tested, and debugged. The models fall into two classes: static prior models and personalized updating models. The static prior models are critical for making sensible predictions before data can be gathered for a specific user.

PopulationPriorModel. The first of the five models, the PopulationPriorModel, predicts the user's activity from the time of day, day of week, and current weather. It makes use of data from a large time-use study, the Leisure-Time Activity Survey from the Japan Statistics Bureau. This data set contains the proportions of the activities performed by about 10,000 people during any fifteen minute period on October 20, 2001. Figure 1 shows an example of the prior distribution derived from this data set.

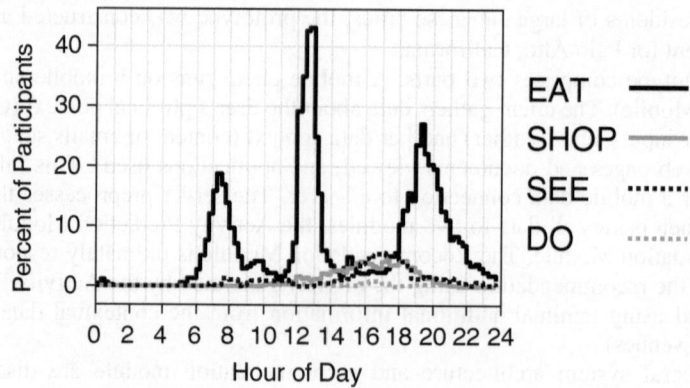

Fig. 1. The fraction of the population engaged in various activities in the data from the Japan Statistics Bureau, as a function of time of day during weekdays. Weekends show more activity diversity.

PlaceTimeModel. The PlaceTimeModel uses both time and location to generate a distribution over activity values. The notion of location used in this model is coarse, characterizing zones within a city as primarily shopping, dining, etc. The backing data used for this model was hand-constructed and verified using data collected from a user study of actual activities (described in Section 4). By default, the model generally predicts EAT (because it is the most likely activity), except in the afternoon, when SHOP is more likely. However, if the user is in a shopping district, then SHOP is the default activity, with EAT only being predicted around noon and in the later evening. SHOP is also predicted at large isolated retail stores. SEE is always predicted around movie theater complexes or performance halls.

UserCalendarModel. The *UserCalendarModel* is the third model. This model determines a set of likely activities from information parsed from the user's electronic communication or from the text in their appointment calendar. The model searches for structured text patterns containing information such as meeting times and names of venues (e.g., "Lunch at 12:30? Joe's Diner?"). Predicted events are extracted and stored on a calendar internal to the model. When the user asks for recommendations around the time of an appointment, this model outputs an activity distribution with a high probability for the activity that corresponds to these plans. If there are no plans associated with the query time, this model outputs a uniform distribution. If messages contain negative information (e.g. "I can't meet for dinner"), the system produces a distribution that is uniform except for the activity that the user is not interested in, which is given a low probability score.

LearnedVisitModel. This model also predicts the user's intended activities from time of day, but unlike the PopulationPriorModel and PlaceTimeModel, this model personalized its predictions to each user by learning from observations of their contextual data history. For example, if a user has a shifted work schedule, and often goes to restaurants at 2:00 pm instead of noon, then the system would infer that 2:00 pm is the user's usual eating time on workdays even though 12:00 pm would be recommended by the prior models.

Learning this model is more difficult than learning a model of online purchases of movies or books. Here, the activities—dining, watching movies or visiting a park—are not directly observable. This model must be learned from indirectly labeled data. We use a database of venues (restaurants, parks, stores, institutions such as schools and libraries, etc.) and the user's GPS trace to determine a set of possible visits to venues. Venue types are then directly mapped to activities.

Unfortunately, inferring a user visit to a venue from a GPS trace is not trivial. Merely having a point near a venue is not sufficient to infer a visit. Points corresponding to the user simply passing by a venue without stopping can be filtered out using a minimum duration metric [14], although short visits may then be missed. Also, current positioning technology is only accurate within 10 meters (30 feet). Because many downtown storefronts are narrow and buildings have multiple floors, many venues may match a single GPS coordinate.

Fortunately, we are ultimately interested not in the specific venue, but in the activity. Activity is more likely to be stable over time and location than any specific venue. We therefore map each candidate venue's type to an activity. So if the user spends time near "Joe's Taco," this would map to a venue type of "restaurant" and activity type EAT. If "Joe's Taco" is near "Bob's Shoes," SHOP might also be a candidate. But evidence for SHOP will be reduced if another day at around the same time the user visits an isolated restaurant, or a restaurant in a food court. By sampling over many days and locations, the stable pattern will emerge.

Formally, we want to estimate a simple model of the form $\Pr(A \mid L, T)$ where A is an activity to be inferred, L is a given location, T is a given time, and V is a (latent) venue. We assume a Bayesian Network in which location is conditioned on venue, venue is conditioned on activity, and activity is conditioned on time. By applying Bayes' Rule, re-introducing the marginalized-over venue, applying the product rule, and applying the independence assumptions of the Bayesian Network, we can decompose $\Pr(A \mid L, T)$ into the probability of a location given a visited venue $\Pr(L \mid V)$, the probability of a venue given an activity and time $\Pr(V \mid A)$, and the prior probability of an activity given a time $\Pr(A \mid T)$.

$$
\begin{aligned}
\Pr(A \mid L, T) \;=\; & \alpha \Pr(L \mid A, T) \Pr(A \mid T) \\
& \alpha \sum_{V} \Pr(L, V \mid A, T) \Pr(A \mid T) \\
& \alpha \sum_{V} \Pr(L \mid V, A, T) \Pr(V \mid A, T) \Pr(A \mid T) \\
& \alpha \sum_{V} \Pr(L \mid V, A) \Pr(V \mid A) \Pr(A \mid T) \\
& \alpha \sum_{V} \Pr(L \mid V) \Pr(V \mid A) \Pr(A \mid T)
\end{aligned}
$$

The location model $\Pr(L \mid V)$ is based on a Gaussian weighting of Euclidean distance from the venue, and is not learned from data. The venue selection model $\Pr(V \mid A)$ is also fixed, and is based on intuitive rules associating venues with activities. $\Pr(A \mid T)$ is learned from a training set $((L_1, T_1), (L_2, T_2), ..., (L_n, T_n))$ without activity labels. For each location, we hypothesize visits to *all* venues. Because the probability that a location is a visit to a venue falls off quickly with distance to the venue we need only consider nearby venues. We employ a spatial data structure to rapidly retrieve relevant venues. Each venue has an associated activity. We then create a new datapoint for each activity label to get $((A_1, L_1, T_1), (A_2, L_2, T_2), ..., (A_m, L_m, T_m))$. Note that one location can generate multiple activity labels. We use this set together with the likelihood function $\Pr(L\,|\,V)\Pr(V\,|\,A)$ to create a set of weighted counts for a standard Dirichlet posterior over activities A conditioned on time and location $\Pr(A\,|\,L,T)$. The variable T is discretized to 15 minute intervals spanning the week. To improve performance, the system precomputes activity distributions for each 15 minute interval of the week.

A similar mechanism indirectly learns user's context specific preferences. For instance, we can look up the attributes of restaurants the user has visited and use these to create counts for the user's cuisine preferences or restaurant type. This allows the system to learn concepts such as the user's preference for fast food at lunch but nice restaurants at dinner.

LearnedInteractionModel. The final model, the LearnedInteractionModel, also constructs a model of the user's typical activities at specific times, but using a different data source from the LearnedVisitModel. The LearnedInteractionModel model looks for patterns in the user's interaction with the mobile device rather than patterns in the user's visits to different physical locations. Magitti lets users override the system's activity prediction when it is incorrect. These override commands are logged, and used to form activity patterns. Like the LearnedVisitModel, this model works well when the user shows repetitive behavior. Data from the LearnedInteraction Model is shifted by fifteen minutes to account for the delay between a request for information and beginning the corresponding activity.

To meet the real time constraints for information delivery, the learning of the LearnedFromVisits model and the LearnedInteractionModel is done separately from the recommendation retrieval. Statistics are compiled into tables indexed directly by time of week so that they can be retrieved quickly and with little overhead.

Activity inferences are made by combining the predictions from all five models. For the learned models, a context-specific confidence measure derived from model counts is used to suppress the learned model influence when it has insufficient data. All models predict activity so there are five possibly differing predictions for the user's current activity at any one time. We use geometric combination of activity distributions provided by these models, inspired by Hinton's Product of Experts [16], in which the distribution from each model is raised to a constant model specific power and then the results are multiplied together. The multiplicative form allows models that are informative (highly peaked) to dominate models that are ambiguous (diffuse).

3.2 Query Context Prediction

Generally, when making an activity prediction, the system uses a context appropriate for immediately useful information: the current location, and a time fifteen minutes into the future. However, the user can override these defaults when planning for a future activity. For instance, a user might leave the office and want to find a restaurant in a specific neighborhood for later in the evening. It would be a mistake for Magitti to recommend currently open restaurants in the office's immediate vicinity.

The query context prediction module learns to predict the context in which the user is actually interested. The context could be the user's current context. Data for learning is gathered, as with the LearnedInteractionModel, from the user's interactions with the Magitti interface. For instance, whenever the user is at the office late in the day, she may manually switch the location context to downtown and time context to 7pm. A mechanism similar to the LearnedVisitModel is used to learn how to infer the queried context from the querying context. This context can then be fed to the activity prediction models when they estimate the activity distribution.

4 User Study

We conducted a user study to evaluate how well the system predicts activities. Eleven participants carried the device for two days each. Participants were recruited from within our organization. The participant pool included researchers as well as administrative staff. To motivate subjects to use the devices we rewarded participants with cash discounts for leisure activities that they engaged in while using the device. We later determined the ground truth of what leisure activities took place through participant surveys, interviews, receipts, and data collected on the device.

Table 1. The five different activity predictors. The predictors combine results from individual models that make separate activity inferences using different data sources.

Activity Predictor	Inputs	Outputs
Baseline	None	Always "EAT"
PopulationPriorModel	Day of Week, Time of Day, Weather	Most common activity using fixed tables
PopulationPriorModel + LearnedVisitModel	Day, Time, Weather, User ID	Product of prior probabilities and probabilities from per-user table.
PlaceTimeModel	Day, Time, Weather, GPS Locations	Activity determined by place-specific rules
PlaceTimeModel + LearnedVisitModel	Day, Time, Weather, GPS Locations, User ID	Product of PlaceTime prior probabilities and per-user profile table probabilities

While participants used the device, their location data and interactions with the device were recorded. Using these data traces, we tested how well different activity prediction mechanisms worked by replaying each trace for each activity predictor. We evaluated the five different activity predictors shown in Table 1. Each predictor contained a different combination of the models listed in Section 3.1. Participants did not use the messaging or appointment capabilities, so we do not include the UserCalendarModel in our analysis results. Furthermore, because users were only using the device for two days, we did not enable the Query Context Prediction mechanism.

4.1 Overall Results

In total, participants performed 45 different leisure-time activities. Participants clearly favored some activities over others: 28 were EAT, 14 were SHOP, one was SEE, two were DO, and none were READ.

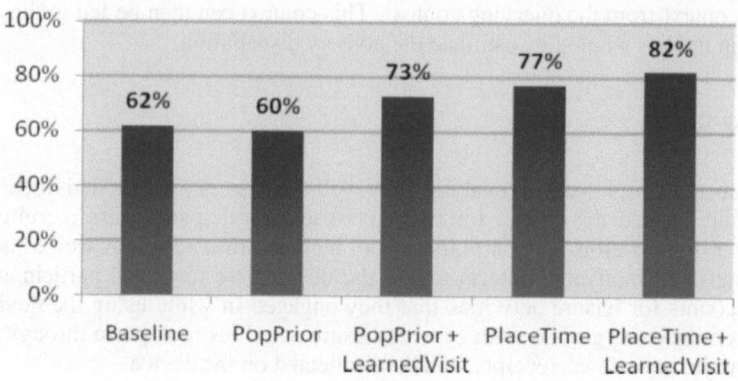

Fig, 1. Overall Results for different activity predictors

Figure 2 shows the overall results for the different activity predictors. The figure reports the percent of activities that were predicted correctly. Generally, the accuracy rises as the predictors incorporated more information and as they adapted to the particular user's behavior patterns. We now consider the performance of each activity predictor in detail.

4.2 Baseline Predictor

The Baseline activity predictor always predicts the same kind of activity. It is an important comparison point, because the baseline prediction can always be made quickly and without any input data. In our user study and the data from the Japan Statistics Bureau, EAT is the most frequent activity, so it determines the baseline. In our user study, 62% of activities are predicted correctly by just predicting EAT.

4.3 Population Prior Predictor

Surprisingly, the PopulationPriorModel performed worse than the baseline, correctly predicting only 60% of the activities in the user study. Although we first suspected that this arose from discrepancies between Japanese behavior and our American participants, inspection of American time-use studies showed little difference. Instead, the poor performance arose because there are a fair number of EAT activities at times that the predictor predicts a different activity. We suspect our user data may be biased towards eat since our recommendation database contained a bias towards restaurants, and because users may have eaten more to take advantage of our subsidies.

4.4 PlaceTime Prior Predictor

The PlaceTimeModel does much better than the PopulationPriorModel, correctly predicting 77% of all activities. Figure 3 shows what happens. The background shading shows the activity prediction for each place, and the striped zones show the number of participants performing each activity at any time. Shopping is much more

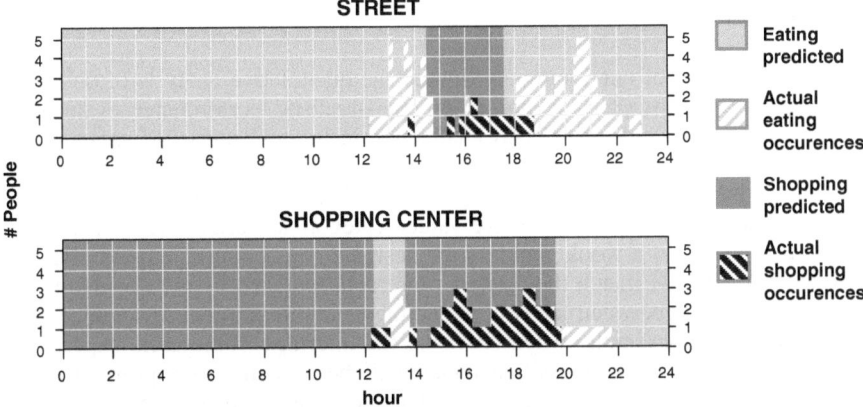

Fig. 2. The PlaceTime prior's performance on the EAT and SHOP activities. Although the time priors are imperfect, they identify activities more accurately than a time-only prior could do.

common at a shopping center than on the urban street, where eating is more common, although time does still play a role. Notice that the PlaceTimeModel still predicts incorrectly sometimes—eating happens in the afternoon on the street and in the shopping center, and shopping happens in one instance during the lunch hour in both places.

4.5   Learning Predictors

The two remaining activity predictors incorporate the learned user models. In a fully deployed system, Magitti would collect data over the course of several weeks and find any repeated patterns. But because of the short duration of the user study, data was very sparse. Training set performance, calculated by building a model from all the data and testing the model's performance again on that same data, raised the PopulationPrior-Model from 60% to 73%, and the PlaceTimeModel from 77% to 82%. However, these figures should only be interpreted as an indication that the learning modules do work— the actual benefits in a deployed system would depend on the prior weights and the regularity in the user's schedule. Other longitudinal activity studies have shown that such regularity does exist, although in amounts that vary from person to person [17].

4.6   Failure Cases

The prediction failures suggest ways that activity might be predicted more accurately. Some single-purpose mid-day snacks were missed by the activity predictors that did not incorporate learning. Multi-purpose trips were generally predicted incorrectly; this might be improved with a model that explicitly handles multiple activities as part of a sequence occurring during a single trip. Finally, one case involved confusion on the user's part. The system mispredicted that he wanted to eat when in fact he wanted to shop, however because it was late, no shops around him were open, so the system assumed otherwise.

5   Discussion

The size and scope of our user study limited the quantitative analysis of our activity inference mechanisms. This is not a surprise—realistic performance evaluation of activity inference systems faces many challenges, including battery life, spotty network coverage, and long study durations between the situations that are being studied. However, our evaluation also led to several qualitative observations worth mentioning.

First, although we selected the five-valued categorical variable representation for activity believing that it would simplify the design, it was not problem-free. First, this representation did not match the activity representation used by the PopulationPrior-Model. We mapped between the two taxonomies, but this introduced some confusing classifications. For example, when browsing the interface, some users expected that "visit museum" would be classified under SEE because it was a primarily visual, while others expected it to be classified as DO, because it involved active choice and exploration.

Another challenge was the mixed-initiative interface design. Although our goal was to minimize the user interaction necessary to get relevant results, we could not predict interest accurately enough to be completely automatic. We did observe several situations in which users needed to manually direct the system's inferences. A longer-running study would illuminate how much of this could be learned by a detailed personal model that had more data about its user.

Yet another issue unique to this domain is the complex relationship between the contextual data and the user's sought-after information. There are other ways in which activity might be predicted, such as pooling data from multiple users, clustering users, and incorporating sequential models. Although we primarily used time and location, more accurate predictions might be possible by using other data streams such data collected from infrastructure sensors or purchase records.

Finally, any system that collects contextual user data must protect users' privacy. This is especially important when such data is being used to make decisions about what information is presented to users. It is important that policies be established about how long data is retained, how data is used, and that users be informed about these policies, and given full control over their data and the ability to opt-in and opt-out whenever they choose.

6   Conclusion

The mobile recommender domain can greatly benefit from artificial intelligence and personalization. The small screen and limited input options limit rich interactions, and thereby create a greater need for personalization. Fortunately, mobile devices provide additional sources of contextual data (such as location) that are currently unavailable on desktops, further strengthening the case for predictive models on mobile devices. Applied correctly, this data can make a big difference in the user experience.

This paper has described the activity inference and learning mechanisms behind such a system. Results from a user study show that both prior information about general population behaviors and personalized user models can improve activity inference accuracy. Prior information that combines place and time is particularly effective, improving the accuracy from 62% to 77% for our prototype. We have also described other techniques that can improve accuracy even further, as well as research challenges to be overcome. We believe that all these results provide evidence that activity inference will play an increasingly important role in recommender systems in the near future.

Acknowledgements. Dai Nippon Printing Co., Ltd. 'Media Technology Research Center' and 'Corporate R&D Division' sponsored this research. We also thank the rest of the Magitti team at PARC, and especially Bo Begole for his suggestions and encouragement.

References

1. Sohn, T., Li, K.A., Griswold, W.G., Hollan, J.: A Diary Study of Mobile Information Needs. In: CHI 2008 (2008)
2. Lamming, M.G., Newman, W.M.: Activity-Based Information Retrieval: Technology in Support of Human Memory. In: Personal Computers and Intelligent Systems (1992)
3. Baus, J., Cheverst, K., Kray, C.: A survey of map-based mobile guides. In: Zipf, A., Meng, L., Reichenbacher, T. (eds.) Map based mobile services - Theories, Methods and Implementations. Springer, Heidelberg (2005)
4. Resnick, P., Varian, H.R.: Recommender systems. Communications of the ACM 40(3) (1997)
5. Adomavicius, G., Tuzhilin, A.: Toward the next generation of recommender systems: a survey of the state-of-the-art and possible extensions. IEEE Transactions on Knowledge And Data Engineering 17(6) (2005)
6. Poslad, S., Laamanen, H., Malaka, R., Nick, A., Buckle, P., Zipf, A.: CRUMPET: Creation of user-friendly mobile services personalised for tourism. In: 3G, London (2001)
7. van Setten, M., Pokraev, S., Koolwaaij, J.: Context-Aware Recommendations in the Mobile Tourist Application COMPASS. In: De Bra, P.M.E., Nejdl, W. (eds.) AH 2004. LNCS, vol. 3137, pp. 235–244. Springer, Heidelberg (2004)
8. Oliver, N., Horvitz, E., Garg, A.: Layered representations for human activity recognition. In: Fourth IEEE International Conference on Multimodal Interfaces (2002)
9. Kern, N., Schiele, B., Schmidt, A.: Multi-sensor Activity Context Detection for Wearable Computing. In: Aarts, E., Collier, R.W., van Loenen, E., de Ruyter, B. (eds.) EUSAI 2003. LNCS, vol. 2875, pp. 220–232. Springer, Heidelberg (2003)
10. Liao, L., Fox, D., Kautz, H.: Extracting Places and Activities from GPS traces Using Hierarchical Conditional Random Fields. The International Journal of Robotics Research (2007)
11. Begole, J.B., Tang, J.C., Hill, R.: Rhythm Modeling, Visualizations and Applications. In: Symposium on User Interface Software and Technology (2003)
12. Krumm, J., Horvitz, E.: Predestination: Inferring Destinations from Partial Trajectories. In: Dourish, P., Friday, A. (eds.) UbiComp 2006. LNCS, vol. 4206, pp. 243–260. Springer, Heidelberg (2006)
13. Bellotti, V., Begole, J., Chi, E.H., Ducheneaut, N., Fang, J., Isaacs, E., King, T., Newman, M.W., Partridge, K., Price, B., Rasmussen, P., Roberts, M., Schiano, D.J., Walendowski, A.: Activity-Based Serendipitous Recommendations with the Magitti Mobile Leisure Guide. In: CHI 2008 (2008)

14. Ducheneaut, N., Partridge, K., Huang, Q., Price, B., Roberts, M., Chi, E., Bellotti, V., Begole, B.: Collaborative Filtering Is Not Enough? Experiments with a Mixed-Model Recommender for Leisure Activities. In: User Modeling, Adaptation, and Personalization (2009)
15. Ashbrook, D., Starner, T.: Learning significant locations and predicting user movement with GPS. In: Sixth International Symposium on Wearable Computers (2002)
16. Hinton, G.E.: Products of Experts. In: Ninth International Conference on Artificial Neural Networks (1999)
17. Eagle, N.: Machine Perception and Learning of Complex Social Systems. Ph.D. diss., Massachusetts Institute of Technology, Cambridge, MA (2005)

Customer's Relationship Segmentation Driving the Predictive Modeling for Bad Debt Events

Carlos Andre Reis Pinheiro and Markus Helfert

School of Computing, Dublin City University,
Glasnevin, Dublin 9, Dublin, Ireland
{cpinheiro,markus.helfert}@computing.dcu.ie

Abstract. This paper covers a comparison between two distinct approaches to neural network modeling. The first one is based on a developing of a single neural network model to predict bad debt events. The second one is based on combined models, building firstly a clustering model to recognize the pattern assigned to the customers, with a particular focus on the insolvency, and then developing several distinct neural networks to predict bad debt. In the second approach, for each group identified by the clustering model one neural network had been constructed. In that way, we turned the quite heterogeneous customer base more homogeneous, increasing the average accuracy for the predictive modeling once several straightforward models were built.

Keywords: Data Mining, Knowledge Discovery, Predictive Modeling, Pattern Recognition, Artificial Neural Networks, Link Analysis, Clustering, Nearest Neighbor, Telecommunications, Customers behavior, bad debt events.

1 Introduction

Data mining have been widely recognized as a powerful tool for many kind of business applications such as fraud detection and direct marketing [1], [2] and [3]. Nevertheless, one of the important issues in data mining, which is roughly discussed in the literature, is data mining deployment actions, i.e. the results of feedback actions taken from the knowledge arisen from data analysis.

This paper presents a case study about development of pattern recognition and predictive models in order to understand and prevent bad debt events. The purpose of this set of models is to avoid financial losses assigned to customers' insolvency [4]. This paper presents a discussion on the importance of business goals understanding in order to direct the choice of algorithms and to offer a better interpretation of the results.

On this case study we compare two distinct approaches, a single neural network model to predict bad debt events and a combined approach based on a clustering and a prediction models. The clustering model was based on link analysis over the customers' relationship records, followed by a clustering approach using the nearest neighbor technique [6]. The clusters found were used to drive the second predictive modeling approach. The predictive models were based on MLP neural networks [5].

G.-J. Houben et al. (Eds.): UMAP 2009, LNCS 5535, pp. 319–324, 2009.

2 Developing the Customer's Behavior Segmentation

Since the customers' behavior was unknown, the first step of the second approach was to build a link analysis over the customers' relationship. The link analysis algorithm has used the call detail records, establishing the network of calls among the customers. Each customer is represented by a node, and a nonparametric clustering method was performed to separate the customers into distinct groups of similarity. The nearest neighbor's technique clusters the nodes based on a specific number of neighbors. This clustering approach uses variable-radius kernels. The link analysis algorithm in this particular case has used ten different neighbor values to find the optimal number of clusters. According to the customer's data provided was found five optimal clusters based on the nearest neighbor technique.

Therefore, the clustering process due to the link analysis has identified five distinct groups, named G1 to G5, according to different profiles assigned to the customer's relationship. As the main focus here is to predict the bad debt events, although the clustering process was established by the relationship among the customer's calls, the relation between population, billing and insolvency, for each group, is shown in Figure 1 as a way to present the clusters distinct characteristics in terms of business perspective.

It is possible to conclude that group G1 presents average usage with relative compromise of payment; group G2 presents average usage with low compromise of payment; group G3 presents low usage with good compromise of payment; group G4 presents high usage with compromise of payment; group G5 presents very high usage with relative compromise of payment.

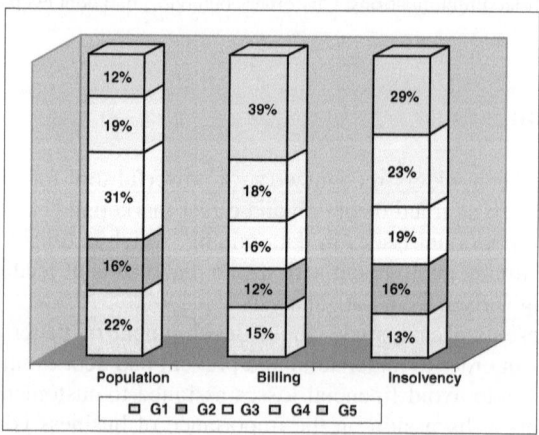

Fig. 1. Comparison of the attributes raised by the clustering model

Analyzing each group individually allows us to raise an important knowledge about the different customer's behaviors and then direct the forward predictive modeling. One of the most important features of the segmented groups is the relation between the billing and the insolvency values according to the delay of payment. Those variables provide a clear understanding of the customers' capacity of paying on each cluster and, therefore, allow us to quantify the insolvency risk. Another important analysis is the relation between the insolvency values and the average payment delay of a certain group. Most part of the large telephone companies work with an extremely tight cash flow, with no gross margin and small financial reserves. As a consequence, for a reasonable period of delay associated with high insolvency values, it is necessary to obtain financial resources in the market. Since the cost of capital in the market is bigger than the fines charged for delay, the company has revenue losses, i.e., even if the company receives the fines, there is a cost to cover the cash flow.

3 Directing the Predictive Model Due to the Clustering Results

The bad debt prediction model was built over the entire data set, including all customers, insolvent or not. In order to build a supervised learning model, customers were classified as "good" (G) or "bad" (B) according to the company business rules. Customer was classified as "bad" if the payment delay was greater than 29 days and as "good" otherwise. The customer base has around 72% of "good" customers and 28% of "bad customers.

The objective of the classifier model is to predict "bad" customers based on their profile, before any payment delay, allowing the company to decide the best prevention action to take, according to the customer groups identified in the previous segmentation models.

The classifier was built as a bagging of neural network classifiers [8], by previously dividing the base into a different of groups with distinct behavior. This procedure has enhanced the overall performance of the classifiers. The five distinct groups raised previously by clustering approach were used to feed the neural network classifier models.

MLP neural network were used in each one of the sub-classifiers [5]. The parameters of each sub-classifier were optimized for their respective data subset. Individual model results of each model, computed by five-fold cross validation are presented in Table 1. The results are presented in terms of the sensitivity ratio for each class, i.e. the ratio between the correctly and the total of instances of each class in the data base and the number of records assigned to each group.

Table 1. Accuracy of the individual classifiers

Group	Records	Good accuracy	Bad accuracy
G1	51,173	84.96	87.37
G2	22,051	82.89	91.12
G3	17,116	85.13	92.14
G4	23,276	82.69	89.04
G5	171,789	81.58	88.36
Average accuracy		84.45	89.60

By developing the classifier model as a bagging of five classifiers, each of it using segmented samples of customers, it is possible to adequate and specify each model individually. This procedure has allowed achieving more accurate predicting models.

For comparison reasons, a single neural network model was developed previously using the same basic configuration, but using the entire database, i.e. without segmentation. This model, not present here in details, reached a sensitivity ratio of 83.95% for class "good", and 81.25% for class "bad".

Comparing the classification model based on a single data sample with the bagging approach, the benefit to the class "good" sensitivity ratio was small, only 0.5%. However, the sensitivity ration achieved for class "bad" with the bagging approach was more than 8% better than the one obtained with the single base, as shown in Table 2.

Table 2. Overall accuracy from the single and combined prediction models

Model approach	Class GOOD	Class BAD
Single	83.95	81.25
Combined	84.45	89.60

Since billing and collection actions are focused on the class of "bad" clients, the gain in the classification ratio of good clients was not very significant, but the gain in the bad clients classification ratio was extremely important, since it helps directing actions more precisely, with less risks of errors and, consequently, less possibility of revenue loss in different billing and collection politics.

4   Establishing the Action Plan According to the Models Score

Due to Brazilian regulations, telecommunications companies are obliged to pay value-added taxes on sales and services when issuing the telephone bills. Independent of whether the client will pay the bill or not, when the bills are issued, around 33% of the total amount is paid in taxes by the company to the government.

The insolvency classification model can be very efficient to predict the customers that will not pay the bill. Therefore, an action inhibiting issuing bills for clients that tend to be highly insolvent can avoid a considerable revenue loss for the company, since it will not be necessary to pay the taxes.

In the classification model development, the customers' trend to become insolvent or not varies according to the confidence values issued. Taking only the range with 95% to 96% of confidence value to the "bad", which means the top hit rate from the model, there are a total of 55,859 customers with high risk to not pay their bills. Since the monthly average billing of these clients is about $47.50, the total possible value to be identified and related to insolvency events is $2,653,303, which corresponds to $875,590 in taxes duties.

The average accuracy level of the combined classifier is 89.6% for the bad class observations that are predicted as really belonging to the bad class. This ratio was obtained from the insolvency classification model based on cross-validation. Then the total of customers whose telephone bills issuing would be correctly inhibited is 50,049. Based on the same billing average, the value relative to non-payment events is about $2,377,328. Hence, the total taxes that can be correctly avoided by inhibiting the telephone bill issuing are about $784,518.

Taking into consideration the model classification error, the population of incorrect predictions is about 5,810 customers, with a billing loss around of $275,975. The value that would be assigned to the tax must not to be considered as loss, and thus must be subtracted from the total amount of billing loss, which is in that case $91,072.

In order to get an estimation of the total of revenue recovering due to tax avoiding, we have to consider the number of bills correctly avoided, and the total of taxes assigned to them, and the number of bills incorrectly inhibited, subtracted the taxes embedded. This estimation was computed on a monthly basis, considering a linear and constant behavior of the insolvent customers, which has actually been happening for the last years. The amount of tax recovery can be estimated as around $599,615 per month.

Table 3. Summary figures assigned to the revenue savings

	Customers	Billing	Taxes
Total	55,589	2,653,303	875,590
True predicted	50,049	2,377,328	784,518
False predicted	5,810	275,795	91,072
Taxes avoided			**599,615**

Considering the same process of billing issue avoided for the single prediction model, developed earlier but not described here in details, which achieved a hit rate of 81% of accuracy, the monthly savings would be around $228,924. The gain in terms of accuracy between both models is just 8% for the bad customer's class. However, the earnings reached in financial terms would achieve more than 160%.

5 Evaluation and Conclusion

This work has shown a real application of data mining techniques for insolvency prevention and revenue recovering. A distinct approach was covered, based on a clustering model for customers' behavior recognition and hence a set of classification models for insolvency prediction based on the bagging data sets according to the segmentation results.

The segmentation model has allowed to structure the knowledge about the customers' behavior according to particulars characteristics, based on which they can be grouped. The segmentation model allowed the company to define specific relationship actions for each of the identified groups, associating the distinct approaches with some highlighted features. The analysis of the different groups identifies the main characteristics of each of them according to business perspectives. The knowledge extracted from the segmentation model, which is extremely analytical, helps to define more focused actions against insolvency creating more efficient collecting procedures.

The classification models have allowed company to anticipate specific events, becoming more pro-active and, consequently, more efficient in the terms of business processes. The deployment of the classification results, even considering an overestimated classifier error, has shown to be significantly compensating as tax recovering policies.

References

1. Berry, M.J.A., Linoff, G.: Data Mining Techniques: for Marketing, Sales, and Customer Support. Wiley Computer Publishing, San Francisco (1997)
2. Fayyad, U.M., Piatetsky-Shapiro, G., Smyth, P., Uthurusamy, R.: Advances in Knowledge Discovery and Data Mining. AAAI Press/The MIT Press, Cambrigde (1996)
3. Abbot, D.W., Matkovsky, I.P., Elder IV, J.F.: An Evaluation of High-end Data Mining Tools for Fraud Detection. In: IEEE International Conference on Systems, Man, and Cybernetics, pp. 12–14. IEEE Press, San Diego (1998)
4. Burge, P., Shawe-Taylor, J., Cooke, C., Moreau, Y., Preneel, B., Stoermann, C.: Fraud Detection and Management in Mobile Telecommunications Networks. In: Proceedings of the European Conference on Security and Detection ECOS 1997, pp. 91–96. IEEE Conference Publications, London (1997)
5. Haykin, S.: Neural Networks – A Comprehensive Foundation. Macmillan College Publishing Company, New York (1994)
6. Bohm, C., Krebs, F.: High Performance Data Mining Using the Nearest Neighbor Join. In: Proceedings of the International Conference on Data Mining, p. 43. IEEE Computer Society, Washington (2002)
7. Ritter, H., Martinetz, T., Schulten, K.: Neural Computation and Self-Organizing Maps. Addison-Wesley, Reading (1992)
8. Deodhar, M., Ghosh, J.: Simultaneos Co-segmentation and Predictive Modeling for Large, Temporal Marketing Data. In: IEEE International Conference on Data Mining Workshops, pp. 806–815. IEEE Press, Pisa (2008)

Supporting Personalized
User Concept Spaces and Recommendations
for a Publication Sharing System

Antonina Dattolo, Felice Ferrara, and Carlo Tasso

University of Udine, Via delle Scienze 206, 33100 Udine, Italy
{antonina.dattolo,felice.ferrara,carlo.tasso}@dimi.uniud.it

Abstract. Current publication sharing systems weakly support creation and personalization of customized user concept spaces. Focusing the attention on the user, SharingPapers, the adaptive publication sharing system proposed in this paper, allows users to organize documents in flexible and dynamic concept spaces; to merge their concept map with a social network connecting people involved in the domain of interest; to support knowledge expansion generating adaptive recommendations. SharingPapers presents a multi-agent architecture and proposes a new way of representing user profiles, their evolution and views of them.

1 Introduction

Over the last decade, the Web has undergone great changes; there is a growing evidence of two parallel worlds, the traditional world constituted by expert and selected contributors and the new Web 2.0-based world, in which each user may become author, tag and share documents with a world wide community.

In this new context, an interesting example is provided by the publication sharing systems [1,2]; unfortunately, these systems weakly support creation and personalization of customized user concept spaces [3], representing them in a static and flat way. This problem has been partly analyzed in Bibsonomy [1], that allows users to organize the tags into hierarchies by exploiting an *if...then* relation; this approach enhances the manual tagging activity, but it does not offer either support for organizing knowledge or for personalized recommendations.

On the other hand, collaborative [4], content [5] and hybrid [6] recommendation frameworks improve searches over the available information bases, but few works (such as [7,8,9]) use the tags for recommending new resources: in [7], the authors use a extension of the PageRank algorithm for ranking resources, tags and users in a folksonomy; in particular, in [8], the authors use hierarchical clustering of tags for personalizing navigational recommendations; in [9], the authors measure the users' similarity considering their past tag activity and inferring tags' relationships based on their association to content.

Nevertheless, such recommendation systems consider only the tags and not the goals and the context of the user's tagging activity.

G.-J. Houben et al. (Eds.): UMAP 2009, LNCS 5535, pp. 325–330, 2009.

In this paper, we present SharingPapers, an adaptive publication sharing system, that allows users: to organize documents in flexible and dynamic concept spaces, using innovative and dynamic data structures (the Nelson's zz-structures [10]); to merge their concept map with a social network connecting people involved in the domain of interest; to support knowledge expansion generating adaptive recommendations. These recommendations are generated analyzing the user's concept space, and evaluating the similarities among them in order to reveal the similarity among goals and perspectives of each user. The paper is organized as follows: in Section 2 we describe the architecture of SharingPapers; then we deepen the discussion about the organization of user concept spaces in Section 3, and we propose a simple schema of recommendations in Section 4. Finally, Section 5 concludes the paper.

2   SharingPapers

SharingPapers presents an agent-based architecture shown in Figure 1.

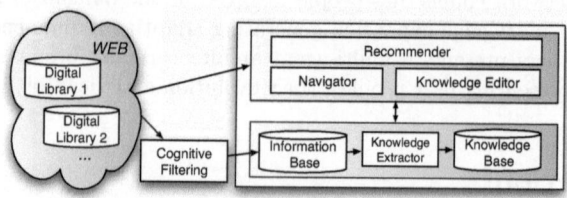

Fig. 1. System architecture

The main modules are:
- the *Cognitive Filtering* module uses the IFT algorithm [11] and specialized agent classes for browsing and accessing a set of external sources (Web sites and digital libraries), looking for relevant documents. The filtering operation is performed according to a set of defined information needs and populates the *Information Base*.
- The *Knowledge Extractor* module is specialized in extracting, from documents present in Information Base, attributes (such as the title of a paper, its authors, its year of publication) and relations (such as the network constituted by co-authors, or by people having a same affiliation, etc.), in order to populate the *Knowledge Base* (see Section 3);
- The *Navigator* module provides views on the Knowledge Base, enabling users to navigate among documents and social networks. Examples of views have been proposed in [12].
- The *Knowledge Editor* module implements the features users can invoke in order to manually modify and re-arrange their personal space, defined as concept space (see definition in Section 3); more specifically, each agent keeps track of the interaction of each user and translates the actions performed by himself into a set of operations on his/her concept space: users can create new entities, add

them to their concept spaces, or connect them with existing entities.

- The *Recommender* module suggests tags, recommends to visit parts of concept spaces (belonging to other users) and calculates personalized rankings on papers.

3   Organizing the Knowledge Base

In our system, the users are represented by their *concept space*: it contains a collection of *papers* and a *social network*.

Papers are connected in an innovative structure by links (indicating, for example, common keywords or tags), while the social network is constituted by users sharing interests and/or contents. A user concept space presents a dynamic structure, evolving in accordance to user behavior (new searches, adding-deleting new contents or tags, etc.).

The **concept space** (Map) related to the user u is formally defined by $M_u = (S_u, En_u, Re_u, Ac_u)$ where: S_u represents its *topological structure*; $En_u = \{\eta_{1_u}, \eta_{2_u}, \ldots\}$ defines its local *environment*; $Re_u = \{\rho_{1_u}, \rho_{2_u}, \ldots\}$ is the finite set of incoming *requests*; $Ac_u = \{\alpha_{1_u}, \alpha_{2_u}, \ldots\}$ is the discrete, finite set of possible *actions*.

In particular, $S_u = (MG_u, T_u, t)$ is a zz-structure, an *edge-colored multigraph* where $MG_u = (V_u, E_u, f)^1$ is a multigraph, in which the set of vertices $V_u = \{P_u, U_u\}$. P_u is the collection of papers of the user u, U_u the set of users connected to u; T_u is a set of colors (T refers to Tag), and $t : E_u \to T_u$ is an assignment of colors (tags) to edges of the multigraph; $\forall x \in V_u$, $\forall k = 1, 2, ..., |T_u|$, $deg^k(x) = 0, 1, 2^2$. Interested readers will find a deeper discussion about zz-structures in [10], [3], and [12]. In Figure 2 (left) is shown a graphical example of a generic M_u.

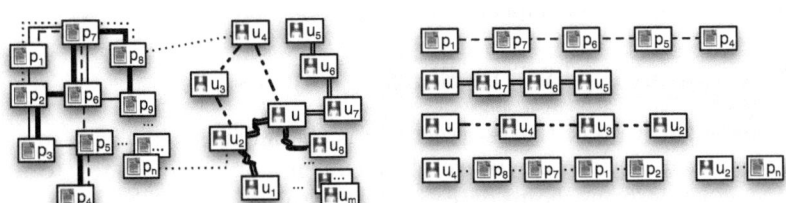

Fig. 2. An example of user concept space (left) and four dimensions of it (right)

$P_u = \{p_1, \ldots, p_n\}$ contains papers of interest for u, while $U_u = \{u, u_1, \ldots, u_m\}$ contains his/her social network; 7 different colors-tags (identified with different types of line style - normal, thick, dashed, double, etc.) are associated to the edges. Each tag identifies a link among vertices; for example, the tag (dashed line) connecting p_1, p_7, p_6, p_5, p_4 represents papers sharing a same tag or topic;

---

[1] Multigraph definition: $MG_u = (V_u, E_u, f)$ is a multigraph composed of a set of vertices V_u, a set of *edges* E_u and a surjective function $f : E_u \to \{\{v, v'\} \mid v, v' \in V_u, v \neq v'\}$.

[2] $deg^k(x)$ denotes the degree (that is, the number of edges incident to x) of color t_k.

the tag (double line) connecting u, u_7, u_6, u_5 indicates co-authors of one or more papers; the tag (long dashed line) connecting users u, u_4, u_3, u_2 groups members of the same research group; the tag (dotted line) connecting users and papers in u_4, p_8, p_7, p_1, p_2 and u_2, p_n identifies the author and a set of his/her papers.

For each color t_k, we may isolate a specific sub-graph of M_u, constituted by the set of vertices V_u and edges $E_u^k \in E_u$, containing edges of the unique color t_k. Each sub-graph of M_u is called *dimension* of color t_k and is denoted by D_u^k. Formally, a dimension $D_u^k = (V_u, E_u^k, f_u, \{t_k\}, t_u)$, with $k = 1, ..., |T_u|$, is a graph such that (1) $E_u^k \neq \emptyset$; (2) $\forall x \in V_u, deg_u^k(x) = 0, 1, 2$.

Using dimensions, the topological structure of M_u can be seen as $S_u = \bigcup_{k=1}^{|T_u|} D_u^k$. In this way, a dimension is defined in terms of one or more connected components, that it, some paths and a set (eventually empty) of isolated cells. For example, four paths present in M_u are shown in Figure 2 (right).

When the user enters in the system for first time, his/her concept space is automatically initialized by a set of dimensions. Papers that the user wrote, cited or tagged are imported in specific dimensions, as well as the papers presented in the events (conferences, journal, workshop) that (s)he attended. Similarly, co-authors and other people involved in the user research activity are also imported in the social network considering common publications, events and organizations. As second step, users can invoke the Knowledge Editor in order to manually modify and re-arrange their concept spaces. In this way, users can create new entities, add them to their concept spaces or connect them with existing entities. In its entirety, the concept space represents the user and model him/her; the interaction with the system is stored in it, generating new dimensions or updating the existing ones. Each dimension groups the resources labelled by the same tag and specifies a user interest, while sets of dimensions are used to identify his/her goals and perspectives. Specialized classes of agents manage the user model and calculate personalized recommendations, as described in the next Section.

4   Recommendations in SharingPapers

An important feature of the zz-structures is the intrinsic simplicity to contextualize information and to retrieve all documents and info related to a given resource, starting from the resource itself. On this feature is based our collaborative approach for recommendations: starting from the set of tags (that is, dimensions), that identify the current user's interests, we apply a four steps process: (1) expanding the set of tags for similarity; (2) comparing the collections of documents, associated to the set of tags; (3) ordering similar collections, assigning them a score of similarity; (4) ordering similar papers, assigning them a score of similarity. Each step enables the system to provide intermediate specific types of recommendation: (1) new tags for selected resources; (2) new similar users; (3) new collections of resources; (4) new specific resources.

In order to simplify our discussion, we identify with t_i a generic topic (tag or set of tags), and with D_u^i the dimension related to the user u, containing only the papers tagged also with t_i. Here, we propose the application of the recommendation mechanism to a specific user dimension D_u^k.

(1) Expanding the set of similar tags. In order to obtain a high recall, we are interested to find tags similar to the starting tag t_k; for this reason, we apply a non-adaptive reasoning for stating tag similarity considering the frequency of association to a certain paper.

Let $w^k(p)$ be the number of times that t_k has been associated to the paper p:

$$w^k(p) = \sum_{u' \in U} w^k_{u'}(p) \text{ where } w^k_{u'}(p) = \begin{cases} 1 \text{ if } deg^k_{u'}(p) \neq 0 \\ 0 \text{ otherwise} \end{cases}$$

$w^k(p)$ is expressed in terms of the number of times that t_k has been associated to the paper p from each generic user u' (that is, $w^k_{u'}(p)$); in particular, $deg^k_{u'}(p) \neq 0$ indicates that the paper p has been tagged with t_k in the concept space of user u'.

Now, we consider a set P of papers, and the vector $\bar{w}^i = (w^i(p_1), \dots, w^i(p_N))$ if $N = |P|$, specified for the generic tag t_i.

In order to measure the similarity between a chosen tag t_k, and another generic t_j, we apply the cosine similarity on related vectors $\bar{w}^k$ and $\bar{w}^j$.

$$tag\_sim(t_k, t_j) = cos(\bar{w}^k, \bar{w}^j) = \frac{\bar{w}^k \cdot \bar{w}^j}{\|\bar{w}^k\| * \|\bar{w}^j\|}$$

This measure allows us to assign a score of similarity to each $t_j \in T$ in respect to t_k. So, we consider top scored tags, T^k, as the most similar tags to the input t_k.

(2) Comparing user dimensions. As second step we compare the dimensions labelled by tags in T^k, evaluating the number of resources that they share; in fact, as stated from traditional collaborative techniques, if two users share a lot of resources (in our system, if their concept spaces contain a common set of resources), there is a greater probability that they have a common information need. The Jaccard similarity coefficient is applied as user similarity metric, $\forall t_j \in T^k, \forall u' \in U$:

$$user\_sim(D^k_u, D^j_{u'}) = \frac{\left| V^k_u \cap V^j_{u'} \right|}{\left| V^k_u \cup V^j_{u'} \right|}$$

This metric compares the dimension of interest for u (that is, D^k_u) with the dimensions of other users and allows us to assign them a score of similarity.

(3) Ordering dimensions. For obtaining an order, which considers both tag and user similarities, we define, $\forall t_j \in T, \forall u' \in U$, the following metric:

$$score^{t_k}_u(t_j, u') = tag\_sim(t_k, t_j) * (user\_sim(D^k_u, D^j_{u'}) + 1)$$

This value can be used for suggesting, to the user u, personalized navigation paths on dimensions defined from other users.

(4) Ordering papers. Finally, we associate a score to each paper present in the chosen dimensions:

$$score_u^{t_k}(p) = \sum_{\forall t_j : deg_{u'}^j(p) \neq 0 \ \ \forall u' \in U} score_u^{t_k}(t_j, u')$$

Top scored resources are suggested.

5 Conclusion

Web 2.0 users share a huge size of user generated content and assign them tags for simplify new searches, but current systems do not provide users with tools for organizing own concept spaces, allowing only a flat organization of them. This paper proposed a concept model focused on a dynamic and flexible organization of user concept spaces, and an adaptive and customized recommendation mechanism. Implementation is currently ongoing and experimental evaluation is planned for the next future.

References

1. Bibsonomy, http://www.bibsonomy.org/
2. Citeseer, http://citeseer.ist.psu.edu/
3. Dattolo, A., Luccio, F.: A new concept map model for e-learning environments. In: Cordeiro, J., et al. (eds.) WEBIST 2008. LNBIP, vol. 18, pp. 404–417. Springer, Heidelberg (2009)
4. Schafer, J., Frankowski, D., Herlocker, J., Sen, S.: Collaborative filtering recommender systems. In: Brusilovsky, P., Kobsa, A., Nejdl, W. (eds.) Adaptive Web 2007. LNCS, vol. 4321, pp. 291–324. Springer, Heidelberg (2007)
5. Pazzani, M.J., Billsus, D.: Content-based recommendation systems. In: Brusilovsky, P., Kobsa, A., Nejdl, W. (eds.) Adaptive Web 2007. LNCS, vol. 4321, pp. 325–341. Springer, Heidelberg (2007)
6. Burke, R.: Hybrid web recommender systems. In: Brusilovsky, P., Kobsa, A., Nejdl, W. (eds.) Adaptive Web 2007. LNCS, vol. 4321, pp. 377–408. Springer, Heidelberg (2007)
7. Hotho, A., Jäschke, R., Schmitz, C., Stumme, G.: Information Retrieval in Folksonomies: Search and Ranking (2006)
8. Shepitsen, A., Gemmell, J., Mobasher, B., Burke, R.: Personalized recommendation in collaborative tagging systems using hierarchical clustering. In: Proc. of the 2nd Int. Conf. on Recommender Systems, Lausanne, Switzerland (2008)
9. Zanardi, V., Capra, L.: Social ranking: Finding relevant content in web 2.0. In: Proc. of the 2nd ACM Int. Conf. on Recommender Systems, Lausanne, Switzerland (2008)
10. Nelson, T.H.: A cosmology for a different computer universe. Jodi 5, 298 (2004)
11. Minio, M., Tasso, C.: User modeling for information filtering on internet services: Exploiting an extended version of the umt shell. In: UM for Information Filtering on the WWW, 5th UM Int. Conf. (1996)
12. Dattolo, A., Luccio, F.: Visualizing personalized views in virtual museum tours. In: Proc. of the Int. Conf. on Human System Interaction, Krakow, Poland, pp. 339–346 (2008)

Evaluating the Adaptation of a Learning System before the Prototype Is Ready: A Paper-Based Lab Study

Tobias Ley[1,2], Barbara Kump[3], Antonia Maas[2], Neil Maiden[4], and Dietrich Albert[2]

[1] Know-Center, Inffeldgasse 21a,
8010 Graz, Austria
tley@know-center.at
[2] Cognitive Science Section, University of Graz, Universitätsplatz 2,
8010 Graz, Austria
{tobias.ley,antonia.maas,dietrich.albert}@uni-graz.at
[3] Knowledge Management Institute, Graz University of Technology, Inffeldgasse 21a,
8010 Graz, Austria
bkump@tugraz.at
[4] Centre for HCI Design, City University London, Northampton Square, College Building,
London, EC1V 0HB, United Kingdom
N.A.M.Maiden@city.ac.uk

Abstract. We report on results of a paper-based lab study that used information on task performance, self appraisal and personal learning need assessment to validate the adaptation mechanisms for a work-integrated learning system. We discuss the results in the wider context of the evaluation of adaptive systems where the validation methods we used can be transferred to a work-based setting to iteratively refine adaptation mechanisms and improve model validity.

Keywords: Adaptive Learning Systems, Evaluation, Task-based Competency Assessment, Learning Need Analysis, Knowledge Space Theory.

1 Evaluating Adaptive Systems in Due Time

Learning systems that adapt to the characteristics of their users have had a long history. Due to the complexity of most adaptive systems, it has been acknowledged that rigorous evaluation is indispensable in order to deliver worthwhile adaptive functionality and to justify the considerable effort of implementation. This is also reflected in the substantial amount of evaluations that have been published so far. Van Velsen et al. [1] present an overview and have noted several limitations in current evaluation practices. A variety of evaluation frameworks have been presented [2], [3], [4], all of which propose to break down the adaptive system into assessable, self-contained functional units.

The core research question when evaluating an adaptive system concerns the appropriateness of the adaptation. Typically, two aspects are distinguished, (a) the *inference mechanisms* and (b) the *adaptation decision*. While endeavors related to (a) seek to answer the question if user characteristics are successfully detected by the adaptive

G.-J. Houben et al. (Eds.): UMAP 2009, LNCS 5535, pp. 331–336, 2009.
© Springer-Verlag Berlin Heidelberg 2009

system, evaluations of (b) ask if the adaptation decisions are valid and meaningful, given selected assessment results.

It is recommended that these two research questions are investigated in an experimental setting using a running system (or prototype) where the algorithms are already implemented [1], [3]. The problem is that in many situations the development cycle of the software product is short and the evaluation might become obsolete as soon as a new version has been developed [4].

For this reason, we are pursuing a multifaceted evaluation approach for adaptive systems. By gathering both field and experimental evidence, we are checking validity of models and appropriateness of the adaptation mechanisms over the course of design, implementation and use of the system in an iterative manner. With this article, we describe an experimental evaluation that seeks to answer the above mentioned research questions in a controlled lab situation but *without* a running prototype, that is, in due time *before* the system is actually developed. After a brief presentation of the results, we will discuss the wider implications of our approach for evaluation research for adaptive systems.

2   Evaluation of an Adaptive Work-Integrated Learning System

Our paper-based evaluation has been conducted in the course of the APOSDLE[1] project. APOSDLE is a system for supporting adaptive work-integrated learning (WIL). With WIL, we refer to learning that happens directly in a user's work context, which is deemed beneficial for maximising learning transfer [5]. APOSDLE offers learning content and recommends experts based on both the demands of the current tasks, as well as the user's state of knowledge with regard to this task. APOSDLE is currently available for five different application domains. The experiment in this article has been conducted for the *requirements engineering* domain.

2.1   Adaptation in APOSDLE

Corresponding to the basic ideas of *competence-based knowledge space theory* [6], the users' knowledge states in APOSDLE are modelled in terms of sets of competencies (single elements of domain related cognitive skill or knowledge). In order to make inferences on a user's competencies, APOSDLE observes the tasks a user has worked on in the past. Each of the tasks is linked to a set of competencies (*task demand*). Taking into account the task demands of all previously performed tasks, their frequency and success, APOSDLE builds the user's instance of the user model by making inferences on the likely state of knowledge. In the following, this procedure shall be termed *task-based competency assessment*.

In order to adapt to the needs of a user in a given situation, APOSDLE performs a *learning need analysis* (also termed competency gap analysis elsewhere): The task demand of a task is compared to the set of competencies of the user. If there is a discrepancy (*learning need*), APOSDLE suggests learning content which should help the user acquire exactly these missing competencies in a pedagogically reasonable

---

[1] APOSDLE (www.aposdle.org) has been partially funded under grant 027023 in the IST work programme of the European Community.

sequence. In order to perform these adaptations, the domain model of APOSDLE contains *tasks* and *competencies* as well as a mapping that assigns required competencies to tasks. A prerequisite relation exists both for competencies and for tasks.

For the present study, the domain model was modelled in terms of the tasks in the requirements engineering domain (e.g. *Complete the normal course specification for a use case*, or *Carry out a stakeholder analysis*), as well as the competencies needed to perform these tasks (e.g. *Understanding of strategic dependency models*, or *Knowledge of different types of system stakeholders*). The model has been constructed, initially validated and refined in a previous study [7].

2.2 Design, Procedure and Hypotheses of the Study

The aim of our study was to test different algorithms for task-based competency assessment and learning need analysis. The participants were a sample of nineteen requirements engineering (RE) students. We had selected eight tasks from two sub-domains of the RESCUE process (Requirements Engineering with Scenarios in User-Centred Environments, [8]). According to the domain model, 22 competencies were required in total to perform well in these eight tasks.

Each student had to work on four exercises which had been constructed to directly map to the tasks from the task model. For example, they were asked to write a use case specification for an iPod, or to carry out a stakeholder analysis for a realtime travel alert system of an underground. The exercises were constructed to be ecologically valid, i.e. that they corresponded well to tasks that would have to be conducted by requirements engineers in a work-based setting. The sequence of exercises was randomized across participants.

Before conducting the exercises, students gave both competency and task self appraisals. Performance in the exercises was measured by marks assigned by a professor of RE. After each exercise, students were asked for an appraisal of their performance for the exercise just conducted. They were also asked to indicate which additional knowledge they would have required to perform better, both in a free answer and a multiple choice format. Answers from the free answer format were later subjected to a deductive content analysis that mapped each free answer to a competency from the domain, or a new one. The multiple choice items contained all competencies assigned to the particular task in the domain model as well as a number of distractors, i.e. other competencies not assigned to that task. Competencies had been reformulated to describe personal learning needs (e.g. *I would need to learn what is a domain lexicon and how to apply it*).

Self appraisal was included in this study as it is a common and economical way to assess competencies or performance in the workplace [9]. In accordance with prior research [10], we expected that self appraisals would correspond to actual task performance (hypothesis 1). The second hypothesis looked at the personal learning needs indicated by the students. We assumed that competencies selected by the students for each task would, in a substantial proportion of cases, correspond to competencies assigned to the task in the domain model. If this were not the case, learning need analysis based on the task-competency assignment in the domain model would not be possible. Lastly, we employed different algorithms for task-based competency assessment and investigated whether they would correspond to competency self appraisal by the students (hypothesis 3).

2.3 Results of the Study

2.3.1 Hypothesis 1: Self Appraisal and Task Performance

A one-way Analysis of Variance which compared the marks received for the exercises between those students that had indicated they were able to perform the task without assistance and those that had indicated otherwise showed that contrary to our expectations there was no relationship between self appraisal *before* task performance and task performance as assessed by the marks received ($F_{(1,69)}$ = .007, ns.). There was, however, a moderate relationship between self appraisal *after* task performance and task performance itself as measured by a Spearman Rank Correlation Coefficient (ρ = -.38, p < .01). It appears that students were not able to realistically predict their performance in the tasks before they conducted the exercise. Their appraisals after task performance, then, were slightly more accurate.

2.3.2 Hypothesis 2: Personal Learning Needs

Asked for their personal learning needs after the exercises, the students were significantly more likely to chose learning needs assigned to the particular tasks (M= 2.63) than distractors (M= 1.06) (t = 5.23; p < .001). This confirms the hypothesis and is an indication of the overall validity of the modeled structures. Similarly, learning needs extracted from student free answers in the content analysis were to a large degree those originally assigned to the particular task (60 vs. 39). Two of the tasks account for more than two thirds of the contradicting answers, namely task 3 (17 contradicting learning needs) and task 4 (11 contradicting learning needs). This gives strong reason to believe that there had been missing competency assignments for these tasks. Particularly, six new competencies that had not been part of the original list were suggested from analyzing the free answers. These include items like *Knowledge about different types of requirements*. These missing competencies may have also led to violations of the prerequisite relation on tasks which were found when comparing the relation to the obtained answer patterns.

2.3.3 Hypothesis 3: Task-Based Competency Assessment

Assessing competencies from the observation of task performance is one of the key benefits of using competence-based knowledge space theory. The usual way to do this is to take the union of all assigned competencies for all successfully mastered tasks. As [11] has shown previously, this method may lead to contradictions, especially in the case where the numbers of competencies assigned to tasks are large, and therefore suggests using both positive as well as negative task performance information. In the present study, we have compared two algorithms to predict the knowledge state of the students from task based information. Three predictors for task information were used (task self appraisal prior to task, task self appraisal after task, and task performance assessed by the expert) and each was correlated with competency self appraisal.

Although in all three cases, correlation coefficients were higher for the algorithm that took negative task performance information into account, the coefficients were of only small magnitude, ranging between ρ=-.017 and ρ=.129 (Spearman Rank Correlation), and with only one becoming significant. We partly attribute these low correlations to the fact that competency self appraisal is probably not a very accurate criterion for the actual knowledge state of our subjects.

3   Discussion and Outlook

The results caution towards the use of self appraisal information as a criterion variable for evaluating the adaptation of a learning system, but also as an input variable for the user model. Self appraisal by our subjects showed to be unrelated to their actual performance. A possible reason for this may be that the students were rather inexperienced in the domain. We assumed this also holds for the case of work-integrated learning, which is in line with [12] who found high validity of self appraisal only for experienced job holders. Also social desirability may have resulted in answer tendencies, as all performance appraisals before task execution were much higher than after.

The results for task-based competency assessment were largely unsatisfying due to low validity of the criterion variable. Future research will show whether our algorithms prove to be more successful than traditional measures. In any case, the question of a valid criterion variable for a knowledge state (which at the same time has ecological validity), will continue to be a challenge in work-based learning.

Checking for personal learning needs has proven to be a promising way to identify parts of the models with low validity (missing competencies in our case). In combination with indicators that estimate violations of the prerequisite relation from answer patters, these methods can be used to iteratively refine models once they are in use.

We are currently planning an extensive summative evaluation of the APOSDLE system and the components contained therein. A purpose of the study reported here was to gain an understanding of how paper-based methods could be applied for evaluating the adaptation of a learning system specifically in the context of adaptive work-integrated learning so that they may be incorporated in a more comprehensive evaluation approach in a field setting. For that reason, all the validation methods employed here can be easily transferred to a setting where the learning system is in operation and provides suggestions for learning needs and learning content during actual task performance. The role of the RE professor in our study could then be taken by supervisors of those working in the tasks. Short and unobtrusive system dialogues after task execution could be used for collecting self appraisal as well as indications of actual personal learning needs from the learners. This information could then be fed back to adaptation designers to iteratively refine the adaptation decision or the underlying domain model, such as suggesting additional competency assignments for particular tasks or missing competencies altogether.

Acknowledgments

The Know-Center is funded within the Austrian COMET Program - Competence Centers for Excellent Technologies - under the auspices of the Austrian Federal Ministry of Transport, Innovation and Technology, the Austrian Federal Ministry of Economy, Family and Youth and by the State of Styria. COMET is managed by the Austrian Research Promotion Agency FFG. Contributions of four anonymous reviewers to an earlier draft of this paper are kindly acknowledged.

References

1. Van Velsen, L., Van Der Geest, T., Klaassen, R., Steehouder, M.: User-centered evaluation of adaptive and adaptable systems: a literature review. The Knowledge Engineering Review 23(3), 261–281 (2008)
2. Brusilovsky, P., Karagiannidis, C., Sampson, D.: The Benefits of Layered Evaluation of Adaptive Applications and Services. In: Weibelzahl, S., Chin, D., Weber, G. (eds.) Empirical evaluation of adaptive systems. Workshop at the UM 2001, pp. 1–8 (2001)
3. Paramythis, A., Totter, A., Stephanidis, C.: A modular approach to the evaluation of adaptive user interfaces. In: Weibelzahl, S., Chin, D., Weber, G. (eds.) Empirical evaluation of adaptive systems: Workshop at the UM 2001, pp. 9–24 (2001)
4. Weibelzahl, S., Lauer, C.U.: Framework for the evaluation of adaptive CBR-systems. In: Vollrath, I., Schmitt, S., Reimer, U. (eds.) Experience Management as Reuse of Knowledge. GWCBR 2001, pp. 254–263. Baden-Baden, Germany (2001)
5. Lindstaedt, S.N., Ley, T., Scheir, P., Ulbrich, A.: Applying Scruffy Methods to Enable Work-integrated Learning. Upgrade: The European Journal of the Informatics Professional 9(3), 44–50 (2008)
6. Korossy, K.: Extending the theory of knowledge spaces: A competence-performance approach. Zeitschrift für Psychologie 205, 53–82 (1997)
7. Ley, T., Ulbrich, A., Scheir, P., Lindstaedt, S.N., Kump, B., Albert, D.: Modelling Competencies for supporting Work-integrated Learning in Knowledge Work. Journal of Knowledge Management 12(6), 31–47 (2008)
8. Maiden, N.A., Jones, S.V.: The RESCUE Requirements Engineering Process - An Integrated User-centered Requirements Engineering Process, Version 4.1. Centre for HCI Design, The City University, London/UK (2004)
9. Hoffman, C., Nathan, B., Holden, L.: A Comparison of Validation Criteria: Objective versus Subjective Performance Measures and Self- versus Supervisor Ratings. Personnel Psychology 44, 601–619 (1991)
10. Mabe, P., West, S.: Validity of Self-Evaluation of Ability: A Review and Meta-Analysis. Journal of Applied Psychology 67, 280–296 (1982)
11. Ley, T.: Organizational Competency Management - A Competence Performance Approach. Shaker, Aachen (2006)
12. Muellerbuchhof, R., Zehrt, P.: Vergleich subjektiver und objektiver Messverfahren für die Bestimmung von Methodenkompetenz am Beispiel der Kompetenzmessung bei technischem Fachpersonal. Zeitschrift für Arbeits- und Organisationspsychologie 48, 132–138 (2004)

Capturing the User's Reading Context for Tailoring Summaries

Cécile Paris and Stephen Wan

CSIRO ICT Centre, Locked Bag 17,
North Ryde, NSW 1670, Australia
{Cecile.Paris,Stephen.Wan}@csiro.au

Abstract. The web has become a major source of information to learn about a topic. With the continuous growth of information and its high connectivity, it is hard to follow only the links that are relevant and not to get lost in hyperspace. Our aim is to support people who read documents in a highly connected information space, helping them remain on focus. Our contextually-aware in-browser text summarisation tool, IBES, does this by capturing users' current interests and providing users with contextualised summaries of linked documents, to help them decide whether the link is worth following.

Keywords: user's interest; tailored summaries; browsing support tool.

1 Introduction

The web has become a major source of information to learn about a topic. With the continuous growth of information and its high connectivity, it is hard to follow only the relevant links and remain focused. While reading a document, people often encounter a promising link, which they decide to follow, only to discover after a quick browse that the document is not relevant to their current needs. Often, to avoid losing their focus, people open the linked document into a new tabbed window to which they return later. In such cases, users usually have many tabs opened. When they finally get to the linked documents to read them, they sometimes wonder why they opened these documents in the first place.

Our aim is to support people who read documents in a highly connected information space. In particular, we want to provide them with support to remain on focus. Our contextually-aware in-browser text summarisation tool, IBES, does this by capturing users' current interests and enabling users to obtain summaries of linked documents to help them decide whether the link is worth following. Then, when they follow a link, the system reminds them of their interest at the time they opened the document. Importantly, the summaries IBES generates are not generic, but rather are tailored to the user's current interests.

It is difficult in the general case and without *a priori* interactions for a system to know a user's interest. We hypothesise that what a user is currently reading reflects his or her immediate interest. We exploit this snapshot of the user's current interest to produce tailored summaries of related documents. We also provide an interface

G.-J. Houben et al. (Eds.): UMAP 2009, LNCS 5535, pp. 337–342, 2009.

enabling them to remain focused on what they are reading and to remember how they reached a specific document.

2 The In-Browser Elaborative Summariser (IBES) System

2.1 Overview

The IBES system is an internet browser[1] plug-in designed to support users browse through a large amount of information in order to learn about a topic. Based on the hypothesis that the user's reading context is a convenient, even if approximate, snapshot of the user's current interest, IBES obtains and captures this information through simple and efficient methods. It essentially notes the current page and the specific sentence of interest through a mouse-over movement: when the user moves the mouse over an anchor text link, this indicates to IBES the specific interest. This information is then exploited to generate a summary of the linked document.

The summary is generated using extraction-based summarisation techniques (cf: [1]) and is tailored to the current reading context. This summary thus acts as a preview of the document in relationship with the current document. It is provided to the user within their reading context, in a popup window. This enables the user to stay in focus. The user can then decide, based on this preview summary, whether the link is worth following or not.

The IBES System is illustrated in Fig. 1 below, using a Wikipedia text. It can be characterised as follows:

- *User Need*: Tell me more about the sentence that I have just read (the linking sentence), using content from the linked document.
- *Possible User Tasks*: Verify the statement just read; Learn more about that proposition; Decide if the linked document is worth reading.
- *Interaction*: The user moves the mouse over the hyperlink. This sets the linking sentence as the user's interest. This is passed to the summariser.
- *System Output*: IBES pops up a window which provides a preview for the linked page. It contains the first sentence of the linked document and a dynamically created summary that is tailored to the current user interest.
- *Interaction*: Having read this preview, the user can go to the linked page (see Fig. 2) or simply close the popup window.

In the example of Fig. 1, the user is reading about Louis Pasteur and moves his mouse on the link for "microbiology" in the sentence: *"He is regarded as one of the three main founders of microbiology, together with Ferdinand Cohn and Robert Koch."* IBES takes this sentence as the user's reading context and generates an extractive summary of the linked page, taking this context into account (the Summary in Context). Here, 6 sentences out of 78 were extracted from the linked page, and all relate to the founding of microbiology. The popup also includes the first sentence of the linked document, which, in Wikipedia, describes the main entity for the article.

---

[1] We currently work with the Firefox browser.

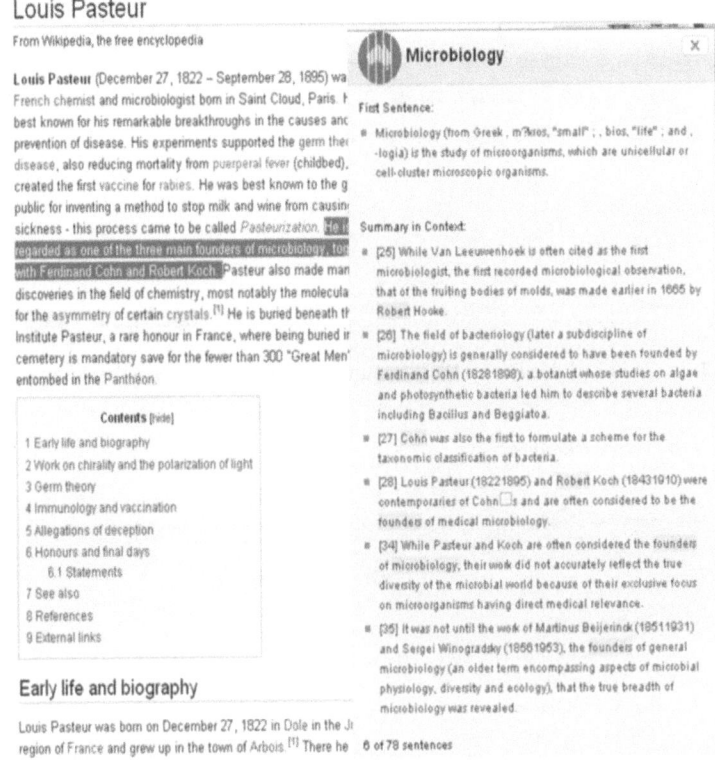

Fig. 1. A summary generated when moving the mouse over "microbiology"

Showing the summary as a popup window in the user's browser page enables readers to keep their focus on what they are reading. Presenting a summary tailored to the reading context enables them to be in a better position to decide whether to follow the link: they can tell from the contextualised summary whether the linked document is likely to be relevant to their current focus, or they might have obtained already the information they were seeking. IBES highlights the relevant words in the contextualised summary. The popup window also contains the link (not shown) so that readers can easily follow it. If the user decides to follow the link, IBES will remind users as to how they reached the new page, thus further supporting users to maintain their focus, and it will provide a link back to that previous reading context. This is illustrated in Fig. 2. Finally, IBES highlights on the linked document the sentences that were included in the Summary in Context for ease of navigation in the page (not shown).

Note that another link to the same document will have a different reading context, and thus a different summary will be generated, as seen in Fig. 3. The reading context is on the profession "microbiologist", and the sentences extracted, this time, are more about the description of the discipline. This summary and that of Fig. 1 only have 1 sentence in common.

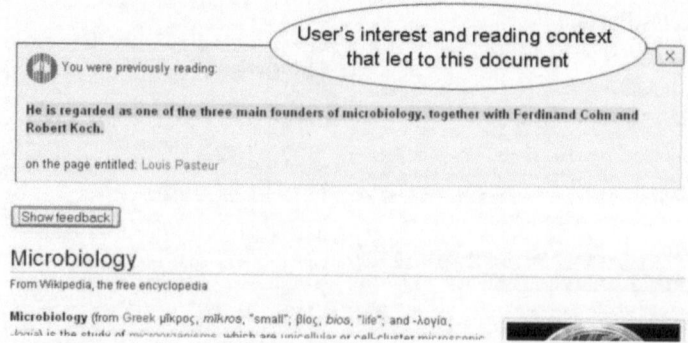

Fig. 2. In the linked document: IBES reminds the user of its original reading context

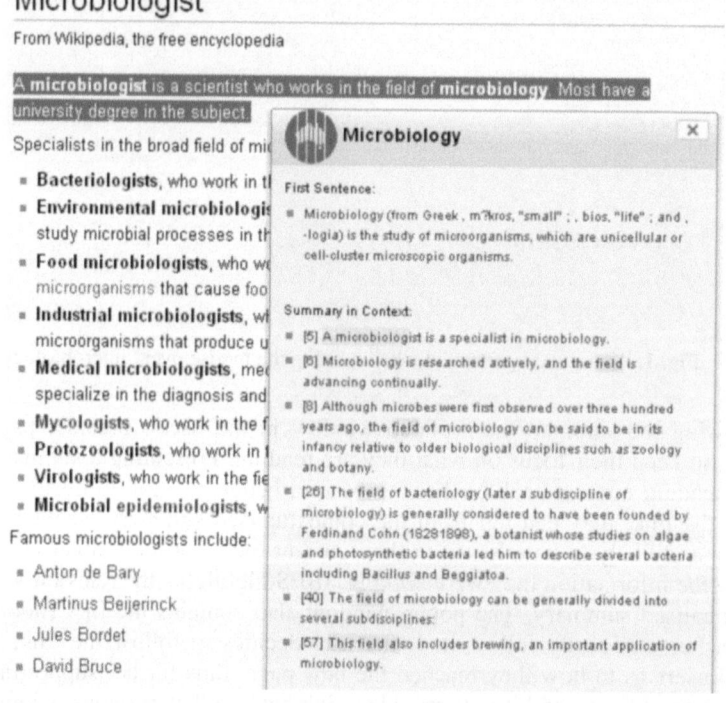

Fig. 3. Another summary of the page "Microbiology", but from a different reading context

2.2 Capturing the User's Interest

IBES considers that the current document represents the general user interest, and the linking sentence the specific one. It captures these two aspects. IBES currently performs only limited language processing (e.g., sentence segmentation). All sentences are represented using a vector space approach [2]. The simplicity of methods like the vector space approach is appropriate in contexts where the user needs to see and understand how the summaries are generated. The linking sentence is also recorded as such, so that IBES can use it to remind users of their original reading context. This method is simple and scalable. It does not require any information about the domain and does not need the identification of the user.

2.3 Generating the Contextualised Summary

When the user moves the mouse over a link, the IBES extension is triggered and provided with three pieces of information:

1. The linking page: the contents of the page being read;
2. The linking sentence: the text of the sentence in which the link is embedded; and
3. The linked page: the contents of the linked page to be summarised.

In extractive summarisation, a document is analysed to find its key words, assumed to represent what the document is about (cf: [1]). Representative sentences containing these words are then selected to form a generic summary of the document. In IBES, instead of choosing the sentences based on the key words of the document, the system chooses sentences that are related to the linking sentence. As mentioned, sentences are represented with vector space approaches. The cosine metric, a simple, scalable and fast method, is used to compare the vector space representation of each sentence in the linked page to the vector for the linking sentence.

3 Related Work

Our work falls under "user-focused" (or topic-focused, or query-focused) summarisation (cf: [3]; also, e.g., [4]) in which a summary takes into account some representation of the user's interests, typically as indicated in a profile or from a question/query. In IBES, users do not have to issue queries, and there is no need for an *a priori* profile. A user's current reading is taken to be his or her current interests. Also, our summaries are not generated in a search context, but as support to the task of browsing through cited documents while reading a specific article.

Amitay and Paris [5] exploited link text for summarisation, recycling human-authored descriptions of links from anchor text to generate web-pages summaries. In our work, we use the anchor text to provide a context for the summary.

Other researchers have studied aspects of graph theory applied to summarisation, e.g., [6, 7], although they do not focus on a live reading context as we do.

Other work has addressed the issue of capturing the user's interest for Web personalistion, e.g., [8, 9]. Our work is more concerned with exploiting user's interests to tailor summaries of related documents and thus can be seen as complementary. We were interested, however, in using as simple a technique as possible to capture the user's interest.

4 Discussion

IBES provides a summary of a document tailored to the user's current reading context within a browser, enabling a reader to get an overview of a linked document without losing his or her focus. Currently, the reading context is taken to be the sentence in which the link occurs. We have done experiments with the size of this window to model the user's interest, but our results so far are inconclusive. We will continue to explore this issue. We will also investigate tracking users' interests over time.

IBES currently works on Wikipedia, but its underlying modules are generic. There are only two features of IBES that are specific to Wikipedia: 1. the inclusion in the preview of the first sentence of the document. We thought that this overall description of the page would be useful in a preview; 2. the module that strips off navigation panels/etc. to provide access to the text proper. We are studying algorithms that would work on arbitrary web pages. Note that we have applied the work to a different data set: scientific articles (linked through citations).

We are designing an end-user evaluation to determine the utility of our context-sensitive summaries. In future work, we intend to explore additional summarisation strategies and the applicability of the tool for other types of document.

Acknowledgments. We would like to thank Julien Blondeau for his work on the system and Nathalie Colineau for her comments on an earlier draft of this paper.

References

1. Mani, I.: Automatic Summarization. John Benjamins Publishing Company, Amsterdam/Philadelphia (2001)
2. Salton, G., McGill, M.J.: Introduction to modern information retrieval. McGraw-Hill, New York (1983)
3. Firmin, T., Chrzanowski, M.J.: An Evaluation of Automatic Text Summarization Systems. In: Manni, I., Maybury, M.T. (eds.) Advances in Automatic Text Summarization, pp. 325–336. MIT Press, Cambridge (1999)
4. Berkovsky, S., Baldwin, T., Zukerman, I.: Aspect-Based Personalized Text Summarization. In: Nejdl, W., Kay, J., Pu, P., Herder, E. (eds.) AH 2008. LNCS, vol. 5149, pp. 267–270. Springer, Heidelberg (2008)
5. Amitay, E., Paris, C.: Automatically summarising web sites: is there a way around it? In: 9th Int'l Conf. on Information and Knowledge Management (2000)
6. Teufel, S., Moens, M.: Summarizing scientific articles: experiments with relevance and rhetorical status. Computational Linguistics 28, 409–445 (2002)
7. Mani, I., Bloedorn, E.: Summarizing similarities and differences among related documents. Information Retrieval 1 (2000)
8. Sia, K.C., Zhu, S., Chi, Y., Hino, K., Tsen, B.: Capturing User Interests by Both Exploitation and Exploration. In: Conati, C., McCoy, K., Paliouras, G. (eds.) UM 2007. LNCS, vol. 4511, pp. 334–339. Springer, Heidelberg (2007)
9. Zhang, H., Song, Y., Song, H.: Construction of Ontology-Based User Model for Web Personalisation. In: The 2007 International Conference on User Modelling, pp. 67–76 (2007)

History Dependent Recommender Systems Based on Partial Matching

Armelle Brun, Geoffray Bonnin, and Anne Boyer

LORIA Laboratory, University Nancy 2, BP 239 54506 Vandœuvre les Nancy
{armelle.brun,geoffray.bonnin,anne.boyer}@loria.fr
http://kiwi.loria.fr

Abstract. This paper focuses on the utilization of the history of navigation within recommender systems. It aims at designing a collaborative recommender based on Markov models relying on partial matching in order to ensure high accuracy, coverage, robustness, low complexity while being anytime.

Indeed, contrary to state of the art, this model does not simply match the context of the active user to the context of other users but partial matching is performed: the history of navigation is divided into several sub-histories on which matching is performed, allowing the matching constraints to be weakened. The resulting model leads to an improvement in terms of accuracy compared to state of the art models.

1 Introduction

Due to the increase of the size of the web and the Internet traffic, users are overwhelmed by the quantity of information available. Personalization and recommendation systems, that predict user attempts and propose resources linked to their tastes, are thus becoming more and more popular.

Several types of recommender systems have been studied, as content-based recommenders, collaborative filtering, etc. In the frame of collaborative web recommender systems, not only the set of resources consulted by all the users has to be used, but the order of consultation of these resources is of major importance and has to be exploited to perform accurate recommendations. State of the art approaches use datamining techniques to perform recommendations, and the web usage mining can be defined as "the automatic discovery and analysis of patterns and clickstream collected as a result of interactions with Web resources" [1]. To discover navigational patterns, sequential association rules (SAR), Markov models (MM), etc. are classically used, among which MM are the most popular due to their accuracy.

In this article, we design a model that takes advantage of all the previous models, in terms of accuracy, robustness, space complexity and coverage. Furthermore, it is anytime, allowing its use in all real-time applications.

Section 2 presents some datamining models used in recommender systems and put forward that partial matching allows high coverage and robustness. Section 3 defines the proposed model. The next section is dedicated to the evaluation of this model. Conclusion and perspectives are put forward in the last section.

G.-J. Houben et al. (Eds.): UMAP 2009, LNCS 5535, pp. 343–348, 2009.

2   Datamining Models for Recommender Systems

This section is dedicated to state of the art of datamining models used to perform history dependent collaborative recommendations. All these models assume that the consultation of a resource depends on the resources that the active user has previously consulted.

2.1   Sequential Association Rules

In the frame of web navigation [2], Sequential association rules (SAR) are used to capture dependences between resources. SAR are of the form $X => Y$ where X (the antecedent) is a sequence of items. Y, called the consequence, is a single resource.

In the recommendation step, if the antecedent of a SAR matches the history of navigation of the active user, we can deduce that the corresponding consequence resource is highly probable and may thus be predicted.

The advantage of SAR is that they are robust to noise: the SAR learned are not necessarily contiguous. Thus the matching step is more permissive than in the case of Markov models described in the next section. The use of SAR leads to a model with a low space requirements. The main drawback of SAR is the time required to learn them and filter out the most relevant ones. Such models also result in a low coverage.

2.2   K-Order and All kth-Order Markov Models

A k-order Markov model (KMM) assumes that the consultation of a resource depends only on the k previously accessed resources, the resources consulted before these k resources are considered as non-informative. Thus, a KMM computes the probability of accessing a resource given the sequence of the k previously accessed resources. Let $S_a = r_{a1}, \ldots, r_{al}$ be the active session, made up of the sequence of resources consulted by the active user u_a. A KMM estimates the probability $p(r_{al+1}|r_{al-k}, \ldots, r_{al})$ for each candidate resource. The resources that are recommended are those that have the highest probability.

Obviously, the higher the value of k is, the most accurate the probabilities are (in the case of a sufficiently large training dataset), and it has been shown [3] that the accuracy of KMM increases with the value of k. However, the higher the value of k is, the larger the number of states to be stored is and the lower the coverage is (as the probability that the history of size k perfectly matches one state of the model decreases).

To cope with the coverage problem, a All-kth-order Markov model (AKMM) has been proposed [4]. In this model, various KMM of different order k are trained and used to make predictions. Predictions are first computed by using a k-order MM, if no prediction can be performed, a $k-1$ order MM is used, etc. until a recommendation can be made. Such models provide a high coverage, but the number of states is dramatically increased.

KMM and AKMM are not robust to noise, as the history of navigation has to perfectly match a state of the model used. KMM and AKMM quickly reach their limits when the order of the models grows: both performance and accuracy decrease due to the size of the training data (probabilities are no more reliable).

2.3 Skipping Based Markov Models

The probabilistic model k-order Skipping Markov Model (KSMM) presented in [5], uses a KMM that allows skipping between the elements of the $k + 1$-tuple, both during training and recommending step. The distance is limited to a predefined value D. Such a model has a low space complexity (similar to a KMM) while using resources at a distance higher than k. A weighting scheme is applied to these $k + 1$-tuples, according to the distance between the resources. The frequency of a $k + 1$-tuple in the training corpus is equal to the weighted sum of all the occurences of this $k + 1$-tuple (within a distance lower than D). The corresponding conditional probabilities are then computed. Let for example the sequence (x, y, t, s, x, y, z). The triplet (x, y, z), occurs twice and the two weighted occurrences are added to the frequency of the triplet.

During prediction step, given the sequence of navigation of the active user $(r_{a1}, \ldots, r_{al})$, the probability of each resource r_{al+1} is computed as follows:

$$P(r_{al+1}|H) = P(r_{al+1}|r_{al-D}, \ldots, r_{al}) = 1 - \prod_{h \in H} 1 - P(r_{al+1}|h) * w(h, H) \quad (1)$$

where h sums over all the sub-histories of size k within the window of size D and $w(h, H)$ is the weight of history h in the whole history H. The probability of a resource r_{al+1} is based on the probability that none of the histories h predicts r_{al+1} as following resource.

This model has the advantage to use long-distance resources while being a low order MM and low complex. This model has been proved to be more accurate with a higher coverage than the corresponding KMM, but has the drawback of not reaching a total coverage (it is however higher than the one of KMM).

2.4 The Advantage of Partial Matching

We have seen that SAR enable the use of long-distance resources in the history as they enable distance between the elements of the history that match the rule; only a sub-part of the history is used: they perform partial matching. This partial matching makes the model robust to noise and enables to perform recommendations even when the whole sequence of navigation of the active user does not perfectly match training data.

The KSMM model also divides the history into sub-histories and performs recommendations by using these sub-histories. Once more, this partial matching is robust to noise: the consultation of additional resources slightly influences the recommendation process, whereas it highly influences the accuracy of KMM and AKMM.

The KSMM model is robust and accurate, due to partial matching, its main drawback is its coverage as matching is performed only on sequences of size k.

Let us remember that a 100% coverage is reached by AKMM due to the use of several KMM models of different order, but is not robust.

We propose here a model that exploits the characteristics of both preceding models (partial matching and several values ok k), resulting in a model having a high coverage and a high accuracy while being robust.

3   A All-kth-Order Skipping Markov Model

To prevent from the coverage problem of the KSMM, while keeping its high accuracy, we decide to create a all-kth order Skipping Markov Model (AKSMM). On the same principle than AKMM, k KSMM models are developed (from order 1 to order k). The KSMM of order k is first used to perform recommendations; if no resource can be recommended (the history of the active user does not match any conditional probability of the model), then order of the model is iteratively decreased until a resource can be recommended.

As the KSMM is more accurate than a KMM, we assume that the AKSMM will be more accurate than a AKMM while having a 100% coverage.

The resulting recommender is robust to noise as it relies on skipping, it has a 100% coverage rate and a low state-space complexity.

4   Experimental Evaluation

4.1   Corpus and Protocol

The dataset used for the evaluation is provided by the Crédit Agricole SA French banking group. It is made up of the logs collected on $3,391$ distinct Web pages (of an intranet of the group) browsed by 815 bank clerks, corresponding to a corpus of $123,470$ anonymous consultations. The corpus has been divided into training and test sets of 90% and 10% respectively.

To assess our models, we use the top-m score. This metric evaluates the average pertinence of recommendation lists. For each history of the test corpus, a recommendation list of size m is built, containing the m most probable resources according to the model. If the resource actually consulted by the user is in the recommendation list, the recommendation is considered as a success. This metric represents the percentage of pertinent recommendations.

We also evaluate the models in term of coverage, *i.e.* the percentage of cases where the model can recommend a resource.

4.2   Experimental Results

Before evaluating the AKSMM in terms of accuracy and coverage, the left part of Table 1 presents performance of KMM and AKMM on our corpus for comparison purpose. The size of the recommendation list is set to the usual value of 10.

We can first notice that, the optimal value of k for KMM is 2 (the recommendation list is computed based on the two previous resources consulted by

Table 1. Accuracy and coverage of KMM and AKMM according to the value of k

	KMM		AKMM		KSMM		AKSMM	
k	Acc.	Cov.	Acc.	Cov.	Acc.	Cov.	Acc.	Cov.
0	31.88	100	31.88	100.0	31.88	100	31.88	100
1	67.38	96.5	64.83	100.0	69.23	99.9	69.21	100
2	**68.14**	**84.4**	**65.16**	**100.0**	**71.21**	**98.8**	**70.81**	**100**
3	61.82	51.0	61.34	100.0	64.98	77.4	67.71	100
4	60.66	27.8	60.51	100.0	53.69	43.7	67.68	100

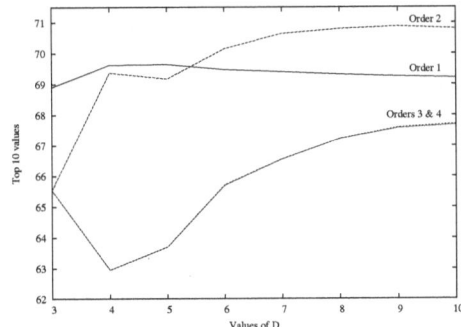

Fig. 1. Accuracy of AKSMM according to the distance D and the order value k

the active user), which leads to the highest accuracy (68.14). The corresponding coverage value is relatively high (84.4%), but is lower than for KMM of lower order. The accuracy of AKMM (that has a constant coverage) increases according to the value of k, until a value of $k = 2$, then accuracy decreases (as does KMM). Let us notice that the accuracy of AKMM with $k = 2$ is lower than KMM with a similar value of k. That is explained by the fact that 15.6% of recommendations have been computed with KMM of order $k < 2$, that have a lower accuracy.

The right part of Table 1 presents the accuracy and coverage of the KSMM and AKSMM with the maximum distance value set to $D = 10$. The value of D has been fixed to 10 as [6] showed that, on the same corpus accuracy of KSMM increased with the value of D and convergence was reached with a value of $D = 10$. As for KMM and AKMM the optimal value of k is 2 that reaches the best accuracy for both models.

In the whole table, we can notice that low order models are not evolved enough to obtain high accuracy values. At the opposite, high order models are too specific for this corpus and do not lead to high accuracy, we face the data sparsity problem. A value of $k = 2$ seems to be the best tradeoff on this corpus.

In order to study the characteristics of AKSMM, Figure 1 presents the accuracy of AKSMM, according to the distance D and the value of k. We can first notice that the accuracy of several models increase according to the size of the window. In the case of AKSMM of order 2, it increases by more than 5 points when the size of the window grows from 3 to 7, a larger window has no influence of the performance. Convergence is reached with a value of D lower than for KSMM. However, the AKSMM of order 1 reaches its optimal accuracy with an even smaller window size. AKSMM of order 3 and 4 also improve their accuracy according to the distance, but their accuracy is lower than the the AKSMM of order 2, once more due to the data sparsity problem.

So, we can conclude that the AKSMM we propose is promising due to its accuracy, coverage, robustness and complexity.

5   Conclusion and Perspectives

In this paper, we focus on context dependent recommender systems. The AKSMM model we design takes advantage of several state of the art models, expecially of skipped-based Markov models and all-kth-order Markov models. It results in a low-order Markov model that has a high coverage. This model has moreover a low space complexity. Experimentations show that the accuracy of this model outperforms those of the other models, while having a 100% coverage. We show that the accuracy increases according to the size of the history used to perform recommendations.

In a future work, we will test this model on larger corpora, to study the model proposed. Moreover, we envisage to design an alternative to the AKMM by using, when necessary, at the same time several models of different order.

References

1. Mobasher, B.: 3. In: Brusilovsky, P., Kobsa, A., Nejdl, W. (eds.) Adaptive Web 2007. LNCS, vol. 4321, pp. 90–135. Springer, Heidelberg (2007)
2. Fu, X., Budzik, J., Hammond, K.: Mining navigation history for recommendation. In: Proc. of the Intelligent User Interfaces Conference, pp. 106–112. ACM Press, New York (2000)
3. Deshpande, M., Karypis, G.: Selective markov models for predicting web-page accesses. In: First SIAM International Conference on Data Mining (2001)
4. Pitkow, J., Pirolli, P.: Mining longest repeating subsequences to predict world wide web surfing. In: USITS 1999: Proceedings of the 2nd conference on USENIX Symposium on Internet Technologies and Systems (1999)
5. Bonnin, G., Brun, A., Boyer, A.: Using skipping for sequence-based collaborative filtering. In: Proceedings of the International Conference on Web Intelligence (2008)
6. Bonnin, G., Brun, A., Boyer, A.: A low-order markov model integrating long-distance histories for collaborative recommender systems. In: Proceedings of the ACM International Conference on Intelligent User Interfaces (IUI 2009), Sanibel Islands, USA, pp. 57–66 (February 2009)

Capturing User Intent for Analytic Process

Eugene Santos Jr.[1], Hien Nguyen[2], John Wilkinson[1], Fei Yu[1], Deqing Li[1],
Keum Kim[1], Jacob Russell[2], and Adam Olson[2]

[1] Thayer School of Engineering
Dartmouth College
8000 Cummings Hall Hanover, NH 03755
[2] Mathematical and Computer Sciences Dept.
University of Wisconsin Whitewater
800 W. Main Street
Whitewater, WI 53190

Abstract. We are working on the problem of modeling an analyst's intent in order to improve collaboration among intelligence analysts. Our approach is to infer the analyst's goals, commitment, and actions to improve the effectiveness of collaboration. This is a crucial problem to ensure successful collaboration because analyst intent provides a deeper understanding of what analysts are trying to achieve and how they are achieving their goals than simply modeling their interests. The novelty of our approach relies on modeling the process of committing to a goal as opposed to simply modeling topical interests. Additionally, we dynamically generate a goal hierarchy by exploring the relationships between concepts related to a goal. In this short paper, we present the formal framework of our intent model, and demonstrate how it is used to detect the common goals between analysts using the APEX dataset.

1 Introduction

We study the problem of modeling an analyst's *intent* to improve the effectiveness of collaboration among intelligence analysts. Our approach offers a way to improve the *diversity* in a collaborative group by looking at the commonalities of the overarching goals that the analysts share instead of specific topics. Most of the existing approaches to modeling users for group collaboration explore the *similarity* of the users' topical interests [6,12]. There are two problems with this approach. First, people with similar interests may get stuck at the same peaks because they view and solve problems similarly [7]. Secondly, topical interests only show *what* the users have in common but do not show *how* the users achieve or use these interests for their tasks. We address these gaps by taking the **first** step to capture the user's intent where the intent is defined as an analyst's goals, commitment to achieve these goals, and actions leading toward these goals. We believe that with this level of understanding of the analyst's intentions, collaboration groups may be better formed with people who are working toward the

G.-J. Houben et al. (Eds.): UMAP 2009, LNCS 5535, pp. 349–354, 2009.

same big goals and different courses of action. Moreover, to improve the effectiveness of collaboration, it is crucial to find people with precise descriptions of their overarching goals and find them early enough to make the collaboration a success.

This problem is challenging because it involves several fields in the design and evaluation of an intent model, including sociology, computer science, and psychology. Two important research questions need to be addressed: (i) What is user intent and how do we capture it?; and (ii) How do we evaluate the effectiveness of the intent model? Our approach differs from existing approaches that capture a user's intent in an information seeking task (such as [1], [2], [4],[3], [9]) in that our model provides information about the *process* of a user's intent as opposed to a simple categorization of intent. This model is different from our previous user modeling approach ([10], [11]) in that the previous model focuses on capturing a user's topical interests as opposed to the process of achieving an overarching goal.

We developed a computational model to capture user intent by analyzing the actions taken by the user as well as the contents of relevant snippets and documents arising from his actions. Our model dynamically creates a goal hierarchy by finding the common concepts shared by directed acyclic graphs representing the relevant information. We capture the information on *What* the user's focus is (his goal), *How committed* he is to a particular goal, and *Which* actions he has taken to achieve this goal.

We demonstrate how our intent model is used to capture an analyst's intent by two simple experiments using the APEX dataset, which was created by the National Institute of Standards and Technology (NIST) to simulate an analytical task in the intelligence community. This collection included 8 analysts, their recorded actions over time, and their final reports. The preliminary assessment shows that our intent model captures the overarching goals more precisely and earlier in the analytical process than the model capturing only a user's interests. This paper is organized as follows: we describe our framework in detail. Next, we present two experiments with four pairs of analysts in the APEX collection. Finally, we present our future work.

2   Our Intent Model

Definition: We define a user's intent (I) as a tuple $I = \{G, A, C\}$ in which G is a set of goals, A is a set of actions to achieve these goals, and C is a set of real value(s) indicating how committed an analyst is to each goal in G. Our definition of intent is consistent with those found in the social sciences [5]. Our goals are characterized by their category and content. The category represents the user's intent generally, such as "Searching for evidence", "Going through a set of documents", while the content represents the detail information, such as "Imar's leaders support nuclear programs." Note that the names in this paper are changed. Based on our definition of intent above, the model needs to provide the information on *What* the analyst's focus is (his goal); *How* committed he is to a particular goal; *How* the analyst is achieving this goal; and finally, *Why* the analyst is trying to achieve this goal. Our aim is to explore the relationships among the components related to goal, actions and commitment to tie them together in the intent framework. Therefore, this model has three inter-related components: *Rationale, Foci* and *Action* networks.

Rationale network: A Rationale network is a directed acyclic graph (DAG) that consists of 2 types of nodes: (i) **Context**: includes concept and relation nodes that are extracted from the content of documents, snippets, annotations generated by an analyst; and (ii) **Goals**: represent what the analyst is aiming for. These goal nodes represent the detail information and are called content-based goal nodes. There are "context" links between context nodes, "support" links between context nodes and goal nodes, and "link-to" links between goal nodes. We construct the Rationale network from a user's query, and relevant snippets and documents as follows: (i) Convert a user's query, snippets or relevant documents into a document graph (DG) representation. The *DG* representation has been used in our prior work for building user models for information retrieval [10], [11]. "Context" links are created between these context nodes. (ii) Insert a content-based goal node into the Rationale network and add the "support" links from this goal node to all the concept nodes generated in Step (i). (iii) Update the Rationale network by finding the common ancestors of the concept nodes that are the children of the newly added goal node with the sets of concept nodes associated with the existing goals. If such an ancestor is found, a goal node is created and the link-to connections are created between the common ancestors and the existing goals. An example extracted from a Rationale network built for APEXF analyst in our experiment shows that the analyst focuses on a common goal of "nuclear program Imar", which are supported by two sub goals "Retain a snippet representing the Grand Aya Ali al-Sistani", and "Searching information on which Imarian clerical leaders debate". These two subgoals, in turns, are supported by context nodes such as "decision maker", "nuclear program", and "grand Aya".

Foci network: A Foci network is a snapshot of the Rationale network with additional information on commitment level and interest list. Each node has a name, a set of weighted interests, and a real number representing the commitment level for the focus. The name of a node in this network is the same as a name of a content-based goal in the rationale network. The set of interests consists of the context nodes which are the children of the corresponding content-based goal in the rationale network. The weight for each interest is the ratio of the frequency of the given interest concept over the total concepts related to the given goal. The commitment is currently computed by a linear function over the frequency and recency of the focus being pursued. The frequency is the ratio of the number of times this goal occurs in the rationale network over the total time slices. The recency is computed as follows: $(1 - (t - t_i))/(t + 1)$ in which t represents the current time slice and t_i represents the latest time slice this goal is active.

Action network: An action network has two components: a long-term component represented in a Hidden Markov Model (HMM) ([8]) and a short-term component represented in a Bayesian network. The HMM contains 3 states and 8 observations representing possible states and actions in an analytical process. The 3 states are "Searching for Evidence", "Going through documents", and "Examining evidence". The 8 observations are "Start application", "Search", "Retain" (triggered when an analyst bookmarks, prints, saves a document, or cuts and pastes information from a document to his/her report), "Access" (triggered when an analyst opens a document to view), "Make Hypothesis", "Associate Evidence" (triggered when analyst links a document or a snippet to a hypothesis), "Assess" (triggered when analyst assesses how relevant a document or snippet to a hypothesis), and "Discard" (triggered when a user discards evidence). The Bayesian network contains category-based goal and action nodes, and the links from category-based goals to actions. A category-based goal node is inferred from the HMM. We use a frequency table to update the conditional probability table for each node in the action network. An example extracted from an action network in one of our experiments shows that the analyst is searching for evidence and has taken several searches on "Imarian clerical community stand on Aya and president Amar's policies with regards to Imarian's civilian and military nuclear program", and "clerics who support Imarian nuclear program".

Intent inference: we determined the intent information as follows: (i) G is determined by finding the nodes in the Foci network with the highest commitment. Set them and their related context nodes in the Rationale network as evidence. (ii) A spreading activation process is performed on Rationale network to find the set of the most active goals. We added those goals to G. (iii) The action nodes that relate to these content-based goals with the corresponding time in the action network, are set as evidence. We perform a belief update and find the category-based goals in the action network with the highest marginal probability.

3   Preliminary Assessment

Our objectives are to show that (i) we capture user intent more precisely in the analytical process compared to the simple interest lists; and (ii) we capture user intent *earlier* in the analytic process compared to the interest-based approach. These objectives help us to get closer to our ultimate goal which is to improve the *diversity* in a collaborative group by looking at the commonalities of the overarching goals shared by intelligence analysts. We use the APEX collection (offered by NIST), which has 8 analysts. Each analyst was requested to assess the two hypotheses: "Where does the Imar clerical community stand on Aya?" and "President Amar's policies with regards to Imar's civilian and military nuclear program?". Their actions are captured and stored in a common repository. There are 5613 events in total.

For the first objective, we choose four pairs of analysts who have different actions (APEXL and APEXC, APEXE and APEXH, APEXL and APEXK,

APEXF and APEXB). The intuition behind this selection is that it addresses the diversity issue by combining people with different actions because they offer different perspectives. We considered Retain and Search events in this experiment. These analysts have different actions because they always belong to different clusters when we use K-means clustering algorithm to cluster their set of queries. Additionally, even though they have the same overarching goals, their final reports have distinct conclusions. In our first experiment, we ran our intent model 7 times. Each time, we used 25 consecutive events from each of the chosen analysts that represented the actions that the analyst has done on December 11, 2007. For each pair of analysts, we defined the precision of our intent model as the ratio between the number of relevant common goals of the two analysts in the pair over the number of common goals. A *common goal* is a goal node that is found in both intent models representing these corresponding analysts. For the interest model, we considered a set of common concepts found in both the interest lists as the set of common goals. We took the set of terms from the two working hypotheses as the ground truth of the analysts' goals. The average of precision for the interest model for these four pairs is 0.43 (sd=0.08), and for the intent model is 0.74 (sd=0.15). The paired t test results reveals that the results are statistically significant (n=4, p-value= 0.0396). In the second experiment, we measured the time at which the common goals of these two analysts were found for our intent model and the model containing only interests. We chose APEXF and APEXB for this experiment. For each analyst, we created our intent model on the fly with the inputs from the set of 40 events and output three components of our intent model for each time slice. We chose 40 events for each analyst (APEXB and APEXF) on December 11, 2007 such that they did not start with the same focus. APEXB started with the question on "nuclear weapon program and Imar" while APEXF asked about "grand Aya". We found out that at time $t=5$, our intent model has precisely picked up the common goals of Imar nuclear program and cleric leaders while at time $t=8$, the interest model has picked up "cleric", "Imar", "nuclear" as interests.

This scenario gives us some insights to develop a more comprehensive evaluation plan in which we divide the set of events for each analyst into a set of sessions and perform similar assessments over the numerations of the set of sessions of all analysts.

4   Conclusion and Future Work

In this paper, we have described the intent model that is used to capture a user's intent in an analytical process. The intent is defined as a set of goals that a user is trying to achieve, a set of actions leading toward the goals, and commitment level that represents how committed the user is to those goals. Our formal framework contains three inter-related components: Rationale, Foci, and Action networks. We develop two simple experiments in which we show that, by capturing the overarching goal of an analyst, it may help precisely describe what he is actually trying to achieve, comparing to listing a set of topics that he currently is focusing on.

There are many interesting and potential directions that we continue to address. In terms of implementation, the generation of a goal description from the set of information including content of relevant documents and query, descriptions of actions and description of the general goal of the analyst is needed to be coherent, logical and informative. We consider some heuristics to fuse several sources of information. In terms of evaluation, we look forward to extending beyond the development of the proof-of-concept scenarios to confirm if the results in our preliminary assessment hold for all analysts on a much more comprehensive evaluation. In addition, we continue to use the APEX dataset and measure how accurate the actions (or a sequence of actions) are predicted. In terms of effectiveness to forming collaboration, we need to define a measure to assess the diversity of a collaborative group and how diversity can improve the effectiveness of collaboration. We plan to find out whether the group consisting of analysts recommended by finding the common intent is more diverse than the group with analysts recommended by the existing approaches such as collaborative filtering, and content-based filtering.

References

1. Baeza-Yates, R., Calderon-Benavides, L., Gonzalez-Caro, C.: The Intention Behind Web Queries. In: Crestani, F., Ferragina, P., Sanderson, M. (eds.) SPIRE 2006. LNCS, vol. 4209, pp. 98–109. Springer, Heidelberg (2006)
2. Broder, A.: A Taxonomy of Web Search. SIGIR Forum 36(2), 3–10 (2002)
3. Jansen, B., Booth, D., Spink, A.: Determining the User Intent of Web Search Engine Queries. In: Proceedings of WWW 2007, Canada, pp. 1149–1150 (2007)
4. Lau, T., Horvitz, E.: Patterns of search: analyzing and modeling Web query refinement. In: Kay, J. (ed.) Proceedings of UM 1999, pp. 119–128. Springer, Heidelberg (1999)
5. Malle, B., Moses, L., Baldwin, D.: Intentions and intentionality: Foundations of Social Cognition. The MIT Press, Cambridge (2003)
6. McDoland, D.W., Ackerman, M.S.: Expertise Recommender: A plexible recommendation system and architecture. In: Proceedings of the CSCW 2000, Philadelphia, PA, pp. 231–240 (2000)
7. Page, S.E.: The Difference: How the Power of Diversity Creates Better Groups, Firms, Schools, and Societies. Princeton University Press, Princeton (2007)
8. Rabiner, R.L.: A Tutorial on Hidden Markov Models and Selected Applications in Speech Recognition. Proceedings of the IEEE 77(2), 257–286 (1989)
9. Rose, D.E., Levinson, D.: Understanding User Goals in Web Search. In: Proceedings of WWW 2004, New York, pp. 13–19 (2004)
10. Santos Jr., E., Nguyen, H., Zhao, Q., Pukinskis, E.: Empirical Evaluation of Adaptive User Modeling in a Medical Information Retrieval Application. In: Brusilovsky, P., Corbett, A.T., de Rosis, F. (eds.) UM 2003. LNCS, vol. 2702, pp. 292–296. Springer, Heidelberg (2003)
11. Santos Jr., E., Nguyen, H.: Modeling Users for Adaptive Information Retrieval by Capturing User Intent. In: Collaborative and Social Information Retrieval and Access: Techniques for Improved User Modeling. IGI Global (2009)
12. Schmitt, C., Dengler, D., Bauer, M.: Multivariate preference models and decision making with the MAUT Machine. In: Brusilovsky, P., Corbett, A.T., de Rosis, F. (eds.) UM 2003. LNCS, vol. 2702, pp. 297–302. Springer, Heidelberg (2003)

What Have the Neighbours Ever Done for Us?
A Collaborative Filtering Perspective*

Rachael Rafter, Michael P. O'Mahony, Neil J. Hurley, and Barry Smyth

CLARITY: Centre for Sensor Web Technologies,
School of Computer Science and Informatics,
University College Dublin, Belfield, Dublin 4, Ireland
{rachael.rafter,michael.p.omahony,neil.hurley,barry.smyth}@ucd.ie

Abstract. Collaborative filtering (CF) techniques have proved to be a powerful and popular component of modern recommender systems. Common approaches such as *user-based* and *item-based* methods generate predictions from the past ratings of users by combining two separate ratings components: a *base estimate*, generally based on the average rating of the target user or item, and a *neighbourhood estimate*, generally based on the ratings of similar users or items. The common assumption is that the neighbourhood estimate gives CF techniques a considerable edge over simpler *average-rating* techniques. In this paper we examine this assumption more carefully and demonstrate that the influence of neighbours can be surprisingly minor in CF algorithms, and we show how this has been disguised by traditional approaches to evaluation, which, we argue, have limited progress in the field.

Keywords: Recommender Systems, Collaborative Filtering, Predictive Accuracy.

1 Introduction

Collaborative filtering (CF) [2] has become a popular recommendation technique and has been applied successfully in many online applications. Different types of CF techniques all share an ability to harness the past ratings of users (over some catalog of items) in order to predict a user's likely rating for an unseen item. In a recommender system, CF techniques can be used to recommend items with high predicted ratings while suppressing items with low predicted ratings.

In this paper we will focus on two common flavours of collaborative filtering, so-called *user-based* and *item-based* based techniques. Given a target user t and a target item i, a rating $r_{t,i}$ is computed as a combination of a *base estimate* (B) and a *neighbourhood estimate*, where the former is generally taken to be the average user or item rating and the latter is some function of the ratings assigned by the target's nearest neighbours, $\mathcal{N}$, see Eq. 1. The neighbourhood estimate is essentially a way to refine the rather blunt, initial base estimate in a way that should improve the accuracy of the resulting prediction.

$$r_{t,i} = B + f(t, i, \mathcal{N}) \tag{1}$$

---

* This work is supported by Science Foundation Ireland under grant 07/CE/I1147.

G.-J. Houben et al. (Eds.): UMAP 2009, LNCS 5535, pp. 355–360, 2009.

User-based and item-based approaches differ principally in the way that they compute and combine the neighbourhood estimates into the overall prediction process. For example, the classic approach to user-based collaborative filtering is presented by [2] and shown in Eq. 2. Here the base estimate is based on the target user's average rating $\bar{r}_t$, and the neighbourhood estimate is based on a weighted-average of the extent to which similar neighbours $u \in \mathcal{N}$ appear to like or dislike the target item. Neighbour similarity, $S_{t,u}$, is usually calculated using Pearson's correlation (comparing target user and neighbour ratings). The extent to which a neighbour likes or dislikes the target item is based on whether their rating for i is greater than or less than their average rating $\bar{r}_u$.

$$r_{t,i} = \bar{r}_t + \frac{\sum_{u \in \mathcal{N}} (r_{u,i} - \bar{r}_u) \times S_{t,u}}{\sum_{u \in \mathcal{N}} |S_{t,u}|} \tag{2}$$

Item-based CF can be presented similarly (see [1]) such that predictions are computed according to Eq. 3. This time the base estimate is the target item's average rating $\bar{r}_i$ across all users and the neighbourhood estimate is based on a weighted-average of the extent to which the user's existing item ratings differ from the average rating received by those items across all users. The similarity $S_{i,j}$ between items i and j is computed using the adjusted cosine metric [3] and the neighbourhood $\mathcal{N}$ consists of each item j previously rated by the user.

$$r_{t,i} = \bar{r}_i + \frac{\sum_{j \in \mathcal{N}} (r_{t,j} - \bar{r}_j) \times S_{i,j}}{\sum_{j \in \mathcal{N}} S_{i,j}} \tag{3}$$

The assumed power of collaborative filtering is derived largely from its neighbourhood estimate which must perturb the base estimate by the *correct magnitude* and in the *correct direction*. It is surprising, to us at least, that there has been no detailed examination of these common collaborative filtering techniques, that focuses on the individual base and neighbourhood estimates.

In this paper we argue that a more principled approach to CF design and evaluation is merited and that it is important to consider more carefully the influence of base and neighbourhood estimates if we are to significantly advance the current state-of-the-art. The main contribution of this paper is an initial analysis of these estimates across three standard CF datasets using both user-based and item-based techniques, with the surprising result that the neighbourhood estimates plays a relatively minor, and often unreliable, prediction role. Moreover, we argue that traditional evaluation methodologies have served only to disguise this effect, and we propose a return to an *analysis of the extremes* as originally proposed by [4], which seems to have been largely forgotten by the community.

2   The Importance of Good Neighbours

In this section we focus on the assumption that underlies user-based and item-based CF–namely, that the neighbourhood estimate, in general, improves the

Table 1. Dataset Statistics

Datatset	# Users	# Items	# Ratings	Sparsity	Rating Scale
MovieLens	943	1,682	100,000	93.695%	1–5
Netflix	24,010	17,741	5,581,775	98.690%	1–5
Book-Crossing	77,805	185,973	433,671	99.997%	1–10

Table 2. Magnitude, correct direction (%) of neighbourhood estimate and overall MAE

	User-based			Item-based		
	Mag.	Cor. Dir.	MAE	Mag.	Cor. Dir.	MAE
MovieLens	0.43	66%	0.73	0.34	64%	0.73
Netflix	0.41	66%	0.7	0.35	67%	0.69
Book-Crossing	0.99	53%	1.53	0.94	63%	1.34

prediction accuracy of the base estimate. We test this assumption on three commonly used, large-scale, real-world datasets: MovieLens (100K)[1], Netflix[2] and Book-Crossing [5][3]. Since the trends observed for MovieLens and Neflix are similar, we at times report on just one. Dataset statistics are given in Table 1.

We first examine the *direction* of the neighbourhood estimate, i.e. how often the base estimate is pushed closer towards the true rating, see Table 2. For MovieLens and Netflix, we find that the neighbourhood estimate produces an adjustment in the correct direction (on average across both user- and item-based CF) in only 63% of cases. This means that 37% of the time, the neighbourhood estimate is actually pushing the prediction from the base estimate in the wrong direction, thus making it less accurate. For the Book-Crossing dataset, user-based CF performs particularly poorly, with only 53% of neighbourhood estimates contributing in the correct direction, and actually performing only slightly better than chance. This implies that CF is contributing to poorer quality predictions in just under half the cases; we will return to this in Section 3 where we will discover more positive results in different regions of the ratings space. The differences in results for user-based CF across the datasets correlate well with dataset sparsity but a deeper analysis is left for future work.

Table 2 also shows the average (absolute) magnitude of shift produced by the neighbourhood estimate. For both MovieLens and Netflix, neighbourhood estimates contribute less than 1/2 point on the 5-point scale. For Book-Crossing, the average magnitude is approximately 1 point on a 10-point scale. Clearly, the ability of the neighbourhood estimate to significantly influence the final prediction is limited. The cumulative distribution functions (CDF) of neighbourhood estimate magnitudes in Figure 1 (a) show that in fact this aspect of the CF algo-

---

[1] http://www.grouplens.org/

[2] http://www.netflixprize.com/

[3] In Netflix, we performed our analysis on a randomly selected 5% of users and associated ratings; for Book-Crossing, we ignored implicit ratings. All results are obtained using 10-fold cross validation to make predictions for randomly selected test ratings.

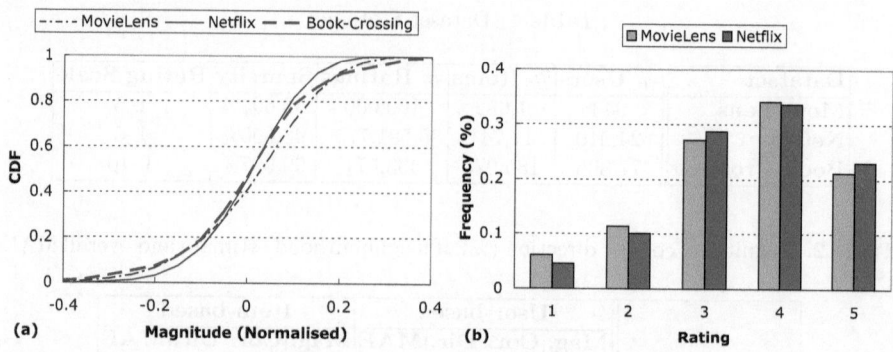

Fig. 1. (a) Cumulative distribution functions showing the magnitude of the neighbour-hood estimate and (b) frequency of ratings in MovieLens and Netflix datasets

rithm has ultimately little influence on the predicted rating. This is true across the three different datasets and both the user- and item-based algorithms.

We can attribute the lack of contribution of the neighbourhood estimate to one of two potential factors. Firstly, since most of the ratings in the datasets fall around the average rating, see MovieLens for example in Figure 1 (b), the required neighbourhood estimate is in fact small. However, we cannot rule out the possibility that CF only appears to be working well because there are many ratings that are close to the average rating. More importantly, the key challenge for the algorithm surely is how it performs when a rating lies closer to the extremes, i.e. when it is rated very high or very low. In the next section, we will examine our results in more detail and look at these cases individually.

3   MAE Evaluation Metric

Prediction accuracy in CF is usually measured using mean absolute error (MAE) across a set of predicted ratings.[4] The MAE data in Table 2, shows that the user- and item-based techniques perform reasonably, with predicted ratings within 20% of true ratings. However these results are misleading and, as first proposed in [4], it is vitally important to consider the distribution of prediction errors at the rating extremes, a fact seemingly often ignored in conventional CF evaluations.

Figure 2 presents a more fine-grained analysis by calculating both the mean and standard deviation of the prediction error at each point on the ratings scale. This time the results tell a very different story. We can immediately see that, while the algorithms perform reasonable well in the mid-range of the ratings scale, they perform very poorly at the extremes, particularly at the low end of the ratings scale. This means that these algorithms are not capable of reliably predicting items that will be loved or hated, with the risk that mediocre items will be recommended in practice. Predictions using the Book-Crossing dataset

---

[4] We focus on MAE here as it is the most common metric used for evaluating prediction accuracy. We leave an analysis of other metrics used, e.g. RMSE, for future work.

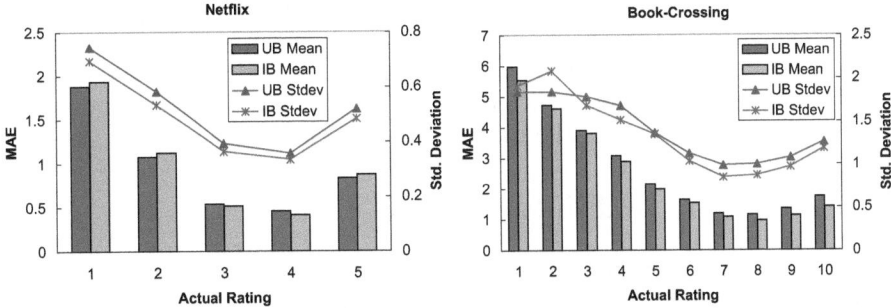

Fig. 2. Mean and standard deviation of prediction error across the ratings scale

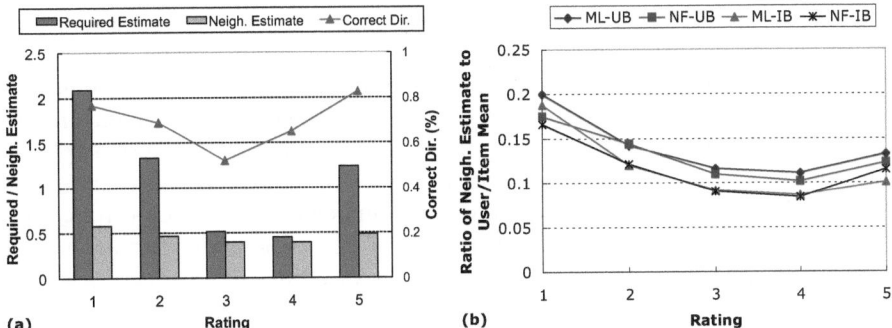

Fig. 3. (a) Difference between the actual and the required neighbour estimate for user-based CF for MovieLens, and (b) ratio of the neighbourhood estimate to base estimate for user- and item-based CF for MovieLens and Netflix

are especially poor, probably due to the high sparsity of this dataset; for example, user-based CF (UB) is only able to predict the rating of a disliked item to within 5 or 6 ratings points on average (and with high variation) on a 10-point scale.

These results suggest that CF is performing poorly exactly when it is most needed: at the extremes. This is reinforced by Figure 3(a), which shows the difference between the required shift needed to make a correct rating prediction, and the actual shift that the neighbourhood estimate delivers in practice (here we focus on user-based CF for MovieLens). At the extremes, the actual shift is far from what is required. Interestingly however, the direction of shift is at least more accurate at the extremes. For example, the shift is in the correct direction about 80% of the time for MovieLens items that are rated as 1 or 5.

In Figure 3(b) we get a sense of this for predictions computed across different ratings, where the ratio of the neighbourhood estimate to the base estimate is plotted. As expected, the relative contribution of the neighbourhood estimate is minor across the ratings scale, but there is an interesting effect at the ratings extremes where neighbours exert a stronger influence. For example, with the MovieLens dataset and user-based CF, there is a neighbourhood-to-base estimate ratio of 0.2 at the first rating point, meaning that the neighbourhood estimate is contributing 20% to the predicted rating. This is twice the contribution that is noted for higher points of the ratings scale, but it is still low.

4   Conclusions and Future Work

CF techniques generate predictions by relying, in part, on the ratings of a neighbourhood of similar users or items. In this paper, we have explored just how important a role neighbours play in prediction; something that has not be examined in detail before. What we have found is surprising. Notwithstanding the significant research that has been invested in neighbourhood selection techniques, the influence of neighbours remains relatively minor (neighbours not usually exerting enough of a shift on the base estimate) and often unreliable (neighbours often shifting the base estimate in the wrong direction). This has a number of important implications. Firstly, as a community, we need to better understand the factors that influence the ability of neighbours to improve a baseline prediction. Secondly, from an evaluation perspective we need to recognise that simple MAE-style evaluations serve only to disguise important prediction errors, especially for extreme ratings. At the very least a more fine-grained error analysis is required in order to highlight the significant variations in error across a given ratings scale. As a final point, we need to emphasise the importance of developing new CF algorithms that offer prediction improvements on extreme ratings because, ultimately, users need to receive reliable recommendations containing items they strongly like and avoiding items they strongly dislike.

References

1. McLaughlin, M., Herlocker, J.: A collaborative filtering algorithm and evaluation metric that acccurately model the user experience. In: Proceedings of the 27th Annual International ACM SIGIR Conference on Research and Development in Information Retrieval, Sheffield, U.K., July 2004, pp. 329–326 (2004)
2. Resnick, P., Iacovou, N., Suchak, M., Bergstrom, P., Riedl, J.: GroupLens: An open architecture for collaborative filtering of netnews. In: Proceedings of ACM Conference on Computer-Supported Cooperative Work (CSCW 1994), August 1994, pp. 175–186. Chapel Hill, North Carolina (1994)
3. Sarwar, B.M., Karypis, G., Konstan, J.A., Riedl, J.: Item-based collaborative filtering recommendation algorithms. In: Proceedings of the 10th International World Wide Web Conference, Hong Kong, May 2001, pp. 285–295 (2001)
4. Shardanand, U., Maes, P.: Social information filtering: Algorithms for automating "word of mouth". In: Proceedings of the ACM SIGCHI Conference on Human Factors in Computing Systems, Denver, Colorado, May 1995, pp. 210–217 (1995)
5. Ziegler, C.-N., McNee, S.M., Konstan, J.A., Lausen, G.: Improving recommendation lists through topic diversification. In: Proceeding of the 14th International World Wide Web Conference, Chiba, Japan (May 2005)

Investigating the Possibility of Adaptation and Personalization in Virtual Environments

Johanna Renny Octavia, Chris Raymaekers, and Karin Coninx

Hasselt University - tUL - IBBT
Expertise Centre for Digital Media
Wetenschapspark 2, 3590 Diepenbeek, Belgium

Abstract. The complex nature of virtual environments customarily hinders users to interact in a natural, intuitive and optimal way. Different user characteristics are hardly taken into account when designing 3D user interfaces for virtual environments. We envision that user interaction in virtual environments can be enhanced by integrating adaptation and personalization into 3D user interfaces. Through our research, we aim to provide adaptive and personalized 3D user interfaces for enhancing user interaction in virtual environments. The establishment of a user model becomes an important first step to facilitate adaptation and personalization to the user. In order to partly construct the user model, we carried out an experiment on 3D target acquisition task with four user groups (differing in experience level and gender). In this paper, we present a general user model that will enable first-time users to benefit instantly from adaptation and personalization in virtual environments.

Keywords: virtual environments, adaptive 3D interfaces, user model.

1 Introduction

The emergence of virtual environments (VE) can be demonstrated by a considerable number of applications in various fields, such as architecture and product design, medical and health care, military, and entertainment. Many of these applications employ highly interactive three-dimensional (3D) user interfaces in order to support performing complex tasks in virtual environments [1]. Users have a high degree of freedom in choosing which interaction technique to use to accomplish a certain task. This may introduce complexity for users and obstruct them from interacting in a natural, intuitive and optimal way.

When designing 3D interaction techniques for virtual environments, different user characteristics (e.g. preferences, abilities, and experience level) are usually not taken into consideration. As a result, many techniques generally work only for a typical user group. When other user groups with different characteristics join in, the VE application may have limited usability. For example, selection techniques using the virtual pointer metaphor such as ray-casting may be less suitable for users with limited motor abilities. User-specificity should be considered in the design of 3D user interfaces to improve the usability of 3D interaction techniques [1].

G.-J. Houben et al. (Eds.): UMAP 2009, LNCS 5535, pp. 361–366, 2009.
© Springer-Verlag Berlin Heidelberg 2009

Research into adaptive user interfaces for virtual environments has received only limited attention. Through our work, we would like to investigate the possibility of adaptation and personalization in virtual environments. This paper describes the conduct of an experiment as an attempt to construct the user model for realizing adaptive and personalized 3D user interfaces.

2   Related Work

Adaptive and personalized interfaces have gained a significant interest in the research community for the past several years. Adaptation and personalization in virtual environments has been explored less often, as interaction in virtual environments (3D interfaces) is more complex than in WIMP applications. Nevertheless, Wingrave et al. [2] and Celentano et al. [3] have looked into adaptivity and personalized interaction in virtual environments by learning user behavior and preferred method of interaction. Both works investigated users individually and not focusing on groups of users.

It is widely accepted that individual differences exist and interfaces should differ to accommodate the diversity among individual user or groups of users. Adaptive user interfaces, which learn a user model from traces of interaction with users, can be considered as one way to accommodate these individual differences and level up users' performance in using an interface. User models contain information and assumptions about users which play an important role in the adaptation process of user interfaces to the needs of different users. There are several approaches in constructing user models: stereotyping/group user models [4] and learning general and individual user models [5]. Little attention has been spent on these user modeling approaches in the context of adaptation and personalization in virtual environments.

3   Experiment

It is our goal to support adaptation and personalization in order to support our users when interacting in a virtual environment. As a first step, we build the user model that will later on be used to assess the adaptation and personalization of interaction techniques. To develop the user model, an experiment was conducted to identify the characteristics of different user groups. We investigated four user groups which are differed by experience level and gender.

3.1   Context

In this experiment, we chose to investigate selection techniques because selection is a fundamental task in virtual environments. We were also interested to investigate user interaction in a virtual environment with controlled variables, such as high density of objects and target occlusion. Therefore, we based the experiment on Vanacken et al. [6] which evaluated several selection techniques for dense and occluded virtual environments. In the study, they found the bubble cursor and the depth ray technique performed best. Therefore in our experiment, we looked into 3D target acquisition task with these techniques.

3.2 Methods

Participants. Sixteen participants ranging from 18 to 31 years old were equally divided into groups of novice females/males and experienced females/males. None of the novice participants had experience with a virtual environment. All participants were right-handed and screened using the Stereo Fly Test SO-001[1] to check their stereoscopic depth perception.

Apparatus. As input device, a Polhemus Fastrak 6 DOF magnetic tracker built in a handheld case was used in this experiment. The tracker was updated at 120 Hz with precision of less than 1mm. The display used was a 2.4 m x 1.8 m polarization projection screen with passive stereo using two DLP projectors. During the experiment, participants stood at the designated position which is about 1 m in front of the screen. Figure 1 illustrates the experiment apparatus.

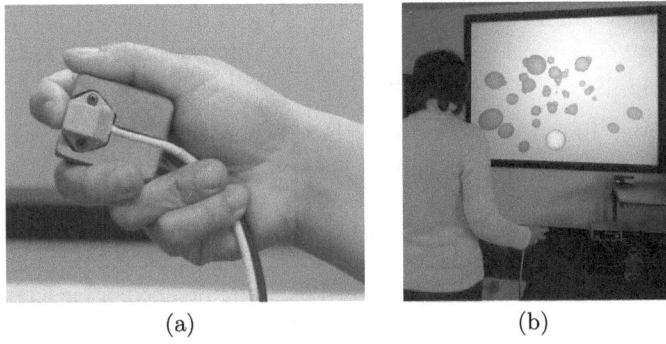

(a)   (b)

Fig. 1. The experiment apparatus: (a) The magnetic tracker (b) The projection screen

Procedure. Randomly pre-generated scenes of the environment were shown on the projection screen. For a more detailed information on the generation of the scenes, please refer to [6]. The scene consisted of a start target (white sphere), a goal target (red cube), and 45 distractor targets (blue spheres). Participants were asked to execute a target acquisition task, which they first selected the start target and then the goal target as fast as possible while minimizing errors.

   Before the experiment, participants were given a description of each technique and a practice session to help them get acquainted with it. After the experiment, participants completed a post-experiment questionnaire administered in Morae[2] and were also interviewed to gather insights about their impression and preference of the techniques.

Design. A repeated measures design was used in this experiment. The independent within-subject variables were: *interaction technique*, IT (bubble cursor, depth ray); *density spacing*, DS (1, 2.5, 5 cm); *visibility condition*, VC (visible,

---

[1] http://www.stereooptical.com/html/stereo-test.html
[2] http://www.techsmith.com/morae

partially occluded, occluded); and *target distance*, TD (15 cm, 25 cm). *Experience level* (novice, experienced) and *gender* (male, female) were independent between-subject variables. Task completion time and subjective feedback were measured.

Each participant completed the experiment in 45 minutes averagely. The experiment session was divided by two techniques, with three blocks applied for each. Within each block, the 18 combinations of DS, VC, and TD were repeated once in a random order, resulting in a total of 36 trials. The order of techniques was counterbalanced across the participants within the user group. Participants were given a short break between the session of the first and the second technique.

3.3   Results

In this paper, we focus our analysis on users' performance and preference. The analysis of these findings were later used as basis to construct the user model. We also observed several identical findings as Vanacken et al. [6] that confirmed the validity of our experiment; these findings will not be discussed further here.

Performance. In our analysis, we excluded the trials in which errors occurred and removed outliers that were more than three standard deviations from the group mean (2.7% of the data).

Repeated measures analysis of variance showed a significant main effect of *experience level* on task completion time ($F_{1,12} = 10.63$, p<0.05). This indicates a difference between novice and experienced participants. Experienced participants perform faster with average completion time of 3.15 s, than novices with 4.23 s.

However, we also found that *experience level* had no significant interaction effects with all of the other independent variables (*interaction technique, density spacing, visibility condition*, and *target distance*). This finding was somehow disappointing since we expected to find that novices perform better than experienced participants (or vice versa) with a particular interaction technique in a certain environment condition.

Based on these findings, we decided to bring the analysis on the individual level and looked at the results of each participant separately. We found that there is a quite distinctive pattern between novices and experienced participants. Among most novices, the difference of task completion times between the bubble cursor (BC) and the depth ray (DR) technique are more pronounced as shown in Figure 2(a). Different from novices, the differences are hardly noticeable among experienced participants as shown in Figure 2(b) .

Preference. In the post-experiment questionnaire, participants were asked to state their preferred technique in a certain environment condition. A chi-square analysis on the number of preferred choices showed no significant effect for *experience level* ($\chi^2(6) = 3.67$, p=0.722) and *gender* ($\chi^2(6) = 7.67$, p=0.264).

However, on the individual level, we found again another interesting pattern between novices and experienced participants. Experienced participants prefer the technique that they also perform better with, so there is a correlation between

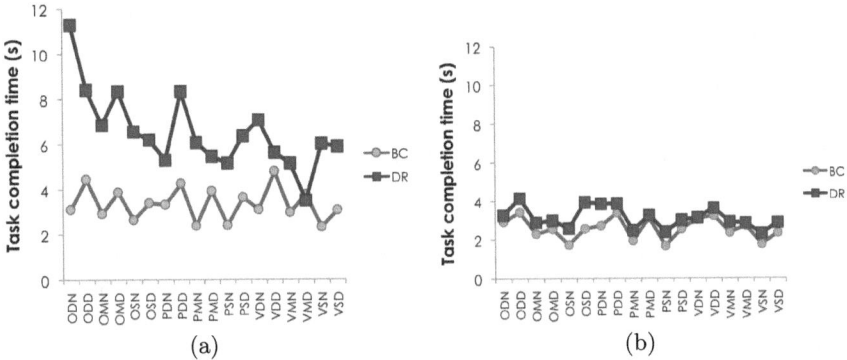

Fig. 2. Completion times by environment conditions: (a) Novice (b) Experienced

Table 1. General user model

Environment condition	Interaction technique
Occluded-Dense-Near (ODN)	Bubble Cursor
Occluded-Dense-Distant (ODD)	Bubble Cursor
Occluded-Sparse-Near (OSN)	Bubble Cursor
Occluded-Sparse-Distant (OSD)	Bubble Cursor
Visible-Dense-Near (VDN)	Bubble Cursor
Visible-Dense-Distant (VDD)	Depth Ray
Visible-Sparse-Near (VSN)	Bubble Cursor
Visible-Sparse-Distant (VSD)	Depth Ray

their performance and preference. This is somewhat different with novices, some prefer the technique which they perform slower with. We also noticed that some participants prefer the last technique they performed, this may show a possibility of preference bias because of recency effect.

General user model. Despite the fact that experienced participants perform better than novices, it was also found that there is no difference between experienced users and novices with regard to selection technique itself. We failed to find any trends and therefore were unsuccessful to construct a group user model. Instead, we proceed with a general user model [5] which is constructed based on the performance and preference of participants as a whole. In order to simplify the conditions for adaptation, we also reduce the number of environment conditions from 18 to 8 conditions. We discarded the partially occluded and middle-dense condition since we found these conditions to be nonsignificant.

Table 1 shows the general user model in summary and provides an explicit information basis about users' performance and preference for 3D target acquisition task in virtual environments. For example when users interacting in dense and occluded virtual environments, the bubble cursor technique can be offered. Then, when users switch to dense and visible virtual environments, the change of selection technique can be offered to depth ray.

4   Conclusions and Future Work

We presented a study in adaptation and personalization as an approach to increase usability in virtual environments. We have illustrated the general user model constructed, which provides information about users' performance and preference for 3D target acquisition task in virtual environments. This model can be beneficial for first-time users who have no prior interaction history.

Overall, this study provides new insights and reveals promising prospects into adaptation and personalization in virtual environments, especially concerning 3D interaction techniques. In addition, exploring other 3D interaction techniques such as navigation or manipulation might be intriguing. However, our priority is to test the general user model and construct individual user models.

Acknowledgments. Part of the research at EDM is funded by the ERDF (European Regional Development Fund) and the Flemish government. We greatly appreciate Lode Vanacken for his abundant help and Joan De Boeck for his valuable insights. We thank all participants for their contribution to the experiment.

References

1. Bowman, D.A., Chen, J., Wingrave, C.A., Lucas, J., Ray, A., Polys, N.F., Li, Q., Haciahmetoglu, Y., Kim, J.S., Kim, S., Boehringer, R., Ni, T.: New directions in 3d user interfaces. International Journal of Virtual Reality 5(2), 3–14 (2006)
2. Wingrave, C.A., Bowman, D.A., Ramakrishnan, N.: Towards preferences in virtual environment interfaces. In: Proceedings of the 8th EGVE, pp. 63–72 (2002)
3. Celentano, A., Nodari, M., Pittarello, F.: Adaptive interaction in web3d virtual worlds. In: Proceedings of the 9th 3D Web, pp. 41–50 (2004)
4. Rich, E.: Users are individuals: individualizing user models. Int. J. Hum.-Comput. Stud. 51(2), 323–338 (1999)
5. Jameson, A., Wittig, F.: Leveraging data about users in general in the learning of individual user models. In: Proceedings of the 17th IJCAI (2001)
6. Vanacken, L., Grossman, T., Coninx, K.: Multimodal selection techniques for dense and occluded 3d virtual environments. Int. J. Hum.-Comput. Stud. 67(3), 237–255 (2009)

Detecting Guessed and Random Learners' Answers through Their Brainwaves

Alicia Heraz and Claude Frasson

HERON Lab, Computer Science Department, University of Montréal,
CP 6128 succ. Centre Ville Montréal, QC, H3T-1J4, Canada
{herazali,frasson}@iro.umontreal.ca

Abstract. This paper describes an experiment in which we tried to predict the learner's answers from his brainwaves. We discuss the efficiency to enrich the learner model with some electrical brain metrics to obtain some important information about the learner during a test. We conducted an experiment to reach three objectives: the first one is to record the learner brainwaves and his answers to the test questions; the second is to use machine learning techniques to predict guessed and random answers from the learner brainwaves; the third is to implement an agent that transmits the prediction results to an Intelligent Tutoring System. 21 participants were recruited, 45827 recording were collected and we reached a prediction accuracy of 96%.

Keywords: Intelligent Tutoring System, Brainwaves, Learning, Guess.

1 Introduction

> "when you can measure what you are speaking about, and express it in numbers, you know something about it; but when you cannot measure it, when you cannot express it in numbers, your knowledge is of a meagre and unsatisfactory kind; it may be the beginning of knowledge, but you have scarcely in your thoughts advanced to the state of Science" Lord Kelvin

Using precise measures to get information from the learner state is a key point in improving the learner model within an Intelligent Tutoring System (ITS). The learner model is an important component within an Intelligent Tutoring System (ITS). By defining efficient metrics related to the learner behavior, an ITS increases its ability to adapt the material to the learner. Many researches in the field of Artificial Intelligence and Cognitive Sciences have contributed to the evolution of the learner model and the tutorial strategies. Thus, to the cognitive model [15] were added other layers like the psychological model [5], the affective model [10] and the motivational model [3] with specific tutorial strategies. To get information about the learner, data collection methods have also evolved from self report [2] to facial expression analysis [13], posture and gestures interpretations [1] to biofeedback measurements [6,7,8]. Recent approaches combine different kinds of information channels to increase the prediction of

G.-J. Houben et al. (Eds.): UMAP 2009, LNCS 5535, pp. 367–372, 2009.

the emotional and cognitive learner states [9]. In the filed of biofeedback measurements, few researches were done and many tracks remain unexplored.

Our previous works focused on using the Electroencephalogram (EEG) and collecting brainwaves during learning tasks [6,7,8]. Results show that the student's affect (Anger, Boredom, Confusion, Contempt, Curious, Disgust, Eureka, and Frustration) can be accurately detected (82%) from brainwaves [7]. We have also conducted an experimentation in which we explored the link between brainwaves and emotional assessment on the SAM scale (pleasure, arousal and domination). Results were promising, respectively with 73.55%, 74.86% and 75.16% accuracy for pleasure, arousal and dominance [8]. Those results support the claim that all rating classes for the three emotional dimensions (pleasure, arousal and domination) can be automatically predicted with a good accuracy through the nearest neighbour algorithm. These results suggest that inducing some brainwave states could help learners increase their ability to concentrate and decrease their stress levels.

This time we are interested in the test period. We want to track the electrical brain activity of a learner when he is answering questions. A learner can guess the right answer or not and when he answers he indicates if he is sure or not. The question of this paper would be then "Can we predict the learner's answer from his brainwaves?"

We believe that the cognitive state has an impact on brainwaves which inform about the learner's answer. In order to investigate this hypothesis, this paper has reached three objectives. The first one was to conduct an experiment to record the electrical brain activity of 23 participants when they were answering 35 questions. The second objective was to use machine learning technique to predict the learners' answer from his brainwaves. The third objective was to complete our previous work and implement an agent to be added to the architecture of a multi-agent system that measures brainwaves and predicts efficient learner's metrics.

1.1 Measuring the Brainwaves

Brain activity is characterized by the production of electrical signals reflected in brain waves. These are of very low voltage and are measured in Hertz or cycles per second. Brainwaves are rapid fluctuations of voltage between parts of the brain that are detectable with an EEG. Bioinformation allows us to reorganize the brain's activities through mental training.

The brainwaves that we measured were categorized into 6 different frequency bands, or types. According to their frequency, the waves are given the following names : delta, theta, alpha, $beta_1$, $beta_2$ and $beta_3$ waves. Each of these wave type correlates with a particular mental state [14]. Table 1 lists the different frequency bands and their associated mental states. The performance of our mind depends on the predominant type of wave at any given moment:

Research has shown that although one brainwave state may predominate at any given time, depending on the activity level of the individual, the remaining five brain states are present in the mix of brainwaves at all times. In other words, while somebody is an attentive state and exhibiting a $beta_2$ brainwave pattern, there also exists in that person's brain a component of $beta_3$, $beta_2$, alpha, theta and delta, even though these may be present only at the trace level.

Table 1. Brainwaves and Mental States

Wave	Frequency	Mental State
Delta	0-4 Hz	Deep sleep. Hypnosis. Increasing immune functions. Physical and mental restructuring.
Theta	4-8 Hz	Deep relaxation. State of meditation. Increase in creativity.
Alpha	8-12 Hz	Mental and muscular relaxation. Positive thought. Improved memory. Assimilation and capacity for study. Improved performance in sport.
Beta$_1$	12-15 Hz	Relaxed focus. Improved attention.
Beta$_2$	15-20 Hz	Vigilance. Logical reasoning. Conscious attention.
Beta$_3$	> 20 Hz	Fully awakened state. Vigilance. Tension-anxiety-stress. Confusion. Irritability. Psychosomatic problems.

2 Study Methodology

Initially, we selected 24 undergraduates from the Computer Science Department at University of Montréal. 3 of them were discarded because their low French language level of comprehension. One day before the experiment, participants were asked to read one time and carefully a set of 7 articles. They were selected from old French newspapers. On the day of the experiment, we recorded the brainwaves of each participant when he was answering the 35 questions related to the 7 texts he read before (Figure 1).

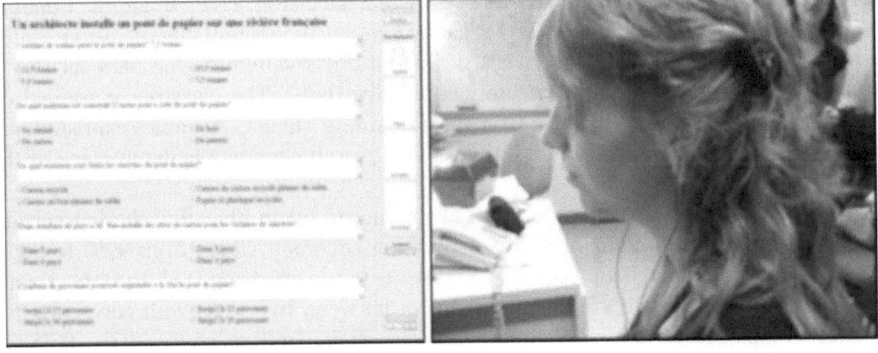

Fig. 1. The Test Interface on the left and the participant wearing Pendant EEG on the right

The EEG used is *Pendant EEG* [12]. Pendant EEG sends electrical signals to the computer via infrared connection. The electrical signal recorded by the EEG is sampled, digitized and filtered to divide it into different frequency bands. Light and easy to carry, Pendant EEG is not cumbersome and can easily be forgotten within a few minutes. The learner wearing Pendant EEG is completely free of his movements: no cable connects him/her to the computer. When asked a question, a participant indicates if he knew the answer or if answers randomly. In both cases, the answer could be right or false. Table 2 shows the whole possibilities. The test duration's varies from 15 to 20 minutes for each participant.

Table 2. Learner's types of answers to the questions

Code	Answer	Meaning
RG	Right: Guessed	The learner knew the answer and he guessed right
RR	Right: Random	The learner did not know the answer but he guessed right
FG	False: Guessed	The learner thinks he knew the answer but he does not
FR	False: Random	The learner did not knew the answer and he guessed false

Over 2 weeks and for a total duration of 30 hours, we collected 45827 recordings in the database. We had 17157 recordings of RG answers, 10803 of FR answers, 5608 of RR answers and 12259 FR answers. Right answers represent 49.68% of the sample. Among of the right answers, 24.63% were a RR answers.

4 Machine Learning: Training and Results

For classification we used WEKA, a collection of machine learning algorithms recommended for data mining problems implemented in Java and open sourced under the GPL [16]. The problem of determining the learner's answer types from the brainwaves amplitudes can be represented as the following mapping function.

$$f\left[Amplitude(\delta,\theta,\alpha,\beta_1,\beta_2,\beta_3)\right] \to answer \qquad (1)$$

Many classification algorithms were tested. The best results were given respectively by the algorithms: Classification via Regression, Decision Tree, Bagging, Random Forest and k-Nearest Neighbour (k=1). Table 3 shows the overall classification results using k-fold cross-validation (k = 10). In k-fold cross-validation the data set (N) is divided into k subsets of approximately equal size (N/k). The classifier is trained on (k-1) of the subsets and evaluated on the remaining subset. Accuracy statistics are measured. The process is repeated k times. The overall accuracy is the average of the k training iterations.

The various classification algorithms were successful in detecting the learner answers' types from his brainwaves. Classification accuracy varies from 90% to 98%. Furthermore, Kappa statistic scores is excellent, they vary from 0.87 to 0.98. Kappa statistic measures the proportion of agreement between two rates with correction for chance. Kappa scores ranging from 0.4 – 0.6 are considered to be fair, 0.6 – 0.75 are good, and scores greater than 0.75 are excellent.

Table 3. Best Accuracies

Algorithm	Accuracy	Kappa Statistic	Mean Absolute Error
Classification Via Regression	90.62%	0.87	0.16
Decision Tree (J48)	91.60%	0.88	0.05
Bagging	96.56%	0.95	0.10
Random Forest	98.36%	0.98	0.04
K-Nearest Neighbor (K=1)	98.57%	0.98	0.01

Table 4. Detailed accuracy by Class

TP Rate	FP Rate	Precision	Recall	F-Measure	Class
0.987	0.008	0.987	0.987	0.987	RG
0.985	0.005	0.984	0.985	0.985	FG
0.981	0.003	0.981	0.981	0.981	RR
0.986	0.005	0.987	0.986	0.986	FR

For the k-Nearest Neighbor (k=1) algorithm, table 4 shows the details of classification accuracy among the 4 classes (the 4 types of the learner's answers).

5 Conclusion and Perspective

This study used machine learning techniques to test the hypothesis: "We can predict the guessed and the random learner's answers from his brainwaves". 21 participants were recruited and 45827 instances were recorded into the database. We used Pendant EEG to measure the brainwaves while the participants were asked to answer some questions related to the texts they read the day before. The participant wearing Pendant EEG is completely free of his movements: no cable connects them to the machine Pendant EEG sends the electrical signals to the machine via an infrared connection. With this infrastructure, we reduced the possible side effect of the material. We acknowledge that the use of EEG has some potential limitations. In fact, any movement can cause noise that is detected by the electrodes and interpreted as brain activity by Pendant EEG. However, we gave very strict instructions to our participants. They were asked to remain silent, immobile and calm. We believe that the instructions given to our participants, their number (21) and the database size (45827 records) were able to considerably reduce this eventual noise. Results are encouraging. In fact, the K-means analyses resulted in accurate predictions 98.57% and the Yuden's J-Index is 98.46%. These results show that we could incorporate an agent into our previous multi-agent system that send this information to an ITS to improve the pedagogical strategy and influence the learner brainwaves for a better results. An ITS should select an adequate pedagogical strategy that adapt to certain learner's mental states correlated to the brainwaves frequency bands in addition to cognitive and emotional states.

Acknowledgments. We acknowledge the support of the FQRSC (Fonds Québécois de la Recherche sur la Société et la Culture) and NSERC (National Science and Engineering Research Council) for this work.

References

1. Ahn, H.I., Teeters, A., Wang, A., Breazeal, C., Picard, R.W.: Stoop to Conquer: Posture and affect interact to influence computer users' persistence. In: Paiva, A.C.R., Prada, R., Picard, R.W. (eds.) ACII 2007. LNCS, vol. 4738, pp. 582–593. Springer, Heidelberg (2007)
2. Anderson, J.R.: Tailoring Assessment to Study Student Learning Styles. In: American Association for Higher Education, vol. (53), p. 7 (2001)

3. Boyer, K.E., Phillips, R., Wallis, M., Vouk, M., Lester, J.: Balancing Cognitive and Motivational Scaffolding in Tutorial Dialogue. In: Woolf, B.P., Aïmeur, E., Nkambou, R., Lajoie, S. (eds.) ITS 2008. LNCS, vol. 5091, pp. 239–249. Springer, Heidelberg (2008)
4. D'Mello, S., Jackson, T., Craig, S., Morgan, B., Chipman, P., White, H., Person, N., Kort, B., el Kaliouby, R., Picard., R.W., Graesser, A.: AutoTutor Detects and Responds to Learners Affective and Cognitive States. In: Workshop on Emotional and Cognitive Issues at the International Conference of Intelligent Tutoring Systems, Montreal, Canada, June 23-27 (2008)
5. Grandbastien, M., Labat, J.M., et al.: Environnements informatiques pour l'apprentissage humain. Éditions, Lavoisier, Paris, France (2006)
6. Heraz, A., Daouda, T., Frasson, C.: Decision Tree for Tracking Learner's Emotional State predicted from his electrical brain activity. In: Woolf, B.P., Aïmeur, E., Nkambou, R., Lajoie, S. (eds.) ITS 2008. LNCS, vol. 5091, pp. 822–824. Springer, Heidelberg (2008)
7. Heraz, A., Razaki, R., Frasson, C.: Using machine learning to predict learner emotional state from brainwaves. In: ICALT, Niigata, Japan (2007)
8. Heraz, A., Frasson, C.: Predicting the Three Major Dimensions of the Learner's Emotions from Brainwaves. International Journal of Computer Science (2007)
9. Kapoor, A., Ahn, H.I., Picard, R.W.: Mixture of Gaussian Processes for Combining Multiple Modalities. In: Oza, N.C., Polikar, R., Kittler, J., Roli, F. (eds.) MCS 2005. LNCS, vol. 3541, pp. 86–96. Springer, Heidelberg (2005)
10. Kort, B., Reilly, R., Picard, R.W.: An Affective Model of Interplay Between Emotions and Learning: Reengineering Educational Pedagogy-Building a Learning Companion. In: Proceedings of International Conference on Advanced Learning Technologies (ICALT 2001), Madison, WI (August 2001)
11. Lang, P.J., Bradley, M.M., Cuthbert, B.N., et al.: International affective picture system (IAPS): Affective ratings of pictures and instruction manual. Technical Report A-6. University of Florida, Gainesville, FL (2005)
12. McMillan Bruce (2006), http://www.pocket-neurobics.com
13. Nkambou, R.V.: Facial expression analysis for emotion recognition in ITS. In: ITS 2004 workshop on Emotional Intelligence proceedings (2004)
14. Norris, S.L., Currieri, M.: Performance enhancement training through neurofeedback. In: Evans, J.R., Abarbanel, A. (eds.) Introduction to Quantitative EEG and Neurofeedback. Academic Press, London (1999)
15. Wenger, E.: Artificial Intelligence and Tutoring Systems. Morgan Kaufmann, Los Altos (1987)
16. Witten Ian, H., Frank, E.: Data Mining: Practical machine learning tools and techniques, 2nd edn. Morgan Kaufmann, San Francisco (2005)

Just-in-Time Adaptivity
through Dynamic Items*

Carsten Ullrich[1], Tianxiang Lu[2], and Erica Melis[2]

[1] Shanghai Jiao Tong University, Shanghai
[2] German Research Center for Artificial Intelligence
Stuhlsatzenhausweg 3, D-66123 Saarbruecken, Germany
ullrich_c@sjtu.edu.cn, Tianxiang.Lu, Melis@dfki.de

Abstract. Adaptive course generation becomes more appropriate for
realistic usage scenarios and more flexible if it includes mechanisms
deciding just-in-time which content, which exercises, which external resources, and which tools to include for an individual student. We developed such a just-in-time delivery framework (called Dynamic Items) that
is used for enhancing the adaptivity of (educational) online material generated by the web-based platform ACTIVEMATH. This paper describes
the framework and discusses several new learning opportunities created
by Dynamic Items for an individual student.

Keywords: E-learning and intelligent learning environments, Tailoring
information presentation to the user, Supporting learning and reflection.

1 Introduction

Course sequencing dynamically selects the most appropriate resource at any moment as defined in [1]. A course is not generated beforehand but step-by-step,
hence it can react to the student's current context. However, this local adaptation, with its transitions from resource to resource makes it hard to convey
information about the structure of a course [2]. Moreover, it prevents the generation of courses which only differ in places, e.g., for a class in school.

In course generation, the course is generated completely before it is presented
to the learner. This has the advantage that the course and its structure can be
visualized to the learner. In addition, the student can navigate freely through the
course. However, our experience shows that a fully personalized course material
that is automatically adapted to an individual learner at *creation* time does not
always satisfy the needs of learners and teacher at *runtime*. Rather, there are
parts and activities in a course which need runtime adaptation, e.g.,

(1) in a classroom, a teacher mostly wants to provide the same material for
every student (important for communication about the material with and among

---

* The described work was supported by the LEACTIVEMATH project, funded under
  by the European Community (Contract Nr. IST-2003-507826) and by ALoE funded
  by DFG (ME 1136/7-1). The authors are solely responsible for its content.

G.-J. Houben et al. (Eds.): UMAP 2009, LNCS 5535, pp. 373–378, 2009.

students) and at the same time wants to take advantage of dynamic adaptation at places (for more or less training and for adjusting the difficulty of problems).

(2) While a student learns his competencies change and, hence, a dynamic selection of learning objects, especially of exercises, makes sense.

(3) For self-regulated learning, a student should be able to include additional learning objects in his personal course on demand.

(4) Similar to an advanced organizer [3], a dynamically generated text (organizer) should prepare the student's mind to what he has to expect and how this is connected to his previous learning.

(5) For access to external tools, the eLearning system should be able to parameterize the call according to the current performance of the student.

To address these issues, we developed the generic framework Dynamic Item for dynamic decisions and implemented it in ACTIVEMATH. It combines adaptive course generation with dynamic features some of which we know from adaptive hypermedia (dynamic selection and sequencing). In the remainder of the article, we describe the Dynamic Item framework and some instances. After the preliminaries, we discuss the principles and the architecture in §3. We also present details of different transformers of Dynamic Items and describe how each serves educational purposes. Finally, conclusions and related work summarize what was achieved and how this differs from other approaches.

2   Preliminaries

ACTIVEMATH [4] is a Web-based intelligent learning platform for mathematics, which has been developed since 2000 at the Saarland University and DFKI. It uses an extension of OMDoc, a knowledge representation for mathematical documents [5] to encode its learning objects. OMDoc consists of different types of elements, such as definition, symbols, example, exercises, text, etc.

The pedagogical knowledge of ACTIVEMATH is implemented in its "tutorial component". Its sub-component "course generator" (CG) [2] generates courses adapted to a particular learner, based on metadata of the learning content as well as information from ACTIVEMATH's student model that is available at generation time. Based on competency values from the student model, the CG searches for appropriate learning objects which satisfy certain constraints. From the search results and depending on learning scenarios it assembles the learning objects and generates a table of contents whose elements are either a predefined learning object or a Dynamic Item.

3   The Dynamic Item Framework

Dynamic Items are abstract learning objects and a parameter specifies their type In contrast to standard OMDoc elements, a Dynamic Item can be dynamically generated by using a context defined by up-to-date pedagogical and user information. A Dynamic Item is always re-generated when executed, i. e., whenever the learner opens a page that contains a Dynamic Item. This property allows to keep the presented information up- to-date.

3.1   Workflow of the Dynamic Item Framework

Fig. 1 shows the workflow of the Dynamic Item framework. It consists of three stages: *generation stage*, *adaptation stage* and *presentation stage*.

Either fetched from a persistent pre-authored content repository or generated by different learning services (see §3.3), an OJDynamicItem element is input to the Dynamic Item transformer. Information about pedagogical goals and constraints processed during course generation are stored within this element. The Transformer takes the Dynamic Item element whenever the student first looks at the page that contains the element and renders the Dynamic Item representation to ordinary OMDoc, taking into account up-to-date user information. The resulting OMDoc elements are then transformed into the presentation format selected by the user e.g., HTML.

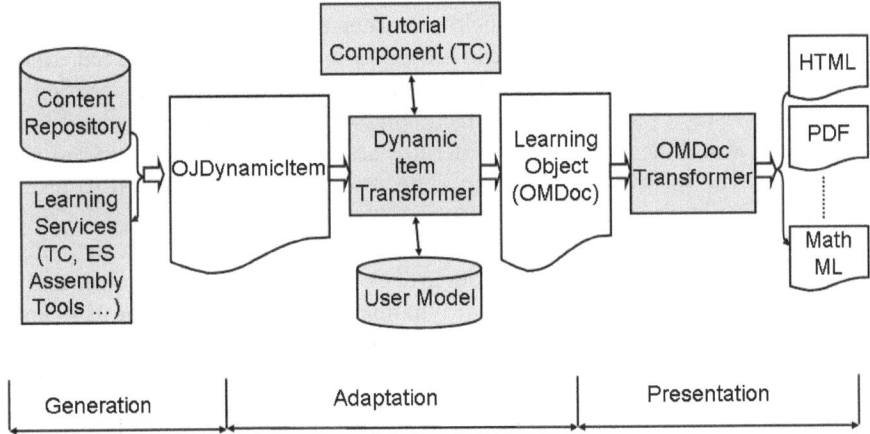

Fig. 1. Workflow of the Dynamic Item Framework

3.2   The Generic Dynamic Item Representation

Dynamic Items are represented by an extension of OMDoc which requires more complex processing than a common OMDoc. It looks as follows.

```
<dynamic-item type="type" servicename="serviceName"
              queryname="queryName">
   <ref xref="r_1" /> ...<ref xref="r_n" />
   <queryparam attribute="p_1" value="v_1" />
     ...
   <queryparam attribute="p_m" value="v_m" />
   <OMOBJ> ...</OMOBJ><OMOBJ> ...</OMOBJ>
</dynamic-item>
```

The *type* specifies the type of a Dynamic Item. Currently, ACTIVEMATH supports the following three types: dynamic tasks, calls to a learning-support service and symbolic representations for text generation. The attributes `servicename` and `queryname` allow for further differentiation, for instance, starting a concept mapping service in exercise or example mode.

The optional children of a Dynamic Item specify information about the context: relevant learning objects (referenced using the `ref` element), mathematical terms in OpenMath format (`OMOBJ`), and additional parameters given as attribute-value pairs (`queryparam`).

3.3   Examples of Dynamic Item Transformers

We implemented various transformers of Dynamic Item in ACTIVEMATH.

(1) *Dynamic Tasks*: these are place holders for a single or a sequence of learning objects that achieves a task. Tasks stand for pedagogical activities, such as training or illustrating a concept. During course generation, the CG selects the appropriate learning objects that help a learner to perform this activity. Using dynamic tasks, course generation can stop at a level that specifies what kind of learning object should be selected but does not specify which ones. When the learner first visits a page that contains a *dynamic task*, the task is passed to the course generator. Then, the course generator assembles the sequence of resources that achieve the task for that student. The student model is queried to provide the current competencies of the learner.

(2) Learning Services: these are place holders for services such as concept mapping tool, an Open Learner Model, a Computer Algebra System, and an Exercise Sequencer (ES) to be called dynamically. For instance, the ES can be driven by different strategies, such as based on competency levels [6] that provides exercises until the student has reached a goal level. ES also provides general feedback depending on the learner's problem solving success (e.g., whether the student has reached a higher competency level).

(3) Dynamic Text Generation (Narrative Bridges): are place holders for dynamically generated template-based narrative bridges. These bridging texts serve the following purposes: (i) they explain the purpose of a course or a section at a level of abstraction higher than the level of single learning object; (ii) they link consecutive sections and provide coherence that a mere sequence of educational resources might lack. The student's profile is used to automatically select the proper language (ACTIVEMATH is a multi-lingual platform) and templates adequate for specific learning context (e.g., middle school or university).

(3) Dynamic External Resources: are place holders for dynamically chosen hyperlinks. Students can easily add an external resources (e.g. entries in Wikipedia) they found and add it to the current course. The assembly tool of ACTIVEMATH [7] uses this functionality to add user-selected content to an assembled course.

(4) Gap Detection: is an application with which authors can request a course generation that characterizes learning objects, which are not yet available but would fit best for a specific set of students. Based on our approach, the gap detection application generates text characterizing the missing learning object for authors instead of inserting the actual learning object. This helps authors to fill gaps in the content.

4   Related Work

Our work is different from Adaptive Hypermedia systems such as AHA! [8]. There, the focus lies on adapting the individual hypertext document. Whenever the user accesses a concept, a set of rules adapts the resulting document. In our approach, the focus lies on the book metaphor: a complete course is generated and navigation is unrestricted so that the user can visit each page of the course any time. In such a setting, our mechanism enables to have part of the course completely generated and parts of it dynamically. Furthermore, unlike in AHA!, a page can contain several concepts. Selector [9] first determines the skills/concepts to be taught and then selects or constructs the required learning object. This is very similar to our approach, with the exception of dynamic tasks which allows our CG to interrupt the planning process and select the specific learning objects at a later. In the following section, we discuss the significant performance improvements made possible by dynamic tasks. KnowledgeTree [10] and its extension ADAPT^2 is a distributed architecture for adaptive e-learning that integrates different learning services. A teacher can author a course and add references to static and dynamic learning objects (service calls). Our framework allows the automatic generation of courses, including the selection of such services. Automatic generation in KnowledgeTree might be possible, too, but to our knowledge has not been investigated. The Medea framework [11] allows integrating different learning environments. Compared to our approach, Medea is more general but also carries some overhead. For instance, to integrate an intelligent service, such a service requires a student model, a set of domain concepts and a set of services implemented as web services.

Compared to existing work, our approach focuses on an abstract representation of service invocation that is easily authorable and that can be created manually by human authors and automatically during course generation.

5   Conclusion

This paper presents a novel approach for just-in-time adaptivity integrated with course generation. It is more general than the common dynamic selection and sequencing of adaptive hypermedia. At generation time only the type and constraints of a Dynamic Item are determined. Dynamic Items enable persistent storage of information about pedagogical goals and constraints processed during course generation. The implementation of the Dynamic Item framework in ACTIVEMATH enables novel features such as dynamic tasks, learning services and dynamic text and link generation.

Due to the very general design of Dynamic Item and its many usages, it is difficult to make a general evaluation of the framework. However, it significantly enhances the performance of ACTIVEMATH, especially the longer the generated courses. Without dynamic tasks, generating a short course (six pages, 37 learning objects) takes less than half a second–an acceptable delay. But generating a long course (80 pages, 365 resources) takes five seconds. In contrast, using dynamic tasks, generating the same long course takes again only half a second. Such consideration are especially important for an actively used system like ACTIVE-MATH, which is used by hundreds of students in several schools.

References

1. Brusilovsky, P., Vassileva, J.: Course sequencing techniques for large-scale web-based education. International Journal of Continuing Engineering Education and Lifelong Learning 13(1/2), 75–94 (2003)
2. Ullrich, C. (ed.): Courseware Generation for Web-Based Learning. LNCS (LNAI), vol. 5260. Springer, Heidelberg (2008)
3. Ausubel, D.: The Psychology of Meaningful Verbal Learning. Grune & Stratton, New York (1963)
4. Melis, E., Goguadze, G., Homik, M., Libbrecht, P., Ullrich, C., Winterstein, S.: Semantic-aware components and services of ActiveMath. British Journal of Educational Technology 37(3), 405–423 (2006)
5. Kohlhase, M.: OMDoc – An Open Markup Format for Mathematical Documents. Springer, Heidelberg (2006)
6. Klieme, E., Avenarius, H., Blum, W., Dbrich, P., Gruber, H., Prenzel, M., Reiss, K., Riquarts, K., Rost, J., Tenorth, H., Vollmer, H.J.: The development of national educational standards - an expertise. Technical report, German Federal Ministry of Education and Research (2004)
7. Homik, M.: Assembly Tool. Deliverable D37, LeActiveMath Consortium (June 2006)
8. Bra, P.D., Smits, D., Stash, N.: Creating and delivering adaptive courses with aha! In: Nejdl, W., Tochtermann, K. (eds.) EC-TEL 2006. LNCS, vol. 4227, pp. 21–33. Springer, Heidelberg (2006)
9. Keeffe, I.O., Brady, A., Conlan, O., Wade, V.: Just-in-time generation of pedagogically sound, context sensitive personalized learning experiences. International Journal on E-Learning 5(1), 113–127 (2006)
10. Brusilovsky, P.: Knowledgetree: a distributed architecture for adaptive e-learning. In: Proceedings of the 13th international World Wide Web conference on Alternate track papers & posters, pp. 104–113. ACM Press, New York (2004)
11. Trella, M., Carmona, C., Conejo, R.: MEDEA: an open service-based learning platform for developing intelligent educational systems for the web. In: Proceedings of Workshop on Adaptive Systems for Web-based Education at 12th International Conference on Artificial Intelligence in Education, pp. 27–34 (2005)

Collaborative Semantic Tagging of Web Resources on the Basis of Individual Knowledge Networks

Doreen Böhnstedt, Philipp Scholl, Christoph Rensing, and Ralf Steinmetz

Multimedia Communications Lab, Technische Universität Darmstadt,
Merckstraße 25, 64283 Darmstadt, Germany
{Doreen.Boehnstedt,Philipp.Scholl,Christoph.Rensing,
Ralf.Steinmetz}@KOM.TU-Darmstadt.de

Abstract. The web is increasingly used as an information source to gain new knowledge but the management of found web pages can be a challenging task. Often social tagging systems are used for resource management. Besides the obvious use of tags – organizing a collection of web resources – they support functionalities like sharing resources with other users and recommendation of further possibly relevant web pages. This paper describes a novel application based on an extended tagging concept that can improve resource management and recommendation. Adding semantic information to tags and tagging fragments of web pages instead of whole web pages enhance the possibilities of well-known tagging applications. Individual knowledge networks are the basis of this tagging concept. A first prototype is developed as proof of concept.

Keywords: Semantic Tagging, Knowledge Networks, Resource Management.

1 Introduction

In this time of fast changing circumstances and new challenges in job and life it is often necessary to learn continuously. It is not feasible anymore to learn for the whole life in advance or attending many advanced trainings. Permanently changing tasks require learning when it is needed. This form of "learning on demand" is a kind of learning where the learning process is self-directed and resources are searched autonomously. Increasingly, the web is the source for new information but the web pages are seldom worked up for learning purposes. There is no teacher who structures the learning process and provides relevant resources. Thus a big challenge is the resource management.

Collaborative tagging systems are one possibility for this sort of knowledge organization [1]. We developed an extended semantic tagging concept which is explained and compared to popular tagging applications in the next section. Our extension of the well-known tagging concept is based on individual knowledge networks as described in section 3 and has some benefits that are described in section 4 e.g. with regard to reflection of the learning process, collaboration, filtering and recommendation. Furthermore we developed a prototype with basic functionalities which is shown in section 5. This paper concludes with a summary and further steps.

G.-J. Houben et al. (Eds.): UMAP 2009, LNCS 5535, pp. 379–384, 2009.

2 Concept of Extended Semantic Tagging

This section shows that collaborative tagging systems are useful to support resource management. Based on evaluating existing applications we developed a concept that enhances the well-known tagging concept towards an extended semantic tagging where not only whole web pages can be tagged but also fragments of web resources. These tags can be specified through a type and linked with other tags.

2.1 Related Systems

In collaborative tagging systems users can label resources with tags that make sense to them to sort the web pages into their own personal resource organization. By aggregating the tags of all users, folksonomies emerge that everyone can profit from. Either the tags are predefined in a controlled vocabulary or they are arbitrary. [2] provides an overview of the collaborative tagging phenomenon/applications and discusses potentials and problems of uncontrolled vocabularies. Unlike organizing web pages into browser bookmark folders or saving in folders on hard disks where users have to decide which folder to choose, in tagging systems they can add more than one keyword. For example, a web page about a comparison between the programming languages Java and Python, could be tagged with the keywords "java", "python", "comparison", "interesting" and can later be easily found again using each one of these tags, whereas in a hierarchical organization the user would have to decide which folder to use.

In the following, four free collaborative tagging applications are described representatively in regard to tagging features: Delicious[1], Faviki[2], Zigtag[3] and CiteULike[4]. They allow users to tag, save, manage and share web pages. CiteULike is specialized in managing and discovering scholarly references. In tag clouds, tags are visualized differently, e.g. in varying sizes based on frequency of use. They serve to browse the own collection or the resources and tags of other users. To be up to date, tags can be subscribed to via RSS feeds or so-called watch lists. If users save a resource, most systems recommend tags, e.g. on the basis of a combination of tags of the user and the folksonomy. In tagging applications it is often possible to build up networks or groups with other users, in order to share bookmarks and to follow group tagging activities. While saving web pages, the Delicious plug-in fills in the title of the web page and text snippets in the page if something is marked. CiteULike offers BibTeX import services for selected publishers while saving articles and users can indicate the reading priority of articles. Faviki und Zigtag use semantic tags. In Faviki, tags must correspond to Wikipedia concepts i.e. tags refer to Wikipedia[5] pages. When tagging a page in Zigtag, users can define a meaning for their tags so that the tags are more than just simple keywords. Semantic tagging can solve the problems of synonyms and homonyms. Based on these tagging features we developed a concept of extended semantic tagging.

---

[1] Delicious, http://www.del.icio.us, Online 2009-01-17
[2] Faviki, http://www.faviki.com, Online 2009-03-15
[3] Zigtag, http://www.zigtag.com, Online 2009-03-15
[4] CiteULike, http://www.citeulike.org, Online 2009-01-17
[5] Wikipedia, http://en.wikipedia.org/wiki/Main_Page, Online 2009-03-15

2.2 Extended Tagging of Web Page Fragments

Tagging is described in [3] as "a way of making sense of many discrete, varied items according to their meaning". Tags which are added to a resource have a semantic meaning for the user who saves the resource – sometimes tags make only sense for the individual depending on the personal situation. Users have diverse motivations to tag. Thus tags can have different functions [4], e.g. expressing opinions like "interesting" or "relevant". Moreover they can be used for identifying persons and topics like "java" or "python". They can be used for goal management as well, for example "writing a paper for UMAP09". These different motivations and functions show that users have a particular concept in mind while tagging, like shown above it can be e.g. a topic. We propose to let users add this concept type while tagging. Therefore we examined possible tag types which are relevant for personal resource management and introduced an extendable type set that contains topic, person, goal, event, location and miscellaneous. In section 5 we show with our prototype that users can add the type easily with little effort.

Furthermore, users should be able to connect tags with tags in order to express relatedness between them. For example, a user discussed an article of a web page with an expert whom he met at a conference. Then the user could tag the article with this person and the person with the name of the conference and he could label the relation between the tags with e.g. "met at". Probably the user will remember the person or the conference later instead of the article title. Because a web page can contain different articles with dissimilar topics, the user is interested in a particular fragment of the page. Thus we propose to link tags to the fragment instead of the URL in contrast to known tagging systems, where tags are bound only to URLs. Moreover, users should not be forced to comply with a predefined typology or structure, but should be able to add information to tags or resources that are considered relevant by them and to decide themselves which and how much information, e.g. to add a deadline to a goal.

3 Individual Knowledge Networks as Basis

Knowledge networks are a good technical basis to realize the concept described in the last section. A knowledge network – also called semantic network – is defined in [5] as "a graphical notation for representing knowledge in patterns of interconnected nodes and arcs". We use the concept *knowledge networks* in this paper to avoid association with formal ontologies. As demanded, each user can configure his knowledge network individually. There are no experts upfront who model the semantic networks. Each user builds up his individual semantic network gradually through tagging resources and adding information. Web page fragments and tags are nodes in the knowledge network and the action of tagging connects the nodes. Relations between tags can have properties as well, e.g. the relation between two goals can have the label "is sub-goal of". Besides managing nodes and relations, knowledge networks can be searched semantically; this means that the knowledge network can use the relations between nodes to answer the search query (see figure 1 right for a more detailed example). The whole concept of our knowledge networks and their usage in learning scenarios is described in [6].

4 Benefits

The extended tagging concept based on individual knowledge networks has some benefits e.g. regarding to reflection, collaboration, filtering and recommendation.

Reflection. Tagging with goals can serve as a simple task management. Users can structure their search and learning process if they specify tags as goals. Users can observe their search progress based on the web resources they have saved and identify knowledge gaps. Thus, a visualization of resources connected to goals can support the reflection of the self-directed learning process.

Collaboration. Users can integrate subsets of other knowledge networks in their own network, so they don't have to switch between the view of the own collection and the whole network – as it is often the case in tagging applications. The integration could be supported with the aid of (semi-)automatic merging algorithms. For example, if a user merges a topic tag with the topic tag of someone else he can be informed if the other user adds new resources. This subscription mechanism is comparable to RSS feeds or watch lists.

Filtering and Recommendation. Often tags fit only to particular contents and recommendation algorithms can provide more precise results if the algorithms work on fragments instead of comparing URLs or whole pages. Folksonomies are increasingly used to suggest further relevant web resources. As described in section 2 tags can have different functions. Recommending could be refined if tag types (like the topic type) are included in the algorithms. Similarity matching algorithms on schema and structure level (like graph matching algorithms) could profit from this additional information. Tag types which make only sense to single individuals like "interesting" could be left out. Semantic searches enhance the possibilities of full-text searches because it can search along relations, e.g. a resource can be found with a location tag – even if the resource doesn't contain the location. While navigating through the knowledge networks it can be helpful to filter particular tag types because filtering reduces the amount of displayed data.

5 Implementation

We implemented an application with basic functionalities of extended tagging as a proof-of-concept. Our prototype system is composed of three parts: a platform for managing the knowledge networks, a client and a web service that handles the access between them. The client is embedded as a plug-in into the sidebar of the web browser Firefox[6] because mostly a web browser is used to search for information in the web. Users can save the current opened web resource in their knowledge network via button or drag and drop. The URL, the title and marked fragments of the web resource are extracted and a screenshot is saved automatically. The client offers a dialog with different input fields – one for each tag type. The users have only to choose the respective text field to specify a tag with a type. By tagging, the according nodes (i.e. tags, tag

---

[6] Mozilla Firefox, http://www.firefox.de, Online 2009-01-10

types and resources) in the knowledge network are linked. Tags are arbitrary and are created automatically, if they haven't existed yet. The tag types are individually extendable; this means that the users can configure a tag type with new properties and thereby new input fields are created in the dialog form.

The sidebar (see figure 1 left) presents additional information when a new web page is opened in the browser, e.g. the user is notified that the web page has already been saved in the own knowledge network or in the network of someone else. In addition, further web resources are recommended that can be relevant for the current search process. Thumbnails of saved resources in the bottom part of the sidebar visualize the current research management progress so that the users can reflect their search process.

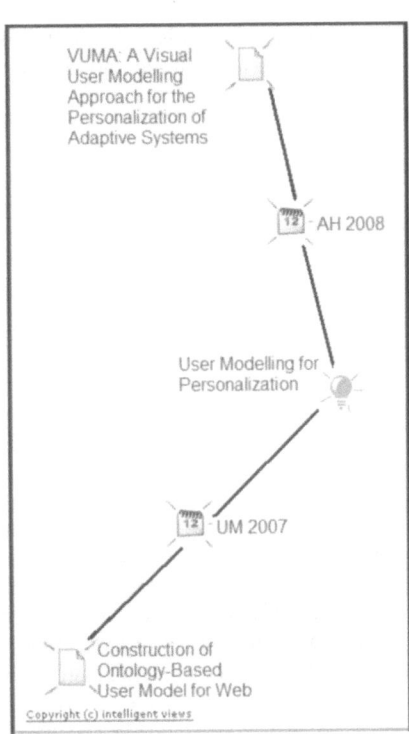

Fig. 1. (left) Screenshot of the sidebar. (right) Screenshot of the Net Navigator showing a subset of a knowledge network. A connection between two resources is inferred over the relations between two conferences covering the same topic.

We use K-Infinity[7] for storing, managing and searching the knowledge networks. This platform has a Knowledge Portal with special features. For example, the users can graphically browse the knowledge network in the Net Navigator, where tag types are marked with different icons. In figure 1 (right), the connection between two resources (page icon) inferred over relations between two conferences (calendar icon) covering the same topic (bulb icon) is shown.

---

[7] Intelligent Views: http://www.i-views.de, Online 2009-01-17

6 Conclusion

This paper introduces a novel extended collaborative tagging concept based on individual knowledge networks where semantic information can be added easily to tagged web pages or fragments of web pages while specifying a type to a tag, linking tags with tags and the possibility to extend tags if needed. This concept enhances the possibilities of collaborative tagging systems with regard to resource management, and despite of its simplicity it can have effects on reflection of learning processes, collaboration, filtering and recommendation. The prototype shows that this extended semantic tagging concept is not only a theoretic construct and the simplicity of its usage will be evaluated soon in a user study. Further steps are improvements of the prototype, for example implementing buddy lists in order to realize different access and visibility permissions in the knowledge network.

Acknowledgments. The project is funded by Hessian State Ministry of Higher Education, Research and the Arts.

References

1. Müller-Prove, M.: Modell und Anwendungsperspektive des Social Tagging. In: Gaiser, B., Hampel, T., Panke, S. (eds.) Good Tags - Bad Tags. Social Tagging in der Wissensorganisation. Medien in der Wissenschaft, Band, vol. 47, pp. 15–22. Waxmann, Münster (2008)
2. Macgregor, G., McCulloch, E.: Collaborative Tagging as a Knowledge Organisation and Resource Discovery Tool. Library Review 55(5), 291–300 (2006)
3. Golder, S., Huberman, B.: Usage patterns of collaborative tagging systems. Journal of Information Science 32(2), 198–208 (2006)
4. Marlow, C., Naaman, M., Boyd, D., Davis, M.: HT06, tagging paper, taxonomy, Flickr, academic article, to read. In: Proceedings of the Seventeenth Conference on Hypertext and Hypermedia, pp. 31–40. ACM Press, New York (2006)
5. Sowa, J.F.: Knowledge Representation: Logical, Philosophical, and Computational Foundations. Brooks Cole Publishing Co., Pacific Grove (1999)
6. Böhnstedt, D., Scholl, P., Benz, B., Rensing, C., Steinmetz, R., Schmitz, B.: Einsatz persönlicher Wissensnetze im Ressourcen-basierten Lernen. In: Seehusen, S., Lucke, U., Fischer, S. (eds.) DeLFI 2008: 6. e-Learning Fachtagung Informatik. Lecture Notes in Informatics, vol. P-132, pp. 113–124. GI (2008)

Working Memory Differences in E-Learning Environments: Optimization of Learners' Performance through Personalization

Nikos Tsianos[1], Panagiotis Germanakos[2,3], Zacharias Lekkas[1], Costas Mourlas[1], George Samaras[2], and Mario Belk[2]

[1] Faculty of Communication and Media Studies, National and Kapodistrian University of Athens, Stadiou Str, GR 105-62, Athens, Hellas
[2] Department of Computer Science, University of Cyprus, CY-1678 Nicosia, Cyprus
[3] Department of Management and MIS, University of Nicosia, 46 Makedonitissas Ave., P.O.Box 24005, 1700 Nicosia, Cyprus
{ntsianos,mourlas}@media.uoa.gr, pgerman@cs.ucy.ac.cy, zlekkas@gmail.com, cssamara@cs.ucy.ac.cy

Abstract. Working memory (WM) is a psychological construct that has a major effect on information processing, thus signifying its importance when considering individual differences and adaptive educational hypermedia. Previous work of the authors in the field has demonstrated that personalization on human factors, including the WM sub-component of visuospatial sketchpad, may assist learners in optimizing their performance. To that end, a deeper approach in WM has been carried out, both in terms of more accurate measurements and more elaborated adaptation techniques. This paper presents results from a sample of 80 university students, underpinning the importance of WM in the context of an e-learning application in a statistically robust way. In short, learners that have low WM span expectedly perform worse than learners with higher levels of WM span; however, through proper personalization techniques this difference is completely alleviated, leveling the performance of low and normal WM span learners.

Keywords: Adaptive Hypermedia, e-Learning, Working Memory, Individual Differences, User Profiling.

1 Introduction

Individuals are characterized by numerous intrinsic traits and states, which relate to their learning performance. Chamorro-Premuzic and Furnham report personality, IQ, fluid intelligence and approaches to learning as predictors of academic performance [1]; state-like individual differences, such as anxiety, have been found to mediate the effect of trait-like differences [2], while Lau and Roeser identified groups of students that exhibit consisted academic performance in relation to their motivation and numerical, verbal and spatial cognitive abilities [3]. Among intelligence and motivation, working memory (WM) is also a predictor of performance [4].

G.-J. Houben et al. (Eds.): UMAP 2009, LNCS 5535, pp. 385–390, 2009.
© Springer-Verlag Berlin Heidelberg 2009

Personalized educational systems have indeed emerged in the field of adaptive hypermedia [5,6,7,8], sharing a common research interest on the construct of learning style. Style is placed between personality and cognition [9], defining classifications of learners (see Cassady's overview of learning style theories [10]); still, neither of the cognitive, motivational or state-like factors influencing academic performance can be adequately addressed in such a generic way.

In an effort to build an adaptive educational system that incorporates psychological constructs that reflect individual differences, both trait and state-like, the authors presented a three-dimensional user representational model, which includes a) cognitive style [11], b) speed of processing, visual attention, WM, and c) emotional processing of the user [12]. Intelligence and fluid intelligence have deliberately been excluded, since it would be very complex to establish personalization rules- according to our opinion off course. Still, it is important to report that WM is correlated to general intelligence, at least to some extent [13,14].

In the context of empirically evaluating this model, personalization on the basis of cognitive style, visual WM and anxiety was proven to increase the performance of learners [15]. Still, the construct of WM was only partially approached and measured, especially when considering that it is one of the main predictors of performance in every aspect of learning [16]. This paper presents the authors subsequent work in the field of WM and personalization.

2   Theoretical Background, Hypotheses, and Implications

One of the predominant theories of WM is Baddeley and Hitch's multicomponent model [17]. According to Baddeley, "the term working memory refers to a brain system that provides temporary storage and manipulation of the information necessary for such complex cognitive tasks as language comprehension, learning, and reasoning" [18].

A brief description of the WM system is that is consisted of the central executive (CE) that controls two slave systems: a) the visuospatial sketchpad and b) the phonological loop. A later addition to the model is the episodic buffer that provides a temporary interface between the slave systems and the long term memory [19]. Both subsystems and the CE, which are generally independent from each other [20], have limited capacity.

The idea of exploring the role of differences in WM in the context of hypertext environments has indeed generated research [21,22], while Cognitive Load Theory is often used when referring to guidelines for designing hypermedia applications, related to WM span [23].

2.1   Hypotheses

Our research hypotheses were formed as follows:

   i)   Are WM measurements tools appropriate for the context of hypermedia learning?
   ii) Do low WM learners perform worse than those with higher levels of storage capacity and CE function in a hypermedia learning environment?

iii) Would it be possible to level low WM learners' performance with their normal WM counterparts' through personalization techniques?

2.2 Classification and Personalization

The classification of users according to the two WM tests (visual memory and CE/verbal storage) was another issue of concern, since it would be possible for a user to perform significantly better in only one of the tests. The system however measured the aggregated performance of users' in both tests, albeit with additional considerations.

It should be clarified that our main concern is to identify users with low WM. The threshold that distinguishes medium from high WM individuals was known for the case of the visual test, but the modified CE/verbal storage test was not tested across a standard population. By conducting a pilot study, we adopted a relative threshold for identifying low WM individuals. Users who scored below the 1/3 of the aggregated score were classified as low WM learners, along with those who scored very low in one of the two tests, assuming that they lack the corresponding WM resources.

As it concerns the low WM personalized condition, the learning content was altered in two ways. Firstly, the simultaneously per webpage presented content was segmented. Fewer learning objects (images and paragraphs of text) were assumed to require less cognitive resources from users with limited storage capacity and attentional control.

The second method of personalization was the annotation of textual objects. This approach is partially derived from studies exploring the relationship of hypertext and WM [21]. Bold text and colors were used for important concepts, links and titles, in an effort to help learners organize information. In a sense, the system imposes on low WM learners a strategy of reading and organizing information; this was related, though not very closely, to the fact that strategies such as rehearsal have a positive effect on low WM learners [24].

3   Experimental Method

3.1 Design and Procedure

The experimental design was a between participants memory test. There were three groups of users: a) a control group of users with normal/high levels of WM, b) a group of low WM users who received the same with the control group on-line course and c) a group of low WM users who received a personalized course. All learning environments were personalized on learners' cognitive style.

The participants were students from the University of Cyprus, with their age varying from 18 to 21 years. The number of valid participants was 80 out of a total of 91 users; 11 were excluded due to very poor performance in the WM tests, which could imply failure to follow the tests' rules.

The subject of the e-learning procedure was an introductory course on algorithms. This course has also been used in our previous experiments, mainly because participants lack any previous knowledge on computer science. Immediately after the completion of the course, participants were asked to take a comprehension on-line test about what they had been taught. Their scores on this test was the dependent variable indicating academic performance.

3.2 Materials

In the case of visuospatial WM span, a tool was already available [25]; it only had to be implemented in the .NET platform of our environment.

The authors however were not aware of an electronic version of a phonological loop span and CE test. For that reason, we were provided with an extended Greek version of the listening sentence recall test of the WMTB-C [26]. For the electronic version of the test we opted for on-screen presentation of written sentences rather than auditory articulation.

This probably leads to a differentiated form of the original test, addressing perhaps different aspects of WM that those originally intended; still, by experimentally assessing the validity of the measurements, we expected that the relative classification of learners would be more appropriate for a web-environment.

4 Results

Low WM learners in the non-personalized condition performed worse, while the mean score of low WM learners in the personalized condition was not only equal but higher than that of the control group (normal/high WM learners). Specifically, low WM learners' score was 52% in the non-personalized and 67.4% in the personalized condition (15.4% increase of performance), while the control group achieved a 63.4% score.

This difference is statistically significant at zero level of confidence: a non parametric analysis of variance was performed, since the assumption of homogeneity of variances was not met: Welch statistic$_{(2,\ 47.980)}$=9.312, p=.000.

Post hoc analysis of variance (Tamhane's T2) revealed that the differences are statistically significant between the non-personalized low WM group and the other two; the personalized low WM group did not differ from the control group.

It should be noted that scoring in the two WM tests was not correlated. This is in line with the fact that the components of Baddeley and Hitch's model are relatively independent; otherwise, the validity of our measurements would be questioned. Additionally, there were absolutely no interactions or correlations of cognitive style with performance in WM tests or scoring.

5 Discussion

According to this research, individual differences in WM may partially predict the performance of users. Profiling users with respect to their WM capacity in order to provide them personalized instruction increased their level of comprehension. Considering that the difference in score reached 15.4%, attributed only to WM, a combined model of individual differences could possibly make a great difference in optimizing learners' performance in educational hypermedia.

There are however some limitations. The personalization rules were based on our assumptions; simple ideas often work, but considering the depth and numerous implications of WM, further research is needed to establish adaptive educational hypermedia design guidelines. Also, it remains ambiguous whether low WM learners where assisted more by the segmentation of the content or the annotation of the text. We also consider that there is still room for improvement in capturing electronically the WM capacity of users.

Nevertheless, our research hypotheses were confirmed, and the notion that WM is a key factor in e-learning was validated; instead of simply acknowledging this effect, it is possible to assist learners effectively, putting into practice the theoretical background of this construct.

References

1. Tomas Chamorro-Premuzic, T., Furnham, A.: Personality, intelligence and approaches to learning as predictors of academic performance. Personality and Individual Differences 44, 1596–1603 (2008)
2. Chen, G., Gully, S.M., Whiteman, J., Kilcullen, R.N.: Examination of Relationships Among Trait-Like Individual Differences, State-Like Individual Differences, and Learning Performance. Journal of Applied Psychology 85(6), 835–847 (2000)
3. Lau, S., Roeser, R.W.: Cognitive abilities and motivational processes in science achievement and engagement: A person-centered analysis. Learning and Individual Differences 18(4), 497–504 (2008)
4. Colom, R., Escorial, S., Shih, P.C., Privado, J.: Fluid intelligence, memory span, and temperament difficulties predict academic performance of young adolescents. Personality and Individual Differences 42(8), 1503–1514 (2007)
5. Cristea, A., Stewart, C., Brailsford, T., Cristea, P.: Adaptive Hypermedia System Interoperability: a 'real world' evaluation. Journal of Digital Information 8(3) (2007), http://journals.tdl.org/jodi/article/view/235/192
6. Papanikolaou, K.A., Grigoriadou, M., Kornilakis, H., Magoulas, G.D.: Personalizing the Interaction in a Web-based Educational Hypermedia System: the case of INSPIRE. User-Modelling and User-Adapted Interaction 13(3), 213–267 (2003)
7. Carver Jr., C.A., Howard, R.A., Lane, W.D.: Enhancing student learning through hypermedia courseware and incorporation of student learning styles. IEEE Transactions on Education 42(1), 33–38 (1999)
8. Gilbert, J.E., Han, C.Y.: Arthur: A Personalized Instructional System. Journal of Computing in Higher Education 14(1), 113–129 (2002)
9. Sternberg, R.J., Grigorenko, E.L.: Are Cognitive Styles Still in Style? American Psychologist 52(7), 700–712 (1997)
10. Cassidy, S.: Learning Styles: An overview of theories, models, and measures. Educational Psychology 24(4), 419–444 (2004)
11. Riding, R.J., Cheema, I.: Cognitive Styles – an overview and integration. Educational Psychology 11(3-4), 193–215 (1991)
12. Germanakos, P., Tsianos, N., Lekkas, Z., Mourlas, C., Samaras, G.: Capturing Essential Intrinsic User Behaviour Values for the Design of Comprehensive Web-based Personalized Environments. Computers in Human Behavior 24(4), 1434–1451 (2008)
13. Colom, R., Abad, F.J., Quiroga, A., Shih, P.C., Flores-Mendoza, C.: Working memory and intelligence are highly related constructs, but why? Intelligence 36(6), 584–606 (2008)

14. Lynn, R., Irwing, P.: Sex differences in mental arithmetic, digit span, and g defined as working memory capacity. Intelligence 36(3), 226–235 (2008)
15. Tsianos, N., Lekkas, Z., Germanakos, P., Mourlas, C., Samaras, G.: User-centered Profiling on the basis of Cognitive and Emotional Characteristics: An Empirical Study. In: Nejdl, W., Kay, J., Pu, P., Herder, E. (eds.) AH 2008. LNCS, vol. 5149, pp. 214–223. Springer, Heidelberg (2008)
16. Alloway, T.P.: Working memory, but not IQ, predicts subsequent learning in children with learning difficulties. European Journal of Psychological Assessment (in press)
17. Baddeley, A.: The concept of working memory: A view of its current state and probable future development. Cognition 10(1-3), 17–23 (1981)
18. Baddeley, A.: Working Memory. Science 255, 556–559 (1992)
19. Baddeley, A.: The episodic buffer: a new component of working memory? Trends in Cognitive Sciences 11(4), 417–423 (2000)
20. Loggie, R.H., Zucco, G.N., Baddeley, A.D.: Interference with visual short-term memory. Acta Psychologica 75(1), 55–74 (1990)
21. DeStefano, D., Lefevre, J.: Cognitive load in hypertext reading: A review. Computers in Human Behavior 23(3), 1616–1641 (2007)
22. Lee, M.J., Tedder, M.C.: The effects of three different computer texts on readers' recall: based on working memory capacity. Computers in Human Behavior 19(6), 767–783 (2003)
23. Kirschner, P.A.: Cognitive load theory: implications of cognitive load theory on the design of learning. Learning and Instruction 12(1), 1–10 (2002)
24. Turley-Ames, K.J., Whitfield, M.M.: Strategy training and working memory task performance. Journal of Memory and Language 49, 446–468 (2003)
25. Demetriou, A., Christou, C., Spanoudis, G., Platsidou, M.: The development of mental processing: Efficiency, working memory, and thinking. Monographs of the Society for Research in Child Development 67(1), 1–155 (2002)
26. Pickering, S., Gathercole, S.: The Working Memory Test Battery for Children. The Psychological Corporation (2001)

Semantic Web Usage Mining: Using Semantics to Understand User Intentions

Till Plumbaum, Tino Stelter, and Alexander Korth

Technische Universität Berlin, DAI-Labor, Germany
{till.plumbaum,tino.stelter,alexander.korth}@dai-labor.de

Abstract. In this paper, we present a novel approach to track user interaction on a web page based on JavaScript-events combined with the Semantic Web standard Microformats to obtain more fine-grained and meaningful user information. Today's user tracking solutions are mostly page-based and lose valuable information about user interactions. To get an in-depth understanding of user's interests and intentions from observing him while interacting on a website, interaction data needs to be tracked on an event rather than on a page basis enhanced with semantic knowledge to understand the user intention. Our goal is to create an easy-to-integrate user tracker that is capable of collecting tracking information of configurable depth and feeding a highly sophisticated user model needed to provide personalized services such as recommendation and search.

Keywords: user modeling, semantic web, microformats, user behavior, user tracking, AJAX.

1 Introduction

In recent years, we experienced two major paradigm shifts coming with the Web 2.0: Improved technical possibilities led to more and more complex and interactive websites and that changed the way users understand and use the Web dramatically. Today, users understand themself as a part of the Web and demand for ways to express their beliefs and thoughts. Therefore, web applications offer more and more ways to allow users to tailor the site according to their needs. Successful examples are MySpace[1] where the user can completely personalize the profile site or Facebook[2], allowing the user to share information with social contacts in several ways. These paradigm shifts, firstly from static to more complex and interactive web applications, and secondly the change of the user role from consumer to producer are accompanied with new requirements on user tracking systems.

In this paper, we introduce a new user tracking approach capable of tracking a user on complex and interactive sites and to preserve the binding of semantic knowledge found on a site while tracking user actions in order to feed

---

[1] http://www.myspace.com
[2] http://www.facebook.com

G.-J. Houben et al. (Eds.): UMAP 2009, LNCS 5535, pp. 391–396, 2009.

a sophisticated user models. Our goal is to extend the process of Web Usage Mining (WUM) to an Semantic Web Usage Mining process (SWUM) to collect fine-grained data from user interactions to provide personalized services such as recommendation and search.

1.1   Requirements and Approach for the User Tracking System

To gain meaningful information on how users interact with web applications, the collected information needs to be more detailed than that provided by tracking the navigation between pages or by analyzing web server log files. The system has to track partial reloads, clicks, mouse movement or input of text. Therefore, an advanced tracking system has to overcome the old request and response paradigm and track information to a greater degree on a JavaScript-event basis. Fig. 1 shows that the tracking of JavaScript-events already provides detailed information about the user interaction, e.g. it is possible to detect in which part of the page a user is active, e.g. scrolling or typing, or if he is idle and thus, allows to build more detailed user model. On top of this, the tracked information can also easily be utilized to perform more in-depth usability tests, e.g. [1] showed that the mouse movement and the viewing direction directly corresponds. Although

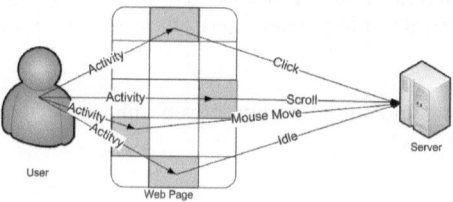

Fig. 1. Level of detail of tracked information based on JavaScript-events

JavaScript-event based tracking allows us to obtain interaction information from complex, interactive web pages, the underlying semantic knowledge and meta information about the user intention behind an action is still lost. To overcome this drawback, we extend the tracking system to collect meta information related to an user action. Therefore, we use the wide spread standard Microformats[3] to describe concepts on web pages. This allows us to connect interrelated information on a web page on the one hand and to describe information on a page in detail on the other hand. Hence, it allows us to obtain more meaningful statements than by just tracking JavaScript-events. Fig. 2 depicts this approach. It shows interrelated information on a Web page which could be obtained by a single user action. The last point relates to the implementation and the willingness of operators and users to use the system. Therefore, the effort for an operator to integrate the tracking system into a Web site must be minimal and the tracking system should not affect the user experience.

---

[3] http://microformats.org/

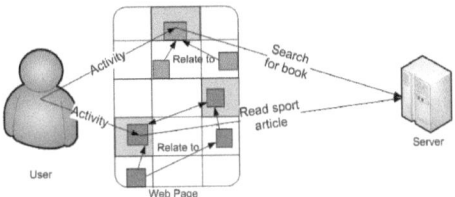

Fig. 2. Level of detail of tracked information based on JavaScript-events enhanced with semantic information

1.2   Related Work

The addressed problems are also discussed in a number of previous publications. In [2], the authors embedded JavaScript code in the web page to track rudimentary actions like the coordinates of the mouse. [3] focus on mining client-side access logs of a single user or client and then incorporates fuzzy logic to generate a usage ontology and to generate personalized usage knowledge from the ontology. With their UsaProxy, [4,5] investigate a solution to track user interaction using standard web technologies to ease usability evaluation of Web applications outside the lab. Therefore, they implemented a HTTP proxy solution to extend passed web pages with JavaScript-events to track user interaction on these pages. In [6], JavaScript-events are associated with concepts providing a context of such an event to be able to adjust the portal accordingly. All relevant UI elements are linked, done via the HTML ID-element, to an concept ontology containing semantic information about the element. The work of [6] is the most similar to our approach. Yet, the approach to use the ID-element is complicated due to the fact that IDs often are generated and that this approach is still a proprietary solution. However, our approach offers important enhancements. The usage of Microformats allows us to add semantic information in a safe way to a web page and since Microformats are an open standard, these semantic information can be used by other applications, too.

2   The Tracking System

In this section, we describe the user tracking system we have implemented consisting of a client and server part. We depict the architecture of the system and explain the functionality of the subparts.

The client performs two major tasks: tracking all actions performed by the user and extracting the semantic information of the web site. In case of a meaningful connection, the semantics are attached to the user actions and sent back to the server. The server receives, processes and persists the data. Both parts are designed to realize an easy integration into existing sites. The tracking server can either be integrated in Java–based web sites or deployed standalone for non-Java systems. The client is integrated by adding an additional JavaScript library to an existing web page. Since JavaScript is the base technology of the Web 2.0, major browser types support it, also it is widely accepted by the users. To ensure a maximum of browser independence, we limited our tracking to ten event types, which are principally supported: *load, unload, click, focus, scroll, mousemove, keypress, change, resize,* and *contextmenu.*

To enable tracking on the client, a single JavaScript object is registered as a handler of these events at the root of the web page. This handler identifies the HTML element which was the target of an event, extracts connected semantics and additionally calculates values that indicate the user activity. The user activity is a measure combining the number of events and view duration of a user on a page. Therefore, the time the user stays on the page is divided in discrete slices. A time slice is considered as an active one, if at least one event was recognized within. The processing of semantic information starts when an event, that indicates a meaningful user activity such as *click*, is triggered. The extraction starts at the target element of the event and parses the DOM tree for Microformats. If a Microformat is found, the semantic data is retrieved. To avoid too much load for the client, the tracked information is bundled and transferred to the server only with *load, unload, click* and *change*-events. The data is encoded in the JavaScript Object Notation (JSON) to minimize data size.

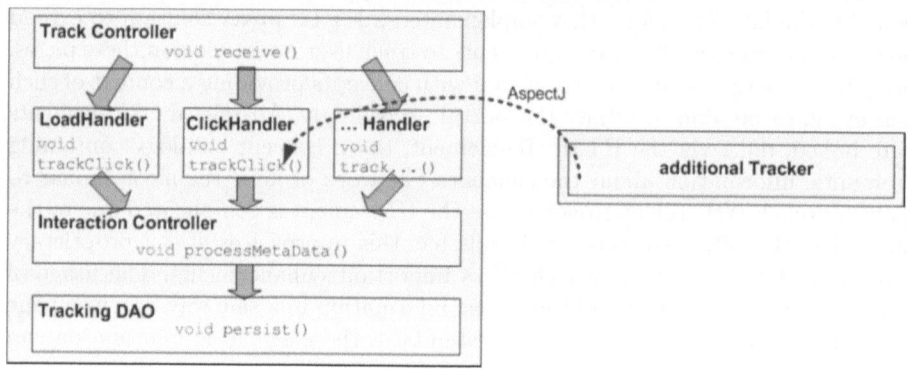

Fig. 3. Tracking server architecture

The server, depicted in Fig.3 consists of four layers. The Track Controller receives the client data and distributes it to the event handler on the next layer. Here, a first combination of event data and semantic information is done. These aggregations, called interaction, indicate composed types, e.g. the *click*-event in combination with a *mousemove*-event is is a *drag* interaction. The *click*-event is also a *selection* if the clicked item contains a Microformat. The third layer, the Interaction Controller, processes the Microformat information. The parsed Microformats in combination with an event type are aggregated to sophisticated interactions, e.g. a *conversion* if the user triggers a *click* on a marked item which is useful to test the usability of a marketing campaign. The bottom layer persists the data. It is also possible to use defined AspectJ pointcuts to enable the Web application to replace or add tracking code according to the applications needs.

3   Evaluation

The first tests were conducted within the Personal Information Assistant(PIA). PIA is a web application that provides functionality to search and organize scientific publications and authors. We chose PIA to integrate and evaluate our tracking system because it makes plentiful use of the Web 2.0 techniques and therefore, most of the interactions will not derive in a navigation to another site, but modify the content of the current site. This allows us to test if the tracking system fulfills the requirement to track complex, volatile and highly interactive sites. The obtained data will show if the system met the requirement to supply fine-grained interaction information. We created a short usage scenario to show the quality and the quantity of collected data which is tracked by our system:

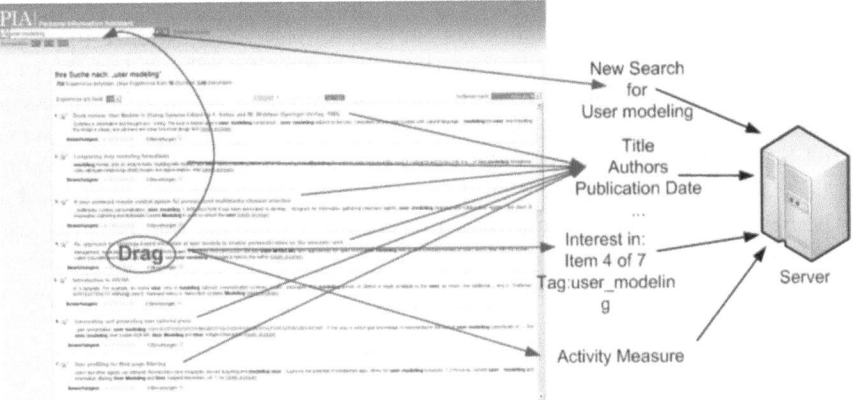

Fig. 4. Tracked information triggered by the drag action

A user searches for publications by typing a keyword into the search field. Afterwards, he scrolls down through the result list to the fourth result and drags it onto the search field to modify the search query. The Microformats *vcard* is used to represent the properties of authors and *hproduct* for the publications. The properties *type* and *title* are matched directly to the similar named properties of *hproduct*, others were defined only for PIA, e.g. the properties *publication-date*, *publication-place*, *author*, *publisher*, *tag* and *abstract*. During the described scenario, the system has tracked three types of interactions: Leaving the start site and entering the result site was represented as an interaction of type *navigation*. An activity indicator was created for each site containing information about the visit duration, number of reloads, total event count and the activity rate. The rate was on both sites noticeable high indicating that there were no breaks in the usage. The next interaction recognized, was of the type *search*. This interaction contained the search string itself as well as the type of creation. The type of creation distinguishes the two searches of the scenario because the second was triggered by drag 'n' drop, which is represented by a separate interaction type.

Fig. 4 depicts the kind of information that is retrieved for a *selection*, which is actually a drag'n'drop action. Not only the dragged item and the belonging properties are tracked, in fact, the drag action triggered the system to include information about on-site user activity, information about surrounding elements and detailed information about the dragged item such as position in the list and information about the target of the drag action and what type of element it is. These extra information are extremely valuable for tasks like Re-Ranking of result lists which is shortly discussed in the conclusion and outlook section.

4   Conclusion and Outlook

In this paper we presented an approach to track user interaction data and preserving semantic knowledge on complex and interactive Web sites. We showed that our approach comes with some major enhancements compared to existing solutions. The usage of Microformats enables an easy integration into existing web sites and allows us to interrelate data on these sites. This allows us to obtain fine-grained information connected with semantic knowledge that opens new chances to personalize web sites. Our next research steps are to model the collected information in a behavior ontology to allow information exchange across applications and to use the collected data to evaluate new Re-Ranking methods of the result list based on the position information of items the user was previously interested in. Another approach is to use the activity data to recognize an user based on his behavior on a web page. Furthermore, user privacy issues will be part of further research.

References

1. Chen, M.C., Anderson, J.R., Sohn, M.H.: What can a mouse cursor tell us more?: correlation of eye/mouse movements on web browsing. In: CHI 2001: CHI 2001 extended abstracts on Human factors in computing systems, pp. 281–282. ACM, New York (2001)
2. Mueller, F., Lockerd, A.: Cheese: tracking mouse movement activity on websites, a tool for user modeling. In: CHI 2001: CHI 2001 extended abstracts on Human factors in computing systems, pp. 279–280. ACM, New York (2001)
3. Zhou, B., Hui, S.C., Fong, A.C.M.: Web usage mining for semantic web personalization. In: Proceedings of Workshop on Personalization on the Semantic Web (PerSWeb), Edinburgh, Scotland, July 2005, pp. 66–72 (2005)
4. Atterer, R., Wnuk, M., Schmidt, A.: Knowing the user's every move: user activity tracking for website usability evaluation and implicit interaction. In: WWW 2006: Proceedings of the 15th international conference on World Wide Web, pp. 203–212. ACM, New York (2006)
5. Atterer, R., Schmidt, A.: Tracking the interaction of users with ajax applications for usability testing. In: CHI 2007: Proceedings of the SIGCHI conference on Human factors in computing systems, pp. 1347–1350. ACM, New York (2007)
6. Schmidt, K.-U., Stojanovic, L., Stojanovic, N., Thomas, S.: On enriching ajax with semantics: The web personalization use case. In: Franconi, E., Kifer, M., May, W. (eds.) ESWC 2007. LNCS, vol. 4519, pp. 686–700. Springer, Heidelberg (2007)

Adaptive Tips for Helping Domain Experts

Alana Cordick and Judi McCuaig

Computing and Information Science,
University of Guelph,
Guelph, Ontario, Canada
{acordick,judi}@uoguelph.ca

Abstract. Workers from all sectors use software applications to complete day-to-day tasks. The mastery of new software applications can be frustrating to users who are otherwise job-experts and can temporarily decrease productivity. Job and task experts are not well served by tutoring approaches that combine instruction about the task with instruction about the tool. This work presents an architecture and prototype implementation that selects timely, task-appropriate hints for expert users as they work with an application to complete real tasks. The architecture maintains models of user and task, as well as a specialized model of tutoring-for-experts that was created by observing human tutors. This research shows that domain experts can be successfully scaffolded with adaptive hints while doing their work and that they endure less cognitive load than users for whom the scaffolding is not adapted to the task.

Keywords: adaptive help, tutoring, expert users, scaffolding.

1 Introduction

Software systems have become increasingly complex over the past few years. Typically, users interact with a handful of applications that facilitate many types of interaction, which increases the work required of the user in order to learn to use the application. One such feature rich applications is the open source development environment, Eclipse[1], which has several completely separate perspectives for development tasks.

However, when users are faced with software change, they do not flock to training courses and manuals to learn about their new software. Rather, 90% of users begin to use the software and learn by trial and error [1]. One possible explanation for the reliance on trial and error is that many people are beginners with respect to the software, not with respect to the task that needs doing. What the task expert needs is the knowledge necessary to be immediately productive with the software, not several hours of programmed instruction.

This paper presents an architecture for a tip/hint system that addresses the learning needs of task experts who are using new software packages. The tip/hint system accommodates the tendency toward trial and error approaches, encouraging the user to

---

[1] www.eclipse.org/

G.-J. Houben et al. (Eds.): UMAP 2009, LNCS 5535, pp. 397–402, 2009.

experiment with software features while trying to help the user minimize errors by pointing out the features most likely to be useful for the subtask being attempted. The architecture uses models of tutoring, user, and task to adapt the provided hints to the users.

2 Tip and Hint Systems for Experts

Eclipse, or any other integrated development environment, provides a unified set of development tools and interfaces for manipulating the code, tools for teamwork, and debugging or error checking code. Eclipse's interface is composed of a set of views, each offering different actions, features, and tools to the user. A grouping of related views forms a perspective, which provides the tools necessary for common task types.

The prototype implementation of the tip/hint architecture focuses on users of the Eclipse Debug Perspective, which provides tools to identify and correct programming errors. Even though the tools are extremely useful, many programmers avoid using the Eclipse Debug Perspective because it is complex and time consuming to learn to use. A proof-of-concept prototype of the tip/hint architecture was created within the Eclipse Debug perspective. Senior computer science students used the environment to debug a program for a memory game. In the experiment, all experimental participants were provided with hints; half of the participants received hints that were adapted using the hint/tip architecture.

2.1 Hint/Tip Architecture

The architecture proposed is shown in Figure 2. The Hint/Tip interface is a separate component from the software being used, the Modeling component, and the Tip Selection component. This architecture provides a loosely coupled design that can be applied in a variety of settings and hardware configurations and not necessarily embedded in the user software.

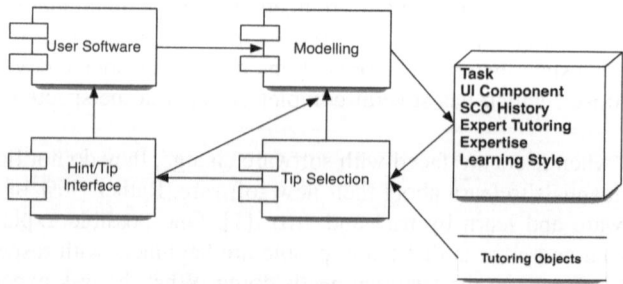

Fig. 1. Hint/Tip Architecture

2.1.1 Tutoring Objects
A good tip and hint system should carefully select instructional materials to match the characteristics of the user and the task, but to do that, the tip/hint system requires an understanding of the available tutoring objects and their expected effect.

Six categories form the core of a hierarchy for describing tutoring objects within the tip/hint architecture. The categories describe the objective of a tutor when providing a particular tutoring object: ask exploratory questions; provide illustrative examples; provide feedback; relate task to existing knowledge; focus the learner on the goal; and provide organizational hints [3].

The tutoring objects in the tip/hint architecture are instantiations of Shareable Content Objects (SCOs) from the Shareable Content Object Reference Model (SCORM) [4].

2.1.2 Models and Modeling

The tip/hint architecture uses models about the user (learning style and expertise), task, a model of tutoring, and a model of hint interface to inform the adaptive algorithm. The modeling component of the architecture is responsible for the maintenance and updating of those models, which can be dynamically updated (task, tutoring object, hint interface, and hint history models in the prototype), or statically added (learning style and expertise models in the prototype) to the model repository.

Models of user: The architecture uses two models of user characteristics: learning style and expertise. The Felder-Silverman learning style model [5] is used because it aligns well with characteristics of adult learners [6].

The learning style model in the tip/hint architecture uses the input aspect of the model (visual/verbal) to select a suitable presentation for tutoring objects. The processing, perception, and understanding aspects of the learning style model are used in tutoring object selection [7].

A dynamic mechanism for identifying the application-expertise of the naïve user is ideal for this architecture, since the user will learn while completing tasks and the adaptive hints should take that learning into account. Machine learning algorithms can use data such as menu selection or mouse movement to classify the expertise of a user [8]. The hint/tip architecture is designed to utilize such a classifier-based predictor of expertise, although the prototype implementation used a static measure of expertise. Experimental participants were prescreened and only those who were good object-oriented (Java) programmers but also novices with respect to the Eclipse Debug Perspective were selected.

Task Model: The task model reflects the possible tasks the user may attempt using the target application. The model then uses information about which task the user is attempting, and which tasks for the overall goal have been completed to dynamically determine the user's current task. While the hint/tip architecture could incorporate any type of task model, this research did not address the problem of automated task modeling.

The task model for the prototype models the five software bugs that users were to find and correct during the experiment. Each bug is modeled as a single task. JUnit[2] tests are used by the modeling component to estimate the completion of each task at any point in time. The prototype modeling component also observes the user's location within source code files to help identify his or her current task.

---

[2] junit.org

Expert Tutoring Model: The model of tutoring used for this research was created through examination of the interactions between human tutors and domain experts who were learning to use new software. The creation of the tutoring model was done using the domain of computer games, and the learners were gaming experts who had never used the target application, an online virtual world. The tutors were both expert gamers and experts with the virtual world. The data from this study was used to construct a belief network for predicting the likelihood that a specific tutoring object is appropriate given the context of the learner.

Table 1. Example beliefs from Expert Tutoring Model

Tutoring Object for Index 2	Tutoring Object Provided previously
	Is Incorrect & Provide Hint to Fix Error
Explicit Correct Acknowledgement	0.2070
Is Incorrect and Provide Hint to Fix Error	0.1724
Is Incorrect and Provides Direction to Fix Error	0.1724
Implicit Incorrect Acknowledgement	0.1034
Implicit Correct Acknowledgement	0.0690
Explicit Incorrect Acknowledgement	0.0690
Is Incorrect and Indicate Error Location	0.0690
Is Incorrect and Provide Error Diagnosis	0.0690
Is Correct and Elaborate	0.0345
Confirmation of Consistency	0.0345

An excerpt from this belief network can be seen in Table 1. The excerpt calculates the suitability of the different types of tutoring objects for the second (and subsequent) interactions with the learner. Suppose that the tip system has provided a hint to help the user complete a problematic task, but has determined that a second hint is required. As can be seen in Table 1, the tutoring object with the highest probability of being a useful next step is the acknowledgement of correctness, which would be given if the user correctly completes the subtask. If the tip system determines that the user needs additional help, the table shows that either providing a second hint, or providing direct instruction has equal predicted usefulness to the user. The completed belief network forms the tutoring model for the prototype implementation.

2.2.3 Tutoring Object Selection
The two-stage selection algorithm chooses an appropriate tutoring object for the learner, using the information contained in the models, and, when possible, suggests a presentation for the tutoring object based on the learner's preferred learning style. The primary selection algorithm uses the task model, tutoring object model, user interface component model, and expertise model to provide search criteria to obtain a list of suitable tutoring objects. The secondary selection algorithm uses the learning style model and a history of tutoring object use to select one object from the list derived by the primary selection algorithm.

The selection algorithm for the prototype uses a Bayesian belief network. First, the user's current task is identified using the task model and sensed data from the modeling component. The algorithm then compares the identified task with the user's previous task. If the tasks are the same, the selection algorithm uses this information to select the next appropriate tutoring objects for sequential support. The primary selection algorithm then uses the tutoring object model to create a list of suitable tutoring objects. Next, the user interface model is used to identify tutoring objects that will assist the user to learn to use the required interface components for the current task, or to direct the user to a more appropriate interface component if necessary. Finally, the expertise model is used to select tutoring objects to match the application and domain expertise of the user.

The secondary selection algorithm chooses the most appropriate tutoring object from the list given the learning style model of the user. If more than one suitable tutoring object remains after considering the learning style, the algorithm selects the one that has been used the least for the current user.

3 Adaptive Hints for Debugging

The Eclipse proof of concept implementation was evaluated with eighteen participants, each of whom was a Java programming expert and a novice with respect to the Eclipse Debug Perspective. The participants were provided with the task of debugging a memory game for which the Eclipse project and source code was provided. Participants were given intentionally buggy code and were told to use the Debug Perspective, the requirements for the game (supplied to them), and their own testing strategies to identify and correct errors in the code. They were not required to use the debugging tools, just the perspective.

Participants were randomly assigned to one of two groups, each of which was provided with hints at regular intervals during the debugging session. The first group (Adaptive Hints Group) was provided with hints selected by the prototype implementation of the hint/tip architecture. The second group (Random Hints Group) was provided with the same hints; however, the presentation order was selected at random.

Each participant's mean weighted-workload was measured using NASA's Task Load Index (TLX)[9]. Each participant's performance was calculated by counting the number of bugs the user corrected, where five was the highest possible score. The Adapted Hints Group demonstrated an overall lower mean weighted-workload, with an average score of 56.45. The Random Hints Group demonstrated an average mean weighted workload score of 74.58. A student t-test confirmed a statistical difference between the two participant groups with a p-value of 0.0312, confirming that the Adapted Support Group had a reduced workload.

The second metric for this experiment was participant performance. Overall the Adapted Hints Group was generally a bit more successful in correcting errors than the Random Hints Group and contained the top three performers. Individuals in the Random Hints Group corrected at most 2 errors, whereas individuals in the Adapted Hints Group corrected up to 4 errors.

A post-experiment survey indicated that Adaptive Hints Group felt the hints primarily targeted the error they were trying to fix whereas the Random Hints Group did not. This is interesting because the hints given to the Random Hints Group had a reasonable chance of being relevant to the task on which the participant was working, since there were only five tasks in the experiment.

4 Discussion

This architecture notably does not require a model of the domain in order to effectively tutor the software user. The domain is immaterial as long as the adaptive tip system has a model of the user's goal, and the required subtasks for meeting that goal with respect to the user's activity within the software package. A domain-independent system is flexible and can easily meet the help requirements of a variety of users. The architecture presented here accommodates the learning style preferences of users, which might permit them to learn to use the software application more quickly than otherwise would be possible. We have demonstrated that an automated tip system can be a useful assistant for expert users who wish to accomplish a particular task with a complex software package, and have provided users with the ability to explore software while accomplishing their goals- trial without error replaces trial and error.

References

1. Marshall, K.: Perspective on Labour and Income: Working With computers, online edition, Statistics Canada. Book Perspective on Labour and Income: Working With computers, Series Perspective on Labour and Income: Working With computers 2 (2001)
2. Kim, J., Gil, Y.: Incorporating tutoring principles into interactive knowledge acquisition. International Journal of Human-Computer Studies 65(10), 852–872 (2007)
3. L. Advanced Distributed, Sharable Content Object Reference Model (SCORM) 2004, 3rd Edition Overview Version 1.0, Report (2006)
4. Felder, R.M., Silverman, L.K.: Learning and Teaching Styles in Engineering Education. Engineering Education 78(8), 674–681 (1988)
5. Knowles, M., et al.: The Adult Learner. Elsevier Inc., Amsterdam (2005)
6. Felder, R.M., Brent, R.: Understanding Student Differences. Journal of Engineering Education 94(1), 57–72 (2005)
7. Hurst, A., et al.: Dynamic detection of novice vs. skilled use without a task model. In: 25th SIGCHI Conference on Human Factors in Computing Systems 2007, CHI 2007, pp. 271–280 (2007)
8. Hart, S.G., et al.: Development of NASA-TLX (Task Load Index): Results of empirical and theoretical research. In: Human Mental Workload, Anonymous, pp. 139–183. North-Holland, Amsterdam (1988)

On User Modelling for Personalised News Video Recommendation

Frank Hopfgartner and Joemon M. Jose

Department of Computing Science
University of Glasgow
Glasgow, United Kingdom
{hopfgarf,jj}@dcs.gla.ac.uk

Abstract. In this paper, we introduce a novel approach for modelling user interests. Our approach captures users' evolving information needs, identifies aspects of their need and recommends relevant news items to the users. We introduce our approach within the context of personalised news video retrieval. A news video data set is used for experimentation. We employ a simulated user evaluation.

1 Introduction

Newspapers, television report broadcasts, the WWW and other media supply the society with a huge allowance of data, an expanding percentage of which is in digital format. However, facing this excessive resource of information sources might overwhelm information consumers. Hence, there is a need for providing personalised access to these data sources. In this paper, we present a personalised video recommender system which is designed to capture the user's evolving interest in multiple facets of news events. Parameters needed to fine tune the personalisation model are determined using a simulation-based evaluation scheme.

The paper is structured as follows: Section 2 provides an overview of related work. In Section 3, we introduce our approach of exploiting user profiles. In Section 4, we present a simulated evaluation and discuss the outcome of the evaluation in Section 5.

2 Related Work

A common approach to capture a user's interests is user profiling. User profiling is the process of learning the user's interest over a long period of time. Chen and Sycara [2] developed a system in which internet users were asked to explicitly judge the relevance of the pages they visit. Exploiting the created user profile of interest, they generate a personalised newspaper containing daily news.

Lee et al. [5] introduced Físchlár-News, a news video recommender system that captured the daily evening news from the national broadcaster's main TV channel. The web-based interface of their system provides a facility to retrieve and to

G.-J. Houben et al. (Eds.): UMAP 2009, LNCS 5535, pp. 403–408, 2009.

recommend news stories to the user based on his interest. The recommendation of Físchlár-News is based on personal and collaborative explicit relevance feedback. The use of implicit relevance feedback as input has not been incorporated.

Though innovative, the above works suffers from some issues: user modelling is done through explicit means, which is not user friendly. Moreover, the users' evolving information need is not modelled, which we aim to address in our approach. Since users tend not to provide explicit relevance feedback, we aim at exploiting implicit user actions while interacting with a recommender system as an indicator of user's interest.

3   Profiling

Our approach to user modelling is to exploit user interaction data to capture the evolving users' interests. Users leave a "semantic fingerprint" when they interact with a result item. We exploit this interaction data to model user interests. Moreover, we include the ostensive evidence to introduce an inverse exponential weighting which will give a higher weighting to stories which have been added more recently to the profile, compared to stories which were added in an earlier stage. For further details, the reader is referred to [3].

In this work, we aim at investigating how this fingerprint can be used for recommendations. Our main research questions are:

1. Is it possible to identify and group stories in the profile belonging to a user's particular interest?
2. How can a user profile be exploited to recommend other news stories in the collection which match a user's interest?

We approach these questions by simulating users' interactions with a news video recommender system. Therefore, we capture daily news bulletins from two different channels and segment these videos into its story units. Moreover, we use OpenCalais[1], a web service provided by Thomson Reuters, to identify the category of each story. This service categorises each story transcript into one or more of the following categories: Business & Finance, Entertainment & Culture, Health, Medical & Pharma, Politics, Sports, Technology & Internet and Other.

Tackling our first research question, we rely on hierarchical agglomerative clustering of stories with the highest story weight at the current iteration. Following Bagga and Baldwin [1], we treat the transcripts extracted from these stories as term vectors and compare them using cosine similarity metric. Unlike their approach, we use the whole transcript rather than sentences linked by coreferences and use the square root of raw counts as our term frequencies rather than the raw counts. We use complete-link clustering since this approach results in more compact clusters. The numbers of clusters k is a parameter. Since each cluster should contain stories associated with an aspect of the user's interest, k should be equal to the number of different interests that a user has.

---

[1] http://www.opencalais.com/

Aiming at our second research question, we investigated how to recommend related stories by exploiting the user's profile. Assuming that each of the k clusters contains stories that cover one or more (similar) aspects of a user's interest, the contents of each cluster can be exploited to recommend more documents belonging to that cluster. The simplest method is to create a search query based on the contents of each cluster and to retrieve stories using this query. We identified three different sources that can be used to create a search query:

- The most frequent terms from all stories within one cluster.
- The most frequent named entities from all stories within one cluster.
- The most frequent nouns from all stories within one cluster.

Extending the second research question, we focus on two different issues: *Which* of these sources provides the user with better recommendations and *what* is the optimal query length? We approach these questions using a simulation-based evaluation scheme, which will be introduced in the following section.

4 Evaluation

In this work, we mimic such user interactions by exploiting the log files of an interactive video retrieval experiment. Underlying assumptions and conditions for this user simulation are discussed in the remainder of this section.

4.1 Interaction Patterns

As we aimed to mimic the actions that potential users of our recommender system could perform, we analysed the log files of a user study [4] performed on a video collection in order to identify statistical user behaviour patterns while interacting with a similar interface. Table 1 shows the probability values obtained from this study.

Table 1. Probability and normal distribution measures for observed action types

Independent Action type	Probability	Dependent Action type	μ	σ
$P(Click\|R); P(Click\|\neg R)$	0.8/0.3	Play Interval (3 sec interval)	2	3
$P(Tooltip\|R); P(Tooltip\|\neg R)$	0.8/0.4	Browsing through keyframes	0.25	1

The left column of the table shows the probabilities associated with standalone actions, i.e. actions that can be triggered independently from others. The action types shown in the right column are dependent on the actions listed in the left column, e.g. as a video cannot be played or navigated if the story has not been expanded by clicking on it in the result list. The most important action type is clicking on a story in the result list, as most of the other actions, except tooltip highlighting, cannot be performed without previously clicking on the story. Once a story was expanded, the user can browse through the shots (represented by their keyframes). The video play duration was also monitored, by triggering a play interval action every three seconds of video playing. The navigation, browsing and play interval actions can be characterised by a Normal Gaussian distribution, with a mean value of μ and a typical deviation of σ. The click action is defined by the probability that a search result is expanded, conditioned to the result document being relevant or not to the task at hand, denoted as $P(Click|R)$ and $P(Click|\neg R)$, respectively.

4.2 User Simulation

User simulations allow us to conduct various combinations of experiments and benchmark different algorithms. In this work, we simulate a user who is interested in four of the six categories determined by OpenCalais. We therefore set $k = 4$, resulting in four clusters which contain the stories associated with the same category. In a first step, we identified four example stories which were broadcast on the first day of the data collection and which belong to one of the given categories of the user's interest and stored them in the user profile. These four stories, one for each cluster, are used as the source for the first query expansion.

In a next step, we simulated a user logging in to the system. Since we want to evaluate how effective the clustering approach is for identifying semantically related stories (our first research question), we had to assume that a user shows an equal interest to all categories over the whole duration of the study. Therefore, we simulated that a user interacted with the results following the previously introduced interaction patterns. Finally, we simulated the user logging out again. This step was repeated for all days of the two months. We aimed to evaluate various parameters of our recommendation approach. Therefore, we repeated the whole simulation several times; for each of the three query sources and for different query lengths.

5 Results

An appropriate measure to answer our first research question is to analyse the coherence of the produced clusters over all iterations. The more coherent each cluster is, the better the performance of the recommendation model for this run. Since we have classified each story into one of six categories, we can use these categories as ground truth to evaluate the coherence of each cluster. For each iteration, we computed how many stories s (in percentage) in each cluster belonged to the same category C as the initial story within this cluster, hence forth referred to as C_s. This can give us an insight into the effectiveness of the clustering approach.

Figure 1 shows the average of C_s across all four categories used in the simulation for different query length. In all cases, we observe a fast drop from the initial 100% cluster coherence. This is expected since our simulation does not include any judgements about relevance: Our simulated user interacts with every result, even with those which are obviously wrong, most of which a real user would not consider clicking on. This results in very noisy data, a drawback in

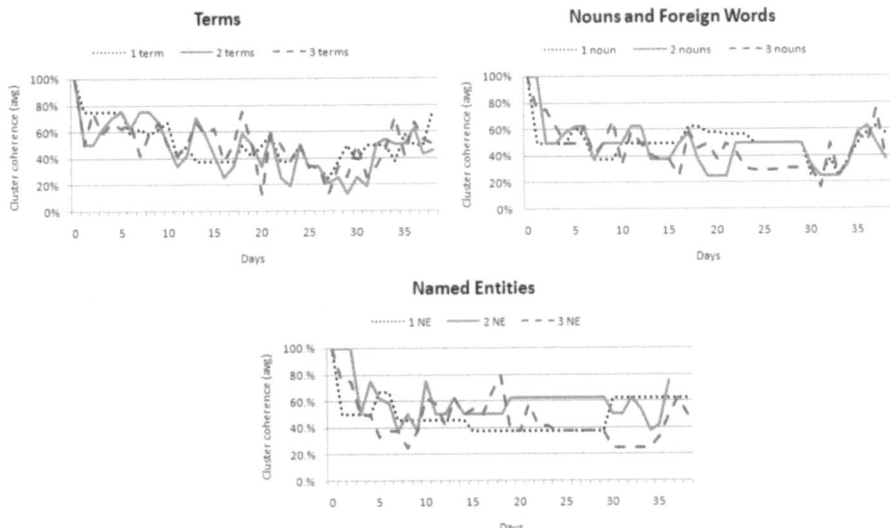

Fig. 1. Simulation results

our simulation. The figure shows similar peaks and tops for various runs, illustrating the effect of changing topics within our collection. The results from the most frequent terms and most frequent nouns seem to be rather random. The runs using named entities for recommendation however provide a more stable coherence, suggesting that named entities are a more promising source on which to base a recommendation technique on.

Table 2. Average coherence over all days

	1	2	3	avg
Terms	0.52	0.48	0.50	0.50
Nouns	0.50	0.48	0.46	0.48
NE	0.49	0.60	0.46	0.52

Table 2 shows the average coherence for each run over all days. The runs using two named entities provide the most coherent clusters, again suggesting that this feature is the most suitable for recommending similar results. This would answer our second research question, what is the best way to exploit the content of the clusters to recommend similar results.

The low percentage of coherent clusters can be partly explained by the high number of unclassified stories within the collection, which results in low values in our evaluation. Moreover, we considered only four out of six possible categories in order to achieve a more realistic user behaviour. This increases the chance to get noisy data though. Therefore, conclusions about the quality of the clusters are not possible, answering the first research question is hence difficult under a simulation-based evaluation scheme. Nevertheless, since all runs are effected by the same problem, the results indicate that our clustering approach can be used to identify similar stories. These findings should be confirmed by a succeeding user experiment where participants are asked to judge the quality of each cluster.

6   Conclusion

In this work, we investigated two different research questions: First of all, we were interested in identifying different aspects within a user's profile. Finally, we wanted to study if these aspects can be exploited to recommend similar stories to the user. Under an interactive evaluation scheme, we would have to rely on a large numer of participants interacting over a long period of time with our system to evaluate these research questions. It is expensive and it would not be possible to benchmark various components. Therefore, we relied on a simulation-based evaluation. This scheme can be used to experiment with various parameters to identify the optimal settings for a personalised video recommender system. Nevertheless, our analysis also highlighted some limitations of a user simulation and argue that some findings should be confirmed by a real user study.

Acknowledgments

This research was supported by the EC under contracts FP6-027122-SALERO and FP6-033715-MIAUCE. It is the view of the authors but not necessarily the view of the community.

References

[1] Bagga, A., Baldwin, B.: Entity-based cross-document coreferencing using the vector space model. In: Proc. Computational Linguistics, pp. 79–85. ACL, Morristown (1998)
[2] Chen, L., Sycara, K.: WebMate: A personal agent for browsing and searching. In: Sycara, K.P., Wooldridge, M. (eds.) Proc. Autonomous Agents, pp. 132–139. ACM, New York (1998)
[3] Hopfgartner, F., Jose, J.M.: Toward an Adaptive Video Retrieval System. In: Advances in Semantic Media Adaptation and Personalization, vol. 2, pp. 113–135. CRC Press, Boca Raton (2009)
[4] Hopfgartner, F., Vallet, D., Halvey, M., Jose, J.M.: Search trails using user feedback to improve video search. In: MM 2008 - Proceedings of the ACM International Conference on Multimedia, Vancouver, Canada, October 2008, pp. 339–348 (2008)
[5] Lee, H., Smeaton, A.F., O'Connor, N.E., Smyth, B.: User evaluation of Físchlár-News: An automatic broadcast news delivery system. ACM Trans. Inf. Syst. 24(2), 145–189 (2006)

A Model of Temporally Changing
User Behaviors in a Deployed
Spoken Dialogue System

Kazunori Komatani, Tatsuya Kawahara, and Hiroshi G. Okuno

Graduate School of Informatics, Kyoto University,
Yoshida-Hommachi, Sakyo, Kyoto 606-8501, Japan
komatani@i.kyoto-u.ac.jp

Abstract. User behaviors on a system vary not only among individuals but also within the same user when he/she gains experience on the system. We empirically investigated how individual users changed their behaviors on the basis of long-term data, which were collected by our telephone-based spoken dialogue system deployed for the open public over 34 months. The system was repeatedly used by citizens, who were each identified by their phone numbers. We conducted an experiment by using these data and showed that prediction accuracy of utterance-understanding errors improved when the temporal change was taken into consideration. This result showed that modeling temporally changing user behaviors was helpful in improving the performance of spoken dialogue systems.

Keywords: Spoken dialogue system, temporal change, real user behavior, habituation, barge-in, deployed system.

1 Introduction

User behaviors are an important factor that should be considered when designing a spoken dialogue system and improving its performance. We empirically investigated how individual users became skilled in using the system. We used long-term data collected by our telephone-based spoken dialogue system [1] used by the general public. We assumed each individual is identified by their telephone number. We analyzed several user behaviors per individual including barge-in rate. A barge-in is a situation in which a user starts speaking during a system prompt and is a characteristic feature of spoken dialogue systems. The barge-in rate reveals in what manner a user uses the system to complete a task.

Our study is characterized by capturing temporal changes of individual users as they acquire experience in using the system. Walker et al. developed a user model that applies to general users and constructed a spoken dialogue system adapted to them [2]. We constructed an individual user model in spoken dialogue systems, based on the classification of Jameson and Wittig [3], after investigating real user behaviors. Another characteristic of our study is that we exploit the barge-in rate as a new profile at the dialogue level. Some studies have used

G.-J. Houben et al. (Eds.): UMAP 2009, LNCS 5535, pp. 409–414, 2009.

dialogue-level features to detect ASR errors [4,5,6]. With respect to the barge-in in spoken dialogue systems, Ström and Seneff discussed how to manage barge-in detection errors [7], and Rose and Kim showed an experimental study how barge-in detection errors affected user utterances [8]. However, the locutionary-act-level phenomenon, barge-in, has not been exploited to detect ASR errors.

We used the barge-in rate to predict errors for "barge-in utterances," where a user barges in with an utterance during the system prompt. We set a window when calculating the barge-in rates to reflect temporally changing user behaviors by discarding their old histories. We show how the prediction accuracy improved when we took the temporal change into consideration.

2   Target Data from Deployed Spoken Dialogue System

We developed the Kyoto City Bus Information System [1] that received user utterances and provided information all by voice. The system locates a bus that a user wants to catch and tells him/her how long it will be before the bus arrives. The system was open to the public and was accessible by telephone, including cellular phones. It operated on a product of Nuance Communications, Inc.

We used data collected by the system between May 2002 and February 2005. The data contained 7,988 valid calls from 671 users. Callers' phone numbers were recorded for 5,927 of the 7,988 calls. We analyzed behaviors of individual users based on these phone numbers. Each utterance was transcribed, and then the language understanding result, whether correct or not, was given manually. We assumed that a language understanding result for an utterance was correct if all content words in its transcription were correctly included in the result. It was regarded as an error if any content words were not correctly recognized in automatic speech recognition (ASR). As with the language understanding results, a task success was also determined manually.

We counted how many times each user called the system. The result is listed in Table 1. Note that the numbers of tasks are not equal to the number of calls multiplied by the number of users because some users completed several tasks during a single call or hung up before completing tasks. We can see a tendency that task success rates were higher as the number of calls per user increased. The number of users who used the system only once during this period was 306, representing 45.6% of total users. Twelve users, meanwhile, called the system over 50 times. All of the twelve phone numbers were those of mobile phones, which are generally not shared, so we can expect that each number corresponds to individuals.

3   Analyzing Temporal Transitions of User Behaviors

Users are expected to change their behaviors, such as how often they barge-in, until they get sufficiently accustomed to the system. We analyzed temporal transitions of user behaviors including barge-in rates. Results for ASR accuracy and task success rate and their relations can be found in [9]. The barge-in rate

Table 1. Number of users per number of calls and their task success rates

# of calls	# of users	Task success rate (%) (#Succeeded/#Tasks)
1	306	76.4 (191/250)
2	130	76.1 (169/222)
3	69	72.1 (124/172)
4	31	71.4 (85/119)
5-9	61	77.0 (285/370)
10-19	39	84.1 (419/498)
20-29	13	92.3 (251/272)
30-39	8	92.7 (229/247)
40-49	2	88.9 (72/ 81)
50-99	6	88.9 (408/459)
100-199	1	94.5 (137/145)
200-299	1	97.1 (298/307)
300-399	1	90.8 (314/346)
400-499	2	95.7 (900/940)
500-599	1	94.2 (491/521)
Total	671	88.4 (4347/4949)

Table 2. Temporal transitions of barge-in rates for frequent users

User ID	$f(1)$	Δ	x_I	MSE
#1	.11	0	-	2.3E-4
#2	.19	0	-	1.9E-3
#3	.60	.60	> 1	6.4E-4
#4	.17	0	-	7.2E-4
#5	.74	.74	.58	4.6E-4
#6	.10	.06	< 0	1.1E-4
#7	.04	.04	.06	1.6E-4
#8	.71	0	-	1.0E-3
#9	.49	.47	.62	4.6E-4
#10	.10	.10	.29	1.3E-4
#11	.15	.04	.13	9.8E-4
#12	.23	0	-	2.6E-3
Average	.30	.17	-	-
Stdev	.24	.26	-	-

MSEs: mean square errors

was defined as the ratio of the number of utterances in which a user barges-in on system prompts and the number of total utterances performed by the user.

Temporal transitions of the barge-in rates for users #1 and #5 are shown in Figure 1 as examples. As a temporal axis, we calculated the ratios using the number of utterances up to a certain point and the number of total utterances by the user, and plotted them on the x-axis. Therefore, $0 < x \leq 1$. Average barge-in rates per user to a certain time x were plotted on the y-axis. The examples show that barge-in rate of user #1 was nearly static, whereas the barge-in rate of user #5 increased as they became used to the system. As highlighted by these examples, variations in barge-in rates depended on individual users.

We then approximated the plotted values by using the following function: $f(x) = c - a \cdot \exp(-bx)$. These parameters were calculated by using the least squares method. We assumed $a \geq 0$. To describe rough shapes of the approximation functions, three values were calculated such as $f(1)$, Δ, and x_I. Here, $f(1)$ represents an average of each measure in this period. Δ was defined as $f(1) - f(0)$, which represents the change of each measure for the user in this period. We calculated x_I as $\{x|\frac{df(x)}{dx} = 0.1\}$, which means that the change of $f(x)$ converges near x_I. Note that x_I is not defined when Δ is zero because there is no change in $f(x)$. Table 2 summarizes temporal transitions of the 12 users who used the system more than 50 times. The table shows that barge-in rates of some users, such as users #3, #5, and #9, increased steeply, whereas the rates of the other users did not change very much. Standard deviations of the averages ($f(1)$) and the amount of change (Δ) were rather large, which showed the diversity of the user behavior.

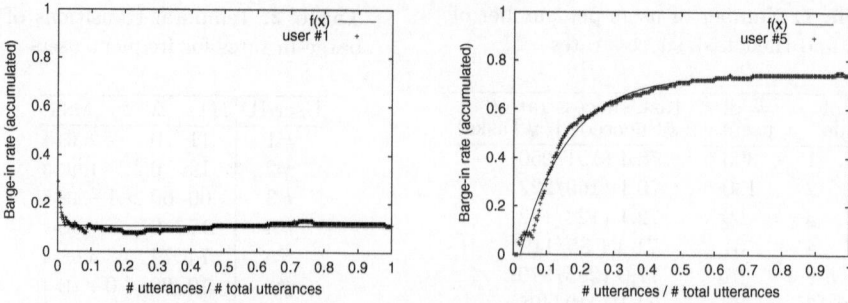

Fig. 1. Temporal transition of barge-in rate for users #1 and #5

4   Predicting Errors by Using Temporally-Changing Barge-in Rate

We conducted an experiment to verify whether the model of temporal change of user behaviors was helpful for improving performance of a spoken dialogue system. We considered the model when predicting utterance-understanding errors of barge-in utterances on the basis of each user's barge-in rate.

Barge-in utterances are prone to containing more ASR errors than those without barge-ins. The barge-in utterances amounted to 26.8% (7,940/29,580) of all utterances, and about half of those contained utterance-understanding errors caused by ASR errors [11]. These were caused by background noise, disfluencies in user utterances, or the user's unfamiliarity with the system. ASR errors often occur in fragments of utterances, especially when novices use the system [10] and cause utterance-understanding errors as a result. An example is when users were not accustomed to the timing when to speak and stopped their utterances when they noticed the system prompt continued. Disfluencies are another reason as Rose and Kim reported that more disfluencies appeared when users barged in compared to when users waited until the prompt ended [8].

4.1   Predicting Errors on the Basis of Barge-in Rate

We had confirmed the relationship between the average barge-in rate per user and the corresponding utterance-understanding accuracy of barge-in utterances [11]. For users whose barge-in rates were high, that is, they frequently barged-in, the utterance-understanding accuracy of barged-in utterances was high. This suggests that the barge-ins were done intentionally. On the other hand, for users whose barge-in rates were low, their utterance-understanding accuracies of such utterances were low, too. This suggests that the barge-ins might be unintentional.

To predict utterance-understanding errors from the barge-in rate, we used a logistic regression model. Denoting a probability that an utterance-understanding result of a barge-in utterance is correct as P, the regression function is written as:

$$P = \frac{1}{1 + \exp(-(a_1 x_1 + a_2 x_2 + b))}.$$

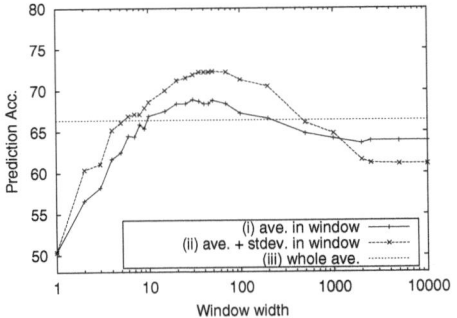

Table 3. Best prediction accuracy and corresponding window width

	(i)	(ii)	(iii)	Maj.
	68.9%	72.3%	66.4%	50.4%
	(w=30)	(w=50)	(-)	(-)

Figures in () are window width.

Fig. 2. Prediction accuracy when window width varies

The independent variables are x_1 and x_2, which represent the average and standard deviation of barge-in rates, respectively. The dependent variable is a binary value indicating whether the utterance-understanding result is correct or not. The coefficients a_1, a_2, and b are obtained after fitting by using training data.

In order to take the temporal transition of user behaviors into consideration, we set a window for calculating barge-in rates at each point of the dialogue. That is, barge-in rates are calculated by using N utterances before the current one. We call this N the window width. When too wide a window is used, the average barge-in rate does not reflect the temporal change of user behaviors. When a window is too narrow, the average barge-in rate is not reliable as a user profile. Standard deviations of barge-in rates are also calculated within the window. Small standard deviations mean that the barge-in rate has already converged, and accordingly its average can be used as a reliable profile.

4.2 Experimental Verification

We set the following three experimental conditions: (i) only used average barge-in rates (x_1), and (ii) used both averages and standard deviations of barge-in rates (x_1, x_2) within each window width. Condition (iii) used the average barge-in rate per individual calculated by using all utterances and did not take into consideration temporal transition of user behaviors.

We calculated the prediction accuracy by using all 7,940 barge-in utterances. The fitting and prediction processes were performed by a 10-fold cross validation. When a window width exceeded the number of all utterances by the user, barge-in rates were calculated by using the all utterances. Figure 2 shows the prediction accuracies when the window width varies. Accuracies and window widths when the best performance was obtained are listed in Table 3. "Maj." in this table means the majority baseline, that is, when all utterances were classified to either binary value.

Prediction accuracies for (i) and (ii) with appropriate window widths were better than (iii) (i.e., when the average of all utterances were used), as shown in Figure 2. The use of the standard deviation, as shown in Condition (ii), also improved the prediction accuracy. The window discarded the users' old histories and thus reflected temporal transitions of their behaviors. Consideration of temporal transitions improved the performance of (i) and (ii), because the barge-in rates were not constant but varied as the users got accustomed to the system, as shown in Figure 1. Figure 2 also shows that prediction accuracy leveled off for window widths larger than around 30. This means that several dozens of utterances at least need to be used to calculate the average barge-in rate. Each call contained 2-6 utterances, so reliable histories are formed when a person used the system more than about 10 times.

As a conclusion, the temporal model was effective and should be considered for improving the system performance. We will further investigate users' actual intentions when they barge in a system prompt. Integration with other measures such as ASR confidences are also included in our future work.

References

1. Komatani, K., Ueno, S., Kawahara, T., Okuno, H.G.: User modeling in spoken dialogue systems to generate flexible guidance. User Modeling and User-Adapted Interaction 15(1), 169–183 (2005)
2. Walker, M., Langkilde, I., Wright, J., Gorin, A., Litman, D.: Learning to predict problematic situations in a spoken dialogue system: Experiments with how may I help you? In: Proc. NAACL, pp. 210–217 (2000)
3. Jameson, A., Wittig, F.: Leveraging data about users in general in the learning of individual user models. In: Proc. IJCAI 2001 (2001)
4. Litman, D.J., Walker, M.A., Kearns, M.S.: Automatic detection of poor speech recognition at the dialogue level. In: Proc. ACL, pp. 309–316 (1999)
5. Gabsdil, M., Lemon, O.: Combining acoustic and pragmatic features to predict recognition performance in spoken dialogue systems. In: Proc. ACL, pp. 343–350 (2004)
6. Bohus, D., Rudnicky, A.: A "k hypotheses + other" belief updating model. In: Proc. AAAI Workshop on Statistical and Empirical Approaches to Spoken Dialogue Systems (2006)
7. Ström, N., Seneff, S.: Intelligent barge-in in conversational systems. In: Proc. ICSLP, pp. 652–655 (2000)
8. Rose, R., Kim, H.: A hybrid barge-in procedure for more reliable turn-taking in human-machine dialog systems. In: Proc. of ASRU, pp. 198–203 (2003)
9. Komatani, K., Kawahara, T., Okuno, H.G.: Analyzing temporal transition of real user's behaviors in a spoken dialogue system. In: Proc. INTERSPEECH, pp. 142–145 (2007)
10. Raux, A., Bohus, D., Langner, B., Black, A., Eskenazi, M.: Doing research on a deployed spoken dialogue system: One year of Let's Go! experience. In: Proc. INTERSPEECH, pp. 65–68 (2006)
11. Komatani, K., Kawahara, T., Okuno, H.G.: Predicting asr errors by exploiting barge-in rate of individual users for spoken dialogue systems. In: Proc. INTERSPEECH, pp. 183–186 (2008)

Recognition of Users' Activities Using Constraint Satisfaction

Swapna Reddy, Ya'akov Gal, and Stuart M. Shieber

School of Engineering and Applied Sciences
Harvard University

Abstract. Ideally designed software allow users to explore and pursue interleaving plans, making it challenging to automatically recognize user interactions. The recognition algorithms presented use constraint satisfaction techniques to compare user interaction histories to a set of ideal solutions. We evaluate these algorithms on data obtained from user interactions with a commercially available pedagogical software, and find that these algorithms identified users' activities with 93% accuracy.

1 Introduction

Computer systems often serve to aid human professionals and care-givers [1]. In these settings, a key requirement is the recognition of user activities, which is important for (1) informing care-givers about user performance, (2) facilitating machine-generated support, and (3) understanding how software is used.

Traditional plan recognition approaches assume agents who form a single, correct plan to achieve their goal. In contrast, flexible software allows users to experiment; users may make mistakes and pursue multiple, interleaving plans. Reasoning about every way that a user can interact in such systems is infeasible.

This paper presents two recognition algorithms for flexible software that use constraint satisfaction techniques to compare user interactions to ideal solutions designed by domain experts. We evaluate our algorithms empirically using a commercially-available pedagogical software, and we show that our methods outperform a recently proposed approach for inferring users' activities [2].

Many past recognition approaches query the user for clarification to reduce the search space of possible plans [3,4]. However, interrupting users impedes their satisfaction and performance, and user replies cannot be assumed correct. Some non-intrusive approaches use machine learning to predict user intentions given past behavior [5,6]. These assumptions do not hold in pedagogical domains, where students continuously solve new problems. Our work is also distinguished from probabilistic approaches that predict future user actions given recent interactions [7,8]. We address a different problem, that of recognizing complete plans given entire interaction histories.

G.-J. Houben et al. (Eds.): UMAP 2009, LNCS 5535, pp. 415–421, 2009.

2   The TinkerPlots Domain

Our study involves TinkerPlots, a commercial software used worldwide to teach students in grades 4 through 8 about statistics and mathematics [9]. TinkerPlots is flexible, providing users with a "construction kit" for data to be modeled, generated, and analyzed in many ways using an open-ended interface [10].

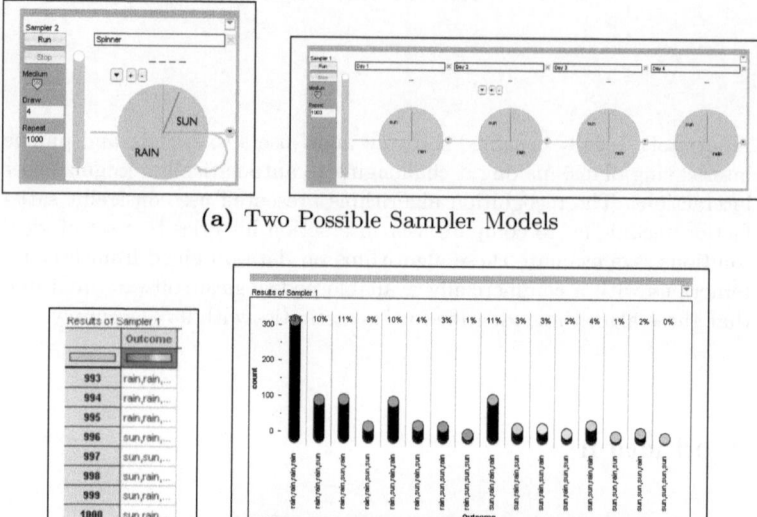

(a) Two Possible Sampler Models

(b) Generating Sampler Data

Fig. 1. Solving the RAIN Problem with TinkerPlots

Our empirical studies focused on four problems for which students used TinkerPlots to estimate probabilities. As an example, we will use one of these problems, called RAIN: "The probability of rain on any day is 75%. Use TinkerPlots to compute the probability that it will rain on the next four consecutive days."

Two approaches to solving RAIN are shown in Figure 1. The first model in Figure 1a shows a sampler containing a "spinner" device with two possible events, "rain" and "sun". The distribution mass, or surface area, of the "rain" event is three times that of "sun". Each spin of this sampler samples the weather for one day. The number of spins is set to four, making the sampler a stochastic weather model for four consecutive days. A second model is shown in Figure 1b. This sampler contains four devices, each modeling a single day, and is spun once. Many other approaches are not shown. Figure 1b shows data as generated by a valid sampler and then organized into a histogram to infer likelihoods.

3   Actions, Recipes and Restrictions

Actions can be basic or complex. *Basic actions* are achieved directly, often with a single mouse or menu operation. TinkerPlots interactions are recorded as a sequence of basic actions, each with an ID and parametrized. Figure 2 shows a partial interaction for creating a device of Figure 1a, with parameters omitted for simplicity. Actions are abbreviated: ADS (Add Device to Sampler), AED (Add Event to Device), AS (Add Sampler), CPD (Change Probability in Device).

$$\ldots, \text{ADS}, \text{AED}, \text{AS}, \text{AED}, \text{CPD}, \text{ADS}, \ldots$$

Fig. 2. Partial Interaction History

Complex actions are achieved indirectly through the completion of other actions, called *sub-actions*, which are themselves basic or complex actions [11]. Examples of complex actions include solving RAIN or fitting data to a plot.

A *recipe* for a complex action contains a set of sub-actions for achieving that complex action and a set of restrictions on those sub-actions [12]. Restrictions may limit the ordering of sub-actions or enforce relations among actions' parameters. We further require recipes to be non-recursive. Figure 3 provides one recipe for the complex action CCD (Create Correct Device), with constraints omitted for simplicity. This recipe includes the basic sub-actions ADS and CPD and the complex sub-action AE (Add Event).

$$\boxed{\text{CCD}} \longrightarrow \text{ADS}, \boxed{\text{AE}}, \boxed{\text{AE}}, \text{CPD}$$

Fig. 3. A Recipe for Creating a Device for the RAIN problem

An *expansion* of a complex action is a set of basic actions and restrictions that constitute completing that complex action. That is, an expansion is a recipe containing only basic sub-actions. Our recognition algorithms consist of two stages: generating all expansions for the desired complex action and comparing each expansion to the interaction history.

To generate all expansions for complex action a, we create a *recipe tree* containing all recipes for a. This structure has two types of nodes: "AND" nodes, whose children represent actions that must be carried out to complete a recipe; and "OR" nodes, whose children represent a choice of recipes for completing an action. The root, action a, is an OR node. For each recipe R_a of a there is an AND child node labeled with the sub-actions of R_a. The children of this AND node are the recipe trees of each sub-action. A partial recipe tree for the CCD action is shown in Figure 4. Dotted leaves denote unfinished sub-trees. The first line of Figure 5a shows the CCD expansion found by selecting the leftmost child at each OR node.

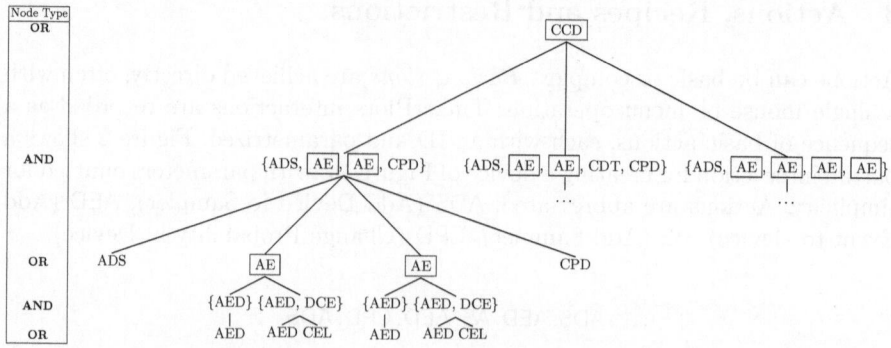

Fig. 4. A Partial Recipe Tree for the Create Correct Device (CCD) Action

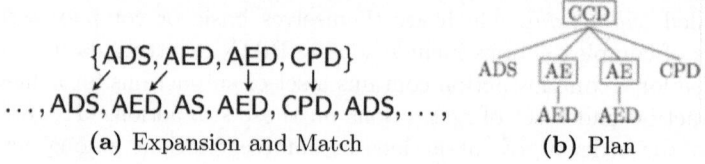

(a) Expansion and Match   (b) Plan

Fig. 5. Expansion, Match, and Plan for the CCD Action

We say that a *match* exists between an interaction and expansion if each action in the expansion can be mapped to a distinct user action with this subset of user actions satisfying all restrictions. Figure 5 shows a match between a CCD expansion and the partial interaction from Figure 2. Note that two user actions, AS and ADS, were deemed redundant based on the match.

Planning is the process by which users use recipes to compose basic and complex actions in order to complete tasks. A *plan* for complex action a is a hierarchical composition of actions such that each complex action is decomposed into sub-actions from a corresponding recipe. The set of basic actions in a plan are an expansion of a. Figure 5b shows one plan for completing the CCD action.

4   From Recipes to Constraint Satisfaction Problems

We now explain how to combine an expansion and user interaction to create a constraint satisfaction problem (CSP). A solution to this CSP gives an explanation of a user's activities by providing a match between the expansion and interaction. A *CSP* is a triple (X, Dom, C). $X = \{x_1, ..., x_n\}$ is a finite set of variables with respective domains $Dom = \{D_1, ..., D_n\}$, each a set of possible values for the corresponding variable, $D_i = \{v_1, ..., v_k\}$, and a set of constraints $\mathcal{C} = \{c_1, ..., c_m\}$ that limit the values that can be assigned to any set of variables.

First, we create variables and domains for our CSP. Let $S = \{s_1, \ldots, s_n\}$ and R be the set of sub-actions and restrictions in the expansion, respectively. Each action in S becomes a unique variable in the CSP.

Each variable's domain is derived from the user's interaction. For each occurrence o_s of action s at index i in the interaction, an element (o_s, i) is added to the domain of s in the CSP. Referring to the interaction of Figures 2 and 5a, the domain of the ADS variable, $Dom(\text{ADS})$, is $\{(\text{ADS}, 0), (\text{ADS}, 5)\}$.

We now create our CSP constraints. For each restriction in R over actions $(s_1, \ldots, s_m) \in S$, we add a constraint over the corresponding CSP variables.

5   Recognition Algorithms

We provide two algorithms that use CSPs to output a plan for complex action a in interaction history h given a database of recipes $\mathcal{R}$. Both algorithms rely on the recipe tree of a to inform their recognition process. The first approach, the Brute-Force algorithm traverses the recipe tree and solves a CSP for every expansion of a or until a match is found. A solution for a CSP provides a match between an expansion and interaction history. The path traversed on the recipe tree to generate that expansion is effectively the user's plan towards completing a task in TinkerPlots.

Use the recipes in $\mathcal{R}$ to construct the recipe tree for complex action a.
Traverse the tree bottom-up. For each OR node representing action s,
   If s has not been cached,
      Use the Brute-Force algorithm to recognize s.
      Cache s as failed or successful.
   If s is cached as failed,
      Prune the parent of s from the tree.
Call the Brute-Force algorithm to recognize a.

Fig. 6. Pruning Recognition Algorithm

The second algorithm is a more sophisticated, bottom-up approach. The Pruning algorithm builds CSPs for sub-actions, pruning nodes from the recipe tree for a if their descendants cannot be explained by the user's interaction. This process narrows the search space of expansions for root action a.

6   Empirical Methodology

We collected interaction histories from 12 adults with backgrounds spanning some high school to some post graduate education. Subject were given identical 30-minute TinkerPlots tutorials and asked to complete four problems in succession. Five of 48 interactions were discarded due to a logging bug causing crucial user actions to be unregistered. Results are based on the remaining 43 instances.

We compared the performance of three recognition algorithms: the Brute-Force and Pruning algorithms and the algorithm proposed by Gal et al. [2], denoted the "Greedy" algorithm. For a plan output by an algorithm to be "correct", a domain expert had to agree on both whether the user solved the problem and which actions played a salient part in the user's solution.[1]

Overall, both CSP algorithms inferred correct solutions for 40 of 43 (93%) interactions, while the Greedy algorithm inferred correct solutions for 27 of 43 (63%) interactions. In all cases, incorrect inferences were "false-negatives," meaning the algorithms were unable to find solutions identified by the domain expert. For the CSP algorithms, all "false-negatives" resulted from limitations of recipe expressiveness, such as the requirement for non-recursive recipes.

For both problems, scalability issues were linked to recipe tree complexity rather than the length of user logs. Correlated to the number of distinct expansions, recipe tree complexity is exponential in both the maximum number of recipes for any action and the maximum number of constituents for any recipe in the recipe database. We find that increased recipe tree complexity for a problem corresponds to increased average run-time. In contrast, the longest user log for each problem experienced among the shortest run-time for that problem, and the average log size for a problem did not correspond to increased average run-time.

User logs ranged in size from 14 to 80 actions, and plans ranged from 16 to 34 actions. The average user log and plan were 35 and 21 actions, respectively. 29 of 43 interactions (70%) contained a solution. Further details and a comparison of both CSP algorithms can be found in a technical report [13].

7   Conclusion and Future Work

This work provided a comprehensive study of the use of constraint satisfaction techniques towards automatic recognition of users' interactions with computer software. Given a comprehensive recipe database, we showed this approach to provide a robust solution. We evaluated our techniques in "real-world" conditions, recognizing users' activities in commercial pedagogical software. These algorithms outperformed a related approach from the literature for inferring user-software interaction. In future work, we wish to evaluate these techniques in other software and to use plans output by our algorithms to construct a collaborative pedagogical agent that generates support to guide student users.

Acknowledgements

This work was supported by NSF grant number REC-0632544. Thanks to Andee Rubin for her great help with the user study and for her paper comments and suggestions. Thanks to Barbara Grosz for her insights and guidance throughout the research and writing processes. Thanks to Elif Yamangil for assisting with the development of the Greedy algorithm, Cliff Konold for helpful discussions, and Craig Miller for developing the TinkerPlots logging facility.

---

[1] To implement our algorithms, we used an open-source test-bed by Gustavo Niemeyer for solving the CSPs, available at: http://labix.org/python-constraint

References

1. Pollack, M.: Intelligent technology for an aging population: The use of AI to assist elders with cognitive impairment. AI Magazine 26(9) (2006)
2. Gal, Y., Yamangil, E., Rubin, A., Shieber, S.M., Grosz, B.J.: Towards collaborative intelligent tutors: Automated recognition of users' strategies. In: Woolf, B.P., Aïmeur, E., Nkambou, R., Lajoie, S. (eds.) ITS 2008. LNCS, vol. 5091. Springer, Heidelberg (2008)
3. Lesh, N., Rich, C., Sidner, C.: Using Plan Recognition in Human-Computer Collaboration, pp. 23–32 (1999)
4. Anderson, J.R., Corbett, A.T., Koedinger, K., Pelletier, R.: Cognitive tutors: Lessons learned. The Journal of Learning Sciences 4(2), 167–207 (1995)
5. Bauer, M.: Acquisition of user preferences for plan recognition. In: Proceedings of the Fifth International Conference on User Modeling, pp. 105–112 (1996)
6. Lesh, N.: Adaptive Goal Recognition. In: Proceedings of the 15th International Joint Conference on Artificial Intelligence, pp. 1208–1214. Morgan Kaufmann, San Francisco (1997)
7. Conati, C., Gertner, A., VanLehn, K.: Using bayesian networks to manage uncertainty in student modeling. Journal of User Modeling and User-Adapted Interaction 12(4), 371–417 (2002)
8. Corebette, A., McLaughlin, M., Scarpinatto, K.: Modeling student knowledge: Cognitive tutors in high school and college. User Modeling and User-Adapted Interaction 10, 81–108 (2000)
9. Konold, C., Miller, C.: TinkerPlots Dynamic Data Exploration 1.0. Key. Curriculum Press (2004)
10. Hammerman, J.K., Rubin, A.: Strategies for managing statistical complexity with new software tools. Statistics Education Research Journal 3(2), 17–41 (2004)
11. Grosz, B., Kraus, S.: The evolution of sharedplans. In: Foundations and Theories of Rational Agency, pp. 227–262 (1999)
12. Pollack, M.: Plans as complex mental attitudes. MIT Press, Cambridge (1990)
13. Reddy, S., Gal, Y., Shieber, S.M.: Recognition of users' activities using constraint satisfaction. Technical Report TR-05-09, Harvard University (2009)

Reinforcing Recommendation Using Implicit Negative Feedback

Danielle H. Lee and Peter Brusilovsky

School of Information Sciences, University of Pittsburgh
135 N. Bellefield Ave., Pittsburgh, PA 15260 USA
suleehs@gmail.com, peterb@pitt.edu

Abstract. Recommender systems have explored a range of implicit feedback approaches to capture users' current interests and preferences without intervention of users' work. However, current research focuses mostly on implicit positive feedback. Implicit negative feedback is still a challenge because users mainly target information they want. There have been few studies assessing the value of negative implicit feedback. In this paper, we explore a specific approach to employ implicit negative feedback and assess whether it can be used to improve recommendation quality.

Keywords: Negative preference, implicit feedback, recommendation.

1 Introduction

Modern recommender systems rely on user feedback to provide high quality recommendations. User feedback communicates information about user interests and it can be provided either explicitly through users' ratings or implicitly through various user activities such as browsing, reading, or bookmarking. While explicit feedback is sometimes considered as more reliable, implicit feedback requires less intervention to users, captures short-term interest, and continuously updates user preference. Modern approaches to implicit feedback analysis make the quality of recommendation based on implicit feedback comparable to those based on explicit feedback. One aspect, however, where implicit feedback still differs from explicit is its predominant positive focus. It has been argued that negative preferences are hard to acquire through implicit channel [3] because users mainly pursue information they consider as interesting. Therefore, there has been little work done to test implicit negative preference to personalize information.

This paper introduces a relatively simple mechanism to infer negative feedback and test the feasibility of the feedback as a way to represent what users want in the context of a job recommender system. In this study, to assess the effectiveness of implicit negative feedback, not only the negative feedback, but two kinds of positive feedback (users' saved jobs and search options) were collected. The collected information was compared with a list of recommended jobs which are evaluated by users as the ground truth. The quality of feedback was measured in several settings – positive preference only, negative preference only and compound preference.

G.-J. Houben et al. (Eds.): UMAP 2009, LNCS 5535, pp. 422–427, 2009.

2   Implicit Feedback as a Way to Indicate User's Preferences

Implicit feedback as a source of information for recommendation has been explored in a range of projects. Some projects [6, 8, 12] utilized browsing history (click-through) to provide personalized search or recommendation Other projects [2, 10] examined time spent on information items and found a strong positive correlation between implicit feedback and time spent.

Implicit feedback techniques were overviewed in [7] and [3]. Both papers showed that almost all personalized systems and approaches rely on positive implicit feedback. In [7], only 4 out of the 27 techniques could be used to represent negative feedback, for instance, deleting, skipping forward, editing existing contents or rating negatively. Even further, none of the studies that are introduced in the paper utilized negative preference in implicit feedback. The same is true for the classification by [3].

The decrease of the discriminative power of positive-only implicit feedback is certainly a concern. Morita and Shinoda's study [10] indicated that the quality of positive-only implicit feedback may decrease with the increased flow of positive judgments. When subjects read a series of related papers, the power of the reading time-based feedback became weaker to discriminate the positive and negative preferences [10]. An empirical study in [4] also suggested that if a recommender system includes one single item that a user dislikes, the system become untrustworthy, even if it provides a set of favorable items as well.

Holland et al. [5] examined the personalization using both positive and negative feedback. Based on users' web log, the user preferences were expressed as a comparison, such as, "A is better than B." This is effective in calculating categorical or numerical preference. Nevertheless, the personalization needed an adequate amount of log data and detecting negative preferences was founded on the assumption that the users know all possible values. If they did not select them, they could be defined as negative. [1] and [11] actively collected negative implicit feedback sources such as skipping or blocking a song. In the former study, only the songs users did not want to hear were taken into account in a recommendation for background music for a group of users. In the later study, the researchers counted for positive and negative preference, and the skipped behavior of users decreased.

3   Job Recommendation Mechanism in Proactive

The study presented in this paper was performed using the recommender system *Proactive* [9], which helps its users to find information technology jobs. The users can explore jobs available in the system by browsing a full list of jobs (which can be sorted by several properties) or searching by keywords and desired job properties (Figure 1). Both full list and search result list offer a summary of each job. Once the job summary looks promising, users can click the job title to see the detailed information in a separate window. If the job is really interesting, they can save (bookmark) the job into "my jobs" list along with a rating (relevant, good, very good). Issuing a query with specific parameters and bookmaking a job case send two kinds of positive feedback to the system, which are used by a job recommender component of *Proactive*. If the job turns out not worthy to save, users just close the window. In the new version of the system we considered this action as implicit negative feedback and used the properties of ignored job cases to elicit negative preferences.

To compare different jobs, *Proactive* uses *job properties* encoded using several taxonomies. Job category and company information are defined by the Yahoo! HotJobs taxonomy. The geographic information of jobs is gathered from Google Map to calculate the neighboring area. Special taxonomies are also defined for educational level, experience, position type and salary levels. Every property is assigned a

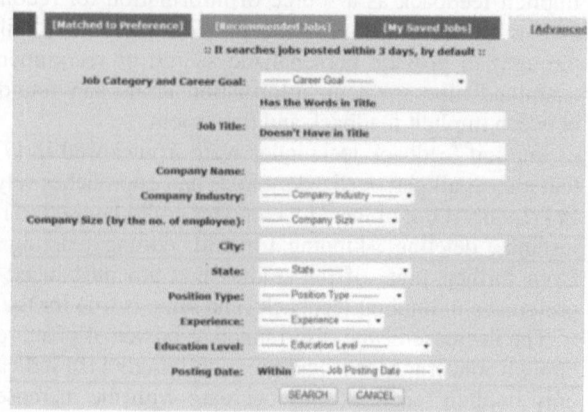

Fig. 1. Advanced Search in *Proactive*

certain weight representing its position in the taxonomy. When jobs are crawled, the properties of each job case are automatically classified using taxonomies and receive the corresponding weight values. To recommend jobs, *Proactive* calculates a distance between each new job case and user *job preference* (profile). The smaller is the distance, the closer is the job to the user preferences [9]. *Proactive* uses the following formula to calculate the distance.

$$\text{Weight Distance } (s_i, c_j) = \frac{\Delta(s_{i1}, c_{j1}) + \Delta(s_{i2}, c_{j2}) + \cdots + \Delta(s_{i8}, c_{j8})}{r_i} \qquad \text{eq. (1)}$$

$$\text{Total Distance } (s, c_j) = \sum_{i=0}^{n} \text{Weight Distance } (s_i, c_j) \qquad \text{eq. (2)}$$

A set of saved jobs represents user's explicit positive preference. In the equations (1,2), s is a saved job and c is a candidate job which are recently added. i take values form 1 to I, where I is the total number of a user's saved jobs and j takes values from 1 to J, where J is the total number of candidate jobs. The weight distance between a saved job and a candidate job counts the distance Δ of each job property in both jobs. s_{il} is the weight value of the first property in ith saved job and c_{jl} is the weight values of the first property in jth candidate job. Every job case has 8 properties (job category, company industry and size, job location, educational level, experience level, salary, and position type). r_i is the ratings of each saved job as additional power. As the equation shows, if two job cases are semantically closer, the weight distance between them is smaller. In addition, as the rating of a saved job is higher, the overall distance gets smaller. Comparison between search options and candidate jobs was also based on this equation. Finally, in order to decide the total distance of a certain candidate job, each weight distance between every saved job and the corresponding candidate job is summed up as shown in eq. (2).

4 The Study

The goal of the reported study was to assess the value of implicit negative feedback. The subjects in this study were 17 Information Science students (10 males, 7 females) at the University of Pittsburgh who expressed interest in looking for information technology-related jobs. The structure of a study session was simple: after a brief introduction of the system, each subject was asked to use the system to find jobs of interest. It was explained that they had to click the job title in either a comprehensive job list or search results list to see job detail. It was also explained that to receive good recommendations, they had to save only interesting jobs. After participants explored the system thoroughly and saved several jobs, the system generated a list of recommended jobs, which were simply the jobs most similar to the saved jobs. Participants had to rate the recommended jobs using three point Likert scale (1 = bad, 3 = neutral, 5 = good). In total, 237 job cases were rated by 17 subjects.

The collected user ratings served as the ground truth for the analysis presented below. During this analysis, we employed users' saved jobs and search options as positive job preferences and jobs that were opened but not saved as negative job preferences. To judge which source of feedback represents user preferences best, we compared weight distance between the ground truth and user preferences elicited using four kinds different groups of sources – one positive feedback source, two positive feedback sources, positive and negative feedback, and compound feedback.

4.1 Positive Preferences

As in the first result, explicit positive feedback – user's saved jobs – was tested to measure how it works well to represent users' preferences. We grouped recommended jobs according to three levels of user evaluation (good-neutral-bad). Then the distances between each group of recommended jobs and the users' saved jobs were compared. If classic explicit positive preferences work well, the distances from user profile to jobs rated as 'good' should be significantly smaller the distances to jobs rated as 'bad'. Unfortunately, there was no significant difference between three groups of recommended jobs and saved jobs, Kruskal-Wallis $H = .595$, $df = 2$, $p = .537$. The result suggests that one kind of positive feedback, even explicit, may not be sufficient to reliably distinguish good and bad jobs.

Table 1. Mean Values of Weight Distance & Mean Difference Tests

Rating / Profile	Good	Neutral	Bad	Sig.
User's saved jobs	47.70	60.67	47.55	.537
User's saved jobs + search options	40.01	42.79	57.66	.477
User's saved jobs + negative prefs	34.09	97.08	78.21	.003*
Compound profile	31.44	94.04	59.40	.005*

Our first attempt to improve the distinguishing power of the user profile was to construct a more precise user profile by adding another source of positive implicit feedback: *search options*. The advanced search interface of *Proactive* (as shown in Figure 1) provides all properties of existing jobs as drop-down menus. Once a user specified the search options, it could be assumed that the user is interested in jobs with these properties. Both saved jobs and search options were compared with recommended jobs respectively using equation (2) and the result distances were summed up together. While the ability of the recommender engine to discriminate good and bad jobs has visibly improved, still, there was no significant difference in weight distance among the level of ratings, Kruskal-Wallis $H = .743$, $df = 2$, $p = .477$. The addition of another source of positive feedback for recommendations wasn't helpful to distinguish good and bad jobs reliably.

4.2   Adding Negative Preferences

As explained, when participants click the job title in a summarized list, they can see job details in a separate window. If they find the job interesting, they can rate and save it to generate recommendations. Otherwise, they just close the window without saving. It can be hypothesized that some of the properties in the job did not match to their interests and the user doesn't want to receive recommendations relevant to the job. Therefore, the properties of the opened but not saved jobs were elicited and added to the user profile. Since there is no way to determine which specific property made the job uninteresting to the user, we counted the job properties as a whole. Since uninteresting jobs had no explicit rating, the ratings were simply marked as 'bad.' The distances between the profile extended with rejected jobs and three groups of ground truth jobs were compared. The result shows significant differences in weight distance among three levels of rating, Kruskal-Wallis $H = 11.951$, $df = 2$, $p = .003$.

Although weight distances evaluated as 'neutral' jobs have the highest values ($M = 97.08$), compared with the weight distance of 'bad' jobs ($M = 78.21$), the weight distance of 'good' jobs are much smaller ($M = 34.09$). Implicit negative preference makes it possible to reliably distinguish 'good' jobs.

4.3   Compound Preferences

As [13] pointed, to suggest better recommendation, it is important to use various methods to see various aspects of users' preferences. Hence, the previous three methods – saved jobs, search options and rejected job cases – were merged to test whether compounded profile outperformed either of the individual methods. There was significant difference in the recommended jobs according to the three levels of ratings using compounded profile, Kruskal-Wallis $H = 10.52$, $df = 2$, $p = .005$. In this method, the results are similar with user profile extended with just uninteresting job cases. The weight distance evaluated as 'neutral' jobs have the highest values ($M = 94.04$), the weight distance of 'bad' jobs are the second highest ($M = 59.40$), and the weight distance of 'good' jobs are the lowest ($M = 31.44$). Compared with the weight distance values only using not-interesting job cases, the mean weight distance of 'good' jobs are smaller, although the mean weight distance of 'bad' jobs also decreased. Therefore, it is concluded that understanding implicit negative preferences can be an effective method to distinguish jobs, which users like and jobs they don't.

5 Conclusion

This study showed how implicit negative feedback affects recommendation quality. Compared with the cases using just positive preferences, the distinction between good and bad jobs was significantly clear when negative preferences were used. As an additional way to reinforce positive preference, search options did not benefit personalization. This study shows that negative preferences, as it was inferred, can increase recommendation quality. In particular, the implicit feedback used in this study can be applied to make recommendation on-the-fly without accumulating a certain amount of information. Due to the semantic infrastructure of the recommender system, it is possible to have richer user profile than the system without semantic structure.

References

1. Chao, D.L., Balthrop, J., Forrest, S.: Adaptive Radio: Achieving Consensus using Negative Preferences. In: Proc. of the 2005 International ACM SIGGROUP Conference on Supporting Group Work, Sanibel Island, Florida, USA (2005)
2. Claypool, M., Le, P., Waseda, M., Brown, D.: Implicit interest indicators. In: Proc. of 6th Conference on Intelligent User Interfaces, pp. 33–40 (2002)
3. Gauch, S., Speretta, M., Chandramouli, A., Micarelli, A.: User Profiles for Personalized Information Access. In: Brusilovsky, P., Kobsa, A., Nejdl, W. (eds.) Adaptive Web 2007. LNCS, vol. 4321, pp. 54–89. Springer, Heidelberg (2007)
4. Golbeck, J.: Trust and Nuanced Profile Similarity in Online Social Networks. ACM Transactions on the Web (to be appeared)
5. Holland, S., Ester, M., Kießling, W.: Preference mining a novel approach on mining user preference for personalized applications. In: Proc. of the 7th European Conference on Principles & Practice of Knowledge Discovery in Databases, Dubrovnik, Croatia (2003)
6. Joachims, T., Granka, L., Pan, B., Hembrooke, H., Gay, G.: Accurately Interpreting Clickthrough Data as Implicit Feedback. In: Proc. of the 17th Annual International ACM SIGIR Conference, Salvador, Brazil, pp. 154–161 (2005)
7. Kelly, D., Teevan, J.: Implicit feedback for inferring user preference: a bibliography. ACM SIGIR Forum 37(2), 18–28 (2003)
8. Kim, H., Chan, P.: Learning Implicit User Interest Hierarchy for Context in Personalization. In: Proc. of the International Conference on Intelligent User Interfaces, Miami, Florida, USA, pp. 101–108 (2003)
9. Lee, D.H., Brusilovsky, B.: Fighting Information Overflow with Personalized Comprehensive Information Access: A Proactive Job Recommender. In: Proc. of the 3rd Conference on Autonomic & Autonomous System, Athens, Greece, pp. 21–26 (2007)
10. Morita, M., Shinoda, Y.: Information Filtering based on User Behavior Analysis and Best Match Text Retrieval. In: Proc. of the 17th ACM SIGIR Conference, Dublin, Ireland, pp. 272–281 (1994)
11. Pamplak, E., Pohle, T., Widmer, G.: Dynamic Playlist Generator Based On Skipping Behavior. In: Proc. of the 6th Conference on Music Information Retrieval, London, UK (2005)
12. Sugiyama, K., Hatano, K., Yoshikawa, M., Uemura, S.: User-Oriented Adaptive Web Information Retrieval based on Implicit Observations. In: Yu, J.X., Lin, X., Lu, H., Zhang, Y. (eds.) APWeb 2004. LNCS, vol. 3007, pp. 636–643. Springer, Heidelberg (2004)
13. Teevan, J., Dumais, S., Horvitz, E.: Personalized Search via Automated Analysis of Interests and Activities. In: Proc. of the 17th ACM SIGIR Conference, Salvador, Brazil, pp. 449–456 (2005)

Evaluating Three Scrutability and Three Privacy User Privileges for a Scrutable User Modelling Infrastructure

Demetris Kyriacou, Hugh C. Davis, and Thanassis Tiropanis

Learning Societies Lab
School of Electronics and Computer Science, University of Southampton
Highfield, Southampton, SO17 1BJ, United Kingdom
{dke06r,hcd,tt2}@ecs.soton.ac.uk

Abstract. This paper describes the evaluation of a Scrutable User Modelling Infrastructure. SUMI is intended to form a service to allow users to share their user models from social e-networking and e-commerce providers to educational systems. The model is scrutable, meaning users can inspect and correct the data that is held about them, and implements privacy policies so that users can control how their models are accessed by other users. This evaluation was conducted with 107 users, which were exposed to a prototype service, for determining whether the proposed scrutability and privacy privileges were acceptable to the users, whether the users were able to achieve the desired outcome, and whether they understood the consequences of their interactions with the system. The conclusions show that the users expressed their general approval of the proposed privileges while making useful suggestions regarding improvements to the presentation and interface to the system.

1 Introduction

Our research has revolved around gathering the requirements for adopting a Scrutable User Modelling Infrastructure (SUMI) for the e-commerce and social e-networking domains, in order to enable exchanging of user models among these domains and educational personalization systems, in an attempt to enrich the various sets of user information which are being used for adaptation purposes. We have focused on three key User Modelling 'ingredients' - interoperability, scrutability and privacy. In this paper we present our work on scrutability and user privacy while attempting to answer the following research question: To what extend is it possible for such an infrastructure to allow users to scrutinize the modelling process and express their data privacy preferences?

2 Key User Modelling Components and Identified Problem

Lifelong User Modelling: User Modelling (UM) is the 'heart' of educational personalization services such as AHA!, which offers adaptive content through fragment variants and adaptive link presentation [1]. By keeping a model for each user, it allows

G.-J. Houben et al. (Eds.): UMAP 2009, LNCS 5535, pp. 428–434, 2009.

unique adaptation and presentation of the available resources based on these models, thus enabling successful interactions between users and personalization systems. Life-long UM was introduced in an attempt to model users' daily-lifelong interactions with several services on the World Wide Web (WWW) while offering to the users the ability to scrutinize and control the whole personalization process [2].

Scrutability: The term scrutability in user modelling signifies that every user's model can be inspected and altered by its owner in order to determine what should be modelled about him/her and how that modelling and following personalization process will be conducted. Scrutable solutions allow users to inspect and alter the value of any single inference that is used for drawing conclusions about them [3].

Privacy-Enhanced Personalization: An area that aims at merging together the techniques and goals of UM with privacy considerations and apply the best possible personalization inside the boundaries set by privacy rules. As the research shows, there is no ideal solution while attempting to combine these two crucial elements. Instead, numerous small enhancements can be implemented, depending on the user and application domains in each case, in order to achieve the best possible solution[4].

Identified Problem: The area of UM is undoubtedly progressing. But, while we find UM in a state of transition, is still been applied single-dimensionally: Most adaptive systems developed, are only using their internal models when offering personalization services to their users. In addition, newly introduced frameworks and architectures, while offering a solution in achieving interoperability across peer systems, do not involve systems beyond the educational domain. Furthermore, User Modelling Servers, a client-server architecture for allowing central information storing and simultaneously data access and retrieval, although are considering and offering scrutability and privacy options to their users, are mostly designed and developed to meet commercial requirements [5]. We are loosing user information, which is flowing on the WWW, because we are not thinking multi-'*domain*'sionally. We can enrich UM if we find a way to model our every day (life-long) interactions with services from the social e-networking and the e-commerce domains, in order to enrich user information sets which are used in the educational domain for personalization purposes. Recent data portability announcements from two key players in the social e-networking domain [6, 7] which revealed these providers' initiatives to pass user data back to their 'owners' have made this multi'*domain*'sional vision even more feasible.

3   SUMI User Evaluation

SUMI's goal is to allow users to gather their various models which they hold with several social e-networking and e-commerce providers, and interact with these models via a SUMI service, using a set of offered scrutability and privacy privileges. Special consideration has been given to collecting the requirements for employing such an infrastructure in an attempt to enrich the current picture in UM [8].

Achieving Interoperability: In this paper we have focused on presenting our work on scrutability and user privacy, thus we will not expand on our solution for achieving interoperability across the social e-networking and e-commerce domains, which is undoubtedly as important as considering scrutability and privacy user privileges. We will just briefly mention that this has been achieved using a 4-category models' architecture which resulted after comparative evaluations of representatives of both domains, a SUMI ontology [9], which uses dictionary concepts to define meaning and a RESTful approach as communication protocol. Providers of user models can describe their data model inside SUMI, in order to allow users to import them in SUMI and for educational services to express interest by subscribing to them.

Proposed Scrutability & Privacy Privileges: In this paper, emphasis is given in our work on scrutability and user privacy which the first user evaluation is based on. More specifically we have proposed:

Three SCRUTABILITY user privileges for SUMI which were exposed to users in the form of three tasks: *Task 1*: Users were asked to add at least one social e-networking and e-commerce model to their SUMI collection. Users were exposed to the 4-category SUMI model's architecture. *Task 2*: In this task users were asked to import the content of their previously added models in two ways, dynamically-meaning real-time HTTP GET requests and retrieval of real-time data from the provider of the user model using the provider's API, and statically-meaning the cache copy that was taken when the last dynamic import request was generated by the user, and will be retrieved from the SUMI database using SQL queries. Network failures or busy network traffics, are some reasons that users could take advantage of the static import option. *Task 6*: During this task users were asked to respond to a request and export the content of one of their models to a group formation system, while inspecting and approving, during the export process, all transaction details.

Three PRIVACY user privileges for SUMI which were exposed to users in the form of three tasks: *Task 3*: During this task, users had to set the privacy status of all 4 categories of at least one of their models using the proposed 3 privacy settings: **public**-others can see that the model exists and anyone can view its content, **private**-others can see that the model exists but they have to place a request to the model's owner for viewing the model's content, and **hidden**-others can not see that the model exists, therefore the model's content is accessed only by the model's owner. *Task 4*: Users had to respond to another user's viewing request and allow the requester to view the content of the requested model. *Task 5*: Users were asked to visit another user's SUMI collection of models and place a request on one private category of that user's models.

Evaluation Objectives: In order to properly evaluate our work, we prepared a prototype SUMI service which has been designed for evaluation and demonstration purposes [10]. The objective of the evaluation was to evaluate if the proposed scrutability and privacy user privileges are appropriate to be offered in SUMI and accepted by SUMI users. For the purposes of this evaluation we have defined the terms "appropriate" and "accepted" as follows: *Appropriate*-Adequate to satisfy a user need; fit for purpose. *Accepted*-Generally approved or recognized. In order to evaluate if the proposed privileges were *appropriate to be offered in SUMI* we took into account the combination of: a) users' *competence* on completing each presented task which exposed the proposed privileges (we compared the actual outcome after the completion of the tasks with the users' answers to the evaluation questions – have they done it VS. do they think they have done it) and b) users' *understanding of the consequences* of their decisions while interacting with each task- thus interacting with the proposed privileges. In addition, in order to evaluate if the proposed privileges were *accepted* by SUMI users we tested users' *acceptance* of the proposed privileges by asking them directly what they think about them and if they would like SUMI to offer them to its users.

Participants & Evaluation Structure: Our target audience was any undergraduate and postgraduate student of any study discipline and age range. Participants were approached via online forums and social networking groups. A sample size of 107 participants was achieved during a 30-day evaluation process. The evaluation consisted of three parts: First, a *pre-questionnaire* allowed us to classify how much users knew about their scrutability and privacy options while interacting with various social e-networking and e-commerce providers on the WWW. Second, *six tasks* exposed to the participants all proposed scrutability and privacy privileges. Users were asked to complete all 6 tasks, while answering some questions during their interaction with each one of them. Furthermore, after the completion of all 6 tasks, users were asked to complete a series of 3-questions-per-task which helped us identify the degree of competence, understanding of consequences, and acceptance for each proposed privilege. Third, a *post-questionnaire* revealed valuable conclusions regarding: how much users valued scrutability and privacy after the completion of the evaluation, users' proposals for any new scrutability and privacy privileges, what users think about SUMI as a service, and finally what users think about the fact that SUMI is keeping a copy of their data while interacting with it.

4   Evaluation Results

Pre-Questionnaire: The pre-questionnaire exposed some useful lessons regarding the users' familiarity with the terms scrutability and user privacy. Results have shown that 89% of students do not know what the term scrutability means, although 38% can easily identify some scrutability privileges once they have been explained to them. Furthermore, 80% of users have found the idea of having scrutability privileges available when interacting with various providers to be a very good idea, which shows the recognition of how important scrutability is to users, once explained to them. User privacy is a term more familiar to users than scrutability. It is something 64% of users understand and recognize when interacting with several providers, although 32% of participants choose not to take advantage of it. But, at the suggestion of not having any privacy privileges available, 91% of users expressed their concerns.

Scrutability & User Privacy Privileges – Comparison of Results: Table 1 summarizes the results and conclusions regarding which privileges have been successful in which category – competence, consequence and acceptance. The ✗ symbol means "not satisfactory", where ✓ marks "success".

Table 1. Results (% of successful responses) & conclusions for the proposed user privileges

	Task1: Adding models	Task2: Importing content	Task6: Exporting content	Task3: Setting privacy status	Task4: Responding to viewing request	Task5: Placing viewing request
Competence	100/100(✓)	79/60(✗)	91/100(✓)	76/68(✗)	88/74(✗)	84/100(✓)
Consequence	77(✗)	67(✗)	60(✗)	100(✓)	100(✓)	79(✓)
Acceptance	89(✓)	100(✓)	94(✓)	100(✓)	99(✓)	83(✓)
During	73	78, 70	72	71	N/A	100

Competence's results show: % of users who answered positively to the question "do you think you have managed to complete the task?" / % of actual successful outcome

Competence: It was clear from the results of the competence questions combined with the results of the during-task questions, that scrutability tasks 1 and 6 and privacy task 5 can be completed successfully by our target audience. It is also clear that scrutability task 2 and privacy tasks 3 and 4, although the responses were satisfactory, users' confidence % did not meet the actual outcome % and this begs the question of how much our presentation format affected these results.

Consequence: A different picture appears when we compare the successful responses on the consequence questions. All 3 tasks of privacy have returned acceptable percentages, where the results for the 3 scrutability tasks show that users require further education regarding those privileges. This can be explained from the fact that all today's social e-networking providers, such as Facebook and MySpace offer similar privacy privileges to their users. On the other hand, scrutability privileges are not so popular among providers thus users do not have the same level of familiarity and knowledge. In addition, some technical terminology which was presented to the users may be found too abstract and difficult to understand.

Acceptance: The most important conclusions were revealed after our comparative evaluation of the results on the acceptance questions. All 6 privileges were accepted by an average of 94% of our targeted audience. The confidence interval for a confidence level of 95% is 4.44. This is a very important conclusion which proves our acceptance hypothesis.

Post-Questionnaire: Finally the post-questionnaire revealed participants' highly positive attitude about the SUMI service which they were exposed to. 92% of users approved our work which was reflected in the evaluation, although 39% of them did not fully agree with the feature of SUMI keeping a copy of their information inside its databases. Two important results of this evaluation can be identified in the participants' responses on the last two questions. 85% and 79% chose the best answer available when asked, *after the completion of the evaluation,* how much they valued scrutability and user privacy respectively. If these percentages were to be compared with the responses in the pre-questionnaire, and specifically with the responses in the questions regarding how much users were familiar with the two terms *before* the evaluation, we observe a significant raise of percentages in both occasions; familiar with scrutability options in pre-questionnaire: 10%, appreciation percentage in post-questionnaire: 85%, familiar with privacy options in pre-questionnaire: 64%, appreciation percentage in post-questionnaire: 79%.

5 Main Conclusion and Future Work

As our results have shown, although the proposed infrastructure meets the requirements to be considered as the solution to the identified problem, technical complexity
and inadequate presentation formats caused the low percentages of successful responses in some tasks. This will be the starting point of our upcoming schedule. In
addition, many useful suggestions came out from the evaluation:

Scrutability: 22% of users raised an important issue when they asked us to find a
way so that subscribed services would inform users how their data would be used
before users deciding if they would go through with the export transaction or not.
Moreover, 43% of users expressed their concerns regarding SUMI keeping a copy of
their information when initiating a dynamic import of their content. Some of them
asked us to introduce an on/off switch so they could set which imported attributes
SUMI will be allowed to keep internally, while others requested the option of deleting
attributes' values from SUMI after inspection of their SUMI collection of models.

User Privacy: The main suggestion we received for user privacy from 37% of the
participants was to allow them to create groups of users and assign a common privacy
status. In addition, 13% of participants requested two more privacy settings, "block"
and "ignore", which could be added to SUMI's current set of privacy settings. Finally,
31% of users wanted to be allowed to take back the viewing access they have granted
to another user when they responded to the viewing request in task 4.

After we go through this already-set agenda, we will conduct a second SUMI user
evaluation in order to properly test any changes we decide to make. Results should
expose a significant improvement of the identified weak areas and the percentages of
successful responses should be higher in order to confidently claim that we have
proven all of our hypotheses.

References

1. De Bra, P., Calvi, L.: AHA: A Generic Adaptive Hypermedia System. In: Proc. of the 2nd
    Workshop on Adaptive Hypertext and Hypermedia, Pittsburgh, pp. 5–12 (1998)
2. Kay, J., Lifelong user models, memory and learning. ResearchChannel.org (2007),
    http://www.researchchannel.org/prog/
    displayevent.aspx?rID=21195&fID=4752 (last retrieved, 29/03/2009)
3. Kay, J.: Scrutable adaptation: because we can and must. In: Wade, V.P., Ashman, H.,
    Smyth, B. (eds.) AH 2006. LNCS, vol. 4018, pp. 11–19. Springer, Heidelberg (2006)
4. Kobsa, A.: Privacy-Enhanced Personalization. Communications of the ACM 50(8), 24–33
    (2007)
5. Fink, J., Kobsa, A.: A Review and Analysis of Commercial User Modeling Servers for
    Personalization on the World Wide Web. User Modeling and User-Adapted Interaction -
    Special Issue on Deployed User Modeling 10, 209–249 (2000)
6. Facebook Developers News, Announcing Facebook Connect,
    http://developers.facebook.com/news.php?blog=1&story=108
    (last retrieved, 29/03/2009)

434   D. Kyriacou, H.C. Davis, and T. Tiropanis

7. Google Inc., Google Friend Connect,
   http://www.google.com/friendconnect (last retrieved, 29/03/2009)
8. Kyriacou, D.: A Scrutable User Modelling Infrastructure for enabling life-long User Modelling. In: Nejdl, W., Kay, J., Pu, P., Herder, E. (eds.) AH 2008. LNCS, vol. 5149, pp. 421–425. Springer, Heidelberg (2008)
9. SUMI Ontology, http://mysumi.org/sumiOntology.owl (last uploaded, 29/03/2009)
10. mysumi.org – SUMI prototype service,
    http://mysumi.org/1stEvaluation.html

User Modeling of Disabled Persons for Generating Instructions to Medical First Responders

Luca Chittaro, Roberto Ranon, Luca De Marco, and Augusto Senerchia

HCI Lab, University of Udine, via delle Scienze. 206,
33100 Udine, Italy
http://hcilab.uniud.it

Abstract. To provide personalized health recommendations concerning disabled persons, an adaptive system needs a detailed user model that can account for the peculiar aspects of the many existing disabilities. This paper describes how we built such a user model and illustrates the Web-based system that allows all interested stakeholders to access and provide user model data.

Keywords: personalized health services, user model, disabled patients, adaptive instructions, first responders.

1 Introduction

Emergency medical services (EMS) rely on well established procedures that apply to the most frequent cases a first responder encounters in her practice, but often do not include special cases concerning (sensory, motor or cognitive) disabled persons. In these cases, first responders may end up applying suboptimal or possibly wrong procedures or lose precious time trying to adapt on-the-fly to the special case. Adaptive systems could thus be employed to generate personalized instructions for medical first responders, taking into account a model of the disabled person involved. For example, an adaptive system could consider the presence of chronic pain or paralysis in specific parts of the body to instruct first responders – while they are traveling in the ambulance to the patient location – about changes to the standard procedures, e.g. the question "Do you feel pain here?" could have to be substituted with "Do you feel more pain than usual here?", and manual procedures to immobilize the patient and to transfer her to a stretcher should treat paralyzed body parts with extra care (e.g., loads and tractions).

In general, to provide personalized health recommendations concerning disabled persons, an adaptive system needs a detailed user model that can account for the peculiar aspects of the many existing disabilities. This paper describes how we built such a user model and illustrates the Web-based system that enables all the identified stakeholders (disabled users, their families, clinicians, and medical first responders) to contribute and receive personalized data and knowledge.

G.-J. Houben et al. (Eds.): UMAP 2009, LNCS 5535, pp. 435–440, 2009.

2 Related Work

Adaptive systems have been applied successfully in medicine to inform patients about their conditions, enable them to take decisions, persuade them to be compliant with care plans. Different diseases, such as diabetes [9], cardiovascular disease [1], cancer [2], and asthma [3], have been addressed. The PULSE project [1] combines patient data acquired from paper-based medical records with adaptive Web-based presentation techniques to provide personalized education materials about cardiovascular risk. The personalized materials address medical and psychosocial aspects together with clinical guidelines to motivate people to take care of their health. The PIGLIT [9,2] system also focuses on health education materials, aiming at providing users with personalized hypertext explanations of their conditions, exploiting information from the patient's health record, a medical knowledge base and a natural language generator.

Many Computer Decision Support Systems (CDSS) have been proposed to support physicians in their activities (for a survey, see [4]), and share with adaptive systems the need for integrating medical knowledge bases, electronic medical records and computer-interpretable clinical guidelines. Relevant patient data can be acquired from Electronic Health Records (EHR), which unfortunately still have usage and adoption issues as discussed in [4]. While EHRs are typically managed by clinicians and staff of health care institutions, the idea of Personal Health Record (PHR) - i.e. an health record that conforms to recognized standards and is managed by the individual – is becoming popular, also thanks to Web-based applications such as Google Health [6] and Microsoft Health Vault [7]. Web-based PHRs are particularly interesting from a personalization point of view, since they offer: (i) standards upon which to build user models and health personalization applications, (ii) more access and control on what personal information is contained in and shared by the PHR, thus contributing to address some of the crucial privacy and trust issues highlighted in [9].

3 Modeling Disabled Users

Identifying and modeling all the impairments of each disabled patient to personalize EMS operations is a challenging task because severely disabled patients can be affected by many different and unrelated conditions which are not taken into account by generic disability stereotypes (e.g., blind, deaf, ...). Moreover, current EHR and PHR standards do not support the detailed specification of disabilities. However, starting from scratch without relying on any standard makes it much more difficult to propose a medical user profile as well as having it adopted by clinicians.

3.1 The International Classification of Functioning, Disability and Health

The International Classification of Functioning, Disability and Health (ICF) [10] is an initiative that is particularly relevant for our project, because it focuses specifically on disabilities. The ICF is the World Health Organization (WHO) international standard for measuring health and disability at both individual and population levels, and is endorsed by all WHO member states since 2001. The ICF organizes information in two parts. Part 1 concerns Functioning and Disability, and is structured into two components:

- *Body Functions and Structures*, to classify functions of body systems (e.g., Mental Functions, Sensory Functions, and Pain) and body structures (e.g., the Nervous System, The Eye, Ear and Related Structures);
- *Activities and Participation*, to cover functioning from both an individual (e.g., Communication, Mobility) and a societal (e.g., Interpersonal Interactions and Relationships) perspective.

Part 2 covers Contextual Factors, and is structured into two components:

- *Environmental Factors*, organized from the individual's most immediate environment (e.g., Products and Technology) to the general environment (e.g. Services, Systems and Policies);
- *Personal Factors*: they include gender, age, race, fitness, lifestyle, habits, coping styles, and other such factors.

Each of the above components consists of various *domains* (e.g. Sensory Functions and Pain is a domain of Body Functions and Structures). Within each domain, *categories* are the units of classification and are arranged hierarchically (e.g. for the domain of Sensory Functions and Pain, examples of nested categories are: Seeing Functions, Quality of Vision, Light Sensitivity). Health and health-related states of an individual are recorded by selecting the appropriate category code and then adding *qualifiers*, which are numeric codes that specify the extent or the magnitude of the functioning or disability in that category, or the extent to which an environmental factor is a facilitator or barrier. For instance, the code b210.4 indicates a complete impairment of seeing functions: the "b" prefix identifies the ICF component of Body Functions, the "210" code identifies the Seeing Functions category of the Sensory Functions and Pain domain, and the ".4" identifies the "complete impairment" value of the impairment category qualifier.

Since the ICF contains over 1400 categories, efforts to facilitate its use in clinical practice are underway. In particular, the ICF Checklist [11] consists of a selection of 125 ICF categories of more frequent use in clinical practice, and provides a questionnaire that can be filled out by a health professional to generate a disability profile of a patient.

3.2 Disabled User Profile (DUP)

In our first meetings with medical experts (3 clinicians working with disabled patients and 1 emergency medicine doctor), the ICF Checklist was identified as a starting point to develop a Disabled User Profile (DUP) that describes the disabilities of an individual which are most relevant in the context of EMS. We asked domain experts to carefully analyze each category of the ICF Checklist and evaluate its appropriateness for the EMS context. The analysis pointed out that the DUP could be built by making some changes and extensions to the ICF Checklist. Our DUP contains:

- Twenty categories[1] of the ICF Checklist, selected by the domain experts based on relevance in the context of EMS.
- Some PHR fields (allergies, medications, diagnoses) to capture medical data not strictly related to disabilities, but relevant in EMS operations for any individual.
- For some specific diagnosis (e.g., autism), additional associated fields (e.g., self injurious or aggressive behavior) recommended by experts.
- Personal data (e.g. social security number, name and surname, address), to identify the disabled person.
- Contact information of relatives and/or representatives to be called or who may call in case of emergency, and a free text field where particular notes about the patient's needs can be stored.

With respect to ICF categories and qualifiers, we made the following changes:

- Since some ICF categories (e.g., b280-Pain, b710-Mobility of joints, b730-Muscle power, b735-Muscle tone, b765-Involuntary movements) do not include the precise identification of the body parts affected by impairments, which is needed for our purposes, we extended them using a 27-parts anatomical representation.
- The qualifiers used to specify the magnitude of an impairment in the different categories have been simplified, by including only 4 of the 7 ICF values: we kept the values *No impairment*, *Moderate impairment*, *Complete impairment* and *Not specified*, while we discarded the values *Mild impairment* and *Severe impairment* to reduce subjectivity in the assignment and interpretation of impairment, and *Not applicable*, since it is useless in our considered categories.
- For the qualifiers of some categories, domain experts identified the need of using specific terms (e.g. Hypoventilation, Normal, Hyperventilation for the category b440 Respiration) to make the values more precise for physicians and first responders, in particular where the above ICF values could lead to ambiguous interpretations (e.g. a Moderate impairment of Blood pressure could mean Hypotension as well as Hypertension).

4   Building and Using DUPs

PRESYDIUM is a Web application that provides a Web Portal allowing disabled users, their relatives and physicians to access DUPs through a user interface that adapts to user category and user disabilities, by exploiting stereotypes. The system also includes a Web Service, which is accessed by EMS center phone operators

---

[1] MENTAL FUNCTIONS: Consciousness, Orientation (time, place, person), Intellectual (incl. Retardation, Dementia), Language; SENSORY FUNCTIONS AND PAIN: Seeing, Hearing, Vestibular (incl. Balance functions), Pain; FUNCTIONS OF THE CARDIOVASCULAR, HAEMATOLOGICAL, IMMUNOLOGICAL AND RESPIRATORY SYSTEMS: Heart, Blood pressure, Respiration (breathing); GENITOURINARY AND REPRODUCTIVE FUNCTIONS: Urination functions; NEUROMUSCULOSKELETAL AND MOVEMENT RELATED FUNCTIONS: Mobility of joint, Muscle power, Muscle tone, Involuntary movements; COMMUNICATION: Communicating with - receiving - spoken messages, Communicating with - receiving - non-verbal messages, Speaking, Producing non-verbal messages; MOBILITY: Walking, Moving around using equipment (wheelchair, skates, etc.).

through a desktop client and by first responders through a mobile client to retrieve tailored instructions for specific patients, EMS personnel (e.g. professional nurses, volunteers) and operational contexts.

PRESYDIUM has been built using the opensource JBoss Web application framework (jboss.org), which includes Drools (jboss.org/drools), a Rule Management System which is used as the personalization engine.

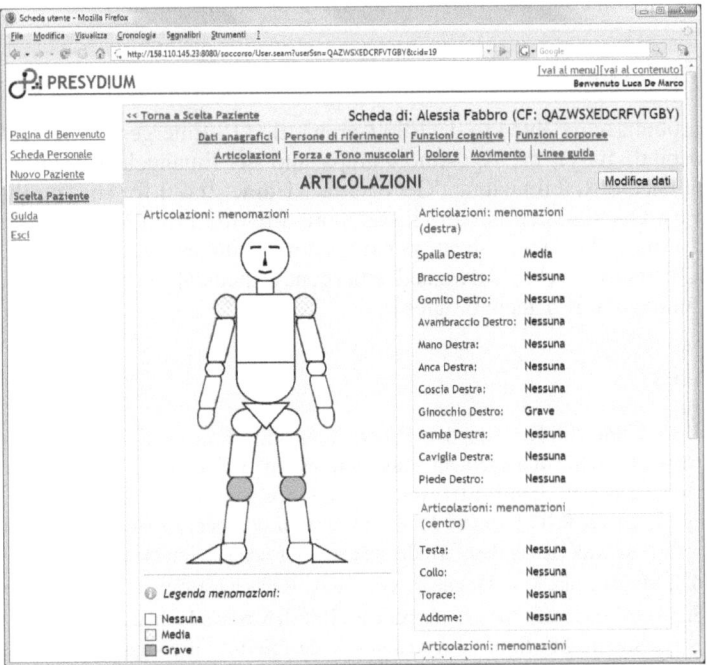

Fig. 1. User interface of the PRESYDIUM Web portal: inspecting a DUP section

The Web portal allows managing DUPs through a shared initiative between physicians, who contribute typical EHR data, and the disabled (or their relatives), who contribute personal information more typical of PHRs. Moreover, disabled users can access their own full DUP so that they can inspect all the data the system stores about them (also to address trust issues). The Web portal adapts the interface of the system (illustrated by the screenshot in Figure 1) by changing the presentation of elements of the user interface (e.g. bigger font size and inverted contrast for users with low vision), and by form adaptations during data entry of a DUP, to show or hide parts of the form (e.g. fields, schematic representations of human body), based on the values entered for specific fields.

Besides usual password-based access, the Web portal supports user identification based on the European Health Insurance Card (the most recent version of which includes a memory that contains identification data and can be read by a PC card reader which in our region is freely distributed to all households).

5 Conclusions

The PRESYDIUM system is currently going through a process of clinical validation. In particular, the present stage of validation is focusing on DUP data entry. A set of reference disabled patients has been selected and each member of a pool of clinicians (with different backgrounds) is separately entering DUPs for all cases. This will allow us both to detect possible misunderstandings in the DUP forms and to analyze consistency among clinicians in filling the DUP of a same patients.

Acknowledgements

We are particularly indebted to dr. Elio Carchietti (118 Emergency Medical Services, Udine Hospital, Italy), dr. Agostino Zampa and dr. Emanuele Biasutti (Istituto di Medicina Fisica e Riabilitazione "Gervasutta", Udine, Italy) for sharing their experience with us. Our research is partially supported by the Friuli Venezia Giulia region under the project "Servizi avanzati per il soccorso sanitario al disabile basati su tecnologie ICT innovative" ("Advanced emergency medical services for the disabled based on innovative ICT technologies").

References

1. Davis, S., Abidi, S.S.R.: Adaptive Patient Education Framework Featuring Personalized Cardiovascular Risk Management Interventions. In: Wade, V.P., Ashman, H., Smyth, B. (eds.) AH 2006. LNCS, vol. 4018, pp. 264–268. Springer, Heidelberg (2006)
2. Cawsey, A., Jones, R.B., Pearson, J.: The evaluation of a personalized health information system for patients with cancer. User Modeling and User-adapted Interaction 10(1), 47–72 (2001)
3. Osman, L.M., Abdulla, M.I., Beattie, J.A.G., et al.: Reducing Hospital Admission through Computer-Supported Education for Asthma patients. British Medical Journal 308, 568–571 (1994)
4. Berlin, A., Sorani, M., Sim, I.: A taxonomic description of computer-based clinical decision support systems. J. of Biomedical Informatics 39(6), 656–667 (2006)
5. Stead, W.W., Herbert, S.L. (eds.): Computational Technology for Effective Health Care: Immediate Steps and Strategic Directions. National Academies Press, Washington (2009)
6. Google Health, http://www.google.com/health
7. Microsoft HealthVault,
   http://www.healthvault.com/Personal/index.html
8. World Health Organization, International Classification of Functioning, Disability and Health, ICF (2001),
   http://www.who.int/classifications/icd/en/index.html
9. Binsted, K., Cawsey, A., Jones, R.B.: Generating Personalised Information using the Medical Record. In: Wyatt, J.C., Stefanelli, M., Barahona, P. (eds.) AIME 1995. LNCS, vol. 934, pp. 29–41. Springer, Heidelberg (1995)
10. Bruyère, S., VanLooy, S., Peterson, D.: The International Classification of Functioning, Disability and Health (ICF): Contemporary literature overview. Rehabilitation Psychology 50(2) (2005)
11. World Health Organization. ICF (International Classification of Functioning, Disability and Health) Checklist,
    http://www.who.int/classifications/icf/training/
    icfchecklist.pdf

Filtering Fitness Trail Content
Generated by Mobile Users

Fabio Buttussi, Luca Chittaro, and Daniele Nadalutti

HCI Lab, Dept. of Math and Computer Science, University of Udine
Via delle Scienze 206, 33100 Udine, Italy
http://hcilab.uniud.it

Abstract. This paper proposes a novel trail sharing system for mobile
devices that deals with context information collected by sensors, as well
as users' personal opinions (e.g., landscape beauty) specified by ratings.
To help the user in finding trails that are more suited to her, the system
exploits a collaborative filtering approach to predict the ratings users
may give to untried trails, and applies a similar approach also to context
information that can significantly vary among users (e.g., lap duration).

1 Introduction

Regularly performing physical activities such as jogging provides a variety of
benefits: it improves physical fitness, it helps to prevent pathologies such as
obesity, it may be an opportunity to meet other people, and it may also be fun.

Since people, especially those who do not exercise regularly, may need support
before, during, and after physical activity, we recently proposed [1,2] a wearable
training system to support users with tailored advice during sessions, and a
visual tool to help them with post-session performance analysis.

This paper focuses instead on a users' need that precedes the actual jogging
activity, i.e. finding trails that satisfy specific requirements such as suitability for
the current physical fitness of the user, possibility to meet other people, purity
of the environment or beauty of the landscape.

While motivating and training people requires knowledge that can be elicited
from domain experts such as physiologists and personal trainers, fulfilling the
above need requires information about the different available trails and their
features, including users' personal opinions on them. Since there are millions
of possible trails spread around the world, it would be very difficult and expensive for a small group of people to collect all the required information. On
the contrary, a Web 2.0 approach would allow a community of users to generate that content, possibly using mobile devices equipped with sensors such as
GPS and heart rate monitor. For this reason, some communities, companies,
and researchers (e.g., [3,4,5]) have proposed trail sharing systems which invite
users to collect context information about themselves (e.g., heart rate) and the
trails where they jog (e.g., waypoints), and share such content with other users
through the Web.

G.-J. Houben et al. (Eds.): UMAP 2009, LNCS 5535, pp. 441–446, 2009.

Position information about trails, represented as the latitude and the longitude of a set of waypoints, has been the first kind of user-generated content considered in the fitness domain. Waypoint information can be enhanced with altitude and timestamp, if available, and can be generated by asking users to manually place the waypoints on a map [3], by automatically collecting position information in the field by means of a GPS device [4], or by combining the two approaches [5].

Besides position, users' heart rate is an important information associated to fitness trails, and is indicative of users' physical fitness as well as trail difficulty. Two of the existing proposals allow to record such information: Nokia Sport Tracker [4] allows users only to manually add average heart rate to the automatically collected position information, while SlamXR [5] can automatically acquire heart rate information, together with synchronized information about position, acceleration, atmospheric pressure, and temperature, by means of a dedicated wrist-wearable device which integrates different sensors.

Unfortunately, existing systems do not consider users' personal opinions on trail features, such as the beauty of the landscape or the purity of the environment. To overcome such limitation, we propose a trail sharing system for mobile devices that deals with data collected by sensors (GPS and heart rate monitor) as well as users' personal opinions, and employs a collaborative filtering approach to help the user in finding the trails that are more suited to her.

2   Our Proposal

The mobile trail sharing system we propose deals with two different types of trail features:

- *Objective features* are those features directly measured by means of sensors or derivable from sensor measurements. Our system exploits (i) a GPS device to collect *waypoints*, (ii) a Bluetooth pulse oximeter to measure users' *heart rate* at each waypoint, and (iii) the internal time of the mobile device to measure the duration of a jogging session (*total duration*) and the duration of a lap (*lap duration*). From the collected information, the system can derive: (i) *total length* (by summing waypoint-to-waypoint distances), (ii) *lap length* (by summing waypoint-to-waypoint distances in a lap), (iii) *mean slope* (by calculating the ratio between the sum of waypoint-to-waypoint differences in altitude and the total length), (iv) *mean speed* (by calculating the ratio between the total length and the total duration), (v) *mean heart rate* (by averaging collected heart rate values), and (vi) *difficulty* (by calculating the ratio between mean heart rate and mean speed). Moreover, the system computes the *popularity* of trails (by considering how many times users jogged there), and the *distance* between a trail and the current location of a user.
- *Subjective features* are those features that depend on users' personal opinions. The system explicitly asks users to specify them using numeric ratings on a 1 to 5 scale. Considered subjective features are: (i) *beauty of the landscape* (e.g., is there anything the user likes to see while jogging such as trees

or rivers?), (ii) *crowding* (e.g., how many people will the user meet while jogging?), (iii) *purity of the environment* (e.g., is there waste or smog around the trail or is it a clean open-air environment?), and (iv) *safety* (e.g., can cars cross the trail? is it a crime-related area?).

We further classify objective features in: (i) *user independent features*, such as waypoints and lap length, and (ii) *user dependent (UD) features*, such as lap duration and difficulty, that can significantly vary according to the user.

Our system provides the user with a mobile tracking application to measure objective features of the trail where she jogs, collect her ratings about trail subjective features, and access a password-protected Web service for sharing trails. Besides storing content, the Web service calculates derivable objective features from the measured ones.

To search for a shared trail, existing systems ask users to specify some objective features. However, a search based only on objective features is not enough to find the trails that are most suited for each individual user, since users may like or dislike trails based on their personal opinions. A real-life scenario where users' opinions are fundamental to find the most suited trail may be the following (Scenario 1): two users (User 1 and User 2), who live in the same town, are looking for a nearby trail with a desired lap length and mean slope. User 1 likes trails with beautiful trees, while User 2 prefers jogging near clean rivers. Among the nearby trails satisfying the specified objective features, there is a trail (Trail T) with several beautiful trees, but no rivers at all. Since existing systems do not consider users' personal opinions, recommended trails for both users will include Trail T. As a result, if both users decide to try that trail, User 1 will appreciate the recommendation, while User 2 will be dissatisfied.

To deal with users' personal opinions, we adopt an approach based on collaborative filtering (see [6] for a recent survey about collaborative filtering), i.e. we collect the ratings that different users give to the subjective features of trails, and exploit such ratings to predict how much each user would like a trail she never tried. More precisely, our system is inspired by the GroupLens architecture [7] and the item-based recommendation algorithm proposed by [8]. We predict the rating a particular user would likely give to a subjective feature of an untried trail by proceeding as follows:

- for each subjective feature f, the system computes, on a regular basis, the adjusted-cosine similarity (Equation 1) between each possible pair of trails (i, j) by considering ratings for f given by the users who have tried both trails (we denote this set of users as $RB_{i,j,f}$) as well as the mean rating of each user $u \in RB_{i,j,f}$ for f (we denote this mean as $\overline{r_{u,f}}$);
- for each user u, trail i, subjective feature f, where u has not rated f of i, the system calculates the rating u would likely give to f of i as the weighted average of the ratings u has given to f of other trails (we denote the set of trails for which u has rated f as $R_{u,f}$), where weights are the adjusted-cosine similarities between i and the other trails for f (Equation 2).

$$AdjCosSim(i,j,f) = \frac{\sum_{u \in RB_{i,j,f}} \left(r_{u,i,f} - \overline{r_{u,f}}\right)\left(r_{u,j,f} - \overline{r_{u,f}}\right)}{\sqrt{\sum_{u \in RB_{i,j,f}} \left(r_{u,i,f} - \overline{r_{u,f}}\right)^2}\sqrt{\sum_{u \in RB_{i,j,f}} \left(r_{u,j,f} - \overline{r_{u,f}}\right)^2}}$$

(1)

$$PredRat(u,i,f) = \frac{\sum_{j \in R_{u,f}} AdjCosSim(i,j,f) \cdot r_{u,j,f}}{\sum_{j \in R_{u,f}} AdjCosSim(i,j,f)}$$

(2)

Applying this technique to Scenario 1 will produce the following results: since users who like trees are likely to give high ratings to the beauty of Trail T (and of other trails with beautiful trees), and users who instead prefer rivers are likely to give low ratings to the beauty of Trail T (and of other trails without rivers), the similarity among T and other trails with beautiful trees and no rivers for the beauty feature will be very high. As a result, the predicted rating of the beauty feature of Trail T for User 1 (who likes trees) will be strongly influenced by the ratings she gave to other trails with beautiful trees and so it is likely to be high. For User 2 (who likes rivers), the predicted rating of Trail T will be influenced by those she gave to other trails without rivers, and is likely to be low. Therefore, if both users query the system for a trail with the specified objective features and a high rating for beauty, recommended trails for User 1 will include Trail T, while recommendations for User 2 will not.

UD features, such as lap duration and difficulty, are strongly dependent on users' physical fitness. As a result, if a user looks for a trail with a particular value for one of these features in existing trail sharing systems, she may be misled by the shown value, since it may have been derived from content collected by users with completely different physical fitness. Consider the following scenario (Scenario 2): an untrained user (User 3) has shared a trail (Trail R) whose lap duration, as measured by her, is 25 minutes, and a well trained user (User 4) is looking for a trail with that particular lap duration. Since existing systems do not personalize recommendations based on users' physical fitness, the recommended trails for User 4 will include Trail R. However, since differently trained users are likely to take an amount of time inversely proportional to their physical fitness to complete a lap of the same trail, User 4 will likely be disappointed after trying Trail R, because she will have taken much less than the shown 25 minutes to complete a trail lap.

To adapt the values of UD features to the individual users, we applied the collaborative filtering technique also to information collected by means of sensors. However, while ratings of subjective features can be considered stable over time, values of UD features are likely to change even within a few months. For example, with appropriate training a user can increase her mean speed or exercise at a lower heart rate without reducing the speed. Therefore, the collaborative filtering technique, which would consider all the collected values, is not well suited for these features. To overcome this problem, we consider only the most recent trails for each user (last 6 months) in the computation of the similarities and the predicted values for UD features, and we invite users to share their information associated to each trail everytime they jog in it. As an additional benefit, regular update allows us to count how many times each user has jogged in each trail, so that we can compute the total number of visits for each trail and determine its popularity.

By applying collaborative filtering to UD features, recommendation in Scenario 2 changes as follows: the system considers lap durations of the same users in different trails to compute the adjusted cosine similarity for the lap duration feature among all the possible pair of trails. Then, the system predicts lap duration of Trail R for User 4 as the weighted average of the values measured for User 4 in similar trails, where weights are the adjusted cosine similarities for the lap duration feature. Since User 4 is more trained than User 3, lap durations measured by her in trails similar to Trail R are likely to be lower than 25 minutes, so predicted lap duration of Trail R for User 4 will be lower than 25 minutes as well. As a result, recommended trails for User 4 will not include Trail R, but other trails whose lap duration is well-suited to User 4's request and physical fitness.

To test the proposed technique, we developed a mobile application (Figure 1) to browse filtered content by specifying a range of values for each feature.

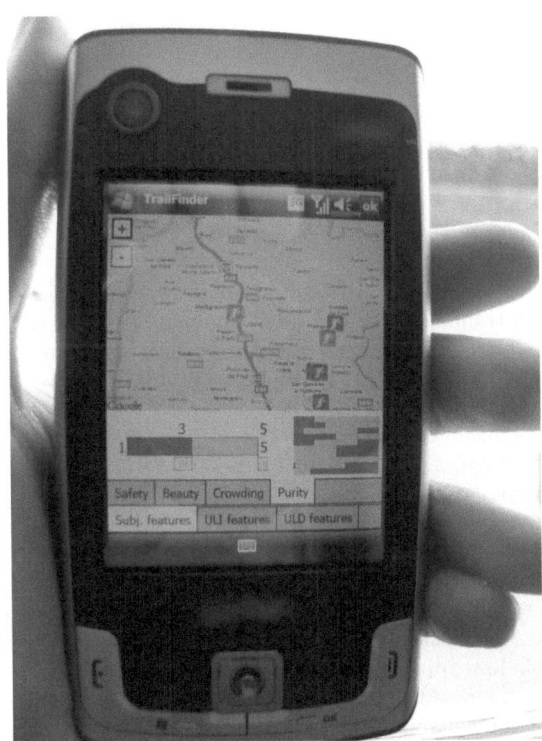

Fig. 1. The proposed mobile application to browse filtered content

3 Discussion and Future Work

As any collaborative filtering system, our system is affected by the cold start problem, i.e. users can be reluctant to share their content and give ratings, expecially during the initial phase after the deployment of the system. Once the system has collected enough content, the users who share more are rewarded with more tailored predictions for their untried trails, but during the initial phase the system may not be able to predict some feature values even for the users who have shared more. To motivate users to share their trails, we are integrating our proposal in a mobile fitness game to provide fun, training, and motivation, while generating content for the trail sharing system.

We will also extend our system to consider more context information. At present, the system filters the content by considering current location and collected information about heart rate and position. Moreover, it implicitly collects also timestamp information about the waypoints, that can be exploited to determine the season and the time of the day. Considering also current season and time of the day in the prediction of ratings will allow the system to further tailor the filtering of the content.

Acknowledgements

We acknowledge financial support from the Italian Ministry of Education, University and Research (MIUR) within the FIRB project number RBIN04M8S8.

References

1. Buttussi, F., Chittaro, L.: MOPET: A context-aware and user-adaptive wearable system for fitness training. Artificial Intelligence in Medicine 42(2), 153–163 (2008)
2. Nadalutti, D., Chittaro, L.: Visual analysis of users' performance data in fitness activities. Computers & Graphics 31(3), 429–439 (2007)
3. Nike, Inc.: Nike+ (2006),
   http://nikeplus.nike.com/nikeplus/index.jhtml?l=mapit
4. Huhtala, Y., Kaasinen, J.: Nokia Sports Tracker (2007),
   http://sportstracker.nokia.com/
5. Counts, S., Smith, M.: Where were we: communities for sharing space-time trails. In: GIS 2007: Proceedings of the 15th annual ACM international symposium on Advances in geographic information systems, pp. 1–8. ACM Press, New York (2007)
6. Schafer, J.B., Frankowski, D., Herlocker, J., Sen, S.: Collaborative filtering recommender systems. In: Brusilovsky, P., Kobsa, A., Nejdl, W. (eds.) Adaptive Web 2007. LNCS, vol. 4321, pp. 291–324. Springer, Heidelberg (2007)
7. Konstan, J.A., Miller, B.N., Maltz, D., Herlocker, J.L., Gordon, L.R., Riedl, J.: Grouplens: applying collaborative filtering to usenet news. Communications of the ACM 40(3), 77–87 (1997)
8. Sarwar, B., Karypis, G., Konstan, J., Reidl, J.: Item-based collaborative filtering recommendation algorithms. In: WWW 2001: Proceedings of the 10th international conference on World Wide Web, pp. 285–295. ACM Press, New York (2001)

Adaptive Clustering of Search Results

Xuehua Shen[1], ChengXiang Zhai[2], and Nicholas J. Belkin[3]

[1] Google Incorporation
[2] Department of Computer Science, University of Illinois at Urbana-Champaign
[3] School of Communication, Information and Library Studies, Rutgers University

Abstract. Clustering of search results has been shown to be advantageous over the simple list presentation of search results. However, in most clustering interfaces, the clusters are not adaptive to a user's interaction with the clustering results, and the important question "how to optimize the benefit of a clustering interface for a user" has not been well addressed in the previous work. In this paper, we study how to exploit a user's clickthrough information to adaptively reorganize the clustering results and help a user find the relevant information more quickly. We propose four strategies for adapting clustering results based on user actions. We propose a general method to simulate different kinds of users and linearize the cluster results so that we can compute regular retrieval measures. The simulation experiments show that the adaptation strategies have different performance for different types of users; in particular, they are effective for "smart users" who can correctly recognize the best clusters, but not effective for "dummy users" who follow system's ranking of results. We further conduct a user study on one of the four adaptive clustering strategies to see if an adaptive clustering system using such a strategy can bring users better search experience than a static clustering system. The results show that there is generally no significant difference between the two systems from a user's perspective.

1   Introduction

The main goal of a search engine is to rank relevant documents above non-relevant ones. There has been a lot of research in developing effective retrieval models to help achieve this goal. However, an equally important goal of a search engine is to present the search results effectively so that a user can find the relevant information from the results quickly. Indeed, most search engines present a ranked list of documents with brief summaries. However, due to the inevitable mismatches between a query and documents, the search results are more often non-optimal. It is quite common that a user may not find any relevant document among the top ranked ones. In such a case, the user would have to go through the many non-relevant documents in the list until eventually finding some relevant ones. Intuitively, a clustering view of the search results would be much more useful in such a case.

Clustering of search results has been shown to be an effective way to present the search results [7,2], and has been adopted by some search engines such as vivisimo [1]. Although clustering of search results has been studied, in most existing work, the clusters are generally not adaptive to a user's interaction with the clustering results. In

---

[1] http://vivisimo.com/

G.-J. Houben et al. (Eds.): UMAP 2009, LNCS 5535, pp. 447–453, 2009.

Scatter/Gather[1,3], the authors proposed that re-clustering can be performed on the user-selected clusters, which can be regarded as attempting to adapt the clustering results to a user. Unfortunately, this is as far as the work goes, and to the best of our knowledge, there has been no work that attempts to seriously study the important question "how to optimize the benefit of a clustering interface for a user." With non-adaptive clustered results, a user would generally select a cluster and examine the results in it. Thus the utility of the results is largely determined by the clustering algorithm. Intuitively, however, the clustering results may be improved as the system sees more user interactions when the user examines the results.

In this paper, we study how to exploit a user's clickthrough information, which is naturally available when a user is interacting with a clustering interface, to adaptively reorganize the clustering results and help a user find the relevant information more quickly. Specifically, we propose four strategies for adapting clustering results based on user actions, which are (1) reranking documents based on a selected cluster, (2) reranking documents based on a viewed document, (3) merging unselected clusters, and (4) promoting "near-miss" documents. Evaluation of the utility of a cluster presentation of results is a challenging task. We propose a general method to simulate different kinds of users and linearize the cluster results so that we can compute regular retrieval measures. The simulation experiments show that the adaptation strategies have different performance for different types of users; in particular, they are effective for "smart users" who can correctly recognize the best clusters, but not effective for "dummy users" who simply follow system's ranking of results. Among the four proposed adaptation strategies, the strategy of reranking based on viewed document is shown to be most effective, but other strategies are also beneficial. We further conduct a user study to see if an adaptive clustering system can bring improved search experience to users, compared with a static clustering system. We focus on the strategy of promoting near-miss documents. The results show that there is generally no significant difference between the two systems from a user's perspective. Specifically, more users say that they like the adaptive system better but users saved more relevant documents with the static interface than with the adaptive interface. Overall, our study shows that adaptive clustering has a good potential for improving search utility for users, but a user may not perceive any significant difference in the system.

2   Four Adaptive Strategies

We propose four strategies for adapting clustering results based on user actions, including reranking documents based on a selected cluster, reranking documents based on a viewed document, merging unselected clusters, and promoting "near-miss" documents.

The first is reranking based on cluster selection. When a user selects a cluster to view, we may infer that the user likes the selected cluster better than un-selected cluster(s). This information is exploited to improve the ranking of documents within a cluster. The information about the selected cluster can be combined with the original query to rerank documents in other (unselected) clusters.

The second is reranking based on document selection. When a user clicks on a document to view after selecting a cluster, the viewed document can presumably provide more information about what the user is interested in to the retrieval system and can thus be exploited to improve search results. The query will be updated with selected document and used to rerank the documents within each cluster.

The third is merging unselected clusters. When the user selects a cluster or views a document, the adaptive clustering algorithm can also restructure the clusters. In [1,3], the retrieval system merges several relevant clusters according to a user's selection. After seeing a user selecting a cluster, it would be reasonable to assume that the user may not be so interested in the partitioning of search results in other clusters. Thus, the retrieval system can merge all unselected clusters into a big cluster and put this big cluster below the selected cluster. Then according to the updated query, the retrieval system can rerank all the documents in the big cluster.

The fourth is promoting "near miss" documents. In this strategy, when the user clicks on a cluster, the adaptive clustering algorithm presents not only the documents in the clicked cluster to the user, but also some (borderline) documents which were originally scattered into unselected clusters. Specifically, the retrieval system would select those documents from each unselected cluster that are most similar to the updated query vector, and then insert these "near miss" documents into the bottom of the selected cluster.

The first and second strategies do not change the cluster structure while the third and fourth do.

3   Simulation Study

Following the use of the simulation strategy in some previous work [3,6], we also use the simulation strategy to evaluate the proposed adapatation strategies. But different from previous work, our simulation distinguishes two different types of extreme users. One is "smart users", who can always make intelligent decisions. Such a user would be assumed to always select the best cluster among several clusters according to the description of the cluster labels and always select a relevant document among a set of documents to view according to the snippet of each document. We simulate the interaction of the smart user as follows. We compute the percentage of relevant documents in each cluster, sort clusters according to the percentage of relevant documents in a cluster. We assume the smart user will select the top (also the best) cluster. We linearize or expand these clusters into a ranked list and evaluate the expanded ranked list with regular retrieval performance measures. We refer to the retrieval performance of this ranked list as the *smart baseline*. After a smart user selects the cluster with the highest percentage of relevant documents, the retrieval system can update the user's information need and rerank documents in each cluster. We evaluate the performance of the new ranked list and refer to the result as the *smart adaptive*. After the documents of the best cluster are presented, the smart user would select the best document in the best cluster to view. We simulate this behavior by selecting the top ranked *relevant* document in the best cluster. Immediately after the smart user selects the best document in the best cluster to view, the retrieval system will further update the user's information need and rerank documents in each cluster again. We refer to this result as the *smart reranking*. The other type of extreme users is "dummy users." A dummy user would always select top ranked cluster and top ranked document to view. Such a user would just passively follow a system's ranked result. In real web search, it is found that a user's behavior has a view bias and clickthrough can be biased according to the presented ranking order by a search engine. The user tends to view or click on documents from the top. As in the case of a smart user, we can also define *dummy baseline*, *dummy adaptive*, and *dummy reranking* similarly. In the real world, a user can be considered as a mixture of smart user and dummy user. We can use the probability of being smart user, which varies from 0.0 (dummy user) to 1.0 (smart user) to control the user interaction behavior.

We use TREC8 ad hoc track data set for empirical evaluation. For each query, we use vector space model to obtain baseline retrieval results. We then use K-Medoids clustering algorithm to cluster the top 100 documents into 6 clusters. We employ a *linearization* method to "convert" any clustering results into a *perceived* ranked list. In each cluster, the documents will be sorted by the retrieval scores. The idea is to simulate the perceived order of documents by a user when the user is browsing a clustering result. This way, we can evaluate a clustering result in the same way as evaluating a regular ranked list of result. We use the mean average precision (MAP), precision at 0.1 (pr@0.1) and 0.2 (pr@0.2) recall levels, and precision at top 10 (pr@10d) and 20 (pr@20d) documents as the evaluation metrics.

Table 1. Experiment Results of Simulation Study

Method	MAP	pr@0.1	pr@0.2	pr@10d	pr@20d
baseline	0.230	0.459	0.355	0.398	0.356
smart baseline	0.283	0.529	0.413	0.531	0.465
smart adaptive	0.282	0.559	0.418	0.539	0.470
smart reranking	0.294	0.580	0.428	0.551	0.467
dummy baseline	0.205	0.410	0.324	0.357	0.318
dummy adaptive	0.196	0.414	0.324	0.349	0.326
dummy reranking	0.202	0.418	0.331	0.353	0.320
regroup adaptive	0.261	0.557	0.401	0.533	0.45
regroup reranking	0.270	0.578	0.407	0.539	0.453
promotion adaptive (q)	0.282	0.561	0.421	0.537	0.457
promotion reranking (q)	0.293	0.583	0.434	0.545	0.460
promotion adaptive (q')	0.287	0.575	0.428	0.527	0.471
promotion reranking(q')	0.291	0.582	0.428	0.549	0.452

Row 3-8 of Table 1 shows the retrieval performance of the experiment results for two types of extreme users at different stages. We can see that for the smart user, the adaptive clustering strategy is effective and the performance of smart baseline is much better than that of baseline. For the smart user, smart reranking is apparently better than smart adaptive and smart baseline while smart adaptive has a better pr@10d than smart baseline does. For the dummy user, however, the adaptive clustering strategy appears to be ineffective. The dummy baseline is not as good as the baseline, which means clustering presentation is not effective for dummy users. Dummy adaptive and dummy reranking have similar performances to dummy baseline. Thus the adaptive clustering representation is generally not effective for the dummy user.

In the cluster regrouping strategy, when the smart user selects one cluster, we will merge other clusters into one cluster so that there will be only two clusters – the active cluster and the unopened cluster. Immediately after the smart user selects a cluster to view, the retrieval system will update the user's information need and use the updated query to rerank the documents in each cluster. We call this result the *regroup adaptive*. When the user selects the best document to view, we can then rerank the documents in each cluster; the corresponding result will be called *regroup reranking*. Row 9-10 of Table 1 shows the retrieval performance of regroup adaptive and regroup reranking. We find that the retrieval performance of regroup adaptive and regroup reranking is not as good as the corresponding smart adaptive and smart reranking.

When we apply the promotion strategy to select a subset of documents from clusters other than the best cluster, we can use the original query to rank and select documents. We can also use the updated query, which is interpolated with the best cluster term vector, to rank and select documents. We tried both queries to promote documents. We promote one document from each cluster other than the best cluster and append it to the bottom of the best cluster. Row 11-14 of Table 1 shows the experiment results using this near miss promotion strategy. We can see that promotion reranking consistently has better retrieval performance than the promotion adaptive strategy. The better performance of promotion reranking over promotion adaptive clearly comes from reranking documents based on the viewed document; this observation is consistent with what we observed in the performance comparison of smart adaptive and smart reranking.

4 User Study

We further conduct a user study by deploying two clustering systems to real users and study whether adaptive clustering strategy can bring better user experience in interacting with the search results than the static clustering strategy. Among the four adaptive clustering strategies, the strategy of promoting "near-miss" strategy has shown some promising results. Thus we use this strategy in the adaptive clustering system.

We implement the clustering result presentation functionality in the UCAIR toolbar [4], which is an Internet Explorer plugin. The adaptive clustering strategy is also implemented in the UCAIR toolbar. Thus we evaluate two systems with clustering result presentation, i.e. Adaptive System (AS) and Static System (SS). We randomly select 6 query topics from TREC8 ad-hoc track topics. After the subjects submit title query to UCAIR toolbar, the UCAIR toolbar will return clustered results to the user by clustering top ranked 100 documents from Google into 6 clusters. We use the centroid document to represent each cluster. Subjects browse clusters and click one cluster to view snippets of documents which belong to the selected cluster. Subjects browse document snippets and then click the most interesting one to view the content of the document. If it is relevant, subjects will save it on the local disk. After a pilot study, 24 subjects partcipated in the formal study.

We collect the exit questionnaires and compare two systems by overall experiences including difference of two systems, helpfulness of systems in completing tasks, easiness of learning to use, easiness of using, and overall preference. The results are listed

Table 2. Comparison of Overall Experience of Two Clustering systems

Comparison	AS is better	SS is better	No difference
Helpfulness	10	6	8
Easy to Learn	1	3	20
Easy to Use	7	2	15
Overall Preference	11	5	8

as Table 2. From Table 2, we can see that System AS is a little better than SS in the aspect of being helpful in completing tasks and easy to use. Both systems are equally easy to learn since their interface is nearly identical. For the overall preference, System AS seems to be better than System SS. However, there is no clear indication that System AS is better than System SS. For more detailed analysis of simulation study and user study, please refer to [5].

5   Conclusion and Future Work

In this work, we explore adaptive clustering presentation in interactive information retrieval and propose four adaptation strategies to improve clustering results based on a user's implicit feedback information. We propose a stochastic way to simulate a user's browsing behavior and propose a method for evaluating clustering results quantitatively based on user simulation. We evaluate the proposed adaptation algorithms with simulation experiments and show that adaptive clustering, especially reranking of documents based on viewed document is effective for smart users who would intelligently identify and view a high precision cluster and pick a relevant document to view, though such strategies are not effective for dummy users who simply follow a system's ranking of clusters and documents. We further conduct a user study to see if an adaptive clustering system can bring improved search utility and/or experience to users, compared with a static clustering system. The results show that there is generally no significant difference between the two systems from a user's perspective. Specifically, more users say that they like the adaptive system better but users saved more relevant documents with the static interface than with the adaptive interface. Overall, our study shows that adaptive clustering has a good potential for improving search utility for users, but a user may not perceive any significant difference in the system.

There are two particularly interesting directions to explore. One direction is to look into other factors to affect the user experience. Although the user study comparing one method of adaptive clustering to static clustering showed no significant user performance or preference differences, this could be due to a variety of factors which we were unable to investigate in this study. Such factors include suitability of the clustering technique to the specific retrieval task; combining user behavior evidence for ranking as well as clustering; and combining several adaptation strategies, rather than using only one. The other one is to do a larger-scale of user study with more topics and multiple iterations of interaction to draw more reliable conclusions.

References

1. Cutting, D.R., Pedersen, J.O., Karger, D., Tukey, J.W.: Scatter/gather: A cluster-based approach to browsing large document collections. In: Proceedings of SIGIR 1992, pp. 318–329 (1992)
2. Dumais, S.T., Cutrell, E., Chen, H.: Optimizing search by showing results in context. In: Proceedings of CHI 2001, pp. 277–284 (2001)
3. Hearst, M.A., Pedersen, J.O.: Reexamining the cluster hypothesis: Scatter/gather on retrieval results. In: Proceedings of SIGIR 1996, pp. 76–84 (1996)
4. Shen, X., Tan, B., Zhai, C.: Implicit user modeling for personalized search. In: Proceedings of CIKM 2005, pp. 824–831 (2005)
5. Shen, X., Zhai, C., Belkin, N.J.: Adaptive clustering of search results in interactive information retrieval. Technical report (2009)
6. White, R.W., Ruthven, I., Jose, J.M., van Rijsbergen, C.J.: Evaluating implicit feedback models using searcher simulations. ACM Transaction of Information System 23(3), 325–361 (2005)
7. Zamir, O., Etzioni, O.: Grouper: A dynamic clustering interface to web search results. In: Proceeding of WWW 1999 (1999)

What Do Academic Users Really Want from an Adaptive Learning System?*

Martin Harrigan[1], Miloš Kravčík[2], Christina Steiner[3], and Vincent Wade[1]

[1] Department of Computer Science, Trinity College Dublin, Ireland
{martin.harrigan,vincent.wade}@cs.tcd.ie
[2] Open Universiteit Nederland, The Netherlands
milos.kravcik@ou.nl
[3] Department of Psychology, University of Graz, Austria
chr.steiner@uni-graz.at

Abstract. When developing an *Adaptive Learning System* (ALS), users are generally consulted (if at all) towards the end of the development cycle. This can limit users' feedback to the characteristics and idiosyncrasies of the system at hand. It can be difficult to extrapolate principles and requirements, common to all ALSs, that are rated highly by users. To address this problem, we have elicited requirements from learners and teachers across several European academic institutions through explorative, semi-structured interviews [1]. The goal was to provide a methodology and an appropriate set of questions for conducting such interviews and to capture the essential requirements for the early iterations of an ALS design. In this paper we describe the methodology we employed while preparing, conducting, and analyzing the interviews and we present our findings along with objective and subjective analysis.

1   Introduction

The development of an *Adaptive Learning System* (ALS) is a challenging task [2, 3]. There exist many prototypical systems with domain-specific adaptive functionality. However, there is no established strategy for incorporating adaptivity in a system. This makes the process of requirements elicitation quite difficult. To address this problem, we have collected and aggregated the needs of users involved in higher education (learners and teachers) in a systematic form through interviews. Our approach is to illustrate the concept of adaptivity during the interviews through a hypothetical scenario involving a learner, a teacher (author and tutor), and a fully-functional ALS. A semi-structured interview allows the interviewees to evaluate an ALS's potential merits, short-comings and usefulness with respect to their individual needs.

Prototypical ALSs are often assessed through user evaluations during or after the system development stage [4, 5]. However, this can frame the user's evaluation; they comment on what has been developed and offer criticisms. Our

---

* This work was performed within the EU FP7 GRAPPLE (Generic Responsive Adaptive Personalized Learning Environment) Project.

G.-J. Houben et al. (Eds.): UMAP 2009, LNCS 5535, pp. 454–460, 2009.

hypothetical scenario is intentionally vague to promote a 'green fields approach'. It is the intention of this work to involve the users before any design or development commences and to later assess the utility of their input through user trials when a system is being developed. An accompanying technical report[1] provides an expanded version of the sections herein, including the full text of the *interview summaries*.

2   The Requirements Elicitation Methodology

Interviewees are first divided into three groups: learners, teachers, and others. An *interview guide and protocol* is produced and distributed to all interviewers to ensure consistency. The interviews are documented in two forms: *interview summaries* (having a narrative character) and *interview data sheets* (for quantitative and statistical analysis). The interview questions are both quantitative (closed questions with a predefined choice of answers) and qualitative (open-ended questions that try to gather information in an unbiased manner).

Before conducting the interviews, a hypothetical scenario involving a learner, a tutor, a content author, and a fully-functional ALS is distributed to the interviewees. The scenario illustrates typical and possible usage of an ALS. It provides the interviewees with a basic understanding of adaptivity. Respondents are encouraged to estimate the relevance of each use case to their own personal context and work. The technical report provides an example of one such scenario. We followed the above methodology when conducting the interviews reported below.

3   The Interviews

There were 27 interviews conducted in June 2008 across seven European institutions (see Table 1). The sample size was predominantly due to the data collection instrument and the involved effort.

Table 1. Summary of the interviews

	Learner	Teacher	Other	Total
Open Universiteit Nederland	2	6	2	10
Technische Universiteit Eindhoven	0	4	0	4
Trinity College Dublin	1	2	0	3
Università della Svizzera Italiana	1	2	0	3
Universität Graz	2	1	0	3
University of Warwick	1	1	0	2
Vrije Universiteit Brussel	1	1	0	2
Total	8	17	2	27

---

[1] https://www.cs.tcd.ie/publications/tech-reports/reports.09/TCD-CS-2009-06.pdf

3.1   Current Usage of Learning Systems

The first section of the interview gauged the current usage of learning systems and ALSs by the interviewees.

A1. Do you use any learning systems? Out of 27 interviewees, 25 were using or had used learning systems. All of the teachers had experience with learning systems. Only two learners indicated that they had no experience. Questions A2-A5 were answered by the 25 interviewees with experience; the remaining questions, unless otherwise indicated, were answered by all 27.

A2. Which learning systems have you used? This was an open-ended question; we did not provide a list of learning systems to choose from. In the case of customized or heavily modified systems, we grouped these under the category 'in-house'. Other than in-house systems, `Moodle` and `Blackboard` were the most popular learning systems (see Table 2). We note that the most popular Open-Source and commercial LMSs feature. This question also provided us with information as regards the number of learning systems in use by each interviewee. On average, each interviewee used two learning systems (`mean` = 2.04, `s.d.` = 1.26). Teachers indicated that they use significantly more learning systems ($t(23) = 2.699$, $p = 0.013$), with teachers listing on average 2.5 (`s.d.` = 2.47) systems and learners listing on average 1.1 (`s.d.` = 0.9) learning systems.

Table 2. The learning systems used by interviewees (in descending order by use)

In-House	13
Moodle	12
Blackboard	9
Sakai	3
WebCT	3
Others (AHA!, ALEKS, Dokeos, Educativa, Ilias)	6

A3. How often do you use a learning system? The majority of the teachers used learning systems daily or once to several times a week, whereas learners used them less frequently.

A4. How long have you been using learning systems? The teachers had long-term experience in using learning systems (13 had many years' experience, 3 had one year's experience, and 1 had several months' experience), whereas learners had considerably less (only 1 has many years' experience, 2 has one year's experience, and 3 had several months' experience).

A5. Do the learning systems you have used so far provide any adaptive features to users? The responses to this question show that the majority of learning systems have no adaptive features (`no` = 15, `yes` = 10). The weak support of adaptation by Open Source and commercial LMSs has been confirmed in the literature [6].

3.2   Adaptivity – Needs and Preferences

The second section of the interview focused more on adaptivity and the purposes and benefits of an ALS (whether the interviewee had previously used one or not).

B1. What do you think are the purposes or tasks for which an ALS is especially suited? Table 3 summarizes the results. The top two answers were individualized teaching and guided, individualized learning. These can be considered the same, but from opposing viewpoints, *i.e.* the teachers' and learners'.

Table 3. The top seven purposes or tasks for which ALSs are especially suited (in descending order by the number of interviewees who said so)

Individualized Teaching	6
Guided and Individualized Learning	5
Details of Technical Material	4
Clearly Defined Knowledge Domains	2
Identification of Strengths and Weaknesses in a Learner	2
Monitoring	2
Procedural and Vocational Training	2

B2. What are the benefits of using an ALS? Do you think adaptivity in a learning system brings added value to the user? The results are summarized in Table 4.

Table 4. The top seven benefits of ALSs (in descending order by the number of interviewees who said so)

Efficiency	11
User Specificity	9
Relevant Learning Material	4
Personalization	3
Re-Usability	3
Learner Motivation	3
Avoids Information and Cognitive Overload	2

B3/B4. I list features that are reported in the literature to function as sources of adaptation, i.e. characteristics of the learner or environment that may be considered by an ALS when adapting to the individual learner. Please indicate your opinion on the importance of adaptation to each of these features on a scale from 1 to 10 (1 being unimportant and 10 being very important). The listed features and the results are shown in Table 5. All adaptation criteria were judged quite important; each criterion reached at least a mean importance of 5. The criteria judged to be the most important were adaptation to learner knowledge (mean = 8.85, s.d. = 1.19) and adaptation to learning goals and tasks (mean = 8.7, s.d. = 1.82). A correlation analysis showed that the judgment of learner knowledge is highly correlated with learning goals and tasks ($r = 0.606$, $p = 0.001$), and features medium correlations with language, learner qualifications, user role, background, and experience in the hyperspace. The importance rating of learner knowledge was not correlated with any other criterion. The least importantly judged aspects, although still characterized by a mean importance of about 5, were background (mean = 5.3, s.d. = 2.37), learner personality (mean = 5.07, s.d. = 2.37), and experience in the hyperspace (mean = 5.0, s.d. = 2.56).

Table 5. Specific features of adaptivity as rated by the interviewees (in descending order by mean ratings)

	No.	Min.	Max.	Mean	S.D.
Learner Knowledge	26	6	10	8.85	1.190
Learning Goals and Tasks	27	4	10	8.70	1.815
Language	26	5	10	7.96	1.455
Platform	26	3	10	7.77	1.583
Interests	27	2	10	7.22	2.136
Learning and Cognitive Style	27	2	10	7.19	2.403
Learner Qualifications	26	3	10	7.15	1.974
User Role	27	1	10	7.00	2.370
Motivation	27	1	10	6.96	2.682
Learner Preferences	27	1	10	6.26	2.474
Location	27	1	10	6.04	2.361
Background	27	1	10	5.30	2.367
Learner Personality	27	1	8	5.07	2.368
Experience in Hyperspace	26	1	10	5.00	2.561

B5/B6. I list dimensions that can be the subject of adaptation, i.e. methods and techniques that may be used for adapting the learning process to the individual learner. Please indicate your opinion on the importance of each of these dimensions on a scale from 1 to 10 (1 being unimportant and 10 being very important). The list of dimensions and the results are shown in Table 6. As was the case for the features of adaptivity, all the dimensions have quite high ratings, with minimum means between 5 and 6. The dimensions judged to be most important were learning activity selection (mean = 8.37, s.d. = 2.02) and content selection (mean = 8.33, s.d. = 2.25) in general – and within this dimension, the techniques of additional explanations (mean = 8.37, s.d. = 1.04) and prerequisite explanations (mean = 8.19, s.d. = 1.98). Furthermore, adaptive testing (mean = 8.22, s.d. = 1.63) was considered very important. The dimensions judged to be least important, but still featuring a medium mean importance score, were hiding (mean = 5.22, s.d. = 2.55) and service provision (mean = 5.85, s.d. = 2.71). Hiding is less popular and desirable in comparison with other techniques within adaptive navigation support. The learner is deprived of information in this way, which was explicitly criticized by some interviewees.

Table 6. Specific dimensions of adaptivity as rated by the interviewees (in descending order by category mean ratings (bold terms) and then individual mean ratings)

	No.	Min.	Max.	Mean	S.D.
Learning Activity Selection	27	1	10	8.37	2.022
Content Selection	27	1	10	8.33	2.253
Additional Explanations	27	7	10	8.37	1.043
Prerequisite Explanations	27	1	10	8.19	1.981
Comparative Explanations	27	5	10	7.56	1.121
Explanation Variants	27	5	10	7.44	1.625
Sorting	27	1	10	7.26	2.177
Problem Solving Support	27	5	10	7.93	1.299
Intelligent Analysis of Solutions	27	5	10	7.74	1.631
Example-Based Problem Solving	27	3	10	7.67	1.687
Interactive Problem Solving Support	27	3	10	7.37	1.822
Assessment	27	1	10	7.89	2.082
Testing	27	3	10	8.22	1.625
Questions	27	1	10	6.52	2.376
Learner Model Matching	27	1	10	7.56	1.888
Collaboration Support	27	3	10	7.78	1.805
Intelligent Class Monitoring	27	6	10	7.70	0.953
Presentation	27	1	10	7.52	2.242
Multimedia Presentation	27	1	10	7.41	2.635
Text Presentation	27	1	10	6.81	1.882
Customization of the Interface	27	1	10	6.63	2.041
Navigation Support	27	1	10	7.33	2.760
Link Generation	27	1	10	7.56	2.225
Sorting	27	1	10	7.04	2.488
Link Annotation	27	1	10	7.00	2.000
Map Annotation	27	1	10	6.96	2.244
Direct Guidance	27	1	10	6.70	2.267
Hiding	27	1	10	5.22	2.547
Service Provision	27	1	10	5.85	2.713

4 Analysis and Conclusions

The views of our interviewees, comprising learners, teachers and others (researchers and developers) can be summarized as follows. They require an ALS that provides individualized teaching and learning. In particular, it should be capable of providing details of technical material that cannot be covered adequately in a class or lecture. They expect such a system to be efficient with respect to the learners, tutors and authors, by providing users with relevant learning material. Table 5 and Table 6 provide a 'most-wanted' list of specific features and dimensions of adaptivity as ordered by their mean ratings.

In addition, ALSs are considered particularly suited to well explored and structured content. However, this is only one part of what a learner needs to learn.

They must also learn more abstract and complex competencies, *e.g.* social and relational skills, creative problem solving (where the 'correct' or 'best' solution is possibly unknown), independent critical thinking, etc. The interviewees propose some areas where an ALS can add value in the academic context: the acquisition of basic knowledge, the acquisition of technical details that are too cumbersome to cover in lectures and classes, adaptive testing of basic knowledge, and language skills. Many interviewees insist that learners should be made aware of the adaptation; they should be able to set adaptation parameters and always feel in control. There is also a potential conflict between a learner's preferred learning style and an optimal learning strategy. It appears to be a delicate trade-off between pleasing the learner and doing what's best for them from a pedagogical standpoint. The accompanying technical report draws some more subjective conclusions from specific remarks and suggestions made by the interviewees.

References

[1] Goguen, J., Linde, C.: Techniques for Requirements Elicitation. In: Proceedings of IEEE International Symposium on Requirements Engineering (RE 1993), pp. 152–164 (1993)
[2] Frosch-Wilke, D., Sanchez-Alonso, S.: Composing Adaptive Learning Systems. In: Proceedings of the 6th IEEE International Conference on Advanced Learning Technologies (ICALT 2006), pp. 360–362. IEEE Computer Society, Los Alamitos (2006)
[3] Tseng, J., Chu, H., Hwang, G., Tsai, C.: Development of an Adaptive Learning System with Two Sources of Personalization Information. Computers and Education 51(2), 776–786 (2008)
[4] Ortigosa, A., Carro, R.: The Continuous Empirical Evaluation Approach: Evaluating Adaptive Web-Based Courses. In: Brusilovsky, P., Corbett, A.T., de Rosis, F. (eds.) UM 2003. LNCS, vol. 2702, p. 146. Springer, Heidelberg (2003)
[5] Paramythis, A., Weibelzahl, S.: A Decomposition Model for the Layered Evaluation of Interactive Adaptive Systems. In: Ardissono, L., Brna, P., Mitrović, A. (eds.) UM 2005. LNCS, vol. 3538, pp. 438–442. Springer, Heidelberg (2005)
[6] Hauger, D., Köck, M.: State of the Art of Adaptivity in E-Learning Platforms. In: Workshop Adaptivität und Benutzermodellierung in interactiven Systemen, ABIS 2007 (2007)

How Users Perceive and Appraise Personalized Recommendations

Nicolas Jones[1], Pearl Pu[1], and Li Chen[2]

[1] Human Computer Interaction Group, Swiss Federal Institute of Technology
{nicolas.jones,pearl.pu}@epfl.ch
[2] Department of Computer Science, Hong Kong Baptist University
lichen@comp.hkbu.edu.hk

Abstract. Traditional websites have long relied on users revealing their preferences explicitly through direct manipulation interfaces. However recent recommender systems have gone as far as using implicit feedback indicators to *understand* users' interests. More than a decade after the emergence of recommender systems, the question whether users prefer them compared to stating their preferences explicitly, largely remains a subject of study. Even though some studies were found on users' acceptance and perceptions of this technology, these were general marketing-oriented surveys. In this paper we report an in-depth user study comparing Amazon's implicit book recommender with a baseline model of explicit search and browse. We address not only the question "do people accept recommender systems" but also how or under what circumstances they do and more importantly, what can still be improved.

1 Introduction and Related Work

Twenty years ago, the classical buying-scheme was that when a user entered a shop, a knowledgeable seller would be available to advise and inform him/her on products. With the emergence of the Internet, online shops started to appear, proposing interfaces where the users had a high level of control, and where actions triggered predictable results. Classical interface have allowed people to express their preferences by browsing along a set of well defined categories. For Books these might be poems, romance or thriller. In addition search tools rapidly appeared allowing users to more quickly navigate to their target items. Later on, recommender systems (RS) were introduced, often relying on explicitly expressed ratings of items. More recently, there has been a lot of research on indirect ways for users to reveal their preferences (e.g. through their purchase history), paving the way to behavioral recommenders. This difference from search & browse to today's behavioral recommenders follows very well a more general and long standing debate, central to the UM community, about automation and direct manipulation which was voiced in [11]: to what extent should users give up control of their interaction with interfaces in favor of depending on intelligent "agents" that learn the likes and dislikes of a user?

In this paper we compare traditional user-controlled interfaces with more recent personalized systems using recommendations. A lot of research has been done on ways for users to reveal their preferences, and experiments such as [10] suggest that when users

G.-J. Houben et al. (Eds.): UMAP 2009, LNCS 5535, pp. 461–466, 2009.

implicitly give feedback, the performance of the RS can be close to the more traditional ones using explicit feedback. But the work is highly incremental and there are no studies directly comparing both extremes. For these reasons, we decided to evaluate how recommendations based on *implicit preference feedback* compare with results provided to users who explicitly reveal their preferences in a traditional *user controlled* way. We chose to conduct this study on Amazon.com [1] and set up a comparative between-group user-study where users were instructed to search for five books. One group of users tested Amazon without the benefit of the RS, by searching and browsing. This represented the baseline measure for the experiment. Two other groups tested Amazon's recommendations which were based on their past purchase history. One group had a small purchase history whereas the second group had a larger profile. The experiment was conducted online and users' opinions were collected through a post-study assessment questionnaire, evaluating multiple dimensions from satisfaction to intention to return.

2   Background and Related Work

In content-based recommenders, users specify their needs explicitly in terms of content or features [8]. Similarly, in user involved RS, ratings are used to determine like-minded users through collaborative filtering. More recently, unit or compound critiquing techniques, rather than single valued ratings, were proposed to improve accuracy [2]. Such direct feedback is the most common interest indicator, offering a fairly precise way to measure users' preferences, but suffers from several drawbacks [3]. These include the fact that a user must stop to enter explicit ratings, which alters browsing and reading patterns. Users may not be very motivated to provide ratings unless this effort is perceived to be beneficial [9], or because the user might not yet know his preferences as he just started to use the system, and often changes them in different contexts [6,8].

In behavior based RS, a user's purchase history or his reading time on a page can be used to infer interests and preferences. In Nichols' seminal paper on implicit rating and filtering [7], he identifies several types of data that can implicitly capture a user's interest, including past purchases, repeated uses, and decisive actions (printing, marking, examining). Since then, several of these indicators have been used like in [10] where Shapira et al. showed that mouse movements normalized by reading time were a good preference indicator, or as in [3] where the time spent on a page is shown as a potentially good indicator. Unfortunately, research work measuring the progress of RS, with few exceptions, has concentrated on improving the accuracy of algorithms, the most common metric being the mean average error (MAE) [5]. The earliest paper evaluating six RS in depth, with real users is [12] where the central concern was to compare the performance and acceptance of such systems against human recommenders (friends). A recent marketing survey [1] reported that consumers strongly preferred sites that provide personalized product recommendations, with 45% claiming that they are more likely to shop at sites with personalized recommendations than at sites without them.

Our work is the first significant in-depth user study that reports on the users' perceptions of today's behavioral recommender systems compared to classical search & browse patterns.

---

[1] We chose Amazon because it has a well-established RS; we have no affiliation with Amazon.

3   Hypotheses

We established three simple hypotheses. First, we expected that, when a user just starts using a website, a user-controlled solution would be more effective at supporting his information needs than an indirect one. If a user has a small purchase history, for example, there is perhaps not enough information to infer his preferences, most certainly resulting in an inadequate recommendation. We thus propose hypothesis H1. Second, we considered how recommendation quality might evolve. When a user controls a search, he may only cover a specific subset of all his preferences, whereas information gathered over time gives a much broader view of these preferences. We highlight this with hypothesis H2 where we fix an arbitrary cut-off level of twenty books. Finally, since an indirect profile should cover multiple aspects of a user's real profile, we hypothesized H3.

H1 for users with a small profile size, search & browse should provide higher recommendation accuracy than indirect feedback.

H2 there exists a profile size as of which indirect feedback should propose a better accuracy than the baseline explicit elicitation.

H3 non-expert users are likely, overall, to significantly benefit from recommendations based on indirect feedback.

4   Real-User Evaluation

The experiment was limited to the domain of *books*. We designed a between-group experiment of three user groups, with 20 users in each: the baseline search & browse group, and two recommendation-receiving groups with small and big purchase profiles respectively. All users were told to find five books to purchase, similar to what they would do on the real website.

4.1   Evaluation Setup and Procedure

We implemented a user study with a wizard-like online web application containing all the instructions, interfaces and questionnaires so that subjects could remotely participate in the in-depth evaluation. The general procedure consists of the following steps.

Step 1. Based on how many books a participant bought in the past on *Amazon* (profile size), he is oriented to the adequate experiment (baseline or recommendations).

Step 2. Basic background information is collected (gender, age, etc.)

Step 3. After reading a brief scenario, the user is given detailed instructions: The tester of the *search & browse* interface is instructed to go to *Amazon.com*, make sure he is not logged in, and then to browse through the available categories of literature, until he finds a book which he likes. The tester of the *implicit RS* system is asked to head to *Amazon.com* and log in to his account. He is then asked to go the "my recommendations" section and to navigate through the book section of the recommendations until he finds a book that he likes.

Step 4. The user starts the experiment. He is asked to select *five* books; for each one, he must fill in a template-questionnaire allowing him to rate the book on the spot.

Step 5. To conclude the study, the user is asked to complete a nine questions assessment questionnaire to evaluate the system he has just tested.

4.2   Measured Variables

All questions in this study are statements to which a user can indicate his level of agreement on a five-point Likert scale, ranging from -2 (strongly disagree) to $+2$ (strongly agree); 0 is neutral. Not having access to Amazon's interaction logs, we recorded users' opinion about the recommendation quality through a template, immediately after selecting each book (novelty, appreciation, intention to buy). Then, once five books had been selected, an overall appreciation was recorded through a set of nine questions, measuring *experience* (satisfaction, effort, trust, confidence, novelty, diversity) and *decision* (acceptance of a recommended book, future usage, sharing with friends). Because of the setup of the experiment, each question was adapted into two variants such as to differentiate between the baseline and recommendation experiments, but tested identical dimensions.

4.3   Participants

The user study was carried out over a period of three weeks and an incentive was proposed. The study was taken by off-campus users (half of the participants), students (7%) and academic researchers in Switzerland. The study collected 60 users, resulting in a sample size of twenty participants per group. There were 17 female and 43 male, with 66% being aged between 25 and 30; 18% were younger, and 15% older. The group of *baseline* users showed slightly less familiarity with Amazon as 25% more users disagreed that they "read a lot of books", and 30% of them had never surfed on Amazon before. We accepted this potential bias as such users have a fresh view of Amazon, less influenced by the evolution of the site.

5   Evaluation Results

Results are reported in Figure 1. An Anova analysis showed that five questions conveyed statistically significant different averages across all three groups of users. The question S2 shows an increase in results from *baseline* elicitation to *recommendation* users with a large profile, who found that the system required less effort (with an average of 1). The *recommendation* users with a small profile scored 0.6 on average. The difference between all three groups is significant ($p = 0.02$). S5, the question on trust, shows the same general tendency, albeit a smaller increase between the first two groups (significant, $p = 0.05$). S3, the confidence about making the best choice, presents a *baseline* average around 0.5 and one of -0.5 for the *recommendation* small group, with the *recommendation* big being amid (significant, $p = 0.02$). Diversity S4 shows a very similar pattern, but with an increased score from the *baseline* users, around 1 (significant, $p < 0.01$). One of the template questions also shows a significant difference: T3, the intention to buy where the *recommendation* small is much lower than both other groups ($p = 0.04$).

For S1, satisfaction, the 0.5 difference between the first two groups is significant ($p = 0.02$). T2, on perceived accuracy, gives much higher averages around 1.0, with a significant difference (t-test, $p = 0.02$) between the two *recommendation* groups. Finally, the special question for *recommendation* users about them having "already used"

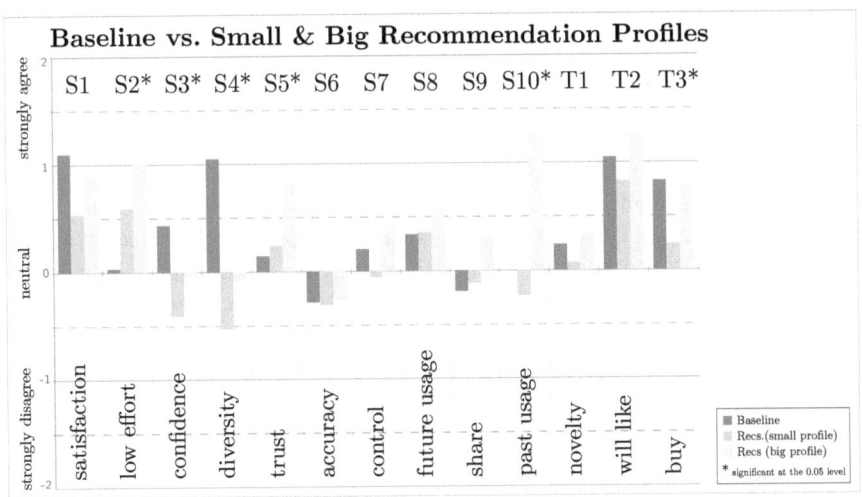

Fig. 1. Detailed Graph of Users' Preferences

this recommendation feature showed S10 the expected trend with a score close to 0 for the *recommendation* small group, and above 1 for the *recommendation* big group (significant, p < 0.01). These results reveal that although a recommender interface provides users with an overall satisfaction and perceived benefits like a lower effort required, most users have to wait until their profile reaches a certain size to enjoy the full benefits.

6   Discussion and Conclusions

Through our hypotheses H1 and H2, we predicted that at first a controlled search would be more accurate but that this would rapidly change, seeing the accuracy of recommendations increase with the profile size. The direct assessments of perceived accuracy, S6 and T2, are not strongly conclusive. This twist-and-turn between hypotheses and results is surprising. However, we would like to point out that if "accuracy" does *not* reveal itself as imagined, other dimensions *do* demonstrate some parallels with the predictions. Elements like confidence and diversity, show us that search & browse methods are more efficient at the beginning, but that larger recommendation profiles actually start to catch up. Nevertheless, and this brings us to H3, there are not many measures where an implicit large profile strongly beats an explicit one (only trust S5 and low effort S2).

The results point out that the two types of interface mechanisms being compared can provide quite similar overall satisfaction for the users. The difference in the amount of effort required to operate in both systems is highly noticed by users, and clearly in favor of the RS (which required lower effort). On the other hand, users clearly found the *baseline* as proposing a much more diverse set of books, which is problematic for the recommender engine. It is also disappointing to see such low scores for the novelty (T1) from the recommender. Measures of confidence show that users are more confident about their choices in the search & browse scheme. However, people are trusting the system's implicitly generated recommendations, as soon as their profile reaches a certain size, which is encouraging. This was further reflected in users' comments. When compared to books that friends might have proposed, neither methods were perceived as being very accurate; nevertheless users' opinions were positive as in all groups they thought they would like the five selected books. Contrary to purchase intentions, decision variables about future usage of the system or introduction to a friend, were not very high on average, but all three showed good correlations with satisfaction.

A decade has passed since the recommender technology was invented [4]. Today's systems based on this technology are in the mainstream practice of e-commerce and social websites. Even though some surveys demonstrate that acceptance and perception of this technology are showing good sings, we should not take them for granted. Our paper demonstrates that investigating users issues pays off, and that several traditional problems remain unsolved. It gives a clear idea how to improve the current technology and points out design guidelines. Additionally, the challenge of motivating initial users until they build a large profile (hence user loyalty) remains.

References

1. Choicestream personalization survey (2007), http://www.choicestream.com/
2. Chen, L., Pu, P.: Evaluating critiquing-based recommender agents. In: AAAI (2006)
3. Claypool, M., Claypool, M., Brown, D., Brown, D., Le, P., Le, P., Waseda, M., Waseda, M.: Inferring user interest. IEEE Internet Computing 5, 32–39 (2001)
4. Goldberg, D., Nichols, D., Oki, B.M., Terry, D.: Using collaborative filtering to weave an information tapestry. Communications of the ACM 35, 61–70 (1992)
5. Herlocker, J.L., Konstan, J.A., Terveen, L.G., Riedl, J.T.: Evaluating collaborative filtering recommender systems. ACM Trans. Inf. Syst. 22(1), 5–53 (2004)
6. Keeney, R.L., Raiffa, H.: Decisions with Multiple Objectives: Preferences and Value Trade-offs. Wiley series in probability and mathematical statistics. John Wiley & Sons, Inc., New York (1976)
7. Nichols, D.M.: Implicit rating and filtering. In: Proceedings of the Fifth DELOS Workshop on Filtering and Collaborative Filtering, pp. 31–36 (1997)
8. Pu, P., Chen, L.: User-involved preference elicitation for product search and recommender systems. AI Magazine 29(4), 93–103 (2008)
9. Resnick, P., Iacovou, N., Suchak, M., Bergstorm, P., Riedl, J.: GroupLens: An Open Architecture for Collaborative Filtering of Netnews. In: Proc. of ACM CSCW 2004, pp. 175–186. ACM, New York (2004)
10. Shapira, B., Taieb-Maimon, M., Moskowitz, A.: Study of the usefulness of known and new implicit indicators and their optimal combination for accurate inference of users interests. In: SAC 2006, ACM, New York (2006)
11. Shneiderman, B., Maes, P.: Direct manipulation vs. interface agents. Interactions 4, 6 (1997)
12. Swearingen, K., Sinha, R.: Beyond algorithms: An hci perspective on recommender systems (2001)

Towards Web Usability: Providing Web Contents According to the Readers Contexts

Mohanad Al-Jabari[1,*], Michael Mrissa[2], and Philippe Thiran[1]

[1] PReCISE Research Center, University of Namur, Belgium
[2] SOC Research Team, LIRIS, University of Lyon 1, France

Abstract. Web usability has been considered as a key issue to the success of the Web. However, Web readers typically face difficulties since Web pages are presented according to the local contexts of Web authors. Web authors and readers follow their own local contexts to represent and interpret Web contents as they originate from different communities. Hence, there is a need to transform Web contents created according to the authors' contexts into the different contexts of their readers.

In this paper, we aim at presenting a solution that provides Web contents according to the reader's context. Our solution is based on an explicit representation of the authors' and readers' local contexts. We rely on RDFa to annotate contents with the author's context and we provide an adaptation process on the client-side that generates contextualized Web contents according to the readers' contexts. We validate our approach through a Firefox extension.

1   Introduction

Recently, the Web has successfully evolved into a "semantic" Web, where *Web authors* can describe Web contents with semantic information such that software applications (e.g., Web browser) can interpret them and hence handle *Web readers'* requests more effectively. For instance, a Web author may describe Web contents such as *events* with semantic information such as *starting date* and *ending date, location*, etc. Accordingly, a reader application can search, aggregate, or export any events with respect to a specific day or a location.

Open Data in XHTML is a bottom-up approach towards the semantic Web (called small-s semantic Web). small-s reuses the current Web as it is and relies on the authors to annotate their contents with semantic metadata, so that the former become machine interpretable. In this field, the main emerging technologies are RDFa and microformats [10]. Our previous work concluded that microformats are inextensible as they propose a finite set of specifications [8].

RDFa provides an abstract solution that aims at expressing RDF statements in XHTML documents. More precisely, RDFa provides a collection of XHTML attributes (reuses existing attributes such as *content* and *rel* and introduces new ones such as *about* and *property*) to embed RDF statements in XHTML, and provides processing rules to extract these statements.

---

* Supported in part by the Programme for Palestinian European Academic Cooperation in Education (PEACE).

G.-J. Houben et al. (Eds.): UMAP 2009, LNCS 5535, pp. 467–473, 2009.

1.1   Web Usability and Local Context

The evolution of the Web raises new challenges, notably regarding *Web usability*. Our understanding of Web usability is derived from the ISO 9241-110:2006[1] specification. Web usability is defined as the effectiveness, efficiency, and satisfaction of the interaction between Web readers and Web pages. *Effectiveness* refers to the extent Web readers interpret Web contents accurately and completely. *Efficiency* refers to the efforts expended (e.g., time) to interpret Web contents effectively. *Satisfaction* refers to the readers' acceptance of the interaction.

In this sense, interactions between Web readers and Web contents are typically ineffective and inefficient. Indeed, authors and readers of Web contents originate from different communities. Web authors follow their local contexts for representing Web contents. This leads to an additional effort for the readers as they need to interpret these contents according to their own local contexts.

By *local context*, we mean a set of common knowledge shared by members of a community [11,2], like common language and common local or cultural conventions, such as measurement units, keyboard configurations and notational standards for writing time, dates, numbers, currency, etc. For instance, let us assume a French reader who needs to register to a summer school course on a Web site which is authored by a British author. In this context, the course price is in British Pound and follows the British currency format (e.g.: 1,234.50). As the French currency is Euro and uses a different format (e.g.: 1 234,50), the course price must be converted from British Pound to French Euro by the reader. Note that the situation can be even worse as the reader can misinterpret the attendance date of the course. For example, he could interpret the attendance date (e.g.: 07/08/2008) as the 7th of August 2008 (following the French format) instead of the 8th of July 2008 (following the British format).

1.2   Objectives

To enhance Web usability, we aim at resolving semantic discrepancies between contexts of Web authors and readers and at adapting context-sensitive contents (called adaptable Web contents) according to readers' contexts.

This paper is structured as follows. Section 2 presents our approach to annotate adaptable Web contents with authors' contexts and adapt them to readers' contexts. Section 3 discusses related works and Section 4 concludes the paper.

2   A Semantic Context-Based Approach with RDFa

This paper proposes a semantic context-based approach that relies on RDFa to annotate and adapt Web contents. This approach firstly introduces a set of adaptable concepts and a set of contextual attributes to specify the semantics of adaptable Web contents and the local contexts of Web authors and Web readers, respectively. Secondly, it exploits the idea of *semantic object*, which was detailed

---

[1] http://www.iso.org/

in [9], to represent adaptable Web contents together with adaptable concepts and contextual attributes. Thirdly, it takes advantages of RDFa technology to annotate adaptable Web contents with these metadata. Finally, we propose an adaptation process implemented as a Firefox extension. This extension adapts the semantic objects according to the readers' contexts.

2.1 Adaptable Concepts and Contextual Attributes

This section distinguishes between adaptable and non-adaptable Web contents. Adaptable Web contents refer to the contents that might be represented and interpreted differently from different authors and readers, according to their local contexts. In order to specify the semantics of adaptable Web contents, we identified in our previous work a list of adaptable concepts [8]. These concepts address the main concerns that rose up from our experience while browsing the Web. Here are some examples:

- **Date/time** are described in different formats, styles, and different time zones according to the user's language and country.
- **Price** are expressed in different formats, currencies[2], VAT rates, etc.
- **Measure units** are used to quantify the values of physical quantities (e.g., weight and length). Countries use different measure systems (e.g., Imperial and Metric systems), different unit prefixes, and different error percentages.
- **Telephone number** identifies telephone endpoint. Based on ITU[3] plan *E*.164, each country has a different *international call prefix* and *country calling code*. Also, each country uses a different telephone number format.

For these concepts, we propose a context ontology that attempts to identify a set of contextual attributes. These attributes make explicit the contexts of Web authors and Web readers. We do not aim at identifying an exhaustive list of contextual attributes, but we try to address the needs of the above adaptable concepts. In this sense, contextual attributes are mainly grouped into two broad categories: *country* and *language*. Each country has a set of local conventions such as currency, value added tax, measure system, etc. Also, each country has many cities, sometimes located in different timezones. The language attribute specifies the local natural language. One country may have one or more communities (e.g., French and Dutch speaking communities in Belgium). Each community usually uses a common natural language and a set of conventions related to that community (e.g., writing formats). Fig. 1 presents an excerpt of the proposed context ontology[4].

2.2 Semantic Object

In [9], *semantic objects* are used to annotate data objects exchanged between Web services with semantic metadata so that it enables automatic data mediation during Web service composition. In our approach, we use our own definition

---

[2] See ISO 4217 for used currency list.
[3] International Telecommunication Union: `http://www.itu.int/`
[4] Context ontology is designed using TopBraid composer[TM] modeling environment.

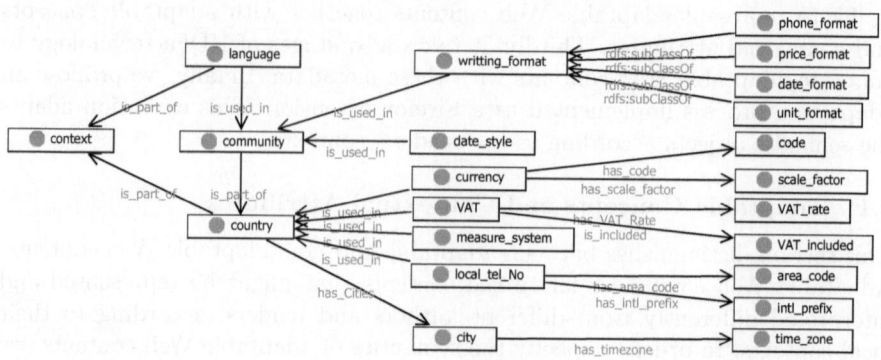

Fig. 1. An excerpt of the Context Ontology

of *semantic object* to annotate adaptable Web contents with a semantic concept and one or more contextual attributes to support automatic adaptation. A semantic object *SemObj* is a 3- tuple represented as follows:

$$SemObj = \langle S, V, C \rangle$$

Where S represents the adaptable concept that the *SemObj* adheres to, V is the physical representation (the value) of the adaptable Web content. C specifies the local context of *SemObj*. This context is represented as a finite set of contextual attributes. In addition, contextual attributes themselves are represented as semantic objects, which may also have contextual attributes. This provides a recursive means for context description. Technically, adaptable concepts and contextual attributes are represented using RDF (See Fig. 2.B[5]).

For the needs of our approach, we categorize contextual attributes into two subsets: *static and dynamic*. Static attributes are the minimum contextual attributes that are used to describe the context of a semantic object and hence, their values must be specified explicitly. On the other hand, dynamic attributes, if they are not specified explicitly, can be inferred from other attributes (static or dynamic) that belong to that semantic object and its contextual attributes.

As an example of a semantic object, Fig. 2.A represents the attendance date of the summer course presented in Section 1.1. *Date* refers to the Date/Time adaptable concept. 08/07/2008 is the value of the attendance date. Finally, *Context* represents the set of contextual attributes. Here, the date *SemObj* has *DateStyle* as *static* attribute; *DateFormat* and *TimeZone* as *dynamic* attributes. The other part of context further describes the context of other semantic objects (*DateFormat, TimeZone*). The value of *DateFormat* is inferred from the *country, language* and *dateStyle* and the value of *TimeZone* is inferred from the *country* and *city*. Fig. 2.B presents the summer course XHTML excerpt annotated with the Date semantic object using RDFa syntax[6].

---

[5] The *namespaces*, inside html tag, represent the URL references of the RDF.

[6] More information available on http://www.w3.org/TR/rdfa-syntax/

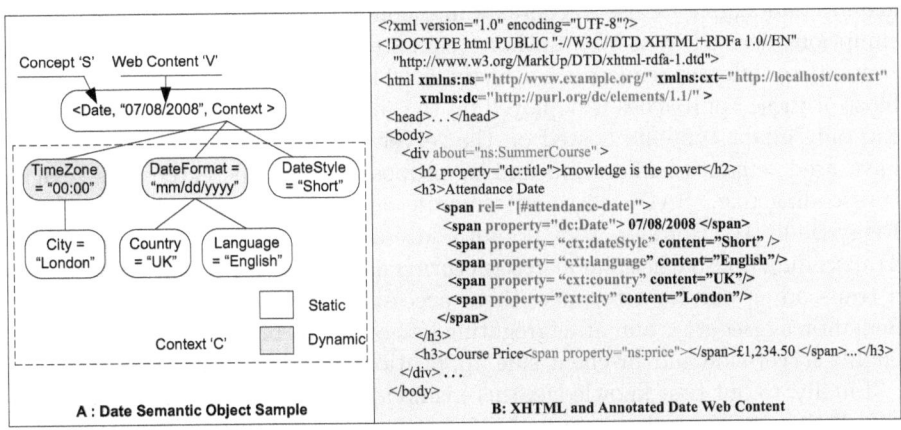

Fig. 2. An excerpt of annotated XHTML Code and Date Semantic Object

2.3 Adaptation of Semantic Objects

Representing Web contents as semantic objects provides a way to adapt a *SemObj* from one local context C to another local context C' (and vice versa). To this end, we specify a conversion function F as follows:

$$F (<S, V, C >, C') = < S, V', C' >$$

F for instance can adapt the above date semantic object (e.g., D) from the British author's context to the French reader's context (e.g., $D1$) as follows.

D =<*Date, 07/08/2008, Timestyle=short, City=London, Country=UK, Lang=EN*>

$D1$ = <*Date, 08/07/2008, Timestyle=short, City=Paris, Country=FR, Lang=FR*>

We implemented an adaptation engine as a Firefox extension. This engine enables the reader to describe his local context and adapts the semantic objects from author's to reader's contexts. In addition, this provides a way to adapt semantic objects from several server-side contents. More details can be obtained at the following address: `http://perso.fundp.ac.be/~maljabar/RDFa/`.

3 Related Work

Space limitations allow us to only discuss some major works related to Web usability, Web adaptation, and semantic contents' annotations. Firstly, enhancing Web usability has been acknowledged as an important issue in many works. However, most initiatives propose practical studies [2] or design guidelines to help enhancing Web usability [11,6]. Secondly, our approach describes the contexts of both Web authors and readers explicitly and adapts the presentation of Web contents according to the reader's contexts. However, most adaptation approaches acquire and aggregate users' contexts into context models, mostly based on assumptions derived from Web authors (e.g., stereotyping), and provide different contents to different readers accordingly [5,4,11]. Also, the adaptation process in most of these approaches is deployed on the server-side. Server-side deployment can only adapt contents hosted on the server-side itself. Finally, several works have used semantic annotation and/or proposed client-side extensions such as transcoding (e.g., SADIe [3]) and semantic aggregators (e.g., Kalpana [7] and Piggy Bank [1]). However, they do not address Web usability and local context. Transcoding approaches aim at restructuring annotated Web contents, based on a transcoding ontology, to make them accessible to visually impaired readers. Semantic aggregators aim at aggregating personal information in RDF form and enable server-side and/or client-side applications to query that information.

Finally, to our best knowledge, there is no approach that uses RDFa to annotate Web contents with contextual information as defined in this paper.

4 Conclusion

This paper presents an approach to enhance the Web usability for Web readers. We explicitly describe the contexts of Web authors and readers with a solution that relies on the notion of semantic object, which includes a tree-structured set of context attributes. Then, we use RDFa to annotate adaptable Web contents with metadata (concepts and context attributes). Hence, Web contents can be adapted into different readers' contexts. We implement an adaptation engine as a Firefox extension. Our future work aims at evaluating Web usability by testing the readers' satisfactions. In addition, we aim at extending our approach to enhance the Web usability of Web authors when they annotate Web contents.

References

1. Ankolekar, A., Vrandecic, D.: Kalpana - enabling client-side web personalization. In: Hypertext. ACM, New York (2008)
2. Barber, W., Badre, A.: Culturability: The merging of culture and usability. In: The 4th Conference on Human Factors and the Web (1998)
3. Bechhofer, S., Harper, S., Lunn, D.: Sadie: Semantic annotation for accessibility. In: Cruz, I., Decker, S., Allemang, D., Preist, C., Schwabe, D., Mika, P., Uschold, M., Aroyo, L.M. (eds.) ISWC 2006. LNCS, vol. 4273, pp. 101–115. Springer, Heidelberg (2006)
4. Brusilovsky, P., Kobsa, A., Nejdl, W. (eds.): Adaptive Web 2007. LNCS, vol. 4321. Springer, Heidelberg (2007)
5. Ceri, S., Daniel, F., Matera, M., Facca, F.M.: Model-driven development of context-aware web applications. ACM Trans. Internet Techn. 7(1) (2007)
6. Gena, C., Weibelzahl, S.: Usability engineering for the adaptive web. In: Brusilovsky, P., et al. (eds.) [4], pp. 720–762
7. Huynh, D., Mazzocchi, S., Karger, D.R.: Piggy bank: Experience the semantic web inside your web browser. J. Web Sem. 5(1), 16–27 (2007)

8. Mrissa, M., Al-Jabari, M., Thiran, P.: Using microformats to personalize web experience. In: IWWOST 2008 Workshop (2008)
9. Mrissa, M., Ghedira, C., Benslimane, D., Maamar, Z.: A context model for semantic mediation in web services composition. In: Embley, D.W., Olivé, A., Ram, S. (eds.) ER 2006. LNCS, vol. 4215, pp. 12–25. Springer, Heidelberg (2006)
10. Torres, E.: Open data in html. In: Xtech Conference (2007)
11. Troyer, O.D., Casteleyn, S.: Designing localized web sites. In: Zhou, X., Su, S., Papazoglou, M.P., Orlowska, M.E., Jeffery, K. (eds.) WISE 2004. LNCS, vol. 3306, pp. 547–558. Springer, Heidelberg (2004)

Plan Recognition of Movement

David N. Chin, Dong-Wan Kang, and Curtis Ikehara

University of Hawaii Dept. of Information & Computer Sciences
1680 East West Rd, POST 317
Honolulu, HI 96822, USA
{chin,dwkang,cikehara}@hawaii.edu

Abstract. Plan recognition of movement by car or foot is generally intractable because of the huge number of potential destinations and routes. However in restricted areas with limited ingress/egress and few places to go such as a military base, plan recognition of movement can be done. The ABM system uses RFID and Lidar to track the movement of vehicles and people, infer their plans/goals, and distinguish threat from normal behavior. ABM represents plans as a series of polygons that abstract important road/terrain features such as intersections and driveways. ABM's keyhole plan recognition algorithm handles unobserved steps caused by insufficient data rates or deficient sensor coverage and handles position inaccuracies due to limited sensor precision or multi-path reflections from buildings. ABM guards privacy by storing only a person's role (e.g., visitor, office worker, grounds keeper) on the military base.

Keywords: plan recognition, RFID, Lidar, movement, behavior analysis.

1 Introduction

If one follows a random car around for a time in any metropolitan area, it is pretty much impossible to tell where that driver is going or why he/she is going there. So whereas plan recognition of user intentions using computers has been commercialized (e.g., Microsoft's Office Assistant [3]), plan recognition of movement has seen little basic research. Previous research in plan recognition of movement includes some work in the robot soccer domain [4, 6, 7] to infer the intention of robot soccer players based on movement relative to the ball and relative to the end lines and possibly relative to other players. Plans include set-plays and tactical movements. Plan recognition for vehicle movement has looked at plans such as passing, preparing to exit, or move into the slower-moving lane based on observations of the relative speeds and positions of vehicles and lanes, vehicle signals, and vehicle acceleration [5]. [2] predicts future traffic jams, but does not consider individual cars. None of these plan recognition systems consider complete end-to-end plans for movement or try to infer why the person is going there.

The ABM (Agent-Based Modeling) system is the first plan recognition system to tackle start-to-end movement plans and goals. ABM is able to infer movement plans because it is applied in the restricted domain of a military base where there are very limited ingress/egress points and few reasonable destinations. ABM is one of three

G.-J. Houben et al. (Eds.): UMAP 2009, LNCS 5535, pp. 474–479, 2009.
© Springer-Verlag Berlin Heidelberg 2009

behavior analysis algorithms implemented for SAIC's BPL (Base Protection Laboratory) project [1] at PMRF (Pacific Missile Range Facility). PMRF is a 5 mile long military base along the southwest shore of Kauai, Hawaii with only two controlled access points, only one of which is open at any time. BPL is a testbed that covers a significant portion of PMRF with various sensors including cameras, RFID tag readers, optical license plate readers, Lidar, microwave, infrared, and seismic sensors. ABM uses data from the RFID sensors, which triangulate the location of the RFID tag and Lidar, which positions objects within range of the lasers to locate vehicles and pedestrians. The ABM algorithm will work with any sensor that gives positional data. ABM infers whether the agent is following a normal or threat plan.

2 Plan Representation

Plans in ABM are represented as a sequence of polygons associated with a goal such as "Going fishing at Major's Bay" (goals are text strings because they are purely for human consumption) and constraints. Polygons are chosen to abstract important features of roads such as intersections, driveways and bridges. Alternative representations such as line segments were considered and rejected because of the nature of the problem. Line segments allow computing the likelihood that someone is following a plan by measuring deviation from the path. This works well in open areas, but in urban areas, people tend to travel on roads and when someone moves off a road, then they are certainly deviating from the plan. On a single lane road, a deviation of 5 meters would be off-road and mean a plan deviation. On the other hand, a deviation of 25 meters from the center of a multi-lane superhighway could still be on the highway and would not be a plan deviation at all. Fig. 1 shows the polygons for the plan of "Going fishing at Major's Bay." The inset shows intersection polygons connected by road segment polygons.

ABM plans also have constraints on agent roles, time/date, environmental conditions, and special events. For example, the plan of "Going to work at Bldg. 282" is only available for agents whose role is "office worker." The plan of "Going to eat at Shenanigans" (a restaurant on base) is only valid shortly before Shenanigans is open up to closing time and only on those days of the week that it is open. The plan of "Going surfing at Major's Bay" is only valid when surf conditions are between 2' (typical high) and 15' (typical low). Surf of 0-1' is too calm for surfing and surf above 15' is too strong for any but a few professionals to surf. The plan of "Watching a missile launch" is only valid for the period right before a launch is scheduled.

ABM's Plan-Base contains plans for both normal base activities and for potential threat activity sequences such as surveillance of potential targets. Normal plans are observed by sensors and their goals are determined by interviewing the travelers. Threat plans are predicted by base security experts. Plans also include observation likelihoods. For normal plans, these are calculated based on how often the plan is actually observed. For threat plans, the security experts estimate the likelihoods.

Fig. 1. Plan for "Going fishing at Major's Bay"

As a vehicle enters the base, the agent is tracked by ABM. Initially the possible plans for the agent includes all plans whose constraints are satisfied. As the agent moves through the base, plans whose steps are not being followed are eliminated until only a single plan is left. It is possible that no plans match when the agent is lost or is pursuing a novel plan. The plans are organized in order of likelihood. ABM can generate alerts to base security if any threat plans match the current path with the degree of alert depending on whether the threat plan is the only matching plan (high alert), the highest likelihood matching plan (medium alert) or just a high likelihood plan (low alert). Alerts can also be generated if no plans match the path at all, indicating a lost visitor or anomalous/erratic behavior.

3   Practical Problems and Solutions

The ABM algorithm needed to be modified to handle certain practical problems due to real world sensor limitations. For example, both RFID and Lidar sensors only gave locations once per second, there were gaps in coverage of sensors, sensors had limited accuracy (up to ±4 meters), sensors were sometimes wildly inaccurate due to multi-path reflections off metal buildings (shifting locations by up to 20 meters) and often gave false readings from wind-blown trees/shrubs.

The limited data rate and gaps in coverage meant that polygons were sometimes skipped in plans. For example, a vehicle traveling at 45 mph would travel 66 feet in one second, much further than the length of many intersections. To limit search, the maximum speed limit of the road plus a percentage was used to predict which polygons might have been skipped. This saved matching about a hundred plan steps in the longer plans. To ease calculations, the length of the polygon in the direction of motion of the plan is included with the plan step.

The limited accuracy meant that locations were sometimes reported as the wrong polygon. For example, if a car is near the edge of a road, then even a small half meter inaccuracy in position can put the car off the road. With road lanes about 3.5 meters wide, the ±4 meters accuracy easily puts a car off road much of the time.[1] ABM solved this problem by looking for all polygons that intersected with a circle centered around the reported location with radius 4 meters using PostGIS. For efficiency, this was done only if the reported polygon did not match any of the currently active plans.

A related problem occurs when a car moves through an intersection. Let's call the four road segments that connect to a four-way intersection N, S, E and W. A car moving from N to S may be reported as being in the E or W road segment instead of in the intersection due to the inaccuracy of the sensors. If there are plans that go from N to E or N to W, then the N to S plans will be eliminated under the assumption that the car has turned right or left, when in fact the car is traveling straight. Following the efficiency optimization of only searching for polygon intersections when no plans match, ABM would not even notice the problem until the following point. To handle this problem, ABM kept plans active until at least two locations did not match the plan and backtracked to check for inaccurately reported polygons if no plans match.

Wildly inaccurate locations and false readings were handled by ignoring location reports that jumped farther than the current speed of the agent would allow.

4 Privacy Concerns

In the USA, people do not like to be under constant surveillance. So even though PMRF already had many surveillance cameras in place before BPL, base personnel had concerns about possible misuse of the additional data. Considerable public relations communications were needed to alleviate their concerns. The BPL system was designed from the start for privacy. The system never records names, identifying numbers or any other information that can be used to trace back to the individual. Even the output of the optical license plate readers is obfuscated with a one-way hash so that the original license plate cannot be reconstructed from the identifier used in BPL. The only information about people stored in the system is their role on the base.

---

[1] This accuracy limitation led to eliminating the distinction between directions on two lane roads, so that all road polygons include both lanes instead of having separate parallel polygons for each direction.

5 Evaluation

ABM can be evaluated using a number of different metrics:

1. Plan-Base Coverage
2. Prediction Accuracy over Time (% time that highest likelihood plan is correct)
3. False Positive Rate
4. Average Alert Response Window
5. Simulated Attack Detection Rate
6. Latency

Because the completeness of the Plan-Base affects how well plan recognition works, an important metric is the percent coverage of the Plan-Base. A key metric is ABM's prediction accuracy over time. The initial prediction may start with a lower accuracy, but as the agent moves through the base, more and more plans should be pruned so accuracy should increase over time. Ideally at some point, only one plan will be active and that should be the correct plan. Because a system that generates too many false alerts will become ignored (only a few is probably too many), another key measure is the false positive rate for alerts. If an alert is generated by simulated attack, an important measure is the time between alert generation and security response onset for thwarting the threat. The alert must come in time for security to respond effectively. The final metric is the latency of ABM, that is, how much time passes between ABM being informed of an agent's position and ABM's output.

Unfortunately not enough normal plan observations have been collected and thus ABM lacks a reasonable plan base of normal plans. So the only metric that can be evaluated currently is Latency. This was evaluated by running ABM, the Blackboard software with the Blitz JavaSpaces JINI software underlying the Blackboard, PostgreSQL for PostGIS geographic database queries and the NetBeans IDE all on a single laptop computer with a single-core AMD Turion 64 2.0 GHz CPU with 2GB of DDR 333 SDRAM. The average time for ABM to process a sensor position report on a test 121 polygon plan was 166 milliseconds, of which 148 ms was taken up by propagation through the Blackboard software. That means ABM itself takes only 18 ms on average to process a position. The timing data also showed a large start-up latency. Removing the first 6 track points lowers the average latency to 98 ms and the ABM portion to 17 ms. ABM's average latency of less than 1/10th second proves that the ABM algorithm is capable of near real-time performance.

5 Future Work

Although ABM has been shown to work with live sensors in real-time, there is still much work to be done to develop the ABM algorithm. The primary task is to analyze and encode normal plans from volunteer data. There is also a need to encode additional threat plans from security experts. Due to the lack of normal data, only one of the evaluation metrics for ABM has been assessed. The other five metrics should also be assessed. Finally, all of the knowledge in ABM is currently laboriously hand-coded. To make ABM deployable, we must address the knowledge acquisition bottleneck with semi-automatic generation of plans for any military base:

1. Use local AutoCAD drawings for layout
2. User-assisted labeling of building/location purposes
3. Knowledge base of where people go, when and why
4. Automatic normal plan generation from observation data
5. User-assisted explanations for unknown normal plans
6. Security/covert-ops domain experts enter threat plans

The idea behind semi-automatic generation of plans is to start with a knowledge-base of where people go on a typical military base, why they go there and when they might go there. Combining this knowledge-base with local AutoCAD drawings and user-assisted labeling of the purposes of buildings and locations on the AutoCAD drawings, ABM could automatically generate normal plans for the specific military base. ABM can verify these auto-generated plans with observation data and seek assistance in classifying plans that do not match any auto-generated plans. Finally, an intelligent user interface could be designed to guide security/covert-ops experts to directly enter threat plans specific to the local base into ABM. With such a knowledge acquisition system, ABM could be deployed on a new military base by personnel without intimate knowledge of the ABM algorithm.

Acknowledgments. This work was partially supported by the Office of Naval Research under contract #N00014-06-C-0718 subcontracted from SAIC.

References

1. Banks, B., Jackson, G.M., Helly, J.J., Chin, D.N., Masters, D., Burger, A., Krebs, W., Smith, T.J., Schmidt, A., Brewer, P., Medd, R.: Using Behavior Analysis Algorithms to Anticipate Security Threats Before They Impact Mission Critical Operations. In: Proceedings of the IEEE International Conference on Advanced Video and Signal based Surveillance, pp. 307–312 (2007)
2. Horovitz, E., Apacible, J., Sarin, R., Liao, L.: Prediction, Expectation, and Surprise: Methods, Designs, and Study of a Deployed Traffic Forecasting Service. In: Proceedings of the Twenty-First Conference on Uncertainty in Artificial Intelligence, pp. 275–283 (2005)
3. Horovitz, E., Breese, J., Heckerman, D., Hovel, D., Rommelse, K.: The Lumière Project: Bayesian User Modeling for Inferring the Goals and Needs of Software Users. In: Proceedings of the Fourteenth Conference on Uncertainty in Artificial Intelligence, Madison, WI, pp. 256–265. Morgan Kaufmann, San Francisco (1998)
4. Marín, C.A., Castillo, L.P., Garrido, L.: Dynamic Adaptive Opponent Modeling: Predicting Opponent Motion while Playing Soccer. In: Alonso, E., Guessoum, Z. (eds.) Fifth European Workshop on Adaptive Agents and Multiagent Systems Proceedings, Paris, France, March 2005, pp. 21–22 (2005)
5. Pynadath, D.V., Wellman, M.P.: Accounting for context in plan recognition, with application to traffic monitoring. In: Proceedings of the Eleventh Conference on Uncertainty in Artificial Intelligence, pp. 472–481. Morgan Kaufmann, San Francisco (1995)
6. Riley, P., Veloso, M.: Recognizing probabilistic opponent movement models. In: Birk, A., Coradeschi, S., Tadokoro, S. (eds.) RoboCup 2001. LNCS, vol. 2377, pp. 453–458. Springer, Heidelberg (2002)
7. Steffens, T.: Feature-based declarative opponent modeling. In: Polani, D., Browning, B., Bonarini, A., Yoshida, K. (eds.) RoboCup 2003. LNCS, vol. 3020, pp. 125–136. Springer, Heidelberg (2004)

Personalised Web Experiences: Seamless Adaptivity across Web Service Composition and Web Content

Ian O'Keeffe and Vincent Wade

Centre for Next Generation Localisation, Knowledge and Data Engineering Group,
School of Computer Science and Statistics, Trinity College Dublin, Ireland
{Ian.OKeeffe,Vincent.Wade}@cs.tcd.ie

Abstract. Users have become accustomed to a web that is more than
an interactive hypermedia but is a complex mix of rich multimedia services and hypermedia content. Users are now contributors and active
participants on the web. However, Pesonalisation technologies, such as
Adaptive Hypermedia, have so far focused almost exclusively on adaptive content delivery resulting in their failure to become a high impact
technologies. The absence of rich multimedia services in the current generation of Adaptive Hypermedia Systems means that they do not live up
to the expectations of users. By providing personalised web experiences
that combine both services and content in a seamless environment such
systems could not only live up to the expectations of users but could
exceed them. This paper presents a system that supports the adaptive
selection and sequencing of both content and services in a unified manner.
By applying techniques used in content based Adaptive Hypermedia to
services with making use of the state of the art in service composition,
this system delivers personalised web experiences that combine adaptively selected and sequenced content and services. The integration of
appropriate content with services can improve the experience of the user
as well as making the activity more efficient.

1 Introduction

Users have become accustomed to a web that is more than an interactive hypermedia but is a complex mix of rich multimedia services and hypermedia content.
Users are now contributors and active participants on the web, communicating
with each other using a range of content sharing and collaborative tools e.g.
Gmail, MSN Messenger, Flickr, YouTube, wikis and blogs. They are no longer
simply consumers of content but are also content creators and publishers.

In this environment, users seamlessly move between interacting with services,
for example voting, rating, annotating, communicating, etc, to content interaction, e.g. viewing, navigating, etc. Furthermore, users frequently combine available services and related content in order to carry out complex activities. An
example of such an activity, within an educational context, is a peer review activity, which not only requires access to appropriate content but also requires

G.-J. Houben et al. (Eds.): UMAP 2009, LNCS 5535, pp. 480–485, 2009.

services to support authoring, submission, annotation and discussion. Not only do these services need to be made available but they must be presented in a specific order according to the requirements of the activity.

Pesonalisation technologies, such as Adaptive Hypermedia [1], have so far focused almost exclusively on the adaptive delivery of interactive content, e.g. AHA! [2], KnowledgeTree [1] and PersonalReader [3]. As we move to next generation web technologies, there is a need to provide a combination of adaptive selection and sequencing of multimedia content with adaptive selection and sequencing of user centric services. We define the notion of a **personalised web experience** (PWE) as an experience that involves the integration of the personalised selection and presentation of content, personalised service adaptation and personalised service composition. Thus the personalised web experience provides a significant engagement of the user in carrying out activities on the web.

Presented in this paper is a radical rethink of Adaptive Engines (AE), where the AE supports adaptive composition of web services as well as multimedia web content. Such next generation AEs effectively generate adaptive service workflows and adaptively compose content, seamlessly integrating the adaptive selection, composition and presentation of content and services. This work builds upon existing AE technology and integrates portal and semantic web business process and planning techniques to support the unified AE.

The rest of this paper is structured as follows, the current state of the art in the adaptive composition of content and services is discussed as well as an analysis of the key differences between content and service composition. This is followed by the design and implementation of a system that combines these techniques to deliver PWEs. Finally, an example use case that has been built using this system is then presented.

2   State of the Art

Adaptive Hypermedia Systems (AHS) can be characterised as systems that dynamically compose multimedia content based on the needs of the user. Such systems often personalise the delivery of content based on the interests of the user, tasks that they are undertaking or contextual information such as network bandwidth or screen size.

Systems such as APeLS [4] and AHA! [2] use separate models to represent the user, application domain, available content and the adaptation rules. These systems are all content centric with no support for the composition of services. Another AHS that does take a step towards addressing this limitation is KnowledgeTree [1]. It supports the integration of 'intelligent content' [5] into the personalised hypermedia that it generates. Pieces of intelligent content are Java applets that are embedded into the content resources used by KnowledgeTree and integrate directly with KnowledgeTree's user modelling service, Cumulate [1]. Although this approach does allow for a richer level of user interaction, it does not allow for the composition of computationally complete services. This would require, for example, support for the parameterisation of the services (both inputs and outputs), the management of the information flow between services and support for error handling.

The techniques used to select and sequence services [8] typically fall into two categories, namely workflow and AI Planning. Workflow based techniques allow services to be composed into a flow of execution that explicitly links services together. Such workflow compositions are typically built manually via rule bases or scripting using technologies such as BPEL [6] and YAWL [7]. Such compositions can be considered to be static as there is limited scope for the workflow sequencing to change and references to the services are explicitly embedded in the workflow. The CAWE framework[11] attempts to apply adaptivity to workflow execution through the use of an abstraction mechanism that allows the workflow to refer to abstract services Information about the user is then used to select appropriate concrete services or pre-existing service compositions on a just in time basis. This approach supports the adaptive selection of services but not the adaptive composition as the workflow remains unchanged.

The second category of composition techniques are those taken from the AI Planning [8] domain. These attempt to dynamically compose services to satisfy a set of goals using techniques such as Hierarchical Task Networks (HTN) [8] or situation calculus. In such systems, the services are modeled in terms of the input parameters, the conditions under which the services can be invoked and the effects that the invocation would have. Examples of systems that compose Web Services (WS) using AI planning techniques include XPlan [9] and Shop2 [10].

3   Comparing Content and Service Composition

Unlike content, the behaviour of services in a composition can also be influenced by the adaptive selection of appropriate parameters. Parameterisation of content, although possible, is very seldom offered. This is in contrast to services, which nearly always have heterogeneous input and output requirements and data flow imperatives. Through parameterisation, it is also possible to provide a level of adaptation with respect to the behaviour and functionality of a service. This provides an additional layer of adaptivity when selecting services in comparison to the selection of content. In order to take advantage of this added flexibility, it is important that the mechanism used to select services is aware of the parameterisation of the available services and is capable of configuring some of these parameters so as to modify the behaviour of the service to better suit the needs of the user.

Another important difference between content and service composition is that service compositions have an explicit information flow between the services. This information flow is fundamental to the correct operation of a service composition. If it is broken in some way then the composition will not behave as intended. There exists an information flow between resources in a content composition. However, this flow is more conceptual as it relates to the sequencing of the topics covered by the content. This information flow, although important, for example in an educational context, is not critical for the system to support as it is typically performed by the user. This is especially illustrated in AHS such as APeLS and AHA! in which users have freedom to jump between different content resources.

In addition to allowing the behaviour of a service to be modified, the parameterisation of services also allows more complex services to be created though the composition of many individual services. The careful management of the information flowing into and out of services can be utilised in order to provide functionalities that were not previously available from existing services.

4   Architecture

A high level view of the system architecture is provided in figure 1. As can be seen from the diagram, the Adaptive Engine is the central component of the system. It is responsible for the reconciliation of the available metadata models through the execution of the narrative (adaptive sequencing rules), which strategically guides the adaptation process. The metadata models describe the available content and services as well as providing information about the learner. The narrative's encapsulation of the strategy for composing a PWE allows a designer to describe the sequencing for a PWE and how it can be adapted.

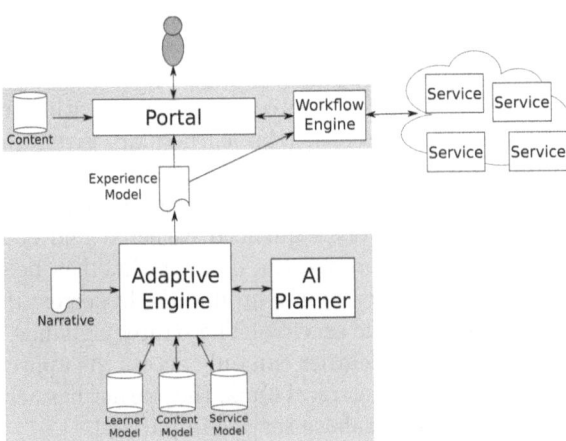

Fig. 1. Diagram representing a high level view of the system architecture

The AE and the narrative that it executes support a basic set of five patterns for describing the sequencing of services. These patterns have been adopted from the work of van der Aalst et al[13] and provide a sufficiently rich range of behaviours to describe the progression between tasks within a PWE. The five patterns supported are: sequence, parallel split, conditional branch, synchronisation and simple merge.

As the AE adaptively sequences the necessary content and services, it makes use of an AI planner to dynamically select appropriate services. The use of the

AI planner allows for the adaptive selection of appropriate services as well as the composition of new services when an appropriate service does not already exist. Service selection can be influenced by the AE as it is responsible for setting the selection criteria for the planner.

As a result of the narrative execution, the AE produces an 'experience model'. This model represents an instantiated PWE in which the appropriate content and services have been identified. In order to make a PWE available to the user, the personalised service composition is instantiated as a BPEL process and deployed to a workflow engine. This brings together the necessary services and controls the users access to those services in order to maintain the sequencing as part of the PWE. The user can then access the PWE through a portal interface that combines the appropriate content and services in a single environment.

5   Case Study

As part of the evaluation of this system, several PWEs were developed. One such PWE was developed based on a personalised eLearning course used to teach undergraduate students. This PWE combines personalised multimedia content covering topics relating to the use of SQL to create, populate and retrieve information from relational databases. The services in this PWE are quiz's that correspond to the different sections of the course. The learner must get a passing score in a quiz before they can move on to the next quiz. In the case of the Database Retrieval quiz, the learner is also provided with an example database service. This service allows the learner to retrieve information from a database on a topic that they are interested in (the learners are given a choice between two subject domains) in order to answer the questions.

The PWE consists of the delivery of personalised content in parallel with services that have been adaptively sequenced, selected and composed for the learner. The learner is free to browse the content that has been selected and sequenced for them so that they can jump around the hypertext document as the wish. This is not the case with the services. The strategy guiding the sequencing of the services requires that the learner can only access the appropriate services. When answering the Database Retrieval Quiz, the learner has access to both the quiz service and the example database service in parallel.

6   Conclusions

This paper discussed how users on the web are moving from being purely content consumers to being active participants in web based activities. Also discussed was how personalisation technologies such as AHS can enhance the user experience by supporting the adaptive selection and sequencing of services as well as content.

To illustrate how this could be achived, this paper considered the issues that a AHS would need to address in order to support this functionality and presented the architecture for a system capable of providing the user with a personalised web experience combining both hypermedia content and multimedia services.

References

1. Brusilovsky, P.: Adaptive Navigation Support. In: Brusilovsky, P., Kobsa, A., Nejdl, W. (eds.) Adaptive Web 2007. LNCS, vol. 4321, pp. 263–290. Springer, Heidelberg (2007)
2. De Bra, P., Smits, D., Stash, N.: The design of aha! In: HYPERTEXT 2006: Proceedings of the seventeenth conference on Hypertext and hypermedia, pp. 171–195. ACM, New York (2006)
3. Henze, N., Krause, D.: Personalized access to web services in the semantic web. In: 3rd International Semantic Web User Interaction Workshop, Athens, Georgia, USA (2006)
4. Conlan, O.: The Multi-Model, Metadata driven approach to Personalised eLearning Services. Ph.D thesis, University of Dublin, Trinity College (2005)
5. Meccawy, M., Brusilovsky, P., Ashman, H., Yudelson, M., Scherbinina, O.: Integrating interactive learning content into an adaptive e-learning system: Lessons learned. In: Richards, G. (ed.) Proceedings of World Conference on E-Learning in Corporate, Government, Healthcare, and Higher Education 2007, Quebec City, Canada, pp. 6314–6319. AACE (2007)
6. Curbera, F., Andrews, T., Dholakia, H., Goland, Y., Klein, J., Leymann, F., Liu, K., Roller, D., Smith, D., Thatte, S., Trickovic, I., Weerawarana, S.: Business process execution language for web services (2003)
7. van der Aalst, W.M.P., Hofstede, T.A.H.M.: YAWL: Yet another workflow language. Information Systems 30(4), 245–275 (2005)
8. Rao, J., Su, X.: A survey of automated web service composition methods. In: Cardoso, J., Sheth, A.P. (eds.) SWSWPC 2004. LNCS, vol. 3387, pp. 43–54. Springer, Heidelberg (2005)
9. Klusch, M., Gerber, A.: Evaluation of service composition planning with owls-xplan. In: WI-IATW 2006: Proceedings of the 2006 IEEE/WIC/ACM international conference on Web Intelligence and Intelligent Agent Technology, Washington, DC, USA, pp. 117–120. IEEE Computer Society, Los Alamitos (2006)
10. Wu, D., Sirin, E., Hendler, J., Nau, D.: Automatic web services composition using SHOP2. In: Workshop on Planning for Web Services (2003)
11. Ardissono, L., Furnari, R., Goy, A., Petrone, G., Segnan, M.: A framework for the management of context-aware workflow systems. In: WEBIST 2007: Proceedings of the third international conference on Web Information Systems and Technologies, pp. 80–87 (2007)
12. Dagger, D., Wade, V., Conlan, O.: Personalisation for all: Making adaptive course composition easy. Journal of Educational Technology and Society 8(3), 9–25 (2005); Special Issue on Authoring of Adaptive Hypermedia
13. van der Aalst, W.M.P., ter Hofstede, A.H.M., Kiepuszewski, B., Barros, A.P.: Workflow patterns. Distributed and Parallel Databases 14(3), 5–51 (2003)
14. Gerevini, A., Saetti, A., Serini, I., Toninelli, P.: Planning in PDDL2.2 domains with LPG-TD (2004)
15. Braun, C., Broberg, J., Mark, C., Freedman, M., Jones, T., Schaeck, T., Tayar, G.: Web Services for Remote Portlets Specification (2003)

Author Index